Lecture Notes in Computer Science

Commenced Publication in 1973
Founding and Former Series Editors:
Gerhard Goos, Juris Hartmanis, and Jan van Leeuwen

T0238093

Editorial Board

Wenyi Zhao   Shaogang Gong
Xiaoou Tang (Eds.)

Analysis and Modelling of Faces and Gestures

Second International Workshop, AMFG 2005
Beijing, China, October 16, 2005
Proceedings

 Springer

Volume Editors

Wenyi Zhao
Vision Technologies Lab
Sarnoff Corporation
Princeton, NJ 08873, USA
E-mail: wzhao@sarnoff.com

Shaogang Gong
Queen Mary, University of London
Department of Computer Science
London E1 4NS UK
E-mail: sgg@dcs.qmul.ac.uk

Xiaoou Tang
Microsoft Research Asia
Beijing Sigma Center
10080 Beijing, China
E-mail: xitang@microsoft.com

Library of Congress Control Number: 2005933260

CR Subject Classification (1998): I.4, I.5, I.3.5, I.2.10, I.2.6, F.2.2

ISSN   0302-9743
ISBN-10   3-540-29229-2 Springer Berlin Heidelberg New York
ISBN-13   978-3-540-29229-6 Springer Berlin Heidelberg New York

Springer is a part of Springer Science+Business Media

springeronline.com

© Springer-Verlag Berlin Heidelberg 2005
Printed in Germany

Typesetting: Camera-ready by author, data conversion by Scientific Publishing Services, Chennai, India
Printed on acid-free paper   SPIN: 11564386   06/3142   5 4 3 2 1 0

Preface

During the last 30 years, face recognition and related problems such as face detection/tracking and facial expression recognition have attracted researchers from both the engineering and psychology communities. In addition, extensive research has been carried out to study hand and body gestures. The understanding of how humans perceive these important cues has significant scientific value and extensive applications. For example, human-computer interaction, visual surveillance, and smart video indexing are active application areas. Aiming towards putting such amazing perception capability onto computer systems, researchers have made substantial progress. However, technological challenges still exist in many aspects.

Following a format similar to the IEEE International Workshop on Analysis and Modeling of Faces and Gestures (AMFG) 2003, this one-day workshop (AMFG 2005) provided a focused international forum to bring together well-known researchers and research groups to review the status of recognition, analysis and modeling of faces and gestures, to discuss the challenges that we are facing, and to explore future directions. Overall, 30 papers were selected from 90 submitted manuscripts. The topics of these papers range from feature representation, robust recognition, learning, and 3D modeling to psychology. In addition, two invited talks were given, by Prof. Kanade and Dr. Phillips. The technical program was organized into four oral sessions and two poster sessions.

This workshop would not have been possible without the timely reviews provided by the members of the Technical Program Committee under a tight schedule.

October 2005

Wenyi Zhao
Shaogang Gong
Xiaoou Tang

Conference Organization

Workshop Chairs

Wenyi Zhao, Sarnoff Corporation, USA
Shaogang Gong, Queen Mary, University of London, UK
Andrew Senior, IBM T.J. Watson Research Center, USA
Xiaoou Tang, Microsoft Research Asia, China

Advisory Committee

Rama Chellappa, University of Maryland, USA
Thomas S. Huang, University of Illinois at Urbana Champaign, USA
Anil Jain, Michigan State University, USA

Local Arrangement Co-chairs

Shuicheng Yan, The Chinese University of Hong Kong, Hong Kong, China
Qingshan Liu, Chinese Academy of Sciences, China

Program Committee

Richard Bowden	Surrey, UK
Kevin Bowyer	Notre Dame, USA
Rama Chellappa	Maryland, USA
Jeff Cohn	Pittsburgh, USA
Robert Collins	Penn State, USA
Tim Cootes	Manchester, UK
David Hogg	Leeds, UK
Anil Jain	Michigan State, USA
David Jacobs	Maryland, USA
Ron Kimmel	Technion, Israel
Josef Kittler	Surrey, UK
David Kriegman	UCSD, USA
Stan Z. Li	NLPR, China
Chengjun Liu	NJIT, USA
Zhichen Liu	Microsoft Research, USA
Gerard Medioni	USC, USA

Baback Moghaddam   MERL, USA
Mark Nixon   Southampton, UK
Jonathon Phillips   NIST, USA
Long Quan   UST, HK
Pawan Sinha   MIT, USA
Matthew Turk   UCSB, USA
David Zhang   HKPU, HK

Table of Contents

3D Modeling

Poster Sessions

Session I

Session II

Facial Expression Analysis

Takeo Kanade

U.A. and Helen Whitaker University Professor, Robotics Institute,
Carnegie Mellon University, Pittsburgh, PA 15213, USA

Abstract. Computer analysis of human face images includes detection of faces, identification of people, and understanding of expression. Among these three tasks, facial expression has been the least studied, and most of the past work on facial expression tried to recognize a small set of emotions, such as joy, disgust, and surprise. This practice may follow from the work of Darwin, who proposed that emotions have corresponding prototypic facial expressions. In everyday life, however, such prototypic expressions occur relatively infrequently; instead, emotion is communicated more often by subtle changes in one or a few discrete features. FACS-code Action Units, defined by Ekman, are one such representation accepted in the psychology community.

In collaboration with psychologists, we have been developing a system for automatically recognizing facial action units. This talk will present the current version of the system. The system uses a 3D Active Appearance Model to align a face image and transform it to a person-specific canonical coordinate frame. This transformation can remove appearance changes due to changes of head pose and relative illumination direction. In this transformed image frame, we perform detailed analysis of both facial motion and facial appearance changes, results of which are fed to an action-unit recogniser.

Modeling Micro-patterns for Feature Extraction

Qiong Yang[1], Dian Gong[1, 2], and Xiaoou Tang[1]

[1] Microsoft Research Asia, Beijing Sigma Center,
100080 Beijing, China
{qyang, xitang}@microsoft.com
[2] Department of Electronic Engineering, Tsinghua University,
100084 Beijing, China
gongd@wmc.ee.tsinghua.edu.cn

Abstract. Currently, most of the feature extraction methods based on micro-patterns are application oriented. The micro-patterns are intuitively user-designed based on experience. Few works have built models of micro-patterns for feature extraction. In this paper, we propose a model-based feature extraction approach, which uses micro-structure modeling to design adaptive micro-patterns. We first model the micro-structure of the image by Markov random field. Then we give the generalized definition of micro-pattern based on the model. After that, we define the fitness function and compute the fitness index to encode the image's local fitness to micro-patterns. Theoretical analysis and experimental results show that the new algorithm is both flexible and effective in extracting good features.

1 Introduction

Feature extraction is one of the most important issues in pattern recognition. In previous studies, people observed that the spatial context in images plays an important role in many vision tasks, such as character recognition, object detection and recognition. So they design micro-patterns to describe the spatial context of the image, such as edge, line, spot, blob, corner, and more complex patterns. Furthermore, it is observed that the regional characteristics of micro-patterns are more robust to shift and scale, so a number of features are developed to calculate the regional characteristics of micro-patterns. These features include:

a) *Orientation Histogram.* This kind of features designs the micro-pattern as directional line or edge, and calculates the histogram of each direction in the region. It has been used as an informative tool for various vision tasks. Sun and Si [1] used orientation histograms to find the symmetry axis in an image. Freeman and Roth [2] developed a method for hand gesture recognition based on the global orientation histogram of the image. Lowe [3] developed a scale-invariant feature from local orientation histograms for object recognition. Levi and Weiss [4] used local edge orientation histograms (EOH) as features to improve performance in object detection as well as face detection. Another example is that Four Directional Line Element (FDLE) [5] has been successfully used for character recognition.

b) *Filter Banks.* In this kind of features, a bank of filters is designed to extract the micro-structural features, and the regional characteristics are computed from the filter

W. Zhao, S. Gong, and X. Tang (Eds.): AMFG 2005, LNCS 3723, pp. 2 – 16, 2005.

response. Goudail et al. [6] designed a series of local autocorrelation filters for face recognition, and the filter response is summed over the global image to form the feature. Wang et al. [7] used the histogram of regulated outputs of Gabor filters for Chinese character recognition in low-quality images.

c) *Local Binary Pattern.* This feature is designed for texture analysis [8], face detection and face recognition [9]. The image is first divided into small regions, from which Local Binary Pattern (LBP) histograms are extracted and concatenated into a single feature histogram to efficiently represent the image.

In all these features, the micro-patterns are intuitively user-designed based on experience, and they are application oriented. The micro-patterns fit for one task might be unfit for another. For example, FDLE [5] is successful in character recognition, but might not achieve the same success in face recognition, since face image is much more complex than the character image so that it cannot be simply represented by directional lines. Another problem is that in some cases, it is difficult for the user to intuitively determine whether the micro-pattern is appropriate unless he refers to the experimental result. A similar problem exists for Gabor features. Although in many papers Gabor has been used to recognize a general object as well as face [10,11,12], the parameters are mainly adjusted by experimental results, and it costs a lot of time and efforts to find the appropriate parameters.

In this paper, we propose a model-based feature extraction approach, which uses Markov random field (MRF) to model the micro-structure of the image and design adaptive micro-patterns for feature extraction. The key idea is motivated by several observations:

First of all, image structure modeling can help us find good features in at least three aspects: 1) Modeling could provide sound theoretical foundations and guide us on how to design suitable micro-patterns. 2) Through modeling, the feature extraction method could be more general, and also more applicable to various applications. 3) Modeling will alleviate the efforts in adjusting parameters. Therefore, we introduce image structure modeling in the stage of feature extraction.

Secondly, Markov field [13,14,15,17,18,19,20,21] provides a flexible mechanism for modeling spatial dependence. If we study the spatial dependence in a local region of the image, it will model the micro-patterns, with different spatial dependency corresponding to different micro-patterns. It is also convenient for representing unobserved complex patterns of images, especially the location of discontinuities between regions homogeneous in tone, texture or depth. Therefore it is possible for using Markov field to model the micro-patterns, not limited to the simple ones, but also the complex patterns. Moreover, the parameters of the model can be statistically learned from samples, instead of intuitively user-designed. Thereby it is more adaptive to the local characteristics of images. Different micro-patterns will be designed for different kinds of images, different attributes of images, and even at different sites of an image, so features will be more flexible, and also more applicable to various applications.

Based on the above observations, we use MRF to extract block-level micro-structural features. We first divide the image into sub-blocks and use MRF to model the micro-patterns in each sub-block. Based on that, we compute the local fitness sequence to describe the image's local fitness to micro-patterns. Then, we extract the modified FFT (fast Fourier transform) feature of the local fitness sequence in each sub-block. Finally, we concatenate these features from all sub-blocks into a long feature vector. The new feature presents a description of the image on three levels: the Markov field model reflects the spatial correlation of neighborhood in a pixel-level; the local fitness sequence in each sub-block reflects the image's regional fitness to micro-patterns in a block level; and the features from all sub-blocks are concatenated to build a global description of the image. In this way, both the local textures and the global shape of the image are simultaneously encoded.

2 Feature Extraction from Micro-structure Modeling

2.1 Markov Random Field Model

Let I represent a $H \times W$ image with S as its collection of all sites, and let $X_s = x_s$ represent some attribute of the image I at site $s \in S$. The attribute may be grayscale intensity, Gabor attribute or other features. Also, we denote the attributes of all other sites in S excluding site s by $X_{-s} = x_{-s}$. The spatial distribution of attributes on S, $X = x = \{x_s, s \in S\}$, will be modeled as a Markov random field (MRF).

Let N_s denote the neighbors of site s, and the r-th order neighborhood is defined to be $N_s^{(r)} = \{t \mid dist(s,t) \leq r, t \in S\}$, where $dist(s,t)$ is the distance between site s and site t. The 1-st and 2-nd order neighborhood structure are displayed in Fig. 1. Because of the local property (i.e. Markovianity: $p(X_s = x_s \mid X_{-s} = x_{-s}) = p(X_s = x_s \mid X_{N_s} = x_{N_s})$), the Markov model is equivalent to the Gibbs random field, so we use the energy function to calculate the probability as follows

$$p(X_s \mid X_{-s}) = p(X_s \mid X_{N_s}) = \frac{1}{\mathcal{T}} \exp\{-E_{\theta_s}(X_s, X_{N_s})\}, \tag{1}$$

where $E_{\theta_s}(X_s, X_{N_s})$ is the energy function at site s which is the sum of energies/potentials of the cliques containing site s, and $\mathcal{T} = \sum_{X_s} \exp\{-E_{\theta_s}(X_s, X_{N_s})\}$ is the partition function. Here, θ_s is the parameter set for site s, so we rewrite $p(X_s \mid X_{N_s})$ into $p_{\theta_s}(X_s \mid X_{N_s})$.

For a pair-wise MRF model, there is $E_{\theta_s}(X_s, X_{N_s}) = H_s(X_s) + \sum_{t \in N_s} J_{st}(X_s, X_t)$, where $H_s(X_s)$ is the "field" at site s, and $J_{st}(X_s, X_t)$ is the "interaction" between site s and site t. Furthermore, if $H_s(X_s) = 0$ and $J_{st}(X_s, X_t) = \frac{1}{(\sigma_{st})^2}(X_s - X_t)^2$, then we get the smooth model and there is $E_{\theta_s}(X_s, X_{N_s}) = \sum_{t \in N_s} \frac{1}{(\sigma_{st})^2}(X_s - X_t)^2$, $\theta_s = \{\sigma_{st}, t \in N_s\}$. If $H_s(X_s) = \alpha_s X_s$, $J_{st}(X_s, X_t) = \beta_{st} X_s X_t$ and $X_s \in \{+1, -1\}, s \in S$, then we get the Ising model and there is $E_{\theta_s}(X_s, X_{N_s}) = \alpha_s X_s + \sum_{t \in N_s} \beta_{st} X_s X_t$, $\theta_s = \{\alpha_s, \beta_{st}, t \in N_s\}$. For simplicity, we write θ_s as θ.

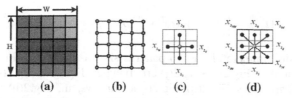

Fig. 1. (a) The image I with the size of $H \times W$. (b) The site set S of the image I. (c) The 1-st order neighborhood structure. (d) The 2-nd order neighborhood structure. Here, H=W=5.

2.2 Feature Extraction

In this section, we will discuss how we extract features based on Markov random field model. Firstly, we propose a generalized definition of micro-pattern, and then we design a fitness function to extract the image's local fitness to micro-patterns.

2.2.1 Generalized Definition of Micro-patterns

Assume that Ω denotes the *micro-pattern*, and $\Omega_\theta(\gamma)$ is defined to be all the pairs of (x_s, x_{N_s}) that satisfy the constraint $g_\theta(x_s, x_{N_s}) = \gamma$ with given θ, i.e. $\{(x_s, x_{N_s}): g_\theta(x_s, x_{N_s}) = \gamma\}$. Here, θ is the parameter set.

$\Omega_\theta(\gamma)$ has the following properties:

1. Given θ, $\{\Omega_\theta(\gamma), \gamma \in \mathcal{R}\}$ describes a series of micro-patterns where $\mathcal{R}$ is the value set of γ.

2. When γ is discrete, $\Omega_\theta(\gamma)$ is characterized by its probability $P(\Omega = \Omega_\theta(\gamma))$; when γ is a continuous variable, $\Omega_\theta(\gamma)$ is characterized by the probability density function $p(\Omega_\theta(\gamma))$.

In this paper, since we use MRF model, we define $g_\theta(x_s, x_{N_s}) = E_\theta(X_s = x_s, X_{N_s} = x_{N_s})$, therefore

$$\Omega_\theta(\gamma) = \{(x_s, x_{N_s}): E_\theta(X_s = x_s, X_{N_s} = x_{N_s}) = \gamma\} \qquad (2)$$

That is, (x_s, x_{N_s}) in the same level of energy belong to the same micro-pattern.

a) When we use the smooth model, i.e. $E_\theta(X_s, X_{N_s}) = \sum_{t \in N_s} \frac{1}{(\sigma_{st})^2}(X_s - X_t)^2$, then

$$\Omega_\theta(\gamma) = \left\{(x_s, x_{N_s}): \sum_{t \in N_s} \frac{1}{(\sigma_{st})^2}(x_s - x_t)^2 = \gamma\right\} \qquad (3)$$

In this sense, Fig. 2(a) and Fig. 2(b) are deemed to be same, while Fig 2(c) and Fig. 2(d) are deemed to be different micro-patterns.

b) When we use the Ising model, i.e. $H_\theta(X_s|X_{N_s}) = \alpha_s X_s + \sum_{t \in N_s} \beta_{st} X_s X_t$ (with 1-st neighborhood), where $X_s \in \{+1, -1\}, \forall s \in S$ and $\theta = \{\alpha_s, \beta_{st}, t \in N_s\}$ is as shown in Fig.2(e), there is

$$\Omega_\theta(\gamma) = \left\{ (x_s, x_{N_s}) : \alpha_s x_s + \sum_{t \in N_s} \beta_{st} x_s x_t = \gamma \right\} \tag{4}$$

This model can discriminate all the 16 patterns shown in Fig.2(f)~Fig.2(u). Among them, Fig.2(f) is a blob, Fig.2(g)~Fig.2(j) are triangles, Fig.2(k)~Fig.2(n) are corners, Fig.2(o)~Fig.2(p) are lines, Fig.2(q)~Fig.2(t) are arrows, and Fig.2(u) is a ring. From the figure, we can see that the above model has strong capability in describing micro-patterns.

In fact, the micro-patterns defined in Eq.(2) is determined by the model parameters once the model form is given. The more parameters the model has, the more micro-patterns it will discriminate. The micro-pattern designed by the model is adaptive to the local characteristics of the image, since the parameters are statistically learned from the training samples. This is quite different from the intuitively user-designed micro-patterns in Gabor [11,12], LBP [8,9], EOH [4] or FDLE [5].

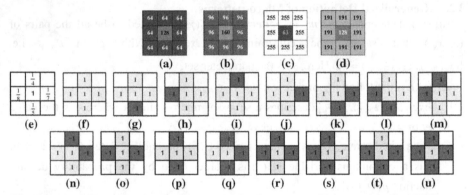

Fig. 2. (a)~(d) Micro-patterns of smooth model. (e) Parameters of Ising model. (f)~(u) Micro-patterns of Ising model.

2.2.2 Fitness Function

Given θ, for any given pair of (X_s, X_{N_s}), we further define the *fitness function* $h_\theta(X_s, X_{N_s})$ as

$$h_\theta(X_s, X_{N_s}) = e^{-\gamma} \big|_{\gamma = g_\theta(X_s, X_{N_s})} \tag{5}$$

Specifically, when $g_\theta(X_s, X_{N_s}) = E_\theta(X_s, X_{N_s})$, there is

$$h_\theta(X_s, X_{N_s}) = e^{-\gamma} \big|_{\gamma = E_\theta(X_s, X_{N_s})} \tag{6}$$

The *fitness index* can be computed by

$$y_{\theta,s} = h_\theta(x_s, x_{N_s}) = e^{-\gamma} \big|_{\gamma = E_\theta(x_s, x_{N_s})} \tag{7}$$

The fitness function detects which micro-pattern the local characteristics of the image at site s fits with. Furthermore, it enlarges the difference between small γ, where there is low potential/energy, and reduces the difference between large γ, where there is high potential/energy.

More importantly, from the definition of micro-pattern (Eq.2) and the Markov random field model (Eq.1), we can derive

$$
\begin{aligned}
P\left(\Omega=\Omega_\theta(\gamma)\right) &= \sum_{X_{N_s}}\left\{P(X_s:E_\theta(X_s,X_{N_s})=\gamma\big|X_{N_s}=x_{N_s})P(X_{N_s}=x_{N_s})\right\} \\
&= \sum_{X_{N_s}}\left\{\left(\sum_{X_s:E_\theta(X_s,X_{N_s})=\gamma}\frac{1}{\mathcal{T}}e^{-\gamma}\right)\cdot P(X_{N_s}=x_{N_s})\right\}, \\
&= \sum_{X_{N_s}}\left\{\frac{1}{\mathcal{T}}\cdot V\cdot e^{-\gamma}\cdot P(X_{N_s}=x_{N_s})\right\} \\
&= Z\cdot e^{-\gamma}
\end{aligned}
\tag{8}
$$

where $\mathcal{T}=\sum_{X_s}\exp\{-E_{\theta_s}(X_s,X_{N_s})\}$ is independent of X_s, V is the number of pairs (X_s,X_{N_s}) which belong to the micro-pattern $\Omega_\theta(\gamma)$ given $X_{N_s}=x_{N_s}$, and $Z=\sum_{X_{N_s}}\left\{\frac{1}{\mathcal{T}}\cdot V\cdot P(X_{N_s}=x_{N_s})\right\}$. Note that both V and $\mathcal{T}$ are only dependent on X_{N_s} and θ, so Z is a constant only dependent on θ. Consequently,

$$
y_{\theta,s}=h_\theta\left(x_s,x_{N_s}\right)\propto P\left(\Omega=\Omega_\theta(\gamma)\big|_{\gamma=E_\theta(X_s=x_s,X_{N_s}=x_{N_s})}\right)
\tag{9}
$$

That is, the fitness index $y_{\theta,s}$ is proportional to the probability of $\Omega_\theta(\gamma)\big|_{\gamma=E_\theta(X_s=x_s,X_{N_s}=x_{N_s})}$. From the perspective of filter design, the fitness function modulates the fitness to the micro-pattern with its probability. It enhances the micro-patterns with low energies which have high probabilities, and depresses those with high energies which have low probabilities. Actually, for a given θ, we design a series of micro-patterns $\{\Omega_\theta(\gamma),\gamma\in\mathcal{R}\}$, and $y_{\theta,s}$ indicates the occurrence probability of the micro-pattern $\Omega_\theta(\gamma)\big|_{\gamma=E_\theta(X_s=x_s,X_{N_s}=x_{N_s})}$ at site s.

The *fitness sequence* can be computed as

$$
y=\left\{y_{\theta,s},s=1,2,...,n\right\},
\tag{10}
$$

where $n=H\times W$ is the number of sites in S.

2.3 Estimation of Model Parameters

The parameters in the MRF Model $\Theta=\{\theta_s,s\in S\}$ are estimated by learning from samples. Suppose there are m independent samples $\{x_j,j=1,2,...,m\}$, where $x_j=\left[x_{j1},x_{j2},...,x_{jn}\right]^T$. The maximum likelihood estimation (MLE) can be treated as the following optimization problem:

$$
\Theta^*=\arg\max_{\Theta}\prod_{j=1}^{m}p_\Theta(X_1=x_{j1},X_2=x_{j2},...,X_n=x_{jn})
\tag{11}
$$

Since there is $p(X_s = x_s | X_{-s} = x_{-s}) = p(X_s = x_s | X_{N_s} = x_{N_s})$, we use the pseudo maximum likelihood estimation (PMLE) for approximation, i.e.

$$\arg\max_{\Theta} \prod_{j=1}^{m} p_{\Theta}(X_1 = x_{j1}, X_2 = x_{j2}, ..., X_n = x_{jn}) \approx \arg\max_{\Theta} \prod_{j=1}^{m} \prod_{s=1}^{n} p_{\theta_s}(X_s = x_{js} | X_{N_s} = x_{jN_s}) \quad , \quad (12)$$

which is equivalent to

$$\Theta^* \approx \arg\max_{\Theta} \sum_{j=1}^{m} \sum_{s=1}^{n} \log\left(p_{\theta_s}(X_s = x_{js} | X_{N_s} = x_{jN_s}) \right) \quad (13)$$

Especially, when we use the smooth model, it can be treated as the following optimization problem: (for generality, we use the continuous form)

$$\arg\max_{\Theta} \sum_{j=1}^{m} \sum_{s=1}^{n} \left\{ -\sum_{t \in N_s} \frac{1}{(\sigma_{st})^2}(x_{js} - x_{jt})^2 - \log\left[\int_a^b e^{-\sum_{t \in N_s} \frac{1}{(\sigma_{st})^2}(x_{js}-x_{jt})^2} dx_{js} \right] \right\} , \quad (14)$$

where $[a,b]$ is the value interval of x_{js}. If we further assume that the Markov random field is homogenous and isotropic, i.e. $\sigma_{st} = \sigma$, $\forall s \in S$, $\forall t \in N_s$, then it is equivalent to find the optimal σ which maximizes the following function:

$$\sum_{j=1}^{m} \sum_{s=1}^{n} \left[-\sum_{t \in N_s} \frac{1}{\sigma^2}(x_{js} - x_{jt})^2 \right] - \sum_{j=1}^{m} \sum_{s=1}^{n} \left\{ \frac{\sqrt{\pi}}{2} \exp\left(\frac{-4\zeta_{js} + (\psi_{js})^2}{4\sigma^2} \right) erf\left(\frac{2x_{js} - \psi_{js}}{2\sigma} \right) \sigma \Big|_{x_{js}=a}^{x_{js}=b} \right\} , \quad (15)$$

where $\psi_{js} = 2\sum_{t \in N_s} x_{jt}$, $\zeta_{js} = \sum_{t \in N_s}(x_{jt})^2$, $erf(x) = \frac{2}{\sqrt{\pi}} \int_0^x \exp(-t^2)dt$. Then we can use the large scale algorithm to find the optimal σ.

3   Algorithm

The new algorithm includes three stages:

1) We first divide the pre-aligned image into C sub-blocks (Fig.3a) with the size of $N \times M$ and the overlapping of $L \times K$. For each sub-block, we independently use MRF to model the attributes $x^{(i)} (i = 1, 2, ..., C)$. For simplicity, we use a homogenous model in the block, i.e. the model parameters are the same in the same block. In the training stage, we learn the model parameters for each sub-block $\theta^{(i)} (i = 1, 2, ..., C)$ from a set of pre-aligned training images $\{x_j^{(i)}, j = 1, 2, ..., m\}$ by using Eq.(16):

$$\theta^{(i)*} \approx \arg\max_{\theta^{(i)}} \sum_{j=1}^{m} \sum_{s=1}^{l} \log\left(p_{\theta^{(i)}}(X_s = x_{js}^{(i)} | X_{N_s} = x_{jN_s}^{(i)}) \right), \text{ where } l = N \times M, i = 1, 2, ..., C \quad (16)$$

Once the parameters are learned, we derive a series of micro-patterns for each block which fits best with the observations from the training samples. In the testing stage, we compute the local fitness sequence of the test image in each sub-block $y^{(i)} (i = 1, 2, ..., C)$ by using Eq.(17).

$$y^{(i)} = \left\{ y_{\theta^{(i)},s}, s=1,2,...,l \right\}, \text{ where } y_{\theta^{(i)},s} = h_{\theta^{(i)}}\left(x_s^{(i)}, x_{N_s}^{(i)}\right) = e^{-\gamma}\Big|_{\gamma = E_{\theta^{(i)}}(x_s^{(i)}, x_{N_s}^{(i)})}, i=1,2,...,C \quad (17)$$

2) After that, we further extract a modified FFT feature (MFFT) of the local fitness sequence in each sub-block to reduce both dimensionality and noise (Fig.3b). The low-frequency components of the local fitness sequence are maintained, while the high-frequency components are averaged. If $y^{(i)}$ denotes the local fitness sequence of the i-th block, and $z^{(i)} = FFT(y^{(i)})$, where $z^{(i)} = \left\{ z_s^{(i)}, s=1,2,...,l \right\}$, then $u^{(i)} = \left\{ u_s^{(i)}, s=1,2,...,k+1 \right\}$, where

$$u_s^{(i)} = \begin{cases} z_s^{(i)}, & s=1,2,...,k \\ \dfrac{1}{l-k}\displaystyle\sum_{t=k+1}^{l} z_t^{(i)}, & s=k+1 \end{cases} \quad (18)$$

and k is the truncation length.

3) Finally, we concatenate $u^{(i)} (i=1,2,...,C)$ from all sub-blocks as follows to form the MRF-based micro-structural feature, whose length is $C\times(k+1)$ (Fig.3b):

$$u = \left[u^{(1)}, u^{(2)}, ..., u^{(C)} \right]^T \quad (19)$$

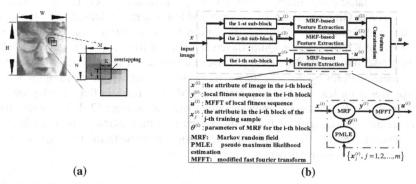

Fig. 3. (a) Block-level representation. (b) MRF-based micro-structural feature extraction.

4 Comparison with Related Works

From above, we can see that, by dividing the pre-aligned image into small sub-blocks and assuming a homogenous model in the block, a series of micro-patterns which fits best with the observations of the block are designed for each sub-block. The occurrence probability of micro-patterns is computed site by site in each sub-block to form a sequence whose MFFT features are extracted to reflect the regional characteristics of its corresponding micro-patterns. All the modified FFT features from all sub-blocks are concatenated together to efficiently represent the image.

The new feature has the following traits:

a) *It is a micro-structural feature.* Compared with the holistic features such as PCA (principal component analysis) [25], the new feature models the local spatial dependence and designs micro-patterns, while the holistic features extract the global characteristics of the image. Therefore, the new feature is more capable in capturing spatial context, which plays an important role in many vision tasks, such as face recognition and character recognition.

b) *It designs adaptive micro-patterns.* Compared with other feature extraction methods based on micro-patterns, such as EOH [4], LBP [8,9], and FDLE [5], the micro-patterns in the new feature are adaptively designed by using MRF model, rather than intuitively user-defined in these previous features. The type of micro-patterns is learned from training samples, so it is adaptive to different images, different attributes, and different sites.

c) *It is a model-based feature.* Compared with learning-based features by designing learning-based filters, such as LFA (local feature analysis) [22] and ICA (independent component analysis) [23], the new feature models the local spatial context directly, and thereby designs finer and more delicate micro-patterns than the previous features. In contrast, the filters in LFA or ICA are actually global feature projection vectors. The locality of filters is obtained by the least independence or least correlation between the filter responses. So it is less expressive in micro-structure than the new feature.

Another related paper might be Liu's work [21]. In that paper, Liu et al. built an inhomogeneous Gibbs model for face shape which is a set of linked key points, and they selected features by finding the optimal set of projection vectors which minimizes the KL divergence. Quite differently, in our paper, we use Markov random field to model the spatial dependence between attributes of neighboring sites, and we design micro-patterns by learning the model parameters from training samples.

Some works on learning image priors using Markov random field can be found in texture analysis [26], image denoising and image inpainting [27]. However, these papers model the statistics of the whole image and they manage to find filters for sparse coding, rather than explicitly defining micro-patterns to extract micro-structural feature as in our paper.

5 Experiments

5.1 Training MRF Model and the Flexibility of MRF Model

To demonstrate the flexibility of the MRF model, we collect 2 training libraries to train the MRF model. The training libraries are from a standard face database: BANCA dataset [24], which contains 52 subjects with 120 images for each subject. Among them, 5 images/subject in Session 1 are used for training models. Using the 260 images, two training libraries are marked as follows. The first library is the grayscale intensity of the 260 faces, which are cropped and normalized to the size of 55×51 based on the automatic registration of eyes. The second library is the Gabor attributes [12] of the same cropped faces, using a bank of Gabor filters with 2 scales and 4 orientations (wave-length: $\lambda_\varphi \in \{6.5, 6.5\sqrt{2}\}$, orientation: $\phi_\mu \in \{0, \pi/4, \pi/2, 3\pi/4\}$).

We use the block-level representation in Sec. 3, and the pseudo maximum likelihood estimation (Eq.17) is utilized to train models respectively on the two libraries. A homogeneous and isotropic smooth model with 1-st order neighborhood structure is independently used for each sub-block as an example. The block size is $M = N = 5$ with $K = L = 2$. The model parameters are shown in Fig. 4. Higher intensity represents larger value, and vice versa.

From the figure, we can see that the MRF model is adaptive and flexible in at least three aspects. Firstly, it is adaptive to the intrinsic pattern of images. It is interesting to note that Fig. 4(b) manifests a facial-style pattern, since the model parameter varies with the local characteristics in the image. Secondly, the model is adaptive to different sites of the image. As Fig. 4(b) shows, the parameter varies with the site of the sub-block, which takes big value when there is big variation in the sub-block, and takes small value when the variation is small. Thirdly, the model is adaptive to different attributes of the image. If we choose the attribute as grayscale intensity, the distribution of model parameter is shown in Fig. 4(b). While if we choose the Gabor attribute, the distribution of parameter is shown in Fig. 4(d), which shows the same characteristic in orientation and scale as the Gabor attribute in Fig. 4(c). All these demonstrate that the new feature is flexible due to the strong flexibility of model.

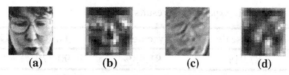

(a)   (b)   (c)   (d)

Fig. 4. Parameters of the MRF model. (a) Grayscale intensity of an example image. (b) Parameters of MRF model on grayscale intensity. (c) Gabor attribute of an example image. $\lambda_{\varphi} = 6.5$, $\phi_{\mu} = \pi / 4$. (d) Parameters of MRF model on Gabor attribute.

5.2 Effectiveness of MRF Modeling in Feature Extraction

To evaluate the effectiveness of our new feature, we conduct tests on two applications, face identification and glasses detection.

5.2.1 Face Identification
In face identification, two groups of experiments are implemented. The first group is conducted to test whether using MRF to model micro-structure on grayscale intensity really helps in identifying faces from different persons. In the tests, we first compare the new feature using MRF model on grayscale intensity with the original grayscale feature, and then compare it with Gabor feature which has been successfully used in face recognition. The second group is conducted to test if this micro-structure modeling could also be useful for Gabor attribute.

The test database is the BANCA dataset [24]. MC test configuration is employed, thereby 5 images/subject in Session 1 are used for training, and the other 35 images/subject in Session 1~4 are used for testing. Each image is preprocessed in the same way as in Sec. 5.1.

In the first group of experiments, three kinds of features are extracted and compared. They are: 1) the original grayscale intensity without MRF modeling (in abbr. Grayscale); 2) the new feature using MRF model on grayscale intensity which has been trained by the first training library in Sec. 5.1 (in abbr. Grayscale+MRF); and 3) the Gabor feature similar to Liu &Wechsler [12] (in abbr. Gabor). Here, the same bank of Gabor filters as in Sec.5.1 is used. Then PCA [25] is applied on the respective three kinds of features for compression and noise suppression. At last, nearest neighborhood decision with L1 distance is used for classification. Here, we set $M = N = 5$, $K = L = 2$, and $k = 3$. Results are given in Fig.5(a) and Table 1.

To further analyze whether the MRF modeling could be useful for Gabor attribute, we extract the new feature using MRF model on Gabor attribute (Gabor+MRF). We use the same scheme in preprocessing, feature compression, and classification as in the first group of experiments. The difference is that a two-stage concatenation is implemented. That is, the MRF-based feature extraction is first implemented on each scale and each orientation of Gabor attribute in each sub-block, and then the features on all scales and all orientations in one block are concatenated into a feature vector for the sub-block. Finally the features from all sub-blocks are concatenated again to form the complete feature set on the whole image. Here, the same bank of Gabor filters as in Sec. 5.1 are used. The MRF model is trained by the second training library in Sec.5.1 with $M = N = 5$, $K = L = 2$, $k = 3$. The original Gabor attribute (in abbr. Gabor) is used as a baseline for comparison. Experimental results are shown in Fig. 5(b) and Table 1.

Table 1. Experimental results on face identification

Feature	Grayscale	Grayscale+MRF	Gabor	Gabor+MRF
Accuracy Rate	87.91%	**91.98%**	90.77%	**93.90%**

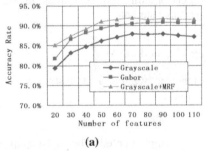
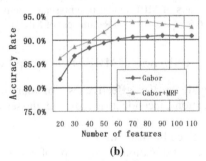

(a)   (b)

Fig. 5. Experiments in face identification. (a) Performance of MRF-based feature on grayscale intensity. (b) Performance of MRF-based feature on Gabor attribute.

From the above experimental results, we can observe three facts:

1) MRF modeling does help improve the performance on face identification. On grayscale intensity, the error rate is reduced by 33.66% after using MRF model. This shows that by using MRF to model the micro-structure in the image, the performance is considerably improved. This is because of two reasons. The first is that MRF is good at modeling spatial dependence between neighboring sites. The second is that the micro-structural features are useful for face identification.

2) If we further compare the three features in the first group of experiments, we can find out that, in our experiments, the MRF-based feature on only grayscale intensity outperforms the Gabor feature, which manifests good performance in many applications. This is important in two aspects. Firstly, although Gabor filter has been widely used in many applications, it remains difficult to find suitable parameters for the method. Compared with Gabor, most of the parameters in the new feature extraction method are learned from training samples, rather than adjusted by experimental results. Secondly, extracting Gabor feature is still time-consuming, however the MRF-based feature extraction on grayscale intensity is much faster.

3) MRF modeling is also useful for Gabor attribute. By using MRF modeling on Gabor attribute, Gabor+MRF achieves the highest performance, 93.90% accuracy rate on the BANCA dataset. This shows that the new feature extraction approach can be applied not only on grayscale intensity, but also on other attributes, if it can be modeled as a Markov field.

5.2.2 Glasses Detection

To further demonstrate the effectiveness of MRF modeling in feature extraction, experiments on glasses detection are also conducted. Images are collected from the complete BANCA dataset, which ranges from constrained scenario to degraded and adverse scenarios. In total, 2769 images of eyes wearing glasses and 3261 images without glasses are collected. Among them, 125 images wearing glasses and 185 images without glasses are used for training, and the remaining images are used for testing. All images are cropped and normalized to the size of 27×51 based on the automatic registration of eyes. Note that in the probe set there is no sun-glasses, and many glasses have no obvious edge, which makes it rather difficult to determine if there are glasses. Example images are shown in Fig.6. Such kind of grayscale images are chosen to test whether the minor change caused by glasses could be detected by the new feature.

(a)   (b)

Fig. 6. (a) Example images of eyes wearing glasses. (b) Example images of eyes with no glasses.

Two groups of comparison are also conducted via similar procedure as Sec. 5.2.1. The block size is $M = N = 5$ with $K = L = 2$. The results are given in Fig. 7 and Table 2, where the overall accuracy rate on both glasses and no-glasses are reported.

From the table and the figures, we can see that although it is rather difficult to detect the minor changes caused by glasses, MRF does help in this challenging task. By using MRF model, the classification accuracy is greatly improved, from 70.61% to 78.11% on grayscale intensity, and 34.30% improvement on Gabor attribute. Again, MRF-based feature on grayscale intensity is better than Gabor feature, and MRF-based feature on Gabor attribute is the best among the 4 kinds of features. This

Table 2. Experimental results on glasses detection

Feature	Grayscale	Grayscale+MRF	Gabor	Gabor+MR
Accuracy Rate	70.61%	**78.11%**	74.84%	**83.47%**

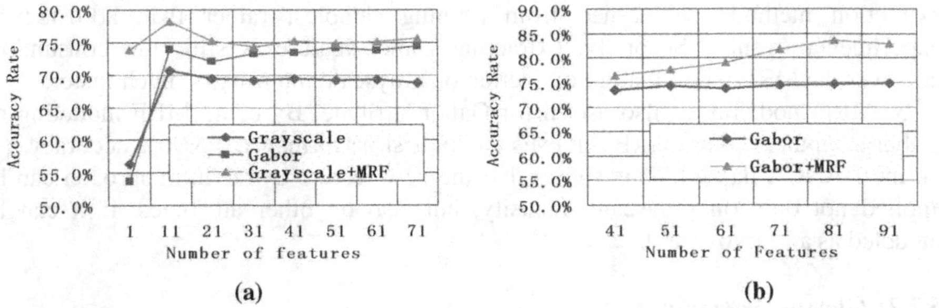

(a)   (b)

Fig. 7. Experiments in glasses detection. (a) Performance of MRF-based feature on grayscale intensity. (b) Performance of MRF-based feature on Gabor attribute.

demonstrates that the new feature extraction approach has good flexibility, and its application is not limited to one single specific area.

6   Discussions

a) Why do we build the model in the sub-block?

There are mainly two reasons. The first is that the regional characteristic in the sub-block is more robust to shift and scale. The second is that it will be much simpler than building the model on the whole image. In the meanwhile, the spatial dependence between two sites generally decreases drastically when their distance exceeds the block size.

b) Why do we use the pseudo-maximum likelihood estimation (PMLE)?

The true maximum likelihood estimation (MLE) can be regarded as a NP-hard optimization problem and it is very hard to find the solution, so PMLE is adopted for approximation. Actually, the estimation from PMLE follows the asymptotic normal distribution whose expectation is the true parameter value.

c) Why do we compare our algorithm with the Gabor feature?

Firstly, Gabor feature has been successfully used in many applications such as face recognition, character recognition, and texture analysis, so we are trying to find some other features beyond Gabor filter. Secondly, most current works find the parameters for Gabor filter through experimental results, which is time-consuming.

7   Conclusions

In this paper, a new algorithm is proposed to use micro-structure modeling for feature extraction, where the micro-structure in the image is modeled by Markov random field, and the model parameters are learned from the training samples. Therefore the micro-patterns are adaptively designed according to the spatial context of images. That is, the micro-patterns are adaptive to various images, various attributes, and various sites.

The paper only discusses methods in feature extraction, rather than feature projection or feature selection. So it can be combined with LDA (linear discriminate analysis) or other discriminant learning algorithms to further improve the discrimination capability of features.

The new algorithm is a model-based feature extraction method. The introduction of Markov random field in the stage of feature extraction enables us to move a step towards modeling micro-patterns for feature extraction. Although this is an initial work, it shows some interesting results:

1) Modeling the micro-structure does help find better features.
2) The new micro-structural feature on grayscale intensity is better than Gabor feature on our experiments, and it is also much faster than Gabor feature.
3) The new algorithm could be applied on various attributes, not only on grayscale intensity, but also on Gabor attribute. It can also be used in a variety of applications, not limited to one single specific area.

Future work will be using better MRF models for feature extraction. Another important direction is more theoretical work on how to extract features based on the model. In addition, we will test the performance of these new algorithms on more applications.

References

1. Sun C. and Si D.: Fast Reflectional Symmetry Detection Using Orientation Histograms. Real-Time Imaging, Vol. 5, 1999, pp. 63-74.
2. Freeman W. and Roth M.: Orientation histogram for hand gesture recognition. Intl. Workshop on Automatic Face- and Gesture- Recognition, June, 1995, pp. 296-301.
3. Lowe D. G.: Object recognition from local scale-invariant features. ICCV, 1999, pp.1150-1157.
4. Levi K. and Weiss Y.: Learning Object Detection from a Small Number of Examples: the Importance of Good Features. CVPR, 2004, pp. 53-60.
5. Kato N., Omachi S., Aso H., and Nemoto Y.: A handwritten character recognition system using directional element feature and asymmetric Mahalanobis distance. PAMI,21(3),1999,pp.258-262.
6. Guodail F., Lange E., and Iwamoto T.: Face Recognition System Using Local Autocorrelations and Multiscale Integration, IEEE Trans. on PAMI, Vol. 18, No. 10, Oct. 1996, pp. 1024-1028.
7. Wang X.W., Ding X.Q., and Liu C.S.: Optimized Gabor Filter Based Feature Extraction for Character Recognition. ICPR, 2002, pp. 223-226.
8. Ojala T., Pietikäinen M., and Mäenpää T.: Multiresolution Gray-scale and Rotation Invariant Texture Classification with Local Binary Patterns. IEEE Trans. PAMI, Vol.24, 2002,pp.971-987.
9. Hadid A., Pietikäinen M., and Ahonen T.: A Discriminative Feature Space for Detecting and Recognizing Faces. CVPR, 2004, pp. 797-804.

10. Feichtinger H. G. and Strohmer T.: Gabor analysis and algorithms: theory and applications. Boston: Birkhauser, 1998.
11. Lades M., Vorbürggen J.C., Buhmann J., Lange J., Malsburg C., Würtz R.P., and Konen W.: Distortion invariant object recognition in the dynamic link architecture.IEEE Trans. Computers, Vol. 42, No. 3, 1993, pp.300-311.
12. Liu C. and Wechsler H.: Gabor feature based classification using the enhanced fisher linear discriminant model for face recognition. IEEE Trans. Image Processing, 11(4),2002, pp.467-476.
13. Chellappa, R. and Jain A.K.: editors. Markov Random Fields: Theory and Application. Academic Press, Inc., 1991.
14. Guyon, X.: Random Fields on a Network. Springer-Verlag, 1995.
15. Li S.Z.: Markov Random Field Modeling in Computer Vision. Springer-Verlag Tokyo, 1996
16. Cox D.R. and Reid N.: A Note on Pseudolikelihood Constructed from Marginal Densities. Biometrika, Vol. 91, 2004. pp. 729-737.
17. Huang R., Pavlovic V., and Metaxas D.N.: A Graphical Model Framework for Coupling MRFs and Deformable Models. CVPR, 2004, pp.739-746.
18. Panjwani D. and Healey G.: Markov Random Field Models for Unsupervised Segmentation of Textured Color Images. IEEE Trans. on PAMI. Vol. 17, No. 10, 1995, pp. 939-954.
19. Dass S.C. and Jain A.K.: Markov Face Models. ICCV, 2001, pp. 680-687.
20. Varma M. and Zisserman A.: Texture classification: are filter banks necessary? CVRR, June 2003, pp. 18-20.
21. Liu C., Zhu S. C., and Shum H.-Y.: Learning inhomogeneous Gibbs model of faces by minimax entropy. ICCV, 2001, pp. 281-287.
22. Penev P. S. and Atick. J. J.: Local feature analysis: a general statistical theory for object representation. Network: Computation in Neural Systems, Vol.7, No.3, Mar 1996, pp. 477-500.
23. Bartlett M, S., Movellan J, R., and Sejnowski T. J.: Face recognition by independent component analysis. IEEE Trans. On Neural Networks. Vol. 13, No. 6, Nov. 2002, pp. 1450-1464.
24. Bailly-Bailliére E., Bengio S., Bimbot F., Hamouz M., Kittler J., Mariéthoz J., Matas J., Messer K., Popovici V., Porée F., Ruiz B., and Thiran J.-P.: The BANCA Database and Evaluation Protocol. AVBPA, 2003, pp. 625-638.
25. Turk M. and Pentland A.: Face Recognition Using Eigenfaces. CVPR, 1991, pp. 586-591.
26. Zhu S., Wu Y., and Mumford D.: Filters, random fields and maximum entropy (FRAME): Towards a unified theory for texture modeling. IJCV, Vol.27, No.2, 1998, pp.107-126.
27. Roth S. and Black M.J.: Fields of Experts: A Framework for Learning Image Priors. To appear in CVPR2005.

Facial Expression Analysis Using Nonlinear Decomposable Generative Models

Chan-Su Lee and Ahmed Elgammal

Computer Science, Rutgers University,
Piscataway NJ 08854, USA
{chansu, elgammal}@cs.rutgers.edu

Abstract. We present a new framework to represent and analyze dynamic facial motions using a decomposable generative model. In this paper, we consider facial expressions which lie on a one dimensional closed manifold, i.e., start from some configuration and coming back to the same configuration, while there are other sources of variability such as different classes of expression, and different people, etc., all of which are needed to be parameterized. The learned model supports tasks such as facial expression recognition, person identification, and synthesis. We aim to learn a generative model that can generate different dynamic facial appearances for different people and for different expressions. Given a single image or a sequence of images, we can use the model to solve for the temporal embedding, expression type and person identification parameters. As a result we can directly infer intensity of facial expression, expression type, and person identity from the visual input. The model can successfully be used to recognize expressions performed by different people never seen during training. We show experiment results for applying the framework for simultaneous face and facial expression recognition.

Sub-categories: 1.1 Novel algorithms, 1.6 Others: modeling facial expression.

1   Introduction

The appearance of a face performing a facial expression is an example of a dynamic appearance that has global and local deformations. There are two interesting components in dynamic facial expressions: face identity (face geometry and appearance characterizing the person) and facial motion (deformation of face geometry through the expression and its temporal characteristics). There has been extensive research related to face recognition [24] emanating from interest in applications in security and visual surveillance. Most of face recognition systems focused on still face images, i.e., capturing identity through facial geometry and appearance. There have been also interests on expression invariant face recognition [15,14,2]. Individual differences of facial expression like expressiveness can be useful as a biometric to enhance accuracy in face recognition [8]. On the other hand, facial expression analysis gain interest in computer vision with applications in human emotion analysis for HCI and affective computing. Most studies of facial expression recognition have focused on static display of intense expressions even though facial dynamics are important in interpreting facial expression precisely [1].

W. Zhao, S. Gong, and X. Tang (Eds.): AMFG 2005, LNCS 3723, pp. 17–31, 2005.

Our objective in this paper is to learn dynamic models for facial expressions that enable simultaneous recognition of faces and facial expressions. We learn a dynamic generative model that factors out different face appearance corresponding to different people and in the same time parameterizes different expressions.

Despite the high dimensionality of the image space in facial expressions, facial motions lie intrinsically on much lower dimensional subspaces. Therefore, researchers have tried to exploit subspace analysis in face recognition and facial expression analysis. PCA has been widely used in appearance modeling to discover subspaces for face appearance variations as in [21,10]. When dealing with dynamic facial expressions, image data lie on low dimensional nonlinear manifolds embedded in the high dimensional input space. Embedding expression manifolds to low dimensional spaces provides a way to explicitly model such manifolds. Linear subspace analysis can achieve a linear embedding of the motion manifold in a subspace. However, the dimensionality of the subspace depends on the variations in the data and not on the intrinsic dimensionality of the manifold. Nonlinear dimensionality reduction approaches can achieve much lower dimensionality embedding of nonlinear manifolds through changing the metric from the original space to the embedding space based on local structure of the manifold, e.g. [17,19]. Nonlinear dimensionality reduction has been recently exploited to model the manifold structure in face recognition, facial expression analysis [3]. However, all these approaches (linear and nonlinear) are data-driven, i.e., the visual input is used to model motion manifolds. The resulting embeddings are data-driven and, therefore, the resulting embedded manifolds vary due to person facial geometry, appearance, facial deformation, and dynamics in facial expressions, which affect collectively the appearance of facial expressions. The embedding of the same facial expression performed by different people will be quite different and it is hard to find a unified representation of the manifold. But, conceptually all these manifolds (for the same expression) are the same. We can think of it as the same expression manifold which is twisted differently in the input space based on person's facial appearance. They are all topologically equivalent, i.e., homeomorphic to each other and we can establish a bijection between any pair of them. Therefore, we utilize a conceptual manifold representation to model facial expression configuration and learn mappings between the conceptual unified representation and each individual data manifold.

Different factors affect the face appearance. There had been efforts to decompose multiple factors affecting appearance from face and facial expression data. Bilinear models were applied to decompose person-dependent factor and the pose-dependent factor as the style and content from pose-aligned face images of different people [20] and facial expression synthesis [4]. Multilinear analysis, or higher-order singular value decomposition [11], were applied to aligned face images with variation of people, illumination and expression factors and applied for face recognition [22]. In this model, face images are decomposed into tensor multiplication of different people basis, illumination basis and expression basis. Facial expressions were also analyzed using multilinear analysis for feature space similar to active appearance model to recognize face and facial expression simultaneously [23]. All these approaches have limitations in capturing nonlinearity of facial expression as the subspaces are expansion of linear subspace of facial images. In addition, all these approaches deal with static facial expressions and do not model dynamics in facial expression.

In this paper, we learn nonlinear mappings between a conceptual embedding space and facial expression image space and decompose the mapping space using multilinear analysis. The mapping between sequences of facial expression and embedding points contains characteristics of the data invariant to temporal variations and change with different people facial expression and different types of facial expressions. We decompose the mapping space into person face appearance factor, which is person dependent and consistent for each person, and expression factor, which depends on expression type and common to all people with the same expression. In addition, we explicitly decompose the intrinsic face configuration during the expression, as a function of time in the embedding space, from other conceptually orthogonal factors such as facial expressions and person face appearances. As a result, we learn a nonlinear generative model of facial expression with modeling dynamics in low dimensional embedding space and decomposing of multiple factors in facial expressions.

Contribution: In this paper we consider facial expressions which lie on a one dimensional closed manifold, i.e., start from some configuration and coming back to the same configuration. We introduce a framework to learn decomposable generative models for dynamic appearance of facial expressions where the motion is constrained to one dimensional closed manifolds while there are other sources of variability such as different classes of expression, and different people, etc., all of which are needed to be parameterized. The learned model supports tasks such as facial expression recognition, person identification, and synthesis. Given a single image or a sequence of images, we can use the model to solve for the temporal embedding, expression type and person identification parameters. As a result we can directly infer intensity of facial expression, expression type, and person face from the visual input. The model can successfully be used to recognize expressions performed by different people never seen in the training.

2   Facial Expression Manifolds and Nonlinear Decomposable Generative Models

We investigate low dimensional manifolds and propose conceptual manifold embedding as a representation of facial expression dynamics in Sec. 2.1. In order to preserve nonlinearity of facial expression in our generative model, we learn nonlinear mapping between embedding space and image space of facial expression in Sec. 2.2. The decomposable compact parameterization of the generative model is achieved using multilinear analysis of the mapping coefficients in Sec. 2.3.

2.1   Facial Expression Manifolds and Conceptual Manifold Embedding

We use conceptual manifold embedding for facial expressions as a uniform representation of facial expression manifolds. Conceptually, each expression sequence forms a one-dimensional closed trajectory in the input space as the expression starts from a neutral face and comes back to the neutral face. Data-driven low dimensional manifolds using nonlinear dimensionality reduction algorithms such as LLE [17] and Isomap [19] vary in different people and in different expression types. Fig. 1 shows low dimensional manifold representation of facial expression sequences when we applied LLE to high dimensional vector representations of image sequences of facial expressions. The facial expression data with twice repetitions of the same type expression are captured and normalized for each person as shown in Fig. 1 (a) and (b). Fig. 1 (c) and (d) show the manifolds found by applying the LLE algorithm. The manifolds are elliptical curves with distortions according to the person face and expressions. Isomap and other nonlinear dimensionality reduction algorithms show similar results. Sometimes the manifold does not show smooth curves due to noise in the tracking data and images. In addition, the embedding manifolds can be very different in some case. It is hard to find representations comparable each manifold for multiple expression styles and expression types. Conceptually, however, all data driven manifolds are equal. They are all topologically equivalent, i.e., homeomorphic to each other, and to a circular curve. Therefore, we can use the unit circle in 2D space as a conceptual embedding space for facial expressions.

A set of image sequences which represent a full cycle of the facial expressions are used in conceptual embedding of facial expressions. Each image sequence is of a certain person with a certain expression. Each person has multiple expression image sequences. The image sequences are not necessarily to be of the same length. We denote each sequence by $Y^{se} = \{y_1^{se} \cdots y_{N_{se}}^{se}\}$ where e denotes the expression label and s is person

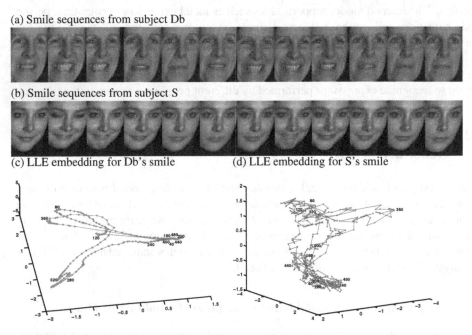

(a) Smile sequences from subject Db

(b) Smile sequences from subject S

(c) LLE embedding for Db's smile   (d) LLE embedding for S's smile

Fig. 1. Facial expression manifolds in different subjects: (a) and (b): Facial expression image sequences. (2 cycles 480 frames):40th, 80th, 120th, 160th, 200th, 240th, 280th, 320th, 360th, 400th, 440th, 480th frames. (c) and (d): Nonlinear manifold embeddings of facial expression sequences by LLE.

face label. Let N_e and N_s denote the number of expressions and the number of people respectively, i.e., there are $N_s \times N_e$ sequences. Each sequence is temporally embedded at equidistance on a unit circle such that $x_i^{se} = [cos(2\pi i/N_{se})\ sin(2\pi i/N_{se})], i = 1 \cdots N_{se}$. Notice that by temporal embedding on a unit circle we do not preserve the metric in input space. Rather, we preserve the topology of the manifold.

2.2 Nonlinear Mapping Between Embedding Space and Image Space

Nonlinear mapping between embedding space and image space can be achieved through raidal basis function interpolation [6]. Given a set of distinctive representative and arbitrary points $\{z_i \in \mathbb{R}^2, i = 1 \cdots N\}$ we can define an empirical kernel map[18] as $\psi_N(x) : \mathbb{R}^2 \rightarrow \mathbb{R}^N$ where

$$\psi_N(x) = [\phi(x, z_1), \cdots, \phi(x, z_N)]^\mathsf{T}, \tag{1}$$

given a kernel function $\phi(\cdot)$. For each input sequence Y^{se} and its embedding X^{se} we can learn a nonlinear mapping function $f^{se}(x)$ that satisfies $f^{se}(x_i) = y_i, i = 1 \cdots N_{se}$ and minimizes a regularized risk criteria. Such function admits a representation of the form

$$f(x) = \sum_{i=1}^{N} w_i \phi(x, z_i),$$

i.e., the whole mapping can be written as

$$f^{se}(x) = B^{se} \cdot \psi(x) \tag{2}$$

where B is a $d \times N$ coefficient matrix. If radial symmetric kernel function is used, we can think of equation 2 as a typical Generalized Radial basis function (GRBF) interpolation [16] where each row in the matrix B represents the interpolation coefficients for corresponding element in the input. i.e., we have d simultaneous interpolation functions each from 2D to 1D. The mapping coefficients can be obtained by solving the linear system

$$[y_1^{se} \cdots y_{N_{se}}^{se}] = B^{se}[\psi(x_1^{se}) \cdots \psi(x_{N_{se}}^{se})]$$

Where the left hand side is a $d \times N_{se}$ matrix formed by stacking the images of sequence se column wise and the right hand side matrix is an $N \times N_{se}$ matrix formed by stacking kernel mapped vectors. Using these nonlinear mapping, we can capture nonlinearity of facial expression in different people and expressions. More details about fitting the model can be found in [6].

2.3 Decomposition of Nonlinear Mapping Space

Each nonlinear mapping is affected by multiple factors such as expressions and person faces. Mapping coefficients can be arranged into high order tensor according to expression type and person face. We applied multilinear tensor analysis to decompose the mapping into multiple orthogonal factors. This is a generalization of the nonlinear style and content decomposition as introduced in [7]. Multilinear analysis can be achieved by higher-order singular value decomposition (HOSVD) with *unfolding*, which is a generalization of singular value decomposition (SVD) [11]. Each of the coefficient matrices $B^{se} = [b_1 b_2 \cdots b_N]$ can be represented as a coefficient vector b^{se} by column stacking (stacking its columns above each other to form a vector). Therefore, b^{se} is an $N_c = d \cdot N$ dimensional vector. All the coefficient vectors can then be arranged in an order-three facial expression coefficient tensor $\mathcal{B}$ with dimensionality $N_s \times N_e \times N_c$. The coefficient tensor is then decomposed as

$$\mathcal{B} = \mathcal{Z} \times_1 S \times_2 E \times_3 F \tag{3}$$

where S is the mode-1 basis of $\mathcal{B}$, which represents the orthogonal basis for the person face. Similarly, E is the mode-2 basis representing the orthogonal basis of the expression and F represents the basis for the mapping coefficient space. The dimensionality of these matrices are $N_s \times N_s$, $N_e \times N_e$, $N_c \times N_c$ for S, E and F respectively. $\mathcal{Z}$ is a core tensor, with dimensionality $N_s \times N_e \times N_c$ which governs the interactions among different mode basis matrices. Similar to PCA, it is desired to reduce the dimensionality for each of the orthogonal spaces to retain a subspace representation. This can be achieved by applying higher-order orthogonal iteration for dimensionality reduction [12].

Given this decomposition and given any N_s dimensional person face vector s and any N_e dimensional expression vector e we can generate coefficient matrix B^{se} by unstacking the vector b^{se} obtained by tensor product $b^{se} = \mathcal{Z} \times_1 s \times_2 e$. Therefore we can generate any specific instant of the expression by specifying the configuration parameter x_t through the kernel map defined in equation 1. Therefore, the whole model for generating image y_t^{se} can be expressed as

$$y_t^{se} = unstacking(\mathcal{Z} \times_1 s \times_2 e) \cdot \psi(x_t) \, .$$

This can be expressed abstractly also in the generative form by arranging the tensor $\mathcal{Z}$ into a order-four tensor $\mathcal{C}$

$$y_t = \mathcal{C} \times_1 s \times_2 e \times_3 \psi(x) \times_4 L \, , \tag{4}$$

where dimensionality of core tensor $\mathcal{C}$ is $N_s \times N_e \times N \times d$, $\psi(x)$ is a basis vector for kernel mapping with dimension N for given x and L is collection of basis vectors of all pixel elements with dimension $d \times d$. We can analyze facial expression image sequence by estimation of the parameters in this generative model.

3   Facial Expression Analysis and Synthesis Using Generative Models

There are two main approaches in representing facial motions for facial expression analysis: model-based or appearance-based. Geometric features are extracted with the aid of 2D or 3D face models in model-based approaches. 3D deformable generic face model [5] or multistate facial component models [13] are used to extract facial features. Active appearance model are employed to use both shape and textures in [10][23]. Our generative model use pixel intensity itself as an appearance representation as we want, not only to analyze, but also to synthesize facial expressions in the image space. The final representation of facial expressions in our generative model, however, is a compact person face vector and an expression vector that are invariant to temporal characteristics and low dimensional embedding that represents temporal characteristics.

The generative model supports both sequence-based and frame-based recognition of facial expressions. Facial expression recognition system can be categorized into frame-based and sequence-based methods [8] according to the use of temporal information. In frame-based methods, the input image is treated independently either a static image or a frame of a sequence. Frame-based method does not use temporal information in the recognition process. In sequence-based methods, the HMMs are frequently used to utilize temporal information in facial expression recognition [5]. In our generative model, the temporal characteristics are modeled in low dimensional conceptual manifolds and we can utilize the temporal characteristics of the whole sequence by analyzing facial expression based on the mapping between the low dimensional embedding and the whole image sequence. We also provide methods to estimate expression parameters and face parameters from single static image.

3.1 Preprocessing: Cropping and Normalizing Face Images

The alignment and normalization of captured faces using a standard face is an important preprocessing in facial expression recognition to achieve robust recognition of facial expressions in head motion and lighting condition change. We interactively select two eyes and a nose tip locations, which are relatively consistent during facial expressions, from one face image for each subject. Based on the selected templates, we perform detection of each template location from subsequent facial image by finding maximum correlation of the template images in the given frame image. We cropped images based on eye locations and nose similar to [14] after affine transformation to align the location of eyes and nose tip to a standard front face. Fig. 2 (a) shows interactively selected two eyes and a nose tip templates. A cropping region is decided after detection of template locations and affine transformation for every new image as shown in (b). Fig. 2 (c) shows normalization results in the sequence where the first frame is used to select templates and (d) in another sequence with different expression of the same subject

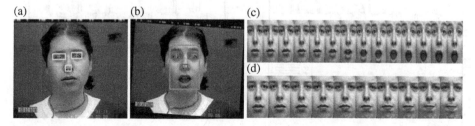

Fig. 2. Cropping and normalizing face images to a standard front face: (a) Selected templates (eyes and a nose tip). (b) Template detection, affine transformation and selected cropping region. (c) A normalized sequence where templates are selected from the first frame. (d) A normalized sequence from another expression of the same person.

without new template selections. We further processed the normalization of brightness when necessary. As a result, we can recognize facial expression robustly with changes of head location and small changes of head orientation from a frontal view.

3.2 Facial Expression Representation

Our generative model represents facial expressions using three state variables of the generative model: person face vector s, expression vector e, and embedding manifold point x, whose dimensions are N_s, N_e and 2 without further dimensionality reduction using orthogonal iteration. The embedding can be parameterized by one dimensional vector as the conceptual embedding manifold, unit circle, is one dimensional manifold in two dimensional space. The total number of dimensions of the parameters to represent a facial image is $N_s + N_e + 1$ after we learn the generative model. Fig. 3 shows examples of person face vectors (a) and expression vectors (b) when we learn the generative model from eight people with six different expressions related to basic emotions from Cohn-Kanade AU coded facial expression database [9], where $N_s = 8$ and $N_e = 6$. Plottings in three dimensional space using the first three parameters of face class vectors (c) and facial expression class vectors (d) give insight to the similarity among different person faces and different facial expression classes. Interestingly, plotting of the first three parameters of six basic expressions in Fig. 3 (d) shows embedding similar to the conceptual distance of six expressions in the image space. The surprise expression class vector is located far from other expressions, which is connected to distinguishable different visual motions in surprise. Anger, fear, disgust, and sadness are relatively close to each other than other expressions since they are distinguished visually using more subtle motions. The expression vector captures characteristics of image space facial expression in low dimensional space.

3.3 Sequence-Based Facial Expression Recognition

Given a sequence of images representing a facial expression, we can solve for the expression class paramter, e, and person face parameter, s. First, the sequence is embed-

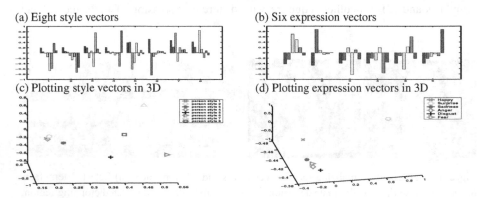

(a) Eight style vectors   (b) Six expression vectors

(c) Plotting style vectors in 3D   (d) Plotting expression vectors in 3D

Fig. 3. Facial expression analysis for eight subjects with six expressions from Cohn-Kanade dataset

(a) Iteration: sadness   (b) Iteration: surprise   (c) Iteration: happy   (d) Iteration: anger

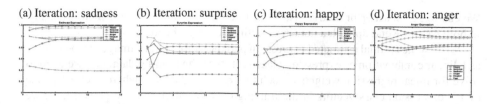

Fig. 4. The convergence of estimated expression parameters in iterations

ded to a unit circle and aligned to the model as described in Sec. 2. Then, mapping coefficients B are learned from the aligned embedding to the input. Given such coefficients, we need to find the optimal s and e, which minimize the error

$$E(s,e) = \|b - \mathcal{Z} \times_1 s \times_2 e\|, \tag{5}$$

where b is the vector representation of matrix B by column stacking. If the person face parameter s is known, we can obtain a closed form solution for e. This can be achieved by evaluating the tensor product $\mathcal{G} = \mathcal{Z} \times_1 s$ to obtain tensor $\mathcal{G}$. Solution for b can be obtained by solving the system $b = \mathcal{G} \times_2 e$ for e which can be written as a typical linear system by unfolding $\mathcal{G}$ as a matrix. Therefore the expression estimation e can be obtained by

$$e = (\mathcal{G}_2)^+ b \tag{6}$$

where $\mathcal{G}_2$ is the matrix obtained by mode-2 unfolding of $\mathcal{G}$ and $+$ denotes the pseudo inverse using singular value decomposition (SVD). Similarly we can analytically solve for s if the expression parameter, e, is known by forming a tensor $\mathcal{H} = \mathcal{Z} \times_2 e$:

$$s = (\mathcal{H}_1)^+ b \tag{7}$$

where $\mathcal{H}_1$ is the matrix obtained by mode-1 unfolding of $\mathcal{H}$.

Iterative estimations of e and s using equations 6 and 7 would lead to a local minima for the error in 5. Fig. 4 shows examples of expression estimation in iteration using new sequences. Y axis shows Euclidian distance between the estimated expression vector and six expression class vectors in the generative model in Sec. 4.1. Usually the estimation parameters of expressions converge into one of expression class vectors within several iterations. Fig. 4 (d) shows a case when more than ten iterations are required to reach stable solution in the estimation of expression vector.

3.4   Frame-Based Facial Expression Recognition

When the input is a single face image, it is desired to estimate temporal embedding or the face configuration in addition to expression and person face parameters in the generative model. Given an input image y, we need to estimate configuration, x, expression parameter e, and person face parameter s which minimize the reconstruction error

$$E(x,s,e) = \| y - \mathcal{C} \times_1 s \times_2 e \times_3 \psi(x) \| \tag{8}$$

We can use a robust error metric instead of Euclidian distance in error measurements. In both cases we end up with a nonlinear optimization problem.

We assume optimal estimated expression parameter for a given image can be written as a linear combination of expression class vectors in the training data. i.e., we need to solve for linear regression weights α such that $e = \sum_{k=1}^{K_e} \alpha_k e^k$ where each e^k is one of K_e expression class vectors in the training data. Similarly for the person face, we need to solve for weights β such that $s = \sum_{k=1}^{K_s} \beta_k s^k$ where each s^k is one of K_s face class vectors.

If the expression vector and the person face vector are known, then equation 8 is reduced to a nonlinear 1-dimensional search problem for configuration x on the unit circle that minimizes the error. On the other hand, if the configuration vector and the person face vector are known, we can obtain expression conditional class probabilities $p(e^k|y, x, s)$ which is proportional to observation likelihood $p(y \mid x, s, e^k)$. Such likelihood can be estimated assuming a Gaussian density centered around $C \times_1 s^k \times_2 e \times_3 \psi(x)$, i.e.,

$$p(y \mid x, s, e^k) \approx N(C \times_1 s^k \times_2 e \times_3 \psi(x), \Sigma^{e^k}).$$

Given expression class probabilities we can set the weights to $\alpha_k = p(e^k \mid y, x, s)$. Similarly, if the configuration vector and the expression vector are known, we can obtain face class weights by evaluating image likelihood given each face class s^k assuming a Gaussian density centered at $C \times_1 s^k \times_2 e \times_3 \psi(x)$.

This setting favors an iterative procedures for solving for x, e, s. However, wrong estimation of any of the vectors would lead to wrong estimation of the others and leads to a local minima. For example wrong estimation of the expression vector would lead to a totally wrong estimate of configuration parameter and therefore wrong estimate for person face parameter. To avoid this we use a deterministic annealing like procedure where in the beginning the expression weights and person face weights are forced to be close to uniform weights to avoid hard decisions about expression and face classes. The weights gradually become discriminative thereafter. To achieve this, we use a variable expression and person face class variances which are uniform to all classes and are defined as $\Sigma^e = T_e \sigma_e^2 I$ and $\Sigma^s = T_s \sigma_s^2 I$ respectively. The parameters T_e and T_s start with large values and are gradually reduced and in each step and a new configuration estimate is computed. Several iterations with decreasing T_e and T_s allow estimations of the expression vector, the person face vector and face configuration iteratively and allow estimations of expression and face from a single image.

3.5 Facial Expression Synthesis

Our model can generate new facial expressions by combinations of new facial expression parameter and person face parameter. As we have decomposed the mapping space that captures nonlinear deformation in facial expressions, the linear interpolation of the face style and facial expression still somewhat captures nonlinearity in the facial expression. In addition, we can control the parameters for person face and facial expression separately as a result of the multilinear decomposition. A new person face vector and a new facial expression vector can be synthesized by linear interpolation of existing person face class vectors and expression class vectors using parameter α_i, and β_j as follows:

(a) Neutral → smile → surprise   (b) Surprise → angry → neutral

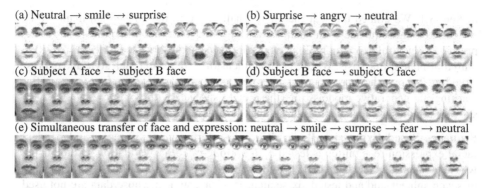

(c) Subject A face → subject B face   (d) Subject B face → subject C face

(e) Simultaneous transfer of face and expression: neutral → smile → surprise → fear → neutral

Fig. 5. Facial expression synthesis: First row: Expression transfer. Second row: Person face transfer during smile expression. Third row: simultaneous transfer of facial expression and person face.

$$e^{new} = \alpha_1 e_1 + \alpha_2 e_2 + \cdots + \alpha_{N_e} e_{N_e} \;,\; s^{new} = \beta_1 s_1 + \beta_2 s_2 + \cdots + \beta_{N_s} s_{N_s} \;, \quad (9)$$

where $\sum_i \alpha_i = 1$, and $\sum_j \beta_j = 1$, and $\alpha_i \geq 0$ and $\beta_i \geq 0$ in order to be linear interpolation in the convex set of the original expression classes and face classes. Here α_i and β_j are control parameters whereas they are estimated in recognition as in Sec. 3.4. We can also control these interpolation parameters according to temporal information or configuration. A new facial expression image can be generated using new style and expression parameters.

$$y_t^{new} = \mathcal{C} \times_1 s_t^{new} \times_2 e_t^{new} \times_3 \psi(x_t) \quad (10)$$

Fig. 5 shows examples of the synthesis of new facial expressions and person faces. During synthesis of the new images, we combine control parameter t to embedding coordinate x and interpolation parameter α and β. In case of Fig. 5 (a), the t changed $0 \to 1$ and new expression parameter $e_t^{new} = (1-t)e^{smile} + te^{surprise}$. As a result, the facial expression starts from neutral expression of smile and animates new expression as t changes and when $t = 1$, the expression become a peak expression of surprise. In case of (b), the t changed $1 \to 0$. In the same way, we can synthesize new faces during smile expressions as in (c) and (d). Fig. 5 (e) is the simultaneous control of the person face and expression parameters. This shows the potential of synthesis of new facial expression in the image space using our generative model.

4   Experimental Results

4.1   Person Independent Recognition of Facial Expression: Cohn-Kanade Facial Expression Data Set

We test the performance of facial expression analysis by our generative model using Cohn-Kanade AU coded facial expression database [9]. We first collected eight subjects with all six basic expression sequences, which are 48 expression sequences whose frame number varies between 11 and 33 to target display. We performed normalization by cropping image sequence based on template eyes and nose images as explained in Sec. 3.1. We embed the sequence into a half circle in the conceptual manifold as we counted the sequence of the data as half of one cycle among neutral → target expression → neutral expression. Eight equal-distance centers are used in learning GRBF with thin-plate spline basis. We used a full dimension to represent each style and expression. Fig. 3 shows the representation of expression vectors and person face vectors after learning the generative models from these eight subjects with six expressions. Fig. 5 shows examples of facial expression synthesis using this generative model.

Sequence-Based Expression Recognition: The performance of person independent facial expression recognition is tested by leave-one-out cross-validation method using whole sequences in the database [9]. We learned a generative model using 42 sequences of seven subjectsand and tested six sequences of one subject whose data are not used for learning the generative model. We tested the recognition performance by selecting the nearest expression class vector after iterations by sequence-based expression recognition in Sec. 3.3. Table 1 shows the confusion matrix for 48 sequences. The result shows potentials of the estimated expression vectors as feature vectors for other advanced classifiers like SVM.

Frame-Based Expression Recognition: Using the generative model, we can estimate person face parameters and expression parameters for a given expression image or sequence of images based on frame-by-frame estimation. We collected additional data that have five different expressions from 16 subjects. We used the generative model learned by eight subjects with six expressions to estimate expression parameters and person face parameters using deterministic annealing in Sec. 3.4. Fig. 6 (a) (b) (c) shows expression weight values α of every frame in three different expression sequences. The weights

Table 1. Person-independent average confusion matrix by sequence-based expression recognition

Emotion	Happy	Surprise	Sadness	Anger	Disgust	Fear
Happy	25%(2)	0	0	37.5%(3)	25%(2)	25%(2)
Surprise	12.5%(1)	62.5%(5)	12.5%(1)	0	0	12.5%(1)
Sadness	0	0	37.5%(3)	25%(2)	12.5%(1)	25%(2)
Anger	12.5%(1)	0	37.5%(3)	50%(4)	0	0
Disgust	12.5%(1)	12.5%(1)	12.5%(1)	25%(2)	12.5%(1)	25%(2)
Fear	0	0	0	50%(4)	0	50%(4)

(a) Happy: (4,8,12,16,20th frames)   (b) Surprise: (2,5,8,11,14th frames)   (c) Sadness: (1,5,9,13,17th frames)

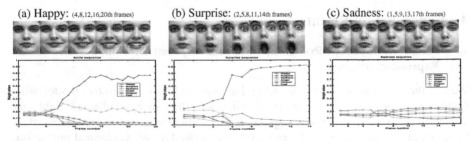

Fig. 6. Estimated expression weights in frame-based estimations

become more discriminative as expressions get closer to target expressions. We can recognize the expression using the maximum weight expression class in every frame. Table 2 shows recognition results when we classified facial expression using maximum expression weight of the last frame from 80 sequences.

Table 2. Person-independent average confusion matrix by frame-based recognition: classification only last frame maximum weight expression

Emotion	Happy	Surprise	Sadness	Anger	Disgust	Fear
Happy	93.3%(14)	0	0	0	0	6.7%(1)
Surprise	0	100%(16)	0	0	0	0
Sadness	0	7.1%(1)	28.6%(4)	7.1%(1)	35.7%(5)	21.4%(3)
Anger	9.1%(1)	0	18.2%(2)	27.3%(3)	45.4%	0
Disgust	9.1%(1)	0	9.1%(1)	18.2%(2)	63.6%(7)	0
Fear	25%(3)	0	8.3%(1)	0	8.3%(1)	58.3%(7)

4.2 Dynamic Facial Expression and Face Recognition

We used CMU-AMP facial expression database which are used for robust face recognition in variant facial expressions [14]. We collected sequences of ten people with three expressions (smile, anger, surprise) by manual segmentation from the whole sequences. We learned a generative model from nine people. The last one person data are used to test recognition of expression as a new person. The unit circle is used to embed each expression sequence.

We used the learned generative model to recognize facial expression, and person identity at each frame from the whole sequence using the frame-based algorithm in section 3.4. Fig. 7 (a) shows example frames of a whole sequence and the three different expression probabilities obtained in each frame (d)(e)(f). The person face weights, which are used to person identification, consistently show dominant weights for the subject face as in Fig. 7 (b). Fig. 7 (c) shows that the estimated embedding parameters

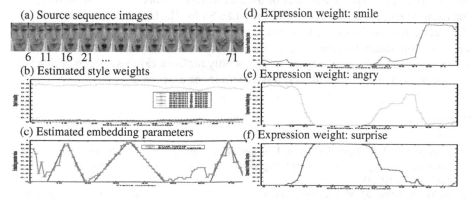

(a) Source sequence images   (d) Expression weight: smile

6 11 16 21 ...   71

(b) Estimated style weights   (e) Expression weight: angry

(c) Estimated embedding parameters   (f) Expression weight: surprise

Fig. 7. Facial expression analysis with partially trained segements

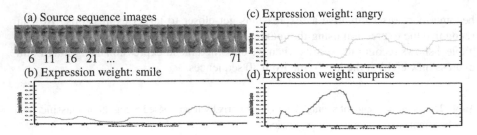

Fig. 8. Expression recognition for a new person

are close to the true embedding from manually selected sequences. We used the learned model to recognize facial expressions from sequences of a new person whose data are not used during training. Fig. 8 shows recognition of expressions for the new person. The model can generalize for the new person and can distinguish three expressions from the whole sequence.

5 Conclusion

In this paper we presented a framework for learning a decomposable generative model for facial expression analysis. Conceptual manifold embedding on a unit circle is used to model the intrinsic facial expression configuration on a closed 1D manifold. The embedding allows modeling any variations (twists) of the manifold given any number factors such as different people, different expression, etc; since all resulting manifolds are still topologically equivalent to the unit circle. This is not achievable if data-driven embedding is used. The use of a generative model is tied to the use of conceptual embedding since the mapping from the manifold representation to the input space will be well defined in contrast to a discriminative model where the mapping from the visual input to manifold representation is not necessarily a function. We introduced a framework to solve facial expression factors, person face factors and configurations in iterative methods for the whole sequence and in deterministic annealing methods for a given frame. The estimated expression parameters can be used as feature vectors for expression recognition using advanced classification algorithms like SVM. The frame-by-frame estimation of facial expression shows similar weights when expression image is close to the neutral face and more discriminative weights when it is near to target facial expressions. The weights of facial expression may be useful not only for facial expression recognition but also for other characteristics like expressiveness in the expression.

References

1. Z. Ambadar, J. W. Schooler, and J. F. Cohn. Deciphering the enigmatic face: The importance of facial dynamics in interpreting subtle facial expressions. *Psychological Science*, 16(5):403–410, 2005.
2. A. M. Bronstein, M. M. Bronstein, and R. Kimmel. Expression-invariant 3d face recognition. In *AVBPA, LNCS 2688*, pages 62–70, 2003.

3. Y. Chang, C. Hu, and M. Turk. Probabilistic expression analysis on manifolds. In *Proc. of CVPR*, pages 520–527, 2004.
4. E. S. Chuang, H. Deshpande, and C. Bregler. Facial expression space learning. In *Pacific Conference on Computer Graphics and Applications*, pages 68–76, 2002.
5. I. Cohen, N. Sebe, A. Garg, L. S. Chen, and T. S. Huang. Facial expression recognition from video sequences: Temporal and static modeling. *CVIU*, pages 160–187, 2003.
6. A. Elgammal. Nonlinear manifold learning for dynamic shape and dynamic appearance. In *Workshop Proc. of GMBV*, 2004.
7. A. Elgammal and C.-S. Lee. Separating style and content on a nonlinear manifold. In *Proc. of CVPR*, volume 1, pages 478–485, 2004.
8. A. K. Jain and S. Z. Li, editors. *Handbook of Face Recognition*, chapter 11. Face Expression Analysis. Springer, 2005.
9. T. Kanade, Y. Tian, and J. F. Cohn. Comprehensive database for facial expression analysis. In *Proc. of FGR*, pages 46–53, 2000.
10. A. Lanitis, C. J. Taylor, and T. F. Cootes. Automatic interpretation and coding of face images using flexible models. *IEEE Trans. PAMI*, 19(7):743–756, 1997.
11. L. D. Lathauwer, B. de Moor, and J. Vandewalle. A multilinear singular value decomposiiton. *SIAM Journal On Matrix Analysis and Applications*, 21(4):1253–1278, 2000.
12. L. D. Lathauwer, B. de Moor, and J. Vandewalle. On the best rank-1 and rank-(r1, r2, ..., rn) approximation of higher-order tensors. *SIAM Journal On Matrix Analysis and Applications*, 21(4):1324–1342, 2000.
13. Y. li Tian, T. Kanade, and J. F. Cohn. Recognizing action units for facial expression analysis. *IEEE Trans. PAMI*, 23(2), 2001.
14. X. Liu, T. Chen, and B. V. Kumar. Face authentication for multiple subjects using eigenflow. *Pattern Recognitioin*, 36:313–328, 2003.
15. A. M. Martinez. Recognizing expression variant faces from a single sample image per class. In *Proc. of CVPR*, pages 353–358, 2003.
16. T. Poggio and F. Girosi. Networks for approximation and learning. *Proceedings of the IEEE*, 78(9):1481–1497, 1990.
17. S. Roweis and L. Saul. Nonlinear dimensionality reduction by locally linear embedding. *Science*, 290(5500):2323–2326, 2000.
18. B. Schlkopf and A. Smola. *Learning with Kernels: Support Vector Machines, Regularization, Optimization and Beyond*. MIT Press, 2002.
19. J. B. Tenenbaum, V. de Silva, and J. C. Langford. A global geometric framework for nonlinear dimensionality reduction. *Science*, 290(5500):2319–2323, 2000.
20. J. B. Tenenbaum and W. T. Freeman. Separating style and content with biliear models. *Neural Computation*, 12:1247–1283, 2000.
21. M. Turk and A. Pentland. Eigenfaces for recognition. *Journal of Cognitive Neuroscience*, 3(1):71–86, 1991.
22. M. A. O. Vasilescu and D. Terzopoulos. Multilinear analysis of image ensembles: Tensorfaces. In *7th European Conference on Computer Vision*, pages 447–460, 2002.
23. H. Wang and N. Ahuja. Facial expression decomposition. In *Proc. of ICCV*, volume 2, pages 958–965, 2003.
24. W. Zhao, R. Chellappa, P. J. Phillips, and A. Rosenfeld. Face recognition: A literature survey. *ACM Comput. Surv.*, 35(4):399–458, 2003.

Kernel Correlation Filter Based Redundant Class-Dependence Feature Analysis (KCFA) on FRGC2.0 Data

Chunyan Xie, Marios Savvides, and B.V.K. VijayaKumar

Department of Electrical and Computer Engineering,
Carnegie Mellon University, Pittsburgh, PA 15213
{chunyanx, kumar}@ece.cmu.edu, msavvid@ri.cmu.edu

Abstract. In this paper we propose a nonlinear correlation filter using the kernel trick, which can be used for redundant class-dependence feature analysis (CFA) to perform robust face recognition. This approach is evaluated using the Face Recognition Grand Challenge (FRGC) data set. The FRGC contains a large corpus of data and a set of challenging problems. The dataset is divided into training and validation partitions, with the standard still-image training partition consisting of 12,800 images, and the validation partition consisting of 16,028 controlled still images, 8,014 uncontrolled stills, and 4,007 3D scans. We have tested the proposed linear correlation filter and nonlinear correlation filter based CFA method on this FRGC2.0 data. The results show that the CFA method outperforms the baseline algorithm and the newly proposed kernel-based non-linear correlation filters perform even better than linear CFA filters.

1 Introduction

Human face recognition is currently a very active research area [1, 2] with focus on ways to perform robust biometric identification. However, face recognition is a challenging task because of the variability of the appearance of face images even for the same subject as it changes due to expression, occlusion, illumination, pose, aging etc. The Face Recognition Grand Challenge (FRGC) [3] has been organized to facilitate the advancement of face recognition processing across the broad range of topics including pattern recognition algorithm design, sensor design, and in general for advancing the field of face recognition.

In this paper, we focus on the face recognition algorithms based on 2D still images. Many algorithms [4-7] have been developed for face recognition from 2D still images. Among the different approaches, spatial frequency domain methods [8-9] have been shown to exhibit better tolerance to noise and illumination variations than many space domain methods. In this paper, we extend the linear correlation filter to the nonlinear correlation filters using kernel methods. The linear and nonlinear correlation filters are tested on the FRGC2.0 data using the redundant class-dependence feature analysis (CFA) approach. In the CFA method, we train a filter bank of correlation filters based on the data from the generic training set, where we have multiple genuine images for each class. The trained filter bank is then used in

W. Zhao, S. Gong, and X. Tang (Eds.): AMFG 2005, LNCS 3723, pp. 32–43, 2005.

validation experiments to extract the discriminant class-dependence features for recognition. The nearest neighbor rule is applied to these features to measure the similarity between target and query images. The algorithm also offers the benefit of computationally efficient training, as when the database size increases there is no need for re-training when a new entry is added to the database.

Kernel tricks have been used with support vector machine (SVM) [10], principal component analysis (PCA) [11], linear discriminant analysis (LDA) [12], kernel spectral matched filter [13] and many other approaches to generate nonlinear classifiers. Motivated by these approaches, we propose in this paper a nonlinear extension of the Equal Correlation Peak Synthetic Discriminant Function (ECP-SDF)[15] filter and the Optimal Trade-off correlation Filter (OTF)[18], obtaining nonlinear correlation filter classifiers for face recognition application. The experimental results show that these nonlinear correlation filters outperform the linear correlation filters in the CFA approach on FRGC2.0 data.

The paper is organized as follows. Section 2 introduces the redundant class-dependence feature analysis method and kernel based nonlinear correlation filters. Section 3 introduces the FRGC2.0 data and Experiments. In Section 4, we show numerical results of the CFA method on the FRGC2.0 data and we discuss the results and outline the future work in Section 5.

2   Redundant Class-Dependence Feature Analysis

Most approaches to face recognition are in the image domain whereas we believe that there are more advantages to work directly in the spatial frequency domain. By going to the spatial frequency domain, image information gets distributed across frequencies providing tolerance to reasonable deviations and also providing graceful degradation against distortions to images (e.g., occlusions) in the spatial domain. Correlation filter technology is a basic tool for frequency domain image processing. In correlation filter methods, normal variations in authentic training images can be accommodated by designing a frequency-domain array (called a correlation filter) that captures the consistent part of training images while de-emphasizing the inconsistent parts (or frequencies). Object recognition is performed by cross-correlating an input image with a designed correlation filter using fast Fourier transforms (FFTs). The advantage of using advanced correlation filter designs is that they offer closed form solutions which are computationally attractive [14].

2.1   Matched Filter (MF) and ECP-SDF Filter

Matched Filters (MFs) [14] are simple correlation filters, which are optimal in the sense that they provide the maximum output signal-to-noise ratio (SNR). However, MFs lose their optimality rapidly when the test image differs from the reference image due to natural variability such as expressions, lighting, pose, etc. For N training images, we need N MFs, one for each training image. The Synthetic Discriminant Function (SDF) approach [15] was proposed to create a composite image that is a linear combination of multiple reference images and the weights for linear combination are selected so that the cross-correlation output at the origin is same for all images belonging to one class. The basic SDF is known as the *equal correlation peak (ECP) SDF* [15]. The objective is to design a composite image **h** such that it generates the same value at the origin of the correlation plane for all training images from the same class. This origin value (loosely referred to as the correlation peak) $c(0,0)$, is the inner product of the training image and the filter to be determined, i.e.,

$$c(0,0) = \mathbf{h}^+ \cdot \mathbf{x}_i = \mathbf{x}_i^+ \cdot \mathbf{h} \tag{1}$$

where $\mathbf{x}_i$ denotes the *i*-th training image and **h** denotes the filter. In most cases, we let $c(0,0)$ be 1 for training images of true class (i.e., authentics) and 0 for the training images of false class (i.e., impostors, assuming that impostor images are available for training). For *N* training images, we can rewrite (1) as

$$\mathbf{X}^+\mathbf{h} = \mathbf{c}^* \tag{2}$$

The ECP SDF assumes that the composite image **h** is a linear combination of the training images and it can be solved as in [14]

$$\mathbf{h} = \mathbf{X}(\mathbf{X}^+\mathbf{X})^{-1}\mathbf{c}^* \tag{3}$$

The ECP SDF filter, however does not incorporate any tolerance to input noise. Also because it is designed solely on the basis of constraints on correlation values at the origin, correlation values elsewhere may be larger and thus the correlation peak may not be the controlled value. If the test input is not centered, then we cannot use it because the correlation output peak is not necessarily the controlled value corresponding to the center of the target. More SDF filters have been developed to address these problems.

2.2 Optimal Tradeoff Filter

Different choices of energy minimization metrics of correlation output lead to correlation filters that address different problems. The *minimum variance synthetic discriminant function* (MVSDF) [16] filter minimizes the correlation output noise energy represented in matrix format as $\mathbf{h}^+\mathbf{C}\mathbf{h}$; where **C** is a diagonal matrix whose diagonal elements $\mathbf{C}(k,k)$ represent the noise power spectral density at frequency *k*. The *minimum average correlation energy* (MACE) [17] filter minimizes the average correlation output energy $\mathbf{h}^+\mathbf{D}\mathbf{h}$ where **D** is the average of $\mathbf{D}_i$, the power spectrum of the *i*-th image, which is also a diagonal matrix whose elements $\mathbf{D}_i(k,k)$ contain the power spectra of the *i*-th training image at frequency *k*. We note that the MACE filter emphasizes high spatial frequencies in order to produce sharp correlation peaks whereas the MVSDF filter typically suppresses high frequencies in order to achieve noise tolerance. Although both attributes are desired, the corresponding energy metrics cannot be minimized simultaneously. The *optimal tradeoff filter* (OTF) [18] is designed to balance these two criteria by minimizing a weighted metric $\mathbf{h}^+\mathbf{T}\mathbf{h}$ where **T**=α**D**+β**C** and $0 \le \alpha, \beta \le 1$. The OTF is obtained as shown in (4) below:

$$\mathbf{h}_{OTF} = \mathbf{T}^{-1}\mathbf{X}(\mathbf{X}^+\mathbf{T}^{-1}\mathbf{X})^{-1}\mathbf{c}^* \tag{4}$$

where $\mathbf{X} = [\ \mathbf{x}_1, \mathbf{x}_2, ..., \mathbf{x}_N\ ]$ is a $d{\times}N$ matrix, and each $\mathbf{x}_i$ is d dimensional vector constructed by lexicographically reordering the 2-D Fourier transform of the i-th training image.

2.3 Redundant Class-Dependence Feature Analysis

When the correlation filters are used for verification, the commonly used method is to correlate the test image with the filter which is designed based on one or more training images, compute PSR value, and to compare it with a preset threshold to decide if the image is authentic or imposter, as shown in Fig. 1.

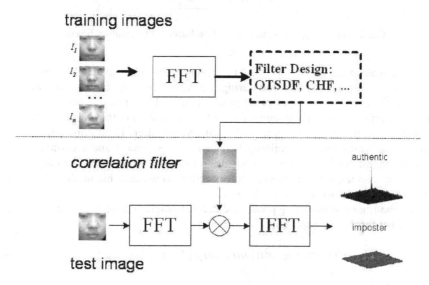

Fig. 1. Commonly used method for still-to-still face verification using correlation filter

There are some problems with this method when applied to the FRGC 2.0 experiments. First, it is not efficient. FRGC2.0 experiment #1 requires that we generate a 16,028x16,028 similarity matrix. For this, we need to design 16,028 correlation filters and compute 16,028x16,028 correlations. It can take a significant amount of time (up to a month using high-power dual processor machines) just to run the whole experiment once. Second, the performance of the filter may not be very good because there is only one genuine image available for training each filter. Third, the generic training set available with FRGC dataset is not being used by the traditional correlation filter synthesis method.

To address these problems, we propose a novel redundant *class-dependence feature analysis* (CFA) method [19] for face recognition using correlation filters. In this method, we train a correlation filter for each subject from the generic training set, and get a bank of subject-dependence correlation filters. All of these filters are used for feature extraction, as shown in Fig. 2. A test image evaluated on all of these filters

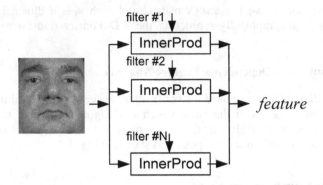

Fig. 2. The concept of feature extraction based on correlation filters

generates a feature vector that is used to represent the test image. Because all of training and test images are centered during the pre-processing stage, we assume that the peak at the correlation output plane is also centered. To make it computationally efficient, we only compute the center value of the correlation output by calculating the inner product of the test image and each synthesized filter. Each component in the feature vector represents the similarity between the test image and a certain subject class. Because all synthetic filters are not orthonormal to each other, the coefficients in the feature vector contain redundant information, so we call this method redundant *class-dependence feature analysis* (CFA).

During the final test matching phase, the nearest neighbor rule is applied to decide the class label for the test image, i.e.,

$$\theta(\mathbf{y}) = \arg \min_{i} \min_{i,j} \left(measure\left(\mathbf{t} - \mathbf{r}_{ij}\right)\right) \qquad (5)$$

where $\mathbf{r}_{ij}$ represents feature vector corresponding the j-th training sample of the i-th class and $\mathbf{t}$ is the feature vector corresponding to the test input $\mathbf{y}$. There are four commonly used similarity measures: the L_1 norm, the Euclidean distance, the Mahalanobis distance and the cosine function. The cosine distance (6) in our experiments has been shown to be the best performance for this method.

$$S_{cos}(\mathbf{r},\mathbf{t}) = \frac{-(\mathbf{r} \cdot \mathbf{t})}{\|\mathbf{r}\|\|\mathbf{t}\|} \qquad (6)$$

There are several attributes of the CFA method worth noting. First, when new classes are added in the generic training set, previously trained correlation filters do not require re-training, we just need to add a new filter which is easy to compute due to the nature of the closed form solution of the OTF. Second, since the filter bank is class-dependence, we expect to observe better performance when the generic training set and the validation sets have more overlapped classes. Finally, under the CFA framework, the class-dependence features can also be extracted by some classifiers other than correlation filters, e.g., support vector machines that can be trained for each individual class.

2.4 Kernel Methods of Correlation Filters

Polynomial correlation filter (PCF) [19] had been developed to generate nonlinear correlation filter classifiers. In PCFs some point nonlinearity transforms (e.g. x^2, x^3, etc.) are applied to each pixel of the image and the filters are developed based on the transformed images to optimize a performance criterion of interest. It is shown [19] that the polynomial correlation filter outperforms the linear correlation filter.

In this paper, we introduce a new method to extend the linear ECP-SDF and OTF correlation filters to non-linear correlation filters using kernel methods. As discussed in Sec. 2.3, in face recognition application, we usually assume that the images are centered and geometrically normalized. In that case, we focus on the inner product of the filter and the tested image. For ECP-SDF filter $\mathbf{h}$ and a test image $\mathbf{y}$, we can get

$$c(0,0) = \mathbf{y}^+\mathbf{h} = \mathbf{y}\mathbf{X}(\mathbf{X}^+\mathbf{X})^{-1}\mathbf{c}^* \tag{7}$$

The only way in which the data appears in the correlation framework is in the form of inner products $\mathbf{x}_i \cdot \mathbf{x}_j$. Suppose we map the data to some other feature space by a non-linear mapping Φ, then the correlation peak value of the ECP-SDF filter becomes

$$c(0,0) = \Phi(\mathbf{y}) \cdot \Phi(\mathbf{X})\big(\Phi(\mathbf{X}) \cdot \Phi(\mathbf{X})\big)^{-1}\mathbf{c}^* \tag{8}$$

The training and test algorithms would depend on the functions of the form $\Phi(\mathbf{y}) \cdot \Phi(\mathbf{X})$. Now if we have a kernel function below

$$K(\mathbf{x}_i, \mathbf{x}_j) = \Phi(\mathbf{x}_i) \cdot \Phi(\mathbf{x}_j) \tag{9}$$

We would only need to use $K(\mathbf{x}_i, \mathbf{x}_j)$ to compute the correlation peak value

$$c(0,0) = K(\mathbf{y}, \mathbf{X})\big(K(\mathbf{X}, \mathbf{X})\big)^{-1}\mathbf{c}^* \tag{10}$$

and we would never need to explicitly know what the Φ mapping is, which saves a lot of computations. This allows us to achieve a nonlinear correlation filter classification boundary in the original image space. Mercer's condition [10] tells us whether or not a prospective kernel is actually an inner product in some space. We use this condition to modify any kernel variations to ensure that this is satisfied.

Next we introduce the method of extend the OTF filter to its nonlinear version. For an OTF filter and a test image $\mathbf{y}$, we can get

$$c(0,0) = \mathbf{y}^+\mathbf{h} = \mathbf{y}\mathbf{T}^{-1}\mathbf{X}(\mathbf{X}^+\mathbf{T}^{-1}\mathbf{X})^{-1}\mathbf{c}^* \tag{11}$$

Note that the difference between (11) and (7) is the diagonal matrix $\mathbf{T}$, where $\mathbf{T}=\alpha\mathbf{D}+\beta\mathbf{C}$, a linear combination of the input noise power spectral density $\mathbf{C}$ and average power spectral of the training images. Since $\mathbf{T}$ is a diagonal and positive definite matrix, it is easy to decompose $\mathbf{T^{-1}} = \mathbf{T^{-\frac{1}{2}}T^{-\frac{1}{2}}}$, then we can rewrite the correlation peak as

$$c(0,0) = \mathbf{y}\mathbf{T^{-\frac{1}{2}}}\mathbf{T^{-\frac{1}{2}}}\mathbf{X}(\mathbf{X^{+}}\mathbf{T^{-\frac{1}{2}}}\mathbf{T^{-\frac{1}{2}}}\mathbf{X})^{-1}\mathbf{c^{*}} = (\mathbf{T^{-\frac{1}{2}}}\mathbf{y})(\mathbf{T^{-\frac{1}{2}}}\mathbf{X})\left(\left(\mathbf{T^{-\frac{1}{2}}}\mathbf{X}\right)^{+}\left(\mathbf{T^{-\frac{1}{2}}}\mathbf{X}\right)\right)^{-1}\mathbf{c^{*}} \quad (12)$$

We can treat $\mathbf{T^{-\frac{1}{2}}}$ as a pre-processing filter and apply it to every training and test image, so we get

$$c(0,0) = (\mathbf{T^{-\frac{1}{2}}}\mathbf{y})(\mathbf{T^{-\frac{1}{2}}}\mathbf{X})\left(\left(\mathbf{T^{-\frac{1}{2}}}\mathbf{X}\right)^{+}\left(\mathbf{T^{-\frac{1}{2}}}\mathbf{X}\right)\right)^{-1}\mathbf{c^{*}} = \mathbf{y'}\mathbf{X'}\left(\mathbf{X'^{+}}\mathbf{X'}\right)^{-1}\mathbf{c^{*}} \quad (13)$$

which is in the same form as in (7) and we can apply the kernel trick as well to obtain the kernel based nonlinear OTF classifier. In Fig. 3 we show an original image and a pre-filtered image by $\mathbf{T}$ with $\alpha=0.1$ and $\beta =1$.

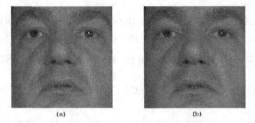

(a)   (b)

Fig. 3. Illustration of image preprocessing: (a) original image and (b) pre-filtered image

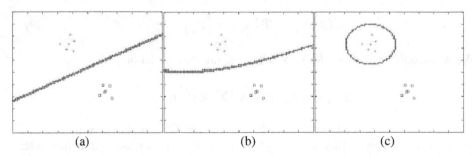

(a)   (b)   (c)

Fig. 4. The illustration of the decision boundary for (a) linear correlation filter, (b) polynomial correlation filter and (c) Gaussian RBF classifier

Some useful kernels include the polynomial kernel in (14) which results in a classifier that is a polynomial of degree p in the data and the Gaussian radial basis function (RBF) kernel in (15) that gives a Gaussian RBF classifier. In Fig. 4 we use a toy example to show the linear correlation filter and polynomial correlation filter and Gaussian RBF classification boundary.

$$K(\mathbf{x}, \mathbf{y}) = (\mathbf{x} \cdot \mathbf{y} + 1)^p \tag{14}$$

$$K(\mathbf{x}, \mathbf{y}) = e^{-\|\mathbf{x} - \mathbf{y}\|^2 / 2\sigma^2} \tag{15}$$

3 FRGC 2.0 Data and Experiments

For the second phase of the face recognition grand challenge FRGC [3] data 2.0 was again collected at the University of Notre Dame. The generic training set contains 222 subjects and consists of 12,776 still images captured in 100 subject sessions from academic year 2002-2003, and the validation set contains 466 subjects and consists of 16,028 controlled still images and 8,014 uncontrolled still images captured in 4007 subject sessions from academic year 2003-2004. The example images from the controlled still image set are shown in Fig. 5. The FRGC experiment #1 is defined to generate a similarity matrix of 16,028x16,028 similarity scores of controlled indoor still images vs. indoor still images and the FRGC experiment #4 is defined to generate a 16,028x8,014 similarity matrix of controlled still images vs. uncontrolled still images. Experiment #1 data set only exhibits some facial expression, minimal illumination variations and minimal pose variations and Experiment #4 data contains severe illumination variations and blurring. Experiment #4 is much harder because the

Fig. 5. Example images from the controlled still set

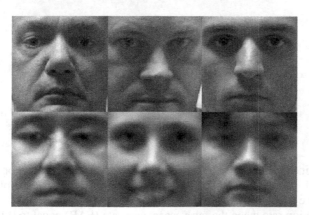

Fig. 6. Example images with illumination variations and blurring from the uncontrolled still set

query images are of poorer quality. More details of all experiments defined in FRGC project can be found in [3].

Fig. 6 shows example images from uncontrolled still set that contains images under severe illumination conditions and images out of focus. We can see that the combination of the illumination, expression, pose variations and the blurring effect makes the recognition task even harder.

4   FRGC Numerical Results

In this paper, we focus on the FRGC2.0 experiment #1 for which we test our proposed algorithms on a controlled 2D still image set of 16,028 images and generate a similarity matrix of size 16,028x16,028. In this paper we show the experimental results of five different algorithms using our proposed CFA approach. The first one is CFA based on the OTF correlation filter with parameters $\alpha=0.001$ and $\beta=1$. The second one is the nonlinear CFA based on the polynomial kernel with polynomial degree parameter $p=2.0$. The third one is the nonlinear CFA based on the fractional power polynomial model [20] with polynomial degree parameter $p=0.9$. Note that when $p=0.9$, a fractional power polynomial does not necessarily define a kernel function, as it might not define a positive semi-definite Gram matrix [20] but the fractional power polynomial models with $0<p<1$ shows better face recognition performance than polynomial kernel with $p>1$ [20] using the same fractional power trick. It is also observed in our experiments. The forth one is the nonlinear CFA based on Gaussian RBF classifier with the variance parameter $\sigma^2 = 3.0$. The last one is also the nonlinear CFA based on Gaussian RBF classifier ($\sigma^2 = 3.0$) plus a preprocessing filter $\mathbf{T}$ ($\alpha=0.1$ and $\beta=1$).

In Fig. 7, we show three OTF correlation filter bases trained on the training data for the linear CFA approach. We generate the CFA feature vectors for all target images and query images by inner product and apply the nearest neighbor rule based on cosine distance to get the similarity matrix.

Fig. 7. Three correlation filter-based CFA basis

For the nonlinear CFA, we use the corresponding kernel functions or models with above specified parameters. We show the verification performance of 5 different algorithms on the FRGC2.0 experiment #1 in table 1 and Fig. 8. In table 1, we reported the face verification rate when the false acceptance rate (FAR) equal to 0.1% which are the result specifications according to FRGC. We compare results of the five algorithms described above to the FRGC baseline result and the traditional correlation filter results.

Table 1. The verification rate at 0.1% FAR of the different methods

Baseline PCA	OTF	CFA Linear Filter	CFA Poly (0.9)	CFA Poly (2.0)	CFA RBF	CFA RBF+OTF
66% [3]	77%	89.9%	91.4%	90.2%	92.5%	93.5%

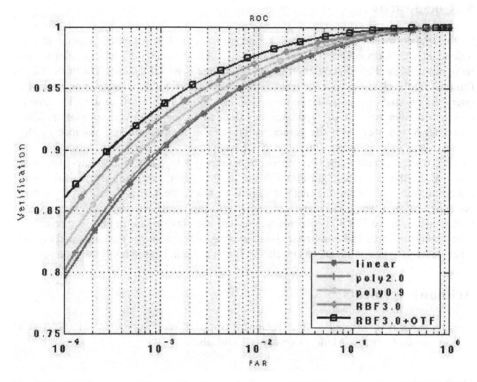

Fig. 8. The ROC curves of the verification performance of 5 different algorithms on FRGC2.0 experiment #1

From table 1 we can see that the CFA approach perform much better than the baseline PCA algorithm and it also performs better than the traditional method of face verification using correlation filter. The nonlinear CFA method generally outperforms the linear CFA method, and the kernel method plus the optimal tradeoff filter perform the best. The ROC curves of these experimental results are shown in Fig. 8.

From Fig. 8 we can see that the nonlinear correlation filters based CFA approach generally outperforms linear correlation filters. The Gaussian RBF classifier based CFA method significantly improves the verification performance over other methods. Moreover, the Gaussian RBF plus the OTF based pre-processing filter further improves the performance; clearly showing the advantages of frequency domain approaches. From our experiments we can also see that there are some parameters to be decided when apply the nonlinear kernel method and/or the linear correlation filters. In this paper, we show the best results of testing on different parameters in our experiments. In our future work, we will investigate the methods on how to theoretically and experimentally select the nonlinear parameter and the correlation filter parameters. We will also investigate other possible kernel functions for nonlinear approaches.

5 Conclusions

In this paper we introduce a novel kernel correlation filter method applied in the redundant class-dependence feature analysis (CFA) approach to perform robust face recognition in the Face Recognition Grand Challenge (FRGC) data set. Under the CFA framework, the class-dependence features can be extracted for each target image and the query image and the nearest neighbor rule is applied for classification. The linear correlation filter based CFA approach is extended to the nonlinear correlation filter based CFA approach with the kernel methods. The verification performance of the linear filter and nonlinear filter based CFA approaches have been tested on the FRGC2.0 experiment#1, and the verification rates (93.5%) are much better than that reported of the baseline algorithm (66%). In the future, we will theoretically and experimentally investigate the method of how to select the kernel function parameters and correlation filter parameters and aim to further improve the face verification performance on the FRGC experiments. We will also investigate the CFA approaches based on other linear and non-linear classifiers (e.g. support vector machine) and extend other different types of advanced correlation filters to kernel based nonlinear filters.

Acknowledgements

This research is sponsored by the Technical Support Working Group (TSWG) and also in part by Carnegie Mellon University's CyLab.

References

1. R. Chellappa, C.L. Wilson, S. Sirohey, "Human and machine recognition of faces: a survey," *Proceedings of the IEEE,* Vol.83 (5), pp705-741 (1995).
2. R. Gross, J. Shi, and J. Cohn, "Quo Vadis Face Recognition?" *Third Workshop on Empirical Evaluation Methods in Computer Vision*, December 2001.
3. P. J. Phillips, P. J. Flynn, T. Scruggs, K. W. Bowyer, J. Chang, K. Hoffman, J. Marques, J. Min, and W. Worek, "Overview of the Face Recognition Grand Challenge," *In Proceedings of IEEE Conference on Computer Vision and Pattern Recognition*, 2005.
4. M. Turk, A. Pentland, "Eigenfaces for Recognition," *Journal of Cognitive Neuroscience*, 3(1), pp71-86, 1991.
5. A. Pentland, B. Moghaddam, T. Starner, "View-Based and Modular Eigenspaces for Face Recognition," *IEEE CVPR,* 1994.
6. P.Belhumeur, J. Hespanha, and D. Kriegman, "Eigenfaces vs Fisherfaces: Recognition Using Class Specific Linear Projection," *IEEE Trans. PAMI*-19(7),(1997).
7. W. Zheng, C Zou, L. Zhao, "Real-time face recognition using Gram-Schmidt orthogonalization for LDA," *ICPR'04*, August, 2004, Cambridge UK, pp. 403-406

8. B.V.K. Vijaya Kumar, M. Savvides, K. Venkataramani, and C. Xie, "Spatial Frequency Domain Image Processing For Biometric Recognition," *Proceedings IEEE International Conference on Image Processing*, pp. 53-56, 2002

9. M. Savvides, B.V.K. Vijaya Kumar, and P.K. Khosla, "'Corefaces'- Robust Shift Invariant PCA based correlation filter for illumination tolerant face recognition," *Proceedings IEEE Computer Vision and Pattern Recognition (CVPR)*, pp. 834-841, June 2004.

10. V. Vapnik, *The nature of statistical learning theory*, Springer-Verlag, New York, 1995.

11. Schölkopf, A. Smola, and K.-R. Müller. "Nonlinear component analysis as a kernel eigenvalue problem," *Neural Computation*, 10:1299-1319, 1998

12. G. Baudat and F. Anouar, "Generalized discriminant analysis using a kernel approach,",*Neural Computation*, vol. 12, pp. 2385-2404, 2000.

13. N. M. Nasrabadi and H. Kwon, "Kernel spectral matched filter for hyperspectral target detection," *Proceedings ICASSP*, 665-668., 2005

14. B.V.K. Vijaya Kumar, "Tutorial survey of composite filter designs for optical correlators," *Appl. Opt.*, 31, 4773-4801, (1992)

15. C.F. Hester and D. Casasant, "Multivariant technique for multiclass pattern recognition," *Appl. Opt.* 21, 4016-4019 (1982)

16. B.V.K. Vijaya Kumar, "Minimum Variance synthetic discriminant functions," *J. Opt. Soc. Am A*, Vol 3, pp1579-1584.

17. A. Mahalanobis, B.V.K. Vijaya Kumar, and D. Casasent, "Minimum average correlation energy filters," *Appl. Opt.* 26, pp. 3633-3630 (1987)

18. P. Refregier, "Filter Design for optical pattern recognition: Multi-criteria optimization approach," *Opt. Lett.*, V.15, 854-856, 1990.

19. Chunyan Xie, Marios Savvides and B.V.K. Vijaya Kumar, "Redundant Class-Dependence Feature Analysis Based on Correlation Filters Using FRGC2.0 Data," *IEEE Workshop on Face Recognition Grand Challenge Experiments in conjunction with CVPR 2005*, San Diego, CA, 21 June 2005

20. B. V. K. Vijaya Kumar and A. Mahalanobis, "Recent advances in composite correlation filter designs," *Asian Journal of Physics*, Vol. 8, No. 4, pp. 407-420, 1999

21. C. Liu, "Gabor-based Kernel PCA with Fractional Power Polynomial Models for Face Recognition", *IEEE Trans. Pattern Analysis and Machine Intelligence*, vol. 26, no. 5, pp. 572-581, 2004

Learning to Fuse 3D+2D Based Face Recognition at Both Feature and Decision Levels

Stan Z. Li, ChunShui Zhao, Meng Ao, and Zhen Lei

Center for Biometrics and Security Research & National Laboratory of Pattern Recognition,
Institute of Automation, Chinese Academy of Sciences,
95, Zhongguancun Donglu Beijing 100080, China
http://www.cbsr.ia.ac.cn/

Abstract. 2D intensity images and 3D shape models are both useful for face recognition, but in different ways. While algorithms have long been developed using 2D or 3D data, recently has seen work on combining both into multi-modal face biometrics to achieve higher performance. However, the fusion of the two modalities has mostly been at the decision level, based on scores obtained from independent 2D and 3D matchers.

In this paper, we propose a systematic framework for fusing 2D and 3D face recognition at both feature and decision levels, by exploring synergies of the two modalities at these levels. The novelties are the following. First, we propose to use Local Binary Pattern (LBP) features to represent 3D faces and present a statistical learning procedure for feature selection and classifier learning. This leads to a matching engine for 3D face recognition. Second, we propose a statistical learning approach for fusing 2D and 3D based face recognition at both feature and decision levels. Experiments show that the fusion at both levels yields significantly better performance than fusion at the decision level.

1 Introduction

Face recognition has attracted much attention due to its potential values for applications as well as theoretical challenges. Many representation approaches have been introduced. Principal Component Analysis (PCA) [1] computes a reduced set of orthogonal basis vector or eigenfaces of training face images. A new face image can be approximated by weighted sum of these eigenfaces. PCA provides an optimal linear transformation from the original image space to an orthogonal eigenspace with reduced dimensionality in the sense of the least mean square reconstruction error. , Linear Discriminant Analysis (LDA) [2] seeks to find a linear transformation by maximizing the between-class variance and minimizing the within-class variance. Independent component analysis(ICA) [3] uses high-order statistics to generate image bases. Elastic bunch graph matching (EBGM) [4,5] uses Gabor wavelets to capture the local structure corresponding to spatial frequency (scale), spatial localization, and orientation selectivity.

Local Binary Pattern (LBP), originally proposed as a descriptor for textures [6], provides a simple yet effective way to represent faces [7,8]. There, the face image is equally divided into small blocks and LBP features are extracted for each blocks to represent the texture of a face locally and globally. Weighted Chi square distance of

W. Zhao, S. Gong, and X. Tang (Eds.): AMFG 2005, LNCS 3723, pp. 44–54, 2005.

these LBP histograms is used as a dissimilarity measure for comparing the two images. The above works have shown that LBP based methods can produces good results for face recognition in 2D images.

Boosting learning with local features have recently been proposed as a promising approach. Jones and Viola [9] propose a general idea of boosting local features and training a classifier on difference between two face image feature vectors (Haar wavelets). Zhang *et al.* present an LBP-based boosting learning algorithm [10]. Such works are for 2D face recognition.

While using 2D intensity images to recognize a face has long history of research [11], recent advances in 3D range sensor has made it possible to overcome some limitations in 2D based face recognition methods such as illumination and pose changes. Early work on 3D face recognition was based on curvature features [12], following this type of work in 3D range image understanding starting from mid-1980's [13]. Later developments in 2D face recognition have influenced 3D face recognition [14].

It may be advantageous to combine information contained in both 2D and 3D data to overcome limitations in 2D or 3D based methods while 2D and 3D images encodes different information. Methods have been proposed to combine information in both modalities into multi-model face biometrics to achieve higher performance [14]. For example, in [15,16], the weighted sum rule is applied to combine the two matching scores. A recent performance evaluation on the 2D and 3D modalities and their fusion has shown that multi-modal 3D+2D face recognition performs significantly better than using either 3D or 2D alone [17].

So far, the fusion of 3D+2D modalities has been at the decision level, using scores from 2D and 3D matchers. The 3D recognition result and the 2D recognition result are each produced without reference to the other modality. It is desirable to explore synergies of the two modalities at the feature level as well [14]. The work presented here explores such synergies in the proposed framework of AdaBoost learning (with LBP feature). This is new for solving the problem of 3D+2D face fusion.

In this paper, we propose a systematic framework for fusing 2D and 3D information at both feature and decision levels. The main contributions are the following: First, we propose to use LBP features as a representation of faces in 3D data. An AdaBoost learning procedure [18,19,20] is then applied for feature selection and classifier learning. Second, with LBP as a unified representation of faces in both 2D and 3D images, we propose to use AdaBoost learning to fuse 2D and 3D information at both feature and decision levels. The same AdaBoost learning procedure as used for 3D face recognition is used for 3D+2D fusion. 3D and 2D LBP histograms are computed, respectively, and then combined into a 3D+2D feature set. AdaBoost is applied to select effective feature from a 3D+2D feature pool, construct weak classifiers based on the selected features, and then combine the weak classifiers into a strong one. Thus, the learning procedure fuses the 3D and 2D modalities at both feature and decision levels. Experiments show that the AdaBoost learning method produces significantly better results than the baseline PCA method. AdaBoost learning based fusion performs significantly better than fusion of PCA based scores. Experimental results clearly demonstrate the advantages of the two level fusion over the exiting decision level fusion such as presented in a recent PAMI paper [17].

The rest of this paper is organized as follows: In section 2, the LBP representation is described. In section 3, we propose an AdaBoost learning method for 3D face recognition. In section 4, we propose the boosting based fusion of 3D+2D modalities. Experimental results are presented in section 5.

2   Feature Representation

Face images are preprocessed so that they are aligned in a predefined way. For 2D data, the alignment and cropping is done according to the eye centers. For 3D data, the face is rotated about the vertical axis so that the nose tip becomes the closest point and then cropped; after that, a median filter is applied to remove high noise; this is followed by hole-filling. Fig.1 shows some examples. LBP features are then extracted from the cropped and preprocessed images.

Fig. 1. 3D (top) and 2D (bottom) face images of a person before (left) and after (right) alignment and cropping

2.1   Local Binary Pattern

The LBP operator was originally introduced by Ojala [6] as texture description. LBP features have performed very well in various applications, including texture classification and segmentation. The basic form of an LBP operator labels the pixels of an image by thresholding the 3×3-neighborhood of each pixel with the center value and considering the result as a binary number. An illustration of the basic LBP operator is shown in Fig.2. Note that the binary LBP code is circular.

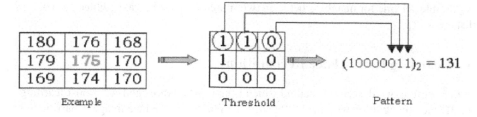

Fig. 2. Calculation of LBP code from 3x3 subwindow (from [8])

The major limitation of the basic LBP operator is its small spatial support area. Features calculated in a local 3×3 neighborhood cannot capture large scale structure that may be the dominant features of some textures. The LBP operator can be extended to use neighborhoods of different size [6]. Another extension to the original operator is to use so called uniform patterns [6]. An LBP is called uniform if it contains at most two bitwise 0-1 or 1-0 transitions. There are 58 uniform LBP code patterns for 8-bits LBP code, and 256-58=198 non-uniform LBP patterns.

2.2   Local Histograms of LBP Code

LBP histograms over local regions provides a more reliable description when the pattern is subject to alignment errors. Considering the uniform LBP scheme, and denoting all the non-uniform LBP patterns with a single bin, then there are a set of $L + 1 = 59$ possible LBP code types for the 8-bit LBP code. Let us denote this set by $\mathcal{L} = \{0, 1, \ldots, L\}$ such that $LBP(x, y) \in \mathcal{L}$, and the local LBP histogram over a block $S_{(x,y)}$ centered at (x, y) by $H_{(x,y)} = (H_{(x,y)}(0), H_{(x,y)}(1), \ldots, H_{(x,y)}(L))$. The histgram can be defined as

$$H_{(x,y)}(\ell) = \sum_{(x',y') \in S(x,y)} I\{LBP(x', y') = \ell\}, \quad \ell \in \mathcal{L} \qquad (1)$$

where $I(\cdot) \in \{0, 1\}$ is an indication function of a boolean condition, and $S(x, y)$ is a local region centered at (x, y) which in our case is a 20x15 block.

The histogram $H_{(x,y)}$ contains information about the distribution of the local micro-patterns, such as edges, spots and flat areas, over the block $S_{(x,y)}$. It effectively gives a description of the face at two different levels of locality: individual LBP labels contain information about the patterns at the pixel-level, whereas the frequencies of the labels in the histogram produce information on regional level [7]. The collection of the histograms at all possible pixels $\{H_{(x,y)} \mid \forall(x, y)\}$, called the global LBP histogram, provides the global level description.

In [7], the face image is partitioned into a number (49) of blocks and a weight is empirically assigned to each block. Denote the corresponding histograms between the probe and a gallery by $H_{(x,y)}^{P}$ and $H_{(x,y)}^{G}$, respectively. Several possible dissimilarity measures are available to compare local two histograms. The following Chi square distance is reported to work better for small sample size [7]:

$$\chi^2(H_{(x,y)}^{P}, H_{(x,y)}^{G}) = \sum_{\ell \in \mathcal{L}} \frac{(H_{(x,y)}^{P}(\ell) - H_{(x,y)}^{G}(\ell))^2}{(H_{(x,y)}^{P}(\ell) + H_{(x,y)}^{G}(\ell))} \qquad (2)$$

A possible scheme for matching between two images is based on a weighted sum of χ^2 distances [7].

3   Learning for 3D Face Recognition

In this section, we describe a method which uses LBP features and AdaBoost learning for 3D face recognition with the LBP features. While in [7], a face image is partitioned into blocks, We consider every block centered at each pixel location. This yields a large number of possible blocks, and hence a large number of local histograms $H_{(x,y)}$. Instead of assigning a weight to each block, we derive the weights using an AdaBoost learning method. As a result of the learning, those blocks which are more discriminative for classification will be assigned larger weights and those which are useless or give conflict information will be assigned near-zero weights. The learning also produces the final classifier.

Face recognition is a multi-class problem. To dispense the need for a training process for faces of a newly added person, we use a large training set describing intra-personal or extra-personal variations [21], and train a "universal" two-class classifier. An ideal intra-personal difference should be an image with all pixel values being zero, whereas an extra-personal difference image should generally have much larger pixel values. However, instead of deriving the intra-personal or extra-personal variations using difference images as in [21], the training examples to our learning algorithm is the set of differences between each pair of local histograms $H_{(x,y)}$ at the corresponding locations. The positive examples are derived from pairs of intra-personal differences and the negative from pairs of inter-personal differences.

With the two-class scheme, the face matching procedure will work in the following way: It takes the probe face image and a gallery face image as the input; computes a difference-based feature vector from the two images; and then calculated a similarity score for the feature vector using some matching function. A decision is made based on the score, to classify the feature vector into the positive class (coming from the same person) or the negative class (different persons). The following presents an AdaBoost learning algorithm for training such a two-class classifier using the positive and negative examples of the 2D or 3D face data.

In AdaBoost learning, we are given a training set of N labeled examples from two classes, $\mathbf{S} = (x_1, y_1), \ldots, (x_N, y_N)$, where x_i is the data $y_i \in \{+1, -1\}$ is the class label. Associated with the training examples is a distribution $w_t = (w_{t,1}, \ldots, w_{t,N})$ which is updated after each learning iteration t. An AdaBoost procedure adjust the distribution in such a way that more difficult examples will receive higher weights. It learns a sequence of T weak classifiers $h_t(x) \in \{-1, +1\}$ and linearly combines it in an optimal way into a stronger classifier

$$H(x) = \text{sign}\left(\sum_{t=1}^{T} \alpha_t h_t(x)\right) \tag{3}$$

where $\alpha_t \in \mathbb{R}$ are the combining weights. We can consider the real-valued number $\sum_{t=1}^{T} \alpha_t h_t(x)$ as the score, and make a decision by comparing the score with a threshold.

An AdaBoost learning procedure, shown in Fig. 3, is aimed to derive α_t and $h_t(x)$. The AdaBoost learning procedure in effect solves the following three fundamental problems: (1) learning effective features from the candidate feature set (step 3), (2) constructing weak classifiers each of which is based on one of the selected features (step 1-3), and (3) combining the learned weak classifiers into a stronger classifier (the output step).

Input: Given labeled examples S;
Set the initial w_1 to the uniform distribution;
For $t = 1, \ldots, T$:
    1. Train a weak classifier $h_j : x \rightarrow \{-1, +1\}$;
    2. Calculate w_t-weighted error
        $e_j = P[h_j(x_i) \neq y_i \mid w_t]$;
    3. Choose $h_k(x)$, such that $e_k < e_j, \forall j \neq k$;
    4. Let $e_t = e_k$.
    5. Choose $\alpha_t = \frac{1}{2} \log \left(\frac{1-e_t}{e_t} \right)$;
    6. Update $w_{t+1,i} \leftarrow w_{t,i} \exp(-\alpha_t y_i h_i(x_i))$;
    7. Normalize w_{t+1} to $\sum_i w_{t+1,i} = 1$;
Output $H(x)$ as in Equ.(3).

Fig. 3. The AdaBoost learning procedure

In our system, a weak classifier is defined based on a single feature (*i.e.* an LBP histogram bin value). A weak classifier gives an output of +1 or -1, by thresholding the feature, at an appropriate threshold value learned with a weak learner procedure. This is unlike the Chi square distance based weak classifiers used in [10]. We find that the bin based weak classifiers can do a better job in both training and testing.

4   Learning to Fuse 2D and 3D

Now we present a method for fusing 2D and 3D information at both feature and decision levels. In the fusion of the 2D and 3D information, we do not make assumptions on how the information is correlated between 2D and 3D nor do we require that there are correspondences between 2D and 3D images. The only requirement is that faces in 2D and 3D images are properly aligned and normalized, respectively, as a result of pre-processing. Then, everything is learned automatically. We use the same AdaBoost learning procedure as above for the 3D+2D fusion as follows:

For every pixel location in an image (2D or 3D), an LBP code is computed. There are $L + 1 = 59$ possible LBP code types. A histogram of 59 bins is calculated, over a local sub-window centered at the pixel, to account for the distributions of the 59 types of features in the sub-window. For each intra-pair or inter-pair of 2D or 3D images, the Chi square distance is computed, according to Eq.(2), to account for the differences of the two corresponding local LBP histograms, and will be used as the feature to measure the dissimilarity between the two local image patches. The distributions of that Chi distances for the positive and negative examples at the local patch are then analyzed by considering all the intra-pairs or inter-pairs. Such statistics are computed over all the image locations and for both 2D and 3D images.

AdaBoost is applied to select most effective features from the complete 3D+2D difference feature set. At each iteration, the best LBP feature is selected, among all the locations for the 2D and 3D images, according to the distributions of the Chi square distances of the LBP histograms, such that the feature provides the best discriminative power. A weak classifier is then constructed by thresholding the Chi square distance. The weak classifiers are then combined into a strong one. This way, the AdaBoost based procedure provides a systematic approach for 3D+2D fusion at both feature and decision levels.

5   Experimental Results

The purpose of the experiments presented below is to compare the proposed boosting learning methods with the baseline PCA methods in their performance for 3D, 2D and 3D+2D face recognition.

5.1   Data Description

A large 3D+2D database is created for the experiments using a Minolta 3D digitizer, which produces a range image and the corresponding color image. The images are taken near-frontal but with varying pose, expression, and lighting changes. The database is composed of 2305 images of persons. It is divided into three sets. The composition of the data for the training, gallery and probe sets is summarized in Table 1. The images are preprocessed and cropped into 138x118 pixels. Figure 4 gives some examples of the preprocessed imaged.

Table 1. Data Composition

3D Data	Num. of Images	Num. of Persons
Train	945	246
Gallery	252	252
Probe	1108	252

2D Data	Num. of Images	Num. of Persons
Train	945	246
Gallery	252	252
Probe	1108	252

Before PCA the pixel vectors are first scaled such that the mean value of the vectors is zero and the standard deviation is one. We choose the top 99 percent of the energy and distance metric is L2. By computing the distance between the images in 2D and 3D set, respectively, we can get two similarity scores matrix. But the performance of the PCA on 2D or 3D is not good enough. Therefore, we fuse the scores to improve the

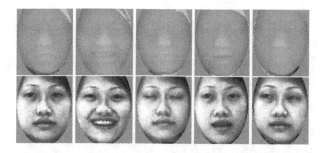

Fig. 4. Examples of 3D images and the corresponding 2D images of a person

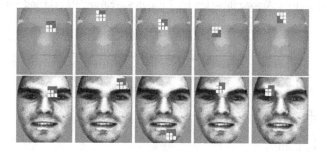

Fig. 5. The first 5 features for 3D (top) and for 2D (bottom) learned by AdaBoost

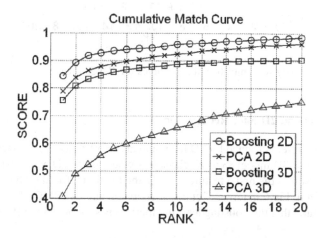

Fig. 6. Cumulative Match Curves for 3D and 2D

classifying performance. Before fusing the scores from each modality, the scores are normalized to [0, 100] and then fused by the sum rule. The weight is computed according to the method being mentioned in [6]. By fusing at decision levels, the performances are improved significantly.

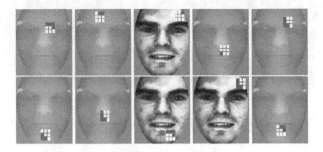

Fig. 7. The first 10 LBP features learned by boosted fusion of 3D+2D, ranked 1 to 10 from left to right, from top to bottom. Among these top 10, 7 features are from 3D data and 3 from 2D.

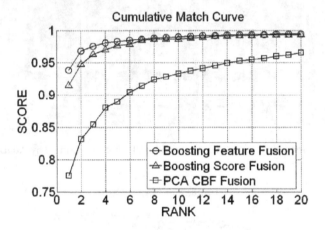

Fig. 8. Cumulative Match Curves for 3D+2D fusion

5.2 Boosted 3D and 2D Face Recognition

An AdaBoost classifier is trained for 3D faces and another trained for 2D faces recognition, separately. The 3D model 83 weak classifiers whereas the 2D model has 170 weak classifiers. Fig.5 shows the first 5 features for 3D and the first 5 for 2D. The comparative results are shown in Fig.6 in terms of cumulative match curves (CMC). From the CMC curves we conclude that the boosting learning method is superior to the PCA method.

5.3 Boosted Fusion of 3D+2D Face Recognition

For 3D+2D fusion, we trained a boosted model selected 97 most significant features. Of the 97 features, 59 are from 3D and 38 from 2D. Fig.7 shows the first 10 features for the 3D+2D fusion. We notice that the first 2 features in the AdaBoost 3D+2D fusion model (Fig.7) correspond to the first 2 features of 3D only model (Fig.5); and that there are more 3D features than 2D ones.

To contrast with the proposed AdaBoost learning fusion scheme, two non-boosting fusion schemes are included: The first is the PCA-based 3D+2D fusion (called "CBF' score fusion, described at the end of Section 3 of [17]), which is the baseline fusion performance. The second uses a sum rule to fuse the two AdaBoost classification scores. The comparative results are shown in Fig.8 in terms of cumulative match curves (CMC). From the CMC curves we conclude that fusing AdaBoost scores performs better than fusing PCA scores; and that fusion at both feature and decision levels by the proposed AdaBoost learning achieves the best performance of the three compared schemes.

6   Conclusion

In this paper, we explore synergies of 3D and 2D modalities by proposing a systematic framework for fusing 2D and 3D face recognition at both feature and decision levels. To our knowledge, this is the first work of this kind and is the main contribution of the paper. Another contribution is the novel LBP+AdaBoost learning method for 3D face recognition. We have demonstrated by experiments the effectiveness of the two contributions in 3D face recognition and in 3D+2D fusion. The successful fusion of 3D+2D at both feature and decision level has verified a conjecture made in [14] that "it is at least potentially more powerful to exploit possible synergies between the the two modalities in the interpretation of the data."

References

1. Turk, M.A., Pentland, A.P.: "Eigenfaces for recognition". Journal of Cognitive Neuroscience **3** (1991) 71–86
2. Belhumeur, P.N., Hespanha, J.P., Kriegman, D.J.: "Eigenfaces vs. Fisherfaces: Recognition using class specific linear projection. IEEE Transactions on Pattern Analysis and Machine Intelligence **19** (1997) 711–720
3. Bartlett, M.S., Lades, H.M., Sejnowski, T.J.: "Independent component representations for face recognition". Proceedings of the SPIE, Conference on Human Vision and Electronic Imaging III **3299** (1998) 528–539
4. Lades, M., Vorbruggen, J., Buhmann, J., Lange, J., von der Malsburg, C., Wurtz, R.P., Konen, W.: Distortion invariant object recognition in the dynamic link architecture. IEEE Transactions on Computers **42** (1993) 300–311
5. Wiskott, L., Fellous, J., Kruger, N., v. d. Malsburg, C.: "Face recognition by elastic bunch graph matching". IEEE Transactions on Pattern Analysis and Machine Intelligence **19** (1997) 775–779
6. Ojala, T., Pietikainen, M., Harwood, D.: "A comparative study of texture measures with classification based on feature distributions". Pattern Recognition **29** (1996) 51–59
7. Ahonen, T., Hadid, A., M.Pietikainen: "Face recognition with local binary patterns". In: Proceedings of the European Conference on Computer Vision, Prague, Czech (2004) 469–481
8. Hadid, A., Pietikinen, M., Ahonen, T.: "A discriminative feature space for detecting and recognizing faces". In: Proceedings of IEEE Computer Society Conference on Computer Vision and Pattern Recognition. Volume 2. (2004) 797–804
9. Jones, M., Viola, P.: "Face recognition using boosted local features". Tech Report TR2003-025, MERL (2003)

10. Zhang, G., Huang, X., Li, S.Z., Wang, Y.: "Boosting local binary pattern (LBP)-based face recognition". In Li, S.Z., Lai, J., Tan, T., Feng, G., Wang, Y., eds.: Advances in Biometric Personal Authentication. Volume LNCS-3338. Springer (2004) 180–187
11. Kanade, T.: Picture Processing by Computer Complex and Recognition of Human Faces. PhD thesis, Kyoto University (1973)
12. Cartoux, J.Y., LaPreste, J.T., Richetin, M.: "Face authentication or recognition by profile extraction from range images". In: Proceedings of the Workshop on Interpretation of 3D Scenes. (1989)
13. Besl, P.J., Jain, R.C.: "Intrinsic and extrinsic surface characteristics". In: Proceedings of the IEEE Computer Society Conference on Computer Vision and Pattern Recognition, San Francisco, California (1985) 226–233
14. Bowyer, K.W., Chang, Flynn, P.J.: "A survey of 3D and multi-modal 3d+2d face recognition". In: Proceedings of International Conference Pattern Recognition. (2004) 358–361
15. Lu, X., Jain, A.K.: "Integrating range and texture information for 3d face recognition". In: Proc. 7th IEEE Workshop on Applications of Computer Vision (WACV'05), Breckenridge, CO (2005)
16. Tsalakanidou, F., Malassiotis, S., Strintzis, M.G.: "Face localization and authentication using color and depth images". **14** (2005) 152–168
17. Chang, K.I., Bowyer, K.W., Flynn, P.J.: "An evaluation of multi-modal 2D+3D face biometrics". IEEE Transactions on Pattern Analysis and Machine Intelligence (2005) to appear
18. Freund, Y., Schapire, R.: "A decision-theoretic generalization of on-line learning and an application to boosting". Journal of Computer and System Sciences **55** (1997) 119–139
19. Schapire, R.: A brief introduction to boosting. In: Proceedings of the Sixteenth International Joint Conference on Artificial Intelligence. (1999)
20. Viola, P., Jones, M.: "Robust real time object detection". In: IEEE ICCV Workshop on Statistical and Computational Theories of Vision, Vancouver, Canada (2001)
21. Moghaddam, B., Nastar, C., Pentland, A.: "A Bayesain similarity measure for direct image matching". *Media Lab Tech Report* No.393, MIT (1996)

A New Combinatorial Approach to Supervised Learning: Application to Gait Recognition

Rong Zhang[1], Akshay Vashist[1], Ilya Muchnik[1,2],
Casimir Kulikowski[1], and Dimitris Metaxas[1]

[1] Dept. of Computer Science
{roni, vashisht, kulikows, dnm}@cs.rutgers.edu
[2] DIMACS Rutgers, The State University of New Jersey,
Piscataway, NJ 08854, USA
muchnik@dimacs.rutgers.edu

Abstract. In many supervised learning problems, objects are represented as a sequence of observations. To classify such data, existing methods build classifiers either based on their dynamics, or the statistics of the observations. However, similar observations shared by most objects are uninformative for identification. In this paper, we present a new approach that identifies similar observations across objects and use only informative data for classification. To do this, we construct a weighted multipartite graph from the training data, with weights representing the similarities between observations from different objects. Identification of uninformative observations is modeled as clustering on this multipartite graph using a combinatorial optimization formulation. Two-level hierarchical classifiers are, then, built using the clustering results. The first layer of the classifiers associates the test observations with a certain cluster, whereas the second level identifies the object within the cluster. Data associated with uninformative clusters are screened out. Final identification for the group of observations is obtained using the majority voting rule only from the informative observations.

We apply our algorithm to the gait recognition problem. The hierarchical classifiers are built in four different feature spaces for silhouette images. Final classification is determined by aggregating results from these four feature spaces. The experimental results show that our method results in improved recognition rates in most cases compared with other previously reported methods.

1 Introduction

In many supervised learning problems, the object of interest is represented as a sequence of observations. For instance, in cytological research, living tissue under a microscope is observed as an ensemble of cell images [1]; and in human motion analysis, an individual's movement is captured by cameras as a sequence of image frames [2]. To distinguish tissue cells, or to identify a person from image sequences, two groups of approaches have been applied to classify these observations. In the first group, the dynamics of all observations from an object, e.g., training a hidden Markov model [3], are employed to capture the characteristics of the subject. In the second group of approaches, static features, such as averages and standard deviations in quadratic discriminant function [4], are used to characterize the subject. These "dynamic" and "static"

W. Zhao, S. Gong, and X. Tang (Eds.): AMFG 2005, LNCS 3723, pp. 55–69, 2005.

features, used to classify the subjects, are obtained through "intra-class" analysis of each individual subject, i.e., without "inter-class" comparing the similarities and differences among observations of different subjects. In many cases, some observations from different subjects are very similar, which do not provide any characteristic information useful for classification. More significantly, including these uninformative frames in the classification process tends to smear the differences among subjects, can lead to a weaker classifier due to the potential confusions. Hence, it is necessary to exclude these uninformative frames to enhance the classification accuracy and robustness.

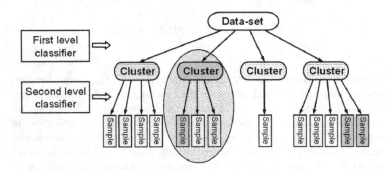

Fig. 1. Outline of the proposed classification framework. The uninformative cluster and the corresponding samples are shown in shadow. Samples from different subjects are color-coded.

A common approach for removing redundant information is feature selection using principle component analysis, independent component analysis etc. [5]. These approaches remove irrelevant features from a given feature set, and thus will modify the feature space for every sample across different objects. However, there has been no systematic research on removing uninformative samples, keeping the feature space representation unchanged.

In this paper, we present a novel combinatorial optimization approach to identify similar observations across subjects, ignoring similarities between frames from the same subject. We construct a multipartite graph structure from observations in the data, where a partite set corresponds to a subject and vertices in a partite set correspond to the samples from an object. Such a graph only specifies similarities between observations from different objects. Then, the problem of identifying similar samples across objects is formulated as a clustering problem on the multipartite graph. We give an efficient algorithm for finding the clusters of uninformative samples.

Subsequently, we build supervised hierarchical classifiers, as illustrated in Fig. 1. The first level classifier performs an assignment of a testing sample to clusters, whereas the second level carries out the actual subject identification.

The above classification framework could be applied to many problems with ensemble data. In this paper, methodological details of this work is demonstrated through the gait recognition problem where objects are the human subjects and the samples correspond to frames/images from the those subjects.

Gait Recognition

To identify a walking subject from an image (frame) sequence, current gait recognition approaches can be classified as either model-based [9,10,11,12,13] or model-free [2,14,15,16,17,18,19,20] based on whether a specific humanoid model is employed. Joint angle trajectories [9,10,11,12,13], body shape parameters [16,19], or other features [2,14,15,17,18,20] extracted from images, were used to represent gait characteristics. When a probe frame sequence is available, the same features are extracted and compared to those in the training data.

Both of these approaches calculate the similarity between the probe sequence and a sequence from any subject in the data, and label the probe sequence as the one with the highest similarity value. However, for subjects represented by silhouette images, or binary images with foreground pixels labeled as 1 and background as 0, very often similar silhouette images occurs among different subjects. Accurate and robust identification can be achieved by training classifiers on frames that are signatures of individual subjects, and excluding the ubiquitously present frames. There is no previous work, to our knowledge, on studying the similarity across frames from different subjects and pinpoint the uninformative ones.

We constructed four feature spaces for silhouette images to formulate of similarity measure between samples. Hierarchical classifiers are built in each feature space. Following classification in each space separately, results in the four feature spaces for all images within the test sequence are aggregated to provide the final classification results.

The organization of this paper is as follows. Section 2 presents a description of the four feature spaces for silhouette images. In Section 3, we present our algorithm for identifying uninformative clusters of similar image frames across subjects. The hierarchical classification process and the aggregation method are described in Section 4. In Section 5, we present the experimental results and discussions, followed by conclusions in Section 6.

2   Feature Spaces for Silhouette Images

The usual inputs in the gait recognition problem are binary silhouette images to eliminate the texture and color information from original images. In this section, we provide a domain-specific feature extraction procedure for the contour points of the human silhouette, and design four different feature spaces for similarity measurement between images. Our classification framework can be applied to other problems by simply modifying the feature spaces.

2.1   Contour Point Detection

Our image features are defined on contour points, as the locations of these points encode a given silhouette image. We design eight filters to detect contour points in silhouette images, as shown in Fig. 2. These detectors are linear filters with various orientations. A foreground point is marked as a contour point only when the convolution between the silhouette image and any of the eight filters is greater than a certain threshold. Compared

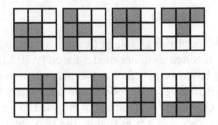

Fig. 2. Eight feature detectors for contour points

Fig. 3. Upper left panel: original silhouette image. Lower left: combined contour point detection results. Second to last columns: responses to the feature detectors in Fig. 2.

with simple morphological operations such as removing foreground pixels whose four-connected neighbors are foreground as well, these detectors can find the outer contour of the silhouette image and also the orientation of the corresponding boundary. Fig. 3 illustrates the results of this contour point detection process. For the silhouette image in the upper left panel, the responses to the eight filters are shown in the second to last columns. Combining these individual filter responses leads to the complete contour point plot shown in the lower left panel of Fig. 3.

2.2 Relative Shape Vector

To measure the relative location of a contour point within the silhouette, we introduce a new shape descriptor, called Relative Shape Vector (RSV). For any point p within a set of contour points C, all other points in the set $C - \{p\}$ should be located in two of the eight overlapping windows as shown in Fig 4(a). Counting the number of contour points located in each window results in an eight-dimensional vector $(c_1(p, C), \cdots, c_8(p, C))$. The RSV for the point p with respect to set C is a normalized version of this vector, defined as follows:

$$RSV(p, C) = (\alpha_1(p, C), \cdots, \alpha_8(p, C)), \tag{1}$$

where $\alpha_i(p, C) = c_i(p, C)/\sum_{k=1}^{8} c_k(p, C), i = 1, \ldots, 8$. The RSVs for contour points A, B, and C in Fig. 4(b) are given in Fig. 4(c). Note that this is similar to the shape context descriptor [21], except that we have a set of overlapping windows and the histogram

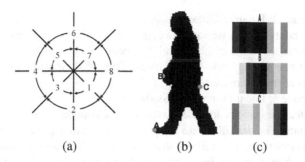

(a)   (b)   (c)

Fig. 4. (a) The eight windows used in Relative Shape Vector calculation. The number inside each section is the window index. (b) Three contour points on a silhouette image. (c) The corresponding eight-dimensional RSVs. Brighter shades means higher value.

is only calculated based on orientations, regardless of distances. Therefore, RSVs preserve redundant information with overlapping windows, and describe less details of the shape by ignoring relative distances, making it less sensitive to changes in the contours.

2.3 The Four Feature Spaces

As the RSV describes the relative location of a given contour point with respect to others, points on different images but at roughly the same relative locations will have similar RSV values. Therefore, grouping in the RSV space results in segmentation of contour points according to their relative locations on a silhouette. Fig. 5 shows the grouping results for two different images using the k-mean algorithm [22], where $k = 13$ is chosen empirically. We see that points at the same relative locations are labeled as the same group. These grouping results enable us to define four feature spaces for the silhouette images:

- Feature Space 1: Gravity Center Distance For each group of points in a given image, we obtain its gravity center. The first feature space contains all distances between different gravity centers, normalized with largest one. With 13 groups, the dimensionality of this feature space is 78.

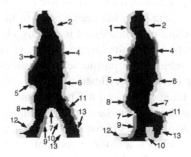

Fig. 5. Grouping results of contour points in two silhouette images. Group numbers are labeled alongside the contour points.

- Feature Space 2: Relative Center Distance
  For each gravity center, we rank its distances to other 12 centers, and obtain two relative distances as the smallest and the second largest distances with respect to the largest one among these 12 distances. This 26-dimensional feature measures relative distances within each image.
- Feature Space 3: Local Orientation Statistics
  The third feature space is designed to capture the boundary orientation information. The orientation of the silhouette image at each contour point is contained in the filter responses to the eight filters shown in Fig. 2. The average response from all points in each group can be interpreted as a histogram of silhouette orientation at the contour points. This 65-dimensional feature captures the local orientation statistics.
- Feature Space 4: Local Shape Statistics
  Another feature we want to capture is the local distribution of contour points within each group. These local shape statistics include the two eigenvalues of the covariance matrix of these points, the ratio of the eigenvalues, and the orientation of the principle components.

The above four feature spaces provide rich descriptions of the shape within a silhouette image and different opportunities for recognition. Similar silhouetted images are close to each other in the feature spaces. Therefore, we are able to cluster images according to their similarities within these four feature spaces.

3   Multipartite Graph Clustering and Filtering

In this section, we describe the clustering method for identifying uninformative frames in a given feature space. Given the representation of frames in a feature space, our goal is to divide the training data frames from multiple subjects into two classes: a set with subject-specific frames, and another with non-subject-specific ones (shared by many subjects). It is likely that filtering out frames that are similar (or uninformative) across subjects would increase the accuracy of classification. Finding such uninformative frames can be cast as a clustering problem on a graph representing similarity between frames from different subjects.

In a traditional clustering scenario, frames close to each other are grouped as a cluster. However, in our problem, similarity between frames from the same subject should not to be considered, as we are only interested in finding clusters containing similar frames from different subjects. Such a similarity structure is captured by a multipartite graph, where we denote a subject as a partite set and frames from a subject as vertices in the corresponding partite set. An illustration of this representation is in Fig. 6, where we show a complete three-partite graph. The multipartite graph representation is suitable because it only considers the similarity relationships between frames from different subjects. The presence of clusters in the multipartite graph reveals the similarity among frames from different objects and those containing very similar frames from a large number of subjects are considered as uninformative.

In graph theory, clusters are related to dense subgraphs called cliques [7]. Therefore, our problem of identifying similar frames across different subjects can be formulated

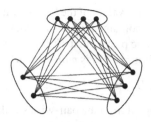

Fig. 6. A complete three-partite graph

as finding cliques in a multipartite graph [6]. However, the maximum clique finding problem, and its various weighted formulations for multipartite graphs, are proven to be NP-complete [8,6]. Due to the sensitivity of the filtering problem and the additional requirement for finding similar frames across different subjects only, existing clustering methods are inadequate. Heuristics are often used to find clusters in data [7] but these heuristic methods are not well suited to our approach since they cannot guarantee finding best multipartite clusters. Therefore, we need an optimization based procedure whose exact solution can be found. In this paper, we propose such a multipartite graph clustering method for finding clusters of uninformative frames. The objective function in our multipartite clustering method have favorable properties which guarantee that a globally optimal solution can be found with an efficient algorithm.

3.1 Multipartite Graph Clustering

For a problem with k subjects in the training data, let V_i, $i \in \{1, 2, \ldots, k\}$ denote a set of vertices which represent frames from subject i. We construct an undirected weighted multipartite graph $G = (V, E, W)$, where $V = \cup_{i=1}^{k} V_i$, and $E \subseteq \cup_{i \neq j} V_i \times V_j$ is the set of weighted, undirected edges connecting vertices from different partite sets. The weight $w_{ij} \in W$ on the edge $e_{ij} \in E$ represents the similarity between the vertices i and j.

Let H denote a subset of V such that H contains vertices from at least two partite. We define a score function $F(H)$ to measure the proximity among elements in H. Then, our multipartite quasi-clique, or a cluster, H^*, is defined as the subset with the largest score value, i.e,

$$H^* = \arg \max_{H \subseteq V} F(H). \tag{2}$$

The efficiency of extracting the optimal set H^* is closely related to the algebraic properties of $F(H)$. When the set function $F(H)$ is *quasi-concave*, i.e,

$$F(H_1 \cup H_2) \geq \min(F(H_1), F(H_2)) \ \forall H_1, H_2 \subseteq V \tag{3}$$

the optimal solution can be efficiently obtained, if $F(H)$ can be efficiently computed. Here, $F(H)$ is designed using a linkage function $\pi(i, H)$ that measures the degree of similarity of the frame $i \in H$ to other frames in H, leading to the following definition:

$$F(H) = \min_{i \in V} \pi(i, V), \forall i \in V \ \forall H \subseteq V \tag{4}$$

In other words, $F(H)$ is the $\pi(i, H)$ values of the least similar (outlier) frame in H. Then, according to (2), the subset, H^* contains frames such that similarity of the least similar frame in H is maximum. It can be proved that $F(H)$ as defined in (4) is quasi-concave if and only if the linkage function $\pi(i, H)$ is *monotonically increasing* [23], i.e,

$$\pi(i, H) \geq \pi(i, H_1) \ \forall i, \forall H_1, \forall H : i \in H_1 \subseteq H \subseteq V \tag{5}$$

The linkage function is constructed from the pair-wise similarity values between frames from different subjects. Besides being monotone increasing, the linkage function should be designed such that $\pi(i, H)$ and hence $F(H)$ can be efficiently computed; this would guarantee a polynomial time procedure to find H^*. At the same time, the linkage function should capture an appropriate notion of similarity so that the optimal solution H^* captures the multipartite quasi-clique nature of relationships between frames contained in H^*. Although a large family of linkage functions satisfying the above requirements exists, we use a simple and intuitive linkage function to demonstrate our approach. If m_{ij} ($\geq o$) is the similarity value between frame i from subject $s(i)$ and frame j from subject $s(j)$ ($s(j) \neq s(i)$), then the linkage function is defined as

$$\pi(i, H) = \sum_{\substack{\ell=1 \\ \ell \neq s(i)}}^{k} \sum_{\substack{j \in H \\ s(j) \neq s(i)}} m_{ij} \tag{6}$$

In other words, the linkage function $\pi(i, H)$ aggregates the similarity between the frame i from subject $s(i)$ and all other frames in H that do not belong to subject $s(i)$.

Table 1. Pseudocode to extract H^*

Step 0: Set $t := 1$; $H_1 := V$; $H^* := V$;
Step 1: Find $M_t := \{i : \pi(i, H_t) = \min_{j \in H_t} \pi(j, H_t)\}$;
Step 2: if $((H_t \setminus M_t = \emptyset) \vee (\pi(i, H_t) = 0 \ \forall i \in H_t))$ STOP.
else $H_{t+1} := H_t \setminus M_t$; $t := t + 1$;
if $(F(H_t) > F(H^*))$ $H^* = H_t$;
go to Step 1.

The algorithm to find the optimal solution H^* is described in Table 1 [23]. This iterative algorithm begins with the calculation of $F(V)$ and the set M_1 containing the subset of frames that satisfy $F(V) = \pi(i, V)$, i.e, $M_1 = \{i \in V : \pi(i, V) = F(V)\}$. The frames in M_1 are removed from V to obtain $H_2 = V \setminus M_1$. At iteration t, it considers the set H_{t-1} as the input, calculates $F(H_{t-1})$, identifies the subset M_t such that $F(H_{t-1}) = \pi(i_t, H_{t-1}), \forall i_t \in M_t$, and removes this subset from H_{t-1} to produce $H_t = H_{t-1} \setminus M_t$. The algorithm terminates at iteration T when $H_T = \emptyset$ or $\pi(i, H_T) = 0 \ \forall i \in H_T$. It outputs H^* as the subset, H_j with the smallest j such that $F(H_j) \geq F(H_l) \ \forall l \in \{1, 2, \ldots, T\}$.

The above formulation gives us one multipartite cluster, however, many such clusters would be present in the multipartite graph. Assuming that these clusters are unrelated to each other, we can use a simple heuristic to find cluster H^*, remove it from the set V, and find another cluster in the remaining set $V \setminus H^*$. This can be applied iteratively to find all the multipartite clusters.

3.2 Determining Uninformative Clusters

There are two criteria for determining which clusters should be labeled as uninformative. First of all, frames within such clusters should be highly similar to each other. Secondly, these clusters should contain frames from most of the subjects.

From the above procedure, similarity among frames within a cluster is given by the score value $F(H^*)$ of cluster H^*. Since this score value is the aggregated similarity between a frame and all other frames in the cluster, it would, in general, be larger for larger clusters. Hence we use the average similarity value of a cluster defined as $F(H^*)/|H^*|$, instead of $F(H^*)$ for estimating homogeneity within a cluster. Clusters with large average similarity values, but containing frames from just a few subjects are actually informative for classification as they characterize the subjects therein. Hence, only those clusters containing frames where most subjects have an average similarity value above a certain threshold are labeled as uninformative.

4 Details of Classification

Clusters obtained in the previous section provide a hierarchical structure for the entire data, based on which we build our classifiers as shown in Fig. 1. The first level is to determine whether a probe frame is informative, whereas identification within each informative cluster is specified in the second level. In addition, for a group of frames from an unknown subject, we aggregate the identification results from all informative ones to reach a final identification.

4.1 Hierarchical Classifiers

There are a number of standard methods available for binary or multi-class classification. Here we use Bayesian logistic regression(BLR) [24] as the first level of our hierarchical classifier structure and the nearest neighbor as the second level classifier.

First Level - Bayesian Logistic Regression. To determine the cluster for a probe frame, we train a binary classifier for each cluster obtained from Section 3. The Bayesian logistic regression (BLR) [24] is applied to achieve state of the art effectiveness while avoiding over-fitting.

Given a training set containing n samples, $s_1, \ldots, s_n$, with corresponding labels $y_1, \ldots, y_n$, the BLR aims at finding the best parameter value which maximizes the conditional probability model of the form

$$p(y = +1|\beta, s_i) = \psi(\beta^T s_i), \quad \text{where} \quad \psi(r) = \frac{exp(r)}{1 + exp(r)}$$

is a logistic regression model, and β is a parameter to be determined through the learning process. We choose Laplace distribution as a prior distribution for each component of β. This sparse favoring prior guarantees most components of β have a 0 or near zero value. Fast and accurate prediction could be achieved through the method provided in [24].

Second Level - Nearest Neighbor. If a probe frame is labeled as an uninformative cluster (the cluster shadowed in Fig. 1), this frame does not contain characteristic information, and will be screened out from classification. The second level of classifier is used only for the frames classified as informative.

Within each informative cluster, there are multiple frames from several subjects. We choose the nearest neighbor method due to its simplicity and low bias.

4.2   Classification Rule

To classify an unknown subject $X = \{(x_{11}, x_{12}, x_{13}, x_{14}), \ldots, (x_{n1}, x_{n2}, x_{n3}, x_{n4})\}$ with n frames where $x_{k.} = (x_{k1}, x_{k2}, x_{k3}, x_{k4})$ is the representation for the frame k in the four different feature spaces, we apply four different classifiers C_1, C_2, C_3 and C_4 in corresponding feature spaces. Let m_{ij} denote the number of informative frames assigned by the classifier C_j to subject i in the training data-set. We integrate the classification results from the individual classifiers for estimating the membership r_i of the unknown subject X to the subject i. We used the ordered weighting assignment (OWA) [25] where weights for each classifier are ordered according to the confidence levels of the classifier. Precisely, for estimating the membership of X to i, the m_{ij}'s, $j = 1, \ldots, 4$ are sorted as $m_{ij_1} \geq \ldots \geq m_{ij_4}$ and ordered weighted assignment, r_i^{OWA} is calculated as $r_i^{OWA} = \sum_{l=1}^{4} w_l m_{ij_l}$. It must be noted that m_{ij_l} is different from m_{ij}. The procedure to find the weights w_l will be described shortly. The final classification r^* for X is obtained as the subject which shows highest level of assignment [26], i.e., $r^* = \arg \max_i r_i^{OWA}$, where i is a subject from the training data.

The weight vector $\mathbf{w} = (w_1, w_2, w_3, w_4)$ used in the above classification rule must satisfy $\sum_{l=1}^{4} w_l = 1$ and $w_l \geq 0 \ \forall l$, where w_l is quantized into ten discrete values, i.e., $w_l \in \{0.1, 0.2, \ldots, 0.9, 1.0\}$. The optimal weights under this restriction are obtained, by exhaustively searching all possible combinations, as the one which maximizes the accuracy of the above classifier under 5-fold cross-validation on the training data.

5   Experimental Results and Analysis

We apply our method to the silhouette images from Human ID Gait Challenge Database collected at the University of South Florida (USF) in May and November 2001. There are a total of 122 subjects in the data, walking on different surfaces (G/C), with different shoes (A/B), with/without carrying a briefcase (BF/NB), and captured with two cameras (R/L) at different times (t_1/t_2). There are 12 carefully designed experiments to test whether identification can be made under different walking conditions, as summarized in Table 2 [27].

The image frames from different subjects are clustered using the multipartite graph clustering procedure described in section 3. On average about 87% of the training data are classified into clusters. Most of the clusters contain frames from a few subjects, therefore, they are considered as informative from classification perspective. Across different feature spaces, we are able to label (on average) about 14% of all frames as uninformative. Figure 7 shows some frames detected as uninformative. As we can see,

Table 2. 12 probe sets with the common gallery of (G, A, R, t_1) containing 122 subjects

Experiment	Probe	Difference
A	G, A, L	View
B	G, B, R	Shoe
C	G, B, L	Shoe View
D	C, A, R	Surface
E	C, B, R	Surface Shoe
F	C, A, L	Surface View
G	C, B, L	Surface Shoe View
H	G, A, R, BF	Briefcase
I	G, B, R, BF	Shoe, Briefcase
J	G, A, L, BF	View, Briefcase
K	G, A/B, R, NB, BF, t_2	Time
L	C, A/B, R, NB, BF, t_2	Surface Time

Fig. 7. A representative instance of uninformative frames from different subjects, in the USF data, within an (uninformative) multipartite cluster

most frames are captured during the mid-swing/mid-stance phase of a gait cycle. This is consistent with our intuition because at this stage of a gait cycle, most body parts overlap with each other and could not show details in the silhouette images.

Further, classifiers are constructed based on the clustering results in the four different feature spaces. The corresponding recognition rates, together with the aggregation results of different feature spaces, are given in Table 3. In addition, Fig. 8 illustrates the aggregation recognition results by the cumulative match score (CMS).

We find that the recognition rates in experiments A and C are consistently better in space 1 (gravity center distance, see section 2.3); however space space 3 (local orientation statistics) provides better recognition in experiments D through L, while space 4 (local shape statistics) seems to capture essential features in experiment B. This suggests that the four feature spaces capture considerably different aspects of the silhouette images, although in most cases, the local orientation statistics is the most relevant feature for recognition. Therefore aggregating results from all four features spaces leads to improved recognition rates, as shown in Table 3 by utilizing all available information.

In Table 4, our results are compared with others reported previously. Our approach considerably outperforms the baseline algorithm [27] in 10 out of the 12 cases, while matching in another one. Our method achieve a much higher recognition rate for experiments K and L, (18% and 15% respectively, comparing to 3% by baseline algorithm), which are the most difficult experiments in the challenge set. The only favorable case

Table 3. Recognition rates for different experiments in each of the four feature spaces as well as the aggregation results

Exp	Space 1	Space 2	Space 3	Space 4	Aggregate
A	70	61	66	52	82
B	81	78	78	83	89
C	69	56	54	63	76
D	19	21	31	20	36
E	36	31	40	34	53
F	12	12	16	13	23
G	22	16	22	16	34
H	32	25	42	25	44
I	40	29	50	40	57
J	25	19	28	20	37
K	12	12	12	12	18
L	6	3	12	9	15

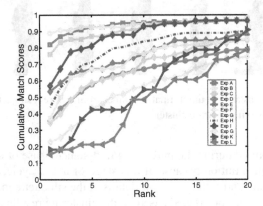

Fig. 8. CMS curves for USF data

for the baseline method is when the subject carries a briefcase in the probe sequence; we attribute this to insufficient information to distinguish subjects when the briefcase contour dominates the subject contour. In comparison to the results from HMM approach [3], our method performs better or equivalently in 5 of the 7 experimental conditions.

We also compare our method with k-nearest neighbor without screening uninformative examples. We choose $k = 5$ in our comparison, and the results show that all of the 12 cases, uninformative frames adversely affect the recognition rate. Further, we employ principle component analysis (PCA), a typical feature selection method, to reduce the feature space before the k-nearest neighbor classification. Though we maintain

Table 4. Comparison of recognition rates of our method with other methods

Exp Id	HMM (UMD) (71 subj.)	Baseline (122 subj.)	kNN (122 subj.)	PCA (122 subj.)	Our work (122 subj.)
A	99	73	75	75	82
B	89	78	78	78	89
C	78	48	56	56	76
D	36	32	34	34	36
E	29	22	40	40	53
F	24	17	16	16	23
G	18	17	22	22	34
H	N/A	61	43	43	44
I	N/A	57	48	48	57
J	N/A	36	32	30	37
K	N/A	3	12	12	18
L	N/A	3	6	6	15

95% total variance of the original data, as we can see, there is no gain in applying PCA, and the recognition rate even decreases in Exp J.

Our method significantly outperforms all other previously reported methods in cases when the subject walks on a different surface or at different time comparing to the training data. This shows our method has more prediction power for unknown walking conditions. Eliminating the common frames across subjects enables us to avoid training on "noisy" (i.e. uninformative from the classification perspective) frames, thereby resulting in a higher recognition rate. In contrast, approaches that attempt to capture strict dynamics of a walking style, such as HMM based methods, cannot isolate the uninformative frames, and hence may perform poorly.

6   Conclusions and Future Work

A new combinatorial framework for supervised classification problem is proposed in this paper. In this framework, the similar samples from a large number of subjects are taken to be uninformative. These uninformative samples are obtained as clusters on a multipartite graph using a novel combinatorial clustering approach. To classify a test subject (probe sequence), its observations (image frames) are first classified as either uninformative or informative; so only the informative frames from the test subject are used for classification.

This framework is applied to the gait recognition problem, and the results demonstrate the efficacy of our method. Currently, we treat sequences of images as a group of frames, without considering the dynamics. However, our framework can be extended to encode the dynamics by introducing another feature space. Furthermore, for color/texture images, different feature spaces should also be developed for other applications. It would be interesting to see the performance of HMMs when they are trained on more informative data for classification.

Acknowledgment

This work is supported by the National Science Foundation under contract numbers 0200983, 0205671, 0313184, and CCR 0325398. In addition, RZ and AV would like to thank the DIMACS Graduate Student Awards for partial support of this work.

References

1. Cheson, B.D.: Chronic Lymphoid Leukemias. Marcel Dekker (2001)
2. Phillips, P., Sarkar, S., Robledo, I., Grother, P., Bowyer, K.: The gait identification challenge problem: Data sets and baseline algorithm. In: CVPR. (2002)
3. Sundaresan, A., RoyChowdhury, A., Chellappa, R.: A hidden markov model based framework for recognition of humans from gait sequences. In: ICIP. (2003)
4. Webb, A.: Statistical Pattern Recognition. Wiley (2002)
5. Comon, P.: Independent component analysis, a new concept? Signal Processing **36** (1994) 287–314
6. Dawande, M., Keskinocak, P., Swaminathan, J.M., Tayur, S.: On bipartite and multipartite clique problems. J of Algorithms **41** (2001) 388–403
7. Everitt, B.S., Landau, S., Leese, M.: Cluster Analysis, 4th edition. Oxford University Press Inc. (2001)
8. Hochbaum, D.S.: Approximating clique and biclique problems. J of Algorithms **29** (1997) 174–200
9. Cunado, D., Nixon, M., Carter, J.: Using gait as a biometric, via phase-weighted magnitude spectra. In: 1st Int. Conf. audio and video based biometric person authentification. (1997)
10. Yam, C.Y., Nixon, M.S., Carter, J.N.: On the relationship of human walking and running: Automatic person identification by gait. In: ICPR. (2002)
11. Tanawongsuwan, R., Bobick, A.: Gait recognition from time-normalized joint-angle trajectories in the walking plane. In: CVPR. Volume II. (2001) 726–731
12. Niyogi, S., Adelson, E.: Analyzing and recognizing walking figures in xyt. In: CVPR. (1994)
13. Zhang, R., Vogler, C., Metaxas, D.: Human gait recognition. In: IEEE Workshop on Articulated and Nonrigid Motion, in conjunction with CVPR'04. (July 2004)
14. Collins, R., Gross, R., Shi, J.: Silhouette-based human identification from body shape and gait. In: International Conference on Automatic Face and Gesture Recognition. (2002)
15. Murase, H., Sakai, R.: Moving object recognition in eigenspace representation: gait analysis and lip reading. Pattern Recognition Letters **17** (1996) 155–162
16. Huang, P., Harris, C., Nixon, M.: Human gait recognition in canonical space using temporal templates. IEE Proceedings - Vision, Image and Signal Processing **146** (1999) 93–100
17. Kale, A., Cuntoor, N., Yegnanarayana, B., Rajagopalan, A., Chellappa, R.: Gait analysis for human identification. In: Proceedings of the 3rd International conference on Audio and Video Based Person Authentication. (2003)
18. Little, L., Boyd, J.: Recognizing people by their gait: the shape of motion. Videre **1** (1996) 1–32
19. Wang, L., Tan, T., Ning, H., Hu, W.: Silhouette analysis-based gait recognition for human identification. IEEE PAMI **25** (2003) 1505–1518

20. Sunderesan, A., Chowdhury, A.K.R., Chellappa, R.: A hidden markov model based framework for recognition of humans from gait sequences. In: IEEE ICIP. (2003)
21. Belongie, S., Malik, J., Puzicha, J.: Shape matching and object recognition using shape contexts. IEEE Transactions on Pattern Analysis and Machine Intelligence **24** (2002) 509–522
22. Tou, J.T., Gonzalezn, R.C., eds.: Pattern Recognition Principles. Addison-Wesley, Norwell, MA (1974)
23. Vashist, A., Kulikowski, C., Muchnik, I.: Ortholog clustering on a multipartite graph. In: Workshop on Algorithms in Bioinformatics (WABI). (2005)
24. Genkin, A., Lewis, D.D., Madigan, D.: Large-scale bayesian logistic regression for text categorization. J of Machine Learning submitted. (2004)
25. Yager, R., Kacprzyk, J., eds.: The Ordered Weighted Averaging Operators: Theory and Applications. Kluwer Academic Publishers, Reading, MA (1997)
26. Kittler, J., Hatef, M., Duin, R.P., Matas, J.: On combining classifiers. IEEE PAMI. **20** (1998) 226–239
27. Sarkar, S., Phillips, P., Liu, Z., Vega, I., Grother, P., Bowyer, K.: The HumanID gait challenge problem: Data sets, performance, and analysis. IEEE PAMI. **27** (2005) 162–177

Learning a Dynamic Classification Method to Detect Faces and Identify Facial Expression

Ramana Isukapalli[1], Ahmed Elgammal[3], and Russell Greiner[2]

[1] Lucent Technologies, Bell Labs Innovations, Whippany, NJ 07981, USA
[2] University of Alberta, Edmonton, CA T6G 2E8, CA
[3] Rutgers University, New Brunswick, NJ 08854, USA

Abstract. While there has been a great deal of research in face detection and recognition, there has been very limited work on identifying the *expression* on a face. Many current face detection projects use a [Viola/Jones] style "cascade" of Adaboost-based classifiers to interpret (sub)images — *e.g.*, to identify which regions contain faces. We extend this method by learning a *decision tree* of such classifiers (DTC): While standard cascade classification methods will apply the same sequence of classifiers to each image, our DTC is able to select the most effective classifier at every stage, based on the outcomes of the classifiers already applied. We use DTC not only to detect faces in a test image, but to identify the expression on each face.

1 Introduction

The pioneering work of Viola and Jones [12] has led to a host of face detectors based on "cascade classifiers", where each classifier is learned by applying Adaboost [4] (or some related algorithm [11,13]) to a database of training images of faces and non-faces. The underlying principle in all these algorithms is to learn multiple classifiers during the training phase, then (at performance time), run these classifiers as a "cascade" on each region (at various resolutions) of the test image — *i.e.*, in a sequence one after another, eliminating non-faces at each stage.

In general, there can be many *sub-clusters* within the class of face images — in particular, perhaps one sub-cluster corresponds to people with the same facial expression while another corresponds to people with some other expression.

Moreover, one of our learned classifiers might do very well on one cluster, but relatively poorly on another. Consider, for example, the examples shown in Figure 1, and notice the positive instances can be grouped into 3 clusters. (Here, imagine every instance labeled "+" corresponds to a HappyFace, "◇" to a SadFace and "□" to an AngryFace". Note all 3 are faces — *i.e.*, should be labeled positively by a face detector.) Now consider two possible classifiers, corresponding to the set of separating lines labeled C_1 (respectively C_2). Neither is perfect. If we are trying to separate only the "+" labeled positive instances from the negative instances, we would get better results using C_1; but if dealing with "◇" labeled or "□" labeled instances, then C_2 would preferred. Of course, this same idea holds for different possible *cascade* of classifiers: different cascades might be preferable for different clusters of images.

W. Zhao, S. Gong, and X. Tang (Eds.): AMFG 2005, LNCS 3723, pp. 70–84, 2005.

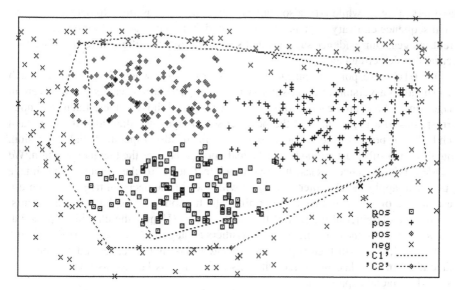

Fig. 1. Two classifiers on set of positive and negative examples. Note various sub-clusters of positive examples.

At performance time, our performance system DTC will scan through an unlabeled image. For each sub-image W, it will (1) quickly sort W to the cluster best able to process this sub-image, and (2) apply to W the classifier cascade appropriate to this cluster. If W passes all of those classifiers, it is declared a "face", and moreover assigned the expression E associated with this cluster. The challenge is learning these two sub-procedures. To do this, we first run the [12] algorithm on a training set whose image regions are labeled only as face (vs non-face), but without any expression data. This produces a set of Adaboost classifiers $\mathcal{C} = \{C_1, \ldots, C_N\}$. We then use these C_is as features, to produce a decision tree that attempts to partition a second labeled training set, which is a collection of images whose faces are each labeled with an expression (as well as non-faces), into sub-collections containing faces with the same expression. At each leaf node of this decision tree we then assemble a sequence of classifiers (each taken from the $\mathcal{C}$ set) to form a cascade appropriate to this cluster. (Note each cluster can have its own classifier sequence.) By construction, the resulting face detection system will not only detect faces, but also associate every such face detected in a test image with an expression.

This framework has two advantages over the standard model of cascade classifiers. First, the standard model can only assign a binary "face vs non-face" label to each subimage. By contrast, our system can return several labels, corresponding to facial expression (as well as "non-face"). Second, while one classifier (or cascade of classifiers) might work well in identifying images in one cluster, that classifier (cascade) might not work well for another. Unfortunately the existing cascade-based detection techniques are *static* and *image-independent*, in that they apply a fixed set of classifiers in a fixed order to *any* image. By contrast, our *dynamic classification technique* DTC can decide which classifier to use at any stage, based on the outcomes of the previous classifiers. That is, while DTC also applies a sequence of classifiers to detect faces, the actual sequence can vary — hence it can apply different cascades of classifiers to different images. Our evidence suggests that such dynamic classifiers have slightly better accuracy in detecting faces.

Our DTC corresponds to an *augmented decision tree*, whose internal nodes each correspond to a version of a classifier (which computes a real-valued score given an image) and whose arcs each correspond to a range of those values. Each leaf node corresponds to a partitioning of the possible sub-images; we then identify with each such leaf node both a further sequence of classifiers and also a specific facial expression. Note that each sub-cluster (and hence the leaf node) identifies the facial expression. We also identify a sequence of classifiers with each leaf node. To classify a test (sub)image I, DTC will apply the classifier associated with root of the decision tree to I, then use the outcome of that classifier to determine which subtree to explore. It then recurs: applying the classifier at the root of that subtree, etc. (Hence, the classifier applied at stage s depends on the outcomes of the classifiers at stage $1, 2, \ldots, s - 1$.) On reaching a leaf node ℓ, DTC will then apply the associated classifier cascade, and accepts I as a face if all of the classifier agree with this claim. If I is labeled as a face, it is also assigned ℓ's facial expression.

Section 2 describes how we produce this DTC system from a collection of labeled images. In particular, this section shows how we use dynamic programming and abstractions to sidestep the serious combinatorial issues — e.g., the exponential number of possible decision trees, and possible cascades.

This section also explains the details of how we build a DTC and how we use it to detect faces and identify the expressions on each detected face. Section 3 evaluates our work in the domain of face detection; Section 4 presents relevant work related to our research.

2   Learning the DTC Classifier

This section describes how we learn our DTC from two sets of labeled images — one training set FLT [1], that identifies the embedded faces (but not the expressions), and a second smaller one, FELT[2], that labels the embedded faces with the associated expressions. Each face image in the FELT set contains a single face that is hand-labeled with one of { sad, fear, surprise, happy, no_expression }.

There are three steps to building the DTC classifier. We first use the standard approach [12] to build a cascade of Adaboost classifiers $\mathcal{C} = \langle C_1, \ldots, C_N \rangle$, based only on the FLT training set; see Section 2.2. We next use the FELT data to produce a fixed-depth decision tree whose nodes each correspond to one of these C_is, with the goal of partitioning the FELT set into sub-clusters of face images with similar expressions; see Sections 2.3. Each leaf node is now identified with a single expression. Third, we add a further fixed-size sequence of classifiers, taken from $\{C_1, \ldots, C_N\}$, to each leaf node; see Section 2.4.

---

[1] Face-Labeled Training set.
[2] Face-Expression-Labeled Training set.

Later, to use DTC to classify some region of an image, we first drop that region into the decision tree, and let it sort itself down to a leaf. We then run the associated sequence of classifiers. If that image "passes" each member of that sequence, it is labeled as a face, and given the expression label associated with the leaf node. Otherwise it is declared a non-face; see Section 2.5.

We give the motivation to our approach first and then present the details of our algorithm.

2.1 Motivation

Figure 1 shows two classifiers C_1 and C_2 that are each, independently, trying to separate positive from negative examples; each line of C_1 (resp., C_2) denotes a linear separator, whose intersection corresponds to the classifier. At a high level, the positive examples can be approximately grouped into three sub-clusters.

Below, we will consider classifiers that map an image into a real "SCO-value" (defined later), not just a bit; see below. A set of N such classifiers therefore map each image into a point in N-dimensional space, and face images can be seen as forming sub-clusters in this space. If we can partition them meaningfully along "$d_1 \ll N$" (a predetermined constant, see below) dimensions, then we can retrieve the sub-clusters. Partitioning the images based on any single classifier C_i is equivalent to finding its projection on the ith dimension in the N dimensional space; we can then split the images based on the classifier's value, into two (perhaps equal) groups. If we take such projections and partition the images repeatedly along d_1 dimensions corresponding to d_1 classifiers, then we can retrieve the (at most 2^{d_1}) sub-clusters.

It is also important to choose the d_1 most effective classifiers. The positive instances in Figure 1 include members of a left-most sub-cluster, labeled "$\diamond$" and a right-most one labeled "$+$".We can see that the positive instances in these two sub-clusters have different ranges for their X–values, while they have a similar range for the Y–value. This means it is easy to separate the left-most cluster from the right-most if we project the data into the X–axis, but this is not true if we consider projection into the Y-axis.

Of the many ways to partition the images, we wanted the partitions that are associated with common facial expressions, based on the images in the FELT dataset. Section 2.3 shows how we build a fixed-depth decision tree, "DTC", using the C classifiers (from the FLT-based cascade) to do this.

Each leaf here corresponds to a single facial expression. We also find a sequence of another d_2 classifiers that are specifically chosen to remove the false positives from the sub-cluster.

2.2 Learning a Cascade of Classifiers

Our implementation first uses Viola-Jones approach [12] to produce a cascade of Adaboost classifiers, $\langle C_1, C_2, \ldots C_N \rangle$: First apply Adaboost to the entire collection of labeled images in the training set FLT to produce a classifier C_1. Let T_1 be the images that C_1 labeled positively. Then apply Adaboost to T_1 to produce the C_2 classifier; then let C_3 be the classifier Adaboost produces when given T_2 (which are the images C_2 labeled positively), and so forth, to produce N classifiers. In our case we tell Adaboost how many linear separators each classifier should use. However, the algorithm decides how many classifiers N it needs to build.

Our DTC will use this *set* of classifiers, but will structure them into a decision tree, rather than simply use them in this sequence.

SCO-Value: Each C_i classifier will reject many of the images. For each image it passes, it will also compute a real-value, as follows: Let $\langle c_i^1, c_i^2, \ldots c_i^k \rangle$ be the linear separators[3] of the boosted classifier C_i and let $c_i^j(W)$ be the outcome of applying c_i^j to a training image W. We define *SCO*-value ("sum of classifier output values"), $V_i(W) = \sum_{j=1}^k c_i^j(W)$ as the sum of the outputs of the linear separators of C_i.

Adaboost is designed to choose the best features from the over-a-hundred-thousand possible candidates. They are likely to fall on salient features specific to faces — like eyes, nose, mouth, etc. Since *SCO*-value uses the outcomes of these classifiers, we anticipate partitioning face images based on these values should group images of similar features into one sub-cluster.

2.3   Building the Basic Decision Tree

Figure 2(a) presents the learning algorithm. It has two goals: first, to partition the images in the FELT set into meaningful sub-clusters of face images with the same face expression, and second, to find the most effective sequence of d_2 classifiers for each sub-cluster.

We first restrict the set of classifiers, paring the list from $\mathcal{C} = \{C_1, \ldots, C_N\}$ down to a smaller set. To do this, we view each of these classifiers *individually*, as if we were planning to use only it to label images. For any classifier C_i and for a specified data set of images S (here, we use FLT.) we compute the score

$$R(C_i, S) \;=\; \ell \times FN(C_i, S) + FP(C_i, S) \tag{1}$$

where $FN(C_i, S_j)$ is the number of false negatives C_i returns over the set S and $FP(C_i, S)$ is the number of false positives in S. (We set $\ell = 10$ in this work, as false negatives are much worse than false positives — as a subsequent classifier may eliminate the false positive, but once any classifier has removed a false negative, it will never be recovered.) We then use only the best $M = 10$ such classifiers.

Next, we produce a depth-d_1 decision tree, whose features each correspond to one of these M classifiers. Its goal is to partition the FELT data, into clusters with the same facial expression. (We used $d_1 = 3$ here.) In general, achieving this objective can be very expensive, as there are several thousands of training images, and a huge number of possible decision trees. We use a two stage divide-and-conquer approach to help sidestep this. First, we use a dynamic programming tableau to learn an optimal depth-d_1 decision tree. Each node at depth d corresponds to the set of images based on the application of a specific sequence of d classifiers. The single depth-0 node $\langle \rangle$ contains all of the images considered, S. To compute the images in the $\langle (C_i, +) \rangle$ node: First let $C_1(S)$ be the subset of S that pass the C_1 classifier; assume these are sorted based on their *SCO*-value

---

[3] Each c_i is a "rectangular feature", the outcome of which is computed using "integral images". See [12] for details.

Learn_DTC(T: FLT TrainingSet, V: FELT TrainingSet)
- Build a cascade of Adaboost classifiers
  $\langle C_1, C_2, \ldots C_N \rangle$ using images in T.
- Let $C_{1:M} = \langle C_1, \ldots, C_M \rangle$ = the M classifiers
  with highest *individual* score on T (Equation 1)
- Build decision tree based on $C_{1:M}$:
  During tree expansion, at depth i
  after applying any C_i from each of *All* sequences
  − Remove each image that C_i classifies as a non-face
  − Partition remaining images into two equal halves
    based on their C_i-based *SCO*-value
  − Apply each C_{i+1} to each half and continue
- Compute utility at each leaf (representing sub-cluster)
- Propagate utility up the tree, for any node n_d
  at depth d
  − $U(n_d) = \max \{U(n_{d+1})\}$
  − Let C_{d+1}^* yield max. utility when applied on n_d
  − Associate C_{d+1}^* with $\mathcal{F}(n_d)$, store $\langle \mathcal{F}(n_d), C_{d+1}^* \rangle$
  − Merge all the δ-equivalent $\mathcal{F}(n_d)$ nodes into one,
    store one classifier C_i^* with the maximum utility
- For each leaf, find best sequence of d_2
  additional classifiers

Use_DTC(I_t : Test Image)
- Set *ratio* = 1.0
- ⋆ For each window W (of 24×24 pixels) within I_t
  ○ For $1 \leq i \leq d_1$
    − Find abstract state $\mathcal{F}(n_i)$ "closest" to W
    − Apply C_i^* associated with $\mathcal{F}(n_i)$
  ○ If $\langle C_1, C_2, \ldots C_{d_1} \rangle$ label the window as a face
    − Find the corresponding sub-cluster, *i.e.*, $\mathcal{F}(n_{d_1})$
    − Apply d_2 classifiers associated with $\mathcal{F}(n_{d_1})$
    − If these d_2 classifiers also label W as a face,
      mark W as a face
- Set *ratio* := *ratio* $\times$ 0.8
  Resize I_t by a factor of *ratio*.
- If I_t.length ≥ 24 and I_t.width ≥ 24, goto ⋆
- For each detected face F_i
  ○ Using images in the matching sub-cluster SC,
    compute $P(E|SC)$ for each expression E.
  ○ Assign expression $E^* =$
    $\arg\max_E \{P(E|SC)\}$ to F_i

Fig. 2. (a) Learning algorithm to discover sub-clusters and find "effective" sequence of classifiers for each sub-cluster; (b) Dynamic classification algorithm

as $\langle w_1, \ldots, w_{m/2}, w_{m/2+1}, \ldots, w_m \rangle$, where $V_1(w_j) > V_1(w_k)$ when $j > k$. Then the $\langle (C_1, +) \rangle$ node contains $\{w_1, \ldots, w_{m/2}\}$, and $\langle (C_1, -) \rangle$ contains $\{w_{m/2+1}, \ldots, w_m\}$.

Similarly $\langle (C_2, +) \rangle$ contains half of the images in $C_2(S)$ — those with the highest $V_2(\cdot)$ values — and $\langle (C_2, -) \rangle$ contains the other half of the $C_2(S)$ images. And so forth for the other $\langle (C_i, \pm) \rangle$ nodes. We can then compute $\langle (C_1, +), (C_2, +) \rangle$ that contains half of the $\langle (C_1, +) \rangle$ images that pass the C_2 classifier, and $\langle (C_1, +), (C_2, -) \rangle$ that contains the other half, etc. We continue for d_1 levels, producing $\binom{M}{d_1} \times 2^{d_1}$ nodes. Each node at depth d_1 corresponds to a sub-cluster; we found that no sub-cluster contained more than 83 images.

We now want to determine the best decision tree within this tableau — the one that leads to the "purest" leaf nodes.

Computing the Utilities, First d_1 Classifiers: Each leaf of the tree represents a possible sub-cluster.. We want the sub-clusters that are as "pure" as possible, which we compute based on the utility

$$ U(S_{d+1}) = K_1 \times \gamma^*_{exp} \times |S_{d+1}| - K_2 \times FN(S_{d+1}) $$

where $|S_{d+1}|$ denotes the number of images in the sub-cluster S_{d+1} (which might include some false positives) and $FN(S_{d+1})$ denotes total false negatives in S_{d+1} (recall this is after applying $\langle C_1, C_2 \ldots C_d \rangle$) and $\gamma^*_{exp} = \max_e \{\gamma_e\}$ where γ_e is the fraction of face images in S_{d+1} with a particular expression $e \in \{$ sad, fear, surprise, no_expression, happy$\}$. (We used the constants $K_1 = 100$ and $K_2 = 10$.) The idea is to assign high utility value to sub-clusters that group face images of the same expression and a low utility value to sub-clusters that have high false negatives. For any internal node S_i we define $U(S_i) = \max_j \{U(S^j_{i+i}\}$ as the maximum utility of its children, $\{S^j_{i+i}\}_j$.

Using these, we propagate the utility up the tree. We collect the $\langle \mathcal{F}(S_i), C^*_i \rangle$ tuples and also the corresponding utilities, for all depths i, $1 \leq i \leq d_1$. $\mathcal{F}(S_i)$ represents the "abstract state" representation of S_1, (see below for the notion of abstract states) C^*_i denotes the classifier that, when applied to S_i, transitions it to another state S^*_{i+1}, with the maximum utility among the children of S_i. For every two states S_i and S_j ($i \neq j$) that are δ-equivalent (see blow for the definition of δ-equivalent states) we retain only one state that has a higher utility and the corresponding classifier.

State Abstraction: At any stage during detection (testing phase) our algorithm first tries to determine the closest matching sub-cluster for each face detected in a test image. To be more precise, after applying classifiers $\langle C_1, C_2, \ldots, C_{i-1} \rangle$ to a window in the image, DTC applies the most appropriate classifier C_i. To choose C_i, we compare the performance of C_i in a "similar situation" on the training data. For that we need to have some kind of a "state representation" that allows us to effectively perform such comparisons *quickly*.

In general, with each node s in the decision tree, we can identify both the sequence of classifiers $\langle C_1, \ldots, C_k \rangle$ on the path from root to s, and also a set of training images S_s that will reach s. We can also identify each s with an abstract state $\mathcal{F}(s) = \langle [V_{min,1}, V_{max,1}], [V_{min,2}, V_{max,2}], \ldots [V_{min,k}, V_{max,k}] \rangle$, for each i, where $[V_{min,i}, V_{max,i}]$ is the range of SCO-values of S_s associated with classifier C_i.

Further, we say two abstractions are "δ-equivalent", written $\mathcal{F}(s_1) \approx_\delta \mathcal{F}(s_2)$, iff:

- s_1 and s_2 have applied the same set of classifiers, not necessarily in the same order.
- For every classifier C_i used in $\mathcal{F}(s_1)$ and $\mathcal{F}(s_2)$, $|V_{min,i}^{(1)} - V_{min,i}^{(2)}| \leq \delta$ and $|V_{max,i}^{(1)} - V_{max,i}^{(2)}| \leq \delta$, where δ is a pre-defined constant. We set $\delta = 70$ throughout this work.

The result of abstraction is that a large number of complex states can be described by a small number of compact state descriptions. Of course, the same abstract state can represent multiple states — it is possible that $\mathcal{F}(s_1) = \mathcal{F}(s_2)$ even if $s_1 \neq s_2$.

2.4   Further Pruning

The d_1 classifiers leading to a leaf node both identify the sub-cluster, and also filter away many, but not all, of the non-faces. We therefore use another set of d_2 classifiers, specific to each leaf node, to help filter out the other non-faces. We noticed that each sub-cluster has just a fraction of the total number of the training data (none had more than 83, from the FELT data of 2672 images). Further, we noticed the number of false positives was not very high (less than 27) for each sub-cluster (see Section 3). So, we select a classifier $C_{d_1+1}^*$ for each state S_d ($d_1 \leq d \leq (d_1 + d_2)$) such that $C_{d_1+1}^*$ has not been used earlier and $C_{d_1+1}^* = \arg\max_{C_{d_1+1}}\{R(S_d, C_{d_1+1})\}$. We apply $C_{d_1+1}^*$, update false positives and false negatives and repeat the process until d_2 such classifiers are found. At performance time, this means our DTC algorithm will use at most a total of $d_1 + d_2$ classifiers for any image, which collectively form the most effective sequence of classifiers for that particular sub-cluster. (Of course, can be different sequences for different images.)

2.5   Detection Using the Dynamic Classifier

The DTC detection algorithm, shown in Figure 2(b), both detects faces within a given image and also identifies the expression of each such face into a sub-cluster. This face detection mechanism is very similar to the cascade classifiers method [12,13], except that it chooses the classifiers dynamically, based on the outcomes of the previous classifiers.

This process examines each 24×24 pixel window in the image; it then rescales and repeats. For each window W, DTC first applies the classifier C_1^* associated with root. This might reject the window W; if so the process terminates (i.e., DTC continues with the next window). Otherwise, DTC computes the SCO-value associated with C_1^* on W and uses this value to decide which subsequent classifier C_2^* to apply. Again this could reject W, but if not, C_2^*'s SCO-value identifies the next classifier C_3^* to apply to W. This can continue for d_1 steps, until W reaches a leaf, ℓ. If so, DTC then runs the sequence of d_2 additional classifiers associated with ℓ, and declares W to be a face only if it passes all of these classifiers. (Here, it had passed all $d_1 + d_2$ classifiers.)

We also identify each detected face W with a facial expression: Recall there are many expression-labeled training images associated with this leaf node ℓ; we assign to W the most common of these expressions.

2.6   Computational Complexity of Learning

Let N be the total number of classifiers and P be the total number of images. We sort the N classifiers based on their utility on the training data and choose M best from them. We expand the tree exhaustively up to a depth of d_1 using the M classifiers. At every depth, we apply a classifier C_d, collect the images classified as faces by C_d as positives, sort them based on the *SCO*-metric of C_d and partition the positive images into two halves[4]. Hence the total complexity of the process is $O(\binom{M}{d_1} \times P \lg(P))$. This is computationally expensive. However, since the number of training images is halved on each branch, this process terminates rapidly. In fact, starting with several thousands of images, we can obtain sub-clusters of size less than 100 by expanding the tree to a depth no greater than 3 or 4, which can be done in a few minutes.[5]

3   Empirical Studies — Face Detection

In this section we show how we apply our ideas to the challenging domain of face detection and show its performance on several images. The training set flt has 1600 images of faces and 2320 images of non-faces[6], each of size 24×24 pixels. The face images include faces of many people, some having glasses, beard and many with different facial expressions, etc. Some training images of faces in FLT are shown in Figure 3(a) The FELT set has a total of 917 face images of the five basic expressions (sad, fear, surprise, no-expression and happy). It also has 2320 non-face images. Some of the face images in FELT are shown in Figure 3(b).

During the training stage, we built a cascade of 21 classifiers using Adaboost, based respectively on { 7 15 30 30 50 50 50 100 120 140 160 180 200 200 200 200 200 200 200 200 200} linear separators. We sort these classifiers based on their score $S(C_i, T)$ on the training data and select the 10 best classifiers. Using the 10 classifiers, we do a depth first search as explained in Section 2.3 up to a depth of $d_1 = 3$ and find sub-clusters. Each sub-cluster included between 26–83 images, some of which could be false positives. The number of false positives was in the range $\{0 ..27\}$, for any sub-cluster. Figure 4 shows face images of the same expression from some interesting sub-clusters that our algorithm learned.

For each sub-cluster we find another sequence $d_2 = 13$ classifiers [7] that have the maximum score on the images of the sub-cluster, as explained in Section 2.3. The $(d_1 + d_2)$ classifiers learned by our algorithm form the most effective sequence for the sub-cluster they are associated with.

To detect faces in any given test image, we use the dynamic detection technique given in Figure 2(b) and explained in Section 2.5. We ran it over 150 images mostly

---

[4] We compute the *SCO*-metric V_j^i of every classifier C_i on every training image I_j and also whether C_i classifies I_j as face or not, *apriori*. So, there are no extra computation during the tree expansion stage.

[5] The training time for building the classification tree on a 1 GHz. computer with 256 Mb. RAM running Windows-2000, using MS Visual C++ was about 5 minutes.

[6] Most of these images were downloaded from the web from popular databases like Olivetti Research & AT&T, Caltech, Yale, JAFFE, PICS, etc.

[7] We set these values after initial experiments on many test images.

(a) Faces in the FLT set

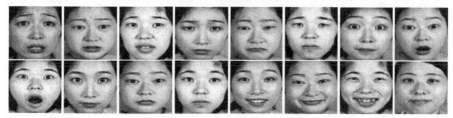

(b) Faces in the FELT set with five different expressions — fear, happy, no expression, sad and surprised

Fig. 3. Face images in the FLT and FELT sets

from Olivetti Research database face images and could successfully identify the expression. Figure 5 shows the performance of our detection algorithm on a number of face images with various expressions. The figure also shows a graph plotting $P(E|SC)$, which indicates the probability of expression E for the detected face. We assign the expression E^* with maximum $P(E|SC)$ to the expression. Note that expressions can be mixed — like happy and surprised, sad and fear and so on. The graph below indicates the probability of each expression.

3.1 ROC Curve

To find out the effectiveness of our face detection algorithm, we ran it on 178 image face images of the MIT-CMU database with a total of over 532 faces and covering

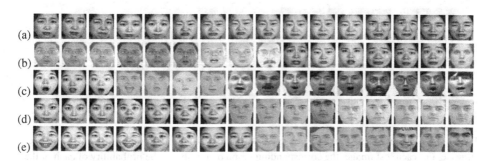

Fig. 4. Various sub-clusters discovered from the FELT data — (a) Sad (b) Fear (c) Surprised (d) No Expression (e) Happy

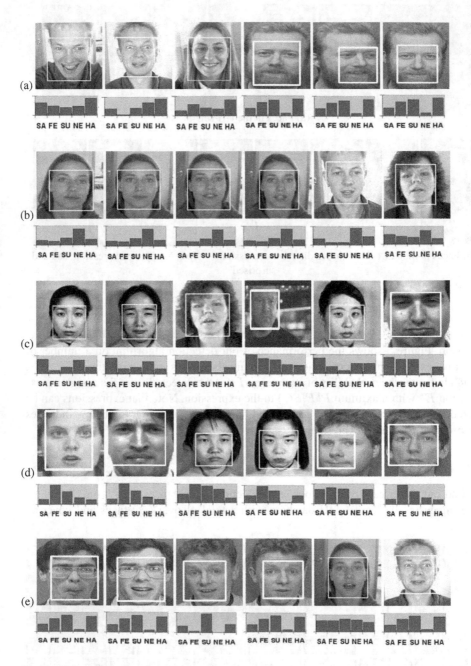

Fig. 5. Performance on several test images — (a) happy (b) no expression (c) sad (d) fear (e) surprise. For each test image, the corresponding graph below shows the probability of each of the five expressions.

Fig. 6. Classification results on sample images from MIT-CMU database

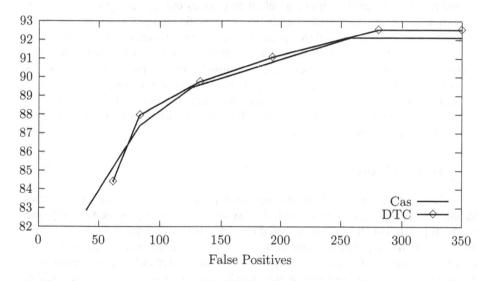

Fig. 7. ROC curve

more than 30 million windows. Figure 6 shows the performance of our algorithm on two images, each with several faces. Figure 7 compares the ROC curves for our face detection algorithm with that of Viola-Jones cascade classification algorithm. [8] Note that Viola-Jones detection method uses 21 classifiers, while our algorithm uses only a subset of 16. Since our algorithm is built using the 21 classifiers of the Viola-Jones algorithm, all the parameters (like the number of linear separators for each classifier, the training data from which they are built) are exactly the same. An important point to note — since our algorithm uses only a subset of the classifiers as Viola-Jones method, it detects every face that Viola-Jones method detects.

---

[8] This is the implementation of the Viola-Jones method [12] by Wu and Rehg.

The main difference is the way they choose the classifiers — Viola-Jones method is static, while our algorithm is dynamic. Our technique can adapt itself to choose the most effective classifier specific to the sub-cluster. Hence, it can apply complex classifiers (with a high number of linear classifiers) very early in the detection process.

The points on the ROC curve are obtained by varying the number of classifiers applied in the range [4–21] for Viola-Jones method and [4–16] for our method. As can be seen from the graph, both the methods seem to have similar performance, with a peak detection rate of 92.5%, while our algorithm does marginally better.

3.2   Efficiency

We ran our Viola Jones algorithm and our algorithm on 400 images of Olivetti Research database face images, each with a size of 92×112 pixels and each image having exactly one face. On average Viola-Jones algorithm took 0.189 seconds per image while our algorithm took 0.243 seconds. The increase in computational time can be attributed to two reasons — our algorithm not only detects faces but also assigns an expression to each detected face, that involves extra computation. Secondly, Viola-Jones algorithm is a static algorithm optimized for speed. It uses boosted classifiers with smaller number (less than 10) of weak classifiers, that are faster to execute, early in the detection process. We cannot detect the best matching sub-clusters (to find out expression) by choosing classifiers statically. Hence, our algorithm may select more complex classifiers (that take more time to execute) in the early stages of detection. However, complex classifier can also prune off several thousands of false positives initially increasing the overall detection efficiency.

4   Previous Work

There has been limited work in identifying face expressions. Liu and others [7,3,2] track facial features and analyze them for facial expressions. Others proposed several other methods [1] almost all of them are based on methods that do a local analysis of facial features, like mouth, eyes, etc. Our work is significantly different from all these — we don't use sequence of images or analyze facial features explicitly, but use training set to group face images of expression into sub-clusters. We associate each detected face with a sub-cluster to identify the expression.

Many researchers have recently proposed several methods for detecting faces in images; see [8,10,9] for a small sample. There has been a lot of interest in the cascade classification methods using classifiers, after the seminal work of Viola and Jones [12,11,13]. All of the cascade classification methods are static — the number of classifiers and the order in which they are applied is fixed; *i.e.*, the same for each instance. Although our approach also uses classifiers, it differs because the order of those sub-classifiers can change for different images. We present an algorithm to learn a dynamic classification method, that decides which classifier to apply to an image based on the outcome of the classifiers already applied. Grossman [5] presented a tree-based detection method, which selects a linear combination of weak classifiers dynamically, based on the outcome of the previous weak classifiers. Our work is also dynamic but differs significantly as we build a classification tree using these subclassifiers in the internal nodes. Moreover, the aim of our work is not only to detect faces but to discover different sub-groups in training images of faces and to associate each face that is detected in a test image to one of these. Thus, it is an extension to simple face detection. [6] addressed related issues in a feature-based face-recognition system by posing the task a "Markov Decision Problem (MDP)". They use dynamic programming to produce an optimal *policy*, π^*, that maps "states" to "actions" (feature detector) for that MDP, then used that optimal policy to recognize faces *efficiently*. We use similar techniques here in this work — we aim to find the best sequence of classifiers here, to detect faces and also each detected face to a sub-cluster.

5 Conclusions

We give future directions to extending this work and present the contributions of our work.

5.1 Directions for Future Work

In this work we use classifiers to achieve two objectives — to detect faces and to group each detected face into one sub-group. There are several interesting extensions to this work; it can extended to partition training images into sub-clusters of faces with and without (external) features like glasses, moustache, etc. The detection system can be used to differentiate people with these features from those without these features.

It will be interesting to try our method on gender classification also. This work can be directly extended to do multiple object detection. Our concept of sub-clusters of faces can be directly correlated to different objects. We can still use a binary (positive and negative) classifier where the training images of all the objects to be detected are positive examples and the rest are negative examples. The training phase of computing the rewards and building a classifier will be quite similar, where the most effective sequence of classifiers will be those that can separate images of different objects into separate clusters. The detection phase will be guided by the dynamic classifier where a classifier with the maximum utility will be selected at each stage.

Finally, we believe that with suitable modifications our approach can be used for gesture recognition, where each sub-cluster corresponds to face images that belong to people with the same gesture.

5.2 Contributions

The main contribution of our work is that it assigns expression to faces during detection. Our training algorithm partitions training images into sub-clusters of similar expressions. During detection, every detected face is matched to one of these sub-clusters to identify the expression. Another novel aspect of our work is that our face detection method is dynamic. We present an algorithm to learn a dynamic classification method that applies the most effective classifier based on the outcome of the previously applied classifiers.

References

1. B. Abboud and F. Davoine Facial expression recognition and synthesis based on appearance model, Signal Processing and Image Communication, Elsevier, Vol. 19, No. 8, pp. 723-740, Sep. 2004
2. J.F. Cohn, T. Kanade, T.K. Wu, Y.T. Lien and A.Zlochower, Facial Analysis: Preliminary analysis of a new image processing based method International Society for Research in Motion, Toronto, 1996
3. J.F. Cohn, A. Zlochower, J. Lien, Y.T. Wu and T.Kanade Automated face coding: A computer vision based method of facial expression analysis Seventh European Conference on Facial Expression, Measurement and Meaning, Salzburg, Austria, 1997.
4. Y. Freund and R.E. Schapire. A decision-theoretic generalization of on-line learning and an application to boosting. *Computational Learning Theory: Eurocolt*, 1995.
5. E. Grossmann. Adatree: boosting a weak classifier into a decision tree. In *IEEE Workshop on Learning in Computer Vision and Patter Recognition*, 2004.
6. R. Isukapalli, and R. Greiner Use of Off-line Dynamic Programming for Efficient Image Interpretation *IJCAI*, Acapulco, Mexico, Aug 2003
7. Y. Liu, K. Schmidt, J.F. Cohn and S. Mitra Facial asymmetry quantification for expression invariant human identification Computer Vision and Image Understanding, pp. 138–151, vol 91, 2003
8. H. Rowley, S. Baluja, and T. Kanade. Neural network-based face detection. *IEEE Transactions on Patten Analysis and Machine Intelligence (PAMI)*, 1998.
9. D. Roth, M. Yang, and N. Ahuja. A snowbased face detector. In *Neural Information Processing Systems (NIPS)*, 2000.
10. H. Schneiderman and T. Kanade. A statistical method for 3d object detection applied to faces and cars. In *International Conference on Computer Vision (ICCV)*, 2000.
11. P. Viola and M. Jones. Fast and robust classification using asymmetric adaboost and a detector cascade. In *Proceedings of the Conference on Computer Vision and Pattern Recognition (CVPR)*, 2001.
12. P. Viola and M. Jones. Rapid object detection using a boosted cascade of simple features. In *Proceedings of the Conference on Computer Vision and Pattern Recognition (CVPR)*, 2001.
13. J. Wu, J.M. Rehg, and M.D. Mullin. Learning a rare event detection cascade by direct feature selection. In *Proceedings of Advances in Neural Information Processing Systems (NIPS)*, 2003.

How to Train a Classifier Based on the Huge Face Database?

Jie Chen[1], Ruiping Wang[2], Shengye Yan[2],
Shiguang Shan[2], Xilin Chen[1,2], and Wen Gao[1,2]

[1] School of Computer Science and Technology,
Harbin Institute of Technology, 150001, China
[2] ICT-ISVISION Joint R&D Lab for Face Recognition,
Institute of Computing Technology, Chinese of Academy of Sciences,
Beijing, 100080, China
{jchen, rpwang, syyan, sgshan, xlchen, wgao}@jdl.ac.cn

Abstract. The development of web and digital camera nowadays has made it easier to collect more than hundreds of thousands of examples. How to train a face detector based on the collected enormous face database? This paper presents a manifold-based method to subsample. That is, we learn the manifold from the collected face database and then subsample training set by the estimated geodesic distance which is calculated during the manifold learning. Using the subsampled training set based on the manifold, we train an AdaBoost-based face detector. The trained detector is tested on the MIT+CMU frontal face test set. The experimental results show that the proposed method is effective and efficient to train a classifier confronted with the huge database.

1 Introduction

Over the past ten years, face detection has been thoroughly studied in computer vision research for its wide potential applications, such as video surveillance, human computer interface, face recognition, and face image database management etc. Face detection is to determine whether there are any faces within a given image, and return the location and extent of each face in the image if one or more faces are present [31]. Recently, the emphasis has been laid on the data-driven learning-based techniques, such as [7, 13, 14, 15, 19, 20, 21, 22, 30]. All of these schemes can be found in the recent survey by Yang [31]. After the survey, the methods based on boosting are much researched. Viola described a rapid object detection scheme based on a boosted cascade of simple features. It brought together new algorithms, representations and insights, which could broaden the applications in computer vision and image processing [23]. And the algorithm has been further developed by other researchers [11, 12, 28].

The performance of these learning-based methods highly depends on the training set, and they suffer from a common problem of data collection for training. It makes easier to collect more than hundreds of thousands of examples with the development of web and digital camera nowadays. How to train a classifier based on the collected immense face database? This paper will give a solution.

W. Zhao, S. Gong, and X. Tang (Eds.): AMFG 2005, LNCS 3723, pp. 85–96, 2005.

In nature, how to train a classifier based on the collected immense face database is a problem of data mining. In this paper we will use the knowledge of the manifold to subsample a small subset from the collected huge face database. Manifold can help us to transform the data to a low-dimensional space with little loss of information, which can enable us to visualize data, perform classification and cluster more efficiently. Recently, some representative techniques, including isometric feature mapping (ISOMAP) [25], local linear embedding (LLE) [17], and Laplacian Eigenmap [1], have been proposed. The ISOMAP algorithm is intuitive, well understood and produces reasonable mapping results [9, 10, 29]. Also, it is supported theoretically, such as its convergence proof [2] and it can recover the co-ordinates [4]. There is also a continuum extension of ISOMAP [32]. A mixture of Gaussians is applied to model a manifold and recover the global co-ordinates by combining the co-ordinates from different Gaussian components [3, 18, 24, 26], or by other methods [27]. To estimate the intrinsic dimensionality, different algorithms also have been considered in manifold learning [8, 16].

The main contributions of this paper are:

1. Subsample a small but efficient and representative subset from the collected huge face database based on the manifold learning to train a classifier.

2. Discuss the effect of outliers on the trained classifier.

3. The performance is instable to train a detector based on the random subsampling face set from a huge database. However, a detector trained based on the subsampled face set by the data manifold is not only stable and but also can improve the detector performance.

4. When we prepare the training set, we should collect more samples along those dimensionalities with larger variances to get a nearly uniformed distribution in the manifold, for example, left-right pose of face more than up-down pose.

The rest of this paper is organized as follows: After a review of ISOMAP, the proposed subsampling method based on the manifold learning is described in section 2. Experimental results are presented in section 3, followed by discussion in section 4.

2   Subsampling Based on ISOMAP

As discussed in [25], for two arbitrary points on a nonlinear manifold (for example, in the "Swiss roll" manifold), their Euclidean distance in the high dimensional input space may not accurately reflect their intrinsic similarity, as measured by geodesic distance along the manifold. Therefore, we use the geodesic distance for subsampling and the geodesic distance can be calculated as in ISOMAP. That is to say, the smaller the geodesic distance between two points is, the more their intrinsic similarity is. When the distance is smaller than a given threshold, one point is deleted as shown in Fig 2.

2.1 ISOMAP Algorithm

The goal of learning the data manifold is to show high-dimensional data in its intrinsic low-dimensional structures and use easily measured local metric information to learn the underlying global geometry of a data set [25].

In the ISOMAP algorithm, firstly, distances between neighboring data points are calculated. The neighborhood can be *knn* -neighborhood. ISOMAP supposes that the data set X lie on a manifold of dimension d and tries to find the global co-ordinates of those points on the manifold. And then an undirected neighborhood graph is constructed.

Secondly, for each pair of non-neighboring data points, ISOMAP finds the shortest path through neighborhood graph, subject to the constraint that the path must hop from neighbor to neighbor. The length of this path (we call it "the estimated geodesic distance") is an approximation to the true distance between its end points (we call it "geodesic distance"), as measured within the underlying manifold. That is to say after embedding the high-dimensional data manifold into low-dimensional structures, we can use straight lines in the embedding to approximate the true geodesic path.

Finally, the classical multidimensional scaling is used to construct low-dimensional embedding.

2.2 The Residual Variance of ISOMAP

The residual variance ($RVar$) of ISOMAP denotes the difference between the Euclidean distance in the d-dimensional Euclidean space and the true geodesic path [25]. The less the value of $RVar$ is, the more approximate between them. The intrinsic dimensionality of the data can be estimated by looking for the "elbow" at which this curve ceases to decrease significantly with added dimensions, i.e., the inflexion of the curve. The relationship between the ISOMAP embedding dimensionality and the residual variance of the 698 face image of [25] is shown in Fig. 1.

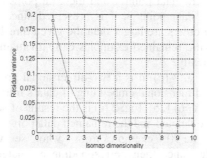

Fig. 1. The residual variance of ISOMAP embedding on the 698 face database of [25]

As discussed in [25], each coordinate axis of the embedding correlates highly with one degree of freedom underlying the original data: left-right pose corresponding to the first degree of freedom, up-down pose corresponding to the second one and lighting direction to the third one. That is to say the scatter of face images in left-right pose is the biggest while the scatter in up-down pose is the smallest among these three factors. We can conclude that, in order to select representative example set, we should pay more attention to the left-right pose variations than the up-down pose.

2.3 Subsampling Algorithm

As discussed in [25], during the manifold learning, we can get the estimated geodesic distance in the high-dimensional space between pairs of the data points. And then they can be used directly to sample by deleting some examples from the database. And the remained examples can still keep the data's intrinsic geometric structure basically. By this means, we can get a small representative subset of the huge data.

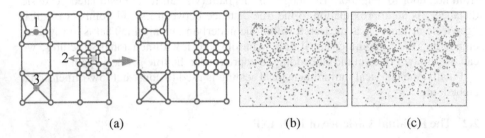

(a)   (b)   (c)

Fig. 2. Subsampling based on the manifold learning. (a) The schematic of subsampling based on the estimated geodesic distance; (b) the manifold of 698 faces; (c) the results of subsampling based on the estimated geodesic distance.

The scheme is demonstrated in Fig. 2 (a). We sort all of the estimated geodesic distances between pairs of points in the high-dimensional space in increasing order. If one of the estimated geodesic distances between an example and others is smaller than a given threshold, it will be deleted while others will be reserved. For example, as shown in Fig. 2 (a), the data point 1 and the data point 2 will be deleted during subsampling. As to the data point 3, it is preserved since the estimated geodesic distance between it and others are larger than the given threshold. From the figure of top right in Fig. 2 (a), the remained examples can still maintain the data's intrinsic geometric structure basically.

As demonstrated in Fig. 2 (b), it is a two-dimensional projection of 698 raw face images where the three-dimensional embedding of data's intrinsic geometric structure is learned by ISOMAP (K=6) [25]. Fig. 2 (c) is the results of subsampling where some data points (in circle) are deleted and the remained data points are still in solid dots.

If we want to subsample 90% examples from a whole set, what we need to do is to delete its 10% examples since their corresponding estimated geodesic distances to others are in the front of the sorted distance sequence.

3 Experiments

3.1 The AdaBoost-Based Classifier

A large number of experimental studies have shown that classifier combination can significantly exploit the discrimination ability comparing with individual feature and classifier. Boosting is one of the common used methods for combining classifiers. AdaBoost, a version of the boosting algorithm, has been used in face detection and is capable of processing images extremely rapidly while achieving high detection rates [23]. Therefore, we use the AdaBoost algorithm to train a classifier. A final strong classifier is formed by combining a number of weak classifiers, which is described in Fig. 3. For the details of the AdaBoost based classifier, please refer to [23].

- Given example set S and their initial weights ω_1;
- Do for $t=1,\ldots\ldots,T$:
  1. Normalize the weights ω_t;
  2. For each feature, j, train a classifier h_j with respect to the weighted samples;
  3. Calculate error ε_t, choose the classifier h_t with the lowest error and compute the value α_t;
  4. Update weights ω_{t+1};
- Get the final strong classifier: $h(x) = \sum_{t=1}^{T} \alpha_t h_t(x)$.

Fig. 3. The AdaBoost algorithm for classifier learning

3.2 Detector Based on the MIT Face Database

The data set is consisted of a training set of 6,977 images (2,429 faces and 4,548 non-faces) and the test set is composed of 24,045 images (472 faces and 23,573 non-faces). All of these images are 19×19 grayscale and they are available on the CBCL webpage [33].

We let $K=6$ when ISOMAP learns the manifold of 2,429 faces in MIT database. By the manifold learning as discussed in [25], we can get the estimated geodesic distance in the high-dimensional space between pairs. And then they can be used directly to sample by deleting some examples from the database.

Note that all of these examples are performed by histogram equalization before the manifold learning. It is because all examples to train a classifier are needed histogram equalization which maps the intensity values to expand the range of intensities.

In order to study the relationship between the distribution of the training set and the trained detector, we subsample the MIT face database by 90%, 80% and 70% (named as ISO90, ISO80, ISO70 later) as discussed in section 2.3. Subsampling by 90% is to say we reserve 90% examples of the database and the same meaning of 80% and 70%. Note that ISO70 is a subset of ISO80 and ISO80 is a subset of ISO90 in fact.

The three subsampled face sets together with the non-face are used to train three classifiers based on the AdaBoost as demonstrated in [23]. And then they are tested on the test set of MIT database. The ROC curves of these three classifiers are shown in Fig. 4. From these ROC curves, one can conclude that all of these three detectors base on ISO90, ISO80 and ISO70 get the comparable performance to the detector

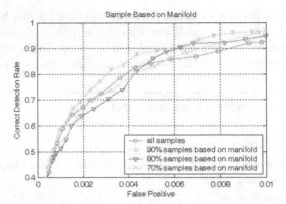

Fig. 4. The ROC curves on the MIT test set using the subsampling face example sets based on the manifold learning and the whole set as training set for a fixed classifier

based on the whole set. It demonstrates that it is reasonable to subsample based on the manifold, i.e. the subsampled subsets ISO90, ISO80 and ISO70 can still maintain the.data's intrinsic geometric structure basically. Further, the detector trained by ISO90 is the best of all and improves the performance of the detector distinctly compared with the detector even by the entire face examples in MIT database. Even the detector trained on ISO70 is a little better than the detector trained on the entire examples. Some possible reasons: the first one is the examples subsampled based on the manifold distribute evenly in the example space and have no examples congregating compared with the whole set; the second is that the outliers in the whole set deteriorate its performance which is to be discussed later.

However, random subsampling from the MIT database is not so lucky. We choose four subsets randomly-subsampled from the MIT database and each subset has the same number of examples as in ISO90. After trained on these four sets, they are also tested on the same test set. The ROC curves are shown in Fig. 5. In this figure, we plot the resulting ROC curves of detectors on the whole set, ISO90, and two randomly chosen subsets. Herein, the curve *"90% examples based on the random subsampling n1"* and the curve *"90% examples based on the random subsampling n2"* represent the best and the worst results of these four random sampling cases. From these ROC curves, one can conclude that the detector based on ISO90 is still the best of all and the results based on random subsampling is much instable. We also think that the evenly-distributed examples and no outliers contribute to this kind of results.

During the ISOMAP learning, we get 30 outliers. Using the examples by ISO90 plus the 30 outliers, we train a classifier also based on AdaBoost. Evaluated on the MIT test set, some resulting ROC curves are shown in Fig. 6. One can find that the detector, based on the ISO90 plus the 30 outliers, will deteriorate its performance. It also denotes that the effects of the evenly-distributed examples on the trained detector are more important than that of the outliers. Integrating these two factors, the detector based on the ISO90 is much better than the detector on the total face set.

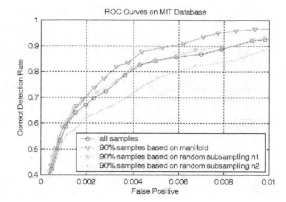

Fig. 5. The ROC curves on the MIT test set using the subsampling face example sets based on the manifold learning, two random sampling sets and the whole set as training set for a fixed classifier

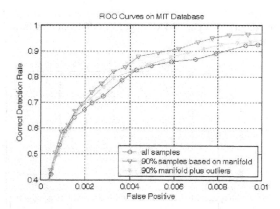

Fig. 6. The ROC curves on the MIT test set using the subsampling face example sets based on the manifold learning, the subsampling sets based on the manifold embedding plus outliers and the whole set as training set for a fixed classifier

3.3 Detector Based on the Huge Database

To compare the performance difference on different training sets further, we also use another three different face training sets. The face-image database consists of 100,000 faces (collected form web, video and digital camera), which cover wide variations in poses, facial expressions and also in lighting conditions. To make the detection method robust to affine transform, the images are often rotated, translated and scaled [6]. Therefore, we randomly rotate these samples up to $\pm 15°$, translate up to half a pixel, and scale up to $\pm 10\%$. After these preprocessing, we get 1,200,000 face images which constitute the whole set. The first group is composed of 15,000 face images which are sampled by the ISOMAP (called ISO15000, here). The second or third group is also composed of 15,000 face images which are random subsampling examples (named Rand1-15000 and Rand2-15000, respectively).

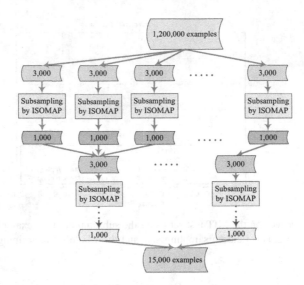

Fig. 7. Subsampling procedure by ISOMAP to get 15,000 examples from 3,000,000 examples

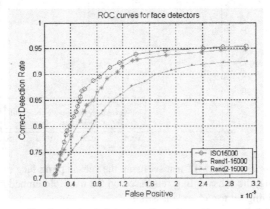

Fig. 8. The ROC curves for the trained detectors, based on the sampled training set by the ISOMAP and the random subsampling training set, tested on the MIT+CMU frontal face test set

It is hard to learn the manifold from 1,200,000 examples by the ISOMAP because it needs to calculate the eigenvalues and eigenvectors of a 1,200,000×1,200,000 matrix. In order to avoid this problem, as demonstrated in Fig. 7, we divide the whole set into 400 subsets and each subset has 3,000 examples. We get 1,000 examples by the proposed method from each subset and then incorporate every three subsampled sets into one subset. With the same procedure, we can get the total 15,000 examples after incorporating all subsampled examples into one set.

In order to avoid destroying the intrinsic structure of the manifold when the whole examples are divided into 400 subsets, we divide the samples in the similar distribution into the same subset. That is to say, the examples vary in poses, facial

Table 1. The detection rates comparison of our system and others

Methods	Detection rate (%)	False alarms
Fröba [5]	89.7	22
Li [11]	90.2	31
Rowley [19]	86.0	31
Schneiderman [21]	94.4	65
Viola [23]	89.7	31
Xiao [28]	88.2	26
Our method	91.28	18

Fig. 9. Output of our face detector on a number of test images from the MIT+CMU frontal face test set and other web images

expressions or lighting conditions are fallen into the different subsets respectively. And this criterion is also applied to incorporate the subsampled sets.

The non-face class is initially represented by 15,000 non-face images. Each single classifier is then trained using a bootstrap approach similar to that described in [22] to increase the number of negative examples in the non-face set. The bootstrap is carried out several times on a set of 13,272 images containing no faces.

The resulting detectors, trained on the three different sets, are evaluated on the MIT+CMU frontal face test set which consists of 130 images showing 507 upright faces [19]. The detection performances on this set are compared in Fig. 8. From these ROC curves one can conclude that the detector based on ISO15000 is the best of all and the results based on random subsampling is also much instable. During the

ISOMAP learning, we get 2,639 outliers. We think that the evenly-distributed examples and no outliers contribute this kind of results, again.

In table 1, the experimental results of our method is compared with the results reported on the same test set — MIT+CMU frontal face test set. We get the detection rate of 91.28% and 18 false alarms with the detector trained on the set ISO15000.

Herein, the results of Fröba [5] and Xiao [28] are read from the ROC curves given in their paper, which might result in a little difference with their real results. In this table, all of the algorithms in [5], [11], [23], [28] are based on boosting, [19] based on neural network, and [21] on Bayes. From the experimental results in table 1, one can conclude that our system outperforms the results achieved by Fröba [5], Li [11], Rowley [19], Viola [23] and Xiao [28]. Although the accuracy is lower than that of Schneiderman [21], our system is approximately 15 times faster. Furthermore, our system has less false detects than that of Schneiderman [21].

However, different criteria (e.g. training time, the number of training examples involved, cropping training set with different subjective criteria, execution time, and the number of scanned windows in detection) can be used to favor one over another, which will make it difficult to evaluate the performance of different methods even though they use the same benchmark data sets [31]. Some results of this detector are shown in Fig. 9.

4 Conclusion

In this paper, we present a novel manifold-based method to subsample a small but efficient and representative training subset from the collected enormous face database. After calculating the geodesic distance by learning the manifold from the collected face database, we subsample the training set in the high dimensional space. An AdaBoost-based face detector is trained on the subsampled training set, and then we test it on the MIT+CMU frontal face test set. Compared with the detector using random subsampling examples, the detector trained by the proposed method is more stable and achieve better face detection performance. We conclude that the evenly-distributed examples, due to the training set subsampled based on the manifold learning, and no outliers, discarded during the manifold learning, contribute to the improved performance.

Acknowledgements

This research is partially sponsored by Natural Science Foundation of China under contract No.60332010, "100 Talents Program" of CAS, ShangHai Municipal Sciences and Technology Committee (No.03DZ15013), and ISVISION Technologies Co., Ltd.

References

[1] M. Belkin and P. Niyogi. Laplacian eigenmaps and spectral techniques for embedding and clustering. In *Advances in Neural Inform. Proc. Systems 14*, pp.585-591. MIT Press, 2002.

[2] M. Bernstein, V. de Silva, J. Langford, and J. Tenenbaum. Graph approximations to geodesics on embedded manifolds. *Technical report, Department of Psychology, Stanford University*, 2000.

[3]   M. Brand. Charting a manifold. In *Advances in Neural Information Proc. Systems 15*, pp. 961-968. MIT Press, 2003.

[4]   D. L. Donoho and C. Grimes. When does ISOMAP recover natural parameterization of families of articulated images? *Technical Report 2002-27, Depart. of Statistics, Stanford University*, 2002.

[5]   B. Froba and A. Ernst, "Fast Frontal-View Face Detection Using a Multi-Path Decision Tree," *In Proceedings of Audio and Video based Biometric Person Authentication*, pp. 921-928, 2003.

[6]   B. Heisele, T. Poggio, and M. Pontil. Face Detection in Still Gray Images. *CBCL Paper #187*. MIT, Cambridge, MA, 2000.

[7]   R. L. Hsu, M. Abdel-Mottaleb, and A. K. Jain, "Face detection in color images," *IEEE Trans. Pattern Anal. Machine Intell.*, pp.696–706, 2002.

[8]   D. R. Hundley and M. J. Kirby. Estimation of topological dimension. In *Proc. SIAM International Conference on Data Mining*, 2003. http://www.siam.org/meetings/sdm03/proceedings/ sdm03_18.pdf.

[9]   O. C. Jenkins and M. J Mataric. Automated derivation of behavior vocabularies for autonomous humanoid motion. In *Proc. of the Second Int'l Joint Conference on Autonomous Agents and Multiagent Systems*, Melbourne, Australia, July 2003.

[10] M. H. Law, N. Zhang, A. K. Jain. Nonlinear Manifold Learning for Data Stream. In *Proc. of SIAM Data Mining*, pp. 33-44, Florida, 2004.

[11] S. Z. Li, L. Zhu, Z.Q. Zhang, A. Blake, H. J. Zhang, and H. Shum. Statistical Learning of Multi-View Face Detection. *In Proc. of the 7th European Conference on Computer Vision*. 2002.

[12] C. Liu, H. Y. Shum. Kullback-Leibler Boosting. *Proceedings of the 2003 IEEE Conf. on Computer Vision and Pattern Recognition (CVPR'03)*. 2003.

[13] C. J. Liu. A Bayesian Discriminating Features Method for Face Detection, *IEEE Trans. Pattern Anal. and Machine Intel.*, pp. 725-740. 2003.

[14] E. Osuna, R. Freund, and F. Girosi, "Training support vector machines: An application to face detection," in *Proc. IEEE Conf. on Computer Vision and Pattern Recognition*, pp. 130–136. 1997,

[15] C. P. Papageorgiou, M. Oren, and T. Poggio, "A general framework for object detection," in *Proc. 6th Int. Conf. Computer Vision*, pp.555–562. 1998,

[16] K. Pettis, T. Bailey, A. K. Jain, and R. Dubes. An intrinsic dimensionality estimator from near-neighbor information. *IEEE Trans. of Pattern Analysis and Machine Intel.*, pp.25-36, 1979.

[17] S. T. Roweis and L. K. Saul. Nonlinear dimensionality reduction by locally linear embedding. *Science*, 290: pp.2323-2326, 2000.

[18] S. T. Roweis, L. K. Saul, and G. E. Hinton. Global coordination of local linear models. In *Advances in Neural Information Processing Systems 14*, pp. 889-896. MIT Press, 2002.

[19] H. A. Rowley, S. Baluja, and T. Kanade. Neural Network-Based Face Detection. *IEEE Tr. Pattern Analysis and Machine Intel.* pp. 23-38. 1998.

[20] H. A. Rowley, S. Baluja, and T. Kanade. Rotation Invariant Neural Network-Based Face Detection. *Conf. Computer Vision and Pattern Rec.*, pp. 38-44. 1998.

[21] H. Schneiderman and T. Kanade. A Statistical Method for 3D Object Detection Applied to Faces. *Comp. Vision and Pattern Recog.*, pp. 746-751. 2000.

[22] K. K. Sung, and T. Poggio. Example-Based Learning for View-Based Human Face Detection. *IEEE Trans. on PAM.* pp. 39-51. 1998.

[23] P. Viola and M. Jones. Rapid Object Detection Using a Boosted Cascade of Simple Features. *Conf. Comp. Vision and Pattern Recog.*, pp. 511-518. 2001.

[24] Y. W. Teh and S. T. Roweis. Automatic alignment of local representations. In *Advances in Neural Information Processing Systems 15*, pp. 841-848. MIT Press, 2003.

[25] B. J. Tenenbaum, V. Silva, and J. Langford. A Global Geometric Framework for Nonlinear Dimensionality Reduction. *Science*, Volume 290, pp.2319-2323, 2000

[26] J. J. Verbeek, N. Vlassis, and B. Krose. Coordinating principal component analyzers. In *Proc. of International Conf. on Artificial Neural Networks*, pp. 914-919, Spain, 2002.

[27] J.J. Verbeek, N. Vlassis, and B. Krose. Fast nonlinear dimensionality reduction with topology preserving networks. In *Proc. 10th European Symposium on Artificial Neural Networks*, pp.193-198, 2002.

[28] R. Xiao, M. J. Li, H. J. Zhang. Robust Multipose Face Detection in Images, *IEEE Trans on Circuits and Systems for Video Technology*, Vol.14, No.1 pp. 31-41. 2004,

[29] M.-H. Yang. Face recognition using extended ISOMAP. In *International Conf. on Image Processing*, pp.117-120, 2002.

[30] M. H. Yang, D. Roth, and N. Ahuja. A SNoW-Based Face Detector. *Advances in Neural Information Processing Systems 12*, MIT Press, pp. 855-861. 2000.

[31] M. H. Yang, D. Kriegman, and N. Ahuja. Detecting Faces in Images: A Survey. *IEEE Tr. Pattern Analysis and Machine Intelligence*, vol. 24, pp. 34-58. 2002.

[32] H. Zha and Z. Zhang. Isometric embedding and continuum ISOMAP. In *International Conference on Machine Learning*, 2003.
http://www.hpl.hp.com/conferences/icml2003/ papers / 8.pdf.

[33] http://www.ai.mit.edu/projects/cbcl/software- dataset / index.html.

Non-rigid Face Modelling Using Shape Priors

Alessio Del Bue, Xavier Lladó, and Lourdes Agapito

Queen Mary University of London, London E1 4NS, UK
{alessio,llado,lourdes}@dcs.qmul.ac.uk

Abstract. Non-rigid 3D shape recovery is an inherently ambiguous problem. Given a specific rigid motion, different non-rigid shapes can be found that fit the measurements. To solve this ambiguity prior knowledge on the shape and motion should be used to constrain the solution. This paper is based on the observation that often not all the points on a moving and deforming surface such as a human face are undergoing non-rigid motion. Some of the points are frequently on rigid parts of the structure – for instance the nose – while others lie on deformable areas. First we develop a segmentation algorithm to separate rigid and non-rigid motion. Once this segmentation is available, the rigid points can be used to estimate the overall rigid motion and to constrain the underlying mean shape. We propose two reconstruction algorithms and show that improved reconstructions can be obtained when the priors on the shape are used on synthetic and real data.

1   Introduction

In this paper we focus on the estimation of the 3D shape and motion of a deformable object such as a human face which is moving rigidly while performing different facial expressions. The face can be thought of as an underlying rigid body undergoing a global rotation and translation while suffering some local non-rigid deformations. Our aim is the simultaneous recovery of motion and 3D non-rigid shape from multiple images exploiting prior knowledge on the structure such as the rigidity of some of the observed points.

In the past years numerous techniques have been proposed to solve the *structure from motion* problem in the case of rigid objects and more recently the framework has also been extended to deal with non-rigid objects. The main challenge in non-rigid structure from motion is to disambiguate the contribution to the image motion given by the shape deformation and that caused by the rigid motion. Bregler et al [3] introduced a representation for non-rigid 3D shape where any configuration can be expressed as a linear combination of basis shapes that define the principal modes of deformation of the object. They proposed a factorization method that exploits the rank constraint on the measurement matrix and enforces orthonormality constraints on camera rotations to recover the motion and the non-rigid 3D shape. Their work can be seen as an extension of Tomasi and Kanade's factorization framework [12] to the case of deformable objects. Torresani et al. [13] extended the method of Bregler et al. to a trilinear optimization problem by minimizing 2D image reprojection error using Alternating Least Squares. Brand [2] proposed an alternative optimization method and added an extra constraint on the basis shapes: the deformations should be as small as possible relative to the rigid shape.

W. Zhao, S. Gong, and X. Tang (Eds.): AMFG 2005, LNCS 3723, pp. 97–108, 2005.
© Springer-Verlag Berlin Heidelberg 2005

The main problem with these approaches stems from the fact that deformation and motion are ambiguous. Given a specific configuration of points on the image plane, different 3D non-rigid shapes and camera motions can be found that fit the measurements. To solve this ambiguity prior knowledge on the shape and motion should be used to constrain the solution. Recently, Xiao et al. [17] proved that the orthogonality constraints were insufficient to disambiguate rigid motion and deformations. They identified a new set of constraints on the shape bases which, when used in addition to the rotation constraints, provide a closed form solution to the problem of non-rigid structure from motion. However, their solution requires that there be K frames (where K is the number of basis shapes) in which the shapes are known to be independent. Non-linear optimization schemes that minimize image reprojection error have also been proposed to refine an initial solution [1,4]. The advantage of these methods is that they provide a maximum likelihood estimate in the presence of Gaussian noise and prior knowledge on any of the model parameters can be easily incorporated to the cost function in the form of penalty terms. The need for incorporating prior information on the motion or shape parameters to avoid the ambiguities inherent to non-rigid shape estimation is also recognised by Torresani et.al. [15,14] who propose an algorithm that learns the time-varying shape of a non-rigid 3D object from uncalibrated 2D tracking data. Temporal smoothness in the object shape can be imposed within their framework which can also deal with missing data.

In this paper we focus on the observation that often not all the points on a moving and deforming surface – such as a human face – are undergoing non-rigid motion. Some of the points are frequently on rigid parts of the structure – for instance the nose – while others lie on deformable areas. Intuitively, if a segmentation is available, the rigid points can be used to estimate the overall rigid motion and to constrain the underlying mean shape by estimating the local deformations exclusively with the parameters associated to the non-rigid component of the 3D model. Our observation is also supported by recent studies on the notion of shape average by Yezzi and Soatto introduced in [18] where the authors precisely separate motion and deformation components for robustly matching, registering and tracking deformable objects.

Our approach first performs rigid and non-rigid motion segmentation on the fully observed image data to separate both types of motion using an automatic measure of deformability of shapes [10]. Once the points have been segmented into the rigid and non-rigid sets we recover the overall rigid motion from the rigid set and we formalise the problem of non-rigid shape estimation as a constrained minimization adding priors on the degree of deformability of each point. We perform experiments on synthetic and real data which validate the approach and show that the addition of priors on the rigidity of some of the points improves the 3D reconstruction.

The paper is organised as follows. In section 2 we describe the non-rigid factorization framework. In section 3 we propose a rigid and non-rigid motion segmentation algorithm. Section 4 presents two alternative algorithms to recover the 3D shape using rigidity constraints on the non-deforming segmented points. Finally, in section 5 we show experiments on synthetic and real data to validate the segmentation algorithm and the 3D reconstruction methods.

2   Non-rigid 3D Modelling Using Factorization

Tomasi and Kanade's factorization algorithm has recently been extended to the case of non-rigid 3D structure, assuming affine viewing conditions [3,2,13,4]. The model used to express the deformations is point-wise and the 3D shape of any specific configuration S is approximated by a linear combination of a set of K basis shapes S_k which represent the principal modes of deformation of the object:

$$S = \sum_{k=1}^{K} l_k S_k \qquad S, S_k \in \Re^{3 \times P} \quad l_k \in \Re \tag{1}$$

where each basis shape S_k is a $3 \times P$ matrix which contains the 3D locations of P object points for that particular mode of deformation. Assuming an orthographic camera model the shape is then projected onto an image frame i giving P image points:

$$\left[\mathbf{x}_{i1} \ \dots \ \mathbf{x}_{iP} \right] = R_i \left(\sum_{k=1}^{P} l_{ik} S_k \right) \tag{2}$$

where each $\mathbf{x}_{ij} = [u_{ij} v_{ij}]^T$ contains the horizontal and vertical image coordinates of the point – referred to the centroid of the object – and R_i encodes the first two rows of the rotation matrix for a specific frame i. If all P points are tracked in F image frames we may construct the measurement matrix W which can be expressed as:

$$W = \begin{bmatrix} \mathbf{x}_{11} & \dots & \mathbf{x}_{1P} \\ \vdots & & \vdots \\ \mathbf{x}_{F1} & \dots & \mathbf{x}_{FP} \end{bmatrix} = \begin{bmatrix} l_{11}R_1 & \dots & l_{1K}R_1 \\ \vdots & & \vdots \\ l_{F1}R_F & \dots & l_{FK}R_F \end{bmatrix} \begin{bmatrix} S_1 \\ \vdots \\ S_K \end{bmatrix} \tag{3}$$

Clearly, the rank of the measurement matrix is constrained to be at most $3K$, where K is the number of deformations. This rank constraint can be exploited to factorize the measurement matrix into a motion matrix $\hat{M}$ and a shape matrix $\hat{S}$ by truncating the SVD of W to rank $3K$. However, this factorization is not unique since any invertible $3K \times 3K$ matrix Q can be inserted in the decomposition leading to the alternative factorization: $W = (\hat{M}Q)(Q^{-1}\hat{S})$. The problem is to find a transformation matrix Q that renders the appropriate replicated block structure of the motion matrix shown in Equation (3) and that removes the affine ambiguity, upgrading the reconstruction to a metric one.

In this paper we address the problem of non-rigid shape estimation and we propose a new solution which incorporates information on the degree of deformability of the 3D points. First we identify the points whose motion can be explained purely by a rigid transformation. This knowledge provides some constraints or priors on the values of the 3D shape which will allow to solve the inherent problem of ambiguity present in the motion and 3D shape in non-rigid factorization.

3   Automatic Rigid and Non-rigid Motion Segmentation

As a first step to 3D structure recovery we propose to separate points in the sequence that exhibit a purely rigid motion from those which are also suffering some non-rigid deformations. To do this we apply a subset selection technique on the non-rigid component of the point trajectories encoded in the measurement matrix W. Subset selection is a technique commonly used in feature selection problems where a group of features is extracted to obtain a robust solution to a particular estimation problem [7].

Under the factorization framework, features are represented by their image point trajectories stored in W. Our goal is to find the set of features whose motion can be modelled exactly as a rigid motion. In this case we formulate the segmentation problem as finding a subset of trajectories W_{rigid} within the measurement matrix such that the following condition is satisfied:

$$rank(W_{rigid}) = 3. \tag{4}$$

The segmentation algorithm follows a *sequential backward selection strategy* [9] by initially considering all the trajectories in the measurement matrix and iteratively deleting one by one those which are contributing most to the rank of the matrix, i.e. the points that exhibit the most non-rigid motion. As the stop criterion for the classification task, we compute the rank of the measurement matrix of the remaining points which will become 3 when only the rigid trajectories are left.

Obviously the rank of the rigid points will not be exactly equal to 3 in the presence of noise. Instead, we have used an automatic method to determine the deformability index of a set of trajectories [10]. This method estimates the value of K – the number of independent basis shapes needed to describe the non-rigid motion – automatically in a non-iterative way. It provides a fixed threshold for comparing the eigenvalues of the matrix to determine the rank. For the case of a 3D rigid body the deformability index K is equal to 1 while in the case of a non-rigid body the index is $3K$ therefore this provides a good selection criterion to separate both sets of trajectories. The complete algorithm is detailed below:

– Initialize $W_{rigid} = W$
– Determine the deformability index K for W_{rigid}

1. Compute $W_{rigid} \simeq UDV^T$ with SVD.
2. Define $S = D^{1/2}V^T$
3. Extract the non-rigid component of the shape matrix $\tilde{S}_{3(K-1)\times P} = \begin{bmatrix} \tilde{S}_1 & ... & \tilde{S}_P \end{bmatrix}$ where each $\tilde{S}_j$ is a $3(K-1) \times 1$ vector which contains the 3D coordinates of the jth 3D point associated to the $K-1$ non-rigid bases.
4. Determine the maximum norm vector: $\tilde{S}_t = \max\{ \| \tilde{S}_1 \|, ... , \| \tilde{S}_P \| \}$.
5. Remove the selected trajectory t from W_{rigid} and determine the new deformability index K.
6. If $K = 1$ stop the iteration.
7. Else, go to step 1.

We have obtained successful rigid and non-rigid motion segmentations on synthetic sequences using this algorithm. The results will be discussed in the experimental section. Note that the method converges to the right solution only if there is a unique set of rigid points such that $K = 1$. In the case where different groups of features satisfy the rank condition the algorithm could converge to the wrong set.

4 Non-rigid Shape and Motion Estimation Using Rigidity Constraints

Once we have segmented the scene into rigid and non-rigid points, we can use the information on the rigidity of the points to constrain the shape estimation. First we define the constraints that arise based on the observation that a generic shape is composed by points with different degrees of deformation. Kim and Hong [8] defined the *degree of non-rigidity* of a point as its degree of deviation from the average shape to classify points into three classes: rigid, near-rigid and non-rigid. Based on this measure they proposed a method to estimate average shape using the degree of non-rigidity to weight the contribution of each point in an iterative certainty re-weighted factorization scheme. In contrast, we use the knowledge that some points of the scene are rigid to construct specific linear constraints which will in turn eliminate the inherent ambiguities present in non-rigid shape estimation.

4.1 Rigidity Constraint

Definition (rigid point). *If the motion of a point p is completely rigid for the entire sequence, the structure referring to the point can be expressed entirely by the first basis (K = 1) called the rigid basis.*

It follows from this definition that a completely rigid point p is entirely parameterized by:

$$\mathbf{S}_p = \begin{bmatrix} \mathbf{S}_{p1} \\ \mathbf{0} \end{bmatrix} \tag{5}$$

where $\mathbf{S}_{p1}$ is a 3-vector which contains 3D coordinates of the rigid component and $\mathbf{0}$ is a $3(K-1)$-vector of zeros. It is possible to reorder the measurement matrix after the detection of all the rigid points by defining the permutation matrix P such that:

$$\mathrm{WP} = \begin{bmatrix} W_{rigid} \,\big|\, W_{nonrigid} \end{bmatrix} = \begin{bmatrix} l_{11}\mathbf{R}_1 & \dots & l_{1K}\mathbf{R}_1 \\ \vdots & & \vdots \\ l_{F1}\mathbf{R}_F & \dots & l_{FK}\mathbf{R}_F \end{bmatrix} \begin{bmatrix} \mathbf{S}_{rigid} & \mathbf{S}_{nonrigid} \\ \mathbf{0} & \end{bmatrix} \tag{6}$$

where $\mathbf{S}_{rigid}$ is a $(3 \times r)$ matrix containing the 3D coordinates of the r rigid points, $\mathbf{S}_{nonrigid}$ is a $(3K \times d)$ matrix containing the 3D coordinates of the K basis shapes for the d deformable points and 0 is a $3(K-1) \times r$ matrix of zeros. Notice that it is now possible to apply Tomasi and Kanade's rigid factorization on the measurement matrix containing the image trajectories of the rigid points W_{rigid} and decompose it into the motion and rigid structure components as:

$$W_{rigid} = \begin{bmatrix} \mathbf{R}_1 \\ \vdots \\ \mathbf{R}_f \end{bmatrix} \mathbf{S}_{rigid} \tag{7}$$

4.2 Non-rigid Shape and Motion Estimation

In this section we solve for the non-rigid shape and motion given the 2D image tracks and incorporating the above constraint on the automatically segmented rigid points. Our approach is to minimize image reprojection error subject to the rigidity of the non-deforming points. The cost function being minimised is:

$$\chi = \sum_{i,j} \| \mathbf{x}_{ij} - \hat{\mathbf{x}}_{ij} \|^2 = \sum_{i,j} \| \mathbf{x}_{ij} - (\mathsf{R}_i \sum_k l_{ik} \mathsf{S}_k) \|^2 \tag{8}$$

where $\mathbf{x}_{ij}$ are the measured image points and $\hat{\mathbf{x}}_{ij}$ the estimated image points. We propose two alternative solutions to this constrained minimization: a linear alternate least squares approach which incorporates the rigidity constraints using Generalised Singular Value Decomposition and a fully non-linear minimization scheme using priors on the rigid shape parameters in a Maximum A Posteriori estimation.

Linear Equality-Constrained Least Squares Using GSVD. First we propose an alternating least squares scheme to minimize the cost function described in equation (8). The algorithm alternates between solving for the basis shapes S and for the configuration weights l_{ik}. The configuration weights are initialised to random values. The scheme can be summarised as follows:

1. Given R_i and l_{ik} equation (3) can be used to estimate S linearly subject to the constraint $\tilde{\mathsf{S}}_p = \mathbf{0}$ for $p \in \Omega$ with Ω being the set of r points considered to be rigid throughout the sequence.
2. Given R_i and S solve for all l_{ik} using linear least-squares.
3. Iterate the above two steps until convergence.

Note that the algorithm does not solve for the overall rigid motion encoded in the rotation matrices R since these are calculated before hand by running the rigid factorization algorithm of Tomasi and Kanade on the rigid points. Rearranging equation (3) the problem of solving for S subject to the rigidity constraint can be expressed as an unconstrained least squares system of the form:

$$\min \| \begin{bmatrix} \mathsf{A} \\ \lambda \mathsf{C} \end{bmatrix} \mathbf{x} - \begin{bmatrix} \mathbf{b} \\ \lambda \mathbf{d} \end{bmatrix} \|_2 \tag{9}$$

where A represents the linear equations, C the linear constraints and $\mathbf{b}$ and $\mathbf{d}$ are the known observations. It is shown [5] that for $\lambda \to \infty$ the final solution lies on the surface defined by $\mathsf{C}\mathbf{x} = \mathbf{d}$ and thus we obtain a linear equality-constrained least squares (LSE) problem:

$$\min \| \mathsf{A}\mathbf{x} - \mathbf{b} \|_2 \tag{10}$$

subject to:

$$\mathsf{C}\mathbf{x} = \mathbf{d} \tag{11}$$

A method to solve the above LSE problem is directly to factorize both A and C using Generalized Singular Value Decomposition (GSVD) (see [6] for details).

Bundle Adjustment Using Priors. The correct approach to non-rigid factorization is to formulate the problem as a non-linear least square estimation minimizing the distance of the reprojection error in the model parameters:

$$\arg \min_{R_i S_k l_{ik}} \sum_{i,j} \| \mathbf{x}_{ij} - \hat{\mathbf{x}}_{ij} \|^2 = \arg \min_{R_i S_k l_{ik}} \sum_{i,j} \| \mathbf{x}_{ij} - (R_i \sum_k l_{ik} S_k) \|^2 \qquad (12)$$

where $\mathbf{x}_{ij}$ are the measured image points and $\hat{\mathbf{x}}_{ij}$ the estimated image points.

This method has the advantage of providing a true maximum likelihood estimate, provided the noise distribution is Gaussian. Besides, prior knowledge on any of the model parameters can be easily incorporated to the error cost function in the form of penalty terms. However, it suffers from the fact that it requires an initialization that is close to the global minimum. Therefore these methods are generally used as a final refinement step.

One of the main advantages of performing a prior segmentation of rigid and non-rigid motion is firstly that the rigid motion (estimates of the rotation matrices R) can be pre-computed by performing rigid factorization on the rigid points. This provides a very good initial estimate for the rotation parameters, which coupled with the priors on the 3D shape help solve the ambiguities.

Our prior expectation is that the points detected as being rigid have a zero non-rigid component and can therefore be modelled entirely by the first basis shape:

$$\mathbf{S}_p = \begin{bmatrix} \mathbf{S}_{p1} \\ \tilde{\mathbf{S}}_p \end{bmatrix} = \begin{bmatrix} \mathbf{S}_{p1} \\ \mathbf{0} \end{bmatrix} \qquad (13)$$

Therefore our expected prior value of the coordinates of the non-rigid bases $\tilde{\mathbf{S}}_p$ is zero in this case. For every rigid point in the scene we model the distribution of $\tilde{\mathbf{S}}_p$ as a Gaussian with a small variance and solve the problem as a Maximum A Posteriori estimation (MAP).

5   Results

5.1   Synthetic Data

The synthetic 3D data consisted of a set of random points sampled inside a cube of size $50 \times 50 \times 50$ units. Five sequences were generated with 8, 16, 32, 64 and 128 non-rigid points sampled inside the cube. Each sequence also included 8 rigid points (the vertices of the cube). Figure 1 shows the 3D data used in each of the five sequences with the rigid points joined up for display purposes. Our aim is to show the performance of our approach under different degrees of non-rigidity. The deformations for the non-rigid points were generated using random basis shapes as well as random deformation weights. Two basis shapes were used and the first basis shape had the largest weight equal to 1. The data was then rotated and translated over 25 frames and projected onto the images using an orthographic camera model and Gaussian noise was added to the image coordinates. The overall rotation about any axis was 90 degrees at most.

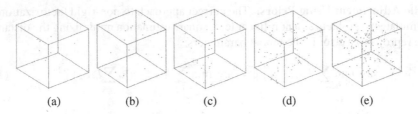

(a)   (b)   (c)   (d)   (e)

Fig. 1. Synthetic sequence. Example of ground truth of the 3D shape with 8 rigid points (vertices of the cube) and (a) 8, (b) 16, (c) 32, (d) 64 and (e) 128 non-rigid points.

Rigid and Non-rigid Motion Segmentation. Figure 4(a) shows results of the motion segmentation algorithm on a sequence using 8 rigid and 32 non-rigid points. The noise level for this particular experiment was set to be $\sigma = 1.5$ pixels. The $-y$ axis of the graph shows the current value of the deformation index (K) and the $-x$ axis represents the total number of total points left at each iteration. The algorithm classifies points according to the current value of K. The first 32 points are selected as non-rigid as their deformability index K is consistently close to 2. When the 33rd point is selected one can observe a sudden drop in the value of K to 1.5 which then tends to 1. This is the cut-off point and the 8 remaining points are correctly classified as rigid.

3D Reconstruction. We have tested 3 reconstruction algorithms: the linear GSVD method, bundle adjustment without priors (MLE) and bundle-adjustment incorporating priors on the 3D structure (MAP). Figure 2 shows the 2D image reprojection error, relative 3D reconstruction error and absolute rotation error using each of the 3 algorithms, for varying ratios of rigid/non-rigid scene points and different levels of measurement noise. It becomes clear that GSVD and MAP outperform MLE thus showing the improved performance when prior information on the shape is incorporated. In fact the GSVD and MAP error curves appear superimposed which shows that they converge to

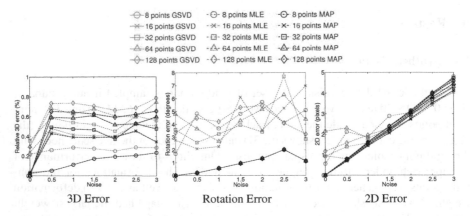

3D Error   Rotation Error   2D Error

Fig. 2. Relative 3D error (%), rms rotation error (deg) and 2D reprojection error for the synthetic experiments for different ratios of rigid/non-rigid points and increasing levels of noise

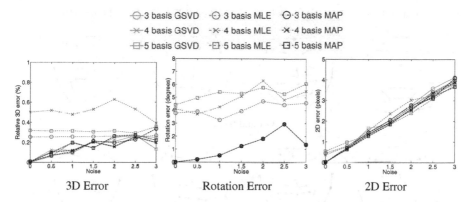

Fig. 3. Relative 3D error (%), rms rotation error (deg) and 2D reprojection error for the synthetic experiments for different numbers of basis shapes and increasing levels of noise

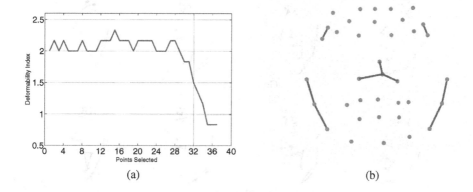

Fig. 4. (a) Deformability index for the automatic segmentation experiment. The graph shows its sudden decrease upon selection of point #33 (the first rigid point). (b) Face data used in the real experiment. Points connected with wireframes show the selected rigid points located on the nose, temples and side of the face.

the same solution, with the main observable difference being the higher speed of convergence for the MAP approach. Note that the MLE approach is not able to compute a correct 3D reconstruction even for the noiseless case showing that the added priors are fundamental to avoid local minima given by ambiguous configurations of motion and deformation parameters.

The number of basis shapes were then varied ($d = 3$, 4 and 5) to test the performance of the algorithm with respect to this parameter. Figure 3 shows the 2D image reprojection error, relative 3D reconstruction error and absolute rotation error obtained with GSVD, MLE and MAP. As expected, the error increases with the number of basis shapes for all 3 algorithms. Once more GSVD and MAP have almost identical performance and provide better results than MLE.

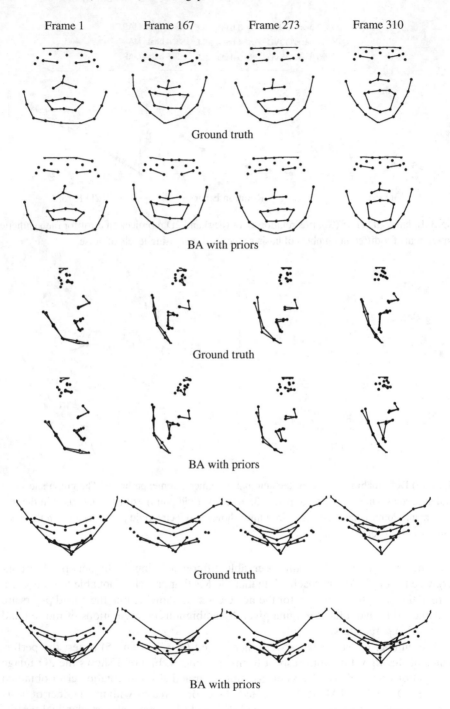

Fig. 5. Front, side and top views of the ground truth and reconstructed face with priors. Reconstructions are shown for frames 1, 167, 273 and 310.

5.2   Real Data

In this experiment we use real 3D data of a human face undergoing rigid motion – mainly rotation – while performing different facial expressions. The 3D data was captured using a VICON motion capture system by tracking the subject wearing 37 markers on the face. The 3D points were then projected synthetically onto an image sequence 310 frames long using an orthographic camera model and noise of variance $\sigma = 0.5$ pixels was added to the image coordinates. In this case the segmentation of points into rigid and non-rigid sets was done manually. Figure 4(b) shows a frontal view of the face where the 14 rigid points – situated on the nose, temples and the side of the face – are marked with circles.

Figure 5 shows the ground truth and reconstructed shape from front, side and top views using the bundle adjustment algorithm incorporating rigidity priors on the non-deforming points. The deformations are very well captured by the model even for the frames in which the facial expressions are more exaggerated. Crucially, the addition of the priors helps remove the ambiguity between the rotational and deformation components.

6   Future Work

We are currently investigating other solutions for rigid and non-rigid motion segmentation using alternative approaches [11,16]. Torresani et al.'s [15] method for learning non-rigid 3D shape from 2D motion using the expectation maximization algorithm could also be used to perform the segmentation.

We also plan to exploit looser rigidity constraints on the shape such as the 3D points behaving rigidly only for a set of frames and to include other priors such as the symmetry of the structure.

Acknowledgements

We acknowledge Dr. Amit K. Roy-Chowdhury for fruitful discussions on the estimation of the deformability index. This work has been partially supported by EPSRC grant GR/S61539/01. Alessio Del Bue holds a Queen Mary Studentship award.

References

1. H. Aanæs and F. Kahl. Estimation of deformable structure and motion. In *Workshop on Vision and Modelling of Dynamic Scenes, ECCV'02, Copenhagen, Denmark*, 2002.
2. M. Brand. Morphable models from video. In *Proc. IEEE Conference on Computer Vision and Pattern Recognition, Kauai, Hawaii*, December 2001.
3. C. Bregler, A. Hertzmann, and H. Biermann. Recovering non-rigid 3d shape from image streams. In *Proc. IEEE Conference on Computer Vision and Pattern Recognition, Hilton Head, South Carolina*, pages 690–696, June 2000.
4. A. Del Bue, F. Smeraldi, and L. Agapito. Non-rigid structure from motion using non-parametric tracking and non-linear optimization. In *Proceedings of the 2004 Conference on Computer Vision and Pattern Recognition Workshop (CVPRW'04) Volume 1*, Washington, DC, USA, 2004.

5. G. H. Golub and C. F. Van Loan. *Matrix Computation*. John Hopkins University Press, 1991. Second Edition.
6. P. C. Hansen. Regularization, gsvd and truncated gsvd. *BIT*, 29(3):491–504, 1989.
7. A.K. Jain and D. Zongker. Feature selection: Evaluation, application, and small sample performace. *IEEE Transactions on Pattern Analysis and Machine Intelligence*, 19(2):153–158, February 1997.
8. T. Kim and K-S Hong. Estimating approximate shape and motion of deformable objects with a monocular view. In *Proc. Asian Conference on Computer Vision*, Jeju Island, Korea, January 2004.
9. J. Kittler. Feature selection and extraction. In T. Y. Young and K. S. Fu, editors, *HPRIP*, pages 59–83, Orlando, FL, 1986. Academic Press.
10. A. Roy-Chowdhury. A measure of deformability of shapes with applications to human motion analysis. In *IEEE Conference in Computer Vision and Pattern Recognition*, volume 1, pages 398–404, June 2005.
11. Y. Sugaya and K. Kanatani. Multi-stage optimization for multi-body motion segmentation. *IEICE Transactions on Information and Systems*, E87-D(7):1935–1942, 2004.
12. C. Tomasi and T. Kanade. Shape and motion from image streams under orthography: A factorization approach. *International Journal in Computer Vision*, 9(2):137–154, 1992.
13. L. Torresani, D. Yang, E. Alexander, and C. Bregler. Tracking and modeling non-rigid objects with rank constraints. In *Proc. IEEE Conference on Computer Vision and Pattern Recognition, Kauai, Hawaii*, 2001.
14. Lorenzo Torresani and Aaron Hertzmann. Automatic non-rigid 3d modeling from video. In *Proc. 8th European Conference on Computer Vision, Prague, Czech Republic*, pages 299–312, May 2004.
15. Lorenzo Torresani, Aaron Hertzmann, and Christoph Bregler. Learning non-rigid 3d shape from 2d motion. In Sebastian Thrun, Lawrence Saul, and Bernhard Schölkopf, editors, *Advances in Neural Information Processing Systems 16*. MIT Press, Cambridge, MA, 2004.
16. R. Vidal and R. Hartley. Motion segmentation with missing data using powerfactorization and gpca. In *IEEE Conference on Computer Vision and Pattern Recognition*, volume 2, pages 310–316, Washington D.C., June 2004.
17. J. Xiao, J. Chai and T. Kanade. A closed-form solution to non-rigid shape and motion recovery. In *Proc. 8th European Conference on Computer Vision, Prague, Czech Republic*, May 2004.
18. Anthony J. Yezzi and Stefano Soatto. Deformotion: Deforming motion, shape average and the joint registration and approximation of structures in images. *International Journal of Computer Vision*, 53(2):153–167, 2003.

Parametric Stereo for Multi-pose Face Recognition and 3D-Face Modeling

Rik Fransens, Christoph Strecha, and Luc Van Gool

PSI ESAT-KUL
Leuven, Belgium

Abstract. This paper presents a new method for face modeling and face recognition from a pair of calibrated stereo cameras. In a first step, the algorithm builds a stereo reconstruction of the face by adjusting the global transformation parameters and the shape parameters of a 3D morphable face model. The adjustment of the parameters is such that stereo correspondence between both images is established, i.e. such that the 3D-vertices of the model project on similarly colored pixels in both images. In a second step, the texture information is extracted from the image pair and represented in the texture space of the morphable face model. The resulting shape and texture coefficients form a person specific feature vector and face recognition is performed by comparing query vectors with stored vectors. To validate our algorithm, an extensive image database was built. It consists of stereo-pairs of 70 subjects. For recognition testing, the subjects were recorded under 6 different head directions, ranging from a frontal to a profile view. The face recognition results are very good, with 100% recognition on frontal views and 97% recognition on half-profile views.

1 Introduction

Over the past decades, the task of automatic face recognition has received considerable attention from the computer vision community. One of the driving forces behind this research is the wide range of commercial and law enforcement applications related to it [16]. Furthermore, the human capability of recognizing faces under variable viewing conditions which include light variations, differences in pose, and the presence or absence of facial features (glasses, beards,...) is remarkable, and keeps on attracting the attention of researchers from different fields.

Given the vast number of face recognition related publications, it is impossible to give a detailed account of past research. Here, we restrict ourselves to a short overview of some landmark papers, where we follow the taxonomy proposed by Zhao *et al.* [16]. For the particular task of face recognition from still images, Zhao *et al.* distinguish between three main categories, being (*i*) holistic matching methods, (*ii*) feature based or structural matching methods and (*iii*) hybrid methods which combine characteristics of both approaches. In the first category, the visual content of the complete face region is used as input for the classification system. The system then extracts a low-dimensional feature vector and compares it to stored examples. Typical examples are the PCA-based Eigenfaces technique [14,11], Fisherfaces [2] and ICA-based representations [1]. In the

W. Zhao, S. Gong, and X. Tang (Eds.): AMFG 2005, LNCS 3723, pp. 109–124, 2005.

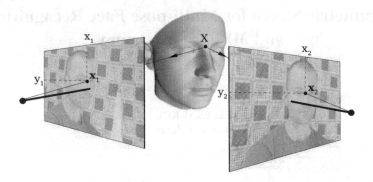

Fig. 1. Geometry of the parametric stereo setting. The 3D-vertices of the face model are projected onto both images, and the model is manipulated to establish stereo correspondence between the image values at the locations of these projections.

second category, the position and appearance of local features like eyes, nose, etc. are determined and a feature vector is built from these descriptors. A typical example is the Elastic Bunch Graph Matching system [15], which uses 'wavelet jets' to encode local appearance. Many successful systems belong to the third category, and use both local and global descriptors. Notable contributions are the modular Eigenfaces approach [12] and the Flexible Appearance Model [10] which uses an ASM-model [8] to encode shape, and PCA to encode image intensities.

The major challenge in automatic face recognition is to develop a system that performs illumination and pose invariant recognition. An interesting approach to illumination invariant recognition is based on the so-called Illumination Cone [3]. One of the most early attempts to solve the multi-pose recognition problem is due to Beymer et al. [4,5]. The method uses a vectorized image representation at each pose, which allows to map the texture information onto a (frontal) reference shape. Arguably the most principled approach to pose invariant recognition makes use of 3D morphable face models. Blanz and Vetter [6] introduced a flexible 3D model learned from examples of individual 3D face data. In [7] a morphable component model is fitted against a multi-pose database of 68 subjects. The resulting shape and texture coefficients form a person specific feature vector, and face recognition is performed by comparing the computed feature vector with a set of stored vectors.

In this paper, we propose a multi-camera approach to face recognition, which addresses the problems of illumination and pose variation. In our setup, two calibrated cameras are used, and the algorithm computes a 3D-shape and texture representation of the face in front of the system. These representations are parametrized by the linear shape and texture coefficients of a 3D-morphable face model. In a first step, the 3D-shape of the face is determined. Rather then first computing a dense depth map of the scene, and then approximating the face related part of this map within the shape-space of the 3D-model, we *directly* fit the morphable 3D-model to the set of stereo-images, hence the name *parametric stereo*. This greatly reduces the degrees of freedom (DOFs) in the depth-from-stereo problem: from one DOF per pixel to the number of shape parameters of the 3D-model plus 6 (the DOFs related to rotational and translational components of the global transformation). Next, the texture from both images are mapped onto the vertices of the 3D-model, and this shape and pose free texture is described in terms of the linear texture model of the 3D-morphable model. The geometry of parametric stereo is shown in Fig.(1).

Using a 3D face model to constraint 3D solutions to possible model realizations is not new. For example, in the context of structure-from-motion, such an approach was followed by Shan *et al.* [13] and Dimitrijevic *et al.* [9]. In structure-from-motion, an uncalibrated video stream is used as input, and the algorithm must simultaneously estimate the unknown camera parameters and the facial model parameters. In [9], for a given video frame, 2D point-correspondences are established in neighboring frames and the camera and model parameters are optimized by means of bundle-adjustment. The minimization criterion is the reprojection error of the 3D-points that are obtained by intersecting the current model hypothesis with the camera rays defined by the 2D-points in the central frame. This criterion is not symmetric w.r.t. the input images, however, the authors argue that the introduced biases cancel each other because many point correspondence pairs are used. In our approach, on the other hand, the cameras are already calibrated and the stereo images are captured simultaneously. This allows us to formulate of a symmetric criterion, which measures the quality of the model fit by color-differences, rather than reprojection distances, of corresponding points.

The advantage of the proposed method, compared to the approach of Blanz and Vetter [7], is that the shape and texture computations are performed separately. Given predominant diffuse or Lambertian reflection, the perceived color of a particular point of the face is the same in all images. Therefore, shape optimization is possible without having to worry about the number of lights in the scene, their intensities and the shadows they cast on the face. Next, in a separate computation, and with knowledge of the facial shape (i.e. surface normal directions), the lighting effects can be compensated for while estimating the coefficients of the linear texture model. In the approach of Blanz and Vetter, on the other hand, all effects have to be accounted for simultaneously, resulting in a formidable optimization problem. Furthermore, the number of lights in the scene has to be specified aforehand. Note that the Lambertian assumption, which underlies the shape-from-stereo approach, is relatively mild, because the stereo solution is computed directly in the 3D model space. Because the modes of the morphable model are global (i.e. changing a parameter alters the global facial appearance), the method can deal with a fair amount of specular reflections which typically occur locally. The stereo-setup also puts strong constraints on the 3D-shape solution which, in principle, should allow for more accurate recognition performance than single image approaches. On the down-side, our approach requires a multi-camera setup. However, in many commercial and law enforcement applications like entrance control, PIN-code verification and surveillance, the employment of multiple cameras is no objection.

The remainder of this paper is organized as follows. In section 2 we briefly introduce the stereo setup and the morphable model, and explain the energy formulation underlying the shape and texture computations. In section 3 we discuss the model initialization and optimization related issues. Section 4 describes the experimental setup and discusses the multi-pose recognition results. We end the paper with some general conclusions and a description of future work.

2 Problem Setting

Suppose we have 2 images $\mathcal{I}_i$, $i \in \{1, 2\}$, which associate a 2D-coordinate $\mathbf{x}$ with an image value $\mathcal{I}_i(\mathbf{x})$. If we are dealing with color images, this value is a 3-vector and for intensity images it is a scalar. The images are taken with 2 cameras of which we know the internal and external calibrations. The cameras are represented by the 3×4 projection matrices $\mathbf{P}_i$:

$$\mathbf{P}_i = \mathbf{K}_i[\mathbf{R}_i^T \mid -\mathbf{R}_i^T \mathbf{t}_i] \, , \tag{1}$$

where $\mathbf{K}_i$, $\mathbf{R}_i$ and $\mathbf{t}_i$ are the camera matrix, rotation and translation of the ith camera, respectively. The projection matrices project homogeneous 3D points $\mathbf{X}^h = [X \, Y \, Z \, 1]^T$ to homogeneous 2D points $\mathbf{x}^h = \lambda[x \, y \, 1]^T$ linearly: $\mathbf{x}^h = \mathbf{P}_i \mathbf{X}^h$. The corresponding image coordinate $\mathbf{x}$ is easily found by dividing out the homogeneous factor. We will denote the overall projection transformation as $\mathbf{x} = \mathcal{P}_i(\mathbf{X})$.

Furthermore, we have a morphable 3D-face model [1] which consists of an orthonormal shape and texture basis. This morphable model is the result of a PCA analysis of a set of 3D-laser scans of human faces. The scans have been brought into correspondence, such that the same vertex of each model corresponds to the same physical point on the face. Let $\mathbf{S}$ be a $3N$-dimensional shape vector which is formed by the concatenation of the N 3D-coordinates of the vertices of the facial model:

$$\mathbf{S} = [X_1 \, Y_1 \, Z_1 \ldots X_N Y_N Z_N]^T \, .$$

Let $\mathbf{T}$ be a $3N$-dimensional texture vector which is formed by the concatenation of the N RGB-color values associated with these vertices:

$$\mathbf{T} = [R_1 \, G_1 \, B_1 \ldots R_N G_N B_N]^T \, .$$

The shape and texture vectors of a particular face can now be realized independently as linear combinations of the so-called *eigen-shapes* $\mathbf{S}_j$ and *eigen-textures* $\mathbf{T}_j$:

$$\mathbf{S} = \overline{\mathbf{S}} + \sum_{j=1}^{m} \alpha_j \mathbf{S}_j, \quad \mathbf{T} = \overline{\mathbf{T}} + \sum_{j=1}^{m} \beta_j \mathbf{T}_j \, . \tag{2}$$

Here, $\overline{\mathbf{S}}$ and $\overline{\mathbf{T}}$ are the average shape and texture vector, and the linear coefficients α_j and β_j constitute the shape and texture description vectors $\boldsymbol{\alpha}$ and $\boldsymbol{\beta}$ which fully characterize the model realization. The effects of the first shape and texture eigenvectors on the average face are visualized in Fig.(2). In what follows, we will use the term *face model* to describe a particular shape and texture combination $(\mathbf{S}, \mathbf{T})$, and we will preserve the term *PCA model* for the generative statistical model (i.e. the collection of shape and texture averages and eigenvectors) itself. Let $\mathbf{X}_k$, $k \in \{1, .., N\}$, be the kth vertex of the face model, then the shape transformation of this vertex is denoted as $\mathcal{S}(\mathbf{X}_k)$.

The 3D-coordinates of the vertices of the face model are defined w.r.t. an object centered coordinate system. The model can be moved around by a rigid body transformation $\mathcal{T}$ applied to each (shape-transformed) vertex of the model:

$$\mathcal{T} \circ \mathcal{S}(\mathbf{X}_k) = \mathbf{R}\big(\mathcal{S}(\mathbf{X}_k) - \mathbf{C}\big) + \mathbf{C} + \mathbf{t} \, , \tag{3}$$

---

[1] USF Human ID 3-D Database and Morphable Faces [6].

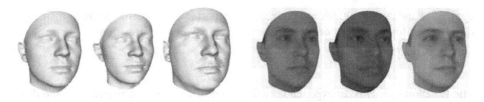

Fig. 2. Textured and untextured renderings of the face model. Left: the average model shape and the effect of the 1st eigen-shape ($\pm 2\sigma$) on the average. Note the changes in scale, as well as the transition from female to male characteristics. Right: the average model texture and the effect of the 1st eigen-texture ($\pm 2\sigma$) on the average.

where $\mathbf{R}$ is a 3×3 rotation matrix, $\mathbf{t}$ is a translation vector, and $\mathbf{C}$ is the geometrical mean of the average face shape. The transformation has 6 free parameters which are jointly denoted as $\boldsymbol{\theta}$. Note that we have not included a scale parameter because the scale variation of human faces is incorporated in the first eigen-shapes of the PCA-model.

Our goal is to estimate a particular set of global transformation, shape and texture parameters ($\boldsymbol{\theta}$, $\boldsymbol{\alpha}$, $\boldsymbol{\beta}$), which best explain the input images $\mathcal{I}_1$ and $\mathcal{I}_2$. We proceed as follows. First, in the *shape recovery* step, we determine the values of $\boldsymbol{\theta}$ and $\boldsymbol{\alpha}$ which establish stereo-correspondence between both input images. Put differently, we wish to find those parameter values, such that for all model vertices $\mathbf{X}$ which are visible in both images, the image color at their respective projections in $\mathcal{I}_1$ and $\mathcal{I}_2$ are as much alike as possible, i.e. $\mathcal{I}_1\big(\mathcal{P}_1 \circ \mathcal{T} \circ \mathcal{S}(\mathbf{X})\big) \sim \mathcal{I}_2\big(\mathcal{P}_2 \circ \mathcal{T} \circ \mathcal{S}(\mathbf{X})\big)$. To reach this objective, we only manipulate the parameter sets $\boldsymbol{\theta}$ and $\boldsymbol{\alpha}$. Next, in the *texture recovery* step, the color information of both images is back-projected onto the face model, giving rise to a shape-free facial texture vector. This is then described as a linear combination of eigen-textures, while simultaneously the effects of ambient and directional lighting are accounted for.

2.1 Shape Computation

If we write $\mathbf{x}_{ik}$ for the projection of the kth vertex of the face model in the ith image, i.e. $\mathbf{x}_{ik} = \mathcal{P}_i \circ \mathcal{T} \circ \mathcal{S}(\mathbf{X}_k)$, the objective function we minimize is the following:

$$E_S = \sum_{k \in \mathcal{V}} w_{S,k} \, \| \mathcal{I}_1(\mathbf{x}_{1k}) - \mathcal{I}_2(\mathbf{x}_{2k}) \|^2 + \lambda_S \sum_{j=1}^{m} \frac{\alpha_j^2}{\sigma_{S,j}^2} , \tag{4}$$

where $\mathcal{V} \subset \{1, .., N\}$ indexes the points which are visible from both images. This energy consists of a data-term, which measures the color difference between the images at corresponding projection positions, and a prior-term, which constraints the shape deformation to reasonable values.

In the data-term, the contribution of the kth color difference is weighted with a vertex specific weight $w_{S,k}$. The purpose of this weight is two-fold. First, it allows us to account for foreshortening effects in the model projection, as a result of which the majority of vertex projections cumulate nearby the contours of the face in both $\mathcal{I}_1$ and $\mathcal{I}_2$. Next, it allows us to assign more importance to the frontal part of the face, i.e. the eyes, nose and mouth regions, which are more important for revealing identity than, say the cheek or forehead regions. We use the following weighting function:

$$w_{S,k} \propto d(\mathbf{X}_k)\, S_k\, \mathbf{n}_k \cdot \mathbf{v} \, . \tag{5}$$

The function $d(\mathbf{X}_k)$ is an exponentially decaying function which depends on the distance (in cylindrical coordinates) from the kth vertex to the center of the face, S_k is the area of the surface patch around the kth vertex, $\mathbf{n}_k$ is the surface normal vector at this vertex and $\mathbf{v}$ is the average viewing direction of both cameras. We include the patch area S_k because the vertices are not evenly distributed over the surface of the model (the 3D-laser sensor samples the facial surface at cylindrical coordinates).

In the prior-term, $\sigma_{S,j}^2$ is the variance (i.e. eigenvalue) associated with the jth eigenshape of the PCA-model. The parameter λ_S, which we take proportional to the sum of all weights in the data-term, allows us to balance the influence of the prior-term relative to the data-term.

2.2 Texture Computation

Let I_{amb}^R, I_{amb}^G, I_{amb}^B be the red, green and blue intensities of the ambient light. Furthermore, let I_{dir}^R, I_{dir}^G, I_{dir}^B be the red, green and blue intensities of the directional (parallel) light, which has direction l. Then the observable color $I_k = [R_k\, G_k\, B_k]^T$ of the kth vertex of the face model can be modeled as follows:

$$R_k = R_{off} + (\overline{R}_k + \sum_{j=1}^{m} \beta_j R_{jk})(I_{amb}^R + I_{dir}^R \mathbf{n}_k \cdot \mathbf{l}) \, , \tag{6}$$

where similar equations hold for G_k and B_k. In this equation, R_{off} is an offset, $\overline{R}_k$ and R_{jk} are the red values of the kth vertex of the average texture and j^{th} eigen-texture, and $\mathbf{n}_k$ is the normal surface vector emanating from the kth vertex. Note that the model texture is used as the reflectance coefficient of a diffuse lighting model. Unlike in [7], we do not add a specular component, because we experimentally observed that the diffuse lighting model is sufficient to account for the lighting effects in our images. Given this color model, the objective function we minimize is the following:

$$E_T = \sum_{k \in \mathcal{V}} \sum_{i=1}^{2} w_{T,k}\, \| \mathcal{I}_i(\mathbf{x}_{ik}) - I_k \|^2 + \lambda_T \sum_{j=1}^{m} \frac{\beta_j^2}{\sigma_{T,j}^2} \, . \tag{7}$$

Like in the shape computation, this energy consists of a data-term, which measures the color difference between the input images and the texture reconstruction, and a prior-term which constraints the texture deformation to reasonable values. The contribution of each vertex color is weighted by a vertex specific weight $w_{T,k}$, which accounts for the aforementioned foreshortening effects, and also allows us to diminish the influence of outliers in the texture reconstruction. These outliers are vertices, for whom the sampled image colors $\mathcal{I}_i(\mathbf{x}_{ik})$ are significantly different. The differences might be caused by wrong shape reconstructions (i.e. image locations where stereo correspondence was not established), but also by specular highlights in either of both images. We use the following weighting function:

$$w_{T,k} \propto w_{S,k} \exp\left(-\frac{1}{2} d_{\mathbf{S}}^2 \big(\mathcal{I}_1(\mathbf{x}_{1k}) - \mathcal{I}_2(\mathbf{x}_{2k})\big)\right), \tag{8}$$

where $d_{\mathbf{S}}^2(\mathbf{x})$ is a squared distance defined by $\mathbf{x}^T \mathbf{S}^{-1} \mathbf{x}$. For $\mathbf{S}$ we take a robust estimate of the covariance matrix of the color differences $\mathcal{I}_1(\mathbf{x}_{1k}) - \mathcal{I}_2(\mathbf{x}_{2k})$.

3 Model Initialization and Optimization

3.1 Model Initialization

Before the shape energy E_S defined in Eq.(4) is optimized w.r.t. the global transformation parameters θ and shape parameters α, the 3D-model needs to be at a reasonable start position. In this paper we assume that we have a set of feature detectors at our disposal, which are able to localize typical facial features (eyes, nose, corners of the mouth, etc.) if they are visible. Furthermore, these detectors provide us with some indication of the spatial uncertainty of the detection. Typically, feature detectors provide a detection value at each location in a certain region of interest, and report the position of maximal detection value. Let $\widehat{\mathbf{x}}_{ip}$ be the estimated position of the pth feature in the ith image, and let $\mathbf{S}_{ip}$ be a 2×2 scatter matrix which characterizes the spatial uncertainty of this estimate. For the feature points of interest, we also know the 3D-coordinates of the corresponding vertex on the morphable model. Let $\mathbf{X}_p$ be the 3D-coordinates of the pth feature, and $\mathbf{x}_{ip} = \mathcal{P}_i \circ \mathcal{T} \circ \mathcal{S}(\mathbf{X}_p)$ be the projection of this point in the ith image. The objective function we minimize is the following:

$$E_I = \sum_{i=1}^{2} \sum_{p=1}^{N_p} \delta_{ip} (\widehat{\mathbf{x}}_{ip} - \mathbf{x}_{ip})^T \mathbf{S}_{ip}^{-1} (\widehat{\mathbf{x}}_{ip} - \mathbf{x}_{ip}), \tag{9}$$

where N_p is the total number of features we consider and $\delta_{ip} \in \{0, 1\}$ is a binary variable which indicates whether or not the pth feature was detected in the ith image. The initial model position is found by minimizing E_I w.r.t. the 6 parameters of θ. If the number of detections is large enough to render a unique solution (e.g. > 3 non-colinear features are detected in both images), it is possible to further optimize E_I w.r.t. the model shape parameters α. Using the same prior as in Eq.(4), the objective function becomes:

$$E_I = \sum_{i=1}^{2} \sum_{p=1}^{N_p} \delta_{ip} (\widehat{\mathbf{x}}_{ip} - \mathbf{x}_{ip})^T \mathbf{S}_{ip}^{-1} (\widehat{\mathbf{x}}_{ip} - \mathbf{x}_{ip}) + \lambda_I \sum_{j=1}^{m} \frac{\alpha_j^2}{\sigma_{S,j}^2}. \tag{10}$$

We minimize this energy by Levenberg-Marquardt iterations. The gradient of E_I w.r.t. the jth global transformation parameter θ_j is given by:

$$\frac{\partial E_I}{\partial \theta_j} = -2 \sum_{i=1}^{2} \sum_{p=1}^{N_p} \delta_{ip} (\widehat{\mathbf{x}}_{ip} - \mathbf{x}_{ip})^T \mathbf{S}_{ip}^{-1} \mathbf{J}_{\mathcal{P}_i} \frac{\partial \mathcal{T}}{\partial \theta_j}. \tag{11}$$

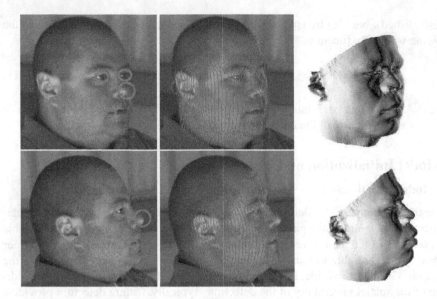

Fig. 3. Model initialization. Left column: the input stereo pair with feature points and their spatial uncertainty. Middle column: the fit of the model guided by the feature points. The fit is relatively accurate, but alignment errors are still visible at the contour of the face. Right column: renderings of the initialized model. The reconstruction is relatively poor, but the main facial features are already visible.

Here, the 2×3-matrix $\mathbf{J}_{\mathcal{P}_i}$ is the Jacobian of the projection function $\mathcal{P}_i$ evaluated at $\mathcal{T} \circ \mathcal{S}(\mathbf{X}_p)$ and $\partial \mathcal{T} / \partial \theta_j$ is a 3-derivative vector evaluated at $\mathcal{S}(\mathbf{X}_p)$. The gradient of E_I w.r.t. the jth shape parameter α_j is given by:

$$\frac{\partial E_I}{\partial \alpha_j} = -2 \sum_{i=1}^{2} \sum_{p=1}^{N_p} \delta_{ip} (\widehat{\mathbf{x}}_{ip} - \mathbf{x}_{ip})^T \mathbf{S}_{ip}^{-1} \mathbf{J}_{\mathcal{P}_i} \mathbf{J}_{\mathcal{T}} \frac{\partial \mathbf{X}_p}{\partial \alpha_j} + 2\lambda_I \frac{\alpha_j}{\sigma_{S,j}^2} , \qquad (12)$$

where the 3×3-matrix $\mathbf{J}_{\mathcal{T}}$ is the Jacobian of the rigid-body transformation evaluated at $\mathcal{S}(\mathbf{X}_p)$, and $\partial \mathbf{X}_p / \partial \alpha_j$ is a 3-derivative vector, which contains the XYZ-values of the jth eigen-shape at the position of $\mathbf{X}_p$. The initialization procedure is graphically illustrated in Fig.(3).

3.2 Shape Optimization

After the model initialization, the 3D face model is in approximate correspondence with both input images. We now proceed with the optimization of the shape energy E_S defined in Eq.(4) w.r.t. the global transformation parameters θ and shape parameters α. The purpose of this optimization is to establish stereo correspondence between both images. The gradient of E_S w.r.t. the jth global transformation parameters θ_j is given by:

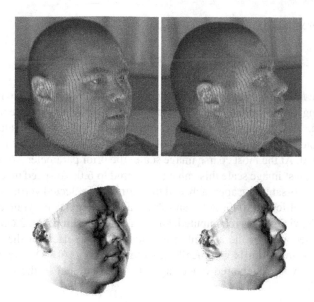

Fig. 4. Shape optimization. Top row: the input stereo-pair with an overlay of the final model shape. Note that, compared to the initialization result in Fig.(3), the accuracy of the fit has improved. Particularly the alignment errors at the contour of the face have largely disappeared. Bottom row: renderings of the untextured model at its final position.

$$\frac{\partial E_S}{\partial \theta_j} = 2 \sum_{k \in \mathcal{V}} w_{S,k} [\mathcal{I}_1(\mathbf{x}_{1k}) - \mathcal{I}_2(\mathbf{x}_{2k})]^T \nabla \mathcal{I}_1 \frac{\partial \mathbf{x}_{1k}}{\partial \theta_j} -$$
$$2 \sum_{k \in \mathcal{V}} w_{S,k} [\mathcal{I}_1(\mathbf{x}_{1k}) - \mathcal{I}_2(\mathbf{x}_{2k})]^T \nabla \mathcal{I}_2 \frac{\partial \mathbf{x}_{2k}}{\partial \theta_j} \tag{13}$$

The image gradients $\nabla \mathcal{I}_i$ are 3×2-matrices and contain the spatial derivatives of the R, G and B-component of $\mathcal{I}_i$ evaluated at positions $\mathbf{x}_{ik}$. The differentials $\partial \mathbf{x}_{ik} / \partial \theta_j$ are 2-vectors defined as follows:

$$\frac{\partial \mathbf{x}_{ik}}{\partial \theta_j} = \mathbf{J}_{\mathcal{P}_i} \frac{\partial \mathcal{T}(\mathcal{S}(\mathbf{X}_k))}{\partial \theta_j} . \tag{14}$$

The gradient of E_S w.r.t. the jth shape transformation parameters α_j can be derived in a similar fashion:

$$\frac{\partial E_S}{\partial \alpha_j} = 2 \sum_{k \in \mathcal{V}} w_{S,k} [\mathcal{I}_1(\mathbf{x}_{1k}) - \mathcal{I}_2(\mathbf{x}_{2k})]^T \nabla \mathcal{I}_1 \frac{\partial \mathbf{x}_{1k}}{\partial \alpha_j} -$$
$$2 \sum_{k \in \mathcal{V}} w_{S,k} [\mathcal{I}_1(\mathbf{x}_{1k}) - \mathcal{I}_2(\mathbf{x}_{2k})]^T \nabla \mathcal{I}_2 \frac{\partial \mathbf{x}_{2k}}{\partial \alpha_j} \tag{15}$$

where the differentials $\partial \mathbf{x}_{ik}/\partial \alpha_j$ are given by:

$$\frac{\partial \mathbf{x}_{ik}}{\partial \alpha_j} = \mathbf{J}_{\mathcal{P}_i}\mathbf{J}_{\mathcal{T}}\mathbf{X}_{jk} \ . \tag{16}$$

Here $\mathbf{X}_{jk}$ is the kth component of the jth eigen-shape. We optimize E_S with conjugate gradient. During optimization, model vertices do not project onto integral positions in $\mathcal{I}_i$, and we use bilinear interpolation to sample pixel and gradient values from the images. To avoid local minima, a pyramidal coarse-to-fine strategy with 3 pyramidal levels is followed. At the most coarse image scale, the prior parameter λ_S is set to 20.0, whereas at the finest image scale this value is lowered to 5.0. To speed up convergence, we use a vertex sub-sampling approach, and the number of selected vertices is increased at every pyramidal level (1000, 2000 and 3000 at the respective pyramid levels). At regular intervals, visibility is recomputed. On a standard desktop (P4, 2.6GHz), it takes on average 35 seconds for the algorithm to converge. The effect of the optimization procedure on the model fit is graphically illustrated in Fig. (4). Different views of a subject, together with untextured renderings of the 3D model in the same pose, are shown in Fig. (7).

3.3 Texture Optimization

After the shape extraction step, the textures from both images are mapped onto the vertices of the 3D-model. The resulting shape and pose free texture is described in terms

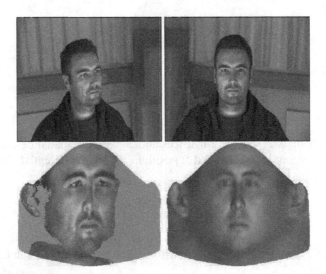

Fig. 5. Texture reconstruction. Top row: the stereo-pair of test view one. Bottom row, left: the average of the textures extracted from both images. The facial regions which are not visible from both images are displayed in gray. Note that the average has remained sharp, which is an indication of the quality of the shape reconstruction. Bottom row, right: the texture reconstruction by the texture model.

of the linear texture model of the 3D-morphable model. This is done by minimizing the energy E_T in Eq.(7) w.r.t. the light source variables and texture coefficients β, where we only take into account the texture of the points which are visible in both images. We optimize E_T with conjugate gradient, and set λ_T to 5.0. An example of a texture reconstruction is shown in Fig.(5).

4 Experiments and Discussion

To validate our algorithm, an extensive image database was built. It consists of stereo-pairs of 70 subjects (35 males, 35 females), recorded from 6 different viewpoints. An example of the stereo-pairs of one subject is shown in Fig.(6). The first viewpoint, which is frontal w.r.t. the stereo-pair, is used as training or enrollment data. An example is shown in the left column of Fig.(6). The shape and texture vectors of these faces are stored in the memory of the recognition system, and all queries are compared to them. The next 5 viewpoints range from a frontal to a profile view w.r.t. the viewing direction of the first camera, in equal steps of $\pi/8$ radians. These views will serve as test data from which query vectors are computed. Note that the first test view, which is frontal, was recorded separately from the training data. The lighting conditions remained constant over the course of the recordings. Lighting is complex with multiple light sources and reflectors in the neighborhood of the subject. From Fig.(6) it can be appreciated that the recorded intensities on the facial part of the image vary considerably over the different viewpoints.

Fig. 6. Stereo-pair database: one face from the stereo database. The first row shows the images from the left camera of the stereo-pair, the second row shows the images taken from the right camera. Left column: the training viewpoint, which shows the subjects in frontal pose w.r.t. the stereo cameras. Columns 2 to 6: the five test views with increasing angle w.r.t. the training view.

For a particular person and particular viewpoint, we then compute the face model parameters (α, β). These are used as a query vector, and all training vectors are sorted according to their distance from the query vector. The distance function we use is a weighted sum of Mahalanobis distances, defined as follows:

$$d(\alpha_1, \beta_1; \alpha_2, \beta_2) = \lambda_\alpha(\alpha_1 - \alpha_2)^T \mathbf{C}_\alpha^{-1}(\alpha_1 - \alpha_2) +$$
$$\lambda_\beta(\beta_1 - \beta_2)^T \mathbf{C}_\beta^{-1}(\beta_1 - \beta_2). \quad (17)$$

Here, λ_α and λ_β are weights which allow us to manipulate the importance of the shape coefficients w.r.t. the texture coefficients, and C_α and C_β are the model covariance matrices of shape and geometry. If the correct person is at the first position of the sorted list of training vectors, we denote this as a correct identification or 'rank-1' match. In the results, we report the percentage of correct identifications for each test viewpoint. We also show the percentage of queries for which the correct person is amongst the first 3 and 5 positions ('rank-3' and 'rank-5' matches). To gain more insight in the roles of shape and texture in the recognition performance, we also report recognition rates when we only use the shape or the texture vectors in the queries. In all experiments, 50 shape and 50 texture components were used. The results are shown in Table (1). From these figures, we immediately see that, except for the frontal test view

Table 1. Recognition rates without coefficient weighting. Top table: recognition rates based on geometry only. Middle table: recognition rates based on texture only. Bottom table: recognition rates based on combined geometry and texture features. Rank-1 matches are indicated in bold.

	test 1	test 2	test 3	test 4	test 5
rank 1	**90.0**	**87.1**	**68.6**	**52.9**	**41.4**
rank 3	92.9	98.6	84.3	71.4	60.0
rank 5	94.3	98.6	90.0	85.7	72.9
rank 1	**91.4**	**67.1**	**30.0**	**17.1**	**11.4**
rank 3	92.9	84.3	44.3	25.7	12.9
rank 5	92.9	90.0	52.9	38.6	17.1
rank 1	**94.3**	**94.3**	**77.1**	**58.6**	**45.7**
rank 3	97.1	95.7	87.1	80.0	62.9
rank 5	97.1	95.7	92.9	85.7	68.6

('test 1'), shape based recognition performs better than texture based recognition. Also, the texture based recognition rates drop sharply when the test views have increasing angle w.r.t. the training view ('test 2,3,...'). Both cues seem to be co-operative, i.e. the results based on both shape and geometry features are better than the results based on the separate features.

In Blanz *et al.* [7], a coefficient weighting method was introduced, which takes into account the variation of model coefficients obtained from different images of the same person. These variations may be due to several reasons. First of all, when the model is fitted against images of the same person but from a different viewpoint, different facial features are estimated with a different accuracy. For example, on the frontal views we can expect an accurate assessment of the width and height of the face. For the 'depth related features' like the profile of nose, the prominence of eyebrows etc..., we can expect a much poorer assessment. On the profile views, on the other hand, the assessment of the width of the face is much more difficult, whereas the profile of the nose can be estimated accurately. Secondly, different lighting conditions can introduce ambiguities in the texture reconstruction, such as skin complexion versus intensity of illumination [7]. We also noticed that there is light-source variation within the eigen-textures of the model. This causes instabilities in the computation of texture coefficients, because the model is able to explain lighting conditions both with its light source variables and its linear model. This probably explains the relatively poor texture based recognition results from Table (1). Finally, if the PCA model is not able to reproduce the faces in the input images, the algorithm will do as well as possible and will distribute the residual error over its coefficients. This distribution is likely to be different for different viewpoints.

To account for these effects, the distance function in Eq.(17) is modified, to suppress directions with high within-person variation in the whitened coefficient spaces. The whitening transformation compensates for the relative magnitude of the coefficients and transforms α and β to $\alpha' = \mathbf{C}_\alpha^{-1/2}\alpha$ and $\beta' = \mathbf{C}_\beta^{-1/2}\beta$, respectively. To suppress directions with high within-person variation, the pooled within-person scatter matrices $\mathbf{W}_\alpha$ and $\mathbf{W}_\beta$ are introduced into the Mahalanobis distances. To estimate $\mathbf{W}_\alpha$ and $\mathbf{W}_\beta$ independently from our test-set, we recorded a training set consisting of stereo-pairs of 30 more subjects (15 males, 15 females). The viewing conditions of this second database are similar, but the lighting conditions are slightly different. Let $N = 30$ and $V = 5$ be the number of persons and number of viewpoints per person in this trainingset. Furthermore, let α'_{ij} and β'_{ij} be the computed (whitened) shape and texture coefficients of the ith person in the jth view point, and let $\langle \alpha'_i \rangle$ and $\langle \beta'_i \rangle$ be the average shape and texture coefficients of the ith person over all V viewpoints, respectively. The weighting matrices are defined as follows:

$$\mathbf{W}_\alpha = \frac{1}{N}\sum_i^N \frac{1}{V}\sum_j^V (\alpha'_{ij} \quad \langle \alpha'_i \rangle)(\alpha'_{ij} - \langle \alpha'_i \rangle)^T$$

$$\mathbf{W}_\beta \quad \frac{1}{N}\sum_i^N \frac{1}{V}\sum_j^V (\beta'_{ij} - \langle \beta'_i \rangle)(\beta'_{ij} - \langle \beta'_i \rangle)^T \,. \tag{18}$$

These matrices estimate the spread of the model coefficients w.r.t. changes in viewpoint, and can be used to identify consistent and inconsistent directions in the shape and texture feature spaces. Taking the shape coefficients as an example, directions α' characterized by a high value of $\alpha'^T\mathbf{W}_\alpha\alpha'$ are inconsistent w.r.t. the viewpoint from which these coefficients are computed, whereas directions α' characterized by a low value of $\alpha'^T\mathbf{W}_\alpha\alpha'$ are relatively stable w.r.t. viewpoint. By incorporating these weights in Eq.(17), the importance of inconsistent directions can be diminished. The new distance function is given by:

$$d(\alpha_1, \beta_1; \alpha_2, \beta_2) = \lambda_\alpha(\alpha_1 - \alpha_2)^T \mathbf{C}_\alpha^{-\frac{1}{2}} \mathbf{W}_\alpha^{-1} \mathbf{C}_\alpha^{-\frac{1}{2}}(\alpha_1 - \alpha_2) +$$

$$\lambda_\beta(\beta_1 - \beta_2)^T \mathbf{C}_\beta^{-\frac{1}{2}} \mathbf{W}_\beta^{-1} \mathbf{C}_\beta^{-\frac{1}{2}}(\beta_1 - \beta_2) \,. \tag{19}$$

The final results are shown in Table (2). The performance boost is quite significant. Especially the recognition rate of the texture-component seems to benefit from the coefficient weighting.

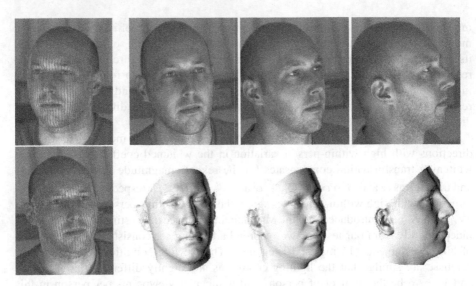

Fig. 7. Shape optimization. Left column: the stereo-pair from which the 3D reconstruction is computed with an overlay of the final model shape. Columns 2,3 and 4: new views of the subject and the untextured renderings of the 3D model at the corresponding positions and orientations.

Table 2. Recognition results with coefficient weighting. Top table: recognition rates based on geometry only. Middle table: recognition rates based on texture only. Bottom table: recognition rates based on combined geometry and texture features. λ_α and λ_β were set to 0.7 and 0.3.

	test 1	test 2	test 3	test 4	test 5
rank 1	**94.3**	**84.3**	**80.0**	**74.3**	**60.0**
rank 3	98.6	95.7	94.3	88.6	75.7
rank 5	100.0	95.7	94.3	91.4	87.1
rank 1	**94.3**	**97.1**	**80.0**	**68.6**	**42.9**
rank 3	95.7	98.6	91.4	82.9	67.1
rank 5	95.7	98.6	97.1	85.7	81.4
rank 1	**100.0**	**98.6**	**97.1**	**91.4**	**82.9**
rank 3	100.0	98.6	98.6	92.9	90.0
rank 5	100.0	100.0	100.0	97.1	92.9

5 Conclusions

We presented a new method for face modeling and face recognition from a pair of calibrated stereo cameras. In the *shape extraction* step, the algorithm builds a stereo reconstruction of the face by adjusting the global transformation and shape parameters of a 3D-morphable face model. Next, in the *texture extraction* step, texture is sampled from the image pair and represented in the texture space of the morphable face model.

The resulting shape and texture parameters are characteristic for the analyzed face, and can subsequently be used for face recognition.

In a face recognition experiment on a stereo database of 70 subjects, we reported recognition rates for 5 different viewpoints. The initial recognition results are reasonable but a decrease in performance is noted for profile views. Particularly the texture feature vector has relatively low discriminative power. However, after weighting the coefficients with the pooled within-person scatter matrices − estimated independently from the test set − detection rates increase significantly. The resulting face recognition system has state-of-the-art performance.

We believe that, with a refinement of the morphable face model, the level of performance can still increase. An obvious improvement is the usage of a component based model with enhanced representative power. Furthermore, we noticed that there is evidence of light-source variation within the eigen-textures of the model, which causes instabilities in the computation of texture coefficients. These variations should be accounted for, prior to PCA-analysis.

Acknowledgments. The authors acknowledge support from EU project Reveal-This and IWT project 020195.

References

1. Bartlett, M. S., Lades, H. M., Sejnowski, T. J., "Independent component representations for face recognition," *Proc. of the SPIE Symposium on Electonic Imaging: Science and Technology*, pp. 528-539, 1998.
2. Belhumeur, P. N., Hespanha, J. P., Kriegman, D. J., "Eigenfaces vs. Fisherfaces: Recognition Using Class Specific Linear Projection," *IEEE Trans. PAMI*, Vol. 19, No. 7, pp. 711-720, 1997.
3. Belhumeur, P., Kriegman, D., "What is the Set of Images of an Object Under All Possible Lighting Conditions?," *IJCV*, Vol. 28, No. 3, pp. 245-260, 1998.
4. Beymer, D., "Face recognition under varying pose," Tech. Rep. 1461. MIT AI Lab, Massachusetts Institute of Technology, Cambridge, MA
5. Beymer, D., "Vectorizing face images by interleaving shape and texture computations," Tech. Rep. 1537, MIT AI Lab, Massachusetts Institute of Technology, Cambridge, MA
6. Blanz, V., Vetter, T., "A morphable model for the synthesis of 3D faces," *SIGGRAPH '99: Proc. of the 26th Annual Conference on Computer Graphics and Interactive Techniques*, pp. 187-194, 1999.
7. Blanz, V., Vetter, T., "Face Recognition Based on Fitting a 3D Morphable Model," *IEEE Trans. PAMI*, Vol. 25, No. 9, pp. 1063-1074, 2003.
8. Cootes, T. F., Taylor, C. J., Cooper, D. H., Graham, J., "Active Shape Models - Their Training and Application," *Computer Vision and Image Understanding*, Vol. 61, No. 1, pp 38-59, 1995.
9. Dimitrijevic, M., Ilic, S., Fua, P., "Accurate Face Models from Uncalibrated and Ill-Lit Video Sequences," *IEEE Proc. Int. Conf. CVPR*, Vol. 2, pp. 1034-1041, 2004.
10. Lanitis, A., Taylor, C. J., Cootes, T. F., "Automatic Face Identification System Using Flexible Appearance Models," *Image Vis. Comput.*, Vol. 13, pp. 393-401, 1995.
11. Moghaddam, B., Pentland, A., "Probabilistic Visual Learning for Object Representation," *IEEE Trans. Pattern Anal. Mach. Intell.*, Vol. 19, pp. 696-710, 1997.

12. Pentland, A., Moghaddam, B., Starner, T., "View-Based and Modular Eigenspaces for Face Recognition," *Proc. Int. Conf. Computer Vision and Pattern Recognition*, pp. 84-91, 1994.
13. Shan, Y., Liu, Z., Zhang, Z., "Model-Based Bundle Adjustment with Application to Face Modeling," *International Conference on Computer Vision*, Vol. 2, p. 644, 2001.
14. Turk, M., Pentland, A., "Eigenfaces for Recognition," *Journal of Cognitive Neuroscience*, Vol. 3, No. 1, 1991.
15. Wiskott, L., Fellous. J.-M., Kruger, N., von der Malsburg, C., "Face Recognition by Elastic Bunch Graph Matching," *IEEE Trans. PAMI*, Vol. 19, No. 7, pp. 775-779, 1997.
16. Zhao, W., Chellappa, R., Phillips, P. J., Rosenfeld, A., "Face recognition: A literature survey," *ACM Comput. Surv.*, Vol. 35, No. 4, pp. 399-458, 2003.

An Investigation of Model Bias
in 3D Face Tracking

Douglas Fidaleo[1], Gérard Medioni[1], Pascal Fua[2], and Vincent Lepetit[2]

[1] Institute for Robotics and Intelligent Systems, University of Southern California
{dfidaleo, medioni}@usc.edu
[2] Computer Vision Laboratory, École Polytechnique Fédérale de Lausanne
{Pascal.Fua, Vincent.Lepetit}@epfl.ch

Abstract. 3D tracking of faces in video streams is a difficult problem that can be assisted with the use of a priori knowledge of the structure and appearance of the subject's face at predefined poses (keyframes). This paper provides an extensive analysis of a state-of-the-art keyframe-based tracker: quantitatively demonstrating the dependence of tracking performance on underlying mesh accuracy, number and coverage of reliably matched feature points, and initial keyframe alignment.

Tracking with a generic face mesh can introduce an erroneous bias that leads to degraded tracking performance when the subject's out-of-plane motion is far from the set of keyframes. To reduce this bias, we show how online refinement of a rough estimate of face geometry may be used to re-estimate the 3d keyframe features, thereby mitigating sensitivities to initial keyframe inaccuracies in pose and geometry. An in-depth analysis is performed on sequences of faces with synthesized rigid head motion.

Subsequent trials on real video sequences demonstrate that tracking performance is more sensitive to initial model alignment and geometry errors when fewer feature points are matched and/or do not adequately span the face. The analysis suggests several indications for most effective 3D tracking of faces in real environments.

1 Introduction

3D tracking of faces in video streams is a difficult problem that can be assisted with the use of a priori knowledge of the structure and appearance of the subject's face at predefined poses. Tracking accuracy, however, is dependent (in part) upon the quality of this knowledge: ie, the underlying 3D accuracy and initial alignment of the tracking model in a selection of key image frames corresponding to the selected poses.

Unfortunately, for many tracking applications it is unreasonable to assume that a model of the tracked subject exists, or that sufficient views of the face are available a priori to optimally align the mesh. As shown in Figure 1, a single generic face is an unsatisfactory prior for all tracking subjects and single-view initialization can mask egregious registration errors. While a model of the subject may be created using global bundle adjustment as in [2], this is a lengthy

W. Zhao, S. Gong, and X. Tang (Eds.): AMFG 2005, LNCS 3723, pp. 125–139, 2005.

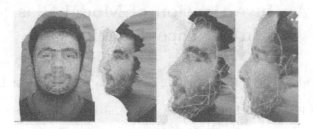

Fig. 1. (left) Improper registration of tracking mesh is not apparent from a single image. (right) Registration errors are dependent on subject's facial structure. With the first subject, errors are concentrated in forehead and chin area. The second subject has a more shallow chin and more pronounced nose bridge making these areas more difficult to align.

offline process. Reasonable results at or near keyframes can be achieved with a relaxed 3D structure (ie, a generic face mesh) but as the subject deviates from the keyframe poses, tracking becomes sensitive to the initial pose alignment. Furthermore, even when accurate keyframe registration and geometry is available, 3D tracking from 2D features can be sensitive to the number and quality of matched features in each image.

The primary goal of this paper is to present a thorough experimental investigation of the tracking performance of a state-of-the-art 3D tracker applied to faces. We validate quantitatively the claims of tracking performance dependence on model accuracy by comparing performance with a variety of meshes on image sequences derived from real faces, but with synthetically generated motion whose parameters are precisely known. We show that it can be better to track with a much weaker prior such as an ellipsoid than to introduce a strong erroneous bias with a misaligned generic "face-like" mesh when optimal keyframe initialization is not possible. In both cases, the suboptimal mesh leads to degraded tracking results when the subject's pose is far from an in-plane translation of the keyframe when compared to an accurate 3D mesh. Additional factors contributing to tracking performance are also investigated, including the number of feature points accurately matched to the keyframe, the total face coverage of the points, and reprojection error.

We also demonstrate that by refining the geometry of the internal tracking model using initial estimates of camera pose, errors in both mesh geometry and alignment are reduced, and tracking performance is enhanced. Beginning with a rough estimate of face geometry we iteratively refine the model online using a simple stereo-based update approach and use the more accurate structure to re-estimate the 3d keyframe features.

The experiments on synthesized motion sequences extend directly to real sequences with the important caveat that due to variable image quality and resolution, the number of accurately matched features can be low. Further investigation on real sequences shows that these effects must be minimized not only for accurate but also stable tracking. The investigation concludes with a set of indications for effective 3D tracking of faces.

We have chosen to use the real-time tracker by [2] for our investigation due to the reported high quality performance, both in speed and accuracy.

2   Previous Work

In most rigid object tracking approaches the pose estimate at a given time is dependent on the estimate at the previous frame. Dubbed *recursive* tracking in [2], the concatenation of motion estimates causes error to be aggregated and can result in considerable tracking drift after several frames.

If the class of tracked objects is restricted (such as, to faces) a priori knowledge of the object properties can be leveraged to improve tracking accuracy and resolve pose ambiguities. 3D model-based tracking introduces this knowledge in the form of the structure, pose, and, in some cases, surface texture of the object. The 3D model is used to regularize feature motion in [6][8][5] [7][11][12].

To eliminate drift, keyframe approaches perform tracking by detection, utilizing information obtained offline such as the known pose of the head in specific frames (keyframes) of the tracking sequence. Input images are matched to existing keyframes and provide accurate pose estimates at or near key poses. Such approaches suffer from tracking jitter and can require several keyframes for robust tracking. In an uncontrolled environment, it may not be possible to accurately establish multiple keyframes.

A critical issue in all 3D model based approaches, is the accurate estimation of the tracking model. In keyframe approaches, accurate pose is also required at keyframes. Indeed, [2] performs optimal pose and model estimation at keyframes using global bundle adjustment. This preprocessing is lengthy and is acceptable for offline tracking, or in situations where the subject to be tracked is known and can be enrolled in the system prior to the tracking phase. However, such effort is impractical for more general "ad-hoc" tracking situations such as surveillance.

View synthesis approaches for rapid model registration can be used to render the appearance of the tracking model at different poses as in [4]. A best-fit search among these views reveals the correct registration parameters. This method performs well when lighting conditions are consistent between the rendered face and the face image. However, like most appearance based approaches is likely to be sensitive to drastic lighting changes and cosmetic changes on the face such as facial hair and makeup.

Most model based trackers assume a rough estimate of face shape such as an ellipsoid in [9][6] and a cylindrical model in [5]. In each of these approaches the initial inaccurate tracking mesh remains static throughout the tracking sequence, introducing considerable error.

In the model-based bundle adjustment work by Shan et.al. [3] a generic face model is allowed to deform to account for both facial deformations and rigid transformation. The number of optimization parameters is reduced by constraining the model points to lie on the surface of a mesh defined by a linear combination of face-metrics. For further performance, the dependence on the 3D model parameters is eliminated using a transfer function that estimates 3d as a projection onto the model surface. Subsequent optimization is performed only over camera parameters and model coefficients. Because the deformed model is constrained to be a linear combination of existing models, model error will be present if the subject's face can not be modeled as such (ie, does not lie in the convex hull of the basis shapes). Though significantly faster than classical bundle adjustment formulations, performance is not realtime. The tracker used in this paper uses a similar approach but ignores model deformation to perform rigid face tracking.

The work most similar to our update approach is [1] where a complex head model is fit to a sequence of face images. After recovering accurate head pose from bundle adjustment on sets of image triplets, stereo matching is performed on image pairs and a generic face mesh is fit to the recovered 3D. In lieu of local bundle adjustment with fixed internal camera parameters Jebara et. al. recursively estimate camera geometry (focal length), mesh structure, and pose [12] within an extended Kalman filter framework [10].

In [11] potentially erroneous feature point matches are eliminated by focusing on a set of optimally trackable feature points where optimality is a function of the determinant of the Hessian at a given feature location and the corresponding surface normal of the point projected onto the model surface.

In contrast to [12] and [11] we separate model update from the internal optimization scheme of the tracker. Mesh vertices are updated using estimates of head pose acquired with the current 3D model. Tracking improves after reinitialization with the updated model. Though the update approach is tested with a specific tracker, maintaining the update outside of the internal tracking mechanism enables augmentation of any existing model based tracker.

3   Rigid 3D Tracking Overview

The starting point for our investigation is the tracker by Fua et. al. that combines a recursive and keyframe based approach to minimize tracking drift and jitter, and reduce the number of keyframes required for stable tracking. This section presents a brief overview of the tracking approach, but the reader is deferred to the original paper [2] for details.

A keyframe in [2] consists of a set of 2d feature locations detected on the face with a Harris corner detector and their 3D positions estimated by backprojecting onto a registered 3D tracking model. The keyframe accuracy is dependent then on both the model alignment in the keyframe image, as well as the geometric structure of the tracking mesh. Especially when the face is far from the closest keyframe, there may be several newly detected feature points not present in any keyframe that are useful to determine inter-frame motion. These points are matched to patches in the previous frame and combined with keyframe points for pose estimation.

The current head pose estimate (or closest keyframe pose) serves as the starting point for a local bundle adjustment. Classical bundle adjustment is typically a time consuming process, even when a reasonable estimate of camera and 3D parameters is provided. However, by constraining the 3D points to lie on the surface of the tracking model, the method is modified to run in real-time without substantial sacrifice in accuracy. When an accurate 3D model of the tracked object is used, reported accuracy approaches that of commercial batch processing bundle adjustment packages requiring several minutes per frame.

Unfortunately, a perfect 3D model of the tracked subject is rarely available to the tracker a priori. As we will show next, tracking performance can degrade drastically when a generic face model is used due to errors in initial alignment. Experiments on real video sequences also exhibit problems due to limited feature point coverage on face images. These issues are somewhat more significant as they are less predictable and can result from an inherent lack of sufficient information in the image.

We first describe the data used in the synthesized and real video experiments and present results and analysis of experiments demonstrating the dependence of tracking accuracy on mesh accuracy and alignment. The mesh update method is detailed and improved tracking results are shown using the updated models. This is followed by an investigation of performance on real image sequences.

4   Test Data

4.1   Synthesized Motion

A set of experiments is performed on sequences of rotating 3D faces. To generate the sequences, textured 3D models of four subjects are acquired using the Face-Vision200 modeling system [14]. For each model, two independent sequences of images are rendered. The first consists of pure rotation about the horizontal (X) axis, and the second, rotation about the vertical (Y) axis. In both cases, the sequences begin with the subject facing the camera and proceed to -15 degrees, then to 15 degrees, and return to neutral in increments of 1 degree. A total of 60 frames is acquired for each sequence. Image dimensions are 484x362.

4.2   Real Video

Two real video sequences are tested for consistency with the synthetic trials. In both cases a subject is instructed to rotate his head from right to left mimicking the synthetic sequences. Ground truth rotation is acquired using commercial bundle adjustment software [15].

5   Investigation of Tracking Model Bias

The tracker utilizes two primary sources to estimate camera pose: prior and observed information. The model prior information is embedded in the keyframes

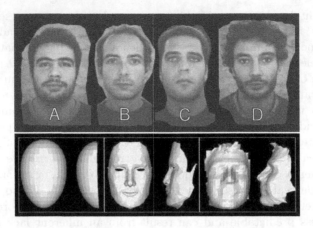

Fig. 2. (top) Four test models. (bottom) Ellipsoid, generic face, and example true mask (for subject A) used for tracking.

and is defined by the tracking mesh, its initial pose, the 2D feature points detected on the face, and their 3D positions estimated by back-projecting to the registered mesh. Observed data consists of 2D feature points detected in non-keyframe images that are matched to the pre-defined keyframe features. Indeed these are fundamental information sources in many 2D-feature-based 3D-trackers, hence the analysis extends beyond the particular choice of tracker in this investigation.

While errors in both the prior and observed data can contribute to tracking inaccuracies, the effects of the latter are negligible in the controlled synthetic sequences. We therefore focus our attention on tracking bias induced by inaccuracies in the model prior and defer the analysis of observed information to the discussion of real sequences later in the paper.

5.1   Investigation 1: Mesh Accuracy

To demonstrate the connection between tracking and model accuracy, tracking results are compared for four different tracking meshes: an ellipsoid, a generic face mask, an updated mesh, and an accurate ("true") 3D model of the subject. The ellipsoid is a weak prior, making no assumptions regarding the location of features on the face such as the eyes, nose, and mouth. The generic face mesh makes stronger assumptions on these features, but other than the manual fitting process (which involves a nonuniform scaling of the mesh) does not account for the true structure of the subject's face. The updated mesh is a refined version of the ellipsoid and makes equally strong assumptions as the generic mask, but derives these assumptions from observed data (discussed in Section 5.3). The true mesh for each subject is derived from the same model used to generate the sequence. The texture is not used, but the geometry is identical, eliminating errors due to geometry inaccuracies. To balance the comparison, each mesh is designed or edited to cover only the face portion of the model as shown.

Figure 3 shows the X component of the recovered rotation compared to ground truth on a representative sequence. Aggregate error for all four subjects is shown in the chart in Figure 4. The average sum of square differences (SSD) is computed with respect to the known ground truth for each degree of freedom.

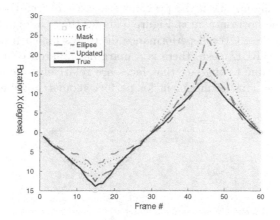

Fig. 3. Recovered X rotation in degrees (vertical axis) versus frame number (horizontal axis) from the tracker for each of the test meshes. Results are from a synthetic sequence with pure rotation about the horizontal axis. Ground truth (GT) shown for comparison.

The largest error consistently occurs with the generic face, and least error with the true mesh. It is evident (and expected) that performance of the tracker improves significantly with the true model geometry. An interesting observation, however, is that the ellipsoidal mesh actually performs better than the face mask in most cases.

An explanation for this is that the mask imposes a stronger (but erroneous) prior on the tracker. Prominent features such as the nose and chin are difficult to align properly using only an aspect change, and in some cases it may not be possible at all given different proportions of human faces. These discrepancies are not significant at small rotations, but become more prominent as the out-of-plane motion increases.

Indeed the example in Figure 3 exhibits tracking performance that is similar for both the ellipsoid and mask within 3-5 degrees of the keyframe. However when more of the face profile is exposed, chin and forehead alignment becomes an issue with the tracker attempting to compensate for the misalignment. Results from the updated mesh are discussed in Section 5.3.

5.2   Investigation 2: Model Registration

Referring back to Figure 1, a mesh that appears properly aligned in a frontal image may actually be grossly misaligned as is apparent in the profile view. This misalignment establishes incorrect a priori information. While the effects of the model bias may be negligible near the original keyframe, as tracking proceeds, the tracker will attempt to resolve the new feature information with the incorrect keyframe information by minimizing reprojection error. As keyframe information is "trusted" to be correct, the result is biased toward an incorrect conclusion. This section provides empirical evidence for this phenomenon with test sequences of intentionally misaligned meshes.

The keyframe alignments of the previous section are perturbed by rotating 5 degrees about the horizontal axis. Figure 5 shows the results of tracking with the misaligned meshes. Overall performance decreases for each of the meshes. In the case of the TRUE mesh, there is a marginal difference in performance. It is expected that due to the fact that faces are relatively smooth continuous surfaces, small deviations in alignment for perfect geometry will embed smaller

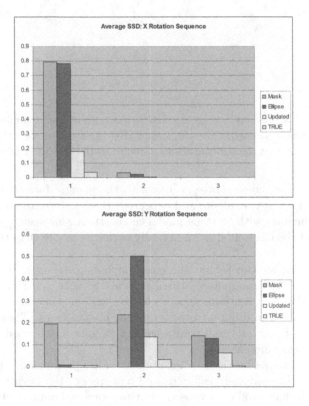

Fig. 4. Average performance over all test subjects on synthetic sequences. Largest error consistently occurs with the generic face. The three groups along the horizontal axis correspond to average rotational tracking errors in X,Y, and Z respectively. Each of the four bars in each group reflects average tracking accuracy (SSD) for one of the four tracking meshes shown in the legend. (top) X-axis rotation (bottom) Y-axis rotation. Units are in degrees.

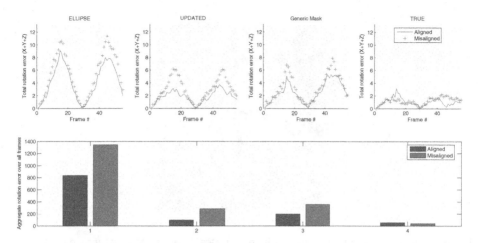

Fig. 5. Results from misalignment experiments. (left) Comparison of tracking error for each image with aligned and misaligned meshes rotated 5 degrees about the horizontal axis. (right) Aggregate error over all frames of sequence.

errors in the prior. Though not tested, larger errors in alignment should induce similar magnitude errors for all face-like meshes.

5.3   Investigation 3: Online Model Refinement

The results in the previous sections demonstrate that despite perfect 3D information, tracking performance can degrade significantly when the model is misregistered in the keyframes. Errors in the geometry of the tracking mesh introduce similar errors. Both of these error sources can be minimized by updating the geometry of an initial tracking model online. Beginning with a rough estimate of the face geometry and we iteratively refine the model and use this more accurate structure to re-estimate the 3D keyframe features thereby reducing the erroneous bias imposed by the misaligned mesh.

Any starting mesh is a candidate for update however an ellipsoid is chosen for its qualitative approximation of face shape without introducing strong assumptions on feature location.

Update Method. The 3D locations of the vertices of the tracking mesh are updated as follows:

The tracker is initialized with a 3D mesh with roughly the same proportions as the subject's face. As shown in the previous section, using a more complicated generic face model does not necessarily improve initial tracking accuracy (and in some cases can hinder it). Rather than risk introducing a strong erroneous bias with a misaligned generic face mesh, we use an ellipsoidal mesh as it assumes nothing about face orientation or location of features. Furthermore, in our current experiments tracking with the ellipsoid provides good pose estimates within

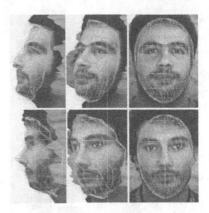

Fig. 6. Updated tracking meshes at different poses. The updated structure conforms well to the subject's face.

a few degrees of the initial keyframe. This baseline is sufficient for incremental improvement of the sparse tracking model.

The ellipsoid mesh is manually aligned with the face in the first frame by applying a translation and nonuniform scaling to the mesh. A single keyframe is generated using this initial registration consisting of the projection matrix P_0, model vertices X_i, and their projections $x_i = \Phi(P_0, X_i)$. A set of "update features" is generated by sampling a $7x7$ window at each x_i.

The tracker provides a new P_t for each image I_t. When a suitable baseline is achieved (3-5 degrees) using the initial tracking model, the update features are matched by correlation in I_t. Using camera estimates P_0 and P_t, straightforward stereo reconstruction [13] is performed at matched features and the new 3D location of model vertices is updated.

The original keyframe mesh is substituted with the updated mesh and a new keyframe is generated. In our current experiments a single update pass is performed. However, the improved tracking results allow multiple passes to be performed to increase the model and tracking accuracy.

Mesh Update Results. We use the method in the previous section to generate updated versions of the ellipsoid for each of the subjects. The synthetic sequences of section 4.1 are re-tracked using the updated models as described. Figure 6 shows the tracking mesh after a single update for two models at initialization and an intermediate stage of tracking. The profile view is generated manually to show the accuracy of the alignment. After a single update, the mesh captures the overall shape and prominent features of the subjects, obviating the need for precise alignment.

Figures 7 and 8 show tracking results for the two sequences of subject A (X and Y rotation respectively). The top row shows the recovered head rotation separated into X, Y, and Z components.

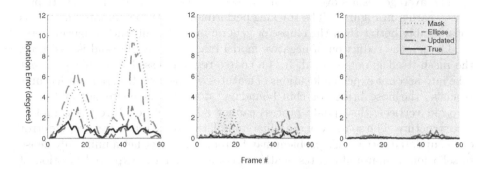

Fig. 7. Absolute tracking error in X, Y, and Z-axis rotation relative to ground truth with synthetic "X-Rotation" sequence. Comparison of results with four tracking meshes.

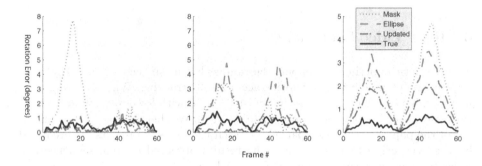

Fig. 8. Absolute tracking error in X, Y, and Z-axis rotation relative to ground truth on with synthetic "Y-Rotation" sequence. Comparison of results with four tracking meshes.

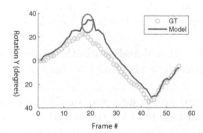

Fig. 9. A real sequence is tracked with the true mesh for the subject. Excellent tracking performance is expected, however the tracker gets stuck in a local minimum at the red circle due to poor feature point coverage.

The average results over all four subjects are summarized on the chart presented earlier in Figure 4. The tracking performance with the updated meshes is considerably better than the ellipse or generic mask for all tracked parameters.

Though the reduction of negative model bias with the ellipsoid is desirable, the mesh itself is not optimal. It is a coarse regular tessellation that does not take into account expected locations of features on the face. If important features (such as the nose bridge or chin boundary) do not happen to fall under the ellipsoid vertices, the update process cannot adequately capture the complete face structure. The sparsity of the ellipse template also increases the average error of the updated mesh. This problem may be remedied by either a uniformly dense tessellation, a non-uniform tessellation accounting for the expected location of important features, or an alternative update approach. The generic face mask is better with respect to tessellation, however it also makes strong assumptions on feature locations, preventing adequate alignment without a nonlinear scaling of the geometry (which requires identification of feature locations such as the eyes, mouth, and nose).

6   Real Video Sequences

The synthetic experiments support the claims that mesh accuracy and keyframe registration play an important role in accurate 3D tracking. When tracking faces in real video sequences, however, we must contend with lower quality input data that may affect the tracker in unpredictable ways. We therefore focus the remainder of the paper on the discrepancies between the expected results (as predicted by the synthetic experiments) and the results observed on real sequences, in order to identify sensitivities in 3D face tracking.

The most surprising case shown in Figure 9 will be the focus of our analysis. This is a clear cut case where the subject is being tracked with the true geometry of his face and should be expected to perform considerably better than the other meshes (as was the case with the synthetic trials). However, it turns out that the tracking accuracy is worse than all but the ellipse. Tracking progresses well up to a point where it appears that the mesh gets locked into an incorrect pose configuration.

The discrepancy between real and synthetic sequences can be explained by the number of accurately matched keyframe feature points and the face coverage they provide.

The number of feature points detected in the high error frames is significantly lower than the best case tracking results. More importantly, the correctly matched keyframe points are clustered on the portion of the face closest to the camera providing poor face coverage and creating pose ambiguity. The tracker minimizes the keyframe point reprojection error, but settles on a local minimum corresponding to a poor tracking estimate. The tracker remains stuck in this local minimum for subsequent frames until more feature points are matched.

Comparing these results to the sequence tracked with the generic mesh, we observe another surprising phenomenon: in this case, the generic mesh performs *better* and doesn't get stuck in the local minimum. It turns out that feature point matching is dependent upon the local surface normal of the tracking mesh at the backprojected feature location. Therefore, given the same input image and 2D keyframe features, it is possible for a different number of points to be matched. Indeed, this is the cause of the discrepancy: While the set of keyframe points matched in the true and generic cases is different throughout the sequence, at the divergence point a single critical feature point is lost while tracking the true mesh. The loss of this point leaves a feature set that covers only a small portion of the face, inducing a less favorable error surface.

6.1 Reprojection Error

In all cases, the tracking performance improves with model accuracy and alignment. A reasonable assumption, therefore, is that overall tracking performance is directly related to feature point reprojection error and a plot of reprojection error over time would be highly correlated with a similar plot of tracking error. Though large tracking errors induce large reprojection errors, the converse is not true: low reprojection error does not necessarily indicate low tracking error. This is due to the fact that as the tracker discards low confidence feature points, it is possible to settle into a minimum configuration where the reprojection error for detected keyframe points is low, but the tracking error is high.

7 Indications

The preceding analysis on controlled, synthesized motion sequences demonstrated a strong dependency between tracking accuracy and mesh geometry and alignment. Trials on real video uncovered a sensitivity to feature point number and coverage. We therefore conclude with a list of issues that should be considered when using and evaluating 3D model based trackers.

MESH COVERAGE: For a detected feature point to be registered as a keyframe point, it must back project onto the mesh at the initialization phase. Tracking meshes with smaller face coverage may miss important potential keyframe points on the outer boundary of the face. Therefore a tracking mask should be maximized to cover as much face area as possible.

IMAGE QUALITY: Despite the fact that the pixel area occupied by the face in the real sequences is larger than the synthetic cases by roughly 30%, on average 5 times fewer feature points are matched on each frame. Care should therefore be taken to either maximize image quality or tune feature detection parameters accordingly.

FEATURE POINTS AND LOCAL MINIMA: Absence or inclusion of a single feature point can cause a dramatic change in the estimated pose. If the tracker gets stuck in a local minimum in the reprojectionerror surface, the pose may remain skewed until a sufficient number of reliable feature points are matched again. These local minima can be avoided or detected by analyzing the proportion of the face covered by the detected feature points.

MODEL REFINEMENT: Tracking accuracy is greatly influenced by mesh geometry and registration errors. If an accurate 3D model of the tracked subject is not available a priori, refinement of the structure online can mitigate both error sources simultaneously.

NON-LOCAL BUNDLE ADJUSTMENT: The experiments in this paper were performed with a single registered keyframe. Given an adequate number and coverage of feature points, it is sufficient to consider only the key and previous frame in the optimization. However, as we have seen, it is possible to get stuck in a local minimum when coverage is poor. Considering additional frames, though increasing the computational burden, is likely to help avoid local minima. This suggests a bundle adjustment framework with a variable size window of frames, dependent on the expected quality of the data (for example, based on feature the current number or coverage of feature points).

8 Conclusions

Using an existing model-based tracker, we have demonstrated the dependence of tracking accuracy on the accuracy of the underlying model geometry and registration. We have shown that a simple stereo based approach to mesh update significantly improves tracking performance. A single update of the model is performed using the narrow baseline camera pose recovered by the tracker.

Updating the mesh eliminates the need for multiple view rotational alignment of the mesh, as the resulting model automatically conforms to the subject's features. Aspect and translation alignment is still needed at initial ellipsoid placement, but this is a much simpler process and can be performed, for example, using the head bounding box information.

The discrepancy between the synthetic and real sequence results are attributed to the sensitivity of the tracker to initial pose alignment and lack of sufficient feature points matched to the keyframes on real sequences. When feature points do not span the entire face region, the pose optimization can get stuck in local mimima on the reprojection error surface corresponding to high pose error. We have provided a set of recommendations based on the investigations that we hope will assist in the development, implementation, and use of 3D tracking methodologies.

Acknowledgments

This work was supported in part by the IC Postdoctoral Fellowship Research Program. This work was also supported in part by the Swiss National Science Foundation.We also thank Luca Vacchetti for generously offering his time and assistance with the face tracker and Jake Mack for helping with data preparation.

References

1. P. Fua, "Using model-driven bundle-adjustment to model heads from raw video sequences," *In Proceedings of the 7th International Conference on Computer Vision,* pages 4653, Corfu, Greece, Sept. 1999.
2. L. Vacchetti, V. Lepetit, P. Fua, "Stable Real-Time 3D Tracking Using Online and Offline Information," *IEEE Trans. Pattern Anal. Mach. Intell.,* 26(10): 1385-1391 (2004).
3. Y. Shan, Z. Liu, and Z. Zhang, "Model-Based Bundle Adjustment with Application to Face Modeling," *International Conference on Computer Vision,* Vancouver, Canada, July 2001.
4. V. Lepetit, L. Vacchetti, D. Thalmann, and P. Fua, "Fully Automated and Stable Registration for Augmented Reality Applications," *International Symposium on Mixed and Augmented Reality,* Tokyo, Japan, September 2003.
5. M. Cascia, S. Sclaroff, and V. Athitsos, "Fast, reliable head tracking under varying illumination: An approach based on registration of texture-mapped 3d models," *IEEE Transactions on Pattern Analysis and Machine Intelligence,* 22(4), April 2000.
6. S. Basu, I. Essa, and A. Pentland, "Motion regularization for model-based head tracking," *International Conference on Pattern Recognition,* 1996.
7. D. DeCarlo and D. Metaxas, "The Integration of Optical Flow and Deformable Models with Applications to Human Face Shape and Motion Estimation," *Computer Vision and Pattern Recognition,* 1996.
8. Schodl, A., A. Haro, and I. Essa, "Head Tracking using a Textured Polygonal Model," *In Proceedings of Perceptual User Interfaces Workshop (held in Conjunction with ACM UIST 1998),* San Francisco, CA., November 1998.
9. A. Azarbayejani, T. Starner, B. Horowitz, and A. Pentland, "Visually controlled graphics," *IEEE Transactions on Pattern Analysis and Machine Intelligence,* 15(6), 1993.
10. A. Azarbayejani and A. Pentland, "Recursive Estimation of Motion, Structure, and Focal Length," *IEEE Transactions on Pattern Analysis and Machine Intelligence,* 17(6), 1995.
11. J. Strom, T. Jebara, S. Basu, and A. Pentland. "Real time Tracking and Modeling of Faces: An EKF-based Analysis by Synthesis Approach," *Proceedings of the Modeling People Workshop at ICCV'99,* 1999.
12. T. Jebara and A. Pentland, "Parameterized Structure from Motion for 3D Adaptive Feedback Tracking of Faces" *IEEE Conference on Computer Vision and Pattern Recognition (CVPR'97),* 1997 .
13. R. Hartley and A. Zisserman, "Multiple View Geometry in Computer Vision," Cambridge University Press, Cambridge, UK, 2000.
14. Geometrix, (http://www.geometrix.com).
15. EoS Systems Inc., (http://www.photomodeler.com).

Facial Expression Representation Based on Timing Structures in Faces

Masahiro Nishiyama, Hiroaki Kawashima, Takatsugu Hirayama, and Takashi Matsuyama

Kyoto University, Yoshida-Honmachi Sakyo, Kyoto 6068501, Japan
{nisiyama, hiroaki, hirayama, tm}@vision.kuee.kyoto-u.ac.jp

Abstract. This paper presents a method for interpreting facial expressions based on temporal structures among partial movements in facial image sequences. To extract the structures, we propose a novel facial expression representation, which we call a *facial score*, similar to a musical score. The facial score enables us to describe facial expressions as spatio-temporal combinations of temporal intervals; each interval represents a simple motion pattern with the beginning and ending times of the motion. Thus, we can classify fine-grained expressions from multivariate distributions of temporal differences between the intervals in the score. In this paper, we provide a method to obtain the score automatically from input images using bottom-up clustering of dynamics. We evaluate the efficiency of facial scores by comparing the temporal structure of intentional smiles with that of spontaneous smiles.

1   Introduction

Facial expression plays an important role in our communication; for instance, it can nonverbally express emotions and intentions to others. Much progress has been made to build computer systems that recognize facial expression for human interfaces. However, these systems have problems; they don't use enough dynamic information in recognition, and the classification of facial expression relies on a fundamental category based on emotions. Most previous systems describe facial expression based on action units (AUs) of the Facial Action Coding System (FACS) developed by Ekman and Friesen [13]. An AU is defined as the smallest unit of facial movement that is anatomically independent and visually distinctive. FACS is a method for describing facial expression on the basis of the combination of AUs. FACS, however, has a major weakness; there is no time component of the description [6]. Furthermore, there may be facial motion that AUs cannot express because they are heuristic motion patterns classified by human. It is also important to decide what categories of facial expression are appropriate as the outputs of facial recognition. Most previous systems categorize facial expression into one of six basic categories (happiness, surprise, fear, anger, disgust, and sadness) [6]. In human communication, however, facial expression is classified into one of the more fine-grained categories by subtle dynamic changes that are observed in facial components: the variety of changes and the timing of

W. Zhao, S. Gong, and X. Tang (Eds.): AMFG 2005, LNCS 3723, pp. 140–154, 2005.

changes. To capture the subtlety of human emotion and intention, automated recognition of subtle dynamic changes in facial expression is needed.

In this paper we assume that (1) dynamic movement of each facial component (facial part) yields changes of facial expression, and that (2) movement of facial parts is expressed based on temporal intervals. We define the intervals as temporal ranges of monotonically changing events that have beginning times, ending times, and labels of motion patterns (modes) as attributes. We provide a framework for recognizing facial expression in detail based on *timing structures*, which are defined as temporal relations among the beginning and ending times of multiple intervals. To extract the timing structures, we propose a novel facial expression representation, which we call a *facial score*. The score is similar to a musical score, which describes the timing of notes in music. Using the score, we can describe facial expressions as spatio-temporal combination of the intervals.

It is important to decide what the definition of modes is in the interval-based description. Whereas AUs are suitable to distinguish emotional facial expression, they sometimes do not preserve sufficient dynamic information (e.g., time-varying patterns) of facial actions. In this paper, we take another approach that determines a set of modes from statistical analysis and describes facial actions based on generative models. This approach extracts modes that have enough dynamic information from the viewpoint of pattern generation, and provides a unified framework that can be used not only for facial expression analysis but for facial expression generation. We propose a bottom-up learning method to find modes from captured real data. In this method, each mode is modeled by a dynamical system that has an ability of generating simple patterns, and the modes are extracted from clustering analysis based on the distances between dynamical systems (see Section 3.3 and 4.2 for details).

In summary, the facial score is characterized as follows:

- It enables us to describe timing structures in faces based on temporal intervals.
- It enables us to use motion patterns extracted from training data in a bottom-up manner as modes of intervals.

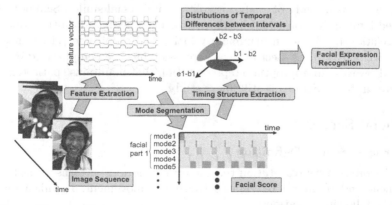

Fig. 1. The overall flow of facial expression recognition using the facial score

Figure 1 depicts the overall flow of facial expression recognition using the facial score: (1) we extract a series of feature vectors that characterize facial expression from a sequence of facial images, (2) we partition the series of feature vectors and extract the modes simultaneously to obtain a facial score, and (3) we extract timing structures from the facial score, which contribute to recognition of the facial expression. Automation of the above process provides for applications in recognizing facial expression, and therefore allows computers to learn to recognize facial expression in detail.

The goal of this paper is to propose a method for automatically obtaining the facial score and to evaluate the efficiency of the facial score for facial expression recognition. We compare the timing structure of intentional smiles with that of spontaneous smiles for the evaluation; in human communication it makes sense to make a distinction between the two smiles, but most previous computer systems have classified these smiles into the same category.

In Section 2, related works are described. In Section 3, facial scores are introduced as representations that describe timing structures in faces. In Section 4, we describe a method for automatically obtaining the facial score from input sequences of facial images. In Section 5, we obtain facial scores automatically from captured real data including intentional and spontaneous smiles, and evaluate the efficiency of the facial scores by the separability between the two smiles. Finally, in Section 6 we conclude our work.

2   Related Works

In psychological experiments, evaluation by playing back facial expressions on videotape to subjects has suggested the following knowledge of dynamic aspects of facial movement. Bassili video-recorded the face that was covered with black makeup and numerous white spots, and found that it is possible to distinguish facial expression to a certain degree of accuracy merely from motion of the white spots by playing back the video [2]. As a study concentrating on a more specific part of facial motion, Koyama, et al. created CG animations with the temporal relation between eye and mouth movement controlled, and showed laughter can be classified into pleasant, unpleasant, and sociable types based on the temporal difference [9]. As a study of analyzing solitary and social smiles, Schmidt, et al. indicated temporally consistent lip movement patterns based on the evaluation of the relationship between maximum velocity and amplitude [11]. Hence, the importance of dynamic aspect in facial expression has been emphasized by many studies. However, an appropriate representation that maintains spatio-temporal structures in facial actions is still under study.

3   Facial Scores

3.1   Facial Scores Definition

A facial score is a representation that describes motion patterns of each facial component and temporal relations between the movement. In this paper we define the following notations:

Facial parts and Facial Part Sets: Facial parts represent isolable facial components. We define facial part sets as $\mathcal{P} = \{P_1, ..., P_{N_p}\}$ where N_p is the number of facial parts described by facial scores. For instance, elements of facial part sets include mouths, right eyes, left eyes, right eyebrows, and left eyebrows.

Modes and Mode Sets: Modes represent monotonically changing events. We define mode sets as $\mathcal{M}^{(a)} = \{M_1^{(a)}, ..., M_{N_{m_a}}^{(a)}\}$ where N_{m_a} is the number of modes of a facial part P_a ($a \in \{1, ..., N_p\}$). For instance, elements of mode sets of a mouth part include "opening", "remain open", "closing", and "remain closed".

Intervals and Interval Sets: Intervals represent temporal ranges of modes. We define interval sets as $\mathcal{I}^{(a)} = \{I_1^{(a)}, ..., I_{N_{k_a}}^{(a)}\}$ where N_{k_a} is the number of intervals into which time series data of a facial part P_a is segmented. Intervals $I_k^{(a)}$ ($k \in \{1, ..., N_{k_a}\}$) have beginning times $b_k^{(a)} \in \{1, ..., T\}$, ending times $e_k^{(a)} \in \{1, ..., T\}$, and labels of modes representing the events $m_k^{(a)} \in \mathcal{M}^{(a)}$ as attributes where T is the number of time series data of a facial part P_a.

Facial Scores: We define a facial score as a set of interval sets of all facial parts $\{\mathcal{I}^{(1)}, ..., \mathcal{I}^{(N_p)}\}$. Figure 2 shows a conceptual figure of a facial score. The vertical axis represents modes of facial parts, and the horizontal axis represents time. The transition of the motion of each facial part is described based on intervals along the temporal axis. In each facial part of the figure, intervals of various colors represent various modes. Thus, the facial score can describe timing structures among motions of facial parts.

3.2   Facial Parts in Facial Scores

To recognize facial expression based on timing structures, we treat the two areas where their movements occur independently as different facial parts. Ekman, *et al.* have revealed that the difference in the facial appearance of basic emotions (happiness, surprise, fear, anger, disgust, and sadness) results from the combination of the three facial areas (around the eyebrows, eyes, and mouth) where their movements can be observed individually in appearance [5]. We use these

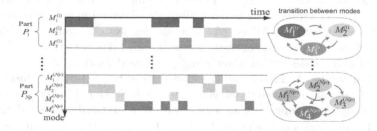

Fig. 2. Facial scores. The vertical axis represents modes of facial parts, and the horizontal axis represents time. The transition of the motion of each facial part is described based on intervals along the temporal axis.

three areas, and furthermore treat areas around the eyebrows and eyes on the left and right as different facial parts because the asymmetric movements of each eyebrow and eye can be observed in real facial expression.

It is important to select useful features that can express subtle changes of movements in the five facial areas. This paper defines feature vectors as coordinates of feature points shown in Figure 5 (a), which can extract information of movement directly. We consider that transient features such as furrows also provide effective information in recognition of subtle facial expression, and that changes of the feature points can represent them indirectly; for instance, movement of feature points on the nose implies nasolabial furrows.

Therefore, we define elements of facial part sets $\mathcal{P}$ as right eyebrow, left eyebrow, right eye, left eye, nose, and mouth. A feature vector $z^{(a)}$ of a facial part P_a is represented by the following $2n_{p_a}$-dimensional column vector:

$$z^{(a)} = \left(x_1^{(a)},\ y_1^{(a)}, ..., x_{n_{p_a}}^{(a)},\ y_{n_{p_a}}^{(a)}\right)^{\top},\qquad(1)$$

where n_{p_a} is the number of feature points of a facial part P_a, and let $\left(x_p^{(a)},\ y_p^{(a)}\right)$ be coordinates of a feature point number $p \in \{1, ..., n_{p_a}\}$.

3.3   Modes in Facial Scores

As we defined in Section 3.1, each complex movement of a facial part is composed of simple motion categories, which we call modes. Therefore, a movement can be partitioned into a sequence of temporal intervals by modes.

Modes are classified into two large categories by the velocity of feature vectors: stationary poses and dynamic movements. For the modes with movement, we use monotonic motions as the lowest-level representation, whereas humans sometimes classify a cyclic motion as one category. Therefore, our facial score represents a cyclic motion as a sequence of monotonic motions. For example, the open and close action of the mouth is represented as the following sequence of four modes: "opening", "remain open", "closing", and "remain closed".

AUs used in FACS are the most common units to describe facial movements. Although AUs are suitable to distinguish emotional facial expressions by their combinations, we do not use AUs as the modes in our facial scores for two reasons. First, a method of AU tracking is still a challenging research topic for computer vision. Second, AUs sometimes do not maintain sufficient dynamic information in facial actions. As a result, AU-based CG animation systems sometimes generate unnatural facial actions. In contrast, our approach takes a bottom-up learning method to find modes rather than using predefined motion categories, as we described in Section 1. That is, all the modes are extracted by the clustering of dynamics from captured real data, as we will see in Section 4.2. For a generative model of simple dynamics in each mode, we use a first-order linear dynamical system. The dynamics of the mode $M_i^{(a)}$ ($i \in \{1, ..., N_{m_a}\}$) in a facial part P_a is represented by the following notation:

$$z_t^{(a)} = F^{(a,\ i)} z_{t-1}^{(a)} + f^{(a,\ i)} + \omega_t^{(a,\ i)},\qquad(2)$$

where $z_t^{(a)}$ is a feature vector at time t, $F^{(a,\ i)}$ is a transition matrix, which differs from other modes' matrices, $f^{(a,\ i)}$ is a bias term, $\omega^{(a,\ i)}$ is a process noise of the system that has a multivariate Gaussian distribution with mean vector 0 and covariance matrix $Q^{(a,\ i)}$.

As a result, each motion transition in each facial part is described based on the transition of linear dynamical systems, which is similar to a switching linear dynamical system [3,8]. Therefore, the proposed model can be considered as a concurrent process of multiple switching linear dynamical systems. We currently do not model the transition probability between modes to reduce the model parameters; however, the transition probability will work as constraints during a mode segmentation process, and can be introduced if specific mode transition patterns appear frequently.

Given a sequence of feature vectors, we find a rough segmentation using zero-crossing points of the velocity as the initialization of the method. Then, we merge the nearest dynamical system pairs iteratively based on agglomerative hierarchical clustering. A linear dynamical system, in general, can generate not only monotonic motions but cyclic or oscillating motions. To extract only the monotonic motions, we propose a method to provide a constraint on eigenvalues of the transition matrices. We will describe the details of the identification and clustering algorithms in Section 4.2.

3.4 Timing Structures in Facial Scores

Using facial scores defined in the previous sections, we can represent temporal relations among motions in facial parts; we refer to the relation as timing structures of the face. In this section, we describe a method to represent and extract timing structures from a facial score.

Representation of Timing Structures: Figure 3(a) shows 13 categories of temporal relations between two intervals I_i and I_j [1,10]. We can classify the relations of the two intervals based on the temporal order of four times b_i, b_j, e_i and e_j, where $b_i(b_j)$ and $e_i(e_j)$ represent the beginning and ending times of the interval $I_i(I_j)$, respectively. Although these categories enable us to represent temporal structures among multiple events, such as overlaps between two intervals, they are insufficient for us to describe the difference of timing structures in facial expressions. We need to concentrate on not only temporal order of events but scales and degree of temporal differences among beginning and ending times of multiple intervals. In this paper, we extend the 13 categories based on multivariate distributions of real-valued variables. Using temporal differences between beginning and ending times, we can represent the first-order timing structure of two intervals as four distributions $H(b_j - b_i), H(e_j - e_i), H(b_j - e_i)$ and $H(e_j - b_i)$, where $H(r)$ is a one-dimensional distribution of variable $r \in \mathrm{R}$. We can also represent the second-order timing structure as six distributions $H(b_j - b_i, e_j - e_i), H(b_j - b_i, b_j - e_i), H(b_j - b_i, e_j - b_i), H(e_j - e_i, b_j - e_i), H(e_j - e_i, e_j - b_i)$ and $H(b_j - e_i, e_j - b_i)$, where $H(r_1,\ r_2)$ is a two-dimensional distribution of variables $r_1,\ r_2 \in \mathrm{R}$. Figure 3(b) shows the example of distribution $H(b_j - b_i,\ e_j - e_i)$,

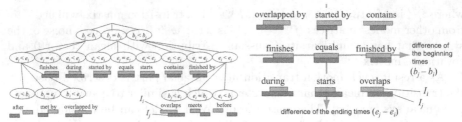

(a) Temporal relations between two intervals (b) Two-dimensional temporal distribution

Fig. 3. (a) An example of two-dimensional distributions of temporal differences between two intervals. The temporal order of beginning and ending times provides 13 relations of the two intervals. (b) The horizontal and vertical axes denote the difference between beginning times $b_j - b_i$ and the difference between ending times $e_j - e_i$ of the two intervals (I_i and I_j), respectively.

where the horizontal and vertical axes represent the difference between the beginning times and the difference between the ending times, respectively. Representations of high-order timing structures become a set of high-dimensional distributions in the same manner. To represent timing structures among more than three intervals, for example the first-order timing structure of three intervals I_i, I_j and I_k, we need 12 one-dimensional distributions $H(b_j - b_i)$, $H(b_k - b_j)$, and so on.

Extraction of Timing Structures from Facial Scores: The selection of interval combinations is necessary for calculating the distributions that are described in the previous paragraphs when we make use of the timing structures for facial expression analysis and recognition. In our experiments in Section 5, we selected the combinations based on the following methods. First, we find combinations of the intervals that belong to each facial part based on temporal distances. The interval in a facial part P_b ($b \neq a, b \in \{1, ..., N_p\}$) that has the nearest distance from an interval $I_k^{(a)}$ in a facial part P_a is calculated as $I_{l^*}^{(b)}$ ($l^* = \arg\min_l \mathsf{IntervalDist}(I_k^{(a)}, I_l^{(b)})$), where IntervalDist is a distance between two intervals that is defined as follows:

$$\mathsf{IntervalDist}(I_k^{(a)}, I_l^{(b)}) = |b_k^{(a)} - b_l^{(b)}| + |e_k^{(a)} - e_l^{(b)}|. \tag{3}$$

Second, we represent the timing structure as two-dimensional distributions. If there are clusters in the calculated distributions, we can define successfully more subtle categories of facial expressions than basic emotional facial expressions.

4 Automatic Acquisition of Facial Scores

In this section, we describe a method for automatically obtaining facial scores with facial image sequences as the inputs.

4.1 Facial Feature Extraction

We track feature points in facial image sequences using Active Appearance Models (AAM) [4]. An AAM contains a statistical model of correlations between shape and grey-level appearance variation. The model can be matched to a target image rapidly and robustly.

To build the model, we require a training set of images marked with feature points. Figure 4 (a) shows an example of a face image labeled with 58 feature points. Let s be a shape vector that represents the coordinate value of feature points. Let g be a grey-level vector that represents the intensity information from the shape-normalized image over the region covered with the mean shape. In the first step, the method applies principal component analysis (PCA) to the data. Any example image can then be approximated using:

$$s = \bar{s} + U_s c_s \; , \; g = \bar{g} + U_g c_g, \tag{4}$$

where $\bar{s}$ and $\bar{g}$ are the corresponding sample mean vectors, U_s and U_g are matrices of column eigenvectors of the shape and grey-level, and c_s and c_g are vectors of shape and grey-level parameters, respectively. In the second step, because there may be correlations between the shape and grey-level variation, the method concatenates the vectors c_s and c_g, applies PCA, and obtains a model of the form

$$\begin{bmatrix} W_s c_s \\ c_g \end{bmatrix} = c = \begin{bmatrix} V_s \\ V_g \end{bmatrix} d = Vd, \tag{5}$$

where W_s is a diagonal matrix of weights for each shape parameter, allowing for the difference in units between the shape and grey-level models, V is a matrix of column eigenvectors, and d is a vector of appearance parameters controlling both the shape and grey-levels of the model.

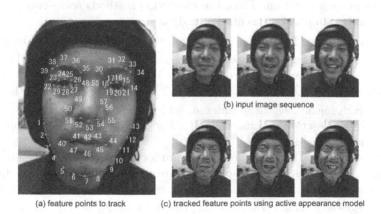

(a) feature points to track   (c) tracked feature points using active appearance model

Fig. 4. (a) A training image to build active appearance models. (b) Part of a captured face image sequence. (c) Part of a face image sequence with tracked feature points.

Note that the linear nature of the model allows us to express the shape vector s and grey-level vector g directly as functions of d:

$$s = \bar{s} + U_s W_s^{-1} V_s d , \quad g = \bar{g} + U_g V_g d. \tag{6}$$

An example image can be synthesized for a given d by generating the shape-free grey-level image from the vector g and warping it using the feature points described by s. During a training phase we learn the relationship between model parameter displacements and the residual errors induced between a training image and a synthesized image.

The matching process for tracking the feature points is provided as an optimization problem in which we minimize the difference between a target image and an image synthesized by the model.

4.2 Modes Extraction

As we postulated in Section 3.3, each mode in the facial expression score is represented by a different linear dynamical system. In this section, we describe a method to find a set of modes that corresponds to a set of dynamical systems. This algorithm is applied to each facial part independently.

Although there are several approaches to find dynamics in training sequences, we propose a bottom-up clustering method to extract modes based on an agglomerative hierarchical clustering approach described in [7]. The method provides useful interfaces such as dendrograms to determine the number of clusters.

First, we introduce a constrained system identification method that restricts an upper bound of eigenvalues in the transition matrix in Equation (2). The method enables us to find a set of modes that represent only monotonic dynamics. Then, we introduce an agglomerative hierarchical clustering of dynamical systems with the definition of distance between two dynamical systems. This algorithm also merges two interval sets that are labeled by the same dynamical system in each iteration. Thus, the clustering methods solve two problems simultaneously: temporal segmentation and parameter estimation.

Constrained System Identification: The parameter estimation of a transition matrix $F^{(a,i)}$ from a sequence of feature vectors $z_1^{(a,i)}, .., z_T^{(a,i)}$ in a facial part P_a becomes an error minimization problem; that is, minimizing squared prediction error vectors during the temporal interval $[1, T]$ that is represented by the mode $M_i^{(a)}$. For convenience, we drop index a, which identifies a facial part, in the remaining of this section because the following clustering method is applied to each part independently.

The key idea to estimate monotonic dynamics is the method to constrain on eigenvalues. If all the eigenvalues are lower than 1, the dynamical system changes state in a monotonic manner (i.e., cyclic or oscillation will not occur and the state converges to a certain value). Using the notation $Z_0^{(i)} = [z_1^{(i)}, ..., z_{T-1}^{(i)}]$ and $Z_1^{(i)} = [z_2^{(i)}, ..., z_T^{(i)}]$, we can estimate matrix $F^{(i)}$ by the following equation:

$$F^{(i)*} = \arg\min_{F^{(i)}} ||F^{(i)} Z_0^{(i)} - Z_1^{(i)}||^2 = \lim_{\delta^2 \to 0} Z_1^{(i)} Z_0^{(i)\top} (Z_0^{(i)} Z_0^{(i)\top} + \delta^2 I)^{-1}, \tag{7}$$

where I is a $2n_{p_a} \times 2n_{p_a}$ unit matrix and δ is a positive real value. Using Gershgorin's theorem in linear algebra, we can determine the upper bound of eigenvalues in a matrix from the elements of the matrix. Therefore, we use a nonzero value for δ that controls the scale of values in the matrix; that is, we stop the limit in the Equation (7) before $Z_0^{(i)\top}(Z_0^{(i)}Z_0^{(i)\top} + \delta^2 I)^{-1}$ converges to a pseudo-inverse matrix of $Z_0^{(i)}$.

Clustering of Dynamics: The clustering algorithm of dynamics (modes) is initialized by a segmentation that partitions the training sequence into motion and stationary pose intervals, which we call the initial interval set. To calculate the initial interval set, we simply divide the training sequence by zero-crossing points of feature velocity (i.e., the first-order difference of feature vectors). In the first step of the algorithm, one dynamical system is identified from each interval in the initial interval set. Then, we calculate the distances for all the dynamical system pairs based on the distance definition in the next paragraph. In the second step, the nearest dynamical systems are merged iteratively based on an agglomerative hierarchical clustering (see Algorithm 1 in Appendix for details). Finally, all the modes are merged to one mode. We determine the number of the modes manually using the obtained dendrogram (i.e., the tree structure that provides the history of the total distance change).

Distance Between Dynamical Systems: We define the distance between two dynamical systems (modes) based on a cross check of the prediction errors between the two modes. In the following equation, we use the notation $z_{t-1}^{(i)}$ and $z_t^{(i)}$, which means that the adjacent feature vectors z_{t-1} and z_t belong to an interval that is represented by mode M_i. The prediction from the vector $z_{t-1}^{(i)}$ to the feature vector of time t by the dynamics of the mode M_j becomes $F^{(j)}z_{t-1}^{(i)}$. Thus, we can calculate the prediction error from $z_t^{(i)}$ as $E_t^{(i|j)} = F^{(j)}z_{t-1}^{(i)} + f^{(j)} - z_t^{(i)}$. Calculating this prediction error for all the adjacent feature vectors in the interval set $\mathcal{I}_i$, which is represented by the mode M_i, we can define the prediction error from M_j to M_i as the following equation:

$$E(M_i||M_j) = \frac{1}{C}\sum_{I_k \in \mathcal{I}_i}\sum_{t=b_k}^{e_k}(E_t^{(i|j)^2} - E_t^{(i|i)^2}), \tag{8}$$

where C is the total interval length of the intervals in the set $\mathcal{I}_i$, which normalizes the sum of prediction error in a time axis. For the distance definition between two modes, we take the average

$$\mathrm{Dist}(M_i, M_j) = \{E(M_i||M_j) + E(M_j||M_i)\}/2, \tag{9}$$

because the two prediction errors, from M_i to M_j and from M_j to M_i, are asymmetric.

5   Experimental Evaluations

We evaluated the efficiency of our representation for a separation of intentional smiles from spontaneous smiles using obtained facial scores from captured data.

Video Capturing: Intentional and spontaneous smiles of four subjects were captured in 240 × 320 at 60 fps as the input image sequences. We used a camera system that was composed of a helmet and a camera fixed in front of the helmet to focus on the analysis of front faces. The camera system enabled us to capture front face images even if head motion occurred. The subjects were instructed to begin with a neutral expression, make a smile, and return to a neutral expression again. Intentional smiles were captured by instructing the subjects to force a smile. Spontaneous smiles were captured by making the subjects laugh. The subjects were instructed to make either smile iteratively in capturing one sequence, so that no sequences included both smiles. Figure 4 (b) shows part of a captured face image sequence.

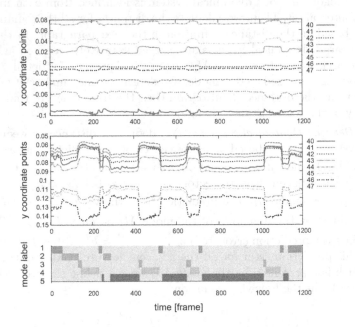

Fig. 5. The correspondence of the mouth part of an obtained facial score from spontaneous smiles with the feature vector series. The vertical axes of the top, the middle and the bottom subfigures represent x-coordinates of feature points, y-coordinates of feature points and modes respectively, and the horizontal axes of each subfigure represent time. The numbers of legends in the top and middle correspond to numbers that represent labels of feature points in Figure 4 (a). For example, the mode 4 and 5 represent "remain open" and "remain closed", respectively.

Automatic Acquisition of Facial Scores: Feature points in the captured face image sequences were tracked using the method in Section 4.1[1]. The number

---

[1] Feature points were tracked using the AAM-API that Stegmann (Technical University of Denmark) developed [12].

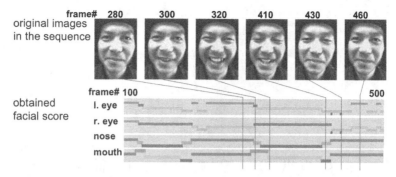

Fig. 6. An example of obtained facial scores from intentional smiles (left and right eyebrows are omitted)

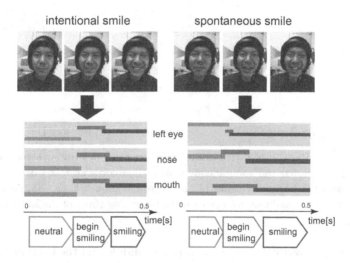

Fig. 7. Comparison of the two facial scores obtained from intentional and spontaneous smiles

of feature points used in the AAM was set to 5 on each eyebrow, 8 on each eye, 11 on the nose, 8 on the mouth, and 13 on the jawline (refer to Figure 4 (a)). Although the jawline was not represented as one of the facial parts, it was used for improving tracking accuracy. Therefore, feature vectors were obtained whose dimensions for each eyebrow, each eye, the nose, and the mouth were 10, 16, 22 and 16 respectively. Figure 4 (c) shows part of a face image sequence with tracked feature points; the frames correspond to the images shown in Figure 4 (b). Comparison of the corresponding images demonstrates extremely precise detection of feature points in changes of facial expression.

The obtained feature vectors of each facial part were segmented into modes using the method in Section 4.2. Consequently, facial scores of intentional and spontaneous smiles were acquired. Figure 5 shows the correspondence of the mouth part of an obtained facial score from spontaneous smiles with the feature

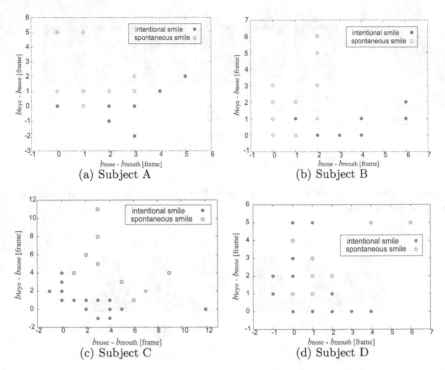

Fig. 8. The two-dimensional distribution that represents the timing structures of the beginning of intentional and spontaneous smiles. The horizontal axis denotes the difference between the beginning times of the nose and mouth $b_{nose} - b_{mouth}$, and the vertical axis denotes the difference between the beginning times of the left eye and nose $b_{leye} - b_{nose}$.

vector series. The vertical axes of the top, the middle and the bottom subfigures represent x-coordinates of feature points, y-coordinates of feature points and modes respectively, and the horizontal axes of each subfigure represent time. Figure 6 shows an example of obtained facial scores from intentional smiles, and the correspondence it with captured image data. These figures demonstrate that movement of smiles can be segmented into the following different modes: "neutral", "begin smiling", "smiling", and "end smiling".

Comparison of Timing Structures in Intentional and Spontaneous Smiles: As an example of comparison of timing structures in intentional and spontaneous smiles, we concentrated on a mode "begin smiling" and examined temporal relations between the beginning and ending times of the mouth, nose and left eye modes (see Figure 7). 20 samples of each smile were prepared. We used a two-dimensional distribution $H(b_{nose} - b_{mouth}, b_{leye} - b_{nose})$, which separated the two smiles with the highest efficiency, where b_{mouth}, b_{nose}, and b_{leye} are the beginning times of the mouth, nose, and left eye, respectively. Figure 8 shows the distributions of four subjects. We see that there are respective clusters in the distribution of the two smiles in case of subject A, B and C, but that there are not any clear clusters in case of subject D. We can find similarity between the distributions of subject A and B. On the other hand, we can find difference between distribution of subject A and C (or subject B and C). Hence, our experimental result suggests that the timing structures extracted from facial scores have individual variation, and the timing structures are effective in discrimination of the two smiles.

6 Conclusion

We proposed a facial score as a novel facial expression representation. The score describes timing structures in faces by assuming that dynamic movement of each facial part yields changes of facial expression. Using the score, we provided a framework for recognizing fine-grained facial expression categories. In our evaluation, the scores were acquired from captured real image sequences including intentional and spontaneous smiles automatically, and we confirmed that movement of facial parts was expressed based on temporal intervals. We suggested the individual variation of the timing structures extracted from facial scores and the efficiency of the timing structures for discrimination of the two smiles.

To emphasize the characteristics of the proposed representation, we focused on only timing structures in this paper. Other features of movement such as scale, speed and duration, which provide further information on recognizing facial expression, should be taken into account in practical systems. We also need to discuss specificity and generality of timing structures: some structures may exist as general features determined by physical muscle constraints, and the other may exist as subject specific features acquired as personal habits. Directions for future works are to tackle these problems and to evaluate the effectiveness of timing structures using a large number of captured sequences.

Acknowledgment. This work is in part supported by Grant-in-Aid for Scientific Research of the Ministry of Education, Culture, Sports, Science and Technology of Japan under the contract of 13224051 and 16700175.

References

1. J. F. Allen. Maintaining knowledge about temporal intervals. *Communications of the ACM*, 26(11):832–843, 1983.
2. J. N. Bassili. Facial motion in the perception of faces and of emotional expression. *Journal of Experimental Psychology: Human Perception and Performance*, 4(3):373–379, 1978.
3. C. Bregler. Learning and recognizing human dynamics in video sequences. *Proc. IEEE Conference on Computer Vision and Pattern Recognition*, pages 568–574, 1997.
4. T. F. Cootes, G. J. Edwards, and C. J. Taylor. Active appearance model. *Proc. European Conference on Computer Vision*, 2:484–498, 1998.
5. P. Ekman and W. V. Friesen. *Unmasking the Face*. Prentice Hall, 1975.
6. I. A. Essa and A. P. Pentland. Facial expression recognition using a dynamic model and motion energy. *Proc. IEEE Int'l Conference on Computer Vision*, pages 360–367, 1995.

7. H. Kawashima and T. Matsuyama. Hierarchical clustering of dynamical systems based on eigenvalue constraints. *Proc. Int'l Conference on Advances in Pattern Recognition (S. Singh et al. (Eds.): LNCS 3686)*, pages 229–238, 2005.
8. Y. Li, T. Wang, and H. Y. Shum. Motion texture: A two-level statistical model for character motion synthesis. *SIGGRAPH*, pages 465–472, 2002.
9. S. Nishio, K. Koyama, and T. Nakamura. Temporal differences in eye and mouth movements classifying facial expressions of smiles. *Proc. IEEE Int'l Conference on Automatic Face and Gesture Recognition*, pages 206–211, 1998.
10. C. Pinhanez and A. Bobick. Human action detection using pnf propagation of temporal constraints. *Proc. IEEE Conference on Computer Vision and Pattern Recognition*, pages 898–904, 1998.
11. K. L. Schmidt, J. F. Cohn, and Y.-L. Tian. Signal characteristics of spontaneous facial expressions: Automatic movement in solitary and social smiles. *Biological Psychology*, 65:49–66, 2003.
12. M. B. Stegmann, B. K. Ersboll, and R. Larsen. FAME - a flexible appearance modelling environment. *Informatics and Mathematical Modelling, Technical University of Denmark*, 2003.
13. Y. Tian, T. Kanade, and J. F. Cohn. Recognizing action units for facial expression analysis. *IEEE Trans. on Pattern Analysis and Machine Intelligence*, 23(2):97–115, 2001.

A   Clustering of Dynamical Systems

Algorithm 1 Agglomerative Hierarchical Clustering
---

for $i \leftarrow 1$ to N **do**
  $M_i^{(a)} \leftarrow$ Identify $\left(I_i^{(a)} \right)$
end for
for all pair$\left(M_i^{(a)},\ M_j^{(a)} \right)$ where $M_i^{(a)},\ M_j^{(a)} \in \mathcal{M}^{(a)}$ **do**
  Dist $(i,\ j) \leftarrow$ CalcDistance $\left(M_i^{(a)},\ M_j^{(a)} \right)$
end for
while $N \geq 2$ **do**
  $(i^*,\ j^*) \leftarrow \arg\min_{(i,\ j)}$ Dist $(i,\ j)$
  $\mathcal{I}_{i^*}^{(a)} \leftarrow$ MergeIntervals $\left(\mathcal{I}_{i^*}^{(a)},\ \mathcal{I}_{j^*}^{(a)} \right)$; $M_{i^*}^{(a)} \leftarrow$ Identify $\left(\mathcal{I}_{i^*}^{(a)} \right)$
  erase $M_j^{(a)*}$ from $\mathcal{M}^{(a)}$; $N \leftarrow N - 1$
  for all pair$\left(M_i^{(a)*},\ M_j^{(a)} \right)$ where $M_j^{(a)} \in \mathcal{M}^{(a)}$ **do**
    Dist$(i^*,\ j) \leftarrow$ CalcDistance $\left(M_{i^*}^{(a)},\ M_j^{(a)} \right)$
  end for
end while

The clustering algorithm is applied to each facial part independently, and extracts modes (simple motion) in the facial part. Suffix (a) in $M^{(a)}$ and $I^{(a)}$ denotes an index of facial part. Identify is a constrained system identification described in Section 4.2, which estimates the mode parameters $\theta_i^{(a)} = \{F^{(a,\ i)},\ f^{(a,\ i)}\}$ from feature vectors in intervals. $\mathcal{I}_i^{(a)}$ is an interval set that comprises intervals labeled by $M_i^{(a)}$. CalcDistance calculates the distance between the two modes based on Equation (9). MergeIntervals merges two interval sets that belong to the nearest modes (dynamical systems).

A Practical Face Relighting Method for Directional Lighting Normalization

Kuang-Chih Lee[1] and Baback Moghaddam[2]

[1] University of Illinois at Urbana-Champaign,
Urbana, IL 61801, USA
[2] Mitsubishi Electric Research Laboratories,
Cambridge, MA 02139, USA

Abstract. We propose a simplified and practical computational technique for estimating directional lighting in uncalibrated images of faces in frontal pose. We show that this inverse problem can be solved using constrained least-squares and class-specific priors on shape and reflectance. For simplicity, the principal illuminant is modeled as a mixture of Lambertian and ambient components. By using a generic 3D face shape and an average 2D albedo we can efficiently compute the directional lighting with surprising accuracy (in real-time and with or without shadows). We then use our lighting direction estimate in a forward rendering step to "relight" arbitrarily-lit input faces to a canonical (diffuse) form as needed for illumination-invariant face verification. Experimental results with the Yale Face Database B as well as real access-control datasets illustrate the advantages over existing pre-processing techniques such as a linear ramp (facet) model commonly used for lighting normalization.

1 Introduction

In computer vision and specifically in face recognition, robust invariance to arbitrary illumination has presented a difficult challenge. Indeed, in large independent US government tests of the leading algorithms (*e.g.,* in FERET [10] and FRVT [9]) improper handling of variable (outdoor) lighting has been a key limiting factor in achieving recognition rates obtained in more controlled laboratory conditions.

In this paper, we address a difficult but routine problem in facial identification as applied to access control and forensic surveillance: we are given a photograph of a possibly unknown individual, appearing in fixed pose (*e.g.,* frontal) which was taken by an uncalibrated camera with unknown intrinsic parameters in an arbitrary scene with unknown and variable illumination. Without any 3D measurement (of subject or environment) and with only the single image provided, we are to match identities by comparing the facial image to that of another in a large database of (frontal) faces in *fixed* lighting (*e.g.,* diffuse or frontal). Equivalently, we must standardize all current and any future images in a growing database in order to simulate a common fixed illumination template suitable for robust pattern matching and illumination-invariant facial identification. Naturally, the canonical choice of illumination would consist of non-directional or

W. Zhao, S. Gong, and X. Tang (Eds.): AMFG 2005, LNCS 3723, pp. 155–169, 2005.
© Springer-Verlag Berlin Heidelberg 2005

diffuse (or at least frontal) lighting that would maximize visibility of all facial features.

Since our focus is on illumination-invariance, we acknowledge that all images have undergone *geometric* normalization prior to analysis: beginning with face detection (*e.g.*, [6]), feature detection (of eyes) followed by rigid transforms (scale, rotation and translation) to align all detected features. In addition, we assume that some form of *photometric* normalization may have already taken place in the form of a non-spatial *global* transform which is a function of intensity only (*e.g.*, gain, contrast, brightness). We also prepare to encounter any number of possible data sources: live video capture, archival photography, web imagery, family photo albums, passport and ID pictures, *etc.*

2   Background

Much of the research on illumination has focused on finding a compact low-dimensional subspace to capture lighting variations. Belhumeur & Kriegman [2] proved that under the Lambertian assumption, the image set of an object under all possible lighting conditions forms a polyhedral "illumination cone" in the image space. Georghiades *et al.* [5] demonstrated applications of this framework to face recognition under variable illumination. Ramamoorthi [11] presented a method to analytically determine the low-dimensional illumination subspace obtained with PCA. Basri & Jacobs [1] represent lighting using a spherical harmonic basis wherein a low-dimensional linear subspace is shown to be quite effective for recognition. Zhang & Samaras [16] have extended this framework with spherical harmonic *exemplars*. Lee *et al.* [7] have empirically found how to arrange physical lighting to best generate an equivalent basis for recognition.

A complementary approach is to generate a lighting invariant signature image. Although this technique cannot deal with large illumination changes, it does have the advantage that only one image per object is required in the gallery. Some of the earlier normalization techniques apply such an approach to face recognition, using histogram equalization or linear ramp subtraction to generate invariant templates [13]. Chen *et al.* [3] demonstrated that the image gradient direction is mostly illumination-insensitive and can be used in a probabilistic framework to determine the likelihood of two images coming from the same object. Zhao & Chellappa [17] took advantage of the near symmetry of faces to compute an illumination invariant prototype image for each individual without recovering albedos. Shashua & Riklin-Raviv [14] assumed that different faces have a common shape but different texture and computed an albedo ratio as an illumination-invariant signature.

In computer graphics, object relighting has received much attention in recent years. An interesting application by Nishino & Nayar [8] is the use of corneal imaging for embedding realistic virtual objects (faces) into a scene, resulting in synthetic faces that are properly lit ("relit") in accordance with the estimated environmental lighting. Another example is the radiance environment

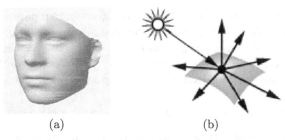

(a)   (b)

Fig. 1. (a) 3D face shape with (b) a Lambertian reflectance model

map technique by Wen *et al.* [15] which renders relatively high-quality relighting of faces using the spherical harmonics approach [12].

For our face verification application however, there is really no need for high-quality graphics rendering or photo-realism. In fact, most 2D face recognition systems in existence today operate at low to moderate resolutions (≈ 100 pixels across the face). Our relighting method can be categorized as an invariant template approach to illumination-invariance as discussed above (although we will also present an equivalent subspace formulation). As with [14] we assume a common underlying 3D shape for all individuals and utilize the albedo or diffuse reflectance (skin texture) as the main source of identity information. This, of course, is in keeping with the fact that most 2D face recognition systems do not measure 3D shape anyway.

Despite our simplifications, we will demonstrate that with low-resolution shape, approximate albedo and simple diffuse reflectance for relighting, it is possible to significantly improve the accuracy of face verification under moderate lighting variations encountered in real access-control operational scenarios. At the very least, it is our hope that others will find this algorithm to be a practical and superior alternative for lighting normalization.

3   Lighting Estimation

We use a Lambertian or "diffuse reflectance" (constant BRDF) illumination model for the face, as shown in Figure 1, despite the fact that sometimes there is some specular reflection (due to secretion of *sebum* oil by sebaceous glands in the skin). Nevertheless, this specular component is not always consistent and therefore of little use in a biometric analysis. Hence, our illumination model consists only of Lambertian and ambient components.

Specifically, let $I(x,y)$ be the intensity at pixel (x,y) corresponding to a point on the surface of a convex object (face or 3D face model) with Lambertian surface reflectance, which is illuminated by a mixture of ambient light and a (single) point light source at infinity $\mathbf{s} \in \mathbb{R}^3$ with intensity $|\mathbf{s}|$. We designate the unit surface normal $\mathbf{s}/|\mathbf{s}|$ as the direction *to* the light source (i.e., pointing out). This direction (*e.g.* in azimuth/elevation angles) is our main estimand of interest. The magnitude of the light source, on the other hand, is of little consequence in our analysis since it can be absorbed by the imaging system parameters modeling gain and exposure. We define $\rho(x, y)$ as the face albedo (or diffuse skin texture) and let $\mathbf{n}(x, y)$ be the unit surface normal of the point on the facial surface that projects onto the pixel $I(x, y)$ in the image (under orthography). Under the simple Lambertian (constant BRDF) model, a pixel's (monochrome) intensity is given by

$$I(x, y) = \alpha \ \{\rho(\mathrm{x}, \mathrm{y})[\max(\mathbf{n}(\mathrm{x}, \mathrm{y})^T \mathbf{s}, 0) + \mathrm{c}]\} \ + \ \beta \tag{1}$$

where α and β represent intrinsic camera system parameters such as lens aperture and gain setting. In our analysis, (α, β) are essentially nuisance parameters which only affect the dynamic range (gain) and offset (exposure bias) of pixel intensity but *not* the lighting direction. Therefore, we can always set (α, β) to their default values of $(1, 0)$ with proper normalization. The parameter c represents the relative strength of the ambient lighting and we will show how it can be estimated in Section 4. The term $\max(\mathbf{n}^T \mathbf{s}, 0)$ above resets negative values of the (Lambertian) cosine factor to zero for surface points that are in shadow.

For simplicity's sake, we are assuming that a single (principal) light source alone is responsible for the majority of the observed directional lighting in the image (diffuse attenuation and/or shadowing) and that any other light sources present in the scene (diffuse or directional) are *non-dominant*, hence their overall contribution can be represented by a global ambient component with relative intensity c in Eq. (1). Nearly all 2D (view-based) face recognition systems are adversely affected by *directional* lighting, but to a much lesser extent by more subtle lighting effects [10]. Therefore, in most cases and for most algorithms the principal directional component is a more critical factor than any other lighting phenomena, especially when the other light sources are non-dominant. Therefore, accounting for this principal illumination factor by effectively "undoing" its effects can enhance verification performance.

Estimation of the principal lighting direction can be carried out with a least-squares formulation with the right simplifying assumptions, especially given the relatively simple illumination model in Eq. (1). More importantly, We can solve this problem rather efficiently (in closed form) with elementary matrix operations and dot-products. Specifically, let $\vec{I}$ be the column vector of pixel intensities obtained by stacking all the nonzero values of $I(x, y)$ and similarly define $\vec{\rho}$ to be the corresponding vectorized albedo map (diffuse texture). [1] We then form a 3-column shape matrix $\mathbf{N}$ by row-wise stacking of the corresponding surface normals. We then form the so-called *shape-albedo* matrix $\mathbf{A} \in \mathbb{R}^{p \times 3}$ where each row $\mathbf{a}$ in $\mathbf{A}$ is the product of the albedo and the unit surface normal in the corresponding row of $\vec{\rho}$ and $\mathbf{N}$. Mathematically, this corresponds to the Hadamard (elementwise) matrix product $\circ$ as $\mathbf{A} = (\vec{\rho} \, \mathbf{1}_{1 \times 3}) \circ \mathbf{N}$.

To solve for the unknown light source we use a matrix equation for least-squares minimization of the approximation error in Eq. (1) in the new vectorized form

---

[1] Without ambient light, zero-valued pixels are most likely in shadow and thus informative only if we use ray-casting to pinpoint the source. In practice, ambient light is always present and we use a nonzero threshold or a pre-set mask for pixel selection.

$$\arg\min_{\mathbf{s}} \; \| \vec{I} - \alpha c \vec{\rho} - \mathbf{A}\mathbf{s} \|^2 \tag{2}$$

which yields the solution

$$\mathbf{s}^* = (\mathbf{A}^T\mathbf{A})^{-1}\mathbf{A}^T(\vec{I} - \alpha c \vec{\rho} - \beta) \tag{3}$$

Note that we are only interested in the unit light source vector $\mathbf{s}^*/|\mathbf{s}^*|$ for its direction and not the magnitude (which depends on the specific camera gain/exposure). Moreover, this estimation problem is well-behaved since it is heavily over-constrained: the number of nonzero elements in $\vec{I}$ ("observations") is on the order of $O(10^3)$ as compared to the 3 unknowns in $\mathbf{s}^*$ (in fact, since we only use the *direction* there are only 2 angular estimands: azimuth & elevation). Estimatation of the principal lighting direction is therefore quite stable with respect to noise and small variations in the input $\vec{I}$. Note that the derived matrix $\mathbf{A}$ comes from a *generic* shape and albedo and hence represents the entire frontal face object class. Assuming that it is adequately representative, there is no need to measure the exact shape (or even exact albedo) of an individual as long as all shapes (and albedos) are roughly equal to first order (*i.e.*, as far as lighting direction is concerned).

Furthermore, The pseudo-inverse $(\mathbf{A}^T\mathbf{A})^{-1}$ in Eq. (3) is directly proportional to the error covariance of the least-squares estimate $\mathbf{s}^*$ under Gaussian noise. If we further define the p $\times$ 3 matrix $\mathbf{P} = \mathbf{A}(\mathbf{A}^T\mathbf{A})^{-1}$ we see that the only *on-line* computation in Eq. (3) is the projection of the input vector $\vec{I}$ on the 3 columns of $\mathbf{P}$ which are linearly independent. In fact, they are basic functions for the *illumination subspace* of our generic face (frontal face class). Moreover, we can always find an equivalent orthogonal basis for this subspace using a QR-factorization: $\mathbf{P} = \mathbf{Q}\mathbf{R}$, where the unitary matrix $\mathbf{Q}$ has 3 orthonormal columns spanning the same subspace as $\mathbf{P}$ and the 3 $\times$ 3 upper triangular matrix $\mathbf{R}$ now defines the quality of the estimates since $\mathbf{R}^{-1}$ is a Cholesky factor (matrix square root) of the error covariance. The QR factorization aids the interpretation and analysis of the estimation in terms of pixels and bases since the input image is directly projected onto the orthonormal basis $\mathbf{Q}$ to estimate the lighting direction (the QR decomposition also saves computation in larger problems). In Section 5 we will show an example of this factorization.

Since $\mathbf{P}$ and $\mathbf{Q}$ are independent of the input data they can be pre-computed once off-line and then stored. Also, the computational cost of using Eq. (3) is quite minimal (requiring only 3 image-sized dot-products) and since the subsequent relighting (see Section 4) is even less expensive (requiring a single dot-product), the lighting normalization process is very practical for real-time implementation (perhaps as part of a much larger face processing system).

3.1   Estimation Analysis

To evaluate our estimation technique we chose the Yale Face Database B which contains images of 10 individuals imaged under 45 different lighting conditions (our tests were performed on all 450 images). Following the protocol established

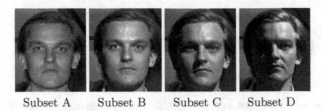

Subset A   Subset B   Subset C   Subset D

Fig. 2. Images of an individual in the Yale Database B under the 4 directional lighting subsets. See [5] for more examples.

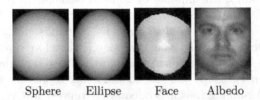

Sphere   Ellipse   Face   Albedo

Fig. 3. Range maps for 3 progressively more complex shapes: a sphere, an ellipse and a generic face (note its smoothness). The effective albedo image is shown on the right.

in [5], the images were grouped into 4 subsets according to lighting direction angle with respect to the camera. The first two subsets cover the range $[0°, 25°]$, the third subset covers $[25°, 50°]$ and the fourth covers $[50°, 77°]$. Figure 2 shows sample images from the four different subsets in the Yale Face Database B.

These 450 images were manually cropped, geometrically aligned as best as possible and down-sampled to size 80×64 and then masked (but no photometric processing was performed). The choice of resolution was partly due to an operational specification (of a pre-existing face verification system) and also due to the challenge of working with a low resolution nearer to the limit at which surface normals can be reliably computed from a (potentially) noisy range map.

For our generic shape model we used the average 3D shape of 138 individuals in the DARPA HumanID database of 3D Cyberware scans [4]. The resulting average 3D face shape, seen in Figure 1(a), was first down-sampled and converted to an 80×64 range map (frontal depth) which was then smoothed using a Gaussian blur in order to reduce any quantization noise in its surface normals. Then, our generic face shape's surface normal map $\mathbf{n}(x, y)$ was computed and registered with the image plane (using the fixed eye positions only) thereby aligning our standardized 2D input image $I(x, y)$ format with the surface normals of our 3D model. As a rough 2nd-order approximation to the generic face shape, we also computed range maps for a comparably-sized sphere and ellipse as shown in Figure 3.

For the average albedo we found it sufficient to use the facial *texture* obtained by averaging images of all 10 individuals in the Yale database with near-frontal lighting (subset A+B). By averaging (integrating) over all illuminations we (approximately) simulate *diffuse* or non-directional lighting. This average texture map was then processed (smoothed, de-noised, *etc.*) and normalized to the range $[0, 1]$ to serve as our generic face albedo. We should note that the albedo plays

Table 1. Mean errors (in degrees) for the underlying shapes used in estimating lighting directions on subsets of the Yale database

LIGHT SOURCE ESTIMATION WITH FRONTAL FACES USING DIFFERENT SHAPES							
Surface Geometry	Mean Errors (in azimuth and elevation)						
	subset **AB**		subset **C**		subset **D**		**ABCD** combined	
	AZ	EL	AZ	EL	AZ	EL	AZ	EL
Sphere	6.4	7.8	10.3	17.2	5.3	24.1	7.1	15.4
Ellipse	1.3	7.5	2.2	17.1	11.2	23.1	4.6	14.9
Face	2.3	4.9	3.0	6.7	5.5	9.2	4.5	5.5

a secondary role (in estimating the illuminant) as compared to the geometry encoded in the surface normals. In fact, without going into the details, we mention that we were able to obtain almost as good estimates even with *constant* albedo. This is indicative of the overall stability (if not perfect accuracy) of this estimation problem. Figure 3 shows the generic face albedo we used for the Yale dataset.

In Table 1 we have summarized the mean estimation errors (in azimuth elevation degrees) for the 3 shapes in Figure 3 (sphere, ellipse, face). All 3 shapes were used to estimate lighting direction of all 450 images in the Yale Face Database B. Each error value reported in the table is the average difference between azimuth and elevation of the ground truth source and the computed lighting directions obtained from $\mathbf{s}^*$ in Eq. (3) with $c = 0$ as there is no ambient component in this dataset. From the totals column in the table (far right) the mean errors over *all* lighting directions are about 5 deg with the generic face and an average of about 10 deg (for both azimuth and elevation) with the sphere and ellipse. For near-frontal lighting (subset A+B) the difference between the two simple shapes and the face is relatively small in terms of the mean error.

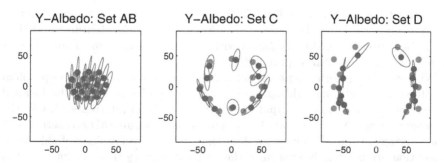

Fig. 4. Yale Database B lighting angle estimation plotted in degrees (elevation *vs.* azimuth). Red dots represent ground truth lighting angles. Blue dots are the mean estimates based on the 10 individuals. Blue dots are also the centers of the error covariances shown as blue ellipses (95% confidence interval). Results are grouped into 3 plots {AB, C, D} based on the 4 subsets shown in Figure 2.

For a more revealing analysis of the face-based results above we must look a bit more closely at the individual estimates. Figure 4 plots the distribution of all lighting estimates for all 10 individuals in the database. By comparing the mean estimates (blue dots) with the ground truth (red dots) we see a high degree of correlation between the two. Furthermore, there is as a surprising degree of accuracy considering all the convenient half-true assumptions made in formulating the solution in Eq. (3). Clearly, the blue error covariance ellipses confirm variation with between individuals as expected (due to differing geometry/albedo) but these estimates are certainly "correct" in the trend, especially with respect to the azimuth. It is only at the most extreme angles (subset D) that we see the estimates "saturate" near a limiting angle of 50 deg (which is most likely due to a lack of resolution in depth and the spatial boundary of the mask).

In Figure 4 we also see, based on the orientation of the error covariances, that the *error* estimate (uncertainty) is much greater along elevation than it is along azimuth. This raises an interesting question: what is limiting the precision of elevation estimates? Since it cannot be a mathematical flaw in our derivation, it must be either the albedo or the shape that we are using to compute the matrix **A** in Eq. (3). To help explain this phenomenon, in Figure 5 we show two separate histograms for the azimuth and elevation of the surface normals in our generic face shape. Note that the variation in azimuth of the surface normals (± 50 deg) is greater than the variation in elevation (± 20 deg). This limited "bandwidth" in the elevation distribution reduces the effective precision of the estimates of elevation (*i.e.,* there are far fewer surface normals with high elevation angles). This is partly due to an intrinsic feature of the shape of the human face, which to a first-order approximation is an upright cylinder or ellipse (both of which span a limited range of elevation) and partly due to the limitation of the smoothed low-resolution face shape we are using (see subset D in particular in Figure 4).

4   Face Relighting

Given an estimate of the input image's directional lighting we can approximately "undo it" by estimating the individual's albedo (diffuse skin texture) and then relight this specific albedo (combined with a generic shape) under any desired illumination (*e.g.,* frontal or pure diffuse).

Whereas both generic shape and albedo were required in the inverse problem of estimating directional lighting, only generic shape is needed in the forward problem of relighting (as the input itself provides albedo information). Clearly, the basic assumption here is that all individuals have the same 3D geometry (that of our average shape). However, we find that moderate violations of this basic assumption are not highly critical to the verification performance since what is actually relighted to generate an invariant template is the facial texture of the individual herself and this texture carries most of the identity information for 2D face recognition. In fact, it is not possible to drastically alter the input image's albedo (skin texture) by using a (slightly) different 3D face shape. Therefore,

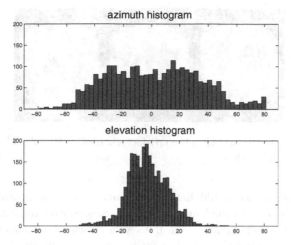

Fig. 5. The histograms of the azimuth and elevation angles of the surface normals of the average (generic) face shape

despite the variations in geometry every individual's identity is mostly preserved as long as their face texture is retained.

Referring back to Eq. (1), once we have a lighting estimate $\mathbf{s}^*$ and our "plug-in" shape (surface normals of the average face) we can directly solve for albedo using

$$\rho^* = \frac{I - \beta}{\alpha(\mathbf{n}^T\mathbf{s}^* + c)}, \quad I \neq 0, \ \mathbf{n}^T\mathbf{s}^* \geq 0. \tag{4}$$

where from hereon we have suppressed the spatial indices (x, y) for all 2D-arrays $(I, \rho$ and $\mathbf{n})$ for the sake of clarity. Notice that the estimated albedo ρ^* at a point (x, y) depends only on the corresponding pixel intensity $I(x, y)$ and the surface normal $\mathbf{n}(x, y)$. Thus, if a scene point is in shadow and there is no ambient illumination $(c = 0)$, I will be zero and $\mathbf{n}^T\mathbf{s}^*$ is negative. If so, the corresponding albedo cannot be estimated with Eq. (4) and a default (average) albedo must be substituted in for that pixel.

The estimated albedo is then relighted in order to generate our invariant (fixed-illumination) template I_o

$$I_o = \alpha_o \left\{ \rho^*[\max(\mathbf{n}^T\mathbf{s}_o, 0) + c_o] \right\} + \beta_o \tag{5}$$

where $\mathbf{s}_o$ denotes the desired template's illumination (defaulted to on-axis frontal lighting) and c_o is the output ambient component. Similarly α_o and β_o designate the output (display/storage) image format parameters.

5   Verification Experiments

To evaluate the performance of our lighting normalization technique in an actual face verification test we used an internal face database belonging to our institution (had we chosen the same Yale Database B which has only 10 individuals,

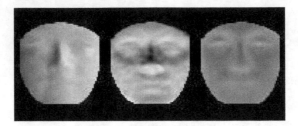

Fig. 6. The orthonormal basis $\mathbf{Q}$ in the QR-factorization of $\mathbf{P} = \mathbf{A}(\mathbf{A}^T\mathbf{A})^{-1}$ in Eq. (3) for internal datasets I & II

our performance results would have been statistically insignificant). Our data comes from an unconstrained and realistic access-control operational scenario inside a large industrial plant. The data was captured on two different days and in two separate locations in the facility with no specific lighting control. Approximately 500 individuals were automatically detected from a surveillance video using an enhanced face/feature-detector based on [6] and then geometrically aligned and cropped to our 80 × 64 image format and stored on disk (no photometric pre-processing was performed).

We put together and processed (by averaging and filtering) a suitably smooth and diffuse average face albedo (texture) for this dataset which is shown in Figure 9(b). Then we computed the corresponding shape-albedo matrix $\mathbf{A}$ in Eq. (3) using the same average 3D shape used with the Yale database in Section 3. Figure 6 shows the orthogonal illumination subspace of this database's generic face. Notice how both the horizontal and vertical lighting directions are decoupled into separate bases. The third basis image is the global intensity or amplitude (recall that we are interested in the two degrees of freedom in azimuth and elevation). The mottled appearance in the 2nd basis image is mostly due to the quantization noise in the surface normals (we did not wish to smooth the surface normals too much and this obviously shows).

Unlike the Yale Database B, our internal dataset *does* have ambient lighting which we can model with the ambient parameter c in Eq. (3. By using a representative set of N training images we can (numerically) estimate the ambient component using the optimality criteria

$$c^* = \arg\min_c \sum_{i=1}^{N} \left| \rho_i(c) - \frac{1}{N}\sum_{i=1}^{N}\rho_i(c) \right|^2 \qquad (6)$$

where $\rho_i(c)$ denotes the albedo of the i-th training image estimated with the relative ambient intensity c in Eq. (3).

We now demonstrate the range of our estimation and relighting capability using a small subset of our internal database which we call Dataset I. This subset has frontal views of 32 individuals under three (maximally) different lighting conditions: frontal lighting (for the gallery images) and left and right directional lighting (for the probe images) both of which are mixed in with some (unknown)

Original Images

Normalized by Linear Ramp

Frontal Relighting using Equation 5

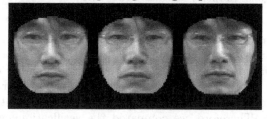

Fig. 7. Comparison of the linear ramp and our relighting method. Three images from different illuminations: frontal, left and right directional lighting (shown left to right).

proportion of ambient illumination. For each lighting condition 10 images of each individual were taken for a total of 960 images.

Figure 7 shows a representative sample of our frontal relighting technique applied to the gallery and probe images (left, then center and right, respectively) of one of the 32 individuals in Database I. The top row shows the original (unprocessed) input images and the bottom row shows our relighting results. Clearly, the directional component of the illumination has been successfully removed and the frontally relit image has been generated in its place (which incorporates an ambient component estimated with Eq. (6). In contrast, the middle row shows the results obtained with *linear ramp* normalization (also known as a "facet model") which fits a plane to the image intensities (using least-squares) which is then subtracted from the input in order to remove the main illumination gradient. The residual image is then normalized back to the original intensity range. The saturation observed is a common feature of linear ramp normalization since this technique can not represent shape variations other than its own implicit Lambertian flat surface. The linear ramp model is also quite susceptible to the specular highlights which can be rather significant outliers in the linear fit. We

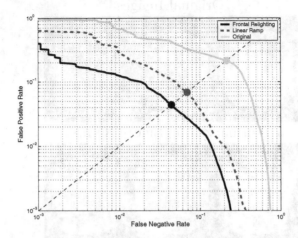

Fig. 8. The ROC curves of the face verification test based on L_2 distance in internal Dataset I. The diagonal (dashed) designates the EER line.

also compared our results to histogram equalization (not shown) but the ROC curve was worse than the linear ramp.

Of course visual inspection of the apparent "good" quality of the relighted images is (for us) a secondary issue (unlike say, in computer graphics). We are primarily interested in improving the *accuracy* of face verification under arbitrary illumination. Therefore, we compared the verification performance of a given algorithm with our relighted images versus with the original (raw) images. We specifically wanted to illustrate a phenomenon which was universal, simple to understand, made the least algorithmic assumptions and could be easily duplicated by others. Therefore, we chose a "model-free" matching metric in the form of simple L_2 norm of the difference between the probe and gallery images or equivalently the Euclidean distance in pixel space. Figure 8 shows the resulting receiver operating characteristic curve (ROC) obtained using the inverse of the L_2 norm as a similarity metric for verification. We see that the commonly reported performance measure, the "equal error rate" (EER), drops from approximately 20% with raw imagery down to 4% with our frontal relighting technique (an improvement by a factor of 5). By comparison, the linear ramp normalization achieves approximately 7% EER. Moreover, the ROC curve for frontal relighting is superior to the linear ramp at every operating point specified by a given pair of false accept rate (FAR) and false reject rate (FRR). Although the improvement trend is quite clear and pronounced in this test, we acknowledge that these results are based on only 32 individuals may not generalize to larger datasets (since it is probably too optimistic).

In order to obtain a more statistically significant performance measure, we assembled the largest collection of images in our internal dataset, called Database II, to accurately calibrate and benchmark the performance advantage provided by using our lighting normalization. Database II consists of a gallery of 3,444

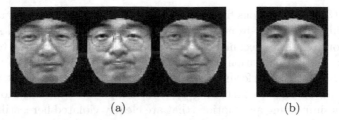

Fig. 9. (a) Database II sample images of an individual in gallery (left) and probes (center and right). Also shown is (b) the mean "albedo" image used.

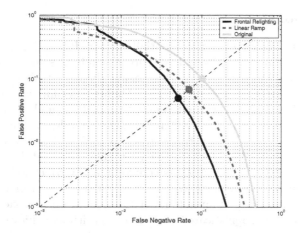

Fig. 10. The ROC of the face verification test based on L_2 distance in internal Dataset II. The diagonal (dashed) designates the EER line. The ROC for histogram equalization (not shown) is similar to that of the linear ramp but slightly worse.

images of 496 individuals and a probe set of 6,663 images of 363 individuals not all of whom are in the gallery (*i.e.*, impostors). Sample images for one individual can be seen in Figure 9. Notice the bright highlights and specular reflection off the spectacles and the relatively overhead (high elevation) lighting direction in the center image (including shadows of the lens and the rims of the glasses on the cheeks). Obviously, the lighting in these images is much more complex than simple directional illumination with Lambertian reflectance.

Figure 10 shows the ROC curve for the verification test with Dataset II. These results were computed based on the statistics of almost 23 million probe-to-gallery matches yielding a relatively high degree of statistical significance. Despite the fact that these images do not contain a single directional lighting component and moreover exhibit some non-Lambertian phenomena (specularity, shadowing, inter-reflection, *etc.*) we see a similar improvement trend with the same rank ordering of performance under the two candidate lighting normalizations performed. Specifically, we see the raw data yield an EER of 10% (lower than the 20% in the previous figure since although the illumination is more complex it is still mostly near-frontal and less extreme than in Figure 7). As seen in the figure, our relighting technique achieves an EER of 5%, compared to 7% with the linear ramp normalization. Considering the size of this test and the subsequent accuracy of the performance estimates (not just the EER but the entire ROC curve) it is perhaps surprising that our simple illumination model which makes a few simplifying assumptions that are clearly violated here, still manages to provide a sizable performance advantage in complex lighting; especially with imagery in which *directional* lighting does not seem (at first glance) to be the main complicating factor adversely affecting the verification performance.

6 Conclusions

The contributions of this paper are essentially two-fold: first, a simple and practical method for estimating the dominant directional light source in a photometrically uncalibrated image of a face (whose exact shape and albedo are basically unknown) and secondly, a fast and efficient relighting technique for normalizing the image for illumination-invariant template matching and recognition. The necessary computations require less than 5 image-sized dot-products.

Furthermore, we have demonstrated the superiority of our technique in experiments with both public datasets such as Yale Face Database B and our own internal datasets of realistic access-control imagery which exhibits complex real-world illumination environments. This performance enhancement is directly due to a tighter clustering of an individual's images in image space, which will very likely help more sophisticated matching algorithms achieve illumination invariance.

Our results demonstrate that (relatively) robust estimation of lighting direction and subsequent normalization are not only possible with simplified calculations but are also quite feasible for online use. The total computational cost for estimation and relighting is only a few dot-products. Consequently, this methodology is a viable alternative for real-time applications while being superior to linear ramp and histogram equalization techniques currently in use.

References

1. R. Basri and D. Jacobs. Lambertian reflectance and linear subspaces. In *Int'l Conf. on Computer Vision*, volume 2, pages 383–390, 2001.
2. P. Belhumeur and D. Kriegman. What is the set of images of an object under all possible lighting conditions. In *Int'l J. Computer Vision*, volume 28, pages 245–260, 1998.
3. H. Chen, P. Belhumeur, and D. Jacobs. In search of illumination invariants. In *Proc. IEEE Conf. on Computer Vision & Pattern Recognition*, pages 1–8, 2000.
4. DARPA. The HumanID 3D Face Database, courtesy of Prof. Sudeep Sarkar, University of South Florida, Tampa Fl. USA.
5. A. Georghiades, D. Kriegman, and P. Belhumeur. From few to many: Generative models for recognition under variable pose and illumination. *IEEE Trans. on Pattern Analysis and Machine Intelligence*, 40:643–660, 2001.

6. M. J. Jones and P. Viola. Fast multi-view face detection. In *Proc. IEEE Conf. on Computer Vision & Pattern Recognition*, 2003.
7. K. C. Lee, J. Ho, and D. Kriegman. Nine points of light: Acquiring subspaces for face recognition under variable lighting. In *Proc. IEEE Conf. on Computer Vision & Pattern Recognition*, pages 519–526, 2001.
8. K. Nishino and S. K. Nayar. Eyes for relighting. In *Proceedings of SIGGRAPH*, 2004.
9. J. Phillips. Face Recogntion Vendor Test 2002 report. Technical report, National Institute of Standards and Technology, March 2003.
10. J. Phillips, H. Moon, S. Rizvi, and P. Rauss. The FERET evaluation methodology for face-recognition algorithms. *IEEE Trans. on Pattern Analysis and Machine Intelligence*, 22(10):1090–1104, 2000.
11. R. Ramamoorthi. Analytic PCA construction for theoretical analysis of lighting variability in images of a lambertian object. *IEEE Trans. on Pattern Analysis and Machine Intelligence*, 24, October 2002.
12. R. Rammamoorthi and P. Hanrahan. A signal processing framework for inverse rendering. In *Proceedings of SIGGRAPH*, 2001.
13. H. Rowley and T. Kanade. Neural network0based face detection. *IEEE Trans. on Pattern Analysis and Machine Intelligence*, 20(1):23–38, 1998.
14. A. Shashua and T. Riklin-Raviv. The quotient image: Class-based re-rendering and recognition with varying illuminations. *IEEE Trans. on Pattern Analysis and Machine Intelligence*, 23(2):129–139, 2001.
15. Z. Wen, Z. Liu, and T. S. Huang. Face relighting with radiance environment maps. In *Proc. IEEE Conf. on Computer Vision & Pattern Recognition*, 2003.
16. L. Zhang and D. Samaras. Face recognition under variable lighting using harmonic image exemplars. In *Proceedings of Computer Vision and Pattern Recognition*, pages 19–25, 2003.
17. W. Y. Zhao and R. Chellappa. Symmetric shape-from-shading using self-ratio image. *Int'l J. Computer Vision*, 45(1):55–75, 2001.

Face Recognition Based on Local Steerable Feature and Random Subspace LDA

Xiaoxun Zhang and Yunde Jia

Department of Computer Science and Engineering,
School of Information Science and Technology,
Beijing Institute of Technology,Beijing 100081, PR China
{zhangxiaoxun, jiayunde}@bit.edu.cn

Abstract. Both local features and holistic features are critical for face recognition and have different contributions. In this paper, we first propose a novel local steerable feature extracted from the face image using steerable filter for face representation. Discriminant information provided by steerable filter is locally stable with respect to scale, noise and brightness changes and it is semi-invariant under common image deformations and distinctive enough to provide useful identity information. We then present a new null space method based on random subspace. Linear Discriminant Analysis (LDA) is a popular holistic feature extraction technique for face recognition. Null Space LDA (NLDA) and Fisherface are adopted to extract global feature in the steerable feature space. Based on random subspaces, multiple NLDA classifiers are constructed under the most suitable situation for the null space. NLDA takes full advantage of the null space, while Fisherface extracts the most discriminant information in the principal subspace. Fisherface classifiers are constructed from the same set of random subspaces for NLDA classifiers. In each random subspace, Fisherface and NLDA share a unique eigen-analysis. There is no redundancy between such two kinds of complementary classifiers. Finally, all of the classifiers are integrated using a fusion rule. Experimental results on different face data sets demonstrate the effectiveness of the proposed method.

1 Introduction

Face recognition has attracted much attention due to its potential values for applications as well as theoretical challenges. To be successful for face recognition, features for classification must be robust to typical image deformations, and highly distinctive to afford identity information [2]. Local features offer advantages with stability to local deformations, lighting variations and expression variations. A variety of local features have been successfully employed in face recognition including Haar-like features [6, 7], Gabor wavelet features [5] and Local Binary Pattern (LBP) features [8]. In this paper, we propose a novel local descriptor based on steerable feature which is robust and distinctive for face recognition. The feature is extracted from face image based on the responses of complex-valued steerable filters. The amplitude and zero-crossings of such filters provide useful information for texture analysis in face recognition. The

W. Zhao, S. Gong, and X. Tang (Eds.): AMFG 2005, LNCS 3723, pp. 170–183, 2005.

major advantage of using steerable feature is the stability with respect to image deformations that typically exist in the face images of the same person, so that similar structure is generally available for classification.

The use of local, band-pass and linear filters is the focus of considerable research on early biological and computational visual processing [3]. Oriented filters are useful in many early vision and image processing tasks. One often needs to rotate the same filter to different angles under adaptive control, or to calculate the filter response at various orientations. Because the synthesis of the rotated filters is analytic and exact, steerable filters offer advantages for image analysis over ad hoc methods which combine oriented filters at different orientations. Physiological data suggest that the response of complex-valued steerable filter may model the basic binocular interaction of simple cells and complex-cell response [3]. Steerable filter has been successfully used for edge detection, shape-from-shading, feature detection, and stereo matching [1, 3, 4]. Steerable filter can capture the local structure corresponding to any orientation in one scale, while discriminative information in the scales-space of face image should be good to improve recognition performance. To further improve the accuracy, steerable filter is implemented with a Gaussian pyramid of face image. Steerable features from multiple scales and orientations are concatenated to an augmented feature vector to represent a face image. Such steerable features are over-complete and redundant. It is prohibitively time-consuming to perform classification in such a high dimensional feature space. Thus, we use AdaBoost method to select a small subset of the most efficient features.

Both holistic features and local features are critical for face recognition and have different contributions [10]. Linear Discriminant Analysis (LDA) is employed to extract holistic feature in the AdaBoosted steerable feature space. However, LDA often suffers from the small sample size problem when dealing with the high dimensional face data. Null Space LDA (NLDA) and Fisherface are two conventional approaches to address this problem. They can respectively extract the most discriminative information from the null space and the principal space. Further, Liu et al. [15] proposed the most suitable situation for the null space, under which all null space contributes to discriminative power. In this paper, we propose a new null space method based on random subspace. Random subspace is generated under this situation. In a random subspace, the NLDA classifier and the Fisherface classifier are constructed sharing a unique eigen-analysis. Finally, the two kinds of complementary classifiers are combined using a simple fusion rule.

Feature extraction, feature selection and classification rule are some crucial issues for face recognition. Our algorithm handles them together. It can effectively solve the small sample size problem. Compared with existing LDA approaches, our method is more stable and efficient.

2 Local Steerable Feature

2.1 Steerable Filters

Steerable filter allows adaptive control over orientation. Steerable filter can be used for a variety of operations involving oriented filters. The oriented filter, rotated to an arbitrary angle, is formed as a linear combination of basis filters. Once the basis filter responses are known, the response of the filter steered (rotated) to an arbitrary angle can easily be found. A similar technique can be used to control the magnitude of the filters. Following Mathews and Michael [1], we consider templates of the form

$$h(x, y) = \sum_{k=1}^{M} \sum_{i=0}^{k} \alpha_{k,i} \frac{\partial^{k-i}}{\partial x^{k-i}} \frac{\partial^{i}}{\partial y^{i}} g(x, y) = \sum_{k=1}^{M} \sum_{i=0}^{k} \alpha_{k,i} g_{k,i}(x, y) \qquad (1)$$

where $g(x, y)$ is an arbitrary isotropic window function and $g_{k,i}(x, y)$ is a basis filter. The filter $h(x, y)$ is steerable. Steerable filter is a class of filters in which a filter of arbitrary orientations is synthesized as a linear combination of a set of basis filters. In other words, the convolution of a 2D signal $f(x, y)$ with any rotated version of $h(x, y)$ can be expressed as

$$f(x, y) * h(x, y; \theta) = \sum_{k=1}^{M} \sum_{i=0}^{k} b_{k,i}(\theta) f_{k,i}(x, y) \qquad (2)$$

where the functions $f_{k,i}(x, y)$ are filtered versions of the signal $f(x, y)$ and can be expressed as

$$f_{k,i}(x, y) = f(x, y) * g_{k,i}(x, y) \qquad (3)$$

The orientation-dependent weights $b_{k,i}(\theta)$ are given by

$$b_{k,i}(\theta) = \sum_{j=0}^{k} \alpha_{k,j} \sum_{l,m \in S(k,j,i)} \binom{k-j}{l} \binom{j}{m} (-1)^{m} \cos(\theta)^{j+(l-m)} \sin(\theta)^{(k-j)+(l-m)} \qquad (4)$$

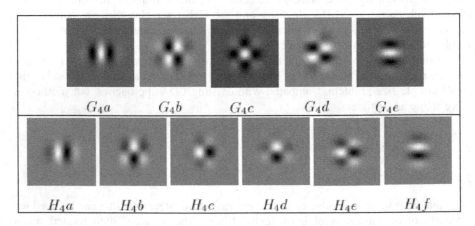

$G_4 a$ $G_4 b$ $G_4 c$ $G_4 d$ $G_4 e$

$H_4 a$ $H_4 b$ $H_4 c$ $H_4 d$ $H_4 e$ $H_4 f$

Fig. 1. X-Y separable basis filters for G4 and H4

where $S(k, i, j)$ is defined as

$$S(k, i, j) = \{l, m \mid 0 \le l \le k - i; 0 \le m \le i; k - (l + m) = j\} \tag{5}$$

Once the $f_{k,i}(x, y)$ are available, $f(x, y) * h(x, y; \theta)$ can be evaluated very efficiently via a weighted sum with its coefficients that are trigonometric polynomials of θ. We use X-Y separable basis filters G4/H4 to extract local steerable features from face images in our algorithm. These basis filters are showed in Figure 1. One important property of steerable filters is that they are X-Y separable [12]. This property allows efficient implement of G4/H4 filters and reduces the filters complexity from $O(N^2)$ to $O(2N)$. Another important property is that the coefficients are either symmetric or anti-symmetric which can be used to further save the computation cost [12].

2.2 Steerable Feature

Steerable feature is a complex representation of local image data that is obtained through the use of steerable filters, tuned to a specific orientation θ. We use the steerable quadrature filter pairs G4/H4 as follows:

$$m(x, y; \theta) = G_4(\theta) * I(x, y) \tag{6}$$

$$n(x, y; \theta) = H_4(\theta) * I(x, y) \tag{7}$$

$$O(x, y; \theta) = m(x, y; \theta) + in(x, y; \theta) \tag{8}$$

where $I(x, y)$ is a 2D gray level face image. $G_4(\theta)$ is the fourth derivative of a Gaussian, and $H_4(\theta)$ is the approximation of Hilbert transform of $G_4(\theta)$. A complex polar representation can be written as

$$O(x, y; \theta) = \rho(x, y; \theta) e^{i\phi(x, y; \theta)} \tag{9}$$

where $\rho(x, y; \theta)$ and $\phi(x, y; \theta)$ are often called instantaneous amplitude and phase to emphasize their local nature. Since the magnitude part of complex response of the steerable filter provides a confidence measure for similarity between face images, it is used as local descriptor in our algorithm. Phase response of the steerable filter is also a good similarity measure, which we report in another paper.

The steerableface, representing one face image, is computed by convoluting it with steerable filters. Figure 2 shows the steerableface representation of a face image with magnitude part corresponding to four orientations $(0°, 45°, 90°, 135°)$ respectively, where $0°$ is vertical. We can see the synthesized texture orientation corresponding to the orientation of steerable filter from the steerableface. In other words, the

Original	Orientation			
Image	0°	45°	90°	135°

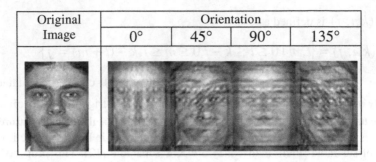

Fig. 2. X-Y separable basis filters for G4 and H4

steerableface of orientation $0°$ shows vertical texture and the steerableface of orientation $90°$ shows horizontal texture, while the steerablefaces of orientation $45°$ and $135°$ show oblique texture. In general, steerableface exhibits distinct spatial locality and orientation properties.

Steerable filter can capture the local structure corresponding to any orientation in a single scale, while recognition performance should benefit from discriminant information in the scales-space of face image. To further improve the accuracy, steerable filter is implemented in a Gaussian pyramid of face image. Gaussian pyramid is constructed by subsampling with a factor of 2 horizontally and vertically at each level. To avoid aliasing, which can happen as a result of down-sampling, we pass the input image through a low-pass anti-aliasing filter. In our algorithm, Gaussian FIR filter is used as an anti-aliasing filter in horizontal and vertical directions. Then each scale of the pyramid is decomposed using oriented quardrature-pair steerable filters G4/H4. Finally, to encompass different spatial frequencies, spatial localities, each face image is represented with an augmented steerable feature vector from multiple scales and orientations in our algorithm. However, such a steerable feature space is high dimensional and redundant. Actually, different facial regions in a face image have different levels of important and discriminant power for face recognition. AdaBoost method provides a simple yet effective stagewise learning approach for feature selection. Without loss of useful facial features, AdaBoost [11] is adopted to select a small number of features with the most discriminant power from a large pool.

3   LDA-Based Methods

Steerable feature is a powerful descriptor for local facial structure, while both holistic features and local features are critical for recognition and have different contributions [10]. LDA is a popular holistic feature extraction technique for face recognition. LDA is used to extract global feature in the steerable feature space. There are many motivations for using features rather than pixels directly. The most common reason is that features can act to encode ad hoc domain knowledge which is difficult to learn using a finite quantity of training data [6].

Let n denote the dimension of the raw sample space and c is the number of classes. The between-class scatter matrix S_b and the within-class scatter S_w are defined as

$$S_b = \sum_{i=1}^{c} N_i (m_i - m)(m_i - m)^T = \Phi_b \Phi_b^T \qquad (10)$$

$$S_w = \sum_{i=1}^{c} \sum_{k \in C_i} (x_k - m_i)(x_k - m_i)^T = \Phi_w \Phi_w^T \qquad (11)$$

where N_i is the number of samples in class $C_i (i = 1,2,...,c)$, N is the number of all the samples, m_i is the mean of all the samples. The total scatter S_t, i.e. the covariance matrix of all the samples, is given by

$$S_t = S_b + S_w = \sum_{i=1}^{N} (x_i - m)(x_i - m)^T = \Phi_t \Phi_t^T \qquad (12)$$

LDA determines a set of projection vectors maximizing S_b and minimizing S_w in the projective feature space. The optimal projection $W = [w_1, w_2,..., w_{c-1}]$ satisfies

$$J(W) = \arg \max_W \frac{|W^T S_b W|}{|W^T S_w W|} \qquad (13)$$

3.1 Fisherface

The optimal projection W can be calculated by the eigenvectors of $S_w^{-1} S_b$. But this method is numerically unstable because it involves the direct inversion of a likely high-dimensional matrix. The most frequently used LDA algorithm in practice is based on simultaneous diagonalization of S_w and S_b,

$$W^T S_w W = I, \qquad W^T S_b W = \Lambda \qquad (14)$$

Most algorithms require S_w being non-singular because the algorithm need to diagonalize S_w at the first step. The above procedure will break down when S_w is singular. It surely happens when the number of training samples is smaller than the dimension of the sample vector, i.e. the small sample size problem. An available solution to the singularity problem is to perform PCA before LDA. However, this step greatly reduces the dimension of both S_w and S_b. It essentially removes null space from both S_w and S_b. So PCA projection potentially loses some significant discriminating information.

3.2 Null Space LDA

A more reasonable method called null space LDA was presented [14], where the optimal projection W should satisfy

$$W^T S_w W = 0, \qquad W^T S_b W = \Lambda \tag{15}$$

i.e. the optimal discriminant vectors must exist in the null space of S_w. In this case, the Fisher criteria in Eqs. (13) definitely reaches its maximum value. However, the computational complexity of extracting the null space of S_w is very high because of its high dimension.

3.3 Null Space LDA in Most Suitable Situation

In most cases,

$$rank(S_t) = \min\{n, \quad N-1\} \tag{16}$$

$$rank(S_w) = \min\{n, \quad N-c\} \tag{17}$$

$$rank(S_b) = \min\{n, \quad c-1\} \tag{18}$$

The dimension of null space of S_w is very large and not all null space contributions to the discriminative ability. Based on this observation, Liu et al [15] presented the most suitable situation for the null space. When n is equal to $N-1$, S_t is full-rank and the dimension of null space of S_t is zero. It follows that all null space of S_w contributes to the discriminative power. Under this situation, only one eigen-analysis is needed to perform on S_w

$$V^T S_w V = D_w \tag{19}$$

where $V^T V = I$, D_w is diagonal matrix sorted in increasing order. Discard those with eigenvalues sufficiently far from 0, and keep $c-1$ eigenvectors of S_w in most cases. Let Y be the first $c-1$ columns of V which spans the null space of S_w, and Z be the last $N-c$ columns of V which spans the principal space of S_w. We have

$$Y^T S_w Y = 0 \tag{20}$$

$$Z^T S_w Z \neq 0 \tag{21}$$

Y and Z span two orthogonal complementary subspaces. There is no redundancy in the context of discriminant information between the two subspaces since they are orthogonal complementary [18].

4 Random Subspace LDA

4.1 Random Subspace NLDA

NLDA is always applicable to the small sample size problem. Any methods that can transform raw samples to $N-1$ dimensional data without adding or losing main information can exploit the full merit of NLDA. In [15], PCA projection and kernel mapping were used to accomplish this transformation. However, recall that PCA may lead to a loss of some significant discriminative information. On the other hand, kernel technique is time-consuming and it is also hard to select an optimal kernel function. In this paper, we propose a new NLDA method based on random subspace (RS-NLDA). A set of random subspaces with $N-1$ dimension are generated by random sampling among the AdaBoosted steerable features, and NLDA classifiers are constructed on the random subspaces. RS-NLDA contains the following steps:

At the training stage,

1)   Apply AdaBoost to the training set to select sufficient steerable features.

2)   Generate K random subspaces $\{R_i\}_{i=1}^{K}$. Each random subspace is constructed from $N-1$ steerable features.

3) K NLDA classifiers $\{C_i^N\}_{i=1}^{K}$ are constructed from the K random subspaces.

At the recognition state,

1)   The steerable feature vector is projected to the K random subspaces and fed to the K NLDA classifiers in parallel.

2)   The outputs of the K NLDA classifiers are fused to make the final decision.

RS-NLDA has several advantages over previous LDA methods. First, random subspace is used to reduce the feature vector dimension, rather than PCA projection or kernel mapping [15]. In this way, the central eigen-decomposition problem is made relatively smaller than traditional LDA approaches. Since eigen-analysis is the most time-consuming in the LDA training, we can save much computation cost.

Second, in our algorithm, random subspaces are completely independent. In comparison, the first 50 base vectors which are used to span the random subspace are identical in Wang and Tang's method [17]. As they mentioned, the random subspaces generated in such a way are not really independent.

Third, the random subspace dimension is determined empirically via extensive search experiments in [17]. By contrast, the optimal dimension of a random subspace is fixed theoretically given a training set.

Fourth, steerable features with AdaBoost selection ensure that the performance of random subspace is not too low. PCA is used to project the high dimension image data to the low dimension subspace prior to construct random subspaces in [17]. As mentioned above, this step arouses a loss of some useful discriminant information. In fact, face images span a nonlinear manifold in the image space [11]. With assumption of Gaussian distribution of original training data, PCA essentially changes the distribution of training samples in the projection subspace.

4.2 Random Subspace LDA

Though NLDA can make full use of the null space, it still discards important discriminative power in the principal subspace. The discriminating information retained by the two subspaces is mutually complementary. To further improve the recognition performance, we construct Fisherface classifiers from the same set of the random subspaces for NLDA classifiers (RS-Fisherface) and combine the two sets of complementary classifiers for final decision (RS-LDA). The main steps of RS-LDA are as follows:

At the training stage,

1) Apply AdaBoost to the training set to select sufficient steerable features.

2) Generate K random subspaces $\{R_i\}_{i=1}^K$. Each random subspace is constructed from $N-1$ steerable features.

3) K NLDA classifiers $\{C_i^N\}_{i=1}^K$ are constructed from the K random subspaces.

4) Based on the same K random subspaces $\{R_i\}_{i=1}^K$, K Fisherface classifiers $\{C_i^F\}_{i=1}^K$ are also constructed.

At the recognition state,

1) The steerable feature vector is projected to the K random subspaces and fed to the K NLDA classifiers and K Fisherface classifiers in parallel.

2) The outputs of the K NLDA classifiers and K Fisherface classifiers are integrated to make the final decision.

Wang and Tang [17] used two different random sampling schemes to improve traditional LDA approaches: sampling feature vectors for Fisherface (random subspace) and sampling training samples for NLDA (bagging). It is clear that Fisherface and NLDA classifiers generated in such a way are not really orthogonal complementary. Our scheme is more reasonable and efficient.

5   Experiments on XM2VTS Database

We first conduct experiments on the XM2VTS face database [13]. There are 295 people, and each person has four frontal face images taken in four different sessions. In our experiments, two face images of each class are selected for training set, and the other two are for gallery and probe respectively. We adopt the recognition test protocol used in FERET [9]. In the following experiments, all the images are scaled to 96×64. Except histogram equalization used for reducing the influence of some extreme illumination, no other pre-processing is performed. Steerable features are extracted from preprocessed face images. The number of steerable features of each sample is 32256 containing four orientations with three scales $(1, 1/4, 1/16)$:

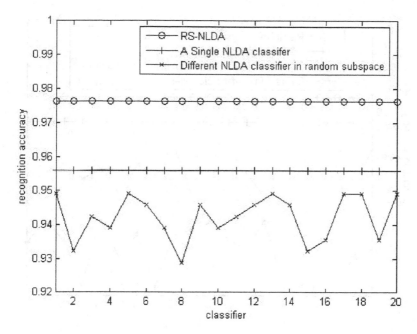

Fig. 4. Recognition accuracy of RS-NLDA on the AdaBoosted steerable feature space

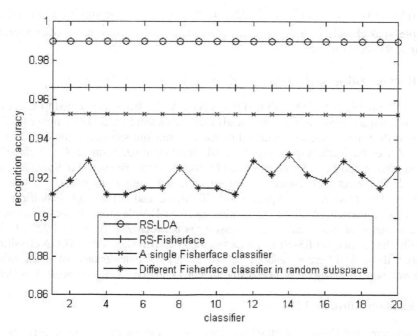

Fig. 5. Recognition accuracy of RS-LDA on the AdaBoosted steerable feature space

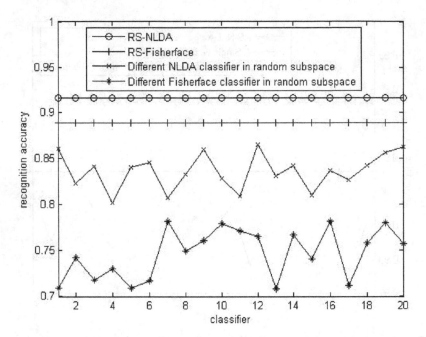

Fig. 6. Recognition accuracy of RS-LDA on the raw steerable feature space

$96 \times 64 \times 4 \times (1 + 1/4 + 1/16) = 32256$. In this paper, we use sum rule to combine multiple weak classifiers. More complex combination algorithms may further improve the algorithm performance.

5.1 Random Subspace NLDA

We first compare RS-NLDA with traditional NLDA. AdaBoost is adopted to select the most discriminative steerable features in advance. Since there are 590 face images of 295 classes in the training set, the optimal dimension of random subspace should be 589. In all, 1178 steerable features are selected via AdaBoost learning. A single NLDA classifier is constructed based on selected features and achieves a recognition rate of 95.93%. Then we randomly select 589 features among the selected features to generate a random subspace. The procedure is repeated for 20 times, and 20 NLDA classifiers are constructed. The result of RS-NLDA combining 20 NLDA classifiers is shown in Figure 4. The accuracy of individual NLDA classifier is between 92.88% and 94.92%. Using sum rule, the accuracy of RS-NLDA achieves 97.63%. This shows that NLDA classifiers constructed from different random subspaces are complementary of each other. Moreover, random subspace is indeed an efficient technique to enforce weak classifiers.

5.2 Random Subspace LDA

We then construct Fisherface classifiers from the same set of random subspaces for NLDA classifiers. A single Fisherface classifier is constructed based on selected steerable features and achieved a recognition rate of 95.25%. The accuracy of each individual Fisherface classifier varies from 91.53% to 92.88%. The recognition rate of RS-Fisherface is 96.61% using sum rule. The accuracy of individual Fisherface classifier is lower than that of each NLDA classifier on the same random subspace. This indicates that the null space of S_w encodes the more significant discriminative information than the principal subspace. Finally, all the NLDA and Fisherface classifiers are integrated to achieve a higher recognition accuracy of 98.98%. Figure5 reports the performance of RS-LDA. Figure 6 depicts the recognition accuracy of RS-NLDA and RS-Fisherface directly random sampling on the raw steerable feature space, rather than on the AdaBoosted steerable feature subspace. It shows that the improved method has a superior performance.

6   Experiments on FERET Database

The proposed method is also tested on the FERET FA/FB sets, which has been widely used to evaluate face recognition methods [9]. There are 1196 images in FA and 1195 images in FB. Each set contains at most one image per person and FA contains different facial expressions with FB. The FA images are used as gallery images and the FB images are used as probes. The training set is also from the training set of FERET database, which includes 1002 images of 429 subjects. The preprocessing procedure for face images is identical with the last experiment. The optimal dimension of each

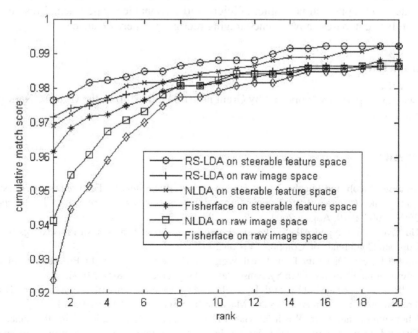

Fig. 7. Recognition accuracy of RS-LDA on the raw image space and the selected steerable feature space

random subspace is 1001. To investigate the effect of steerable feature on recognition performance, RS-LDA on the raw face image space is also performed. Totally, AdaBoost selected 2002 steerable features and original pixels respectively for constructing the random subspaces. We compare RS-LDA with NLDA and Fisherface. The rank curves of all the methods are shown in Figure 7. We achieve a high recognition rate of 97.66%. It can be observed that all of the methods based on steerable feature space outperform that on the raw image space. Steerable feature is a powerful local descriptor for face structure. On the other hand, both RS-NLDA and RS-Fisherface are superior to NLDA and Fisherface. It confirms that NLDA or Fisherface are not sufficient to discriminate the complex data consisting of many classes like human faces.

7   Conclusions

Local descriptor is popular in the field of face recognition. We propose a novel local steerable feature extracted from the face image using steerable filter. Furthermore, steerable filter is implemented in the scales-space to encode more discriminate information.

Subspace discriminant analysis involves two aspects: 1) Extract the most discriminative features from each subspace. 2) Exploit as much the complementary discriminative information as possible. In this paper, NLDA and Fisherface classifiers are constructed from the same set of random subspaces and integrated using a fusion rule. All the random subspaces are constructed under the most suitable situation for the null space. Our approach is simple, efficient and reasonable. Experimental results on multiple face databases show an encouraging recognition performance.

Acknowledgements

This work was partially supported by Grant no. (60473049) from the Chinese National Science Foundation.

Reference

1. Mathews Jacob, and Michael Unser. Design of Steerable Filters for Feature Detection Using Canny-Like Criteria. IEEE Transations on Pattern Analysis and Machine Intelligence, 26(8): 1007-1019, August 2004.
2. Gustavo Carneiro and Allan D.Jepson. Phase-based Local Features. In Proceedings of the Europen Conference on Computer Vision 2002.
3. David J.Fleet. Disparity from Local Weighed Phase-Correlation. In Proceedings of the International Conference On Systems, Man and Cybernetics. 48-54 , 1994.
4. William T. Freeman and Edward .H. Adelson, The design and use of steerable filters. IEEE Transations on Pattern Analysis and Machine Intelligence, 13(9): 891-906, 1991.
5. Chengjun Liu and Harry Wechsler. Gabor Feature Based Classification Using the Enhanced Fisher Linear Discriminant Model for Face Recognition. IEEE Transations on Image Processing. 11(4): 467-476 2002.

6. Paul Viola, Michael Jones. Rapid Object Detection using a Boosted Cascade of Simple Features. IEEE Proceedings of the IEEE Conference on Computer Vision and Pattern Recognition, 2001.
7. Michael J.Jones, Paul Viola. Face Recognition Using Boosted Local Features. In International Conference on Computer Vision, October 2003
8. Timo Ahonen, Matti Peitikainen, Abdenour Hadid and Topi Maenpaa, Face Recognition Based on the Appearance of Local Regions. International Conference on Pattern Recognition, 2004.
9. P.Jonathon, Phillips, Heyonjoon Moon, Syed A.Rizvi, and Patrick J.Rauss. The FERET evaluation methodology for face-recognition algorithms. IEEE Transations on Pattern Analysis and Machine Intelligence 22(10): 1090-1104, 2000.
10. W. Zhao, R. Chellappa, A. Rosenfeld, and P.J. Phillips, (2000), "Face Recognition: A Literature Survey," UMD CAR Technical Report CAR-TR 948.
11. LeiZhang, Stan Z. Li, ZhiYiQu, Xiangsheng Huang. Boosting Local Feature Based Classifiers for Face Recognition. In proceedings of the IEEE conference on Computer Vision on Pattern Recognition, 2003.
12. Ahmad Darabiha, Jonathan Rose, W.James Maclean. Video-Rate Stereo Depth Measurement on Programmable Hardware. In proceedings of the IEEE conference on Computer Vision on Pattern Recognition, 2003.
13. K.Messer, J.Matas, J.Kittler, J.Luettin, and G.Maitre, "XM2VTSDB: The Extended M2VTS Database". Processings of Internatinal Conference on Audio- and Video-Based Person Authentication. P. 72-77, 1999.
14. L.F. Chen, H.Y.M. Liao, J.C.Lin, M.T.Ko, and G.J.Yu, "A New LDA-based Face Recognition System Which Can Solve the Small Sample Size Problem", Pattern Recognition, Vol. 33, No. 10, 2000
15. Wei Liu, Yunhong Wang, Stan Z. Li, Tieniu Tan. Null Space-based Kernel Fisher Discriminant Analysis for Face Recognition. IEEE International Conference on Automatic Face and Gesture Recognition(FG), May. 2004.
16. Peter N.Belhumer, Joao P.Hespanha, and David J.Kriegman. "Eigenfaces vs. Fisherfaces: Recognition using Class Specfic Linear Projection". IEEE trans. On PAMI, Vol. 19, No.7, pp. 711-720, July 1997.
17. Xiaogang Wang and Xiaoou Tang. Random Sampling LDA for Face Recognition. In proceedings of the IEEE conference on Computer Vision on Pattern Recognition, 2004.
18. S.Z. Li, X.W. Hou, and H.J. Zhang. "Learning Spatially Localized, Part-Based Representation". IEEE Conf. on Computer Vision and Pattern Recognition, 2001.

Online Feature Selection Using Mutual Information for Real-Time Multi-view Object Tracking

Alex Po Leung and Shaogang Gong

Department of Computer Science,
Queen Mary, University of London, London, E1 4NS
{alex, sgg}@dcs.qmul.ac.uk

Abstract. It has been shown that features can be selected adaptively for object tracking in changing environments [1]. We propose to use the variance of Mutual Information [2] for online feature selection to acquire reliable features for tracking by making use of the images of the tracked object in previous frames to refine our model so that the refined model after online feature selection becomes more robust. The ability of our method to pick up reliable features in real time is demonstrated with multi-view object tracking. In addition, the projective warping of 2D features is used to track 3D objects in non-frontal views in real time. Transformed 2D features can approximate relatively flat object structures such as the two eyes in a face. In this paper, approximations to the transformed features using weak perspective projection are derived. Since features in non-frontal views are computed on-the-fly by projective transforms under weak perspective projection, our framework requires only frontal-view training samples to track objects in multiple views.

1 Introduction

Much effort has been made to solve the problem of real-time object tracking over the years. However, tracking algorithms still suffer from fundamental problems including drifts away from targets [4] (partially due to change of viewpoint), inability to adapt to changes of object appearance, dependence on the first frame for template matching [5], instability to track objects under deformations (e.g. deformed contours), the inefficiency of Monte Carlo simulations for temporal tracking [6], and reliance on gradients by active contours [7], i.e. problems with similar intensities on the background and the object, or high gradient edges on the object itself. These problems are due to the complexity of the object dynamics. We also have to deal with difficult tracking conditions which include illumination changes, occlusions, changes of viewpoint, moving cameras and non-translational object motions like zooming and rotation.

Recent techniques use more complex and descriptive representations for tracking [8], [9], [10], [11]. A more descriptive representation may reduce the dependency on temporal information for tracking. There are a number of advantages to use a more descriptive representation. It makes tracking more robust in cluttered scenes. Less constrained physical state trajectories such as those containing discontinuities may also be tracked. If the representation can encode the appearance of the object more discriminatively, it allows the tracking of objects largely relying on framewise detections without

W. Zhao, S. Gong, and X. Tang (Eds.): AMFG 2005, LNCS 3723, pp. 184–197, 2005.

much temporal analysis, such as Viola-Jones detector-based tracking [8]. However, it is both difficult and expensive to obtain statistics to build a 3D model for object detection or tracking while 2D appearance models such as [17], [3], [9] and [11] have been very successful. When multi-views are considered, a huge amount of data is needed for each view for the training for a particular object. Such a huge dataset is impractical to create and it is also computationally expensive to train such a multi-view model. It is hard to obtain thousands of samples in each view and train a system for weeks or even months to track a particular object.

In this paper, a technique to track non-rigid objects in changing views with only frontal-view training samples is developed. Non-frontal views are deduced from frontal-view samples by geometric transformations. Using weak perspective projection, our method can track objects with a roughly flat surface such as faces or cars. It is obvious that, even for a roughly flat surface, there could be some uneven structures such as the nose on a face. We further use Mutual Information for online feature selection to acquire reliable features which are the relatively flat in our case. Our implementation picks up flat features in real time for multi-view object tracking.

Haar-like features selected by AdaBoost [3] can model non-rigid objects under different lighting conditions. We explore the possibility to devise a tracking algorithm using Haar-like features selected by AdaBoost as the representation [3]. Kalman filters are adopted to track the state variables after projective warping in every frame. They are used to temporally confine the parameter space of the transform. Our tracker is able to track non-rigid objects and the initialization of tracking is completely automatic. A single appearance model for both detection and tracking means a smooth transition from detection to tracking. No assumption on color is made in our model.

In the rest of this paper, Section 2 presents our proposed methods to compute warped Haar-like features. A technique for online feature selection using Mutual Information is proposed in Section 3. Section 4 presents experiments to test our proposed framework. Conclusions and future work are given in Section 5.

2 Projective Warping of Rectangle Features

Viola and Jones [3] make use of an intermediate representation for images called the integral image or summed-area table [12] to obtain the sum of pixel values for rectangle features with no more than four array references. The integral image is vital to computational efficiency for computing rectangle features. However, features are no longer rectangular after projective transforms. Therefore, we cannot calculate the features directly from the integral image. We propose to use a generalization of the method to calculate the features while we can still use the integral image. The generalization was proposed originally by Glassner [13] for texture mapping. It computes the average pixel value within a quadrilateral to an arbitrary degree of accuracy using the integral image with additional computation depending on the accuracy required. Glassner approximates a non-rectangular shape by rectangles. Two methods can be used to do this: additive and subtractive synthesis. Arbitrarily accurate features can be obtained and the integral image can still be used to retain the efficiency of the original appearance model.

An alternative way is to approximate projective transforms. This method makes the computation much more efficient. A planar projective transformation is a transformation with eight free parameters. A search in the parameter space could be computationally very expensive. An advantage to approximate projective transforms is to reduce the dimensionality of the parameter space. High dimensionality leads to expensive computation and sparsity of data which prevents the search from finding the correct set of parameters. A common approach is to approximate projective transforms by considering weak perspective projection such as planar affine transforms. For a planar affine transform, the number of free parameters is reduced from eight to six.

2.1 Approximating Projective Transforms

We may use weak perspective projection to approximate the perspective projection of rectangle features such as Haar-like features. Let us consider a rectangle feature with corners P_i' where $i = 1$ for the top left, 2 for the top right, 3 for the bottom right and 4 for the bottom left.

$$P_i = R_o P_i', \tag{1}$$

where $R_o = R_{o1}(\alpha)R_{o2}(\beta)R_{o3}(\gamma)$ is the rotation of the object and P_i are the corners after rotating the feature. We consider tracking the out-of-plane rotations of an object (i.e. pitch and yaw):

$$P_i = R_{o1}(\alpha)R_{o2}(\beta)P_i'. \tag{2}$$

The rotational matrix R_o for the object rotation with pitch and yaw is $R_{o_1}(\alpha)R_{o_2}(\beta) =$

$$\begin{bmatrix} cos\beta & 0 & sin\beta \\ sin\alpha sin\beta & cos\alpha & -sin\alpha cos\beta \\ -cos\alpha sin\beta & sin\alpha & cos\alpha cos\beta \end{bmatrix}.$$

The corner of a rectangle feature after the pitch and yaw rotations in world coordinates is, therefore,

$$X_w = cos\beta X_w', \tag{3}$$

$$Y_w = sin\alpha sin\beta X_w' + cos\alpha Y_w', \tag{4}$$

where (X_w', Y_w') is the corner before rotations in world coordinates. Note that we rotate the object symmetrically by locating it on the x-y plane and its center to be in the origin in world coordinates so $Z_w' = 0$ and, under weak perspective,

$$\bar{Z}_w \approx 0. \tag{5}$$

A rectangle feature can be on any part of the object. Thus, $\bar{Z}_w$ is not exactly zero. In homogeneous coordinates, the matrix equation of perspective projections can be written

$$\begin{bmatrix} x_1 \\ x_2 \\ x_3 \end{bmatrix} = M \begin{bmatrix} X_w \\ Y_w \\ Z_w \\ 1 \end{bmatrix},$$

where $x = \frac{x_1}{x_3}, y = \frac{x_2}{x_3}$ are in image coordinates and

$$M = \begin{bmatrix} -fr_{11} & -fr_{12} & -fr_{13} & fR_1^T T \\ -fr_{21} & -fr_{22} & -fr_{23} & fR_2^T T \\ r_{31} & r_{32} & r_{33} & -R_3^T T \end{bmatrix}.$$

where R_i, $i = 1, 2, 3$, is a three dimensional vector formed by the i-th row of the matrix R. Under weak perspective projection,

$$x_{wp} = \frac{x_1}{x_3} \approx \frac{fR_1^T(T - P_w)}{R_3^T(\bar{P}_w - T)},$$

$$y_{wp} = \frac{x_2}{x_3} \approx \frac{fR_2^T(T - P_w)}{R_3^T(\bar{P}_w - T)}.$$

Let $R = I$, i.e. there is no rotation between the world coordinates and the camera coordinates. Thus,

$$x_{wp} \approx -\frac{f(X_w - T_X)}{\bar{Z}_w - T_Z}, \qquad y_{wp} \approx -\frac{f(Y_w - T_Y)}{\bar{Z}_w - T_Z}.$$

Using Equation 5, a corner in image coordinates under weak perspective projection is then

$$P_{i_{wp}} = \begin{bmatrix} \dfrac{f(X_w - T_X)}{T_Z} & \dfrac{f(Y_w - T_Y)}{T_Z} & f \end{bmatrix}^T. \tag{6}$$

By combining Equations 3, 4 and 6, a corner after the rotations of the object becomes

$$P_{i_{wp}} = \begin{bmatrix} \dfrac{f(cos\beta X_w' - T_X)}{T_Z} \\ \dfrac{f(sin\alpha sin\beta X_w' + cos\alpha Y_w' - T_Y)}{T_Z} \\ f \end{bmatrix}$$

under weak perspective projection in image coordinates. Let us assume there is only the pitch rotation or the yaw rotation and the two rotations don't occur at the same time. That means either $\alpha = 0$ or $\beta = 0$. So, $sin\alpha sin\beta X_w' = 0$. In reality, especially for face tracking, it is natural to assume the object to rotate either with the pitch or the yaw. Therefore, when α becomes large, $\beta \approx 0$, or when β becomes large, $\alpha \approx 0$. Hence, $sin\alpha sin\beta X_w' \approx 0$ and

$$P_{i_{wp}} = \begin{bmatrix} \dfrac{f(cos\beta X_w' - T_X)}{T_Z} & \dfrac{f(cos\alpha Y_w' - T_Y)}{T_Z} & f \end{bmatrix}^T.$$

Notice that, since x_{wp} in the above is independent of Y_w' and y_{wp} independent of X_w' after rotations, a rectangle feature after rotations is still rectangular under weak perspective. The width and height of the rectangle feature after rotations in image coordinates are

$$x_{2_{wp}} - x_{1_{wp}} = \frac{f\,cos\beta(X_{2_w}' - X_{1_w}')}{T_Z}, \text{ and}$$

$$y_{1_{wp}} - y_{4_{wp}} = \frac{f\,cos\alpha(Y'_{1_w} - Y'_{4_w})}{T_Z}.$$

The aspect ratio of the rectangle feature η after the rotations α and β becomes $\frac{cos\beta}{cos\alpha}\eta_0$, where $\eta_0 = (X'_{2_w} - X'_{1_w})/(Y'_{1_w} - Y'_{4_w})$ is the aspect ratio before rotations.

This shows that, under weak perspective projection, the projective warping of a rectangle feature can be approximated by simply varying the aspect ratio of the rectangle feature. It gives us an extremely efficient means to track a rotating object. Only the aspect ratio η, the scale s and the centroid location (x_l, y_l) need to be tracked.

3   Feature Selection

It is both difficult and expensive to obtain statistics to build a 3D model for object detection or tracking. For face detection and tracking, different people have their own 3D face shapes. 2D appearance models cannot be trained easily to cope with view variations due to both the lack of the huge amount of labelled data for multi-views and the computational cost of training.

We use projective warping to transform learned Haar-like features. However, not all features are roughly flat. Therefore, the warping can introduce tracking errors due to the linearity of projective transformation if a measure of feature "goodness" is not evaluated on-the-fly. The best features which are approximately flat need be selected in real time after projective transforms have been made. We make use of the images of the object which has been tracked in previous frames to refine our model so that the refined model after online feature selection becomes more robust to track the object in different views.

3.1   The Mutual Information

We use Mutual Information to select approximately flat features which should be reliable for projective warping as the object rotates. The mutual information measures the statistical dependence between two variables. It has been shown to be a very effective measure for selecting a small set of relevant features from a large set of potential features very quickly [16].

We have a set of features selected by AdaBoost for objects in single view. Redundancy between features is not considered because redundancy is eliminated during the AdaBoost training. Hence, for computational efficiency, we simply use the mutual information instead of the conditional mutual information [16] considered to take into account redundancy between features. For continuous probability distributions, the mutual information is defined as

$$\mathcal{I}(i) = \int_{x_i} \int_y p(x_i, y) log \frac{p(x_i, y)}{p(x_i)p(y)} dx dy.$$

It is hard and inefficient to estimate the continuous distributions $p(x_i, y)$, $p(x_i)$ and $p(y)$ [18] for Feature i. Instead of estimating the distributions of the features directly, we use the output of the weak classifiers [3]. The statistical dependence of the weak classifer output of a feature and the output of the AdaBoost cascade [3] is determined by the mutual information. Both of the outputs are Boolean values so we can use the discrete form of the mutual information $I(i) =$

$$\sum_{x_i} \sum_{y} P(X = x_i, Y = y) log \frac{P(X = x_i, Y = y)}{P(X = x_i)P(Y = y)}.$$

Given a finite training set, one using frequency counts can only obtain an estimate of the mutual information as follows:

$$\hat{I}(i) = \frac{log\ n}{n} \sum_{x_i y} n_{x_i y} log \frac{n_{x_i y}}{n_{x_i} n_y},$$

where n is the total number of occurrences and $n_{x_i y}$, n_{x_i} and n_y are respectively the numbers of occurrences of the pair (x_i, y), x_i and y. Hutter [2] obtained the distribution, expectation value and variance of the mutual information by using a Bayesian approach. The expectation value defined as follows containing a correction term, $\frac{(r-1)(s-1)}{2n}$, is a more accurate estimate for the mutual information:

$$E\{I(i)\} = \sum_{x_i y} \frac{n_{x_i y}}{n} log \frac{n_{x_i y} n}{n_{x_i} n_y} + \frac{(r-1)(s-1)}{2n} + O(n^{-2}).$$

When the tracked face is frontal, all features learned by AdaBoost are almost equally discriminative. However, the more the face rotates, the lower the mutual information of an uneven feature gets due to the linearity of projective transformation. On the contrary, for an ideally flat feature, the mutual information remains the same as the face rotates. Thus, as we transform the features geometrically under weak perspective, features relatively flat are more stable for tracking and, thus, associate with small variations in the mutual information (i.e. small variances) when the view is changing. Instead of finding a set of features with the largest mutual information, we should look for a set of features with the smallest corresponding variances of the mutual information so that features more stable and, therefore, flat are selected. To measure the stability of a feature, the variance of the mutual information [2] is $Var\{I(i)\} =$

$$\frac{1}{n} \sum_{x_i y} \frac{n_{x_i y}}{n} \left(log \frac{n_{x_i y} n}{n_{x_i} n_y} \right)^2 - \frac{1}{n} \left(\sum_{x_i y} \frac{n_{x_i y}}{n} log \frac{n_{x_i y} n}{n_{x_i} n_y} \right)^2$$

$$+ O(n^{-2}).$$

It to the order of n^{-1} can be written

$$\frac{(log\ n)^2}{n^2} \left(\sum_{x_i y} n_{x_i y} \left(log \frac{n_{x_i y}}{n_{x_i} n_y} \right)^2 \right.$$

$$\left. - \frac{1}{n} \left(\sum_{x_i y} n_{x_i y} log \frac{n_{x_i y}}{n_{x_i} n_y} \right)^2 \right).$$

When we compare the variances of the mutual information of the features, the scaling factor $\frac{(log\ n)^2}{n^2}$ can be ingored. Thus, to select the most reliable features, we compare

$$\sum_{x_i y} n_{x_i y}\left(log\frac{n_{x_i y}}{n_{x_i}n_y}\right)^2 - \frac{1}{n}\left(\sum_{x_i y} n_{x_i y}log\frac{n_{x_i y}}{n_{x_i}n_y}\right)^2.$$

In other words, we select the most reliable or stable features by picking up the smallest corresponding variances of the mutual information of the features. Additionally, for the strong classifier of AdaBoost, we set the weight of Feature i, $\alpha_i = 0$ to reject Feature i so that the weights of the majority vote remain the same except for the rejected features.

4   Experimental Results

We use the MIT-CBCL face dataset [14] which consists of 6,977 cropped images (2,429 faces and 4,548 nonfaces). The resolution of the images is 19×19 and slightly lower than 24×24 used by Viola and Jones [3].

After the Viola-Jones detector initializes our tracker, four Kalman filters are separately used to track the aspect ratio η, the scale s and the centroid location of the object (x_l, y_l). A 5-stage cascade of AdaBoost [3] is used in our experiments. There are only 127 features in the 5 stages. The 5 stages separately compute 2, 7, 20, 50 and 50 features.

Experiment 1 (see Figure 1) shows a video (Video Sequence 1) with $|\beta| < 90°$. It shows that faces with relatively large $|\beta|$ could also be tracked. It is clear that the side views share some common features with the frontal view after projective transforms. Experiment 2 (Figure 2) shows tracking a non-frontal male face outdoors with a

Fig. 1. Experiment 1 - Tracking a non-frontal female face in real-time. The figure shows example images from an indoor sequence (Video Sequence 1).

Fig. 2. Experiment 2 - Tracking a non-frontal male face in real-time. The figure shows example images from an outdoor sequence with a moving hand-held camera (Video Sequence 2).

Table 1. Comparisons of Our Experiments

Experiment Number	MI Feature Selection Used	Warping Used	Video Sequence Number	Number of Frames Tracked
1	Yes	Yes	1	500 (End of Sequence)
2	Yes	Yes	2	526 (End of Sequence)
3	No	Yes	1	431 (Background)
4	No	No	1	17 (Non-Frontal View)
5	No	Yes	2	499 (Partial Occlusion)
6	No	No	2	141 (Non-Frontal View)

moving hand-held camera (Video Sequence 2). Both experiments demonstrate that our tracker can track deformable objects from different viewpoints, i.e. faces with different expressions in different views in this case. In order to evaluate the performance of our

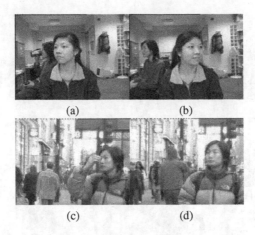

(a)   (b)

(c)   (d)

Fig. 3. Notice that all tracking failures in our experiments are due to the fact that no subwindow is classified to be a face in several consecutive frames. (a) and (c) show the failure of the tracker after tracking respectively 431 frames in Experiment 3 due to the background and 499 frames in Experiment 5 due to a partial occlusion. No feature selection is used. The tracker is significantly less robust without online MI feature selection. In (b) and (d), Experiment 4 and Experiment 6 show the failure of the tracker due to view changes after respectively tracking 17 frames and 141 frames. In Experiments 4 and 6, neither feature selection nor geometric transformation is used. The tracker is only able to track very few frames in the sequences without online MI feature selection and geometric transformation.

Fig. 4. Experiment 7 - Two trackers are initiated to track both the person in the foreground and the person wearing glasses in the background. The resolution of the face in the background is approximately 19×19 as shown in the magnified image. The tracker loses the face in the last frame due to the large quantization errors of projective warping when the out-of-plane rotation angle β is large with the low resolution.

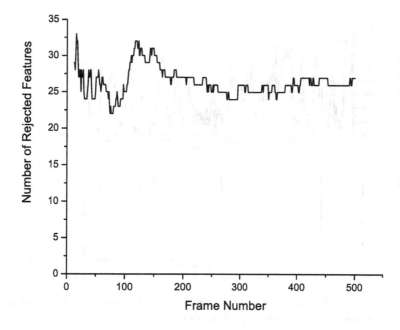

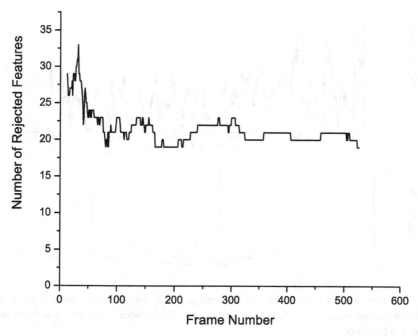

Fig. 5. In Experiment 1 (top figure) and Experiment 2 (bottom figure), the number of features rejected by the variance of the mutual information becomes stabilized after approximately the initial two hundred frames

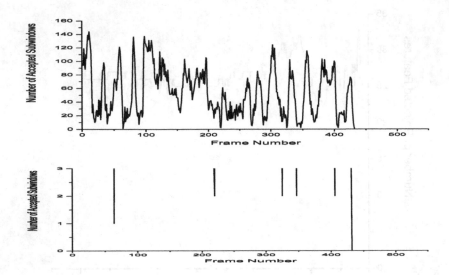

Fig. 6. The above are the same figure with different scales. In Experiment 3, the tracker without online MI feature selection loses the face at Frame 432.

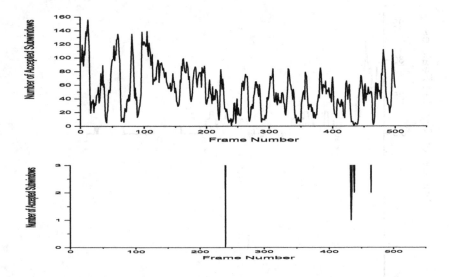

Fig. 7. The above are the same figure with different scales. In Experiment 1, the number of accepted subwindows is much less likely to go below 3 than it is without online MI feature selection as shown in Figure 6.

warping method and the proposed Mutual Information (MI) feature selection technique, additional four experiments (3, 4, 5 and 6) are performed using the two videos used in Experiment 1 and Experiment 2. Figure 3 shows tracking failures in our experiments

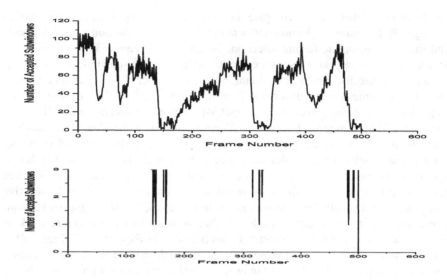

Fig. 8. The above are the same figure with different scales. In Experiment 5, the tracker without online MI feature selection loses the face at Frame 500.

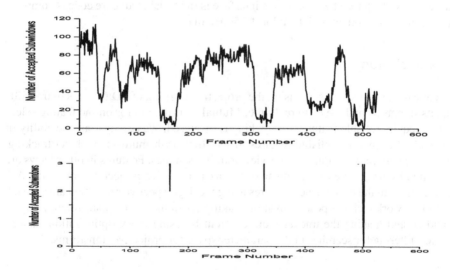

Fig. 9. The above are the same figure with different scales. In Experiment 2, the number of accepted subwindows is much less likely to go below 3 than it is without online MI feature selection as shown in Figure 8.

and Table 1 shows the comparisons of those experiments. In Figure 5, the number of features rejected by the variance of the mutual information is shown to be stabilized after the initial two hundred frames in Experiments 1 and 2. Furthermore, the number of subwindows accepted by the cascade of AdaBoost, to a certain extent, indicates the stability of the tracker. So, we compare the numbers of subwindows accepted during tracking with MI feature selection and without MI feature selection to better understand the effect of online feature selection. Besides, since Figure 3 shows all of the tracking failures in our experiments are due to the fact that no subwindow is classified to be a face, we are also interested in seeing when the number of subwindows classified to be a face becomes low. Figures 6 and 7 are the plots of the numbers of subwindows accepted during tracking respectively without MI feature selection and with MI feature selection for Video Sequence 1. Moreover, Figures 8 and 9 are the plots of the numbers of subwindows accepted during tracking respectively without MI feature selection and with MI feature selection for Video Sequence 2. We found that, when the number of subwindows becomes zero, the tracker does not necessarily fail because of the Kalman filters. However, when the number of subwindows becomes zero in several consecutive frames, the tracker usually fails. As we can see in Figures 6, 7, 8 and 9, the tracker with our proposed online MI feature selection method is much less likely to lose track of the face when the number of subwindows goes below 3. In Experiment 7 (Figure 4), a tracker is initiated to track a person wearing glasses in the background. The resolution of the face is approximately 19×19 in order to evaluate tracking with low-resolution images. Our tracker can track low-resolution faces provided that the out-of-plane rotation angle β is not very large to avoid high quantization noise.

In our current experiments, the tracking frame rate is 7.4 frames per second with the frame size 320×240. The code for the interface is in Matlab. Our core code is compiled by gcc on Cygwin on an AMD Athlon 1.68GHz machine.

5   Conclusion

We have demostrated a system using the projective warping of 2D features to track 3D objects in non-frontal views in real time. Mutual Information for online feature selection to acquire reliable features for tracking is proposed. We demonstrate the ability of our method to pick up reliable features in real time with multi-view object tracking. Our framework requires only frontal-view training samples. Features in other views are computed by projective transforms under weak perspective projection on-the-fly. Approximations to the transformed features using weak perspective projection are derived.

Future work includes pose estimation making use of the out-of-plane rotation angles α and β, and making the tracker more efficient by using noisy optimization such as implicit filtering for searches in the parameter space for projective transforms.

References

1. R. Collins, Y. Liu and M. Leordeanu, "On-Line Selection of Discriminative Tracking Features," *PAMI*, 2005.
2. M. Hutter, "Distribution of Mutual Information", *Advances in Neural Information Processing Systems*, 14 (2002) 399-406.
3. P. Viola and M. Jones, "Robust real-time object detection," *IJCV*, 2002.
4. I. Matthews, T. Ishikawa and S. Baker, "The Template Update Problem," *PAMI(26)*, No. 6, 2004, pp. 810-815.

5. F. Jurie and M. Dhome, "Hyperplane Approximation for Template Matching," *IEEE PAMI 24(7)*, 996-1000, 2002.
6. S. Arulampalam, S. Maskell, N. Gordon and T. Clapp, "A tutorial on particle filters for on-line non-linear/non-gaussian bayesian tracking," *Transaction of Signal Processing*, 50(2):174-188, 2002.
7. M. Isard and A. Blake, "CONDENSATION – conditional density propagation for visual tracking," *IJCV*, 29, 1, 5–28, (1998).
8. G. Shakhnarovich, P. A. Viola and B. Moghaddam, "A Unified Learning Framework for Real-Time Face Detection and Classification," *IEEE FG*, pp. 14-21, May 2002.
9. S. Avidan, "Support Vector Tracking," *PAMI(26)*, No. 8, August 2004, pp. 1064-1072.
10. O. Williams, A. Blake and R. Cipolla, "A Sparse Probabilistic Learning Algorithm for Real-Time Tracking," *ICCV*, Nice, France, 2003.
11. M. J. Black and A. Jepson, "EigenTracking: Robust matching and tracking of articulated objects using a view-based representation," *ICCV*, 26(1), pp. 63-84, 1998.
12. F. Crow, "Summed-Area Tables for Texture Mapping," *SIGGRAPH*, Pages 207-212, July, 1984.
13. A. Glassner, "Adaptive Precision in Texture Mapping," *SIGGRAPH*, 20, 4, August 1986, pp. 297-306.
14. CBCL Face Database #1, MIT Center For Biological and Computation Learning, http://www.ai.mit.edu/projects/cbcl.
15. P. Sinha, "Qualitative representations for recognition," *In Lecture Notes in Computer Science, Springer-Verlag*, LNCS 2525, pp 249-262, 2002.
16. F. Fleuret, "Fast Binary Feature Selection with Conditional Mutual Information", *Journal of Machine Learning Research*, 5 (2004) 1531-1555.
17. H. Schneiderman and T. Kanade, "Object Detection Using the Statistics of Parts", *IJCV*, v.56 n.3, p.151-177, February-March 2004.
18. K. Torkkola, "Feature Extraction by Non-Parametric Mutual Information Maximization", *Journal of Machine Learning Research*, 3(Mar):1415-1438, 2003.

A Binary Decision Tree Implementation
of a Boosted Strong Classifier

S. Kevin Zhou

Siemens Corporate Research, Integrated Data Systems Department,
755 College Road East, Princeton, NJ 08540
{kzhou}@scr.siemens.com

Abstract. Viola and Jones [1] proposed the influential rapid object detection algorithm. They used AdaBoost to select from a large pool a set of simple features and constructed a strong classifier of the form $\{\sum_j \alpha_j h_j(x) \geq \theta\}$ where each $h_j(x)$ is a binary weak classifier based on a simple feature. In this paper, we construct, using statistical detection theory, a binary decision tree from the strong classifier of the above form. Each node of the decision tree is just a weak classifier and the knowledge of the coefficients α_j is no longer needed. Also, the binary tree has a lot of early exits. As a result, we achieve an automatic speedup that always makes the rapid Viola and Jones algorithm rapider.

1 Introduction

Viola and Jones [1] proposed the influential rapid object detection algorithm. There are three key contributions of the Viola and Jones algorithm. The first is to use the integral image that enables fast computation of Harr-like simple features [2]. The second is to invoke the AdaBoost algorithm [3] to select a small set of crucial features from a large set. The final contribution is to train a cascade of strong classifiers that eliminates negative examples as quickly as possible.

A strong classifier is constructed based on weak classifiers. A weak classifier $h_j(x)$, consisting of a simple feature $f_j(x)$, a threshold θ_j, and a parity p_j indicating the direction of the inequality sign, produces a binary decision

$$h_j(x) = \begin{cases} 1 \text{ if } p_j f_j(x) < p_j \theta_j \\ 0 \text{ otherwise} \end{cases} \tag{1}$$

The final strong classifier is $h(x)$ of the following form

$$h(x) = \begin{cases} 1 \text{ if } g(x) = \sum_{j=1}^{J} \alpha_j h_j(x) \geq \frac{1}{2} \sum_{j=1}^{J} \alpha_j \\ 0 \text{ otherwise} \end{cases} \tag{2}$$

Following the spirit of the Viola and Jones algorithm [1], many variants and extensions have been proposed in the literature. Naturally, the Viola and Jones algorithm [1] can be modified in each of the three contributions.

- *Modifying the feature set.* Since the work of Viola and Jones [1], various new types of Harr-like have been proposed: diagonal features [4,5], rotated features [6],

W. Zhao, S. Gong, and X. Tang (Eds.): AMFG 2005, LNCS 3723, pp. 198–212, 2005.

center-surrounded features [6]. In the article of Zhang *et al.* [7], the Gabor wavelets features were used for face recognition. Lienhart *et al.* [8] even used small CART features.

- *Modifying the AdaBoost algorithm.* In Voila and Jones [9], the asymmetric AdaBoosting algorithm was proposed to handle the unbalanced nature of the positive and negative training sets. In the work by Li and Zhang [10], the FloatBoost algorithm was used as a substitute of AdaBoost to achieve an even lower classification error. The effect of three versions of AdaBoost (Discrete AdaBoost, Real AdaBoost, Gentle AdaBoost) were compared by Lienhart *et al.* in [8].
- *Modifying the cascade structure.* The cascade structure can be regarded as a degenerate decision tree. Full decision tree was trained by Li and Zhang [10] to perform multiview face detection more efficiently. A similar detection tree approach were found in the work of Lienhart *et al.* [11]. Also, in [12], Sun *et al.* trained the cascade while taking in account perturbation bias.

However, the core idea of using the strong classifier that consists of weak classifiers remains intact. In this paper, we examine the strong classifier in detail. In particular, we investigate the computational speed of the strong classifiers themselves, assuming that they have been trained by some means.

1.1   A General Form of the Strong Classifier

We focus on a very general form of the strong classifier that arises from the AdaBoost algorithm. It is worth emphasizing that our analysis is not only applicable to the Viola and Jones detection algorithm, and can be used in a wide range of applications where the AdaBoost algorithm is used.

- The weak classifier can be of an arbitrary form.

$$h_j(x) = \begin{cases} T & \text{if certain condition holds} \\ F & \text{otherwise} \end{cases} \tag{3}$$

In the above, the weak classifier produces a binary decision of true (+1) or false (0).
- The strong classifier threshold is adjustable for various purposes [1]. We denote the arbitrary threshold as θ. As mentioned above, usually the strong classifier threshold obtained from an AdaBoost algorithm is set to $\frac{1}{2}\sum_{j=1}^{J}\alpha_j$.
- Because of the additive nature of the weighted sum $g(x) = \sum_{j=1}^{J}\alpha_j h_j(x)$, without loss of generality, we can always pre-sort the weights α_i such that $\alpha_1 > \cdots > \alpha_J > 0$. We will show that the tie case such as $\alpha_j = \alpha_{j+1}$ is a special case of our treatment and can be easily handled by merging two cases. The fact that $\alpha_j > 0$ arises from the AdaBoost algorithm. According to the AdaBoost algorithm [1], $\alpha_j = log\frac{1-e_j}{e_j}$ where e_j is the probability of error. Usually, e_j is smaller than 1/2 and hence $\alpha_j > 0$. If $e_j \geq 1/2$, there is no need for further boosting because adding this feature only degrades the final performance.

Now, the strong classifier has a very general form

$$h(x) = \begin{cases} T & \text{if } g(x) = \sum_{j=1}^{J}\alpha_j h_j(x) \geq \theta \\ F & \text{otherwise} \end{cases} \tag{4}$$

A further generalization is to allow the functions $h_j(x)$ to output discrete values (not necessarily just a binary decision of true and false). However, this is not considered here.

1.2   Proposed Approach

Calling upon the classical detection theory [13,14], we will show that the strong classifier of the above form (4) is equivalent to a binary decision tree. To be more exact, given a strong classifier, we are able to construct a binary decision tree that has the same detection and false alarm rates. To have an intuition how it works, by simply treating the weak classifiers $h_j(x)$ as boolean inputs, one can arrive at a boolean output for $h(x)$. In other words, we can easily construct a lookup table for a strong classifier. It turns out that the lookup table can be summarized by a binary decision tree.

The binary decision tree possesses three properties. First, each node of the binary decision tree is just a weak classifier and its binary decision guides what to proceed. The second property is that, once the tree is constructed, the knowledge of the coefficients α_j can be thrown away. So, there is no need to compute multiplications like $\alpha_j h_j(x)$ and sum up the terms $\alpha_j h_j(x)$. Third, the binary tree has a lot of early exits, which implies that only the weak classifiers before exit need evaluation. The above three properties guarantee an automatic speedup that always makes the *rapid* Viola and Jones algorithm even *rapider*.

The binary decision tree corresponding to the strong classifier should not be confused with the cascade of the strong classifiers since the latter is also treated as a degenerate binary decision tree with each node being a strong classifier. Our intention is to replace the strong classifier at each stage of the cascade with a binary decision tree, not the cascade structure. After replacing the strong classifiers at all stages, the cascade of strong classifiers can be regarded as a true binary decision tree with each node being a weak classifier. Also, the binary decision tree structure derived from the strong classifier does not prevent us from using a decision tree for the weak classifier as in [15]. In this case, we have a true decision tree corresponding to the boosted strong classifier.

In [16], Grossmann directly learned a decision tree that can be analyzed in the framework of Adaboost. He also observed that the tree structure reduces computational cost. We here propose a technique that converts a boosted strong classifier to a binary decision tree that improves computational speed as well.

1.3   Paper Organization

Sections 2 and 3 study the strong classifier with two weak classifiers and three weak classifiers, respectively. Many insights are derived from the detailed discussion. Section 4 addresses a general strong classifier with more than three weak classifiers. Section 5 presents the experiments.

Table 1. Rates for the weak classifier $h_j(x)$

	$p(h_j(x) = T)$	$p(h_j(x) = F)$
$x \in \mathcal{P}$	$1 - a_j$	a_j
$x \in \mathcal{N}$	b_j	$1 - b_j$

1.4 Notation

To simplify our analysis, we assume that all weak classifiers are statistically independent[1]. Further, we assume that each weak classifier $h_j(x)$ has its own detection rate $(1 - a_j)$ and false alarm rate b_j. Table 1 summarizes the rates associated with the weak classifier $h_j(x)$, where $\mathcal{P}$ denotes the positive set and $\mathcal{N}$ the negative set.

We use the notation $\langle \mathcal{S}_J \rangle$ to denote a strong classifier that combines J weak classifiers or simple refer to it as the strong classifier $\langle \mathcal{S}_J \rangle$. We are often interested in conducting a case study. We use the notation $\langle \mathcal{S}_{J,n} \rangle$ to denote the nth case of the strong classifier $\langle \mathcal{S}_J \rangle$, or simply refer to it as the strong classifier $\langle \mathcal{S}_{J,n} \rangle$.

Sometime we isolate, from a 'mother' strong classifier, a 'child' strong classifier that combines a subset of weak classifiers that belongs to the 'mother' strong classifier. Therefore, there is a need to specify the weak classifiers used by the 'child' strong classifier. We use the notation $\langle \mathcal{S}_{j,n} |_{\{\text{weak classifier IDs}\}} \rangle$. For example, the strong classifier $\langle \mathcal{S}_{2,3} |_{\{4,5\}} \rangle$ means the 3rd case of the 'child' strong classifier using two weak classifiers, the 4th and 5th ones, belonging to the 'mother' strong classifier.

2 Strong Classifier $\langle \mathcal{S}_2 \rangle$

We start from a simple case of combining $J = 2$ weak classifiers with $\alpha_1 > \alpha_2 > 0$. The possible $g(x)$ values are given in Table 2. Note that $\theta_{11} > \theta_{10} > \theta_{01} > \theta_{00}$. There are five cases of interests.

Table 2. Possible $g(x)$ values of combining $J = 2$ weak classifiers

$h_1(x)$	$h_2(x)$	$g(x)$
T	T	$\theta_{11} = \alpha_1 + \alpha_2$
T	F	$\theta_{10} = \alpha_1$
F	T	$\theta_{01} = \alpha_2$
F	F	$\theta_{00} = 0$

---

[1] It should be noted that we assumed the statistical independence among the weak classifiers for simplicity of illustration. The assumption of independence is only needed for calculating the detection and false alarm rates of the strong classifier. Therefore our case study analysis presented above still holds even when the weak classifiers are dependent. One evidence is that the ROC curve for strong classifier $\langle \mathcal{S}_2 \rangle$ always consists of five points, whether the two weak classifiers are independent or not.

Table 3. Rates for all five cases of the strong classifier $\langle S_2 \rangle$

$\langle S_{2,1} \rangle$	$p(h(x) = T)$	$p(h(x) = F)$
$x \in \mathcal{P}$	0	1
$x \in \mathcal{N}$	0	1
$\langle S_{2,2} \rangle$	$p(h(x) = T)$	$p(h(x) = F)$
$x \in \mathcal{P}$	$(1 - a_1)(1 - a_2)$	$a_1 + a_2 - a_1 a_2$
$x \in \mathcal{N}$	$b_1 b_2$	$1 - b_1 b_2$
$\langle S_{2,3} \rangle$	$p(h(x) = T)$	$p(h(x) = F)$
$x \in \mathcal{P}$	$1 - a_1$	a_1
$x \in \mathcal{N}$	b_1	$1 - b_1$
$\langle S_{2,4} \rangle$	$p(h(x) = T)$	$p(h(x) = F)$
$x \in \mathcal{P}$	$1 - a_1 a_2$	$a_1 a_2$
$x \in \mathcal{N}$	$b_1 + b_2 - b_1 b_2$	$(1 - b_1)(1 - b_2)$
$\langle S_{2,5} \rangle$	$p(h(x) = T)$	$p(h(x) = F)$
$x \in \mathcal{P}$	1	0
$x \in \mathcal{N}$	1	0

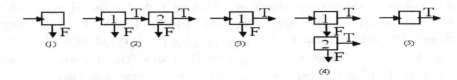

Fig. 1. The binary decision trees for all five cases of the strong classifier $\langle S_2 \rangle$

2.1   Case Study

Below, we examine each case separately. The detection and false alarm rates for all cases are listed in Table 3. The binary decision trees for all cases are shown in Figure 1.

- Strong classifier $\langle S_{2,1} \rangle$: $\theta_{11} < \theta$. This is an all-fail case, i.e., the strong classifier fails all possible x.
- Strong classifier $\langle S_{2,2} \rangle$: $\theta_{10} < \theta \le \theta_{11}$. The only way to pass the strong classifier is to pass both weak classifiers. Thus, the corresponding decision tree is just a cascade of two weak classifiers. Only when the first weak classifier is passed is the second weak classifier triggered.
- Strong classifier $\langle S_{2,3} \rangle$: $\theta_{01} < \theta \le \theta_{10}$. Passing the strong classifier is equivalent to passing the first weak classifier and the second weak classifier is completely useless! Hence, we automatically save the computation of evaluating the second weak classifier.
- Strong classifier $\langle S_{2,4} \rangle$: $\theta_{00} < \theta \le \theta_{01}$. The only way to fail the strong classifier is to fail both weak classifiers. Thus, the corresponding decision tree is also a cascade of two weak classifiers. However, only when the first weak classifier is failed is the second weak classifier triggered.
- Strong classifier $\langle S_{2,5} \rangle$: $\theta < \theta_{00}$. This is an all-pass case, i.e., the strong classifier passes all possible x.

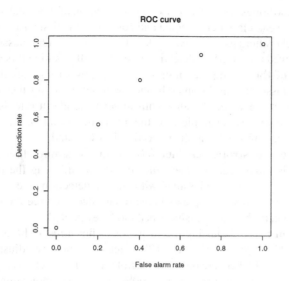

Fig. 2. A typical ROC curve for the strong classifier $\langle \mathcal{S}_2 \rangle$

Table 4. The XOR problem

$h_1(x)$	$h_2(x)$	$h(x)$
T	T	F
T	F	T
F	T	T
F	F	F

The above 5 cases can be summarized using a receiver operating characteristic (ROC) curve plotted in Figure 2 (with $a_1 = 0.2$, $a_2 = 0.3$, $b_1 = 0.4$, $b_2 = 0.5$). The ROC curve consists of a set of discrete points. As the detection rate increases, the false alarm rate increases too.

2.2 Discussion

The following issues are worthy of further clarification.

[XOR problem]. The XOR problem means that Table 4 or similar thing holds. The XOR problem might result in a very complicate binary decision tree so that there is no computational saving available. However, this cannot happen to the strong classifier $\langle \mathcal{S}_2 \rangle$ because, if the second row holds, then the $h(x)$ function in the first row must take a true value owing to the additive nature of the $g(x)$ function.

[Tie $\alpha_1 = \alpha_2$]. If $\alpha_1 = \alpha_2$, the strong classifier $\langle \mathcal{S}_{2,3} \rangle$ never exists. We only consider cases 1, 2, 4, and 5.

[Strong classifier threshold $\theta = \frac{1}{2}(\alpha_1 + \alpha_2)$]. When the strong classifier threshold is $\theta = \frac{1}{2}(\alpha_1 + \alpha_2)$, the strong classifier $\langle \mathcal{S}_{2,3} \rangle$ is applied, which means that the first stage of the Voila and Jones cascade that uses a combination of two weak classifiers can be replaced by one weak classifier. In Voila and Jones [1], the first strong classifier of a cascade of strong classifiers uses two weak classifiers and its strong classifier threshold is adjusted to achieved a near 100% detection rate. We will examine this point next.

[Design issue of the strong classifier $\langle S_{2,2} \rangle$]. In this strong classifier, the order of the two weak classifiers can be interchanged without affecting the final decision. In practice, we select the weak classifier with lower false alarm rate as the first one because this way the negative example exits the binary decision tree more quickly. For the positive example, both weak classifiers need to be evaluated.

[Design issue of the strong classifier $\langle S_{2,4} \rangle$]. In this strong classifier, the order of the two weak classifiers can be interchanged without affecting the final decision. In practice, we select the weak classifier with higher detection rate as the first one because this way the positive example exits the binary decision tree more quickly. For the negative example, both weak classifiers need to be evaluated.

[100% **detection rate**]. Adjusting the strong classifier threshold θ is equivalent to running on the ROC curve. To achieve a 100% detection rate by adjusting θ as suggested in [1], theoretically there are only one feasible way, that is, choosing the classifier $\langle S_{2,5} \rangle$. However, the false alarm rate is also 100% in this case, indicating that the classifier $\langle S_{2,5} \rangle$ is useless in practice. Therefore, adjusting the strong classifier threshold in principle is a dangerous practice to achieve 100% detection. The strong classifier $\langle S_{2,4} \rangle$ is the practical choice with the highest detection rate and moderate false alarm rate.

Ultimately, the detection rate of the strong classifier depends on the detection rates of the weak classifiers. If the weak classifier classifiers all have 100% detection rate, the strong classifiers from $\langle S_{2,2} \rangle$ to $\langle S_{2,4} \rangle$ all have 100% detection rate. In practice, we will choose the strong classifier $\langle S_{2,2} \rangle$ owing its lower false alarm rate and its early exit for negative examples. Therefore, adjusting the weak classifier thresholds is a more feasible approach to achieving 100% detection rate.

3   Strong Classifier $\langle S_3 \rangle$

We now consider combining $J = 3$ weak classifiers with $\alpha_1 > \alpha_2 > \alpha_3 > 0$. The possible $g(x)$ values are given in Table 5. Note that $\{\theta_{111}, \cdots, \theta_{000}\}$ are in a descending order except the order ambiguity between θ_{100} and θ_{011}. If $\alpha_1 > \alpha_2 + \alpha_3$, then $\theta_{100} > \theta_{011}$. There are ten cases of interests.

3.1   Case Study

Below, we examine each case separately. Similarly, we can compute the detection and false alarm rates for all cases. The binary decision trees for all cases are shown in Figure 3.

- Strong classifier $\langle S_{3,1} \rangle$: $\theta_{111} < \theta$. This is an all-fail case, i.e., the strong classifier fails all possible x.
- Strong classifier $\langle S_{3,2} \rangle$: $\theta_{110} < \theta \leq \theta_{111}$. The only way to pass the strong classifier is to pass all three weak classifiers. The strong classifier $\langle S_{3,2} \rangle$ is a cascade of three

Table 5. Possible $g(x)$ values of combining $J = 3$ weak classifiers

$h_1(x)$	$h_2(x)$	$h_3(x)$	$g(x)$
T	T	T	$\theta_{111} = \alpha_1 + \alpha_2 + \alpha_3$
T	T	F	$\theta_{110} = \alpha_1 + \alpha_2$
T	F	T	$\theta_{101} = \alpha_1 + \alpha_3$
T	F	F	$\theta_{100} = \alpha_1$
F	T	T	$\theta_{011} = \alpha_2 + \alpha_3$
F	T	F	$\theta_{010} = \alpha_2$
F	F	T	$\theta_{001} = \alpha_3$
F	F	F	$\theta_{000} = 0$

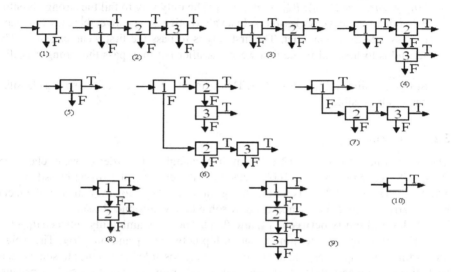

Fig. 3. The binary decision trees for all 10 cases of the strong classifier $\langle S_3 \rangle$

weak classifiers or a cascade of the first weak classifier and the strong classifier $\langle S_{2,2}|_{\{2,3\}} \rangle$.

- Strong classifier $\langle S_{3,3} \rangle$: $\theta_{101} < \theta \leq \theta_{110}$. The way to pass the strong classifier is to pass the first two weak classifiers. This reduces to the strong classifier $\langle S_{2,2}|_{\{1,2\}} \rangle$. An alternative way is to view the strong classifier $\langle S_{3,3} \rangle$ as a cascade of the first weak classifier and the strong classifier $\langle S_{2,3}|_{\{2,3\}} \rangle$.
- Strong classifier $\langle S_{3,4} \rangle$: $\max(\theta_{100}, \theta_{011}) < \theta \leq \theta_{101}$. The way to pass the strong classifier is to first pass the first weak classifier and then the strong classifier $\langle S_{2,4}|_{\{2,3\}} \rangle$. Therefore, the strong classifier $\langle S_{3,2} \rangle$ is a cascade of the first weak classifier and the strong classifier $\langle S_{2,4}|_{\{2,3\}} \rangle$.
- Strong classifier $\langle S_{3,5} \rangle$: $\min(\theta_{100}, \theta_{011}) < \theta \leq \max(\theta_{100}, \theta_{011})$ and $\theta_{100} = \max(\theta_{100}, \theta_{011})$. The way to pass the strong classifier is to simply pass the first weak classifier. Also, the strong classifier $\langle S_{3,5} \rangle$ can be viewed as a cascade of the first weak classifier and the strong classifier $\langle S_{2,5}|_{\{2,3\}} \rangle$.

- Strong classifier $\langle \mathcal{S}_{3,6} \rangle$: $\min(\theta_{100}, \theta_{011}) < \theta \leq \max(\theta_{100}, \theta_{011})$ and $\theta_{011} = \max(\theta_{100}, \theta_{011})$. There are two ways to pass the strong classifier. The first way is to pass the strong classifier $\langle \mathcal{S}_{3,4} \rangle$. The second is to first fail in the first weak classifier (this is allowed!) but then pass the strong classifier $\langle \mathcal{S}_{2,2} | \{2,3\} \rangle$.
- Strong classifier $\langle \mathcal{S}_{3,7} \rangle$: $\theta_{010} < \theta \leq \min(\theta_{100}, \theta_{011})$. There are two ways to pass the strong classifier. The first way is to pass the first weak classifier. The second is to first fail in the first weak classifier but then pass the strong classifier $\langle \mathcal{S}_{2,2} | \{2,3\} \rangle$.
- Strong classifier $\langle \mathcal{S}_{3,8} \rangle$: $\theta_{001} < \theta \leq \theta_{010}$. There are two ways to pass the strong classifier. The first way is to pass the first weak classifier. The second is to first fail in the first weak classifier but then pass the second weak classifier or the strong classifier $\langle \mathcal{S}_{2,3} | \{2,3\} \rangle$.
- *Strong classifier* $\langle \mathcal{S}_{3,9} \rangle$: $\theta_{000} < \theta \leq \theta_{001}$. The only way to fail the strong classifier is to fail all three weak classifiers. In an alternative perspective, there are two ways to pass the strong classifier. The first way is to pass the first weak classifier. The second is to first fail in the first weak classifier but then pass the strong classifier $\langle \mathcal{S}_{2,4} | \{2,3\} \rangle$.
- Strong classifier $\langle \mathcal{S}_{3,10} \rangle$: $\theta < \theta_{000}$. This is an all-pass case, i.e., the strong classifier passes all possible x.

3.2 Discussion

The same issues (such as XOR problem, interchanging the order of weak classifiers for specific strong classifiers, 100% detection rate, etc.) for the strong classifier $\langle \mathcal{S}_2 \rangle$ addressed in section 2.2 exists for the strong classifier $\langle \mathcal{S}_3 \rangle$. However, most of them can be similarly treated. Here we address only some newly introduced issues.

[**Order ambiguity between** θ_{100} **and** θ_{011}]. The order ambiguity between θ_{100} and θ_{011} arises from the undetermined relationship between α_1 and $\alpha_2 + \alpha_3$. The weight pre-sorting can only automatically fix orders of all possible $g(x)$ values to some extent (in fact sub-exponentially!). In practice, we would prefer the case $\theta_{100} > \theta_{011}$ because it provides a far simpler binary decision tree. However, the experimental results seldom present this. We will return to this point in section 4.

[**Recursive tree construction**]. As we have mentioned in the case study and illustrated in Figure 3, all the binary decision trees corresponding to the strong classifier $\langle \mathcal{S}_3 \rangle$ can be constructed as follows: The top node contains the first weak classifier, followed by the strong classifier $\langle \mathcal{S}_2 | \{2,3\} \rangle$ (with different case numbers though). In other words, we can construct the tree recursively. This idea applies to the strong classifier with an arbitrary value of J. We will examine this in detail in Section 4.

4   Strong Classifier $\langle \mathcal{S}_{J>3} \rangle$

A complete analysis of the strong classifier $\langle \mathcal{S}_{J>3} \rangle$ becomes tedious. Especially when J takes a very big value, the tree could be complex. Below, we present a general comprehension of the asymptotic behavior of the tree corresponding to the strong classifier $\langle \mathcal{S}_{J>3} \rangle$. We also address the same issue from an information theory perspective.

[**Number of cases**]. As we have seen before, the tree structure is completely determined by the weight coefficients α and the strong classifier threshold θ. A different choices of α and θ might yield a completely different tree. Unfortunately, the number of all possible trees (or cases) grows exponentially with the number of weak classifiers J. It roughly equals to $O(2^{J+1})$. This number can estimated as follows. If there is no order ambiguity, there are $O(2^J)$ cases (exactly $2^J + 1$ cases). The case with order ambiguity also grows as $O(2^J)$ because the unambiguous cases that can be eliminated by the condition $\alpha_1 > \ldots > \alpha_J > 0$ is $o(2^J)$. It should be noted that the case study is introduced for theoretic analysis only. In practice, when only one configuration of α and θ is available, there is no need to store all cases.

[**Tree construction**]. The tree for the strong classifier $\langle S_{J,n} \rangle$ can be constructed recursively, as illustrated in Figure 4. First test the first weak classifier. If true, test the next binary decision tree corresponding to the strong classifier $\langle S_{J-1,n_1} \rangle$ (with case number n_1); if false, test the next binary decision tree corresponding to $\langle S_{J-1,n_0} \rangle$ (with case number n_0). Therefore, at each node, we only need to remember two case numbers. Similarly, the tree can be constructed backward, starting from the nth weak classifier.

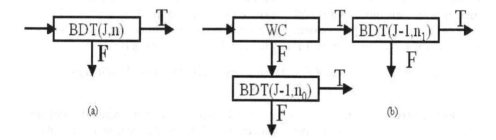

Fig. 4. Recursive construction of the decision tree. (a) Decision tree corresponding to the strong classifier $\langle S_J \rangle$. (b) The equivalent decision tree constructed using the first weak classifier followed two decision tree corresponding to the strong classifiers $\langle S_{J-1,n_1} \rangle$ and $\langle S_{J-1,n_0} \rangle$.

[**Tree complexity**]. It seems that the constructed tree can be rather complicated because it may exhaust all possible nodes of a binary decision tree. However, in practice, we found that many nodes disappears because of the additive nature of the strong classifier and there is no XOR problem.

[**Information**]. In summary, the decision tree is just another way of storing the same amount of information. Therefore, we did not gain or loss any information. To be more specific, the information of the strong classifier $\langle S_J \rangle$ lies in the J weighting coefficients α_j, the strong classifier threshold θ, and the comparison to determine the final classification result, whereas the information of the decision tree lies in the tree structure. Because of the discrete nature of the weak classifier responses (true or false), the binary decision tree encodes more than one configuration of the weights α and the threshold θ. Therefore, the binary decision trees partition the complete information space covering all possible configurations of weights α and strong classifier threshold θ into a finite number of subsets. Also, binary decision tree helps visualize and interpret the results.

5   Classification Experiment

We compared the binary decision tree implementation with other two methods. The default method is to first calculates the value $g(x)$ and then compares it with θ. The fast exit algorithm [12] utilized the additive nature of the function $g(x) = \sum_{j=1}^{J} \alpha_j h_j(x)$. Denote the sum up to k by $g_k(x) = \sum_{j=1}^{k} \alpha_j h_j(x) = g_{k-1}(x) + \alpha_k h_k(x)$. The fast exit algorithm uses the following two facts:

1. If $g_k(x)$ is already larger than the threshold θ, we can safely declare x as positive.
2. If $g_k(x) + \sum_{j=k+1}^{J} \alpha_j$ is already smaller than θ, we can safely declare x as negative.

The essence is to check at each weak classifier if we can exit the whole strong classifier quickly.

5.1   The First Experiment

In this experiment, we used 3724 frontal face patches of size 24×24 (in fact 1862 images with their mirrors) and 6231 negative examples sampled from natural images to boost a strong classifier consisting of 5 weak classifiers. Some training images are shown in Figure 6. This boosted strong classifier has the following form:

$$2.550h_1(x) + 1.606h_2(x) + 1.288h_3(x) + 1.274h_4(x) + 1.096h_5(x).$$

[**Exp. 1, strong classifier 1**]. When we take the strong classifier threshold as default, i.e. $\theta = 3.907$, we achieves a detection rate of 97.3% at the cost of a false alarm rate of 5.89% on the training data. The corresponding binary decision tree is shown in Figure 5(a).

[**Exp. 1, strong classifier 2**]. When adjusting the strong classifier threshold to pass all training positive samples, the threshold is set to $\theta = 1.287$ and the false alarm rate

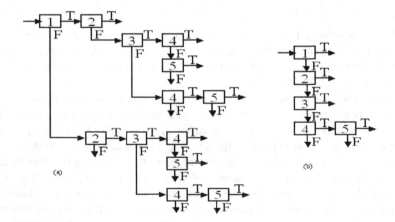

Fig. 5. Two binary decision trees corresponding the first stage strong classifier in the face detector with two different strong classifier thresholds

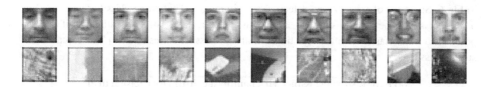

Fig. 6. Example of positives (the top row) and negatives (the bottom row) of size 24×24 in the training data set

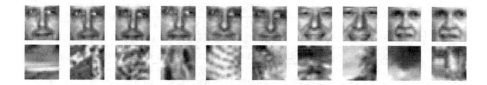

Fig. 7. Example of positives (the top row) and negatives (the bottom row) of size 24×24 in the first testing data set

Fig. 8. Two testing images of size 1024×768 in the second testing data set

increases to 82.4%! The corresponding binary decision tree is shown in Figure 5(b), which is nothing but the following: to fail the strong classifier is to fail the first 3 weak classifiers and then fail either of the 4th and 5th weak classifiers.

We used the above strong classifier to classify two test datasets. (i) The first testing data set contains 4858 positives (2429 images with their mirrors) and 8569 negatives. This data set is downloaded from the MIT CBCL website [17] and used in [18] for face detection. The original image size is 19×19 and we normalized it to 24×24 using a bicubic interpolation. Sample images in this testing data set are shown in Figure 7. Note that the face images are shifted, rotated, and scaled version of the same object that is not explicitly learned in the training stage. (ii) The second testing data set exhaustively sampled 7740000 negatives from 10 images of size 1042×768 known to be no face inside. Two such images are shown in Figure 8. This is used for testing negative rejection at a large scale.

Table 6. Summary of various face detection algorithms. (a) The strong classifier composed of 5 weak classifiers before adjusting the strong classifier threshold. (b) The strong classifier composed of 5 weak classifiers after adjusting the strong classifier threshold. (c) The cascade of 3 strong classifiers.

(a) Exp. 1, strong classifier 1	Default	Fast exit	Binary decision tree
Detection(train)	97.3%	97.3%	97.3%
False alarm (train)	5.89%	5.89%	5.89%
Duration	64.80 s	40.16 s	36.98 s
Detection (test1)	94.2%	94.2%	94.2%
False alarm (test1)	9.07%	9.07%	9.07%
Duration	26.91 s	16.86 s	15.17 s
False alarm (test2)	16.4%	16.4%	16.4%

(b) Exp. 1, strong classifier 2	Default	Fast exit	binary decision tree
Detection(train)	100%	100%	100%
False alarm (train)	82.4%	82.4%	82.4%
Duration	64.67 s	34.56 s	29.12 s
Detection (test1)	99.96%	99.96%	99.96%
False alarm (test1)	75.8%	75.8%	75.8%
Duration	26.88 s	17.59 s	15.93 s
False alarm (test2)	46.4%	46.4%	46.4%

(c) Exp. 2	Default	Fast exit	Binary decision tree
Detection(train)	99.98%	99.98%	99.98%
False alarm (train)	2.78%	2.78%	2.78%
Duration	991 s	561 s	86.8 s
Detection (test1)	98.0%	98.0%	98.0%
False alarm (test1)	8.41%	8.41%	8.41%
Duration	349 s	253 s	32.5 s
False alarm (test2)	12.3%	12.3%	12.3%

It is obvious from Table 6(a) and (b) that the binary decision tree is the fastest algorithm for the first dataset, almost two times faster than the default method. The fast exit algorithm is more efficient than the default method, only a bit slower than the binary decision tree. However, here we only used one strong classifier. When a cascade of strong classifier is used as shown later, the decision tree implementation is much faster than the fast exit algorithm. As expected, in the terms of the detection and false alarm rates, the binary decision tree yields the exactly same results as the default and fast exit algorithms.

5.2   The Second Experiment

In this experiment, we mimicked a detection scenario and tested the computation of the cascade of strong classifiers. We followed the negative selection to training the strong classifier cascade as in [1]. We used the same 3724 positives and selected negatives from web images whenever needed. For simplicity, we trained a cascade of three strong classifiers with 5, 10, and 200 weak classifiers at each stage. We constructed the binary decision trees for the first two stages and used the fast exit algorithm for the third stage.

Table 6(c) compares the performance of different algorithms. This experiment truly manifests the computational advantage of the binary decision tree. It is significantly faster than the other two implementation. It is more than ten times faster than the default method and more than six times faster than the fast exit algorithm!

6 Conclusions

We presented a computational improvement to the rapid Viola and Jones algorithm [1]. The improvement arises from the fact that a binary decision tree is derived from a boosted strong classifier and the tree has a lot of early exits. In addition, each node of the tree is just a weak classifier and the knowledge of the coefficients α_j can be discarded once the tree is constructed. Our experiments demonstrated that the binary decision tree implementation is indeed rapider.

Acknowledgement

The author thanks Binglong Xie for providing the face database used for training.

References

1. Viola, P., Jones, M.: Rapid object detection using a boosted cascade of simple features. IEEE Computer Society Conference on Computer Vision and Pattern Recognition **1** (2001) 511–518
2. Papageorgiou, C., Oren, M., Poggio, T.: A general framework for object detection. IEEE International Conference on Computer Vision (1998) 555–562
3. Freund, Y., Schapire, R.: A decision-theoretic generalization of on-line learning and an application to boosting. (Computation Learning Theory: Eurocols) 23–27
4. Jones, M., Viola, P.: Face recognition using boosted local features. IEEE International Conference on Computer Vision (2003)
5. Jones, M., Viola, P.: Fast multi-view face detection. IEEE Computer Society Conference on Computer Vision and Pattern Recognition (June 2003)
6. Lienhart, R., Maydt, J.: An extended set of harr-like features for rapid object detection. IEEE International Conference on Image Processing **1** (2002) 900–903
7. Zhang, L., Li, S., Qu, Z., Huang, X.: Boosting local feature based classifier for face recognition. First IEEE International Workshop on Face Processing in Video (2004)
8. Lienhart, R., Kuranov, A., Pisarevsky, A.: Empirical analysis of detection cascades of boosted classifiers for rapid object detection. The 25th Pattern Recognition Symposium (2003) 297–304
9. Viola, P., Jones, M.: Face and robust classification using asymmetric adaboost and a detector cascade. Neural Information Processing Systems 14 (2001)
10. Li, S., Zheng, Z.: Floatboost learning and statistical face detection. IEEE Trans. Pattern Analysis and Machine Intelligence **26** (2004) 1–12
11. Lienhart, R., Liang, L., Kuranov, A.: A detector tree of boosted classifiers for real-time object detection and tracking. IEEE International Conference on Multimedia and Expo (July 2003)
12. Sun, J., Rehg, J.M., Bobick, A.: Automatic cascade training with perturbation bias. In: CVPR. (2004)

13. Casella, G., Berger, R.L.: Statistical Inference. Duxbury (2002)
14. Poor, H.: An Introduction to Signal Detection and Estimation. Springer-Verlag (1994)
15. Friedman, J., Hastie, T., Tibshirani, R.: Additive logistic regression: a statistical view of boosting. Annals of statistics **28** (2000) 337–374
16. Grossmann, E.: Adatree: Boosting a weak classifier into a decision tree. In: IEEE Workshop Learning in Computer Vision and Pattern Recognition. (2004)
17. CBCL Face Database #1, MIT Center for Biological and Computational Learning, http://www.ai.mit.edu/projects/cbcl.
18. Sung, K., Poggio, T.: Example-based learning for view-based human face detection. IEEE Trans. Pattern Analysis and Machine Intelligence **20** (1998) 39–51

Robust Facial Landmark Detection
for Intelligent Vehicle System

Junwen Wu and Mohan M. Trivedi

Computer Vision and Robotics Research Laboratory,
University of California, San Diego, La Jolla, CA 92093, USA
{juwu, mtrivedi}@ucsd.edu

Abstract. This paper presents an integrated approach for robustly loca
ting facial landmark for drivers. In the first step a cascade of probability
learners is used to detect the face edge primitives from fine to coarse, so
that faces with variant head poses can be located. The edge density descriptors and skin-tone color features are combined together as the basic
features to examine the probability of an edge being a face primitive. A
cascade of the probability learner is used. In each scale, only edges with
sufficient large probabilities are kept and passed on to the next scale.
The final output of the cascade gives the edge primitives that belong to
faces, which determine the face location. In the second step, a facial landmark detection procedure is applied on the segmented face pixels. Facial
landmark candidates are first detected by learning the posteriors in multiple resolutions. Then geometric constraint and the local appearance,
modeled by SIFT descriptor, are used to find the set of facial landmarks
with largest matching score. Experiments over high-resolution images
(FERET database) as well as the real-world drivers' data are used to
evaluate the performance. A fairly good results can be obtained, which
validates the proposed approach.

1 Introduction

Facial landmark localization is an important research topic in computer vision.
Many human computer interfaces require accurate detection and localization of
the facial landmarks. The detected facial landmarks can be used for automatic
face tracking [1], head pose estimation [2] and facial expression analysis [3]. They
can also provide useful information for face alignment and normalization [4], so
as to improve the accuracy of face detection and recognition. In computer vision
area, the facial landmarks are usually defined as the most salient facial points.
Good facial landmarks should have sufficient tolerance to the variations from
the facial expressions, lighting conditions and head poses. Eyes, nostrils and lip
corners are the most commonly studied facial landmarks.

In literature, many research efforts have been undertaken for solving this
problem. The Bayesian shape model presented in [5] and [6] model the facial
landmarks as the control points. The Bayesian shape model is modeled by the
contour, which gives a set of geometric constraints on the facial landmarks. Together with the local appearance, the geometric configuration determines the

W. Zhao, S. Gong, and X. Tang (Eds.): AMFG 2005, LNCS 3723, pp. 213–228, 2005.

location of the facial landmarks. Face bunch graphs [7] represent the facial landmarks by "Gabor Jet". A graph structure is used to constrain the "Jets" under certain geometric configuration. The facial landmarks are located by an exhaustive search for the best matching graph. In [8], Feris et. al. used a two-level hierarchical Gabor Wavelet Network (GWN). In the first level, a GWN for the entire face is used to locate the face region, find the face template from the database and compute the appropriate transformation. In the second level, other GWNs are used to model the local facial landmarks. The facial landmarks are located under the constraint from the full-face GWN. In [9], the authors first use Viola and Jone's object detector [10] to locate the facial landmark candidates and then a shape constraint is imposed on the detected candidates to find the best match. In [11] and [12], the algorithms focused on the eye detection, which is realized by a more accurate feature probability learning. Different statistical models are proposed to serve this purpose. However, most algorithms are designed for feature detection in frontal face. When large head pose variation presents, the performance deteriorates largely.

In this paper, we present an integrated approach to locate the facial landmarks under variant head poses in a complicated background. More specifically, we applied this algorithm on drivers' video from an in-car camera. In the following sections, we discuss the details of the algorithm. In section 2, we give the framework of the algorithm. In section 3, the pose invariant robust face detector is presented. In section 4, the two-level scheme of the facial landmark detection inside the face region is discussed. In section 5, experimental results are shown to validate the effectiveness of our approach. Section 6 concludes our presentation.

2   Algorithm Framework

The application scenario of intelligent vehicle system requires a robust algorithm to accommodate the variations in illumination, head pose and facial expressions. Locating the facial landmarks in an unconstrained image is not an easy job. Some feature points from the cluttered background may possess the similar local texture as the facial landmarks, causing false detections. Limiting the search window within the face region would help reduce the false alarm. Therefore, we first locate the faces. Considering the *pose-invariant* requirement, local low-level primitives are used as the basic features. Edge density descriptor [13] is a good local texture representation. It has certain tolerance to the background noise while preserving local textures. However, local texture descriptor alone cannot remove the ambiguous background patterns. Skin-tone color features [14] are combined together for better performance. At different scales, the extracted texture information is different. In a smaller scale, more local details are represented; while more global structural information is obtained in a larger scale. A cascade of probability learners is used to detect the face edge primitives from fine to coarse, using the combination of the edge density descriptors and the skin-tone color features. The rectangular area that includes the most face edge primitives determines the face location. For the ease of the successive processing, in the detected face region we further segment the face pixels using K-means clustering of the color features. Only the segmented face pixels can be the facial landmark candidates. It is worth to mention that in [15], Froba et. al also used the edge features for face detection. However, the use of global template requires well alignment of the images, which is not a trivial job.

Facial landmarks are constrained by their geometric structure. Given the face pixels, geometric configuration together with the local appearance determines the location of facial landmarks. Similar as [9], a coarse-to-fine scheme is proposed. We use the local Gabor wavelet coefficients. Each pixel is represented by its neighborhood's wavelet coefficients. In the first level, the posterior for each face pixel of being a facial landmark is computed. Additive logistic regression is used to model this posterior. Gabor filters can de-correlate the images into features from different frequencies, orientations and scales. Features from one resolution determine one posterior map. The de-correlated features have more dependencies so that the posterior learning can be more accurate. The accumulative posteriors give the overall posterior map, from which the local maxima are determined as the facial landmark candidates. In the second level the false candidates are rejected. A global geometric constraint together with local appearance model using SIFT feature descriptor is used.

3   Face Detection

A background pixel may appear the similar local textures as the facial landmarks. To remove such ambiguity, we confine the search window of facial landmarks within face regions. In an in-car driver video sequence, as show in Fig. 1, there are large variations in the illumination as well as in the head pose. Many existing techniques were designed for single-view face detection. For example, the Viola and Jone's face detector [10] based on the Harr-type features can get a very good accuracy for frontal face detection, however, the performance is not as good if large head pose variation presents. It is because the appearance of the face image changes a lot under different pose positions, a single view model is not sufficient to catch the change. Using pose-invariant local features can solve the problem. Color features are good candidates, but color features alone are not consistent enough under large illumination change. Local primitive features, such as edges, corners, are also pose invariant. Inspired from the wiry object detection work in [13], we use the edge density descriptor together with the skin tone technique. A concatenation of probability learners is used to find the edge primitives that belong to the face region, so as to determine the face pixels. We use additive logistic regression model for the probability. AdaBoost is used to learn the logistic regression model. Fig. 2 gives the flowchart of the face detector. The detector is proceeded from a smaller scale to a larger scale. In each scale, only the detected face edge primitives are remained and passed on to the next scale. The edge primitives obtained from the last scale are the detected face edges.

Fig. 1. Examples of frames from a driver's video captured inside the car

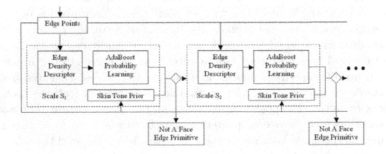

Fig. 2. Flowchart of the face detection algorithm

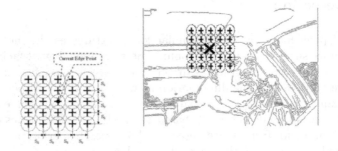

Fig. 3. Illustration of the local edge density descriptor. The left image: the central black dot shows the current edge point to be processed; the edge probes are located at the positions indicated by the crosses. The right image: illustration of applying the edge density descriptor on the image.

3.1   Edge Density Descriptor

Fig. 3 illustrates how to construct the local edge density descriptors. The descriptors are formed under different scales $S_k \in \{S_1, S_2, \cdots, S_K\}$. Smaller scale can give a more detailed description; while larger scale can get a better representation of the global context. For a given edge point $\mathbf{p}_c$, the edge density under scale S_k is described by a set of edge probes $\{E_k(\delta_1, \delta_2)\}(\delta_1 = -d, \cdots, d, \delta_2 = -d, \cdots, d)$. The edge probe $E_k(\delta_1, \delta_2)$ is located around $\mathbf{p}_c$ with horizontal distance $\delta_1 S_k$

and vertical distance $\delta_2 S_k$. The edge probe $E_k(\delta_1, \delta_2)$ evaluates the density of the edges in its neighborhood using a Gaussian window:

$$E_k(\delta_1, \delta_2) = \sum_{\mathbf{p} \in \{\mathbf{PI}_e\}} \exp\{-\frac{\|\mathbf{p} - \mathbf{p}_\delta\|^2}{\sigma^2}\}; \tag{1}$$

where $\{\mathbf{PI}_e\}$ is the set of coordinates of all edge points. $\mathbf{p}_\delta$ is the position of the edge probe $E(\delta_1, \delta_2)$:

$$\mathbf{p}_\delta = \mathbf{p}_c + (S_k\delta_1, S_k\delta_2).$$

3.2 Probability Learning

Given the edge density descriptor $\mathbf{E}_k = \{E_k(\delta_1, \delta_2)\}$, the probability that the edge point belongs to the face region is denoted as $P(\text{face}|\mathbf{E}_k)$. AdaBoost is used to learn this probability. As one of the most important recent developments in learning theory, AdaBoost has received great recognition. In [16], Friedman et. al indicated that for binary classification problem, boosting can be viewed as an approximation to additive modeling on the logistic scale using maximum Bernoulli likelihood as an criterion.

If the probability can be modeled using logistic regression as follows:

$$\frac{P(\text{face}|\mathbf{E}_k)}{P(\text{non} - \text{face}|\mathbf{E}_k)} = e^{C(\mathbf{E}_k)}; \tag{2}$$

where $C(\mathbf{E}_k)$ is a function of the edge density descriptor $\mathbf{E}_k$ and:

$$P(\text{face}|\mathbf{E}_k) + P(\text{non} - \text{face}|\mathbf{E}_k) = 1.$$

This can also be rewritten as:

$$P(\text{face}|\mathbf{E}_k) = \frac{e^{C(\mathbf{E}_k)}}{1 + e^{C(\mathbf{E}_k)}}. \tag{3}$$

If $C(\mathbf{E}_k)$ takes the form $C(\mathbf{E}_k) = \sum_{t=1}^{T} \alpha_t c_t(\mathbf{E}_k)$, this probability model becomes an additive logistic regression model. In [16], it shows that AdaBoost actually provides a stepwise way to learn the model up to a scale factor of 2, which is:

$$P(\text{face}|\mathbf{E}_k) = \frac{e^{C(\mathbf{E}_k)}}{e^{C(\mathbf{E}_k)} + e^{-C(\mathbf{E}_k)}}. \tag{4}$$

Now $c_t(\mathbf{E}_k)(t = 1, \cdots, T)$ becomes the hypotheses from the weak learners.

3.3 Skin Tone Prior

Edge density probe catches the texture information in a local neighborhood; while the probability learning procedure gives the similarity between the observed edge primitives and the known facial landmarks. However, certain background points may have similar local textures as the facial landmarks. Regional color features in different scale are used as priors to help reject the ambiguous patterns from the background.

HSV space is a well-used color space for skin-tone segmentation due to hue feature's relative consistency to skin-colors [14]. We also use hue color here. Since the color feature for a single pixel is not stable enough, we use regional color features instead. Given an edge point $\mathbf{p}_c$, we denote the hue value of its $\xi S_k \times \xi S_k (\xi < 1)$ neighborhood as $\mathbf{h}_k = (h_1, h_2, \cdots, h_{N_k})$. The distribution of the regional skin color feature is:

$$P(\mathbf{h}_k) = P(\|\mathbf{h}_k\|)P(\tilde{\mathbf{h}}_k\|\|\mathbf{h}_k\|);$$

where $\tilde{\mathbf{h}}_k = \frac{(h_1, h_2, \cdots, h_{N_k})}{\|\mathbf{h}_k\|}$ is the normalized hue vector. $\|\mathbf{h}_k\|$ represents the average hue value in the neighborhood, while $\tilde{\mathbf{h}}_k$ evaluates the variations. We neglect the dependency between $\|\mathbf{h}\|_k$ and $\tilde{\mathbf{h}}_k$, so that

$$P(\mathbf{h}_k) = P(\|\mathbf{h}_k\|)P(\tilde{\mathbf{h}}_k). \tag{5}$$

Due to the reflectance and noise on the face, the dependency between $\tilde{\mathbf{h}}_k$ and $\|\mathbf{h}_k\|$ is weak. Hence this assumption is reasonable. A Gaussian mixture is used to model $P(\|\mathbf{h}_k\|)$:

$$P(\|\mathbf{h}_k\|) = \sum_{k_i} \omega_{k_i} \mathcal{N}(\|\mathbf{h}_k\|; \mu_{k_i}, \sigma_{k_i}).$$

A Gaussian in the subspace is used to model the probability of $\tilde{\mathbf{h}}_k$:

$$P(\tilde{\mathbf{h}}_k) = \exp\{-\frac{\|\mathbf{U}_k(\tilde{\mathbf{h}}_k - \mathbf{m}_k)\|^2}{\sigma_k'^2}\};$$

where $\mathbf{U}_k$ is the PCA subspace transformation matrix and $\mathbf{m}_k$ is the mean vector from the training samples. Fig. 4 gives some example of the skin-tone segmentation. We use the images from internet to learn the skin-color model.

Fig. 4. The regional color features in different scales. Leftmost: the original image. Middle right: the color feature from the second scale. Middle left: the color feature from the fourth scale. Rightmost: the color feature from the sixth scale.

3.4   Face Edge Primitive and Face Detection

The edge density descriptor extracts the image features from different abstract levels. Accordingly, we use a local-to-global strategy to detect the face edge primitives. At each scale S_k, if:

$$P(\text{face}|\mathbf{E}_k) \times P(\mathbf{h}_k) > \theta_k, \tag{6}$$

the edge point is determined as a candidate of the face edge primitive. In the next scale, only the face edge candidates from the previous scale are processed. Six scales are used. Fig. 5 gives an example of the face edge primitive detection procedure.

An edge filter is used to locate the face region from the detected face edge primitives. The face region is the one that includes the most face edge primitives. At each pixel, the edge filter output is the number of the face edge primitives falling inside the rectangle box centered at the pixel. The location of the edge filter maximum indicates the location of the face. Fig. 6 gives an example of the edge filter output. If more than one maximum exist, we use the mean of the maxima to locate the face.

Fig. 5. Example of the detected face primitives at each scale. Top left: the original video frame. Top middle: black box shows the detected face. Top right: original edge map. Bottom left: the detected candidates of face edge primitives at the second scale; bottom middle: the detected candidates of face edge primitives at the fourth scale; bottom right: the detected candidates of face edge primitives at the last scale.

Fig. 6. The example of edge filter output

Fig. 7. An example of the face pixel segmentation result. First image: detected face; Second image: segmented face pixels (white color: face pixels); Third image: refined face pixel mask; Fourth image: segmented face pixels.

For the ease of the facial landmark localization procedure, we further segment the face points in the detected face region from the background. All pixels are clustered into H clusters by K-means clustering in the hue space. We use $H = 10$ as the initial number of clusters. During the clustering, the clusters with close means are merged. Since face pixels dominates in the detected face region, the largest cluster corresponds to the face pixels. Morphographic operation is used to smooth the segmentation. The face components, eg. eyes and mouth, have different color distributions. Morphographic operation might not be able to connect them with the face pixels. Hence for every background patch, we need to determine if it is a face component. If most pixels around the background patch are face image, this background patch is a face component and correspondingly the pixels in the background patch are actually face pixels. Fig. 7 gives an example of the face pixel segmentation procedure. White pixels indicate the face points.

4   Pose Invariant Facial Landmark Detection

We use a two-step scheme to detect the facial landmarks. In the first level, candidates of the facial landmarks are found as the maxima in the posterior map. In the second level, geometric constraint as well as local appearance are used to find the facial landmarks.

4.1   First Stage: Finding Facial Landmark Candidates by Posterior Learning

We use Gabor wavelets to decompose the images into different scales and orientations. Gabor wavelets are joint spatial-frequency domain representations. They extract the image features at different spatial locations, frequencies and orientations. The Gabor wavelets are determined by the parameters $\mathbf{n} = (c_x, c_y, \theta, s_x, s_y)$, as shown in the following equation:

$$\Psi_{\mathbf{n}}(x,y) = e^{-\frac{1}{2}[s_x((x-c_x)\cos\theta-(y-c_y)\sin\theta)]^2+[s_y((x-c_x)\sin\theta+(y-c_y)\cos\theta)]^2}$$
$$\times \sin\{s_x((x - c_x)\cos\theta - (y - c_y)\sin\theta)\}. \tag{7}$$

c_x, c_y are the translation factors, s_x, s_y are the scaling factors and θ denotes the orientation. Here only the odd component is used.

Gabor wavelets actually model the local property of a neighborhood. We use the wavelets coefficients of the local neighborhood around the given pixel to estimate its probability of being a facial landmark. Gabor wavelet transform partially de-correlate the image. Wavelet coefficients from the same Gabor filter output have more dependency. Consequently, if we only use the wavelet coefficients from one Gabor filter, the probability estimation can be more accurate. Since we have no prior information to tell which filter output contains more discriminant information for classification, the posteriors are estimated in every resolution. Posteriors for all pixels form a posterior map. These posterior maps from all filter output are combined together to give the final probability estimate.

Let the feature vector for point $\mathbf{p}_c$ be $\{\mathbf{x_s}\}(s = 1, \cdots, S)$. The probability that pixel $\mathbf{p}_c$ belongs to a facial landmark is:

$$P(l|\mathbf{x}_s) = \prod_{s=1}^{S} \beta_s P(l|\mathbf{x}_s); \tag{8}$$

where s-th is the filter index; β_s is the confidence for the posterior estimated from the s-th filter output and $l \in \{\text{Facial Feature}_1, \cdots, \text{Facial Feature}_n, \text{Background}\}$.

Similarly, we use the additive logistic regression model for the posterior. Let $P(l = i|\mathbf{x}_s)$ be the probability that $\mathbf{x}_s$ is the i-th facial landmark, which is modeled as:

$$P(l = i|\mathbf{x}_s) = \frac{e^{2F(\mathbf{x}_s)}}{1 + e^{2F(\mathbf{x}_s)}}, F(\mathbf{x}_s) = \sum_t \alpha_t f(\mathbf{x}_s). \tag{9}$$

AdaBoost is used to learn $F(\mathbf{x}_s)$. The AdaBoost training procedure also provides us a measure for the discriminant ability of each filter output. The objective function of AdaBoost, also that of the additive logistic regression model, is to minimize the expectation of $e^{-l \cdot f(\mathbf{x}_s)}$. If the features from these two classes do not have enough discrimination information, $\sum_m e^{-l^{(m)} \cdot f(\mathbf{x}_s^{(m)})}$ over the testing samples will be large. Cross-validation provides a way to evaluate $E[e^{-l \cdot f(\mathbf{x}_s)}]$ empirically, which is the mean value of $\sum_m e^{-l^{(m)} \cdot f(\mathbf{x}_s^{(m)})}$ over different testing sets:

$$\hat{E}[e^{-l \cdot f(\mathbf{x}_s)}] \propto \frac{\sum_{t=1}^{T} \sum_m e^{-l^{(m)} \cdot f(\mathbf{x}_s^{(m)})}}{T}. \tag{10}$$

We use this estimate as the confidence on the posterior learned from current resolution.

$$\beta_s = \frac{T}{\sum_{t=1}^{T} \sum_m e^{-l^{(m)} \cdot f(\mathbf{x}_s^{(m)})}}. \tag{11}$$

The probability map is updated at each filter output by using Equation. 8. For each facial landmark, we can get an individual probability map. The overall probability map is the summation of these individual probability maps. Fig. 8 gives an example of the probability map learning procedure for the left eye corner, where the probability map updating procedure is shown. The desired facial landmark is highlighted after the probability updating. Local maxima on

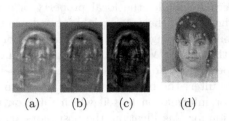

(a)   (b)   (c)   (d)

Fig. 8. The posterior updating procedure. Fig.8(a)-8(c): updated probability maps of using 2, 4, 6 Gabor filter output respectively. Fig.8(d): Candidates for the left eye corner (marked with the red points).

the overall probability map are computed and those local maxima with sufficient high probabilities are selected as the candidates for the facial landmark. The red crosses in Fig. 8(d) show the candidates for the left eye corner. A refinement step by the geometric configuration is used in the next step to remove the false detection.

4.2   Second Stage: Refinement by Geometric and Appearance Constraints

The first level gives a set of facial landmark candidates. In the second level, the detection is refined using the geometric constraints and the local textures.

The geometric configuration is described by the pairwise distances between facial landmarks. The connectivity between different facial landmarks, denoted by $\mathcal{G}$, are predefined. Fig. 9 gives an example of the predefined connectivity, where the facial landmarks include eye pupils, nostrils and lip corners. The dotted red lines show the connection between features. If feature $\mathbf{p}_1$ and $\mathbf{p}_2$ are connected, $g(\mathbf{p}_1; \mathbf{p}_2) = 1$; otherwise $g(\mathbf{p}_1; \mathbf{p}_2) = 0$. Let $\mathcal{T}$ be a combination of the landmark candidates. Considering the situation that some facial landmarks may not be visible due to occlusions, we allow the combination that includes less facial landmarks than defined. We use Gaussian function $\mathcal{N}(x; \mu, \sigma)$ to model the geometric configuration: the distance between the i-th and the j-th facial landmarks is modeled by $(\mu_{ij}^x, \sigma_{ij}^x)$ and $(\mu_{ij}^y, \sigma_{ij}^y)$. μ_{ij}^x and μ_{ij}^y are the means of

Fig. 9. Facial landmarks and the geometric constrains

the corresponding horizontal distance and the vertical distance respectively. σ_{ij}^x and σ_{ij}^y are the corresponding variances. For the combination $\mathcal{T}$, if $\mathbf{p}_i = (x_i, y_i)$ and $\mathbf{p}_j = (x_j, y_j)$ are candidates for the i-th and j-th features respectively, their distance is constrained by:

$$\mathcal{J}(\mathbf{p}_i; \mathbf{p}_j) = \mathcal{N}(x_i - x_j; \mu_{ij}^x, \kappa\sigma_{ij}^x)\mathcal{N}(y_i - y_j; \mu_{ij}^y, \kappa\sigma_{ij}^y)g(\mathbf{p}_i; \mathbf{p}_j). \qquad (12)$$

κ is the relaxation factor. We set $\kappa = 1.5$ in our implementation. The overall geometric matching score for the combination $\mathcal{T}$ is:

$$\mathcal{S}(\mathcal{T}) = \sqrt{q}\prod_i^N \prod_j^N \mathcal{J}(\mathbf{p}_i, \mathbf{p}_j); \qquad (13)$$

where $q = \sum_i^N \sum_j^N g(\mathbf{p}_i; \mathbf{p}_j)$ is the number of the connections between feature candidates. Only a small number of possible combinations can get sufficient high geometric matching score. A nearest neighbor classifier based on the SIFT feature [17] descriptor is used afterwards to find the final result.

Assume $\mathcal{T}_p$ is a combination with sufficient high geometric score and is composed by N features. For each facial landmark candidate, we compute its SIFT feature descriptor, which is $\mathbf{f}_1, \cdots, \mathbf{f}_N$. From the training samples, we can get a dictionary of the corresponding SIFT feature descriptors for both positive and negative samples. For the i-th feature, the dictionary for the positive sample is Ω_i^p and that for the negative samples is Ω_i^n. The best match is found by:

$$\mathcal{T}_p^\star = \arg\min_{\mathcal{T}_p} \sum_{i=1}^N \frac{\min_{\mathbf{f}^p \in \Omega_i^p} \| \mathbf{f}_i - \mathbf{f}^p \|}{\min_{\mathbf{f}^n \in \Omega_i^n} \| \mathbf{f}_i - \mathbf{f}^n \|}. \qquad (14)$$

The facial landmark can be determined accordingly from $\mathcal{T}_p^\star$. Fig. 10 gives a detection example of the facial landmarks defined in Fig. 7.

(a) First example.   (b) Second example.

Fig. 10. Examples of the facial landmarks localization results. Fig.10(a) and Fig.10(b) give two examples. In both Fig.10(a) and Fig.10(b), the leftmost images: the overall posterior maps; the middle images: the candidates of the facial landmarks; the rightmost images: the final detected facial landmarks.

5   Experimental Evaluation

In this paper we presented an integrated approach for facial landmark detection in complicated background. More specifically, we apply the approach for analyzing driver's videos from an in-car camera. As described above, our algorithm has two steps. The first one is to segment the face pixels and the second is to locate the facial landmarks from the segmented face pixels. We evaluated these two steps separately, and then some combined results are shown.

5.1   Experimental Evaluation on Face Localization

We use an in-car camera facing the driver to get the testing videos. 5 subjects are tested. The drivers were asked to drive naturally. There were illumination changes caused by the weather, shadow and road conditions. For each subject

Fig. 11. Examples of the face detection results for different subjects. The black boxes show the detected faces.

Table 1. Accuracy of the face localization results

Video	Person1	Person2	Person3	Person4	Person5
Accuracy	$\frac{377}{400}$	$\frac{325}{400}$	$\frac{356}{400}$	$\frac{332}{400}$	$\frac{326}{400}$

Fig. 12. Examples of the correctly detected eye features

12000 frames are collected, which are sub-sampled by every 30 frames to get the testing images. Hence, we have 400 frames per subject as the testing set. Examples of the detecting results are shown in Fig. 11. (Some subjects wear a camera on the head for data collecting.) The detection accuracy is summarized in table 1.

5.2 Experimental Evaluation on Facial Landmark Localization

In this section, the performance for facial landmark localization is evaluated. Subjects from grayscale FERET database [18] in different poses were used for evaluation. Images from FERET database have high resolutions. The images are obtained under controlled illuminations that have certain variations and the subjects assume variant poses from -90° to 90°. We use left eye landmarks, which include the two eye corners and eye pupil center, for the evaluation. Locating such eye landmarks accurately is not an easy job. 70 subjects are used for testing. Each subject takes 5 different poses. In our testing, we only takes the images with poses from -60° to 60°. A different set of images from the FERET database is used as the training samples. For every feature, there are 250 positive training samples and 1000 negative training samples. For one image, if more than two eye landmarks can be located correctly, this is called a correct detection. The algorithm gives an accuracy of 90.9%. Fig. 12 gives some examples of the eye landmark localization results. The red markers indicate the left corner. The blue ones indicates the pupils. The green markers indicate the right corner. Not every eye feature can be detected. However, the location of the missing features can easily be inferred from the geometric configuration.

5.3 Facial Landmark Detection in In-car Video

The facial landmarks to be detected are shown in Fig. 7. We only allow up to 2 facial landmarks missing. The algorithm is tested on the subjects without sunglasses. In Fig. 13, more examples of the results are shown. Experiments indicate that the extreme case of the profile views cannot get satisfied results due to severe occlusion. This can actually be solved by succeed feature tracking procedure.

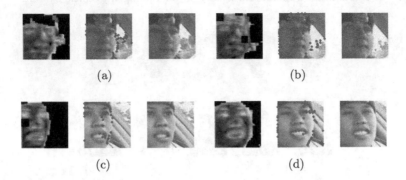

(a)   (b)

(c)   (d)

Fig. 13. Examples of the located facial landmarks. For Fig.13(a)-13(d), the first images: the overall probability map for all face pixels; the second images: the detected facial landmark candidates; the third images: detected facial landmarks. Blue markers show the detected facial landmarks.

6   Conclusion

In this paper we proposed an integrated approach for facial landmark localization in complicated background, especially for drivers' video. Edge density descriptors at different scales are combined with skin-color segmentation to detect the face edge primitives, so as to segment the faces regions. A cascade of probability learners exploiting AdaBoost is used. At each scale, the probability of being a face edge primitive is modeled by an additive logistic regression model. AdaBoost is used to learn the model. Edges that have sufficient large probabilities are determined as the face edges. The position that contains most face edges gives the bounding box of the faces. K-means clustering in the hue space is applied to segment the face pixels from the bounding box, which confines the facial landmarks searching window. The facial landmark localization uses a two-level scheme. In the first level, Gabor wavelets de-correlate the images into features from different resolution. In each resolution, AdaBoost is used to learn the posterior modeled by the additive logistic regression model. Facial landmark candidates are obtained from the probability map. Different combinations of these candidates are input into the second level for refinement. Only the combinations that have high matching score to the geometric configurations are kept. Nearest neighborhood matching using the SIFT features is used afterwards to get the final facial landmark locations. We use FERET data as well as the data from real in-car environment to evaluate the performance. A fairly good results can be obtained. However, the performance for subjects with sub-glasses is still not satisfied due to the difference in local appearance.

Acknowledgement

Our research was supported in part by grants from the UC Discovery Program and the Technical Support Working Group of the US Department of Defense.

The authors thank them for providing the support. The authors also thank our other sponsors in providing the test-bed for collecting the data. The authors are thankful for the assistance and support of our colleagues from the UCSD Computer Vision and Robotics Research Laboratory, especially Joel Mccall for providing the data and other research support.

References

1. C. Hu, R. S. Feris and M. Turk. *Real-time View-Based Face Alignment Using Active Wavelet Networks*, in Proceedings of ICCV'2001 International Conference on Computer Vision, Workshop on Analysis and Modeling of Faces and Gestures, Nice, France, October 2003.
2. B. Braathen, M. S. Bartlett, and J. R. Movellan. *3-D Head Pose Estimation from Video by Stochastic Particle Filtering*, in Proceedings of the 8th Annual Joint Symposium on Neural Computation, 2001.
3. F. Bourel,C. C. Chibelushi and A. A. Low. *Robust Facial Expression Recognition Using a State-Based Model of Spatially-Localised Facial Dynamics*, in Proceedings of the Fifth International Conference on Automatic Face and Gesture Recognition, pp. 106 -111, Washington D.C., USA, 20 - 21 May 2002.
4. F. Liu, X. Lin, S. Z Li and Y. Shi. *Multi-Modal Face Tracking Using Bayesian Network*, in Proceedings of IEEE International Workshop on Analysis and Modeling of Faces and Gestures. Nice, France. 2003.
5. Z.Xue, S. T. Li and E. K. Teoh. *Bayesian shape model for facial feature extraction and recognition*, Pattern Recognition, vol. 36, no. 12, pp. 2819-2833, December 2003.
6. Y. Zhou, L. Gu and H.J.Zhang. *Bayesian Tangent Shape Model: Estimating Shape and Pose Parameters via Bayesian Inference*, in Proceeding of The IEEE Conference on Computer Vision and pattern Recognition (CVPR 2003), Wisconsin, USA, June 16-22, 2003.
7. L. Wiskott, J.-M. Fellous, N. Kr uger and C. von der Malsburg. *Face recognition by elastic bunch graph matching*, IEEE Transactions on Pattern Analysis and Machine Intelligence, vol. 19, no. 7, pp. 775-779, May 1997.
8. R. Feris, J. Gemmell, K. Toyama and V. Krueger. *Facial Feature Detection Using A Hierarchical Wavelet Face Database*. Microsoft Research Technical Report MSR-TR-2002-05, January 2002.
9. D. Cristinacce and T.F. Cootes. *Facial Feature Detection using ADABOOST with Shape Constraints*, In Proceedings of the British Machine Vision Conference (BMVC2003), Vol.1,pp.231-240.
10. P Viola and M. Jones. *Robust Real-time Object Detection*, In Proceedings of the Second International Workshop on Statistical and Compu tational Theories of Vision - Modeling, Learning and Sampling. Jointed with ICCV2001.
11. H.Schneiderman. *Learning a Restricted Bayesian Network for Object Detection*, In Proceedings of the IEEE Conference on Computer Vision and Pattern Recognition (CVPR), 2004.
12. Junwen Wu and Mohan M. Trivedi. *A Binary Tree for Probability Learning in Eye Detection*, In Proceedings of the IEEE Workshop on Face Recognition Grand Challenge Experiments (FRGC'05), in conjunction with CVPR 2005, San Diego, CA, June 21, 2005.

13. O. Carmichael and M. Hebert. *Shape-Based Recognition of Wiry Objects*, IEEE Transactions on Pattern Analysis and Machine Intelligence. Vol. 26, No. 12, December 2004, pp. 1537-1552.

14. H. Wu, Q. Chen, and M. Yachida. *Face detection from color images using a fuzzy pattern matching method*, IEEE Transactions on Pattern Analysis and Machine Intelligence. Vol. 21, No. 6, pp. 557-563. June 1999.

15. B. Froba and C. Kublbeck. *Robust face detection at video frame rate based on edge orientation features*, In Proceedings of the 5th International Conference on Automatic Face and Gesture Recognition. pp. 327-332. May 2002.

16. J. H. Friedman, T. Hastie. and R. Tibshirani. *Additive Logistic Regression: a Statistical View of Boosting*. Annals of Statistics. Vol. 28. pp. 337407.

17. David G. Lowe, *Distinctive image features from scale-invariant keypoints*, International Journal of Computer Vision, 60, 2 (2004), pp. 91-110.

18. P. J. Phillips and H. Moon and S. A. Rizvi and P. J. Rauss, "The FERET Evaluation Methodology for Face Recognition Algorithms," IEEE Trans. Pattern Analysis and Machine Intelligence, Volume 22, October 2000, pp. 1090-1104.

Pose-Encoded Spherical Harmonics for Robust Face Recognition Using a Single Image

Zhanfeng Yue[1], Wenyi Zhao[2], and Rama Chellappa[1]

[1] Center for Automation Research, University of Maryland,
College Park, MD 20742, USA
[2] Vision Technologies Lab, Sarnoff Corporation,
Princeton, NJ 08873, USA

Abstract. Face recognition under varying pose is a challenging problem, especially when illumination variations are also present. Under Lambertian model, spherical harmonics representation has proved to be effective in modelling illumination variations for a given pose. In this paper, we extend the spherical harmonics representation to encode pose information. More specifically, we show that 2D harmonic basis images at different poses are related by close-form linear combinations. This enables an analytic method for generating new basis images at a different pose which are typically required to handle illumination variations at that particular pose. Furthermore, the orthonormality of the linear combinations is utilized to propose an efficient method for robust face recognition where only one set of front-view basis images per subject is stored. In the method, we directly project a rotated testing image onto the space of front-view basis images after establishing the image correspondence. Very good recognition results have been demonstrated using this method.

1 Introduction

Face recognition is one of the most successful applications of image analysis and understanding. In spite of recent advances, robust face recognition under variable lighting and pose remains to be a challenging problem. This is due to the fact that we need to compensate for both significant pose and illumination change at the same time. It becomes even more difficult when only one training image per subject is available. Recently, methods have been proposed to handle the illumination problem when only one training image is available, for example, a statistical learning method [13] based on spherical harmonics representation [1,9]. In this paper, we propose to extend the harmonics representation to encode pose information. That is, all the harmonic basis images of a subject at various poses are related to the front-view basis images via close-form linear combinations. Moreover, these linear combinations are orthonormal. This suggests that recognition methods based on projection onto the harmonic basis images [1] for rotated testing images can be made very efficient. We do not need to generate a new set of basis images at the same pose as that of the testing images. In stead, we can directly use the existing front-view basis images without changing the matching score defined in [1].

W. Zhao, S. Gong, and X. Tang (Eds.): AMFG 2005, LNCS 3723, pp. 229–243, 2005.
© Springer-Verlag Berlin Heidelberg 2005

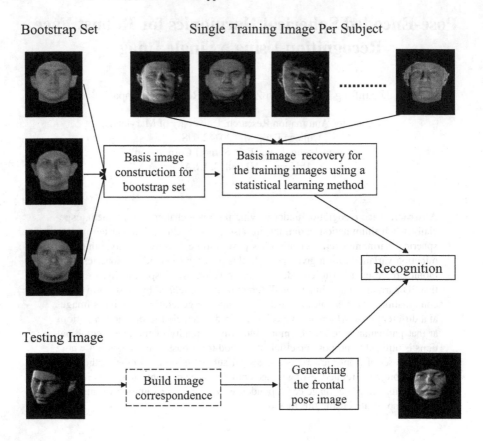

Fig. 1. The flow chart of the proposed face recognition system

We propose an efficient face recognition method that needs only one set of basis images per subject for robust recognition of faces under variable illuminations and poses. The flow chart of our face recognition system is shown in Fig. 1. We have a single training image at the frontal pose for each subject in the training set. The basis images for each training subject are recovered using a statistical learning algorithm [13] with the aid of a bootstrap set consisting of 3D face scans. For a testing image at a rotated pose and under an arbitrary illumination condition, we first establish the image correspondence between the testing image and the training images. The frontal pose image is then warped from the testing image. Finally, a face is identified for which there exists a linear reconstruction based on basis images that is the closest to the testing image.

The remainder of the paper is organized as follows: Section 2 introduces the related work. The pose-encoded spherical harmonic representation is presented in Section 3 where we prove that the basis images at a rotated pose is a linear combination of the basis images at the frontal pose. Section 4 presents the complete face recognition system. Specifically, in Section 4.1 we briefly summarize a statistical learning method to recover the basis images from a single image when the pose is fixed. Section 4.2 describes the recognition algorithm, and the system performance is demonstrated in Section 4.3. We conclude our paper in Section 5.

2   Related Work

Either pose variations or illumination variations may cause serious performance degradation for existing face recognition systems. [17] examined these two problems and reviewed some approaches to solving them. The early effort to handle illumination variations was to discard the first few principal components, which packs most of the energy caused by illumination variations [2]. In this method, the testing image must have the same pose as the training images. In [3], a template matching scheme was proposed to handle pose variations. It needs many different views per person and no lighting variations are allowed. Approaches to face recognition under pose variations [8][6] avoid the correspondence problem by storing multiple images at different poses for each person. View-based eigenface methods [8] explicitly code the pose information by constructing an individual eigenface for each pose. [6] treats face recognition across poses as a bilinear problem and disentangles the face identity and the head pose.

Few methods consider both pose and illumination variations at the same time. The synthesis method in [7] can handle both illumination and pose variations by reconstructing the face surface using the illumination cone method under fixed pose and rotating it to the desired pose. A set of training images are required for each subject to construct the illumination cone. [16] presented a symmetric shape-from-shading (SFS) approach to recover both shape and albedo for symmetric objects. This work was extended in [5] to recover the 3D shape of a human face using a single image. In [15], a unified approach was proposed to solving the pose and illumination problem. A generic 3D model was used to establish the correspondence and estimate the pose and illumination direction. [12] presents a pose-normalized face synthesis method under varying illuminations using the bilateral symmetry of the human face. A Lambertian model was assumed and single light source was considered. [18] extends the photometric stereo algorithms to recover albedos and surface normals from one image under unknown single distant illumination conditions.

Recent work on spherical harmonics representation has been independently conducted by by Basri et al. [1] and Ramamoorthi [9]. It has been shown that the set of images of a convex Lambertian object obtained under a wide variety of lighting conditions can be approximated accurately by a low dimensional linear subspace. The basis images spanning the illumination space for each face can be rendered from a 3D scan of the face [1] or estimated by applying PCA to a number of images of the same subject under different illuminations [9]. Following the statistical learning scheme in [10], Zhang et al. [13] showed that the basis images spanning this space can be recovered from just one image taken under arbitrary illumination conditions when the pose is fixed.

To handle both pose and illumination variations, 3D morphable face model has been proposed. By far the most impressive face synthesis results were reported in [4] followed with very high recognition rates, where the shape and texture of each face is represented as a linear combination of a set of 3D face exemplars and the parameters are estimated by fitting a morphable model to the input image. In order to handle illumination more effectively, a recent work [14] incorporates spherical harmonics into the morphable model framework. Most of the 3D morphable model approaches are computationally intense because of the large number of parameters that need to be optimized.

3 Pose-Encoded Spherical Harmonics

The spherical harmonics are a set of functions that form an orthonormal basis for the set of all square-integrable functions defined on the unit sphere [1]. It can be shown that the irradiance can be approximated by the combination of the first nine spherical harmonics for Lambertian surfaces. Any image of an object under certain illumination conditions is a linear combination of a series of basis images $\{b_{mn}\}$. In order to generate the basis images for the object, 3D information is required as shown in Appendix A.

For a fixed pose, spherical harmonics representation has proved to be effective in modelling illumination variations, even in the case when a bootstrap set of 3D models and only one training image per subject are available [13]. In the presence of both illumination and pose variance, two possible approaches can be taken. One is to use 3D morphoable model to reconstruct the 3D model from a single training image and then build spherical harmonic basis images at the pose of the testing image for recognition [14]. Another approach is to require multiple training images at various poses in order to recover the new set of basis images at each pose. However, multiple training images are not always available and 3D morphoable model method could be computationally expensive. As for efficient recognition of a rotated testing image, a natural question to ask is: can we represent the basis images at different poses using one set of basis images at a given pose, say, the front-view pose? In this section, we address this question by showing that 2D harmonic basis images at different poses are related by close-form linear combinations. This enables an analytic method for generating new basis images at different poses from basis images at one pose.

Assuming that the testing image is at a different pose (rotated view) as the training images (usually frontal view), we aim to derive the basis images at the rotated pose from the basis images at the frontal pose, assuming that the correspondence between the rotated view and the frontal view has been built. The general rotation can be decomposed into three concatenated rotations around the X, Y and Z axis, namely elevation, azimuth and roll, respectively. Roll is an in-plane rotation that can be handled much easily and will not be discussed here. The following theorem states that the basis images at the rotated pose is a linear combination of the basis images at the frontal pose, and the transformation matrix is a function of the rotation angles only.

Theorem 1. Assume a rotated view is obtained by rotating a front-view head with an azimuth angle $-\theta$. With the correspondence between the frontal view and the rotated view, the basis images B' at the rotated pose are related to the basis images B at the frontal pose in the following linear form:

$$
\begin{cases}
b'_{00} = b_{00} \\[4pt]
\begin{bmatrix} b'_{10} \\ b'^{e}_{11} \\ b'^{o}_{11} \end{bmatrix}
=
\begin{bmatrix} \cos\theta & -\sin\theta & 0 \\ \sin\theta & \cos\theta & 0 \\ 0 & 0 & 1 \end{bmatrix}
\begin{bmatrix} b_{10} \\ b^{e}_{11} \\ b^{o}_{11} \end{bmatrix} \\[24pt]
\begin{bmatrix} b'_{20} \\ b'^{e}_{21} \\ b'^{o}_{21} \\ b'^{e}_{22} \\ b'^{o}_{22} \end{bmatrix}
=
\begin{bmatrix}
1-\frac{3}{2}\sin^2\theta & -\sqrt{3}\sin\theta\cos\theta & 0 & \frac{\sqrt{3}}{2}\sin^2\theta & 0 \\
\sqrt{3}\sin\theta\cos\theta & \cos^2\theta-\sin^2\theta & 0 & -\cos\theta\sin\theta & 0 \\
0 & 0 & \cos\theta & 0 & -\sin\theta \\
\frac{\sqrt{3}}{2}\sin^2\theta & \cos\theta\sin\theta & 0 & 1-\frac{1}{2}\sin^2\theta & 0 \\
0 & 0 & \sin\theta & 0 & \cos\theta
\end{bmatrix}
\begin{bmatrix} b_{20} \\ b^{e}_{21} \\ b^{o}_{21} \\ b^{e}_{22} \\ b^{o}_{22} \end{bmatrix}
\end{cases}
\tag{1}
$$

If there is an elevation angle $-\beta$ other than the azimuth angle $-\theta$, the basis images B'' for the newly rotated view are related to B' in the following linear form:

$$
\begin{cases}
b''_{00} = b'_{00} \\[4pt]
\begin{bmatrix} b''_{10} \\ b''^{e}_{11} \\ b''^{o}_{11} \end{bmatrix}
=
\begin{bmatrix} \cos\beta & 0 & \sin\beta \\ 0 & 1 & 0 \\ -\sin\beta & 0 & \cos\beta \end{bmatrix}
\begin{bmatrix} b'_{10} \\ b'^{e}_{11} \\ b'^{o}_{11} \end{bmatrix} \\[24pt]
\begin{bmatrix} b''_{20} \\ b''^{e}_{21} \\ b''^{o}_{21} \\ b''^{e}_{22} \\ b''^{o}_{22} \end{bmatrix}
=
\begin{bmatrix}
1-\frac{3}{2}\sin^2\beta & 0 & \sqrt{3}\sin\beta\cos\beta & \frac{-\sqrt{3}}{2}\sin^2\beta & 0 \\
0 & \cos\beta & 0 & 0 & \sin\beta \\
-\sqrt{3}\sin\beta\cos\beta & 0 & \cos^2\beta-\sin^2\beta & -\cos\beta\sin\beta & 0 \\
-\frac{\sqrt{3}}{2}\sin^2\beta & 0 & \cos\beta\sin\beta & 1-\frac{1}{2}\sin^2\beta & 0 \\
0 & -\sin\beta & 0 & 0 & \cos\beta
\end{bmatrix}
\begin{bmatrix} b'_{20} \\ b'^{e}_{21} \\ b'^{o}_{21} \\ b'^{e}_{22} \\ b'^{o}_{22} \end{bmatrix}
\end{cases}
\tag{2}
$$

For proof of this theorem, please see Appendix B.

The basis images at various poses can be generated from a set of basis images at the frontal pose using the linear relationship in (1) and (2). Although in theory new basis images can be generated from a rotated 3D model inferred by existing basis images since basis images actually capture the albedo (b_{00}) and the 3D surface normal ($b_{10}, b^{e}_{11}, b^{o}_{11}$) of a given human face. The procedure of such 3D recovery is not trivial in practice, let alone the computational cost. Now we have proved that the procedure of first rotating objects and then recomputing basis images at a desired pose can be *totally* avoided.

It is easy to see that the coefficient matrices in (1) and (2) are block diagonal, thus preserving the energy on each band $n = 0, 1, 2$. Moreover, the orthonormality of the coefficient matrices helps to further simplify the computation required for recognition of the rotated testing image as shown in Section 4.2.

We synthesized the basis images at arbitrary rotated poses from those at the frontal pose using (1) and (2), and compared them with the ground truth in Fig. 2. The first row through the third row are the results for subject 1, with the first row showing the basis images at the frontal pose generated from the 3D scan, the second row showing the synthesized basis images at the rotated pose (azimuth angle $\theta = -30°$, elevation angle $\beta = 20°$), and the third row showing the ground truth of the basis images at the rotated pose. Rows four through six are the results for subject 2, with the fourth row showing the

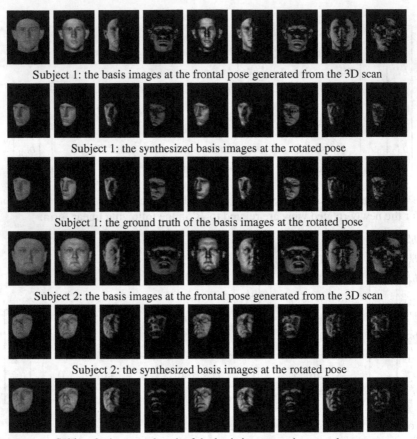

Subject 1: the basis images at the frontal pose generated from the 3D scan

Subject 1: the synthesized basis images at the rotated pose

Subject 1: the ground truth of the basis images at the rotated pose

Subject 2: the basis images at the frontal pose generated from the 3D scan

Subject 2: the synthesized basis images at the rotated pose

Subject 2: the ground truth of the basis images at the rotated pose

Fig. 2. Results of the synthesized basis images at the rotated pose. The first row through the third row are the results for subject 1, with the first row showing the basis images at the frontal pose generated from the 3D scan, the second row showing the synthesized basis images at the rotated pose (with the azimuth angle $\theta = -30^o$ and the elevation angle $\beta = 20^o$), and the third row showing the ground truth of the basis images at the rotated pose. Rows four through six are the results for subject 2, with the fourth row showing the basis images at the frontal pose generated from the 3D scan, the fifth row showing the synthesized basis images at another rotated pose (with the azimuth angle $\theta = -30^o$ and the elevation angle $\beta = -20^o$) and the last row showing the ground truth of the basis images at the rotated pose.

basis images at the frontal pose generated from the 3D scan, the fifth row showing the synthesized basis images for another rotated view (azimuth angle $\theta = -30^o$, elevation angle $\beta = -20^o$), and the last row showing the ground truth of the basis images at the rotated pose. As we can see from Fig. 2, the synthesized basis images at the rotated poses have no noticeable difference with the ground truth.

4 Face Recognition Using Pose-Encoded Spherical Harmonics

In this section we present an efficient face recognition method using pose-encoded spherical harmonics. Only one training image is needed per subject and high recognition performance is achieved even when the testing image is at a different pose from the training image and under an arbitrary illumination condition.

4.1 Statistical Models of Basis Images

We briefly summarize a statistical learning method to recover the harmonic basis images from only one image taken under arbitrary illumination conditions, as shown in [13].

We build a bootstrap set with 50 3D face scans and the texture information from Vetter's 3D face database [19], and generate 9 basis images for each face model. For a novel d-dimensional vectorized image I, let B be the $d \times 9$ matrix of basis images, α a 9 dimensional vector and E a d-dimensional error term, we have $I = B\alpha + E$. It is assumed that the pdf's of B are Gaussian distributions and the sample mean vectors $\mu_b(x)$ and the sample covariance matrixes $C_b(x)$ are estimated from the basis images in the bootstrap set. Fig. 3 shows the sample mean of the basis images estimated from the bootstrap set.

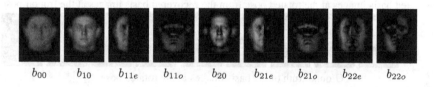

$$b_{00} \quad b_{10} \quad b_{11e} \quad b_{11o} \quad b_{20} \quad b_{21e} \quad b_{21o} \quad b_{22e} \quad b_{22o}$$

Fig. 3. The sample mean basis images estimated from the bootstrap set

The problem of estimating the basis images B and the illumination coefficients α is a coupled estimation problem because of its bilinear form. It is simplified by estimating α in a prior step with kernel regression and using it consistently across all pixels to recover B. K bootstrap images $\{J_k\}_{k=1}^{K}$ with known coefficients $\{\alpha_k\}_{k=1}^{K}$ are generated from the 3D face scans in the bootstrap set. Given a new image i_{tra}, the coefficients α_{tra} can be estimated as

$$\alpha_{tra} = \frac{\sum_{k=1}^{K} w_k \alpha_k}{\sum_{k=1}^{K} \alpha_k} \tag{3}$$

where $w_k = exp[-\frac{1}{2}(D(i, J_k)/\sigma_k)^2]$ and $D(i, J_k) = \|i - J_k\|_2$, σ_k is the width of the k-th Gaussian kernel which controls the influence of J_k on the estimation of α_{tra}. All $\{\sigma_k\}_{k=1}^{K}$ are pre-computed in a way such that ten percent of the bootstrap images are within $1 \times \sigma_k$ at each σ_k. The sample mean $\mu_e(x, \alpha)$ and the sample variance $\sigma_e^2(x, \alpha)$ of the error term $E(\alpha)$ are also estimated using kernel regression, similar to (3).

Given a novel face image $i(x)$, with the estimated coefficients α, the corresponding basis images $b(x)$ at each pixel x are recovered by computing the maximum a posteriori (MAP) estimate, $b_{MAP}(x) = argmax_{b(x)}(P(b(x)|i(x)))$. Using Bayes rule:

I b_{00} b_{10} b_{11e} b_{11o} b_{20} b_{21e} b_{21o} b_{22e} b_{22o}

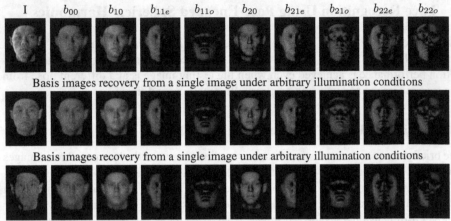

Basis images recovery from a single image under arbitrary illumination conditions

Basis images recovery from a single image under arbitrary illumination conditions

Basis images recovery from a single image under arbitrary illumination conditions

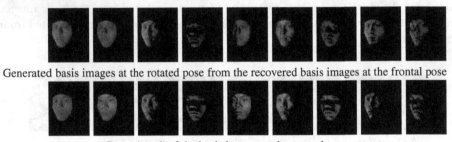

Generated basis images at the rotated pose from the recovered basis images at the frontal pose

Ground truth of the basis images at the rotated pose

Fig. 4. Rows one though three show the basis images recovery from a single training image, with the first column showing different training images I under arbitrary illumination conditions for the same subject and the rest 9 columns showing the reconstructed basis images. Row four shows the generated basis images at the rotated pose from the recovered basis images at the frontal pose, and the fifth row show the ground truth of the basis images at the rotated pose.

$$b_{MAP}(x) = argmax_{b(x)} P(i(x)|b(x)) P(b(x))$$
$$= argmax_{b(x)} \left\{ \mathcal{N}\left(b(x)^T \alpha + \mu_e, \sigma_e^2\right) \times \mathcal{N}\left(\mu_b(x), C_b(x)\right) \right\} \quad (4)$$

Taking logarithm, and setting the derivatives of the right hand side of (4) (w.r.t $b(x)$) to 0, we get $A * b_{MAP} = T$, where $A = \frac{1}{\sigma_e^2}\alpha\alpha^T + C_b^{-1}$ and $T = \frac{(i-\mu_e)}{\sigma_e^2}\alpha + C_b^{-1}\mu_b$. By solving this linear equation, $b(x)$ of the subject can be recovered.

Combining Section 3 and Eq. (4), we illustrate in Fig. 4 the procedure of generating the basis images at a rotated pose (azimuth angle $\theta = -30^o$) from a single training image at the frontal pose. In the first part of Fig. 4, rows one though three show the basis images recovery from a single training image, with the first column showing different training images I under arbitrary illumination conditions for the same subject and the remaining 9 columns showing the reconstructed basis images. In the second part of Fig. 4, row four shows the generated basis images at the rotated pose from the recovered basis images at the frontal pose, and the fifth row shows the ground truth of the basis images at the rotated pose. As we can see from the plots, the basis images recovered from different training images of the same subject look very similar, although not perfect.

4.2 Recognition

For recognition, we follow a simple yet effective algorithm given in [1]. A face is identified for which there exists a weighted combination of basis images that is the closest to the testing image. Let B be the set of basis images at the frontal pose, with size $d \times r$, where d is the number of pixels in the image and r the number of basis images used. We use $r = 9$ as it is a natural choice capturing 98 percent of the energy of all the model's images [1]. Every column of B contains one spherical harmonic image. These images form a basis for the linear subspace, though not an orthonormal one. A QR decomposition is applied to compute Q, a $d \times r$ matrix with orthonormal columns, such that $B = QR$ where R is an $r \times r$ upper triangular matrix.

For a testing image I_{test} at a rotated pose, we can efficiently generate the set of basis images B' at that pose for each training subject from Section 3. The orthonormal basis Q' of the space spanned by B' can be computed by QR decomposition. The distance from the testing image I_{test} to the space spanned by B' is computed as $d_{match} = \|Q'Q'^T I_{test} - I_{test}\|$. However, this algorithm is not efficient overall because the set of basis images B', or the orthonormal basis Q', has to be generated for each training subject at the pose of an arbitrarily rotated testing image. The question is that can we have an overall efficient recognition method. The answer is yes based on the following lemma:

Lemma 2. The matching distance d_{match} of a rotated testing image I_{test} based on the basis images B' at that pose is the same as the matching distance of a geometrically synthesized front-view image I_f based on the basis images B.

Let C be the transpose of the combined coefficient matrices in (1) and (2), we have $B' = BC = QRC$ by QR decomposition. Applying QR decomposition again to RC, we have $RC = qr_{RC}$ where $q_{r \times r}$ is an orthonormal matrix. We now have $B' = Qqr_{RC} = Q_q r_{RC}$ by assuming $Q_q = Qq$. Since Q_q is the product of two orthonormal matrices, it forms a valid orthnormal basis for B'. Hence the matching distance is $\|Q_q Q_q^T I_{test} - I_{test}\|$. Now $Q_q Q_q^T = Qqq^T Q^T = QQ^T$ since q is orthonormal. Hence the final matching distance is $\|QQ^T I_{test} - I_{test}\|$. Recall this implies that the cross-pose correspondence between Q (B) and I_{test} has been established. To make this explicit, we use I_f, a geometrically warped front-view version of I_{test}, in the equation.

In brief summary, we now have a very efficient solution for face recognition to handle both pose and illumination variations as only one image I_f needs to be synthesized.

The remaining problem is that how the frontal pose image I_f is warped from I_{test}. Apparently the correspondence between the frontal pose and the rotated pose has to be established for the testing image. Finding correspondence is always challenging. Most of the approaches to handle pose variations utilized manually picked sparse features to build the dense cross-pose or cross-subject correspondence. For I_{test} at an arbitrary pose, 63 designed feature points (eyebrows, eyes, nose, mouth and the face contour)

Fig. 5. Building dense correspondence between the rotated view and the frontal view using sparse features. The first and second image show the sparse features and the constructed meshes on the mean face at the frontal pose. The third and fourth image show the picked features and the constructed meshes on the given testing image at the rotated pose.

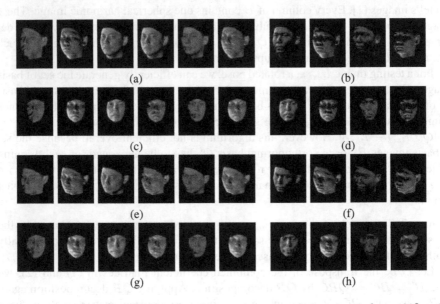

(a)   (b)

(c)   (d)

(e)   (f)

(g)   (h)

Fig. 6. (a) shows the testing images of a subject at the pose with the azimuth $\theta = -30°$ under different lighting conditions (($\gamma = 90°, \tau = 10°$), ($\gamma = 30°, \tau = 50°$), ($\gamma = 40°, \tau = -10$), ($\gamma = 20°, \tau = 70°$), ($\gamma = 80°, \tau = -20°$) and ($\gamma = 50°, \tau = 30°$) from left to right). The testing images of the same subject under some extreme lighting conditions (($\gamma = 20°, \tau = -70°$), ($\gamma = 20°, \tau = 70°$), ($\gamma = 120°, \tau = -70°$) and ($\gamma = 120°, \tau = -70°$) from left to right) are shown in (b). (c) and (d) show the generated frontal pose images from the testing images in (a) and (b) respectively. The testing images at another pose (with $\theta = -30°$ and $\beta = 20°$) of the same subject are shown in (e) and (f), with the generated frontal pose images shown in (g) and (h) respectively.

were picked. A mean face from the training images at the frontal pose and the corresponding feature points were used to help to build the correspondence between I_{test} and I_f. Triangular meshes on both faces were constructed and barycentric interpolation inside each triangle was used to find the dense correspondence. The number of feature

Table 1. The correct recognition rates at two rotated pose under various lighting conditions

Illumination condition	Correct recognition rate at the pose $\theta = -30°$ using our approach	Correct recognition rate with the training images at the same pose available	Correct recognition rate at the pose $\theta = -30°, \beta = 20°$ using our approach	Correct recognition rate with the training images at the same pose available
$(\gamma = 90°, \tau = 10°)$	94%	94%	94%	94%
$(\gamma = 30°, \tau = 50°)$	92%	100%	96%	100%
$(\gamma = 40°, \tau = -10°)$	90%	100%	92%	100%
$(\gamma = 70°, \tau = 40°)$	94%	100%	100%	100%
$(\gamma = 80°, \tau = -20°)$	80%	96%	86%	94%
$(\gamma = 50°, \tau = 30°)$	94%	100%	100%	100%
$(\gamma = 20°, \tau = -70°)$	86%	96%	94%	100%
$(\gamma = 20°, \tau = 70°)$	86%	92%	96%	96%
$(\gamma = 120°, \tau = -70°)$	42%	76%	62%	78%
$(\gamma = 120°, \tau = 70°)$	58%	84%	84%	86%

points needed in our approach is comparable to the 56 manually picked feature points in [14] to deform the 3D model. Fig. 5 shows the feature points and the meshes on the mean face at the frontal pose and on a testing image at a rotated pose.

4.3 Recognition Results

We conducted the recognition experiments on Vetter's 3D face model database [19] for the sake of controllability and the convenience of comparison. There are totally 100 3D face models in the database, wherein 50 of them were used as the bootstrap set and the other 50 were used to generate training images. We synthesized the training images under a wide variety of illumination conditions with the 3D scans of the subjects. For each subject, only one frontal view image was stored as training image and used to recover the basis images B using the algorithm in Section 4.1. The orthonormal basis Q of the space spanned by B was obtained by applying QR decomposition to B. For a testing image I_{test} at an arbitrary pose, the frontal pose image I_f was synthesized by warping I_{test}, and the recognition score was computed as $\|QQ^T I_f - I_f\|$.

We generated the testing images at different poses from the training images by rotating the 3D scans and illuminated them with various lighting conditions (represented by slant angle γ and tilt angle τ). Fig. 6 (a) shows the testing images of a subject at the pose with the azimuth angle $\theta = -30°$ and under 6 different lighting conditions. We also did experiments under some extreme lighting conditions as shown in Fig. 6 (b). The corresponding frontal pose images were synthesized as shown in Fig. 6 (c) and (d) respectively. The correct recognition rates obtained by using $\|QQ^T I_f - I_f\|$ for all these illumination conditions are listed in column 2 of Table 1. The testing images at another pose (with $\theta = -30°$ and $\beta = 20°$) of the same subject are shown in Fig. 6 (e) and (f), with the generated frontal pose images shown in Fig. 6 (g) and (h) respectively and the correct recognition rates listed in column 4 of Table 1.

As an comparison, we also conducted the recognition experiment on the same testing images assuming that the training images at the same pose are available, as most of the approaches suggested. By recovering the basis images B at that pose using the algorithm in Section 4.1 and computing $\|QQ^T I_{test} - I_{test}\|$, we achieved the correct recognition rates as shown in column 3 and column 5 of Table 1 respectively, in correspondence with the two poses mentioned above. As we can see, the recognition rates using our approach are comparable to those when the training images at the rotated pose are available.

We have to point out that if the the testing image has a large pose variation from the frontal pose, it is inevitable that part of the face is self-occluded (Fig. 6). To have good recognition result, only the visible part of the face is used for recognition. Accordingly, only the visible parts of the basis images at the frontal pose are used as well.

5   Discussions and Conclusion

We have presented an efficient face recognition method to handle arbitrary pose and illumination from a single training image per subject using pose-encoded spherical harmonics. With a pre-built 3D face bootstrap set, we use a statistical learning method to obtain the spherical harmonic basis images from a single training image. We then show that the basis images at a rotated pose is a linear combination of the basis images at the frontal pose. For a testing image at a different pose from the training images, recognition is accomplished by comparing the distance from a warped version of the testing image to the space spanned by the basis images of each model. Experimental results show that high recognition rate can be achieved when the testing image is at a different pose and under an arbitrary illumination condition. We are planning to conduct experiments using the proposed approach on larger databases such as the CMU-PIE [11] database.

In the proposed method and existing methods where only one training image is available, finding the cross-correspondence between the training images and the testing image is inevitable. If the testing image is at a pose around the Y-axis only, a simpler method can be used to find the self-correspondence of the testing image by exploiting the bilateral symmetry of the human face. As a result, we do not need to build the cross-subject correspondence between the testing image and the training images. Unfortunately, automatic computation of these correspondences is not a trivial task and manual operation is required in existing methods. We are looking into possible solutions to address this issue.

References

1. R. Barsi and D. Jacobs, "Lambertian Reflectance and Linear Subspaces," *IEEE Trans. PAMI*, Vol. 25(2), pp. 218–233, Feb. 2003.
2. P. Belhumeur, J. Hespanha and D. Kriegman, "Eigenfaces vs. Fisherfaces: Recognition Using Class Specific Linear Projection," *IEEE Trans. PAMI*, Vol. 19, pp. 711–720, July, 1997.
3. B. Beyme, "Face Recognition Under Varying Pose," *Tech. Report 1461, MIT AI Lab*, 1993.
4. V. Blanz and T. Vetter, "Face Recognition based on Fitting a 3D Morphable Model," *IEEE Trans. PAMI*, Vol. 25(9), pp. 1063–1074, Sept. 2003.

5. R. Dovgard and R. Basri, "Statistical Symmetric Shape from Shading for 3D Structure Recovery of Faces," *ECCV*, 2004.
6. W. Freeman and J. Tenenbaum, "Learning Bilinear Models for Two-Factor Problems in Vision," *Proceedings, IEEE Conference on CVPR*, Puerto Rico, pp. 554–560, June, 1997.
7. A. Geoghiades, P. Belhumeur, D. Kriegman, "Illumination-Based Image Synthesis: Creating Novel Images of Human Faces Under Differing Pose and Lighting," *Proceedings, Workshop on Multi-View Modeling and Analysis of Visual Scenes*, pp. 47–54, 1999.
8. A. Pentland, B. Moghaddam, and T. Starner, "View-based and Modular Eigenspaces for Face Recognition," *Proceedings, IEEE Conf. on CVPR*, pp. 84–91, June, 1994.
9. R. Ramamoorthi, "Analytic PCA Construction for theoretical Analysis of Lighting Variability in Images of A Lambertian Object," *IEEE. PAMI*, Vol. 24(10), pp. 1322–1333, Oct. 2002.
10. T. Sim and T. Kanade, "Illuminating the Face," *Tech. Report CMU-RI-TR-01-31*, Robotics Institute, CMU, 2001.
11. T. Sim, S. Baker and M. Bsat, "The CMU Pose, Illumination, and Expression (PIE) Database of Human Faces," *AFGR*, pp. 46–51, 2002.
12. Z. Yue and R. Chellappa, "Pose-Normailzed View Synthesis of a Symmetric Object Using a Single Image," *ACCV*, 2004.
13. L. Zhang and D. Samaras, "Face Recognition Under Variable Lighting Using Harmonic Image Examplars," *CVPR*, Vol. I, pp. 19–25, 2003.
14. L. Zhang, S. Wang and D. Samaras, "Face Synthesis and Recognition from a Single Image under Arbitrary Unknown Lighting using a Spherical Harmonic Basis Morphable Model," *CVPR*, to appear, 2005.
15. W. Zhao and R. Chellappa, "SFS Based View Synthesis for Robust Face Recognition," *Int. Conf. on Automatic Face and Gesture Recognition*, 2000.
16. W. Zhao and R. Chellappa, "Symmetric Shape-from-Shading Using Self-ratio Image," *Int. Journal Computer Vision*, Vol. 45, pp. 55–75, 2001.
17. W. Zhao, R. Chellappa, J. Phillips and A. Rosenfeld, "Face Recognition: A Literature Survey," *ACM Computing Surveys*, Dec. 2003.
18. S. Zhou, R. Chellappa and D. Jacobs, "Characterization of human faces under illumination variations using rank, integrability, and symmetry constraints," *ECCV*, 2004.
19. "3DFS-100 3 Dimensional Face Space Library (2002 3rd version)", University of Freiburg.

Appendix A: Harmonic Basis Images

The harmonic basis image intensity of a point p with surface normal $n = (n_x, n_y, n_z)$ and albedo λ can be computed as (5), where $n_{x^2} = n_x n_x$. $n_{y^2}, n_{z^2}, n_{xy}, n_{xz}, n_{yz}$ are defined similarly. $\lambda . * t$ denotes the component-wise product of λ with any vector t.

$$b_{00} = \frac{1}{\sqrt{4\pi}}\lambda, \ b_{10} = \sqrt{\frac{3}{4\pi}}\lambda. * n_z, \ b_{11}^e = \sqrt{\frac{3}{4\pi}}\lambda. * n_x, \ b_{11}^o = \sqrt{\frac{3}{4\pi}}\lambda. * n_y,$$

$$b_{20} = \frac{1}{2}\sqrt{\frac{5}{4\pi}}\lambda. * (2n_{z^2} - n_{x^2} - n_{y^2}), \ b_{21}^e = 3\sqrt{\frac{5}{12\pi}}\lambda. * n_{xz}, \ b_{21}^o = 3\sqrt{\frac{5}{12\pi}}\lambda. * n_{yz},$$

$$b_{22}^e = \frac{3}{2}\sqrt{\frac{5}{12\pi}}\lambda. * (n_{x^2} - n_{y^2}), \ b_{22}^o = 3\sqrt{\frac{5}{12\pi}}\lambda. * n_{xy} \tag{5}$$

Appendix B: Proof of Theorem 1

Assume that (n_x, n_y, n_z) and (n'_x, n'_y, n'_z) are the the surface normals of point p at the frontal pose and the rotated view respectively. (n'_x, n'_y, n'_z) is related to (n_x, n_y, n_z) as

$$
\begin{bmatrix} n'_x \\ n'_y \\ n'_z \end{bmatrix} = \begin{bmatrix} \cos\theta & 0 & \sin\theta \\ 0 & 1 & 0 \\ -\sin\theta & 0 & \cos\theta \end{bmatrix} \begin{bmatrix} n_x \\ n_y \\ n_z \end{bmatrix} \tag{6}
$$

where $-\theta$ is the azimuth angle.

By replacing (n'_x, n'_y, n'_z) in (5) with $(n_z \sin\theta + n_x \cos\theta, n_y, n_z \cos\theta - n_x \sin\theta)$, and assuming the correspondence between the rotated view and the frontal view has been built, we have

$$
b'_{00} = \frac{1}{\sqrt{4\pi}}\lambda, \ b'_{10} = \sqrt{\frac{3}{4\pi}}\lambda. * (n_z \cos\theta - n_x \sin\theta),
$$

$$
b'^e_{11} = \sqrt{\frac{3}{4\pi}}\lambda. * (n_z \sin\theta + n_x \cos\theta), \ b'^o_{11} = \sqrt{\frac{3}{4\pi}}\lambda. * n_y,
$$

$$
b'_{20} = \frac{1}{2}\sqrt{\frac{5}{4\pi}}\lambda. * (2(z\cos\theta - n_x \sin\theta)^2 - (n_z \sin\theta + n_x \cos\theta)^2 - n_y^2),
$$

$$
b'^e_{21} = 3\sqrt{\frac{5}{12\pi}}\lambda. * (n_z \sin\theta + n_x \cos\theta) * (n_z \cos\theta - n_x \sin\theta),
$$

$$
b'^o_{21} = 3\sqrt{\frac{5}{12\pi}}\lambda. * n_y (n_z \cos\theta - n_x \sin\theta),
$$

$$
b'^e_{22} = \frac{3}{2}\sqrt{\frac{5}{12\pi}}\lambda. * ((n_z \sin\theta + n_x \cos\theta)^2 - n_y^2),
$$

$$
b'^o_{22} = 3\sqrt{\frac{5}{12\pi}}\lambda. * (n_z \sin\theta + n_x \cos\theta)n_y \tag{7}
$$

Rearranging, we get

$$
b'_{00} = b_{00}, \ b'_{10} = b_{10}\cos\theta - b^e_{11}\sin\theta, \ b'^e_{11} = b^e_{11}\cos\theta + b_{10}\sin\theta, \ b'^o_{11} = b_{11},
$$

$$
b'_{20} = b_{20} - \sqrt{3}\sin\theta\cos\theta b^e_{21} - \sqrt{\frac{5}{4\pi}\frac{3}{2}}\sin^2\theta(n_z^2 - n_x^2),
$$

$$
b'^e_{21} = (\cos^2\theta - \sin^2\theta)b^e_{21} + 3\sqrt{\frac{5}{12\pi}}\sin\theta\cos\theta(n_z^2 - n_x^2),
$$

$$
b'^o_{21} = b^o_{21}\cos\theta - b^o_{22}\sin\theta,
$$

$$
b'^e_{22} = b^e_{22} + \cos\theta\sin\theta b^e_{21} + \sqrt{\frac{5}{12\pi}\frac{3}{2}}\sin^2\theta(n_z^2 - n_x^2),
$$

$$
b'^o_{22} = b^o_{22}\cos\theta + b^o_{21}\sin\theta. \tag{8}
$$

As shown in (8), $b'_{00}, b'_{10}, b'^e_{10}, b'^o_{11}, b'^o_{21}$ and b'^o_{22} are in the form of linear combination of the basis images at the frontal pose. For b'_{20}, b'^e_{21} and b'^e_{22}, we need to have $(n_z^2 - n_x^2)$ which is not known. From [1], we know that if the sphere is illuminated by a single directional source in a direction other than the z direction the reflectance obtained would be identical to the kernel, but shifted in phase. Shifting the phase of a function distributes its energy between the harmonics of the same order n (varying m), but the overall energy in each order n is maintained. The quality of the approximation, therefore, remains the same. This can be verified by $b_{10}'^2 + b_{11}'^{e2} + b_{11}'^{o2} = b_{10}^2 + b_{11}^{e2} + b_{11}^{o2}$ for the order $n = 1$. Noticing that $b_{21}'^{o2} + b_{22}'^{o2} = b_{21}^{o2} + b_{22}^{o2}$, we still need $b_{20}'^2 + b_{21}'^{e2} + b_{22}'^{e2} = b_{20}^2 + b_{21}^{e2} + b_{22}^{e2}$ to preserve the energy for the order $n = 2$.

Let $P = 3\sqrt{\frac{5}{12\pi}}\sin^2\theta(n_z^2 - n_x^2)$ and $Q = 3\sqrt{\frac{5}{12\pi}}\sin\theta\cos\theta(n_z^2 - n_x^2)$, we have

$$b_{20}' = b_{20} - \sqrt{3}\sin\theta\cos\theta b_{21}^e - \frac{\sqrt{3}}{2}P,$$
$$b_{21}'^e = (\cos^2\theta - \sin^2\theta)b_{21}^e + Q,$$
$$b_{22}'^e = b_{22}^e + \cos\theta\sin\theta b_{21}^e + \frac{1}{2}P. \qquad (9)$$

Then

$$b_{20}'^2 + b_{21}'^{e2} + b_{22}'^{e2}$$
$$= b_{20}^2 + b_{21}^{e2} + b_{22}^{e2} + \frac{3P^2}{4} - 2\sqrt{3}\sin\theta\cos\theta b_{20}b_{21}^e - \sqrt{3}b_{20}P + 3\sin\theta\cos\theta P + Q^2$$
$$+2(\cos^2\theta - \sin^2\theta)b_{21}^e Q + \frac{P^2}{4} + 2\sin\theta\cos\theta b_{22}^e b_{21}^e + b_{22}^e P + \sin\theta\cos\theta P$$
$$= b_{20}^2 + b_{21}^{e2} + b_{22}^{e2} + P^2 + 4\sin\theta\cos\theta b_{21}^e P + (b_{22}^e - \sqrt{3}b_{20})(P + 2\sin\theta\cos\theta b_{21}^e)$$
$$+Q^2 + 2(\cos^2\theta - \sin^2\theta)b_{21}^e Q$$

Having $b_{20}'^2 + b_{21}'^{e2} + b_{22}'^{e2} = b_{20}^2 + b_{21}^{e2} + b_{22}^{e2}$ and $Q = P\frac{\cos\theta}{\sin\theta}$, we get

$$P^2 + 2\sin\theta\cos\theta b_{21}^e P + (b_{22}^e - \sqrt{3}b_{20})(P\sin^2\theta + 2\sin\theta\cos\theta b_{21}^e) = 0$$

and then $(P + 2\sin\theta\cos\theta b_{21}^e)(P + \sin^2\theta(b_{22}^e - \sqrt{3}b_{20})) = 0$.

The two possible roots of the polynomial gives $P = -2\sin\theta\cos\theta b_{21}^e$ or $P = -\sin^2\theta(b_{22}^e - \sqrt{3}b_{20})$. Taking $P = -2\sin\theta\cos\theta b_{21}^e$ into (9) gives $b_{20}' = b_{20}$, $b_{21}'^e = -b_{21}^e$, $b_{22}'^e = b_{22}^e$, which is apparently incorrect. Therefore, we have $P = -\sin^2\theta(b_{22}^e - \sqrt{3}b_{20})$ and $Q = -\cos\theta\sin\theta(b_{22}^e - \sqrt{3}b_{20})$. Substituting them in (9) we get

$$b_{20}' = b_{20} - \sqrt{3}\sin\theta\cos\theta b_{21}^e + \frac{\sqrt{3}}{2}\sin^2\theta(b_{22}^e - \sqrt{3}b_{20}),$$
$$b_{21}'^e = (\cos^2\theta - \sin^2\theta)b_{21}^e - \cos\theta\sin\theta(b_{22}^e - \sqrt{3}b_{20}),$$
$$b_{22}'^e = b_{22}^e + \cos\theta\sin\theta b_{21}^e - \frac{1}{2}\sin^2\theta(b_{22}^e - \sqrt{3}b_{20}). \qquad (10)$$

Using (8) and (10), we can write the basis images at the rotated pose in the matrix form of the basis images at the frontal pose, as shown in (1).

Assume there is an elevation angle $-\beta$ after the azimuth angle $-\theta$ and denote (n_x'', n_y'', n_z'') as the surface normal for the new rotated view, we have

$$\begin{bmatrix} n_x'' \\ n_y'' \\ n_z'' \end{bmatrix} = \begin{bmatrix} 1 & 0 & 0 \\ 0 & \cos\beta & -\sin\beta \\ 0 & \sin\beta & \cos\beta \end{bmatrix} \begin{bmatrix} n_x' \\ n_y' \\ n_z' \end{bmatrix} \qquad (11)$$

Repeating the above derivation easily leads to the linear equations in (2) which relates the basis images at the new rotated pose to the basis images at the old rotated pose.

Advantages of 3D Methods for Face Recognition Research in Humans

Chang Hong Liu[1] and James Ward[2]

[1] Department of Psychology, University of Hull,
Hull, HU6 7RX, United Kingdom
C.H.Liu@hull.ac.uk
[2] Department of Computer Science, University of Hull,
Hull, HU6 7RX, United Kingdom
J.W.Ward@dcs.hull.ac.uk

Abstract. Research on face recognition in humans has mainly relied on 2D images. This approach has certain limitations. First, observers become relatively passive in face encoding, although in reality they may be more spontaneous in exploring different views of a 3D face. Moreover, the volumetric information of a face is often confined to pictorial depth cues, making it difficult to assess the role of 3D shape processing. This paper demonstrates that 1) actively exploring different views of 3D face models produces more robust recognition memory than passively viewing playback of the same moving stimuli, 2) face matching across 2D and 3D representations typically incurs a cost, which alludes to depth-cue dependent processes in face recognition, and 3) combining multiple depth cues such as stereopsis and perspective can facilitate recognition performance even though a single depth cue alone rarely produces measurable benefits.

1 Introduction

Research on face recognition in humans has mainly relied on 2D pictures. An implicit assumption of this approach is that face recognition in pictures reveals the truth about face recognition in general. While the resemblance between a real face and its photographic representation is hardly in question, face recognition in the real world may employ additional information that is not available in a 2D representation. The most obvious difference between a real face and a photograph is their depth information. Whereas a photograph contains only monocular depth cues, a face in reality contains both monocular and binocular depth cues. This rich depth information may allow more precise encoding of facial surface geometry.

Furthermore, unlike photographic images, faces and observers in reality are rarely stationary. Although increasing numbers of researchers use dynamic face stimuli [21], a crucial difference between perception of a face in motion pictures and a face in reality remains. Perception of a real face is an interactive process in the sense that the relative motion of the face and its observer determines resulting viewpoint of the face. The observer may from time to time actively engage in this interaction to deliberately register certain desired facial features. This means that face perception in reality in-

W. Zhao, S. Gong, and X. Tang (Eds.): AMFG 2005, LNCS 3723, pp. 244–254, 2005.
© Springer-Verlag Berlin Heidelberg 2005

volves the observer's head movements and locomotion. Research methods based on 2D images do not allow researchers to assess the role of this active process.

In this paper, we will review how these issues are tackled by some recent studies that employed 3D face models and visualization methods. Before that, we will briefly review some prior research that has pioneered the use of 3D methods in psychology.

1.1 Using 3D Face Models

Despite their limitations, photographic materials are still considered as better alternatives to life models in behavioral research. The main reason that life models have never become a popular choice is that they are susceptible to extraneous variables. Photographs allow much better control of variables such as pose, lighting, and facial expression, although at expense of poorer applicability of the research to real-world face recognition.

The use of 3D models offers a promising solution to the problems facing 2D images and life models. When 3D laser-scanned models are shown in virtual environments, for example, they not only can mimic reality more closely, but also allow a

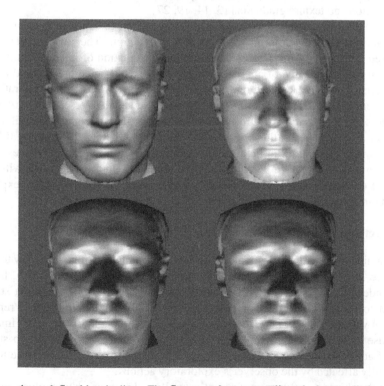

Fig. 1. Face shape defined by shading. The first row shows a top-lit and a bottom-lit face. The second row shows a bottom-lit face in a stereo pair. Bottom-lit faces are more difficult to recognize. Although this is sometimes attributed to disruption of 3D shape reconstruction from shading, stereopsis does not rectify this difficulty [20].

similar level of control over experimental variables. In the early days when the 3D method was first used in behavioral research, however, it was the potential to manipulate certain variables in face recognition that attracted most attention.

Laser-scanned faces were used in numerous studies since the early 1990s. Unlike photographs, laser-scanned models allow separation of 3D surface information from color or pigmentation information. Using this advantage, Bruce and her colleagues studied contributions of shading and surface information in face perception without presence of color or facial textures [3, 4, 5, 11, 12, 25]. Fig. 1 shows images of an example face defined by shading information alone. Although shape-from-shading is an important source of information for human face recognition, the effectiveness of this information is limited to top-lit faces [17]. The disadvantage of bottom-lit faces cannot be corrected by stereo cues, showing that shape-from-shading overrides shape-from-stereo in face processing [18].

The relative contributions of face shape and texture can be assessed by using 3D morphing techniques, where face shape and texture are selectively normalized onto an average [23, 24]. Similar techniques also allow separation of motion from shape or texture gradients from shading, making it possible to measure the contribution of non-rigid motion and texture gradients [13, 14, 19, 27].

The studies described so far have mainly attempted to separate out contributions from various sources of information in face perception. Their use of 3D methods involved reduction of information such that the information of interest could be studied in isolation. This line of approach, however, needs to be complemented by a synthetic approach, whereby different sources of information are combined rather than subtracted. Clearly, 3D models can be comfortably adapted to research in either direction. It is the combination of information that makes 3D models more credible substitutes for live models. It allows researchers to assess whether there is any difference between face recognition in pictures and face recognition in reality. At present, relatively fewer attempts have been made in this direction. In this paper, we will present some of our recent studies that were aimed to explore the roles of active exploration and 3D information commonly found in real-world face perception.

1.2 Methods of Stimulus Presentation

To examine the role of active exploration in face recognition, it is necessary to present 3D face models in real time for observer-face interaction. Most research, however, pre-renders 3D faces under the desired image conditions. For example, a study designed to measure the effect of pose change on face recognition would render 3D faces in various views. The rendered scenes are captured and saved as 2D images for later use in planned experiments. However, this method is not suitable to study the role of active exploration, because the views of a face in such a study have to be dynamically affected by the observer's exploratory actions.

We developed a software tool recently to allow the observer to explore views of a 3D face with a joystick [26]. The software is a user interface between the MATLAB programming environment and graphics libraries that operates directly on 3D face models and creates the desired image conditions in real time. Instead of retrieving pre-rendered images, joystick feedback or simple MATLAB commands are used to control simulated rigid motion of a 3D face model.

Unlike the pre-rendering method, the interactive feature reduces the difference between real faces and face images used in laboratory settings.

2 Active Exploration Improves Recognition Performance

Very little is known about whether spontaneous and active exploration of stimuli plays a role in visual cognition. The issue has only been investigated in computer generated novel objects [10]. Observers in the active condition explored the objects with a track ball during the training session, whereas those in the passive condition simply viewed the playbacks of the rotated objects generated by the active observers. It was found that active observers recognized trained objects more quickly than passive observers. However, there was no difference between the accuracy scores of the two conditions. The study leaves two unanswered questions. First, it is not clear whether recognition of a novel class of objects is readily applied to that of a familiar class of objects. Even if the answer is positive, it is still unclear whether recognition for a class of birds, for example, would be similar to recognition of faces. Unlike any other class of objects, faces are discriminated at individual level without deliberate training. Second, and perhaps more importantly, it is not clear whether recognition accuracy could be affected by active exploration. Accuracy is arguably a more important measure of identification in forensic and social settings. It is certainly also a more critical measure of face recognition in engineering.

We conducted a series of experiments aiming to answer these questions. We used a standard recognition task in a yoked design. The task involved remembering eight faces presented once at the learning session, and later identifying them at the test session where the trained faces were mixed with eight new ones. Observers in the active condition explored views of faces via a joystick, whereas observers in the passive condition simply viewed the replay of the same sequence of face stimuli generated by the active observers. The range of possible views for exploration is shown in Fig. 2. The initial view of each face was determined randomly from this range. Three experiments were conducted in which the condition of active exploration was varied.

2.1 Active Exploration at Both Training and Test Sessions

In the first experiment, active observers were allowed to explore the faces during both training and test sessions of the task. Active observers also decided how long they wished to explore each face at each trial before moving onto the next trial. Passive observers viewed the same views for the same length of time as the active observers. A total of 101 undergraduate students were randomly assigned to the two conditions.

It was found that the active condition produced better recognition accuracy ($M = 83.5\%$, $SD = 16.4$) than the passive condition ($M = 73.5\%$, $SD = 19.7$), $F(1, 99) = 10.59$, $p < .002$. The result shows that human observers acquire more robust recognition memory of faces when they are able to interactively control the views of faces.

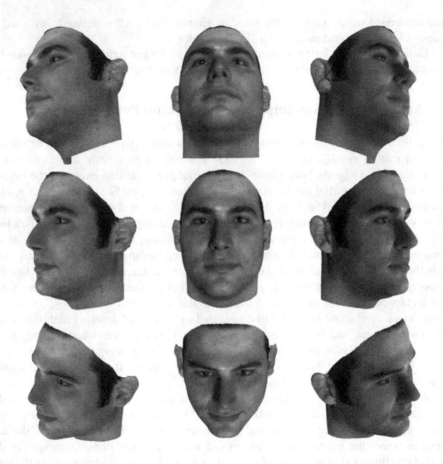

Fig. 2. Limits of rotation (x = ±55°, y = ±30°) from the frontal view in the center. The laser-scanned face database used in the present study was obtained from University of South Florida.

2.2 Active Exploration Only at Training Session

The advantage of active exploration found in the first experiment could either be due to spontaneous control of training views or correlations between the explored views at training and test. In order to determine whether active exploration at training could by itself produce better recognition performance, we ran the second experiment where active participants could explore views of faces only during the training session. A total of 80 undergraduate students participated. Other aspects of the experiment were identical to the first experiment.

The results showed again that the active condition scored higher on recognition accuracy ($M = 79.1\%$, $SD = 16.0$) than the passive condition ($M = 72.3\%$, $SD = 18.6$), F $(1, 78) = 4.66$, $p < .03$, although the mean difference between the two conditions was somewhat lower than that of the first experiment. The result shows that the advantage of the active condition cannot be simply due to correlations of the face views explored at training and test.

2.3 Active Exploration Only at Training Session Within a Fixed Duration

Both experiments described so far allowed active observers to decide the duration of face stimuli on the display. Because preferred inspection time may well differ from one observer to another, the inability to decide the length of inspection time in the passive condition may have been a disadvantage that contributed to the different performance between the two conditions. To investigate this possibility, we ran another experiment where the time to explore each face was fixed at 10 s such that observers in both conditions inspected the faces for the same duration. This specific duration was based on the data from the first experiment where observers on average spent 10.6 s (SD = 5.7) learning each face. Again, observers in the active condition only explored the views of faces during the training session. A total of 60 undergraduate students were tested. Other aspects of the experiment were the same as before.

Results again favored the active condition (M = 81.5%, SD = 8.9) over the passive condition (M = 75.6%, SD = 12.8), F (1, 58) = 4.22, p < .05. This experiment thus rules out the possibility that the advantage of the active condition in the previous experiments was merely due to the free control of preferred learning duration in that condition.

These experiments present the first converging evidence that actively explored face views during learning can improve the accuracy of face recognition memory.

3 Relevance of 3D Shape Information in Face Processing

Both image-based and model-based approaches to face recognition have been developed in engineering over the past decades (see [8] and [28], for a review). A key difference between these two approaches is whether they involve face processing based on volumetric information. The psychological status of these approaches remains largely unknown. Although shading and motion related effects reported in psychology are often attributed to 3D shape processing, studies to date have not yet found convincing evidence that the brain encodes 3D volumetric information of faces for recognition.

The obvious way to test the hypothesis that 3D information is used in face processing is to assess to what extent 3D cues assist face recognition. Research to date has failed to find any use of some key 3D information, such as stereopsis [18, 20] and linear perspective [15, 16]. Although stereo is often considered a more reliable cue for 3D shape than shading and other cues [6], it is shading information that prior research has found to be far more important in face recognition. For example, faces in line drawings that are devoid of shading information are more difficult to recognize than photographs [3, 7]. Stereopsis, on the other hand, hardly produces any measurable effect on face recognition. If face recognition does rely on reconstruction of 3D surface, such a result would appear rather surprising. Intuitively, the 3D shape of a face should be more easily perceived with stereo information. For example, the height of a nose from a frontal view of a face can only be accurately estimated when this information is available. The diminished importance of stereo information has prompted the conclusion that the visual system mainly uses 2D information for face processing [18]. Shading is merely treated as a 2D pattern rather than a cue to 3D shape.

However, two questions remain. First, if 2D information plays a key role in face processing, is a 3D face simply encoded as a collection of 2D images just like the way a face in photographs would be encoded? Second, can certain combinations of 3D cues facilitate face recognition even though each of these cues alone fails to do so? We addressed the first question by looking at how well faces can be identified across their 2D and 3D representations and the second question by measuring how the combination of stereo with linear perspective affects recognition performance.

3.1 Transfer Between 2D and 3D Representations

Matching a 2D face image to a 3D face requires ignoring unmatched depth cues. If a 3D face is simply encoded as 2D images, there should be no cost for such matching. To determine whether face recognition is affected by differences between 2D and 3D representations, we conducted two experiments where the dimensionality of the images used at training and test were either congruent or incongruent [20]. We used two congruent conditions. In the congruent stereo condition, both images of a face used at training and test were presented with stereo information. In the congruent mono condition, both of these images were presented without stereo information. In the incongruent condition, one of the images was presented with stereo, and the other without, and vice versa.

Face images at training and test were always presented in two different views (full-face and 3/4) to avoid matching based on trivial image similarity alone. Both stereo and mono images were observed through shutter glasses. One experiment employed a standard recognition task with a between-subject design. The task was to decide whether the faces presented at the test session had been shown at the training session. Another experiment was a matching task using a within-subject design. The task was to decide whether two sequentially displayed images were of the same person.

Both experiments found significant main effects, $F(2, 187) = 4.16, p < .02$, and $F(2, 112) = 6.85, p < .001$, for the recognition and matching experiments respectively. Bonferroni post-hoc tests showed that the congruent stereo condition produced a significantly higher accuracy ($M = 74.3\%, SD = 10.0$) than the incongruent condition ($M = 68.8\%, SD = 10.7$) in the recognition experiment. In the matching experiment, the accuracy scores in both congruent conditions ($Ms = 86.0$ and $85.7\%, SDs = 8.3$ and 7.7, respectively, for the congruent stereo and congruent mono conditions) were significantly higher than that in the incongruent condition ($M = 82.3\%, SD = 9.4$). No difference was found between results of the congruent stereo and congruent mono conditions in either experiment.

3.2 Combination of Depth Cues May Facilitate Face Recognition

Evidence to date appears to deny any usefulness of 3D information in face processing. Nevertheless, it remains possible that the usefulness of this information depends on certain combinations of cues. We recently tested this hypothesis in a recognition task where face stimuli with several levels of perspective transformation were either presented in stereo or without stereo. Faces were trained and tested at different distances simulated on a computer screen. As Fig. 3 shows, the 2D projections of facial features and the configuration of a face can be quite different from two camera distances. In a relatively large perspective transformation such as in Fig. 3A, the projection from the near camera not only results in a larger image overall, but also produces quite considerable differences in 2D shape. It has visibly larger internal facial features such as the nose and eyes, and smaller peripheral features such as the neck and fading ears than the image projected from the far camera distance. In order to perceive the correspondence between the two projections despite their image differences, the observer needs to compensate for the differences caused by perspective transformation.

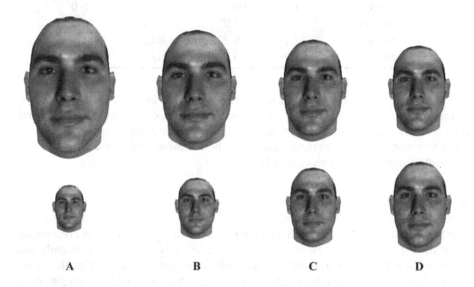

Fig. 3. Four levels of perspective transformation between training and test. A. Large transformation. B. Medium transformation. C. Small transformation. D. No transformation.

We used four levels of perspective transformation which ranged from large to no transformation. The mean visual angles subtended from the vertical extent of the faces (defined by the length from the top edge of the forehead to the tip of the chin) to the observer at these distances are shown in the second and third columns of Table 1. Each face was trained at a far distance and later tested at a near distance or vice versa. Each observer performed the task twice using two different sets of faces, once with stereo and once without. The order of the two conditions was counterbalanced.

Results for the mono and stereo condition under perspective transformation are shown in the last two columns of Table 1. We found a significant main effect of perspective transformation, $F(3, 185) = 27.54$, $p < .001$. Namely, the greater the distance between the training and test face locations, the more difficult it is to identify the two images as the same person. However, when stereo information was available, recognition performance was less affected by perspective transformation, $F\,(3, 185) =$ 13.72, $p < .001$. Overall, recognition in the stereo condition was 5% better than the mono condition. Even at a small perspective transformation, the stereo condition produced better performance. The stereo advantage diminished when perspective transformation was not present.

Table 1. Percentage accuracy as a function of perspective transformation and presence of stereopsis

Perspective Transformation	Face Size		Mean Accuracy (%)	
	Near	Far	Mono	Stereo
Large	31.7°	9.9°	63.8	70.9
Medium	25.8°	12.9°	66.7	74.4
Small	22.1°	16.7°	80.2	84.3
None	19.5°	19.5°	87.2	87.5

The results show that stereo information can play a role in face processing but only when it is combined with certain other 3D cues. Clearly, not all combinations of depth cues facilitate recognition performance. For example, recognition using shading information alone is similar to recognition using both shading and stereo information as demonstrated in this and prior studies [18].

4 Conclusions

The benefits of 3D methods in behavioral research of face perception were recognized since the early infancy of the technology. However, it is not till quite recently that these methods have been applied to more realistic settings. Using 3D methods, our studies have revealed a number of previously unknown facts about face recognition in humans. First, we found that actively exploring views of a face can lead to improved learning and more robust recognition memory of that face. Second, our results showed that although faces trained and tested in 2D images produce equivalent recognition performance to faces trained and tested in 3D images, transfer from 2D to 3D or vice versa results in reduced recognition performance. Last, stereopsis can enhance face recognition when combined with linear perspective.

These findings show that face recognition may rely on more resources in reality than most research has suggested so far. These resources have not been fully investigated due to the limitations of 2D face images used in laboratory research. However, these unexplored territories can now be more systematically examined using 3D methods.

Our results show that using 3D faces in virtual environments leads to better identification performance. This may have promising implications for forensic applications. Currently, 2D mug shots and video parade systems are still dominant in this field. Simulated 3D environments offer an eyewitness the opportunity to explore any arbitrary views of a suspect in a police lineup parade, along with depth cues that are more compatible with real environments. Because recognition of unfamiliar faces is highly view or image dependent [9], being able to explore a face in various pose conditions should improve the chance of successful identification.

Understanding the benefits of 3D information in human face recognition should help engineers to determine what kind of face recognition software is useful to human users. If 3D models facilitate face recognition, it would be sensible to develop software capable of 3D face synthesis from video or photographic images for use in eyewitness identification.

Apart from practical implications, our research on the role of 3D information in face recognition was aimed to shed some light on the psychological basis of the image-based and model-based theories. Consistent with some prior findings [15, 16, 18], our recent research suggests that 3D information plays a relatively minor role in human face perception. There may be few processes in the brain for reconstruction of 3D structures, or at least such reconstruction is not necessary. However, it has also become clear that the human visual system does employ 3D information for face processing and this can at times improve or optimize recognition performance. Indeed, the utility of the 3D information may have been underestimated given that systematic research on the effects of combination of 3D cues has just started. Whether other combinations of depth cues such as motion parallax and stereopsis affect face recognition will become issues for future research.

Acknowledgement

This research was supported by the British Academy and the Nuffield Foundation.

References

1. Braje, W.L., Kersten, D., Tarr, M.J., Troje, N.F.: Illumination effects in face recognition. Psychobiology, Vol. 26, (1998) 371–380
2. Bruce, V., Burton, A.M., Hanna, E., Healey, P., Mason, O., Coombes, A., Fright, R., Linney, A.: Sex discrimination: How do we tell the difference between male and female faces? Perception, Vol. 22, (1993) 131–152
3. Bruce, V., Hanna, E., Dench, N., Healey, P., Burton A.M.: The importance of "mass" in line drawings of faces. Applied Cognitive Psychology, Vol.6, (1992) 619–628
4. Bruce, V., Healey, P., Burton, M., Doyle, T., Coombes, A., Linney, A.: Recognising facial surfaces. Perception, Vol. 20, (1991) 755–769
5. Bruce, V., Langton, S.: The use of pigmentation and shading information in recognising the sex and identities of faces Perception, Vol. 23, (1994) 803–822
6. Bülthoff, H.H.: Shape from X: Psychophysics and computation. In: Landy, M.S., Movshon, J.A. (Eds.): Computational Models of Visual Processing. The MIT Press Cambridge MA (1991) 305–330
7. Davies, G., Ellis, H. D., Shepherd, J.: Face recognition accuracy as a function of mode of representation. Journal of Applied Psychology, 63, (1978) 180–187
8. Hallinan, P.L., Gordon, G.G., Yuille, A.L., Giblin, P., Mumford, D.: Two- and Three-Dimensional Patterns of the Face. A. K. Peters Limited Natick MA (1999)
9. Hancock, P.J.B., Bruce, V., Burton, A.M.: Recognition of unfamiliar faces. Trends in Cognitive Sciences, Vol. 4, (2000) 330–337

10. Harman, K.L., Humphrey, G.K., Goodale, M.A.: Active manual control of object views facilitates visual recognition. Current Biology, Vol. 9, (1999) 1315–1318
11. Hill, H., Bruce, V.: The effects of lighting on the perception of facial surfaces. Journal of Experimental Psychology: Human Perception and Performance, Vol. 22, (1996) 986–1004
12. Hill, H., Schyns, P.G., Akamatsu, S.: Information and viewpoint dependence in face recognition Cognition, Vol. 62, (1997) 201–222
13. Hill, H., Jinno, Y., Johnston, A.: Comparing solid body with point-light animations. Perception, Vol. 32, (2003) 561–566
14. Knappmeyer, B., Thornton, I.M., Bülthoff, H.H.: The use of facial motion and facial form during the processing of identity. Vision Research, Vol.43, (2003) 1921–1936
15. Liu, C.H.: Is face recognition in pictures affected by the center of projection? IEEE International Workshop on Analysis and Modeling of Faces and Gestures, (2003) 53–59
16. Liu, C.H., Chaudhuri, A.: Face recognition with perspective transformation. Vision Research, Vol. 43, (2003) 2393–2402
17. Liu, C.H., Collin, C.A., Burton, A.M., Chaudhuri, A.: Lighting direction affects recognition of untextured faces in photographic positive and negative. Vision Research, Vol. 39, (1999) 4003–4009
18. Liu, C.H., Collin, C.A., Chaudhuri, A.: Does face recognition rely on encoding of 3-D surface? Examining the role of shape-from-shading and shape-from-stereo. Perception, Vol. 29, (2000) 729–743
19. Liu, C.H., Collin, C.A., Farivar, R., Chaudhuri, A.: Recognizing faces defined by texture gradients. Perception & Psychophysics, Vol. 67, (2005) 158–167
20. Liu, C.H., Ward, J., & Young, A.W.: Transfer between 2D and 3D representations of faces. Visual Cognition. (in press)
21. O'Toole, A.J., Roark, D., Abdi, H.: Recognizing moving faces: A psychological and neural synthesis. Trends in Cognitive Sciences, Vol. 6, (2002) 261–266.
22. O'Toole, A.J., Edelman, S., Bülthoff, H.H.: Stimulus-specific effects in face recognition over changes in view-point. Vision Research, Vol. 38 (1998) 2351–2363
23. O'Toole, A.J., Price, T., Vetter, T., Bartlett, J.C., Blanz, V.: Three-dimensional shape and two-dimensional surface textures of human faces: The role of "averages" in attractiveness and age. Image and Vision Computing Journal, Vol. 18, (1999) 9–19
24. O'Toole, A.J., Vetter, T., Blanz, V.: Three-dimensional shape and two-dimensional surface reflectance contributions to face recognition: An application of three-dimensional morphing. Vision Research, Vol. 39, (1999) 3145–3155
25. Troje, N.F., Bülthoff, H.H.: Face recognition under varying poses: The role of texture and shape. Vision Research, Vol. 36, (1996) 1761–1771
26. Ward, J., Liu, C.H.: VRVision: A new tool for the display of 3D images in behavioural research. Behavior Research Methods, Instruments, & Computers. (in press)
27. Watson, T.L., Johnston, A., Hill, H.C.H., Troje, N.: Motion as a cue for viewpoint invariance. Visual Cognition. (in press)
28. Zhao, W., Chellappa, R., Rosenfeld, A., Phillips, J. Face recognition: A literature survey. Technical Report, CS-TR4167R, University of Maryland (2002)

The CMU Face In Action (FIA) Database

Rodney Goh[1], Lihao Liu[1], Xiaoming Liu[2], and Tsuhan Chen[1]

[1] Electrical and Computer Engineering Department,
Carnegie Mellon University, Pittsburgh 15213, USA
{rhgoh, llihao, tsuhan}@andrew.cmu.edu
[2] GE Global Research, one research circle, New York 12308, USA
liux@research.ge.com

Abstract. Our team has collected a face video database named the CMU Face In Action (FIA) database. This database consists of 20-second videos of face data from 180 participants mimicking a passport checking scenario. The data is captured by six synchronized cameras from three different angles, with an 8-mm and 4-mm focal-length for each of these angles. We performed the collection in both a controlled, indoor environment and an open, outdoor environment for each participant. Our data collection was taken in three sessions over a period of ten months. We aimed for a three month separation between sessions for each participant. We expect the database to be useful for analysis and modeling of faces and gestures.

1 Introduction

There are many existing databases containing face images under controlled conditions, FERET [1], CMU PIE [2], ORL [3], Yale Database [4], UMIST [5]. However, as more and more researchers begin working on video-based face recognition as opposed to traditional image-based face recognition, there is a greater demand for a database of human faces in video sequences. With such a database, the benefits of video-based face recognition can be explored.

Fig. 1. Sample images of the Face In Action database taken from the three 8-mm focal-length cameras. Here we show 10 intermittent frames among the 600 JPEG images to give a clear idea of our face video data.

W. Zhao, S. Gong, and X. Tang (Eds.): AMFG 2005, LNCS 3723, pp. 255–263, 2005.
© Springer-Verlag Berlin Heidelberg 2005

We have collected such a face video database, calling it CMU Face In Action (FIA) database (Figure 1). The collection was performed for 180 participants in both indoor and outdoor environments, three times per participant, over a ten month period. We captured our videos from three different angles, with two different focal-lengths for each angle. For each of these 20-second videos, participants were asked to mimic a passport checking scenario, providing a large range of gestures, facial expressions, and motions.

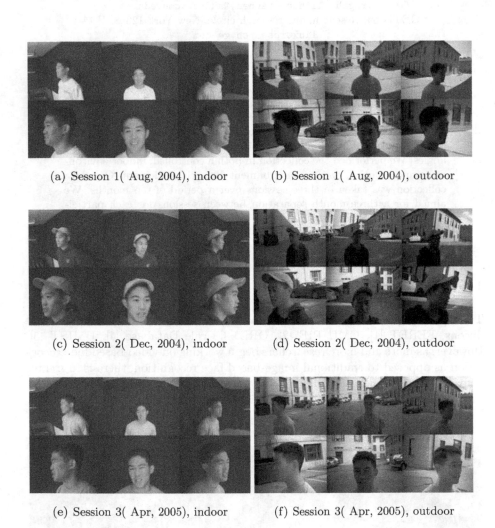

(a) Session 1(Aug, 2004), indoor   (b) Session 1(Aug, 2004), outdoor

(c) Session 2(Dec, 2004), indoor   (d) Session 2(Dec, 2004), outdoor

(e) Session 3(Apr, 2005), indoor   (f) Session 3(Apr, 2005), outdoor

Fig. 2. Frame number 300 of 600 for the indoor (left) and outdoor (right) scenarios from all three sessions. User-dependent gestures and expression variations are expected.

2   Database Variation

In face database collection, one samples the face in multiple dimensions, such as pose, illumination, expression, aging, etc. In our CMU FIA capturing system, we sampled in the following dimensions: motion, pose, image resolution, illumination and variations over time.

Motion and pose were left participant-dependent. In order to vary image resolution, we utilized two focal lengths for each angle from which we captured. To sample variations over time, we conducted our data collection in three sessions, aiming for three months separation between sessions. Illumination was varied by our two different environments: a controlled, indoor environment and an open, outdoor environment. The indoor environment was fixed with a blue background and fluorescent lighting. The outdoor environment utilized natural lighting, that could be affected by season and climate as seen as Figure 2. The variables that remained constant between these environments were the data rate and quality of the videos, camera angles, procedure, and the face of each participant. The poses for each sequence will have varied, as they are dependent to the participant. The sequences from the outdoor scenario can be used to study how well a video-based face recognition system performs in a natural setting.

2.1   Equipment

For our video collection, we utilized six OEM-style IEEE-1394 board level Dragonfly cameras (Figure 3) from Point Grey Research Inc. [6], along with their corresponding synchronizing mechanisms. The cameras utilize the Sony ICX424 sensor, which has a maximum resolution of 640x480 pixels and 24-bit true color images (RGB), and a maximum frame rate of 30 Hz. The cameras were put on adjustable arms of two identical aluminum carts, one used in our indoor scenario and the other for our outdoor scenario. One IEEE-1394 bus can process a data stream from a maximum of three cameras, based on the data rate of 640x480 pixels at 30 frames per second. Therefore, we utilized two separate buses, each responsible for synchronizing three cameras. Since we were aiming to synchronize

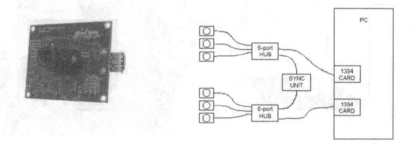

Fig. 3. The Dragonfly camera from Point Grey Research Inc. (left). The Synchronization Unit (right) plays the role of synchronizing two IEEE-1394 buses.

all six cameras together for our database, and only three cameras may be synchronized on one bus, we attached the two buses, each processing three cameras, into a separate camera synchronization unit, which then serves to synchronize the two groups together. Based on our experiences, the speed of the hard drive, rather than the CPU speed, is the bottleneck of the capturing system. We used more memory as cache to compensate for the latency of the hard drive. Even so, we occasionally encountered "out of sync" frames. For the purpose of our database, out of a total 600 frames, we made sure to keep this number of "out of sync" frames to under 60 in the indoor scenario, and under 150 in the outdoor scenario. In most cases, we had no "out of sync" frames.

2.2   Positioning

As shown in Figure 4, we have built a cart for mounting the capturing system. There are six cameras on the C-shape arm whose height can be adjusted manually from 1.5 meters to 1.7 meters according to the different height of each participant. All of the cameras point to the same center spot from a distance of 0.83 meters. We placed a red cross mark on the floor at this center spot as a reference point for our participants. Since the C-shape arm can be adjusted vertically by the linear bearing according to the height of the subject, the face is essentially captured by three pairs of cameras with the same vertical angle, but three different horizontal angles (-72.6 , 0 , 72.6) respectively. The six cameras were arranged into three pairs. For each pair of cameras, one camera was set to an 8-mm focal-length, which results in a face area of around 300 x 300 pixels, and the other to a 4-mm focal-length, which results in a face area of around 100 x 100 pixels. The video sequence with larger face area can be used for applications demanding high-resolution face images, such as 3D reconstruction, while the sequence with smaller face area presents face data closer to the size used in video surveillance applications and gesture analysis. Two carts were used for

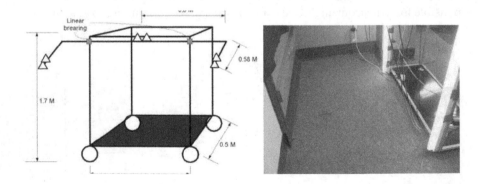

Fig. 4. A simple diagram of our cart to show exact dimensions and the location of our cart

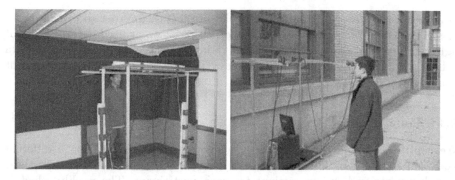

Fig. 5. Snapshots of data collection in progress for the indoor (left) and outdoor (right) scenarios

capturing our data, one in a controlled indoor environment, and the other in an open outdoor environment, as seen in Figure 5. The indoor cart was always kept in the same location, whereas the outdoor cart, for concern of security and weather damage, was moved for each day that data was collected. Therefore, the location of the outdoor cart may have varied by a few feet day to day, on the occasion that the view was blocked by parked cars in the area. The red cross reference and cart were adjusted accordingly.

2.3   Illumination

In the indoor scenario, we had a controlled environment with a blue background made from a felt material, and fluorescent bulb lighting. In addition to standard overhead, office lighting, a 40 inch, 40 watt Phillips "Soft White" fluorescent bulb was affixed on either side of the cart, as well as to the top of the cart,

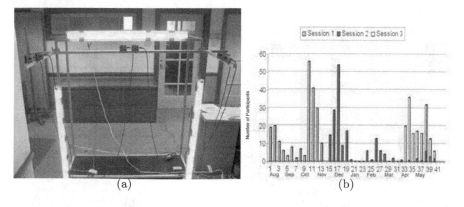

Fig. 6. (a) The positioning of the fluorescent lighting for the indoor scenario and (b) Our collection schedule represented in a bar graph, separated into sessions by color

pointed directly forward from the cart (Figure 6 (a)), in order to provide sufficient lighting for our video. In the outdoor scenario, we utilized natural daylight
lighting, that was dependent upon the variant weather and season. The data
collection did not take place during heavy precipitation, in order to save our
equipment from water damage.

2.4   Time Variance

We captured data in three sessions, each session occurring during a different
season: Late summer/fall, winter, and spring. Our goal was to have a three
month separation between sessions for each participant. The weekly schedule
for all three sessions is shown in Figure 6 (b). We began collecting data for
session one in August, 2004. Session two began in the beginning of November,
2004. Session three began in the middle of March, 2005. The total collection
spanned 10 months, or 40 weeks. The overlap between sessions two and three
are attributed to a large amount of precipitation and cold weather during the
months of session two, delaying our data collection for that session. The specific
dates of each participants' collections has been documented.

3   Collection Procedure and Calibration

To simulate real-world face motion and gestures, we asked each of the participants to mimic a passport checkpoint at an airport, as shown in Figure 7 (a).
Each participant was asked to begin from the side of the cart, walk in and stand
on the red cross mark in front of the the cart, and simulate the gestures and
conversation typical of a passport check. After about 20 seconds, the participant
was asked to exit back off to the side. Each session consisted of two similar runs,
one taking place with the indoor scenario and one in the outdoor. There was no
audio recorded.

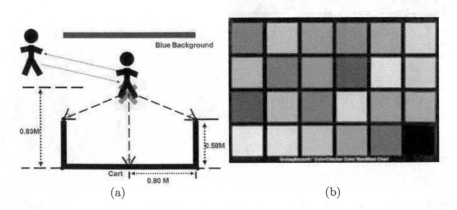

(a)   (b)

Fig. 7. (a) A diagram illustrating participants' procedure and (b) ColorChecker Color
Rendition Chart

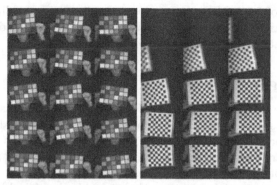

Fig. 8. Sample images of color (left) and camera (right) calibration data. Here we show 15 intermittent frames for the front camera.

In order to ensure color consistency among all the cameras, daily color calibration data was taken. We waved a GretagMacbeth^{TM} [7] ColorChecker Color Rendition Chart (Figure 7 (b)) in the area where a participant's face would be. This chart measures 8.5 x 11 inches and contains an array of 24 scientifically designed colored squares. Six cameras captured the continuously moving chart simultaneously. The color calibration data was taken at 20 frames per second for 5 seconds. Figure 8 shows sample images of our color calibration data. This color calibration data was taken for each day that we collected face data.

We also captured camera calibration data for each subject, using a 9x9 black and white checkerboard. Similarly to the color chart, the checkerboard was waved at the location that was clearly visible from all cameras. We captured the calibration data at 7 frames per second for 6.5 seconds. Also, Figure 8 shows sample images of our camera calibration data. The color calibration and camera calibration data were only collected in the indoor scenario.

4   Database Organization

4.1   Data

We used the maximum resolution and data rate available to us through the Dragonfly cameras, which is 640x480 pixels at 30 frames per second. Each video sequence is 20 seconds long. Our video sequences, which are taken in raw .AVI format, are converted into raw .PGM images for every frame captured. Giving consideration to the large amount of disk space required, we converted the frames to JPEG format with 90% quality. Each image consumes about 100 kb of hard disk space. Thus the total required storage space for our database is ≈ 380GB for only the .JPEG files. We must also put into consideration the space required for the daily color calibration data and the camera calibration data for each subject. Daily color calibration takes up ≈ 5 GB and camera calibration takes up ≈ 15 GB. Thus, the total storage for the participants' images, daily color calibration, and participants' camera calibration is 400 GB. The raw .AVI files require a space of 1.02 GB per participant, leading to an additional required space of 180 participants, 1100 GB. Therefore, the total required disk space for our complete database is 1100GB+400GB = 1500 GB.

4.2 Demographics

We captured the first session of CMU FIA for 214 participants, 180 of whom returned for the second session, of whom 153 returned for a final, third session. Of these participants for the first session, 38.7% are female and 61.3% are male. The youngest participant is 18 years old. The oldest participant is 57 years old. The mean age of the participants is 25.4 years old. In addition, we recorded whether or not each participant wears glasses and/or has facial hair. This data, along with gender and age, is also documented.

5   Possible Usage

The CMU FIA database, with different kinds of variations such as pose, illumination, expression, aging, and etc. is beneficial to the task of recognizing human faces. The CMU FIA database is especially helpful to pose and face gesture variation related research, which is the most difficult to model [8]. Given the variety of variation we were sampling in the CMU FIA database, we suggest that CMU FIA can be used in the following studies:

- Video-based face recognition.
- Pose invariant face recognition [9].
- Three-dimensional face reconstruction from multiple views or from a video sequence.
- Face recognition with respect to image resolution.
- Outdoor illumination invariant face recognition.
- Face recognition over periods of time.
- Face and facial gesture modeling and analysis.

6   Summary and Availability

We have collected a face video database named CMU FIA database. By mimicking the passport checking scenario, six synchronized cameras capture human faces simultaneously from three different poses. We have performed the collection in both indoor and outdoor environments three times, in order to capture the face variance over time. Our data is open to all those interested in using it for research purposes. Those interested may contact Tsuhan Chen (tsuhan@cmu.edu) and send us one or several hard drives. The disk space for only the JPEG images is about 400 GB. The raw .AVI files require an additional 1100 GB.

References

1. P. Jonathon Phillips, Hyeonjoon Moon, Syed A. Rizvi, and Patrick J. Rauss, "FERET (Face Recognition Technology) Recognition Algorithm Development and Test Results". *Army Research Lab technical report 995*, October 1996.
2. Terence Sim, Simon Baker, and Maan Bsat, "The CMU Pose, Illumination, and Expression Database". *IEEE Transactions on Pattern Analysis and Machine Intelligence , Vol. 25, No. 12 pages 1615 - 1618*, December 2003.
3. ORL Face Database. http://www.uk.research.att.com/facedatabase.html
4. Athinodoros S. Georghiades, Peter N. Belhumeur, and David J. Kriegman , "From Few to Many: Illumination Cone Models for Face Recognition under Variable Lighting and Pose". *IEEE Transaction Pattern Analysis Machine Intelligence, Vol. 23, No 6, pages 643 - 660*, 2001.
5. Daniel B. Graham, and Nigel M. Allinson, "Characterizing Virtual Eigensignatures for General Purpose Face Recognition". *recognition. In H. Wechsler, P. J. Phillips, V. Bruce, F. Fogelman- Soulie, and T. S. Huang, editors, Face Recognition: From Theory to Applications, Vol. 163 of NATO ASI Series F, Computer and Systems Sciences, pages 446 - 456*, 1998.
6. Point Grey Research Inc. http://www.ptgrey.com/
7. GretagMacbeth AG. http://www.gretagmacbeth.com/
8. Xiaoming Liu, and Tsuhan Chen, "Online Modeling and Tracking of Pose-Varying Faces in Video". *Video Proceedings of IEEE International Conference on Computer Vision and Pattern Recognition* , June 2005.
9. Xiaoming Liu, and Tsuhan Chen, "Video-based Face Recognition Using Adaptive Hidden Markov Models". *Proceedings of IEEE International Conference on Computer Vision and Pattern Recognition* , Madison, Wisconsin, June 2003.

Robust Automatic Human Identification Using Face, Mouth, and Acoustic Information

Niall A. Fox[1], Ralph Gross[2], Jeffrey F. Cohn[2], and Richard B. Reilly[1]

[1] Dept. of Electronic and Electrical Engineering,
University College Dublin, Belfield, Dublin 4, Ireland
niall.fox@ee.ucd.ie, richard.reilly@ucd.ie
http://ee.ucd.ie/mmsp/
[2] Robotics Institute, Carnegie Mellon University,
5000 Forbes Ave, Pittsburgh, PA 15213
rgross@cs.cmu.edu, jeffcohn+@cs.cmu.edu

Abstract. Discriminatory information about person identity is multimodal. Yet, most person recognition systems are unimodal, e.g. the use of facial appearance. With a view to exploiting the complementary nature of different modes of information and increasing pattern recognition robustness to test signal degradation, we developed a multiple expert biometric person identification system that combines information from three experts: face, visual speech, and audio. The system uses multimodal fusion in an automatic unsupervised manner, adapting to the local performance and output reliability of each of the experts. The expert weightings are chosen automatically such that the reliability measure of the combined scores is maximized. To test system robustness to train/test mismatch, we used a broad range of Gaussian noise and JPEG compression to degrade the audio and visual signals, respectively. Experiments were carried out on the XM2VTS database. The multimodal expert system out performed each of the single experts in all comparisons. At severe audio and visual mismatch levels tested, the audio, mouth, face, and tri-expert fusion accuracies were 37.1%, 48%, 75%, and 92.7% respectively, representing a relative improvement of 23.6% over the best performing expert.

1 Introduction

Biometrics is a field of technology devoted to verification or identification of individuals using physiological or behavioral traits. Verification, a binary classification problem, involves the validation of a claimed identity whereas identification, a multi-class problem, involves identifying a user from a set of enrolled subjects; and becomes more difficult as the number of enrollees increases. In audio-video processing, the video modality lends itself to two experts, the face expert and the visual speech expert (referred to as the mouth expert here).

Deployed person recognition systems are generally unimodal. Face based identification is susceptible to pose/illumination variation, occlusion, and poor image quality [1], [2]. Audio-based identification achieves high performance when the signal-to-noise ratio (SNR) is high. Yet, the performance degrades quickly as the test

W. Zhao, S. Gong, and X. Tang (Eds.): AMFG 2005, LNCS 3723, pp. 264–278, 2005.

SNR decreases (referred to as a train/test mismatch), as shown in [3] and elsewhere. Visual speech based person identification under performs audio and face based experts, and is not thought of as a stand-alone person recognition expert.

To combat these limitations of unimodal audio-video based experts, a multimodal fusion approach can be adopted. This can both improve robustness and overall performance. The audio, face, and mouth modalities contain non-redundant, complementary information about person identity. For example, it was reported in [2] that the performance of the FaceIt face recognizer [4] is extremely sensitive to eye occlusion (dark sunglasses), yet the effect of mouth occlusion (scarf) was significantly lower. This provides motivation for combining the FaceIt and mouth experts, i.e. combining an expert emphasizing eye information with an expert emphasizing mouth information. Also, it is expected that, for person identity, audio and video information are complementary.

In order to exploit this complementary information, issues arise, such as how to account for the reliabilities of the modalities and at what level to carry out the fusion. Only a few studies have investigated the combination of audio, face, and temporal mouth information for the purpose of person recognition [5], [6], [7]. The majority of studies are bi-modal, employing either the audio and face modalities, [8], or, the audio and temporal mouth modalities (ignoring face) [3], [9], [10].

The audio, mouth, and face experts were combined for person recognition in [5], [6], [7]; yet none of these studies employed expert weights that adapt automatically to local test conditions. In [5], fusion was carried out at the decision level, thus no individual expert reliability information could be considered. The weighted sum rule was employed in [7], however, the weights could only be varied using manual supervision. In [6], the weights were global and set empirically. To the best knowledge of the authors, no person recognition system exists, that combines the audio, mouth, and face experts in an automatic unsupervised manner, while adapting to the local performance of each expert.

The aim of this study was to develop a tri-expert person recognition fusion system, combining audio, mouth sequence, and face information in an automatic unsupervised manner. Specifically the tri-expert information was to be combined, such that the fused system provided improved performance beyond existing systems, exhibiting higher robustness to mild through adverse test levels of both audio and visual (face and mouth) noise (train/test mismatch). Therefore, to fully fulfill the aims of this study, the contribution from each source of information to the final decision must be weighted dynamically by taking the current reliability of each source into account.

This paper is organized as follows. Sections 2 and 3 describe how person identification based on audio, mouth features, and face was performed. Section 4 investigates classifier fusion and develops the proposed fusion strategy. In Section 5, the audio-video corpus employed and its' augmentation for the specific experiments is described. In Section 6, we present results of extensive evaluations examining individual expert performance and fusion performance. The results are discussed in Section 7 and finally in Section 8, conclusions from the results are drawn.

2 Audio Identification

Audio based speaker identification is a mature topic, [11]. Standard acoustic methods are employed here. For the feature extraction, the audio signal was divided into frames using a Hamming window of length 20 ms, with an overlap of 10 ms. Mel-frequency cepstral coefficients (MFCCs) of dimension 16 were extracted from each frame [12]. The energy [12] of each frame was also calculated and used as a 17th static feature. Static features refer to features extracted from individual audio frames that do not depend on other frames. Seventeen first order derivatives or delta features were calculated using W_D adjacent static frames, where W_D is the delta window size. The delta frames were appended to the static audio features to give an audio feature vector of dimension 34. These are calculated using HTK [12], employing a W_D value of five frames. Cepstral mean normalization [12] was performed on the audio feature vectors (to each audio utterance).

A text dependent speaker identification methodology was tested. For text dependent modeling [13], the same utterance is spoken by the subject for both training and testing. It was employed, as opposed to text independent modeling [11], due to its suitability to the database used in this study (see Section 5). The N subject classes S_n, $n=1,2,...,N$, are represented by N speaker hidden Markov models (HMMs) denoted by λ_n, $n=1,2,...,N$. The speaker utterance that is to be classified is a sentence, which is represented by a sequence, O_A, of feature vectors or observations denoted by,

$$O_A = \{o_1, o_2, ... o_t, ..., o_{T_A}\}, \tag{1}$$

where o_t is the speech frame at time t and T_A denotes the number of observations. For HMMs, the output scores are in *log-likelihood* form, denoted by $ll(O_A|\lambda_n)$.

3 Video Based Identification

Visual speech based speaker recognition differs from face recognition in two major ways. Firstly, face recognition employs the entire face area, conversely, visual based speaker recognition employs a region of interest about the speakers' mouth, where most of the speech information is contained. Secondly, for face recognition, a gallery of *static* face images forms a template, whereas for visual based speaker recognition, it is attempted to model the temporal characteristics of the visual speech signal.

3.1 Mouth Features Expert

It has been consistently shown in several visual speech studies, that pixel based features outperform geometric features [14], [15]. Geometric features/lip-contours require significantly more sophisticated mouth-tracking techniques compared to just locating the mouth region of interested (ROI) for pixel-based features. This may be difficult, particularly when the visual conditions are poor. Pixel based features employ linear transforms to map the image ROI into a lower dimensional space, removing the redundant information while retaining pertinent speech information. Many types of transforms are examined in the literature, including the *discrete cosine transform* (DCT) [14], [16], *discrete wavelet transform* (DWT) [14], and *principal component analysis* (PCA) [15]. The DCT is one of most commonly employed image transforms. It has good de-correlation and energy compaction properties and has been found to outperform other transforms [15]. The visual mouth features were extracted from the mouth ROI, which consists of a 49×49 color pixel block (see Fig. 3). To account for varying illumination conditions across sessions, the gray scale ROI was histogram equalized and the mean pixel value was subtracted. The two dimensional DCT was applied to the pre-processed gray scale pixel blocks.

Considering that most of the information of an image is contained in the lower DCT spatial frequencies, the first 15 non-zero DCT coefficients were selected, using a mask that selects the coefficients in a tri-angular fashion (upper-left region of the transform matrix) [14]. This gives the static features. The visual sentences were modelled using the same HMM methodology as described for the audio sentences. Dynamic features (frame derivatives of the static features) were employed in previous studies, but exhibited very poor robustness to video degradation, compared to using just static features [17], and were not employed here. We have T_V visual observations (generally $T_A \approx 4xT_V$) and a sequence, O_M, of visual mouth speech feature vectors or observations denoted by,

$$O_M = \{o_1, o_2, ..., o_t, ..., o_{T_V}\}. \tag{2}$$

Each mouth expert HMM gives the *log-likelihood* $ll(O_M|\lambda_n)$, that the observation sequence O_M was produced by the nth mouth expert model λ_n.

3.2 Face Expert

Most current face recognition algorithms can be categorized into two classes, image template-based or geometry feature-based. The template-based methods compute the correlation between a face and one or more model templates to estimate the face identity. Statistical tools such as Support Vector Machines (SVM) [18], Linear Discriminant Analysis (LDA) [19], [20], Principal Component Analysis (PCA) [21], [22], Kernel Methods [23], and Neural Networks [24] have been used to construct a suitable set of face templates. While these templates can be viewed as features, they mostly capture global features of the face images. Facial occlusion is often difficult to handle in these approaches.

The geometry feature-based methods analyze explicit local facial features, and their geometric relationships. Cootes et al. have presented an active shape model in [25] extending the approach by Yuille [26]. Wiskott et al. developed an elastic bunch graph matching algorithm for face recognition in [27]. Penev et. al [28] developed PCA into Local Feature Analysis (LFA) which is the basis for the commercial face recognition system FaceIt. LFA addresses two major problems of PCA. The application of PCA to a set of images yields a global representation of the image features that is not robust to variability due to localized changes in the input. Furthermore the PCA representation is non topographic, so nearby values in the feature representation do not necessarily correspond to nearby values in the input. LFA overcomes these problems by using localized image features in form of multi-scale filters. The feature images are then encoded using PCA to obtain a compact description.

FaceIt was among the top performing systems in a number of independent evaluations [1], [2], [29]. It has been shown to be robust against variations in lighting, facial expression and lower face occlusion. Each of the registered N subjects is represented by a face template λ_n. Unlike for the audio and mouth experts employed here, FaceIt gives a *confidence score*, rather than a log-likelihood, denoted here by $l(O_F|\lambda_n)$, i.e. the likelihood that the face observation O_F belongs to the nth face template λ_n. For FaceIt, the set of N templates, λ_n, $n=1...N$, receives maximum and minimum scores of ten and zero respectively, i.e. $l(O_F|\lambda_n) \in [0,10]$.

4 Classifier Fusion

The fusion of audio and video information falls into two broad categories, *early integration* and *late integration* [13]. Early-integration consists of concatenating the feature vectors, from the different modalities, to give a combined larger dimensional feature vector. This has the disadvantage of high dimensionality and the inability to take the reliability of the individual modalities into account. Furthermore, features from some experts may not be suitable or even available for fusion with speech-based features, e.g. the FaceIt face recognizer.

Late integration can occur at the *score* level or at the *decision* level; and has several advantages: a) late integration involves lower data dimensions than early integration, b) early integration is less robust to sensor failure, c) for late integration, it is more straightforward to add new experts, d) late integration allows the fusion of modalities possessing different temporal synchrony e.g. face and audio.

A significant amount of information is lost when the expert confidence scores are mapped to the class labels (decisions). This is why that, if the individual expert reliabilities are to be considered, fusion should occur at the *score* and not the *decision* level, as the score level information is crucial for discerning the reliability of each expert. For *decision* fusion, the number of classifiers should be higher than the number of classes. This is reasonable for person verification. For person identification, the number of classes is large, rendering decision fusion unsuitable.

Two typical methods of combining the output scores from the N_E experts are the *product* and the *sum* rules [30]. The *product rule* consists of multiplying the N_E scores together. It is sensitive to expert errors; in the extreme case, if any single expert produces a close to zero score for a specific class; the combined score for that class will be close to zero. The *sum rule* is less sensitive to expert errors and will outperform the product rule when the expert errors are large. The robustness of the sum rule to expert errors was shown theoretically and verified experimentally in [30].

Experts scores can take many forms such as posteriors, likelihoods, and distance measures. Non-normalized scores cannot be integrated sensibly in their raw form, as it is impossible to fuse incomparable numerical scales. The min-max technique shifts and scales the scores into the range *[0,1]*. Given a set or a list of N scores $\{S_n\}_{n=1...N}$ corresponding to N class labels the normalized score is calculated as:

$$S_n^{'} = \left(\frac{S_n - S_{min}}{S_{max} - S_{min}} \right), \quad S_n^{'} \in [0,1], \tag{3}$$

where S_{max} and S_{min} are the maximum and minimum scores from the set $\{S_n\}$. While been straightforward to implement the min-max norm, has been found to have comparable performance to more complicated methods [31], hence, it was used for experiments reported here. Its' poor robustness to outlier scores can be circumvented (in the person identification scenario) by considering only the top M ranked scores for normalization. This omits the worst (outlier) expert scores.

4.1 The Proposed Method

The fusion strategy was first developed for fusing any two experts, and was then extended to include an additional third expert. Each expert provides a list of N likelihoods: $\{l(O_m|\lambda_n)\}_{n=1...N}$ with $m \in \{A, M, F\}$. These are ranked into descending order and normalized into the range $[0,1]$ using Eqn. (3), applied to only the top M scores. Using a high value for M may retain the worst s(outlier) scores, which could unfairly skew the distribution. A very low value, would result in information loss; the limit been $M=1$, where all confidence information has been lost. Tests showed that the system performance degraded for $M<50$ and $M>100$. A value for M of 75 was employed for this study[1]. This value may depend on N, the number of classes. The set of M *ranked* normalized scores is denoted by $\{S(O_m|\lambda_i)\}_{i=1...M}$. We have the *weighted sum rule* (for the specific case of two experts):

$$S(O_1,O_2|\lambda_i) = \sum_{m=1}^{N_E} \alpha_m \cdot S(O_m|\lambda_i) = \alpha_1 \cdot S(O_1|\lambda_i) + \alpha_2 \cdot S(O_2|\lambda_i), \qquad (4)$$

where $S(O_1,O_2|\lambda_i)$ represents the combined likelihood that the observations O_1 and O_2 were produced by the subject class λ_i; and α_m is the weight of the mth expert, subject to the constraints that $\sum \alpha_m=1$ and $0 \leq \alpha_m \leq 1$ for $m=1...N_E$. Given that the weights α_m are variable, some sort of reliability measure must be devised, which takes the confidence associated with each expert into account, and is used to determine the α_m values.

Expert reliability parameters can be calculated at the *signal* or at the *score* level. Signal based reliability measures are generally acoustic based [32] which have the disadvantage of having no corresponding video reliability measure. Even if an observation signal is of high quality, the expert may still give a misclassification for two (non-exhaustive) reasons: 1) the correct subject class may be indistinguishable for the given expert, and may be consistently misclassified, 2) the model/template for the correct subject may be a poor representation. A signal based reliability measure cannot take these into account. The distribution of the set of expert confidence scores contains information not only about the integrity of the observation signal, but also the reliability of that experts' decision. Taking these points into account, it is better to calculate the reliability measure based on the expert scores.

If the highest ranked class receives a high score and all of the other classes receive relatively low scores, then the confidence level is high. Conversely, if all the classes receive similar scores, the confidence is low. Various metrics exist, which can be used to capture this confidence information. Examples include, score *entropy* [32], *dispersion* [32], *variance* [9], and *difference* [9]. For a test observation vector O_m, we

---

[1] The overall performance did not vary significantly for $50<M<100$.

have the set of M ranked normalized scores $\{S(O_m|\lambda_i)\}_{i=1...M}$. The difference, ξ, between the two highest ranked confidence scores is calculated as

$$\xi_m = S(O_m \mid \lambda_1) - S(O_m \mid \lambda_2), \tag{5}$$

where λ_1 and λ_2 are the subject classes achieving the highest and second highest ranks respectively, and m denotes the expert. This metric was employed for this study.

A mapping between the reliability estimates and the expert weightings is required. In [16], [32] a sigmoidal mapping was used to map the reliability estimates to the fusion weights. The sigmoidal parameters require training, which is difficult when the amount of audio-visual data is scare, and may be specific to the noise type. Another option is to form bins of evaluation reliability values and the corresponding α_m values (found by exhaustive search), effectively a lookup table, but again this requires extensive training. Considering the small amount of audio-visual training data generally available, it was decided to use a non-learned approach to map the reliability estimates to the α_m values. This was carried out as follows:

For each specific identification trial (user interaction), the system is presented with two expert observations, O_1 and O_2.

1. The two experts each generate a set of N match scores, $\{l(O_1|\lambda_n)\}$ and $\{l(O_2|\lambda_n)\}$, which are normalized to give the sets of M ranked scores $\{S(O_1|\lambda_i)\}_{i=1...M}$ and $\{S(O_2|\lambda_i)\}_{i=1...M}$.
2. The fusion parameter α_2 is varied from 0 to 1 in steps of 0.05. For each of these α_2 values, the expert score lists $\{S(O_1|\lambda_i)\}$ and $\{S(O_2|\lambda_i)\}$ are combined using Eqn. (4) (with $\alpha_1=1-\alpha_2$), to give the combined set of N scores $\{S_{12,n}\}=\{S(O_1,O_2|\lambda_n)\}_{n=1...N}$. We have N, not M, S_{12} scores here because the sets of M normalized scores arising from experts 1 and 2 will in general correspond to different sets of M subject classes; some of the N S_{12} scores will be zeroed valued.
3. The combined score set is subsequently normalized as before, to give $\{S(O_1,O_2|\lambda_i)\}_{i=1...M}$, and the combined score reliability estimate, denoted by ξ_{12}, is calculated, as in Eqn. (5). ξ_{12} can be thought of as a linear weighted combination of the individual expert reliabilities ξ_1 and ξ_2 because

$$\xi_{12} = S(O_1, O_2 \mid \lambda_1) - S(O_1, O_2 \mid \lambda_2) \tag{6}$$
$$= \alpha_1 \cdot S(O_1 \mid \lambda_1) + \alpha_2 \cdot S(O_2 \mid \lambda_1) - \alpha_1 \cdot S(O_1 \mid \lambda_2) - \alpha_2 \cdot S(O_2 \mid \lambda_2)$$
$$= \alpha_1 \cdot \xi_1 + \alpha_2 \cdot \xi_2,$$

where λ_1 and λ_2 are the subject classes achieving the highest and second highest ranks respectively, as before. However, the ξ_{12} value is calculated using Eqn. (5) and not Eqn. (6) because the set of scores $\{S_{12,n}\}$ is normalized, and hence Eqn. (6) does not hold exactly.

4. We choose the α_2 value that maximizes ξ_{12} for the given test according to Eqn. (7), to give the fusion parameters α_{2opt} and $\alpha_{1opt} = 1-\alpha_{2opt}$. The maximum ξ_{12} value should correspond to the combined scores of highest confidence, i.e. maximizes the score separation between the highest ranked class and the other classes. Finally, we combine $\{S(O_1|\lambda_i)\}$ and $\{S(O_2|\lambda_i)\}$ as in Eqn. (4) (using α_{1opt} and α_{2opt}), to form the combined score list $\{S_{12,n}\}_{opt, n=1,...,N}$ which is used to make the final identification decision.

$$\alpha_{2opt} = \arg \max_{\alpha_2 \in [0,1]} \{\xi_{12} | \alpha_2\}. \tag{7}$$

It should be noted that the above procedure is carried out for every identification trial, and thus the fusion weights are determined online and automatically in an unsupervised manner. Also, O_1/O_2 above can represent any of $m \in \{A, M, F\}$. For illustration, Fig. 1 gives four examples of the specific case of fusing the scores arising from audio and mouth observations. The four examples show that the weight selection procedure has the ability to adapt the weights to the reliability of each expert.

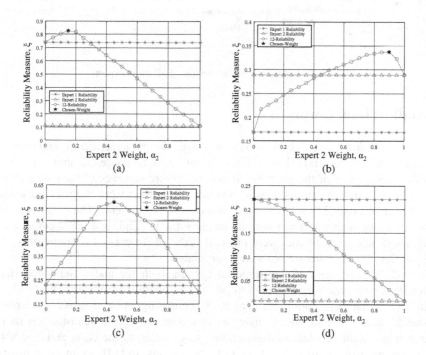

Fig. 1. The variation of the combined score reliability estimate w.r.t. α_2; and the individual expert reliability estimates are shown for four scenarios: (a) expert 1 is more reliable (selected $\alpha_{2opt} = 0.15$), (b) expert 2 is more reliable ($\alpha_{2opt} = 0.9$), (c) experts 1 and 2 have similar reliabilities ($\alpha_{2opt} = 0.5$), and (d) expert 2 has a very low reliability ($\xi_2 = 8 \times 10\text{-}4$), and $\alpha_{2opt} = 0$

4.2 Fusion of the Three Experts

The bi-expert fusion method developed above can be employed to combine the output scores from any pair of person identification experts. In order to carry out tri-expert fusion of the audio, mouth, and face experts, a cascade approach is employed. Firstly, the two visual based experts (face and mouth) are combined, thus giving N *"face-mouth"* scores. This is shown in the first block of Fig. 2, where *"N Score Integration"* refers to the general bi-expert fusion block as described above. It is intuitive to fuse the two visual experts initially, as a noisy visual observation signal is likely to affect both the face and mouth experts; in which case, the audio scores can still be weighted highly to counteract this. The *"face-mouth"* scores are subsequently fused with the N audio scores to give a tri-expert identification decision. We will now describe the fusion experiments that were carried out using the proposed method.

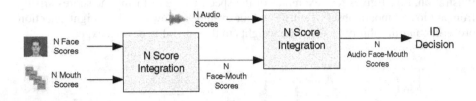

Fig. 2. Flow diagram for the fusion of all three experts

5 Audio-Visual Corpus

The XM2VTS audio-visual database [19] was used for the experiments, and consists of video data recorded from 295 subjects in four sessions, spaced monthly. The first recording per session of the phonetically balanced third sentence (*"Joe took father's green shoe bench out"*) was used. Some sentence recordings were clipped. Due to this and other errors, only 248 subjects were used for the experiments. The position of the mouth ROI was determined by manually labeling the left and right labial corners and taking the center point. Frames were manually labeled for every 10th frame only; the ROI positions for the other frames were interpolated.

To test the robustness of the proposed system, both the audio and video (face sequence) test signals were degraded to provide a train/test mismatch. Ten levels of audio and visual degradation were applied; emulating mild to adverse train/test mismatch noise levels, which may be encountered in a realistic operating environment. Additive white Gaussian noise was applied to the clean audio at SNR levels ranging from 48 dB to 21 dB in 3 dB decrements. In [14], an image transform based approach was used to carry out visual word recognition. The system demonstrated robustness to JPEG compression, with no significant drop in performance until JPEG quality factors (QF) levels fell below 10. For our study, in order to account for practical video conditions, the video frame images were compressed using JPEG compression. We tested ten levels of JPEG QF, i.e.

$$QF \in \{50, 25, 18, 14, 10, 8, 6, 4, 3, 2\}, \tag{8}$$

where a QF of 100 represents the original uncompressed image. The compression was applied to each video frame individually. The mouth ROI was then extracted from the compressed images. Manually labeled mouth coordinates were employed, so that any drop in performance would be due to mismatched testing rather than poorer mouth tracking. The variation of the face and corresponding mouth ROI images w.r.t. JPEG QF is shown in Fig. 3. JPEG blocking artifacts are evident at the lower QF levels.

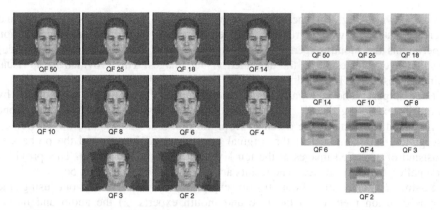

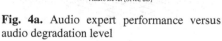

Fig. 3. Ten levels of JPEG compression and corresponding mouth ROI images

6 Experiments and Results

The proposed tri-expert system was applied to closed-set person identification. It can also be applied to the more general problem of open-set person recognition.

Audio Expert: The HMMs were trained/tested using HTK [12]. The first three sessions were used for training and the last for testing. A prototype HMM consists of the initial parameters. Since there are only three training utterances per subject, there was insufficient training data to train a speaker HMM directly from a prototype model. For this reason, a background HMM was trained using three of the sessions for all N subjects, and was used to initialize the training of the speaker models. All models were trained on the clean speech and tested on the various SNR levels. This provides for an audio train/test mismatch. The num+ber of HMM states that maximized the audio accuracy was found empirically to be eleven (with a mix of two Gaussians per state). Fig. 4 shows how the audio expert performs w.r.t. audio degradation. A maximum accuracy of 97.6% was achieved at 48dB, with dropped to 37.1% at 21 dB.

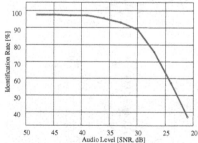

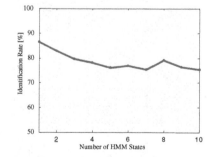

Fig. 4a. Audio expert performance versus audio degradation level

Fig. 4b. Mouth expert performance versus number of HMM states

Mouth Expert: The effect of the number of HMM states on the performance of the mouth expert was initially tested. One Gaussian per state was used. The result of this is shown in Fig. 4b. The mouth expert performed best with just one state and decreased steadily with increasing number of states. For the visual degradation experiments the mouth expert HMMs were trained on the "clean" (uncompressed) visual images and tested on the degraded visual images. This provided for a visual train/test mismatch. The results are given in Table 1 and Fig. 5c.

Face Expert: The face gallery set, comprising of three images, was formed by arbitrarily extracting the 9th image frame from the first three sessions. The probe images used for testing were obtained from the fourth session (again, the 9th frame). The gallery sets consisted of the original uncompressed images and the probe sets consisted of degraded images at the ten levels of JPEG compression. This provided for a gallery/probe mismatch. The results are given in Table 1 and Fig. 5c.

Fusion Experiments: Four fusion experiments were carried out using the proposed fusion method: 1) the face and mouth experts, 2) the audio and mouth experts, 3) the audio and face experts, and 4) the audio, face, and mouth experts. The face, mouth, and *face-mouth* fusion performance w.r.t. JPEG QF mismatch is given in Table 1 and Fig. 5c. For the three audio-visual fusion experiments, ten levels of both visual (JPEG QF) and audio (dB) degradation were examined. The results for these experiments are given in Fig. 5 and Table 2, with the *audio-mouth* results in Fig. 5a, the *audio-face* results in Fig. 5b, and the *audio-face-mouth*, results in Fig. 5d.

Table 1. The mouth, face, and face-mouth fusion accuracies for the ten levels of JPEG QF

JPEG QF	50	25	18	14	10	8	6	4	3	2
Mouth [%]	85.9	85.1	84.3	84.3	82.7	80.2	79.4	60.5	50.8	48.0
Facelt [%]	98.8	98.8	99.6	99.6	98.8	98.8	98.0	91.9	85.9	75.0
Mouth-Facelt [%]	100.0	99.2	100.0	100.0	100.0	100.0	100.0	98.4	92.7	87.5

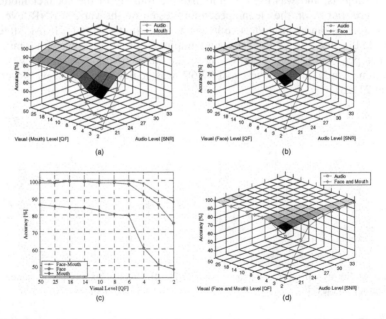

Fig. 5. The accuracies for the fusion of: (a) the audio and mouth experts, (b) the audio and face experts, (c) the face and mouth experts, and (d) the audio, face, and mouth experts

Table 2. The accuracies for the mouth (M), face (F), audio (A), and the fusion of: (a) the face and mouth experts (FM), (b) the audio and mouth experts (AM), (c) the audio and face experts (AF), and (d) the audio, face, and mouth experts (AFM)

QF			dB	33	30	27	24	21
			A	93.1	89.1	75.8	57.3	37.1
8	M	80.2	AM	98.8	97.6	96.0	91.1	86.3
	F	98.8	AF	99.6	99.6	99.6	99.6	99.6
	FM	100.0	AFM	100.0	100.0	100.0	100.0	100.0
6	M	79.4	AM	98.8	97.2	94.4	89.9	85.1
	F	98.0	AF	99.6	99.6	99.6	99.2	98.8
	FM	100.0	AFM	100.0	100.0	100.0	100.0	100.0
4	M	60.5	AM	97.6	96.4	91.1	84.7	76.6
	F	91.9	AF	99.2	99.2	08.0	90.8	96.4
	FM	98.4	AFM	99.6	99.2	98.8	98.4	98.4
3	M	50.8	AM	97.6	95.6	91.9	81.5	72.6
	F	85.9	AF	99.2	98.8	97.2	94.8	93.1
	FM	92.7	AFM	99.2	98.8	98.4	97.6	96.4
2	M	48.0	AM	97.2	95.2	91.1	80.6	71.4
	F	75.0	AF	98.8	97.2	93.1	89.9	86.3
	FM	87.5	AFM	97.6	97.2	96.4	95.6	92.7

7 Discussion

With regard to the specific experiments, the audio expert performed very well under near "clean" testing conditions, however the accuracy roll off w.r.t. SNR is very high. For the mouth expert experiments, the fact that the static visual features performed best with just one state indicates that HMMs may not be required to model visual speech, rather, a Gaussian mixture model (GMM) approach [11] would be sufficient. The best mouth expert accuracy is 85.9%. A reasonable level of robustness to video degradation is exhibited; with an accuracy of 48.2% at a QF of 2.

It was expected that FaceIt, a commercial system, employing features located throughout the entire face would outperform an expert employing features extracted from just the mouth ROI. The face expert outperformed the mouth expert at all levels of train/test mismatch. The highest face expert accuracy of 98.8% is 15% higher (relative) than the highest mouth expert accuracy of 85.9%. The face expert also exhibits higher robustness to JPEG compression, when compared to the mouth expert, with accuracies exceeding 98%, for all test mismatch levels exceeding a QF of 4. At the highest mismatch QF level of 2, the face expert accuracy was 75%, and the mouth expert accuracy was 48%. The superior performance of FaceIt is more impressive when considering that the FaceIt gallery consists of only three images, whereas the mouth expert model has the advantage of *"seeing"* three sequences of video frames and hence more variation in the subjects' appearance. The robustness of the face expert against JPEG compression is in line with results from the Face Recognition Vendor Test 2000 [1], where similar observations were made.

For the fusion of the face and mouth experts, a perfect *face-mouth* accuracy of 100% is achieved at several levels of JPEG QF mismatch. Also, the *face-mouth* accuracies are higher than either of the face or mouth expert accuracies for all levels of JPEG QF mismatch, i.e. enhancing fusion. The most significant improvements are yielded for the higher levels of mismatch, for example at the lowest QF level of 2, the *face-mouth*, face, and mouth accuracies are, 87.5%, 75%, and 48% respectively, representing a 17% relative improvement over the face expert alone. The improved *face-mouth* performance indicates that the mouth features complement the facial

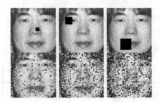

Fig. 5. Some examples of randomly occluded images and noisy images

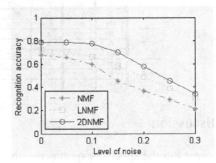

Fig. 6. Comparison of recognition accuracy of NMF, LNMF and 2DNMF under different size of occlusions (left) and different level of noises (right)

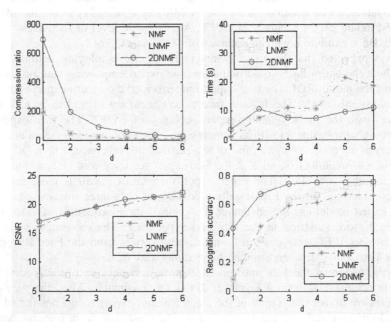

Fig. 7. Comparisons of performances of NMF, LNMF and 2DNMF under different number of bases. For NMF and LNMF, number of bases is $d*d$, while for 2DNMF the both numbers of row and column bases are $2d$.

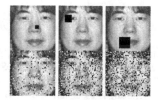

Fig. 5. Some examples of randomly occluded images and noisy images

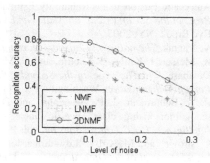

Fig. 6. Comparison of recognition accuracy of NMF, LNMF and 2DNMF under different size of occlusions (left) and different level of noises (right)

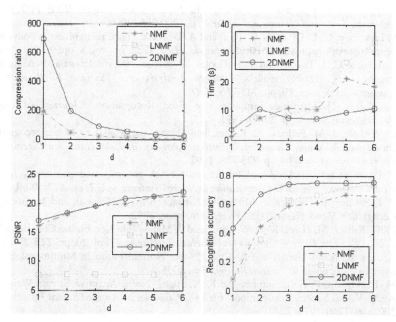

Fig. 7. Comparisons of performances of NMF, LNMF and 2DNMF under different number of bases. For NMF and LNMF, number of bases is $d*d$, while for 2DNMF the both numbers of row and column bases are $2d$.

[14] G. Potamianos, H. Graf, and E. Cosatto, "An Image Transform Approach for HMM Based Automatic Lipreading," in *Proc. of the IEEE Int'l Conf. Image Processing*, Chicago, vol. 3, pp. 173-177, 1998.

[15] I. Matthews, G. Potamianos, C. Neti, and J. Luettin, "A Comparison of Model and Transform-based Visual Features for Audio-Visual LVCSR," in *proc. of the IEEE Int'l Conf. on Multimedia and Expo*, pp. 825-828, 2001.

[16] N. A. Fox, R. Gross, P. de Chazal, J. F. Cohn, and R. B. Reilly, "Person Identification Using Automatic Integration of Speech, Lip, and Face Experts," in *ACM SIGMM workshop on Biometrics Methods and Applications*, Berkley, CA., pp. 25-32, 2003.

[17] N. A. Fox, B. A. O'Mullane, and R. B. Reilly, "Audio-Visual Speaker Identification via Automatic Fusion using Reliability Estimates of both Modalities," in *to appear in the Proc. of the 5th Int'l Conf. on Audio- and Video-Based Biometric Person Authentication*, Rye Brook, NY, 2005.

[18] V. Vapnik, *The nature of statistical learning theory*: Springer Verlag, 1995.

[19] K. Messer, J. Kittler, J. Luettin, and G. Maitre, "XM2VTSDB: "The Extended M2VTS Database"," in *The Proc. of the Second Int'l Conf. on Audio and Video-based Biometric Person Authentication*, Washington D.C., pp. 72-77, 1999.

[20] P. N. Belhumeur, J. P. Hespanha, and D. J. Kriegman, "Eigenfaces vs. Fisherfaces: recognition using class specific linear projection," *Pattern Analysis and Machine Intelligence, IEEE Transactions on*, vol. 19, pp. 711-720, 1997.

[21] L. Sirovich and M. Kirby, "Low-dimensional procedure for the characterization of human faces," *Journal of the Optical Society of America A. 4*, pp. 519-524, 1987.

[22] M. Turk and A. Pentland, "Eigenfaces for Recognition," *Journal of Cognitive Neuroscience*, vol. 3, pp. 71-86, 1991.

[23] Y. Li, S. Gong, and H. Liddell, "Support vector regression and classification based multi-view face detection and recognition," in *Proc. of the Fourth IEEE Int'l Conf. on Automatic Face and Gesture Recognition*, pp. 300-305, 2000.

[24] S. Lawrence, C. L. Giles, A. C. Tsoi, and A. D. Back, "Face recognition: a convolutional neural-network approach," *Neural Networks, IEEE Tran. on*, vol. 8, pp. 98-113, 1997.

[25] A. Lanitis, C. J. Taylor, and T. F. Cootes, "Automatic interpretation and coding of face images using flexible models," *Pattern Analysis and Machine Intelligence, IEEE Transactions on*, vol. 19, pp. 743-756, 1997.

[26] A. Yuille, "Deformable Templates for Face Recognition," *Journal of Cognitive Neuroscience*, vol. 3, pp. 59-70, 1991.

[27] L. Wiskott, J.-M. Fellous, N. Kuiger, and C. von der Malsburg, "Face recognition by elastic bunch graph matching," *Pattern Analysis and Machine Intelligence, IEEE Transactions on*, vol. 19, pp. 775-779, 1997.

[28] P. Penev and J. Atick, "Local feature analysis: A general statistical theory for object representation," *Network: Computation in Neural Systems*, vol. 7, pp. 477-500, 1996.

[29] P. J. Phillips, P. Grother, P. Michaels, D. Blackburn , E. Tabassi, and M. Bone, "Face Recognition Vendor Test 2002," Evaluation report 2002.

[30] [30]J. Kittler, M. Hatef, R. P. W. Duin, and J. Matas, "On Combining Classifiers," *IEEE Transactions on Pattern Analysis and Machine Intelligence*, vol. 20, pp. 226-239, 1998.

[31] A. Jain, K. Nandakumar, and A. Ross, "Score Normalization in Multimodal Biometric Systems," *to appear in Pattern Recognition*, 2005.

[32] M. Heckmann, F. Berthommier, and K. Kristian, "Noise Adaptive Stream Weighting in Audio-Visual Speech Recognition," *EURASIP Journal on Applied Signal Processing*, vol. 2002, pp. 1260-1273, 2002.

AdaBoost Gabor Fisher Classifier for Face Recognition

Shiguang Shan[1], Peng Yang[2], Xilin Chen[1], and Wen Gao[1,3]

[1] ICT-ISVISION JDL for Face Recognition, Institute of Computing Technology,
Chinese Academy of Sciences, Beijing, 100080, China
{sgshan, xlchen, wgao}@jdl.ac.cn
http://www.jdl.ac.cn/project/faceId/index_en.htm
[2] Department of Computer Sciences at Rutgers, The State University of New Jersey, USA
peyang@eden.rutgers.edu
[3] School of Computer Science and Technology, Harbin Institute of Technology,
150001 Harbin, China

Abstract. This paper proposes the AdaBoost Gabor Fisher Classifier (AGFC) for robust face recognition, in which a chain AdaBoost learning method based on Bootstrap re-sampling is proposed and applied to face recognition with impressive recognition performance. Gabor features have been recognized as one of the most successful face representations, but it is too high dimensional for fast extraction and accurate classification. In AGFC, AdaBoost is exploited to select optimally the most informative Gabor features (hereinafter as AdaGabor features). The selected low-dimensional AdaGabor features are then classified by Fisher discriminant analysis for final face identification. Our experiments on two large-scale face databases, FERET and CAS-PEAL (with 5789 images of 1040 subjects), have shown that the proposed method can effectively reduce the dimensionality of Gabor features and greatly increase the recognition accuracy. In addition, our experimental results show its robustness to variations in facial expression and accessories.

1 Introduction

Automatic Face Recognition (AFR) research has been motivated by both its scientific values and wide potential applications in public security, law enforcement, and video surveillance. Relevant research activities have significantly increased, and much progress has been made during the past few years [1,2,3]. However, most current systems work well only under constrained conditions, even requiring the subjects highly cooperative. Therefore, the general problems in AFR remain unsolved, especially under the practical unconstrained conditions.

The performance of a face recognition system depends not only on the classifier, but also on the representation of the face patterns. Generally speaking, a good representation should have such characteristics as small within-class variation, large between-class variation, and being robust to transformations without changing the class label [4]. Furthermore, its extraction should not depend much on the manual operation. Intuitively, one should derive face representation from the 3D face shape and skin reflectance if we could recover the above intrinsic information from a given 2D face image. Unfortunately, it is an ill-posed problem in computer vision. Therefore, most current famous face recognition methods derive face representation

W. Zhao, S. Gong, and X. Tang (Eds.): AMFG 2005, LNCS 3723, pp. 279–292, 2005.
© Springer-Verlag Berlin Heidelberg 2005

directly from the 2D face image matrix. The obvious disadvantages of 2D image representation lie in its sensitivity to the changes in the extrinsic imaging factors such as viewpoint and lighting.

Another popular strategy to represent face pattern exploits some transformations of the 2D image. Typical transformations include the Fourier transform [5], various wavelets, among which Gabor wavelets have been widely accepted by researchers in AFR community [6,7,8,9], mostly because the kernels of Gabor wavelet are similar to the 2D receptive field profiles of the mammalian cortical simple cells and exhibit desirable characteristics of spatial locality and orientation selectivity [10, 11]. Previous works on Gabor features have also demonstrated excellent performance. Typical methods include the Dynamic Link Architecture (DLA) [6], Elastic Graph Matching (EGM) [7], Gabor Wavelet Network (GWN) [8], and Gabor-Fisher Classifier (GFC) [9].

EGM represents a face as a labeled graph [7]. Each vertex of the graph corresponds to a predefined facial landmark with fixed high-level semantics, and labeled by the multi-scale, multi-orientation Gabor *Jet* computed from the image area centered at the vertex landmark. And the edge of the graph represents the connection between the two vertices landmarks and labeled by the distance between them. After the construction of the graph, identification can be achieved by the elastic matching between the reference graph and the probe one. By selecting facial landmarks carefully, elastic graph can well model the local facial features as well as their configuration. Therefore, it makes the most of the local features as well as the overall facial configuration. Nevertheless, the high complexity of graph construction and matching may have prevented its further application. In addition, imprecise landmarks localization may also influence its recognition performance.

One straightforward way to exploit Gabor features for AFR is proposed by Liu [9]. In Liu's method, Gabor features of multi-scale and multi-orientation for each pixel in the normalized face images (with the eyes aligned) are firstly computed and concatenated to form a high-dimensional Gabor features, which is then uniformly down-sampled to a low-dimensional feature vector, and further reduced dimension by Principle Component Analysis (PCA), and discriminated by enhanced Fisher Discriminant Analysis for final face identification [9]. This method is simple and does not need to localize more facial landmarks except the two eyes. Liu has experimentally shown the excellent performance of such a method. However, the uniform down-sampling procedure would not only reduce the dimension of the high-dimension dense Gabor features, but also reject a great number of informative Gabor features and reserve many redundant ones, which would do harm to the final classification.

Aiming at the above-mentioned problem of GFC, this paper proposes to optimally select informative Gabor features to keep from losing discriminant Gabor features and introducing redundant ones by the simple down-sampling procedure. We originally apply AdaBoost to face recognition as a feature selection tool to reduce the dimension of Gabor features. The Gabor features selected by AdaBoost are further processed by Fisher discriminant as the final classifier. Our experiments on two large-scale face databases, FERET and CAS-PEAL, have shown that the proposed AGFC method can efficiently reduce the dimension of the original Gabor features, and the final recognition performance has also been improved.

2 Related Works

2.1 Gabor Features

Gabor wavelets model quite well the receptive field profiles of cortical simple cells, and they can capture salient visual properties such as spatial localization, orientation selectivity, and spatial frequency characteristic. Gabor filters extract both the overall and the subtle spatial frequency features in some local image area with multiple scales and multiple orientations, magnifying like a microscope all the features implied in the changing of gray-level intensity. Therefore, 2D Gabor filters enhance the low-level image features such as the peaks, valleys, and ridges. So, the eyes, the nose and the mouth, as well as the other salient local features like naevi, dimples, and scars, are enhanced as key features for the following discrimination of different faces. The Gabor wavelet representation also facilitates recognition without correspondence (hence, little need for manual annotations) because it captures the local structure corresponding to spatial frequency (scale), spatial localization, and orientation [9]. As a result, the Gabor wavelet representation of face images is robust to mis-alignment to some degree as Shan et al report in [12].

Lades et al. pioneered the use of Gabor wavelets for face recognition using the DLA framework, which is then expanded to EGM by Wiskott et al. [7]. The commonly used Gabor filters in face recognition area is defined as followings [6, 7, 9, 11]:

$$\psi_{u,v}(z) = \frac{\| k_{u,v} \|^2}{\sigma^2} e^{(-\| k_{u,v} \|^2 \| z \|^2 / 2\sigma^2)} \left[e^{i k_{u,v} z} - e^{-\sigma^2/2} \right], \tag{1}$$

where u and v define the orientation and scale of the Gabor kernels, $z = (x, y)$, $\|.\|$ denotes the norm operator, and the wave vector $k_{u,v}$ is defined as follows:

$$k_{u,v} = k_v e^{i\phi_u}, \tag{2}$$

where $k_v = k_{max} / f^v$ and $\phi_u = \pi u / 8$ with k_{max} be the maximum frequency, and f be the spacing factor between kernels in the frequency domain. In face recognition area, researchers commonly use 40 Gabor wavelets with five scales $v \in \{0,1,2,3,4\}$ and eight orientations $u \in \{0, \cdots, 7\}$ and with $\sigma = 2\pi$, $k_{max} = \frac{\pi}{2}$, and $f = \sqrt{2}$.

Convolving the image with these 40 Gabor kernels can then generate the Gabor features. Thus, for each pixel position in the face image, 40 complex values can be calculated. Note that, because the phase information of the transform is time-varying, generally, only its magnitudes are used to form the final face representation. Evidently, this will result in a feature with a dimension of 40 times of the original face images size, which is too high dimensional in pixel-wise dense sampling case. Therefore, GFC down-sampled the Gabor features, while in this paper learning method is used to select the most informative ones.

2.2 Adaptive Boosting (AdaBoost)

Boosting has been proposed to improve the accuracy of any given learning algorithm. In Boosting one generally creates a classifier with accuracy on the training set greater than an average performance, and then adds new component classifiers to form an ensemble whose joint decision rule has arbitrarily high accuracy on the training set [4]. In such a case, we say that the classification performance has been "boosted". In overview, the technique train successive component classifiers with a subset of the entire training data that is "most informative" given the current set of component classifiers [4].

AdaBoost (Adaptive Boosting) is a typical instance of Boosting learning. In AdaBoost, each training pattern is assigned a weight that determines its probability of being selected for some individual component classifier. Generally, one initializes the weights across the training set to be uniform. In the learning process, if a training pattern has been accurately classified, then its chance of being used again in a subsequent component classifier is decreased; conversely, if the pattern is not accurately classified, then its chance of being used again is increased [4]. In each iteration, one draws a training set at random according to the weights, and then trains a component classifier C_k on the patterns selected. Next one increases weights of those training patterns misclassified by C_k and decrease weights of the patterns correctly classified by C_k. Patterns chosen according to this new weights are used to train the next classifier, C_{k+1}, and the process is iterated to a predefined error rate or enough component classifiers have been constructed [4]. In this way, AdaBoost focuses on the informative or "difficult" patterns. The final classifier is a linear combination of the component classifiers. According to the idea, Freund and Schapire first proposed the concrete algorithms of Adaboost [13].

In 2001, Viola and Jones proposed a modified AdaBoost algorithm and applied it to face detection successfully [14]. In Viola's AdaBoost, the component classifier (or so-called weak classifier) has been designed by one individual weak Haar-like feature. AdaBoost learning is adopted to combine these weak classifiers. Therefore, in some sense, in Viola's AdaBoost, weak classifier is somewhat equivalent to weak feature. For the specific face detection problem, Viola has designed a fast algorithm to exact a huge number of rectangle (Haar-like) features from a small candidate window region, a few of which are then selected and combined to form a strong classifier by AdaBoost learning. By far, AdaBoost-based face detection has been recognized as the most successful one for face detection task [15]. Viola has also applied the similar method to pedestrian detection and achieved similar success. By using AdaBoost for selecting Gabor features, this paper originally applies AdaBoost to face recognition successfully.

3   AdaBoost Gabor Fisher Classifier

The great success of AdaBoost on face detection has motivated our interest in applying AdaBoost to face recognition. Considering the success of Gabor features in face recognition area, we have previously proposed to design an AdaBoost classifier by using the Gabor representation as the original feature set [16]. Unlike our previous work in [16], this paper re-considers AdaBoost as a feature selection tool and Fisher Discriminant Analysis is exploited as the final classifier. To apply AdaBoost to multi-class AFR problem, the "dual difference class", i.e., intra-personal and extra-personal differences are introduced to convert the multi-class problem into a binary classification problem [17]. Given a training set, the two difference classes are first computed, and then AdaBoost is trained on them to select those most informative ones (named by AdaGabor features) from all the original high-dimensional pixel-wise dense Gabor features. The resulting AdaGabor features are then further reduced in dimensionality by PCA, and then fed into the Fisher Discriminant Analysis for final classification.

3.1 Intra-personal and Extra-personal Difference

To exploit AdaBoost for face recognition, we have to convert the multi-class problem to a binary one. Typical methods include one-to-one and one-to-rest, which need to construct $C(C-1)/2$ and C classifiers respectively, where C is the number of persons to be recognized. Both of them are very complex, and inconvenience when we need to enroll new persons. To solve this problem, we have adopted the intra-personal and extra-personal difference method proposed by Moghaddam and Pentland [17]. Given two images in a training set coming from the same face, their feature vector difference would be put into the intra-personal difference class, otherwise, their difference will be labeled as an extra-personal difference. In this way, face recognition problem is reformulated as a binary classification problem to determine which class the difference between the probe image and any gallery one belongs to. Therefore, AdaBoost can be applied straightforwardly to learn the separation super-surface.

3.2 Gabor Features Selection Using Chain AdaBoost Learning Based on Bootstrap Re-sampling

Inevitably, given a training set, the intra-personal/extra-personal difference method will result in the heavy unbalance between the amount of intra-personal (hereinafter as "positive") and extra-personal (hereinafter as "negative") difference samples. For instance, assume there are m persons with k samples for each person in the training set, the amount of intra-personal and extra-personal difference samples would be $N^+ = C_m^1 C_k^2 = mk(k-1)/2$ and $N^- = C_m^2 C_k^1 C_k^1 = k^2 m(m-1)/2$ respectively. So, their ratio is $R = N^- / N^+ = k(m-1)/(k-1)$. Let $m=500$ and $k=5$, then N^+ and N^- will be $5,000$ and $3,118,750$ respectively with their ratio be 624. Obviously, such huge amount of negative samples will lead to severe memory problem for the learning process. In addition, the heavy unbalance between the positive and negative samples will also influence the design of the final classifier. One simple way to deal with this problem is sampling part of the negative set randomly. However, random sampling would not necessarily guarantee inclusion of the most representative ones. To solve this problem, we further turn to the idea of bootstrap and propose a re-sampling strategy to construct a chain AdaBoost. The abstract procedure of the methods is described in Algorithm 1.

Alg.1 *Chain AdaBoost Learning Based on Bootstrap Re-sampling of Negative Examples*

Input: $\{(\Delta_1, y_1),...,(\Delta_n, y_n)\}$ be the whole training set, with $\Delta_i \in D$ be the difference pattern, and $y_i \in Y = \{0,1\}$ its label ('1' denotes Intra-personal difference and '0' denotes extra-personal difference.)

Initialize: (1) All the positive exemplas form the positive training set S^+, which is remain unchanged during the whole learning procedure. (2) Randomly choose a predefined amount of negative exemplas to form the initial negative training set S_0^-. And assume $N^+ = \|S^+\|, N^- = \|S^-\|$ be the amount of positive and negative exemplas respectively. In our experiments, N^- is set to be 7 times of N^+.

For $l = 1, \cdots, L$

Begin

(1) Initialize the weights for each training exemplum.

$$w_{1,i} = \begin{cases} \dfrac{1}{2N^+} & y_i = -1 \\ \dfrac{1}{2N^-} & y_i = 0 \end{cases} \tag{3}$$

(2) Call AdaBoost procedure to learn the current level AdaBoost classifier C_l using the current training set:

$$C_l(\Delta) = sign(\sum_{t=1}^{T_l} \alpha_t h_t(\Delta) - \frac{1}{2}\sum_{t=1}^{T_l} \alpha_t) \tag{4}$$

where T_l is the number of weak classifiers learned in this level AdaBoost, which can be adjusted by controlling the learning accuracy, and $\alpha_t = \log \beta_t^{-1}$ be the combination weight of the t-th weak classifier in the AdaBoost. For the meaning of other symbols, please refer to the AdaBoost algorithm in [14] for details.

(3) Then, combine the C_l with the previous classifiers to form the lth strong classifier Hl:

$$H_l(\Delta) = sign(H_{l-1}(\Delta) + C_l)$$
$$= sign(\sum_{t=1}^{T} \alpha_t h_t(\Delta) - \frac{1}{2}\sum_{t=1}^{T} \alpha_t) \tag{5}$$

where $T = \sum_{j=1}^{l} T_j$.

(4) Re-sampling the negative exemplas to form the next generation of negative training set:

a) Set S^- be a null set, $S^- = \phi$.

b) Randomly take out one negative exemplum, Δ_k, from the left negative training set. If Δ_k is classified incorrectly by the classifier,

$$H_l^{\xi_l}(\Delta_k) = sign(\sum_{t=1}^{T} \alpha_t h_t(\Delta_k) - \frac{1}{2}\xi_l\sum_{t=1}^{T} \alpha_t), \tag{6}$$

it is selected and added into the next generation negative exemplas set, $S^- = S^- \cup \{\Delta_k\}$. The classifier described by Equ.6 is a loose version of H_l, where $\xi_l < 1$ and increase gradually with the increase of l.

c) Repeat the above b-step until the size of S^- becomes the predefined number N^- .

End

So, finally H_L is the final classifier:

$$H_L(x) = sign(\sum_{t=1}^{T} \alpha_t h_t(x) - \frac{1}{2}\sum_{t=1}^{T} \alpha_t) \tag{7}$$

where $T = \sum_{j=1}^{L} T_j$, T_j is the number of weak classifier for the jth AdaBoost.

Though the above chain AdaBoost learning algorithm finally establishes a strong classifier discriminating the intra-personal and extra-personal difference that can be used for both face identification and verification, unfortunately, our experiments have shown that its performance for face recognition is not as satisfactory as expected. Therefore, in this paper, we have re-considered its usage as an excellent *feature selection* or *dimension reduction* tool to solve the high dimension problem when using Gabor features for face recognition. From the learning procedure, one can see that each weak classifier is constructed from one single Gabor feature using the simplest linear perceptron. This implies that the Gabor features selected to construct the weak classifiers should be the most informative ones. Therefore, in this sense, AdaBoost has selected a small quantity from all the Gabor features, i.e., AdaBoost has completed a feature selection or dimension reduction procedure. For convenience, we call the T Gabor features selected by the above-mentioned chain AdaBoost learning procedure *AdaGabor* features. These AdaGabor features are then further reduced in dimensionality by PCA and then fed into Fisher linear discriminant analysis for the final face identification.

3.3 FDA of AdaGabor Features

In face recognition research, Fisher Discriminant Analysis (FDA) has been recognized as one of the most successful methods [18]. In FDA, the original face representation is transformed to a new FDA subspace where the between-class scatter is maximized, while the within-class scatter is minimized by maximizing the Fisher separation criterion.

When designing a Fisher classifier, one has to deal with the within-class scatter matrix carefully, because it may be singular. To avoid the singularity problem, PCA is conducted to further reduce the dimensionality of the AdaGabor features to be less than $N-C$, where N is the number of training examples, and C is the number of classes. The PCA transformed features are then fed into the final FDA for classification.

4 Experiments and Analysis

4.1 Description of the Testing Database

To evaluate the proposed method with some statistically salient comparisons, we choose the FERET and CAS-PEAL face database, both of which contain more than 1000 subjects with several face images for each subject.

FERET Face Database [2]

The Facial Recognition Technology (FERET) database was collected at George Mason University and at US Army Research Laboratory facilities as part of the FERET program, sponsored by the US Department of Defense Counterdrug Technology Development Program. The lists of images used in training, gallery and probe sets are distributed along with the database CD. Note that the FERET face database has strictly distinguished the testing set (composed of Gallery and Probe sets) from the training set. Table.1 shows the structure of the FERET face database we use to evaluate our method. We have tested our method on the largest probe set FB with 1195 images of different subject. Note that the training set we use is a near-frontal face subset of the standard FERET training set, in which only the near-frontal face images in the standard FERET training CD are included.

Table 1. Structure of the FERET face database used in our experimental evaluation

Database		#Persons	#Images	Note
Training Set		429	1002	All near-frontal faces in the standard FERET training set
Test Set	Gallery	1196	1196	Standard FERET gallery with Near-frontal faces
	FB Probes	1195	1195	Near-frontal faces with different expressions from those in Gallery.

CAS-PEAL-R1 Face Database [19]

CAS-PEAL face database is constructed by the Joint R&D Laboratory for Advanced Computer and Communication Technologies (JDL) of Chinese Academy of Sciences (CAS), under the support of the Chinese National Hi-Tech (863) Program. The CAS-PEAL face database contains 99,594 images of 1040 individuals (595 males and 445 females) with varying Pose, Expression, Accessory, and Lighting (PEAL). CAS has recently released part of the database named by CAS-PEAL-R1 face database, which consists of 30,900 images of 1040 Chinese and is divided into a frontal subset and a pose subset. In the release CAS-PEAL-R1 CD, the authors have also suggested a standard evaluation prototype, which has specified the images that compose the

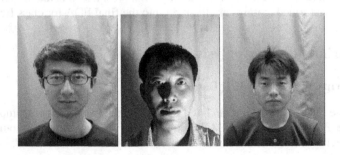

Fig. 1. Frontal face examples in the CAS-PEAL-R1

training set, the gallery, and the probe sets. This paper has strictly followed the CAS-PEAL-R1 evaluation protocol as illustrated in Table 2. Some example images are shown in Figure 1.

Table 2. Structure of the CAS-PEAL-R1 face database used in our experimental evaluation

Datasets	Traini ng set	Gallery	Probe sets (frontal)				
			Exp	Acc	Bac	Dis	Age
#Subject	300	1040	377	438	297	275	66
#Images	1,200	1040	1,570	2,285	553	275	66

Preprocessing
For both FERET and CAS-PEAL-R1 face database, the coordinates of the eyes in all the face images have been provided, which can be used as the ground-truth alignment. In our experiments, faces are normalized as shown in Fig.2. Faces are firstly cropped out, as Fig.2 (c), by placing the two eyes at fixed locations specified with h, t, b be 0.64, 0.43, and 1.85 respectively. A mask is then overlapped on the face region to eliminate the background and the hairstyle. Eventually, all faces are warped to the size of 64x64 as shown in Fig.2 (d) from their original form as in Fig.2 (b).

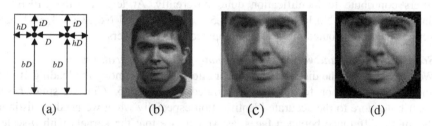

(a)   (b)   (c)   (d)

Fig. 2. Face normalization method in our experiments

4.2 Analysis of the Selected AdaGabor Features

As we have analyzed, the AdaGabor features should be the most informative features discriminating different faces. To observe their characteristics intuitively, we conducted experiments on FERET training set to obtain 1000 AdaGabor features. Some of their statistics are given below.

The Most "Discriminant" Gabor Features
Figure 3 shows the leading 4 most "discriminant" AdaGabor feature obtained through the Chain AdaBoost learning procedure, in which their Gabor kernels are overlapped to a face image for intuitive understanding. From the figure, one can easily see the position, scale and orientation of the corresponding Gabor kernel. It seems that these four Gabor kernels have coarsely positioned at the two eyes, the nose, and the mouth. One may have expected the first two exactly coincide with the two eye centers, but the experimental results have conflict with this expectation. We suppose the precise alignment of the two eyes in the processing stage should answer for the phenomenon, since this may have greatly decreased the difference between eyes.

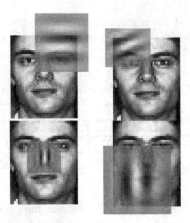

Fig. 3. The Four Leading AdaGabor features

Frequency analysis of the 40 Gabor kernels in the AdaGabor features
Figure 4 illustrates the frequency of the 40 Gabor kernels in the leading 1000 AdaGabor features. From the figure 4, we can safely conclude that different Gabor filters contribute to identification quite differently. At least for the FERET face database case, the No.1 (u=0, v=0), No.5 (u=4, v=0), and No.13 (u=4, v=1) Gabor kernels have contributed more when compared with the others.

Scale distribution and variation of the leading AdaGabor features
We also reviewed the distribution and variation of scales among the leading 100, 500, and 1000 AdaGabor features, as illustrated in Figure 5. Clearly, smaller scales contribute more to the accurate identification especially when we need to distinguish the subtle difference between faces, as we can see that the kernels with 0-scale are about 1/3 in the 1000 AdaGabor features. This is also coinciding with our basic intuition.

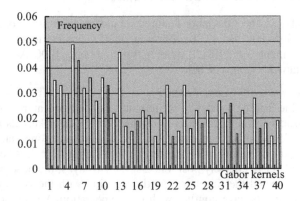

Fig. 4. Distribution of 40 Gabor kernels in the Leading AdaGabor features

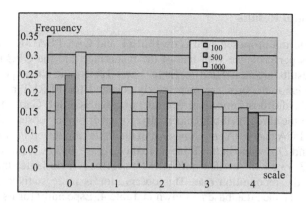

Fig. 5. The scale distribution and variation of the leading AdaGabor features

Orientation distribution and variation of the leading AdaGabor features
Different orientations also contribute differently to the classification. Figure 6 shows the distribution and variation of orientations among the leading 100, 500, and 1000 AdaGabor features. It seems that the orientation distribution is somewhat uniform. However, the vertical Gabor kernels (with $v=4$) have extracted stronger features, while those with 45 degree ($v=2$ and $v=6$) are relatively weaker.

4.3 Methods for Comparison

We have implemented two algorithms, Fisherface and Liu's GFC, to compare with the proposed AGFC. In GFC, the down-sampling factor is 16, that is, the 16 Gabor Jets in a 4×4 rectangle are averaged to calculate one Jet. So, for the original normalized 64 pixels by 64 pixels face image, the dimension after down sampling is $15 \times 15 \times 40 = 9,000$. These 9000 Gabor features are then analyzed by PCA to further reduce its dimension to 500 for further Fisher discriminant analysis.

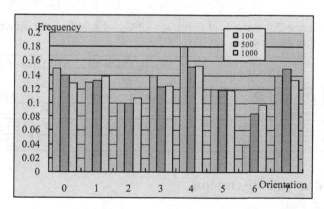

Fig. 6. The orientation distribution and variation of the leading AdaGabor features

4.4 Experimental Results

We then evaluate the proposed AGFC on FERET and CAS-PEAL-R1 face database, and compare its performance with that of the Fisherface and the GFC methods. The experimental results are illustrated in Table 3 and Table 4. In the experiments, 1884 and 2500 AdaGabor features are respectively selected for FERET and CAS-PEAL database by the AdaBoost procedure from the original 163,840 Gabor features. Note that to compare the three methods impartially, for each probe subset, all the possible dimensions for PCA and FDA (D_{pca} and D_{fda} in the table) are tested to find the optimal one. The D_{pca} and D_{fda} value in the Table 4 are the average for the 5 subsets.

From Table 3, one can see that our AGFC performs a little better than Fisherface and GFC from the recognition rate. This observation is more statistically salient on the CAS-PEAL-R1 face database as shown in Table 4. Especially for its "Expression" and "Accessory" cases, AGFC has achieved much higher recognition rate compared with Fisherface and GFC, which indicates that the AGFC is much more robust to the variations in facial expression and accessories.

Except its advantage in recognition accuracy compared with Fisherface and GFC, more importantly, our AGFC has greatly reduced the dimensionality of the original face features for classification. This will greatly facilitate the design of the classification as well as the real world face recognition systems, since we need not to compute all the Gabor features as GFC. So, a more fast and accurate face recognition system can be easily implemented using AGFC after the training stage.

Table 3. Performance Comparisons of Fisherface, GFC, and the AGFC on FERET face database fb subset

Methods	Dimensions			Recognition rate on FERET fb
	D_{ori}	D_{pca}	D_{fda}	
Fisherface	4096	300	210	94.4%
GFC	9000	500	250	96.3%
AGFC	1884	250	200	97.2%

Table 4. Performance Comparisons of Fisherface, GFC, and AGFC on the different subsets of CAS-PEAL-R1 face database

Methods	Dimension			Recognition rate on different CAS-PEAL Subsets (%)				
	D_{ori}	D_{pca}	D_{fda}	Exp	Acc	Bac	Age	Dis
Fisherface	4096	400	210	80.2	71.0	97.5	77.3	97.5
GFC	9000	500	250	92.9	85.1	98.9	93.9	100.0
AGFC	2500	250	200	98.2	87.5	99.6	97.0	99.3

5 Conclusion and Discussion

This paper has investigated the dimensionality reduction of high dimensional Gabor features and proposed a novel AdaBoost Gabor Fisher Classifier (AGFC) for robust face recognition by successfully applying the popular AdaBoost to face recognition as an effective feature selection tool to select the most informative Gabor features for discriminating different faces. In order to apply AdaBoost to multi-class problem, the intra-personal and extra-personal difference strategy is exploited to convert face recognition problem to a binary classification problem, then a chain AdaBoost learning algorithm is proposed based on Bootstrap re-sampling to make full use of the huge amount of extra-personal difference samples. Thus, thousands of informative AdaGabor features are selected for further Fisher discriminant analysis. In the experimental parts, we analyzed the distribution of the selected AdaGabor features, and compared the performance of the proposed AGFC with Fisherface and GFC on two large-scale face databases, FERET and CAS-PEAL-R1, which has impressively indicated the advantages of the AGFC.

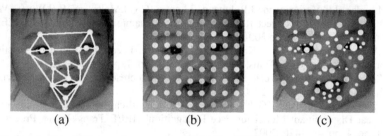

(a)   (b)   (c)

Fig. 7. Intuitive difference between the EGM, the GFC, and the proposed AGFC

The intuitive difference in Gabor sampling of the EGM, the GFC, and the proposed AGFC is illustrated in Figure 7. In EGM, predefined facial landmarks with canonical positions can subsequently shift and adapt to the input face geometry, and all the 40 Gabor features (5 scales combing 8 orientations) are computed for each landmark. However, for GFC, after aligning the two eye centers, all the 40 Gabor filters are convoluted with the image at each vertex of a uniform grid. Evidently, both of them rely on the subjective selection of "informative" Gabor features. But in our AGFC method, the Gabor filters (in terms of its position, the orientation and the scale) to be exploited for identification are learned by the AdaBoost, which can be regarded as an objective standard.

Our future work would focus on the further investigation of the AdaGabor features. Also, we are trying other feature selection tools and comparing their performance with AdaBoost-based method.

Acknowledgements

This research is partially sponsored by Natural Science Foundation of China under contract No.60332010, "100 Talents Program" of CAS, ShangHai Municipal Sciences and Technology Committee (No.03DZ15013), and ISVISION Technologies Co., Ltd.

References

[1] R.Chellappa, C.L.Wilson, S.Sirohey, Human and Machine Recognition of faces: A survey, Proceedings of the IEEE, vol.83, no.5, 1995

[2] P.J.Phillips, H.Moon, etc. "The FERET Evaluation Methodology for Face-Recognition Algorithms," IEEE Trans. on Pattern Analysis and Machine Intelligence, Vol.22, No.10, pp1090-1104, 2000

[3] P.J.Philips, P.J.Grother, R.J.Micheals, D.M.Blackburn, E.Tabassi, and J.M.Bone, Face Recognition Vendor Test 2002: Evaluation report, Technical Report, NISTIR 6965, National Institute of Standards and Technology, 2003, http://www.frvt.org.

[4] R.O.Duda, P.E.Hart, D.G.Stork, Pattern Classification, Second Edition, John Wiley & Sons Inc. 2001

[5] J.Lai, P.C.Yuen, G.C.Feng, Face recognition using Holistic Fourier Invariant Features", Pattern Recognition, 34(1), 95-109, 2001

[6] M.Lades, J.C.Vorbruggen, J.Buhmann, J.Lange, C.v.d.Malsburg, R.P.Wurtz, W.Konen, Distortion Invariant Object Recognition in the Dynamic Link Architecture, IEEE Trans. On Computers, 42(3), pp 300-311, 1993

[7] L.Wiskott, J.M.Fellous, N.Kruger, C.v.d.Malsburg, Face Recogniton by Elastic Bunch Graph Matching, IEEE Trans. On PAMI, Vol.19, No. 7, pp775-779, 1997

[8] V. Krueger. Gabor wavelet networks for object representation. . DAGM Symposium, Kiel, Germany, 9, 13-15, 2000.

[9] C.Liu and H.Wechsler: "Gabor Feature Based Classification Using the Enhanced Fisher Linear Discriminant Model for Face Recognition", IEEE Trans. Image Processing, vol. 11, no. 4, pp. 467-476, 2002.

[10] J.G. Daugman, "Uncertainty Relation for Resolution in Space, Spatial Frequency, and Orientation Optimized by Two-Dimensional Visual Cortical Filters," J. Optical Soc. Amer., vol. 2, no. 7, pp. 1,160-1,169, 1985.

[11] T. S. Lee. Image Representation Using 2d Gabor Wavelets. IEEE Trans. Pattern Analysis and Machine Intelligence, 18(10):959--971, 1996

[12] S.Shan, W.Gao, Y.Chang, B.Cao, P.Yang, Review the Strength of Gabor features for face recognition from the angle of its robustness to mis-alignment, Proceedings of ICPR2004, vol.I, pp338-341, 2004

[13] Y.Freund and R.E. Schapire. A decision-theoretic generalization of on-line learning and an application to boosting. J. Comput. Syst. Sci., 55(1):119--139, 1997

[14] Paul Viola, M.Jones, Rapid Object Detection using a Boosted Cascade of Simple, Proceedings of CVPR2001, vol.I, pp511-518, 2001

[15] S.Z.Li, ZhenQiu Zhang. "FloatBoost Learning and Statistical Face Detection". IEEE Transactions on Pattern Analysis and Machine Intelligence, Accepted, 2004.

[16] P.Yang, S.Shan, W.Gao, S.Z.Li, D.Zhang, Face Recognition Using Ada-Boosted Gabor Features, Proceeding of the 6th IEEE International Conference on Automatic Face and Gesture Recognition, pp356-361, Korea, May, 2004

[17] Baback Moghaddam, Tony Jebara, Alex Pentland, Bayesian Face Recognition, Pattern Recognition Vol.33 (2000), pp1771-1782, 2000

[18] P. N. Bellhumer, J. Hespanha, and D. Kriegman. Eigenfaces vs. fisherfaces: Recognition using class specific linear projection. IEEE Transactions on Pattern Analysis and Machine Intelligence, Special Issue on Face Recognition, 17(7): 711--720, 1997

[19] W.Gao, B.Cao, S.Shan, et al. The CAS-PEAL Larege-Scale Chinese Face Database and Evaluation Protocols, Technical Report JDL-TR-04-FR-001, Joint Research&Development Laboratory, CAS, 2004. http://www.jdl.ac.cn/peal/index.html

Automatic 3D Facial Expression Analysis in Videos

Ya Chang[1], Marcelo Vieira[2], Matthew Turk[1], and Luiz Velho[2]

[1] Computer Science Department, University of California,
Santa Barbara, CA 93106
{yachang, mturk}@cs.ucsb.edu
[2] Instituto de Matemática Pura e Aplicada, Est. Dona Castorina,
110 Jardim Botânico, 22460-320, Rio de Janeiro, RJ, Brazil
{mbvieira, lvelho}@impa.br

Abstract. We introduce a novel framework for automatic 3D facial expression analysis in videos. Preliminary results demonstrate editing facial expression with facial expression recognition. We first build a 3D expression database to learn the expression space of a human face. The real-time 3D video data were captured by a camera/projector scanning system. From this database, we extract the geometry deformation independent of pose and illumination changes. All possible facial deformations of an individual make a nonlinear manifold embedded in a high dimensional space. To combine the manifolds of different subjects that vary significantly and are usually hard to align, we transfer the facial deformations in all training videos to one standard model. Lipschitz embedding embeds the normalized deformation of the standard model in a low dimensional generalized manifold. We learn a probabilistic expression model on the generalized manifold. To edit a facial expression of a new subject in 3D videos, the system searches over this generalized manifold for optimal replacement with the 'target' expression, which will be blended with the deformation in the previous frames to synthesize images of the new expression with the current head pose. Experimental results show that our method works effectively.

1 Introduction

Facial expression analysis and synthesis is an active and challenging research topic in computer vision, impacting important applications in areas such as human-computer interaction and data-driven animation. We introduce a novel framework for automatic facial expression editing in 3D videos. The system recognizes the expressions and replaces them by expression mapping functions smoothly. We expect to use this 3D system in the future as the core element of a facial expression analysis that takes 2D video input.

3D information is becoming widely used in this field [1-3]. A combination of image texture and 3D geometry can be used to considerably reduce the variation due to pose and illumination changes. Recent technical progress allows the capture of accurate dense 3D data in real time, which enables us to build a 3D expression database for learning the deformation space of human faces. The data capture system was de-

W. Zhao, S. Gong, and X. Tang (Eds.): AMFG 2005, LNCS 3723, pp. 293–307, 2005.
© Springer-Verlag Berlin Heidelberg 2005

veloped by [4]. A coarse mesh model is fitted to track the inter-frame point motion and a dense mesh is used for synthesis of new expressions.

The nonlinear expression manifolds of different subjects share a similar structure but vary significantly in the high dimensional space. Researchers have proposed many approaches, such as locally linear embedding (LLE) [5] and Isomap [6] to embed the nonlinear manifolds in a low dimensional space. Expression manifolds from different subjects remain difficult to align in the embedded space due to various causes: (1) subjects have different face geometries; (2) facial expression styles vary by subject; (3) some persons cannot perform certain expressions; and (4) the whole expression space is large including blended expressions, so only a small portion of it can be sampled. Considering these factors, bilinear [7] and multi-linear [8] models have been successful in decomposing the static image ensembles into different sources of variation, such as identity and content. Elgammal and Lee [9] applied a decomposable generative model to separate the content and style on the manifold representing dynamic objects. It learned a unified manifold by transforming the embedded manifolds of different subjects into one. This approach assumes that the same kind of expression performed by different subjects match each other strictly. However, one kind of expression can be performed in multiple styles, such as laughter with closed mouth or with open mouth. The matching between these styles is very subjective.

To solve this problem, we built a generalized manifold that is capable of handling multiple kinds of expressions with multiple styles. We transferred the 3D deformation from the models in the training videos to a standard model. Sumner and Popovic [10] designed a special scheme for triangle meshes where the deformed target mesh is found by minimizing the transformation between the matching triangles while enforcing the connectivity. We added a temporal constraint to ensure the smooth transfer of the facial deformations in the training videos to the standard model. This model is scalable and extensible. New subjects with new expressions can be easily added in. The performance of the system will improve continuously with new data.

We built a generalized manifold from normalized motion of the standard model. Lipschitz embedding was developed to embed the manifold to a low dimensional space. A probabilistic model was learned on the generalized manifold in the embedded space as in [11].

In this framework, a complete expression sequence becomes a path on the expression manifold, emanating from a center that corresponds to the neutral expression. Each path consists of several clusters. A probabilistic model of transition between the clusters and paths is learned through training videos in the embedded space. The likelihood of one kind of facial expression is modeled as a mixture density with the clusters as mixture centers. The transition between different expressions is represented as the evolution of the posterior probability of six basic expression paths. In a video with a new subject, the deformation can be transferred to the standard model and recognized correctly.

For expression editing, the user can define any expression mapping function F: $R^6 \rightarrow R^6$, where the domain and range are the likelihood of one kind of facial expression. We currently use 3D videos as input data. Many algorithms [12,13] have been

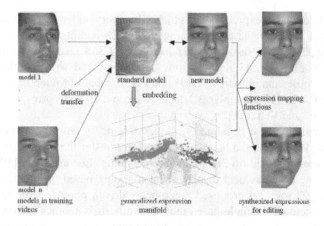

Fig. 1. System diagram

proposed to fit 3D deformable models on 2D image sequences. So the next step will be to take 2D videos as input with a system (such as [13]) used as a preprocessing module.

When the expression in the domain of F is detected, the system will search over the generalized manifold for an optimal replacement in the 'range' expression. The deformation of the standard model is transferred back to the subject, and blended with the facial deformation in the previous frame to ensure smooth editing. Fig. 1 illus trates the overall system structure.

The main contributions of this paper are the following: (1) We constructed a 3D expression database with good scalability. (2) We proposed and defined a generalized manifold of facial expression. Deformation data from different subjects complement each other for a better description of the true manifold. (3) We learned a probabilistic model to automatically implement the expression mapping function.

The remainder of the paper is organized as follows. We present the related work in Section 2. We then describe how to construct the 3D expression database in Section 3. Section 4 presents how to build generalized expression manifold. Section 5 discusses the probabilistic model. Section 6 presents the experimental results. Section 7 concludes the paper with discussion.

2 Related Work

Many researchers have explored the nature of the space of facial expressions. Zhang et al. [14] used a two-layer perceptron to classify facial expressions. They found that five to seven hidden perceptrons are probably enough to represent the space of facial expressions. Chuang et al. [15] showed that the space of facial expression could be modeled with a bilinear model. Two formulations of bilinear models, asymmetric and symmetric, were fit to facial expression data.

There are several publicly available facial expression databases: Cohen-Kanade facial expression database [16] provided by CMU has 97 subjects, 481 video sequences with six kinds of basic expressions. Subjects in every video began from a neutral expression, and ended at the expression apex. FACS coding of every video is also provided. The CMU PIE database [17] includes 41,368 face images of 68 people captured under 13 poses, 43 illuminations conditions, and with 3 different expressions: neutral, smile, and blinking. The Human ID database provided by USF has 100 exemplar 3D faces. The exemplar 3D faces were put in full correspondence as explained by Blanz and Vetter [1].

Facial animation can be generated from scratch, or by reusing existing data. Noh and Neumann [18] proposed a heuristic method to transfer the facial expression from one mesh to another based on 3D geometry morphing. Lee and Shin [19] retargeted motions by using a hierarchical displacement mapping based on multilevel B-spline approximation. Zhang [20] proposed a geometry-driven photorealistic facial expression synthesis method. Example-based motion synthesis is another stream of research. Ryun et al. [21] proposed an example-based approach for expression retargeting. We improve the deformation transfer scheme in [10] by adding temporal constraints to ensure smooth transfer of source dynamics.

We were inspired by the work of Wang et al. [3]. The main difference is that we build a generalized expression manifold by deformation transfer, which is capable of handling multiple expressions with multiple styles. The probabilistic model also takes the blended expression into consideration and enables automatic expression editing.

3 3D Expression Database

To our knowledge, there is no 3D expression database publicly available, so we built our own 3D database by capturing real-time range data of people making different facial expressions. The database includes 6 subjects and 36 videos, with a total of 2581 frames. Each subject performed all six basic expressions from neutral to apex and back to neutral. The range data were registered by robust feature tracking and 3D mesh model fitting. We intend to make the database publicly available with more subjects in the near future.

3.1 Real-Time 3D Scanner

To construct a high quality 3D expression database, the capture system should provide high quality texture and geometry data in real-time. Quality is crucial for accurate analysis and realistic synthesis. Real-time is important for subtle facial motion capture and temporal study of facial expression.

The system used for obtaining 3D data [4] is based on a camera/projector pair and active stereo. It was built with off-the-shelf NTSC video equipment. The key of this system is the combination of the color code (b,s)-BCSL [22] with a synchronized video stream.

The (b,s)-BCSL code provides an efficient camera/projector correspondence scheme. Parameter b is the number of colors and s is the number of patterns to be projected. Two patterns is the minimum, giving the best time coherence compromise.

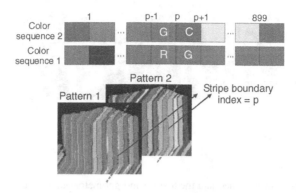

Fig. 2. Decoding stripe transitions

The complementary patterns are used to detect stripe transitions and colors robustly. Our system applies six colors that can be unambiguously detected through zero-crossings: RGBCMY. In our experiments, we use a (6,2)-BCSL code that features two patterns of 900 stripes.

To build camera/projector correspondence, we project a subsequence of these two patterns onto the scene and detect the projected stripe colors and boundaries from the image obtained by a high-speed camera. The four projected colors, two for each pattern, detected close to any boundary are uniquely decoded to the projected stripe index p (Fig. 2). The correspondent column in the projector space is detected in $O(1)$ by using (6,2)-BCSL decoding process. The depth is then computed by the camera/projector intrinsic parameters and the rigid transformation between their reference systems.

We project every color stripe followed by its complementary color to facilitate the robust detection of stripe boundaries from the difference of the two resulting images. The stripe boundaries become zero-crossings in the consecutive images and can be detected with sub-pixel precision. One complete geometry reconstruction is obtained after the projection of the pattern 1 and its complement followed by pattern 2 and its complement.

The (6,2)-BCSL can be easily combined with video streams. Each 640x480 video frame in NTSC standard is composed of two interlaced 640x240 fields. Each field is exposed/captured in 1/60 sec. The camera and projector are synchronized using genlock. For projection, we generate a frame stream interleaving the two patterns that is coded with its corresponding complement as fields in a single frame. This video signal is sent to the projector and connected to the camera's genlock pin. The sum of its fields gives a texture image and the difference provides projected stripe colors and boundaries. The complete geometry and texture acquisition is illustrated in Fig. 3.

This system is suitable for facial expression capture because it maintains a good balance between texture, geometry and motion detection. Our videos were obtained by projecting 25-35 stripes over the face and the average resolutions are: vertical = 12 points/cm and horizontal = 1.25 points/cm (right bottom window of Fig. 4). We used a Sony HyperHAD camera and an Infocus LP-70 projector.

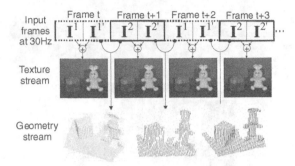

Fig. 3. Input video frames, and the texture and geometry output streams at 30 fps

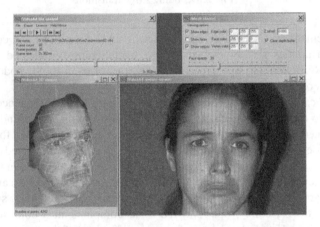

Fig. 4. An example of 3D data viewer with fitted mesh

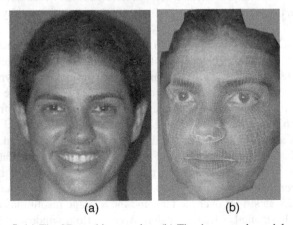

(a)   (b)

Fig. 5. (a) The 2D tracking results. (b) The dense mesh model.

3.2 3D Data Registration

The acquired range data need to be registered for the following analysis. The range points are first smoothed by radial basis functions (RBF). We build a coarse mesh model with 268 vertices and 244 quadrangles for face tracking. A coarse generic model is fitted manually at the first frame. A robust feature tracker from Nevengineering [23] provides the 2D positions of 22 prominent feature points. The mesh's projection was warped by the 22 feature points. The depth of the vertex was recovered by minimizing the distance between the mesh and the range data [24].

An example of the 3D viewer is shown in Fig. 4. The left bottom window shows the range data with the fitted mesh. The right bottom window is the texture image with the projected 3D points. Fig. 5 (a) shows the texture image with the 22 tracked feature points. Fig. 5 (b) shows the dense mesh with 4856 vertices and 4756 quadrangles. The dense model is used for the synthesis of new expressions.

4 Generalized Expression Manifold

We built the generalized expression manifold by transferring the facial deformations in the training videos to a standard model. The standard model serves as the interface between the models in the training videos and models in the testing videos. The generalized manifold, that is the expression manifold of the standard model, includes all information in the training videos. The more training data we have, the better it approximates the true manifold. We can define expression similarity on this manifold and use it to search the optimal approximation for any kind of expression. The expression synthesis will involve only the standard model and target model.

4.1 Deformation Transfer with Temporal Constraints

Sumner [10] proposed a novel method to transfer the deformation of the source triangle mesh to the target one by minimizing the transformation between the matching triangles while enforcing the connectivity. This optimization problem can be rewritten in linear equations:

$$\min_{v_1...v_n} \| c - Ax \|_F^2 \tag{1}$$

where the matrix norm $\| \bullet \|_F$ is the Frobenius norm, or the square root of the sum of the square matrix elements. $v_1,...,v_n$ is the vertex of the unknown deformed target mesh. x is a vector of the locations of $v_1,...,v_n$. c is a vector containing entries from the source transformations, and A is a large sparse matrix that relates x to c, which is determined by the undeformed target mesh. This classic least-square optimization problem has closed form solution as

$$Sx = b, \text{ where } S = A'A, b = A'c. \tag{2}$$

The result is unique up to a global translation. We fix the rigid vertex, such as inner eyes corners to resolve the global position. x can be split as $x = [xf'\quad xm']'$ where xf corresponds to the fixed vertex, and xm to all the other vertices. Thus

$$c - Ax = c - [Af\quad Am] * \begin{bmatrix} xf \\ xm \end{bmatrix} = c - Af * xf - Am * xm = d - Am * xm$$

Our goal is to transfer the deformation of a training subject in a video sequence to a standard face smoothly. The vertex v_i at frame t is represented as $v_i^t, i = 1,...,n; t = 1,...,k$. k is the length of the video. We add a constraint for temporal coherence and the optimization problem becomes

$$\min_{v_1^1...v_n^1,...,v_1^k...v_n^k} \sum_{t=1,...,k} \| d^t - Am * xm^t \|_2^2 + \sigma \| \frac{\partial xm^t}{\partial t} \|_2^2 \qquad (3)$$

where σ is the weight for temporal smoothing. c^t is the source transformation at frame t, $d^t = c^t - Af * xf$.

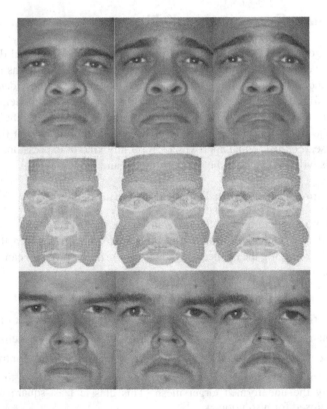

Fig. 6. Example of deformation transfer with texture synthesis. The first row is the texture image of the source video at frames 1, 12, and 24. The second row is the dense mesh of the target face with transferred deformation. The first image of the third row is the texture image of the undeformed target model. The second and the third images are the corresponding synthesized faces by the deformed dense mesh.

This problem can be solved in a progressive way by approximating

$$\frac{\partial xm^t}{\partial t} = xm^t - xm^{t-1},$$

where xm^0 is the vertex locations of the undeformed target mesh.

Eq. (3) can be rewritten as

$$\min_{v_1^1 \ldots v_n^1, \ldots, v_1^k \ldots v_n^k} \sum_{t=1,\ldots,k} \| Q * xm^t - p^t \|_2^2 \tag{4}$$

where

$$Q'Q = Am'^* Am + \sigma I$$

$$Q' p^t = Am'^* d^t + \sigma * xm^{t-1}$$

σ is chosen to guarantee $Am'^* Am + \sigma I$ is symmetric positive matrix. Q always exists, while it is not needed to solve Q explicitly. Eq. (4) has a closed solution: $Q'Q * xm^t = Q' p^t$. For efficiency, we compute and store the LU factorization of $Q'Q$ only once.

We separate the motion of the tracked source mesh into a global transformation due to head movement and a local deformation due to facial expression. The local deformation is used for facial expression (deformation) transfer.

Fig. 6 shows an example of transferring the source mesh to the target mesh with synthesized texture data.

4.2 Lipschitz Embedding

We get the deformation vectors of the standard model as $x^{s,t} \in R^{n*3}, t = 1, \ldots k$, where n is the number of vertices; s is the number of videos and k is the length of the video. We normalize the duration of every video by re-sampling the deformation vectors at equal intervals. The interpolation is implemented by a cubic spline. We build the manifold by using the coarse mesh such that expression can be recognized quickly. The dense mesh of the standard model is saved for synthesis of the new expression.

Lipschitz embedding [25] is a powerful embedding method used widely in image clustering and image search. For a finite set of input data S, Lipschitz embedding is defined in terms of a set R of subsets of S, $R = \{A_1, A_2, \ldots, A_k\}$. The subsets A_i are termed the reference sets of the embedding. Let $d(o; A)$ be an extension of the distance function d to a subset $A \subset S$, such that $d(o, A) = \min_{x \in A}\{d(o, x)\}$. An embedding with respect to R is defined as a mapping F such that $F(o) = (d(o; A_1); d(o; A_2); \ldots, d(o; A_k))$.

For our experiments, we used six reference sets, each of which contains only the deformation vectors of one kind of basic facial expression at its apex. The embedded space is six dimensional. The distance function in the Lipschitz embedding should reflect the distance between points on the manifold. We use the geodesic manifold distance [5] to preserve the intrinsic geometry of the data. After we apply the Lipschitz embedding with geodesic distance to the training set, there are six basic paths in the embedded space, emanating from the center that corresponds to the neutral image. The images with blended expression lie between the basic paths.

An example of the generalized expression manifold projected on its first three dimensions can be found in the middle of the second row of Fig. 1. Points with different colors represent embedded deformation vectors of different expressions. Anger: red; Disgust: green; Fear: blue; Sad: cyan; Smile: pink; Surprise: yellow. In the embedded space, expressions can be recognized by using the probabilistic model described in the following section.

5 Probabilistic Model on the Generalized Manifold

The goal of the probabilistic model is to exploit the temporal information in video sequences in order to recognize expression correctly and find the optimal replacement for expression editing.

5.1 Model Learning

On the standard model, assume there are K videos sequences for each kind of basic expression S, $S = \{1,...,6\}$. The embedded vector for the ith frame in the jth video for expression S is $I_{s,j,i} \in R^6$, $j = \{1,..., K\}$. By K-means clustering technique, all points are grouped into clusters $c^n, n = 1,..., r$. We compute a cluster frequency measure

$$T_{n1,n2} = \#(I_{s,j,i} \in c^{n1} \& I_{s,j,i+1} \in c^{n2}, j = 1..K, S = 1..6)$$

$T_{n1,n2}$ represents how many time the situation occurs in all videos that one frame belongs to cluster c^{n1} and its next frame belongs to cluster c^{n2}. The prior $p(c^{n2} | c^{n1})$ is learned as

$$p(c^{n2} | c^{n1}) = \begin{cases} \delta, T_{n1,n2} = 0 \\ T_{n1,n2} * scale , otherwise \end{cases}$$

where δ is a small empirical number. Scale and δ are selected such that $\sum_{n2} p(c^{n2} | c^{n1}) = 1$.

The prior $p(c | S)$ is assigned according to the expression intensity of the cluster center, varying from 0 to 1. By Bayes' rule,

$$p(S | c) = \frac{p(c | S) p(S)}{\sum_{S} p(c | S) p(S)}.$$

For time series $t = 0,1,...$, the transition between different expressions can be computed as the transition between the clusters:

$$p(S_t | S_{t-1}) = \sum_{n1,n2} p(S_t | c_t = c^{n2}) p(c_t = c^{n2} | c_{t-1} = c^{n1}) p(c_{t-1} = c^{n1} | S_{t-1})$$

Due to the small variation within a cluster, S_{t-1} and S_t are conditionally independent given c_{t-1}.

5.2 Expression Recognition

Given a probe video, the facial deformation is first transferred to the standard model, and the deformation vector is embedded as $I_t, t = 0,1,...$. The expression recognition can be represented as the evolution of the posterior probability $p(S_{0:t} | I_{0:t})$.

We assume statistical independence between prior knowledge on the distributions $p(c_0 | I_0)$ and $p(S_0 | I_0)$. Using the overall state vector $x_t = (S_t, c_t)$, the transition probability can be computed as:

$$p(x_t | x_{t-1}) = p(S_t | S_{t-1})p(c_t | c_{t-1}) \tag{5}$$

We define the likelihood computation as follows

$$p(I | c, S) \propto \exp[-\frac{1}{2\sigma_c^2}d(I, u_c)] p(c | S)$$

where u_c is the center of cluster c, σ_c is the variation of cluster c.

Given this model, our goal is to compute the posterior $p(S_t | I_{0:t})$. It is in fact a probability mass function (PMF) since S_t only takes values from 1 to 6. The marginal probability $p(S_t, c_t | I_{0:t})$ is also a PMF for the same reason.

Using Eq. (5), the Markov property, statistical independence, and time recursion in the model, we can derive:

$$p(S_{0:t}, c_{0:t} | I_{0:t}) = p(x_{0:t} | I_{0:t}) = p(S_0, c_0 | I_0)\prod_{i=1}^{t} \frac{p(I_i | S_i, c_i)p(S_i | S_{i-1})p(c_i | c_{i-1})}{p(I_i | I_{0:i-1})}$$

By marginalizing over $c_{0:t}$ and $S_{0:t-1}$, we obtain Equation (6):

$$p(S_t | I_{0:t}) = \int_{c_0} \int_{S_0} ... \int_{c_{t-1}} \int_{S_{t-1}} \int_{c_t} p(c_0 | I_0)p(S_0 | I_0) *$$
$$\prod_{i=1}^{t} \frac{p(I_i | S_i, c_i)p(S_i | S_{i-1})p(c_i | c_{i-1})}{p(I_i | I_{0:i-1})} dc_t dS_{t-1} dc_{t-1}...dS_0 dc_0 \tag{6}$$

which can be computed by the priors and the likelihood $p(I_i | S_i, c_i), i = 1,..., t$. This provides us the probability distribution of the expression categories, given the sequence of embedded deformation vectors of the standard model.

5.3 Expression Editing

The user can define the any expression editing function F as needed. $F: R^6 \rightarrow R^6$.

$$F(p(S = 1),..., p(S = 6)) = [q_1, q_2,..., q_6]$$

where $\sum_{i=1}^{6} q_i = 1$, q is the new likelihood of one kind of facial expression. For example, if we want to edit all sadness (S=1) videos to anger (S=2), the mapping function can be defined as

$$F (p (S=1), p (S=2), ..., p (S=6))=$$
$$[p (S=2), p (S=1), ..., p (S=6)], \text{ when } p (S=1) > \gamma. \tag{7}$$

This function will increase the likelihood of anger when the sadness is detected, that is, its likelihood is above a threshold γ.

The system automatically searches for the embedded vector with likelihood that is closest to the "range" expression. It first looks for the cluster whose center has the closest likelihood. In that cluster, the point closest to the embedded vector of the input frame is selected. We transfer the corresponding deformation vector back to the model in the new video. The deformation vector is blended with the deformation at the previous frame to ensure smooth editing. The synthesized 2D image uses the head pose in the real input frame and the texture information of the dense model.

6   Experimental Results

We collected 3D training videos from 6 subjects (3 males, 3 females). Every subject performed six kinds of basic expressions. The total number of frames in the training videos is 2581. We use Magic Morph morphing software to estimate the average of the training faces, and we use that average as the standard model. The standard model only contains geometrical data, no texture data. It will approach the "average" shape of human faces when the number of training subjects increases.

Fig. 7 includes some examples of the mesh fitting results. We change the viewpoints of 3D data to show that the fitting is very robust. A supplementary video is available at http://ilab.cs.ucsb.edu/demos/AMFG05.mpg. This video gave a snapshot of our database by displaying the texture sequences and 3D view of the range data with the fitted mesh at the same time.

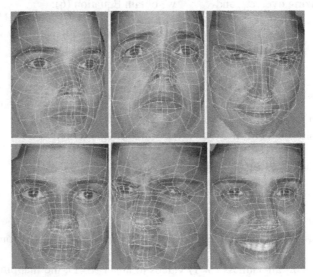

Fig. 7. Mesh fitting for training videos. Images in each row are from the same subject. The first column is the neutral expression. The second and third columns represent large deformation during the apex of expressions.

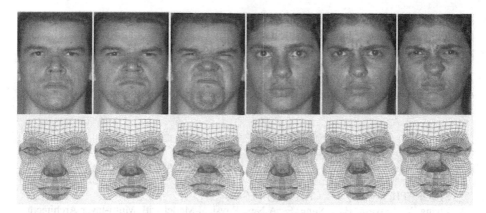

Fig. 8. Two different styles of the anger in training videos transferred to the standard mesh model. The first row and second row is images of anger and the corresponding deformed standard mesh model. The first to the third column is one style of anger at frame 1, 6, and 29. The fourth to sixth column is another style of anger at frames 1, 20, and 48.

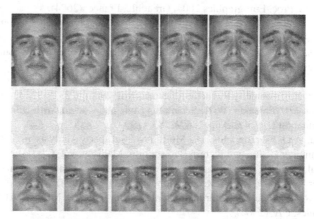

Fig. 9. Expression editing examples. First row is from the input video of sadness. We define the expression mapping function as Eq. 7. The second row is the deformed dense mesh by our algorithm. The third row is the output: the first image is unchanged, the following images are synthesized anger faces by the expression mapping function.

Fig. 8 shows examples of deformation transfer. The motions of the training videos are well retargeted on the standard model.

Fig. 9 is an example of expression editing. The system recognized the sadness correctly and synthesized new faces with anger expression correspondingly.

7   Conclusion

We introduced a novel framework for automatic facial expression analysis in 3D videos. A generalized manifold of facial expression is learned through a 3D expression database. This database provides a potential to learn the complete deformation space of human faces when more and more subjects are added in. Expression recognition and editing is accomplished automatically by using the probabilistic model on the generalized expression manifold of the standard model.

The current input is 3D videos. We plan to take 2D video input by using a system like [13]. The output video is a synthesized face with a new expression. How to separate and keep the deformation due to speech and merge the synthesized face smoothly with the background in videos [26] are important topics for the future research.

References

1. Blanz, V. and Vetter, T.: A Morphable Model for the Synthesis of 3D Face. ACM SIGGRAPH, Los Angeles, CA, (1999) 187-194.
2. Zhang, Y., Prakash, E.C., Sung, E.: A New Physical Model with Multi-layer Architecture for Facial Expression Animation Using Dynamic Adaptive Mesh. IEEE Transactions on Visualization and Computer Graphics, 10(3):339-352, (2004).
3. Wang, Y., Huang, X., Lee, C., Zhang, S., Li, Z., Samaras, D., Metaxas, D., Elgammal, A., Huang, P.: High Resolution Acquisition, Learning and Transfer of Dynamic 3-D Facial Expressions. Proc. Eurographics 2004, Grenoble, France, (2004).
4. Vieira, M.B., Velho, L., Sá, A., Carvalho, P.C.: A Camera-Projector System for Real-Time 3D Video. IEEE Int. Workshop on Projector-Camera Systems, San Diego, CA, (2005).
5. Roweis, S., Saul, L.: Nonlinear Dimensionality Reduction by Locally Linear Embedding. Science, 290; 2323-2326, (2000).
6. Tenenbaum, J.B., Silva, V. de, Langford, J.C.: A Global Geometric Framework For Nonlinear Dimensionality Reduction. Science, vol. 290, pp. 2319-2323, (2000).
7. Tenebaum, J.B., Freeman, W.T.: Separating Style and Content with Bilinear Models. Neural Computation J., Vol. 12, pp. 1247-1283, (1999).
8. Vasilescu, A.O., Terzopoulos, D.: Multilinear Subspace Analysis for Image Ensembles. Proc. Computer Vision and Pattern Recognition, Madison, WI, (2003).
9. Elgammal, A., Lee, C.: Separating Style and Content on a Nonlinear Manifold. Proc. Computer Vision and Pattern Recognition, Washington, (2004).
10. Sumner, R., Popovic, J.: Deformation Transfer for Triangle Meshes. ACM SIGGRAPH, Los Angeles, CA, (2004).
11. Chang, Y., Hu, C., Turk, M.: Probabilistic Expression Analysis on Manifolds. Proc. Computer Vision and Pattern Recognition, Washington, (2004).
12. Vacchetti, L., Lepetit, V., Fua, P.: Stable Real-time 3D Tracking Using Online and Offline Information. IEEE Trans. on Pattern Analysis and Machine Intelligence, 26 (2004) 1385–1391.
13. Goldenstein, S.K., Vogler, C., Metaxas, D.: Statistical Cue Integration in DAG Deformable Models. IEEE Trans. on Pattern Analysis and Machine Intelligence, 25 (2003) 801–813.
14. Zhang, Z., Lyons, M., Schuster, M., Akamatsu, S.: Comparison Between Geometry-based and Gabor-wavelets-based Facial Expression Recognition Using Multi-layer Perceptron: IEEE Conf. on Automatic Face and Gesture Recognition, Nara, Japan, (1998).
15. Chuang, E., Deshpande, H., Bregler, C.: Facial Expression Space Learning. Pacific Graphics, (2002).
16. Kanade, T., Cohn, J., Tian, Y.: Comprehensive Database for Facial Expression Analysis. IEEE Conf. on Automatic Face and Gesture Recognition, (2000) 46-53.

17. Sim, T., Baker, S., Bsat, M.: The CMU Pose, Illumination, and Expression Database. IEEE Trans. on Pattern Analysis and Machine Intelligence, 25 (2003) 1615-1618.
18. Noh, J., Neumann, U.: Expression Cloning. ACM SIGGRAPH, Los Angeles, CA, (2001).
19. Lee, J., Shin, S.Y.: A Hierarchical Approach to Interactive Motion Editing for Human-like Figures. ACM SIGGRAPH, Los Angeles, CA, Los Angeles, CA, (1999) 39-48.
20. Zhang, Q., Liu, Z., Guo, B., Shum, H.: Geometry-Driven Photorealistic Facial Expression Synthesis. SIGGRAPH Symposium on Computer Animation, (2003).
21. Pyun, H., Kim, Y., Chae, W., Kang, H.W., Shin, S.Y.: An Example-Based Approach for Facial Expression Cloning. Siggraph Symposium on Computer Animation, (2003).
22. Sá, A., Carvalho, P.C., Velho, L.: (b,s)-BCSL: Structured Light Color Boundary Coding for 3D photography. Int. Fall Workshop on Vision, Modeling, and Visualization, (2002).
23. www.nevengineering.com
24. Sederberg, T.W., Parry, S.R.: Free-Form Deformation of Solid Geometric Models. ACM SIGGRAPH, pp. 151-159, Dallas, TX, (1986).
25. Bourgain, J.: On Lipschitz Embedding of Finite Metric Spaces in Hilbert Space. Israel J. Math., 52 (1985) 46-52.
26. Blanz, V., Scherbaum, K., Vetter, T., Seidel, H.: Exchanging Faces in Images. Proc. Eurographics, Grenoble, France, (2004).

Real-Time Modeling of Face Deformation
for 3D Head Pose Estimation

Kenji Oka and Yoichi Sato

Institute of Industrial Science, The University of Tokyo,
4-6-1 Komaba, Meguro-ku, Tokyo, 153-8505, Japan
ysato@iis.u-tokyo.ac.jp

Abstract. We propose a new technique for simultaneously executing
face deformation modeling and 3D head pose estimation. Previous methods for estimating 3D head pose require a preliminary training stage for
the head model, and cannot start tracking the head pose until this stage
is complete. In contrast, our proposed method can acquire and refine a
user's deformable head model in parallel with tracking the user's head
pose. This allows progressive improvement in the accuracy of the estimation of head pose and face deformation.

Our technique consists of three main steps. In the first step we estimate the 3D head pose using a head model that is obtained automatically. The second step finds true positions of feature points by using
the resulting poses of the first step. Finally, the basis vectors of face
deformation are calculated from the true positions of feature points to
acquire a new deformable head model as a linear combination of the basis
vectors.

The iteration of the three steps refines the deformable head model,
thus improving the accuracy of head pose estimation progressively. The
improvement has been successfully demonstrated via experiments.

1   Introduction

Tracking of 3D head pose is regarded as an important topic in computer vision.
So far a number of researchers have developed methods for estimating 3D head
pose. Many of those methods employ a rigid model that can only deal with
3D translation and rotation [1, 7, 14, 16, 20, 17]. Actually, the human face is often deformed significantly due to various factors, for example, change of facial
expression, which causes deterioration of accuracy or failure of tracking.

This has motivated work that uses a model to represent deformation of a user's
face, that is, a deformable head model. Black and Yacoob segment the human
face into rigid parts and deformable parts, and estimate head pose and face
expression with the segmented model [2]. Several researchers use 3D deformable
surface models, for example mesh models, for estimating fine deformation of a
user's face [10, 6, 3, 18, 5]. Recently, the Active Appearance Model (AAM) and
similar methods have been studied by many researchers. Matthews and Baker
presented good survey on AAM [15]. While those methods have the potential for

W. Zhao, S. Gong, and X. Tang (Eds.): AMFG 2005, LNCS 3723, pp. 308–320, 2005.

good estimation, some sort of 3D geometrical model, for example the deformable head model itself, must be prepared with manual feature extraction or 3D laser scanning. An approach for solving this problem is automatic tracking of several feature points, and then analyzing the coordinates of the tracked points for acquiring basis shape vectors of face deformation. In this approach, Gokturk et al. utilizes the Principal Component Analysis (PCA) [8], and Del Bue et al. makes use of the non-rigid factorization technique [4].

The previously proposed methods that use a deformable head model as described above have a common problem: they require a preliminary stage to acquire the head model. Those methods cannot start real-time tracking of 3D head pose before completing that stage, and they do not have a framework for refining the deformable head model using estimation results.

In this paper, we propose a new method for acquiring and refining a user's deformable head model in parallel with estimating the user's head pose in real time. This means that our method requires no cumbersome preparation for constructing a head model. The method for acquiring a deformable head model consists of three steps. In the first step we estimate the 3D head pose and the face deformation using a head model that is obtained automatically. Second, we find true positions of feature points by using the resulting poses of the first step. Finally, the basis vectors of face deformation are calculated from the true positions of the feature points to acquire a new deformable head model as a linear combination of the basis vectors. Since the newly acquired model is used for the next estimation of the 3D head pose and face deformation, our method can progressively improve the accuracy of estimating pose and deformation.

The main contributions of our study are summarized in the following three points: 1) real-time estimation of 3D head pose without a preliminary training stage, 2) real-time refinement of a deformable head model, and 3) progressive improvement of the accuracy of estimating head pose and face deformation. The improvement has been successfully demonstrated via experiments.

The reminder of this paper is organized as follows. In Section 2, we describe our method for estimating head pose and face deformation. We then propose a method for acquiring a deformable head model in Section 3. We show the experimental results of our method in Section 4. Finally, we conclude this paper in Section 5.

2   Real-Time Estimation of 3D Head Pose with Deformable Head Model

In this section, we describe our method for estimating 3D head pose and deformation from image inputs from two calibrated cameras[1], the left camera and the right camera, that incorporate a deformable head model.

---

[1] Although we assume a two-camera configuration here, we can increase the number of cameras without altering the algorithm of our proposed method.

2.1   Deformable Head Model

In our method, the head model has K feature points, and each feature point consists of two components: the 3D position in the model coordinate system fixed to a user's head at the frame t, and two small image templates. Let M_t be the $3K$-dimensional shape vector that consists of 3D coordinates of K feature points in the model coordinate system. Also, T_L and T_R are defined as the image template sets for the left camera and the right camera respectively. Here, K is set to 10 to represent these ten feature points: the inner and outer corners of both eyes, both corners of the mouth, both nostrils, and the inner corner of both brows.

The shape vector M_t of our deformable head model is formulated as:

$$M_t = \bar{M} + \mathcal{M} a_t \tag{1}$$

where $\bar{M}$ is the mean shape vector, $\mathcal{M}$ is the $3K \times B$ basis shape matrix, which consists of B columns of the basis shape vectors, and a_t is a B-dimensional coefficient vector of $\mathcal{M}$. Here, the shape M_t is represented as a linear combination of the constant basis shape vectors corresponding to the columns of $\mathcal{M}$ in a similar way to other methods [8, 15, 5]. The limited size of B, $B = 5$ in this method enables us to represent the face deformation by a small number of parameters in a_t, We will describe how the basis matrix $\mathcal{M}$ and the mean vector $\bar{M}$ are obtained later in Section 3.

2.2   Particle Filter for Estimating Head Pose and Face Deformation

During tracking we produce successive estimation of a $(6 + B)$ dimensional state vector $x_t = (p_t^{\mathrm{T}}, a_t^{\mathrm{T}})^{\mathrm{T}}$ for each image frame t. Here, p_t is the translation and the rotation from the world coordinate system to the model coordinate system. For pose estimation we make use of the deformable head model and the particle filtering technique.

A particle filter [9] represents the probability density function (PDF) of a state as a set of many discrete samples, each sample with a corresponding weight. Hence, this sample set can approximate an arbitrary PDF including non-Gaussian ones. Our method uses the sample set $\{(s_t^{(i)}; \pi_t^{(i)})\}(i = 1 \ldots N)$, which consists of N discrete samples $s_t^{(i)}$ in the $(6 + B)$ dimensional state space and their corresponding weights $\pi_t^{(i)}$.

The main flow of our estimation method is shown in Fig.1. We first generate N new samples $\{s_t^{(i)}\}$ based on the sample set $\{(s_{t-1}^{(i)}; \pi_{t-1}^{(i)})\}$ and the following motion model on the assumption of a uniform straight motion of a user's head between each pair of successive image frames:

$$s_t^{(i)} = s_{t-1}' + \tau v_{t-1} + \omega \tag{2}$$

where s_{t-1}' is a chosen sample from $\{(s_{t-1}^{(i)}; \pi_{t-1}^{(i)})\}$, τ is the time interval between frames, v_{t-1} represents the velocity of the pose that is calculated at the end of

> ## Estimation of Head Pose and Deformation
> 1. generate new samples $\{s_t^{(i)}\}$ from $\{s_{t-1}^{(i)}; \pi_{t-1}^{(i)}\}$
> 2. determine weights $\{\pi_t^{(i)}\}$
>   a. calculate a score $c_t^{(i)}$ using $N_h(s_t^{(i)})$
>   b. calculate weight $\pi_t^{(i)}$ from the score
> 3. apply resampling to sample set $\{s_t^{(i)}; \pi_t^{(i)}\}$
> 4. aggregate samples to have a result x_t

Fig. 1. Flow of estimating head pose and deformation

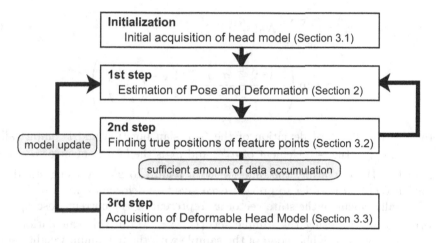

Fig. 2. Flow of acquiring deformable head model

the previous estimation step $t-1$, and ω is system noise. In addition, ω is a $(6+B)$ dimensional Gaussian noise vector with a zero mean, and the upper-left 6×6 elements of its covariance matrix corresponding to the pose parameters are adaptively controlled depending on the velocity of the head. We have found that such control of system noise improves the robustness against sudden abrupt motion while maintaining the high accuracy of estimating head pose at the same time [17]. On the other hand, the rest of the covariance matrix is a diagonal matrix whose diagonal elements are represented by a B-dimensional constant vector β. Each element of β is proportional to the corresponding element of the standard deviation vector μ of a_t which is calculated by PCA as explained in Section 3.3.

After we obtain new samples $\{s_t^{(i)}\}$ we compute the weight $\pi_t^{(i)}$ by evaluating each sample $s_t^{(i)}$ based on the set of current input images.

Given a sample $s_t^{(i)}$, we apply the normalized correlation-based function $N_h(s_t^{(i)})$ with the following processes. In this function, the shape of the head model is first deformed by the deformation elements $a_t^{(i)}$ of $s_t^{(i)}$ using Eq.(1). The deformed shape is then translated and rotated depending on the pose elements $p_t^{(i)}$ of $s_t^{(i)}$. After the 3D feature points of the transformed shape are projected onto the image plane h, the sum of matching scores is calculated between the neighboring region of each projected 2D point and the corresponding template included in the template set T_h by normalized correlation. The sum is given as the output of $\mathcal{N}_h(s_t^{(i)})$.

We apply $\mathcal{N}_h(s_t^{(i)})$ to all image planes h to produce a total score $c_t^{(i)}$ (Eq.(3)). We then calculate the weight $\pi_t^{(i)}$ from the total score $c_t^{(i)}$ using a Gaussian function as in Eq.(4). Finally, each weight $\pi_t^{(i)}$ is normalized so that the sum of the $\pi_t^{(i)}$ is equal to 1.

$$c_t^{(i)} = \sum_{h \in \{L,R\}} \mathcal{N}_h(s_t^{(i)}) \tag{3}$$

$$\pi_t^{(i)} \propto \exp\left(-\frac{\left(2K - c_t^{(i)}\right)^2}{2\sigma^2} - \frac{1}{2}\sum_{b=1}^{B}\left(\frac{a_{t,b}^{(i)}}{\mu_b}\right)^2\right) \tag{4}$$

Here, σ is the standard deviation of the Gaussian function and is empirically set to 3.0, $a_{t,b}^{(i)}$ is the b-th element of $a_t^{(i)}$, and μ_b is the b-th element of μ. Note that in Eq.(4) we multiply the function with regard to $a_t^{(i)}$ by using standard deviation vector μ in order to prevent excessive face deformation.

We finally calculate the state vector x_t representing the current pose p_t and deformation a_t by using the sample set $\{(s_t^{(i)}; \pi_t^{(i)})\}$. In this calculation, we aggregate only the neighborhood of the sample with the maximum weight using the following equation:

$$w_t^{(i)} = \begin{cases} 1 \text{ if } \|s_t^{(i)} - s_t^{(M)}\| < d \\ 0 \text{ else} \end{cases} \tag{5}$$

$$x_t = \frac{\sum_{i=1}^{N} s_t^{(i)} \pi_t^{(i)} w_t^{(i)}}{\sum_{i=1}^{N} \pi_t^{(i)} w_t^{(i)}} \tag{6}$$

where $\pi_t^{(M)}$ is the maximum of $\{\pi_t^{(i)}\}$, and $s_t^{(M)}$ is the sample corresponding to $\pi_t^{(M)}$. In the current implementation, the value of d is empirically determined.

We also calculate the velocity v_t of x_t for the estimation of the next frame:

$$v_t = \frac{x_t - x_{t-1}}{\tau} \tag{7}$$

where the last B elements of v_t corresponding to face deformation are set to 0, because the variation of the face deformation parameters does not match well with the assumption of uniform straight motion.

2.3   Halfway Partitioned Sampling

We could obtain the new sample set $\{(s_t^{(i)}; \pi_t^{(i)})\}$ using the procedure described above. Actually, instead of the procedure described above, we apply the following sampling and weighting method which is similar to the partitioned sampling technique [13] in principle. We call this sampling technique *the halfway partitioned sampling*.

According to our observations, the motion of the human head and face can be categorized into two typical situations: rigid transformation of head pose with little face deformation, and face deformation with little transformation of head pose. For efficiently handling such situations, we first apply the drift of the pose elements from Eq.(2) to just half of the total samples; to the other half, we apply only the deformation elements' operation from Eq.(2). Then we determine the weights of those samples by Eq.(3) and (4).

After that, we apply a standard resampling technique, that is total resampling in the all dimensions, to the sample set $\{(s_t^{(i)}; \pi_t^{(i)})\}$ to improve the accuracy of the PDF. Even if face deformation and rigid transformation occur simultaneously, our method can handle such cases owing to this resampling process.

3   Method for Acquiring Deformable Head Model

In this section, we explain the method for acquiring the deformable head model of a user's head. This method consists of an automatic initialization step and three model acquisition steps as shown in Fig.2.

In the automatic initialization step, we construct the rigid head model as the initial head model. This initialization step is described in Section 3.1. After the initialization, we execute the three steps for acquiring a deformable head model. At the first step, we estimate the 3D head pose p_t and face deformation a_t from input images in real time, as described in Section 2. In the second step, we find the true positions of feature points in each input frame by using p_t and a_t, as described in Section 3.2. Finally, in the third step, we calculate the mean shape vector $\bar{M}$ and the basis shape matrix $\mathcal{M}$ in Eq.(1) by using the PCA as described in Section 3.3.

The new deformable head model is then used for the next estimation of 3D head pose and face deformation in the first step. This framework allows progressive improvement of the accuracy for estimating head pose and face deformation in parallel with refining a user's deformable head model.

3.1   Initial Acquisition of Head Model

The initialization step automatically constructs a 3D rigid model of a user's head. In this step, we utilize the OKAO vision library developed by OMRON Corporation [12]. This library is used for detecting a face and 6 facial feature points, that is, the inner and outer corners of both eyes, both corners of the mouth, from input images. The other feature points are detected as the distinct features [19] satisfying certain geometrical relations given *a priori*.

We first try to detect those feature points from the left image, and then search for the corresponding points based on epipolar constraints from the right image. After that, the 3D shape M is calculated based on triangulation, and the 3D shape and image template set T_L, T_R are registered together.

Note that we cannot estimate the deformation vector a_t when we have only the rigid model just after this initialization step. In such situation, a_t is set to zero vector.

3.2   Finding True 3D Positions of Feature Points

The purpose of this step, the second step of acquiring a deformable head model, is to find the true 3D positions of feature points from each input image frame. For constructing an accurate deformable head model, we have to collect the exact positions of each feature point. However, these positions do not necessarily coincide with the positions given in M_t which are calculated from Eq.(1) and the estimated a_t.

For this purpose, we make use of the feature tracking technique [11, 19]. Let M'_t be the $3K$-dimensional vector that represents the true 3D coordinates of K feature points in the model coordinate system. For reliably finding M'_t, we refer to p_t and a_t which are estimated in the first step (Section 2).

At first, we define a function $\mathcal{P}_h$ that first transforms M'_t by the head pose p_t and then projects the transformed points onto the image plane h:

$$m_{h,t} = \mathcal{P}_h(p_t, M'_t) \tag{8}$$

where $m_{h,t}$ is a $2K$-dimensional vector that consists of the 2D coordinates of K projected points. We also define a K-dimensional intensity vector $I^h_t(m_{h,t})$ whose k-th element is the intensity of the k-th 2D position represented by $m_{h,t}$ in the input image frame t from the camera h.

By using those definitions, we produce the energy function E^I_t to minimize as follows:

$$E^I_t = \sum_{\substack{\text{ROI} \\ h \in \{L,\, R\}}} \left\{ \begin{array}{l} \rho \| I^h_t(m_{h,t}) - I^h_{t-1}(m_{h,t-1}) \|^2 \\ + \| I^h_t(m_{h,t}) - I^h_1(m_{h,1}) \|^2 \end{array} \right\} \tag{9}$$

Here, the first term in Eq.(9) is the standard energy function representing the difference between the K Regions Of Interest (ROIs) in the current image I^h_t and their corresponding ROIs in the previous image I^h_{t-1}. In contrast, the second term works for the minimization of the difference between the current image I^h_t and the first image I^h_1. This term is useful for avoiding the drift of feature points as used also in [8]. In addition, ρ is a constant for determining the ratio between the effect of the first term and that of the second term. In the current implementation, ρ is empirically set to 4, and the size of ROI is 16×16.

We also introduce the additional term E^M_t based on the estimated shape M_t. This term plays a very important role for preventing failure of tracking the feature points especially when a user's head pose changes significantly.

$$E_t^M = \|M_t' - M_t\|^2 \tag{10}$$

This function means that we find each point of M_t' in the neighboring region of each point of M_t. Such method for finding the point reduces significantly the probability of losing tracking of feature points. Furthermore, as the deformable head model is refined more accurately, the minimization of E_t^M becomes more effective for finding the correct 3D coordinates of feature points.

Hence, we minimize the following energy function for the purpose of finding M_t':

$$E_t = E_t^I + \epsilon E_t^M \tag{11}$$

where ϵ is a constant, and it is empirically set to 2000.

M_t' is then found by minimizing E_t in a similar way to [8]. That is, we calculate the difference $dM_t' = M_t' - M_{t-1}'$ successively in each input frame. This is achieved by setting the derivative of E_t with respect to dM_t' to 0.

While the technique described above yields a good tracking result M_t', the components caused by rigid transformation are occasionally involved in M_t'. This might lead to incorrect deformable head models that cannot appropriately distinguish face deformation from rigid transformation.

For this reason, we need to eliminate the components of transformation involved in M_t' in a similar way to the method used in [15]. We first calculate the mean shape $\bar{M}'$ of the series from M_1' to M_{t-1}'. Then, we apply 3D translation and rotation to M_t' so that the sum of the square distance between the corresponding points of M_t' and $\bar{M}'$ is minimized. While this operation can eliminate the unwanted components due to rigid transformation, it might have an adverse affect on the correctly calculated M_t'. Therefore, we apply this operation only if necessary: when the distance between M_t' and M_t exceeds the constant threshold.

3.3 Acquisition of Deformable Head Model by PCA

In the third step of acquiring a deformable head model, we calculate the mean shape vector $\bar{M}$ and the basis shape matrix $\mathcal{M}$ in Eq.(1). Our method applies the PCA to the accumulated correct shape set $\{M_t'\}$; then uses the first B basis vectors to form $\mathcal{M}$ for representing face deformation in a similar way to the method by Gokturk et al. [8] This contributes to preventing unfeasible deformation of the human face as well as reducing the number of dimensions of the state vector x_t.

Here, we briefly describe how to acquire $\bar{M}$ and $\mathcal{M}$. To be precise, $\{M_t'\}$ consists of only the shape M_t' when a user is facing toward the cameras judging from the estimated pose p_t; this is because we desire to use as reliable data as possible for acquiring the deformable head model. We first calculate the mean shape vector $\bar{M}$ from $\{M_t'\}$. Then, in $\{M_t'\}$, we count the M_t' satisfying the condition where the distance between M_t' and $\bar{M}$ exceeds the predetermined threshold. If this number exceeds the predetermined number L ($L = 600$ in the current implementation), we apply the PCA to $\{M'_t\}$. This condition is necessary for judging whether $\{M'_t\}$ includes sufficient amount of shape deformation. By the PCA-based operation, we obtain the basis shape matrix $\mathcal{M}$ and the B-dimensional standard deviation vector μ, each of whose elements represents the standard deviation of its corresponding column of $\mathcal{M}$. μ is equivalent to the standard deviation of distribution of a_t in Eq.(1). Thus, μ is used for determining the variance of random noise in Eq.(2) and the weight of each sample in Eq.(4).

4   Experimental Evaluation

We have conducted experiments to evaluate the performance of our proposed method. Our system consists of a Windows-based PC with Intel Pentium4 3.0-GHz and two CCD black-and-white digital video cameras connected via IEEE-1394. Each image frame was captured at the resolution of 640×480. The size of image templates for normalized correlation was set to 16×16, and a set of 1000 samples was used for particle filtering. Our method runs at 30 frames per second with this configuration, including the 1st step and the 2nd step of Fig.2. In addition, the 3rd step of Fig.2, that is, the PCA-based calculation of the shape vectors, can also execute at very short execution time without spoiling real-time performance (30fps) of the proposed system.

We prepared an image sequences of a user moving his head pose with occasional face deformation. This image sequence was 60 seconds long and therefore contained 1800 frames. By using the first 1200 frames, the user's deformable head model was acquired with our proposed method. Then, we estimated the 3D head pose and face deformation from the last 600 image frames using the acquired deformable head model. For the first approximately 150 out of 600 image frames, the user's head moved by rigid transformation accompanied by little face deformation. After that, the user moved his head accompanied by face deformation, for example, opening and closing his mouth.

For comparison, we also conducted head pose estimation from the same 600 image frames using the rigid head model. This rigid head model was acquired from the initialization step in Section 3.1. We compared those two estimation results.

Fig.3 shows the estimation results using the rigid head model and the deformable head model. In this figure, the thin lines show the results with the rigid head model, and the thick lines represent the ones using the deformable head model. For the first 150 frames, both estimation results are similar each other. This means the deformable head model can estimate rigid transformation without generating unwanted face deformation. On the other hand, we can see the clear difference between both results for the remaining 450 frames. As shown in this figure, the results using the deformable model are far more stable than the ones using the rigid model. Hence, the deformable head model constructed by our proposed method has the capability to handle the face deformation in contrast to the rigid head model.

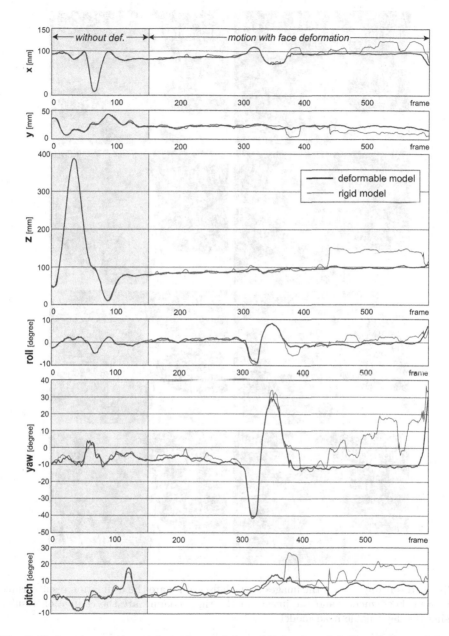

Fig. 3. Estimation results with rigid and deformable head model. Translation consists of x, y, and z: x represents the horizontal motion, y shows the vertical motion, z corresponds to the depth-directional motion. Rotation consists of *roll*, *yaw*, and *pitch*: *roll* is the rotation around the axis toward the front, *yaw* corresponds to the pan-directional rotation, and *pitch* represents the tilt-directional rotation.

Fig. 4. Resulting images: the images of the left column are the estimation results using the rigid head model, and the images of the right column are the estimation results using the deformable head model

Fig.4 shows the resulting images. In this figure, we have drawn the model co-ordinate axes corresponding to the estimated 3D head pose, and the 2D points onto which the estimated shape M_t is projected. The left column of the figure is the results using the rigid head model, and the right column shows the results using the deformable head model. Also from those results, we can confirm that our deformable head model handles face deformation successfully.

We can see the video of this experiment on the Web. [2] This video demonstrates the stability of pose estimation with our deformable head model.

5   Conclusions

In this paper, we proposed a new method for acquiring and refining a user's deformable head model in parallel with estimating the user's 3D head pose in real time. The main contributions of our study are summarized in the following three points: 1) real-time estimation of 3D head pose without a preliminary training stage, 2) real-time refinement of a deformable head model, and 3) progressive improvement of the accuracy of estimating head pose and face deformation. The improvement has been successfully demonstrated via experiments. We believe that this work is the first example to achieve simultaneous execution of face deformation modeling and 3D head pose estimation in real-time.

For further study, we are planning to use the Candid Covariance-free Incremental PCA (CCIPCA) [21] that allows basis vectors to be updated at each input image frame.

Acknowledgment

A part of this work was supported by Grants-in-Aid for Scientific Research from the Ministry of Education, Culture, Sports, Science and Technology in Japan (No. 13224051). We also thank Omron Corporation for providing the OKAO vision library used in our method.

References

1. Azarbayejani, A., Starner, T., Horowitz, B., Pentland, A.: Visually controlled graphics. IEEE Trans. Pattern Analysis and Machine Intelligence, Vol. 15, No. 6. (1993) 602–605
2. Black, M.,Yacoob, Y.: Tracking and recognizing rigid and non-rigid facial motions using local parametric models of image motion. Proc. IEEE ICCV '95. (1995) 374–381
3. DeCarlo, D., Metaxas, D.: Optical flow constraints on deformable models with applications to face tracking. Int. J. Computer Vision, Vol. 38, No. 2. (2000) 99–127
4. Del Bue, A., Smeraldi, F., Agapito, L.: Non-rigid structure from motion using non-parametric tracking and non-linear optimization. Proc. IEEE CVPRW 2004, Vol. 1: Articulated and Non-Rigid Motion. (2004)
5. Dornaika, F., Davoine, F.: Head and facial animation tracking using appearance-adaptive models and particle filters. Proc. IEEE CVPRW 2004, Vol. 10: Real-Time Vision for Human-Computer Interaction. (2004)

---

[2] http://www.hci.iis.u-tokyo.ac.jp/~oka/AMFG2005.html

6. Fua, P.: Using model-driven bundle-adjustment to model heads from raw video sequences. Proc. IEEE ICCV '99, Vol. 1. (1999) 46–53
7. Gee, A., Cipolla, R.: Fast visual tracking by temporal consensus. Image and Vision Computing, Vol. 14. (1996) 105–114
8. Gokturk, S., Bouguet, J., Grzeszczuk, R.: A data-driven model for monocular face tracking. Proc. IEEE ICCV 2001, Vol. 2. (2001) 701–708
9. Isard, M., Blake, A.: Condensation– conditional density propagation for visual tracking. Int. J. Computer Vision, Vol. 29, No. 1. (1998) 5–28
10. Jebara, T., Pentland, A.: Parametrized structure from motion for 3D adaptive feedback tracking of faces. Proc. IEEE CVPR '97. (1997) 144–150
11. Lucas, B., Kanade, T.: An iterative image registration technique with an application to stereo vision. Proc. Int. Joint Conf. Artificial Intelligence. (1981) 674–679
12. Lao, S., Kozuru, T., Okamoto, T., Yamashita, T., Tabata, N., Kawade, M.: A fast 360-degree rotation invariant face detection system. Demo session of IEEE ICCV 2003. (2003)
13. MacCormick, J., Isard, M.: Partitioned sampling, articulated objects, and interface-quality hand tracking. Proc. ECCV 2000, Vol. 2. (2000) 3–19
14. Matsumoto, Y., Zelinsky, A.: An algorithm for real-time stereo vision implementation of head pose and gaze direction measurement. Proc. IEEE FG 2000. (2000) 499–504
15. Matthews, I., Baker, S.: Active appearance models revisited. Int. J. Computer Vision, Vol. 60, No. 2. (2004) 135–164
16. Morency, L., Rahimi, A., Darrell, T.: Adaptive view-based appearance models. Proc. IEEE CVPR 2003, Vol. 1. (2003) 803–810
17. Oka, K., Sato, Y., Nakanishi, Y., Koike, H.: Head pose estimation system based on particle filtering with adaptive diffusion control. Proc. IAPR MVA 2005. (2005) 586–589
18. Shan, Y., Liu, Z., Zhang, Z.: Model-based bundle adjustment with application to face modeling. Proc. IEEE ICCV 2001, Vol. 2. (2001) 644–651
19. Shi, J., Tomasi, C.: Good features to track. Proc. IEEE CVPR '94. (1994) 593–600
20. Vacchetti, L., Lepetit, V., Fua, P.: Stable real-time 3D tracking using online and offline information. IEEE Trans. Pattern Analysis and Machine Intelligence, Vol. 26, No. 10. (2004) 1380–1384
21. Weng, J., Zhang, Y., Hwang, W.: Candid Covariance-Free Incremental Principal Component Analysis. IEEE Trans. Pattern Analysis and Machine Intelligence, Vol. 25, No. 8. (2003) 1034–1040

An Integrated Two-Stage Framework
for Robust Head Pose Estimation

Junwen Wu and Mohan M. Trivedi

Computer Vision and Robotics Research Laboratory,
University of California, San Diego, La Jolla, CA 92093, USA
{juwu, mtrivedi}@ucsd.edu

Abstract. Subspace analysis has been widely used for head pose estimation. However, such techniques are usually sensitive to data alignment and background noise. In this paper a two-stage approach is proposed to address this issue by combining the subspace analysis together with the topography method. The first stage is based on the subspace analysis of Gabor wavelets responses. Different subspace techniques were compared for better exploring the underlying data structure. Nearest prototype matching using Euclidean distance was used to get the pose estimate. The single pose estimated was relaxed to a subset of poses around it to incorporate certain tolerance to data alignment and background noise. In the second stage, the uncertainty is eliminated by analyzing finer geometrical structure details captured by bunch graphs. This coarse-to-fine framework was evaluated with a large data set. We examined 86 poses, with the pan angle spanning from $-90°$ to $90°$ and the tilt angle spanning from $-60°$ to $45°$. The experimental results indicate that the integrated approach has a remarkably better performance than using subspace analysis alone.

1 Motivation and Background

Head pose can be used for analyzing subjects' focus of attention in "smart" environment [1][2][3]. Head pose is determined by the pan angel β and the tilt angle α, as shown in the right image of Fig. 1. For applications in driver assistance systems, accuracy and robustness of the head pose estimation modular is of critical importance [3]. Besides focus analysis, head pose estimation is also a very useful front-end processing for multi-view human face analysis. The accurate pose estimate can provide necessary information to reconstruct the frontal view face for a better facial expression recognition [4]. Pose estimation can also help select the best view-model for detection and recognition [5][6].

Over the past several years, head pose estimation has been an active area of research. If there are multiple images available, pose position in the 3D space can be recovered using the face geometry. The input could be video sequences [3][4][7][8] as well as multi-camera output [9][10]. Following techniques have been proposed: feature tracking, including tracking the local salient features [4][8] or the geometric features [3][7]; studying the joint statistical property of image intensity and the depth information [9][10]. With only static images

W. Zhao, S. Gong, and X. Tang (Eds.): AMFG 2005, LNCS 3723, pp. 321–335, 2005.

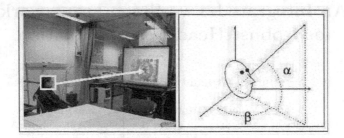

Fig. 1. Illustration of head pose estimation in focus analysis

available, the 2D pose estimation problem has presented a different challenge. Pose can only be determined in certain degrees of freedom (DOF), instead of the full 6 DOF as the 3D one does. 2D pose estimation can be used as the front-end for multi-view face analysis [5][11]; as well as to provide the initial reference frame for 3D head pose tracking. In [12], the author investigated the dissimilarity between poses by using some specific filters such as Gabor filters and PCA. This study indicates that identity-independent pose can be discriminated by prototype matching with suitable filters. Some efforts have been put to investigate the 2D pose estimation problem [5][6][11][13][14] and they are mainly focused on the use of statistical learning techniques, such as SVC in [5], KPCA in [11], multi-view eigen-space in [14], eigen-space from *best* Gabor filter in [13], manifold learning in [6] etc. All these algorithms are based on the features from entire faces. Although the identity information can be well-suppressed, one main drawback of such techniques is that they are sensitive to the face alignment, background and scale. Some researchers also explored the problem by utilizing the geometric structure constrained by representative local features [15,16]. In [15], the authors extended the bunch graph work from [17] to pose estimation. The technique provides the idea to incorporate the geometric configuration for the 2D head pose estimation. However, the study is only based on 5 well-separated poses. The other poses not included can be categorized into these 5 poses by extensive elastic searching. Although this benefits the multi-view face recognition problem, it is not suitable for head pose estimation in a fine scale, since the elastic searching introduces ambiguity between similar poses. In [16], Gabor wavelets network, or GWN, which is constructed from the Gabor wavelets of local facial features, was used to estimate the head pose. One drawback is that it requires selected facial features to be visible, hence not suitable for head pose estimation with wide angle changes.

In this paper, our aim is to get a robust identity independent pose estimator over a wide range of angles. We propose a two-stage framework which combines the statistical subspace analysis together with the geometric structure analysis for more robustness. The main issue we want to solve is the robustness to data alignment and background. More details are discussed below.

2   Algorithm Framework

The proposed solution is a two-stage scheme in a coarse-to-fine fashion. In the first stage, we use subspace analysis in a Gabor wavelet transform space. Our study indicates that statistical subspace analysis is insufficient to deal with data misalignment and background noise, however, the noise does not drive the estimate far from its true value. Therefore, we can assume that the true pose locates in a subset of $p \times p$ neighboring poses around the estimate with a high accuracy. We use the subset of poses as the output from the first stage. This is similar to a fuzzy decision. The first-stage accuracy is evaluated accordingly: if the true pose locates in the $p \times p$ subset around the estimate, the estimate is determined as a correct one. Since geometric structure of the local facial features has the ability to provide the necessary detail for a finer pose assessment, in the second stage, we use a structural landmark analysis in the transform domain to refine the estimate. More specifically, we use a revised version of the face bunch graph [17]. The diagrams in Fig. 2 outline this algorithm.

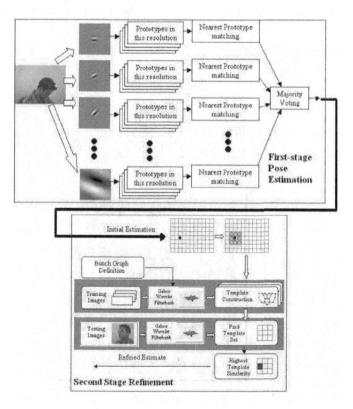

Fig. 2. Flowchart of the two-stage pose estimation framework. The top diagram is for the first-stage estimation and the bottom one is for the second-stage refinement. The output of the first stage is the input of the second stage.

To get a comprehensive view of the underlying data structure, we study four popular subspaces so that the best subspace descriptors can be found: Principle Component Analysis (PCA) [18]; Kernel Principle Component Analysis (KPCA) [19]; Multiple class Discriminant Analysis (MDA) [18] and Kernel Discriminant Analysis (KDA) [20,21]. Results show that analysis in the kernel space can provide a better performance. Also, discriminant analysis is slightly better than PCA (please refer to Table 1). To refine the estimate from the first-stage, *semi-rigid* bunch graph is used. Different from the face recognition task solved in [17], we only need to recover the identity-independent head pose. In [17], an exhaustive elastic graph searching is used so as to find the fiducial points that contains subjects' identity. However, the distortion in the geometric structure caused by the exhaustive elastic search would introduce ambiguity for close poses. Furthermore, for pose estimation, we do not require exact match of the fiducial points since the nodes from Gabor jets are actually able to describe the neighborhood property. That is the reason we use the "semi-rigid" bunch graph, in which the nodes can only be individually adjusted locally in legitimate geometrical configurations. We use multiple bunch graphs per pose to incorporate all available geometric structures. The reason is that the geometric

Table 1. First-stage multi-resolution subspace analysis results evaluated under different p

	p=1	**p=3**	p=5
PCA	36.4	**86.6**	96.9
MDA	40.1	**88.0**	97.3
KPCA	42.0	**90.2**	99.2
KDA	50.3	**94.0**	97.9

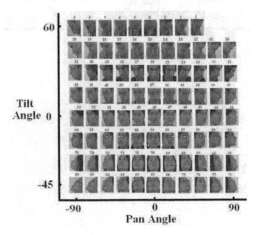

Fig. 3. Examples of the image set. The top two poses are not discussed because of lacking of enough samples.

structure captured by a single model graph is not subject-independent. Simply averaging is not sufficient to describe all subjects. Since the first stage estimation restricts the possible candidate in a small subset, the computational cost is still reasonable.

The data span pan angles from $-90°$ to $90°$ and tilt angle from $-60°$ (head tilt down) to $45°$ (head tilt up). 86 poses are included, as shown in Fig. 3.

3   Stage 1: Multi-resolution Subspace Analysis

Gabor wavelet transform is a convolution of the image with a family of Gabor kernels. All Gabor kernels are generated by a mother wavelet by dilations and rotations. Gabor wavelets provide a good joint spatial frequency representation. DC-free version of the Gabor wavelets can suppress the undesired variations, such as illumination change. Also, optimal wavelets can ideally extract the position and orientation of both global and local features [22]. Only magnitude responses are used in our algorithm since the phase response is too sensitive.

3.1   Subspace Projection

The wavelet features suffer from high dimensionality and no discriminant information are extracted. Subspace projection is used to reduce the dimensionality as well as extracting the most representative information. In this paper, we compare four popular subspaces for better discovering the underlying data structure, which are PCA, MDA and their corresponding nonlinear pair. For the clarity of presentation, in the following sections, the data set is denoted as $\{\mathbf{x}_i\}_{i=1,\cdots,N}$ with C classes. Samples from c-th class are denoted as $\mathbf{x}_{c,i}, i = 1, \cdots, N_c$, where $N = \sum_{c=1}^{C} N_c$ and $\{\mathbf{x}_i\}_{i=1,\cdots,N} = \cup_{c=1}^{C}\{\mathbf{x}_{c,j}\}_{j=1,\cdots,N_c}$.

Linear Subspace Projection. PCA aims to find the subspace that describes most variance while suppresses known noise as much as possible. PCA subspace is spanned by the principal eigenvectors of the covariance matrix, which is:

$$\mathbf{\Sigma} = \frac{1}{N} \sum_{i=1}^{N} (\mathbf{x}_i - \boldsymbol{\mu})(\mathbf{x}_i - \boldsymbol{\mu})^{\mathrm{T}}; \tag{1}$$

where $\boldsymbol{\mu}$ is the sample mean: $\boldsymbol{\mu} = \frac{1}{N} \sum_{i=1}^{N} \mathbf{x}_i$. The principal components are computed by solving the following eigen-decomposition problem:

$$\mathbf{\Sigma V} = \mathbf{\Lambda V}; \tag{2}$$

where $\mathbf{\Lambda}$ is the diagonal matrix whose non-zero entries are the eigenvalues λ_i of $\mathbf{\Sigma}$. $\mathbf{V}$ is the matrix from eigenvectors. λ_i indicates the information preserved on the corresponding eigenvector direction. By picking the eigenvectors with the largest eigenvalues the information lost is minimized in the mean-square sense.

While PCA looks for a projection subspace with minimal information lost, discriminant analysis seeks a projection subspace efficient for classification. The basic idea is to find a projection, in which the within class data are compactly represented while the between class data are well-separated. We use a multiple class discriminant analysis as introduced in [18]. The within-class scatter matrix $\mathbf{S}_W$ is used to evaluated the data compactness, defined as follows:

$$\mathbf{S}_W = \sum_{c=1}^{C} \sum_{i=1}^{N_c} (\mathbf{x}_{c,i} - \boldsymbol{\mu}_c)(\mathbf{x}_{c,i} - \boldsymbol{\mu}_c)^{\mathrm{T}}; \tag{3}$$

with $\boldsymbol{\mu}_c = \frac{1}{N_c} \sum_{i=1}^{N_c} \mathbf{x}_{c,i}$ as the class mean. The separability between data from different classes is evaluated by the between-class scatter matrix as follows

$$\mathbf{S}_B = \sum_{c=1}^{C} N_c (\boldsymbol{\mu}_c - \boldsymbol{\mu})(\boldsymbol{\mu}_c - \boldsymbol{\mu})^{\mathrm{T}}; \tag{4}$$

where $\boldsymbol{\mu} = \frac{1}{N} \sum_{i=1}^{N} \mathbf{x}_i$ is the overall sample mean. The subspace is found by Fisher's criterion, which maximize the Raleigh coefficient:

$$\mathcal{J}(\mathbf{V}) = \frac{\mathbf{V}^{\mathrm{T}} \mathbf{S}_B \mathbf{V}}{\mathbf{V}^{\mathrm{T}} \mathbf{S}_W \mathbf{V}}. \tag{5}$$

This turns out to be an eigen-decomposition problem. The solution can be found by solving the generalized eigen-decomposition problem $\mathbf{S}_B \mathbf{v}_i = \lambda_i \mathbf{S}_W \mathbf{v}_i$.

PCA and MDA provide powerful linear techniques for data reduction. However, most interesting data in real world assume certain non-linearities that linear projection can not model. This inspires the use of kernel machine, which explores the non-linearity of the data space. The extended nonlinear alternative, KPCA [19,23] and KDA [20], are used.

Kernel Machine: KPCA and KDA. In [11] the use of KPCA for modeling the multi-view faces in the original image space was presented. Assuming data non-linearly distributed, we can map it onto a new higher dimensional feature space $\{\boldsymbol{\Phi}(\mathbf{x}) \in \mathcal{F}\}$ where the data possess a linear property. The mapping is $\boldsymbol{\Phi} : \mathbf{x} \mapsto \boldsymbol{\Phi}(\mathbf{x})$. KPCA is realized by a linear PCA in the transformed space $\mathcal{F}$. The covariance matrix now becomes:

$$\boldsymbol{\Sigma} = \frac{1}{N} \sum_{i=1}^{N} (\boldsymbol{\Phi}(\mathbf{x}_i) - \boldsymbol{\Phi}(\boldsymbol{\mu}))(\boldsymbol{\Phi}(\mathbf{x}_i) - \boldsymbol{\Phi}(\boldsymbol{\mu}))^{\mathrm{T}}. \tag{6}$$

Sample mean $\boldsymbol{\Phi}(\boldsymbol{\mu}) = \frac{1}{N} \sum_{i=1}^{N} \boldsymbol{\Phi}(\mathbf{x}_i)$. Only dot product $\boldsymbol{\Phi}(\mathbf{x}_i) \bullet \boldsymbol{\Phi}(\mathbf{x}_j)$ is involved, hence no explicit function is needed for the mapping $\boldsymbol{\Phi}$. Define the kernel as

$$\mathcal{K}(\mathbf{x}_i; \mathbf{x}_j) \equiv \boldsymbol{\Phi}(\mathbf{x}_i) \bullet \boldsymbol{\Phi}(\mathbf{x}_j)$$

and the Gram matrix $\mathbf{K}$ as a $N \times N$ matrix with its entry: $\mathcal{K}(\mathbf{x}_i; \mathbf{x}_j), (i, j = 1, \cdots, N)$. The Hilbert space assumption constrains $\mathbf{v}$'s solution space within the span of $\{\mathbf{\Phi}(\mathbf{x}_1), \cdots, \mathbf{\Phi}(\mathbf{x}_N)\}$, which means $\mathbf{v} = \sum_i \alpha_i \mathbf{\Phi}(\mathbf{x}_i)$ $(\boldsymbol{\alpha} = [\alpha_1, \cdots, \alpha_N]^T)$. The linear PCA problem in space $\mathcal{F}$ gives:

$$\mathbf{K}'\boldsymbol{\alpha} = N\lambda\boldsymbol{\alpha}, \tag{7}$$

where $\mathbf{K}'$ is the slightly different version from $\mathbf{K}$ by removing the feature's mean:

$$\mathbf{K}' = (\mathbf{I} - \mathbf{e}\mathbf{e}^T)\mathbf{K}(\mathbf{I} - \mathbf{e}\mathbf{e}^T); \tag{8}$$

$\mathbf{e} = \frac{1}{\sqrt{N}}[1, 1, \cdots, 1]^T$.

The eigen-decomposition of the Gram matrix provides an embedding that captures the low-dimensional structure on the manifold. Hence, a better generalization ability can be achieved. In our implementation, we use the traditional Gaussian kernel.

The same as KPCA, KDA processes data in the transformed space $\mathcal{F}$. Hilbert space is assumed so that k-th projection direction is: $\mathbf{w}_k = \sum_{i=1}^{N} \alpha_i^{(k)} \mathbf{\Phi}(\mathbf{x}_i)$. Introduce the kernel $\mathcal{K}(\mathbf{x}_i; \mathbf{x}_j) = \mathbf{\Phi}(\mathbf{x}_i) \bullet \mathbf{\Phi}(\mathbf{x}_j)$ and define an additional kernel matrix $\mathbf{K}_c$ as a $N \times N_c$ matrix whose entry is $\mathcal{K}(\mathbf{x}_i; \mathbf{x}_{c,j})$ $(i = 1, \cdots, N, j = 1, \cdots, N_c)$. Now the scatter matrices can be represented by:

$$\mathbf{W}^T\mathbf{S}_B\mathbf{W} = \mathbf{W}^T \sum_{c=1}^{C} N_c(\boldsymbol{\mu}_c - \boldsymbol{\mu})(\boldsymbol{\mu}_c - \boldsymbol{\mu})^T\mathbf{W}$$

$$= \mathbf{V}^T\left(\sum_{c=1}^{C} \frac{\mathbf{K}_c\mathbf{1}_c\mathbf{K}_c^T}{N_c} - \frac{\mathbf{K}\mathbf{1}\mathbf{K}}{N}\right)\mathbf{V}; \tag{9}$$

$$\mathbf{W}^T\mathbf{S}_W\mathbf{W} = \sum_{c=1}^{C} \sum_{i=1}^{N_c} (\mathbf{x}_{c,i} - \boldsymbol{\mu}_c)(\mathbf{x}_{c,i} - \boldsymbol{\mu}_c)^T$$

$$= \mathbf{V}^T\left(\sum_{c=1}^{C} \mathbf{K}_c\mathbf{K}_c^T - \sum_{c=1}^{C} \frac{\mathbf{K}_c\mathbf{1}_c\mathbf{K}_c^T}{N_c}\right)\mathbf{V}. \tag{10}$$

where $\mathbf{1}$ is an $N \times N$ matrix with all 1 entries and $\mathbf{1}_c$ is an $N_c \times N_c$ matrix with all 1 entries. The new projection matrix is $\mathbf{V} = [\boldsymbol{\alpha}_1, \cdots, \boldsymbol{\alpha}_m]$ with $\boldsymbol{\alpha}_k = [\alpha_1^{(k)}, \cdots, \alpha_N^{(k)}]^T$. The Raleigh's coefficient now becomes:

$$\mathcal{J}(\mathbf{V}) = \frac{\mathbf{V}^T(\sum_{c=1}^{C} \frac{1}{N_c}\mathbf{K}_c\mathbf{1}_c\mathbf{K}_c^T - \frac{1}{N}\mathbf{K}\mathbf{1}\mathbf{K})\mathbf{V}}{\mathbf{V}^T(\sum_{c=1}^{C} \mathbf{K}_c\mathbf{K}_c^T - \sum_{c=1}^{C} \frac{1}{N_c}\mathbf{K}_c\mathbf{1}_c\mathbf{K}_c^T)\mathbf{V}}. \tag{11}$$

Similar as its linear alternative, KDA projection is pursued by maximizing the Raleigh's coefficient.

In Fig. 4 and Fig. 5, 2D toy examples are used to illustrate the four subspace analysis methods. In Fig. 4, the original 2D data are projected onto the 1D PCA and LDA subspace as shown. LDA can well-separate the data while PCA cannot. In Fig. 5, we illustrate the separation abilities for nonlinear data set. All four

Fig. 4. Illustrative example of PCA and LDA subspace representation. The data from two classes are shown in red and blue individually. Left: original data; middle: projected data from PCA subspace; right: the projected data from LDA subspace.

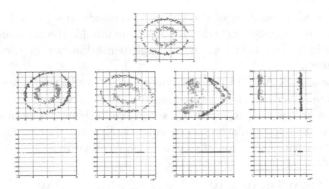

Fig. 5. Illustrative examples of the subspace representation for nonlinear data. Red color and blue color indicate samples from different classes. First row: the original data. Row 2-3: transformed data (top: 2D space; bottom: 1D space). From column 1 to column 4: PCA, LDA, KPCA, KDA. Kernel: same Gaussian kernel.

subspace projections are compared on a binary 2D toy data set. As can be seen, PCA and LDA are not able to produce a more discriminating representations due to the non-linearity of the data, whereas the KPCA and KDA transform the data into two well-separated clusters.

3.2 Prototype Matching

We use the nearest prototype matching for the first stage classification. Each pose is represented by a set of subspaces, each of them computed from filter responses in one resolution. In each subspace the prototype from class mean is found as a template. Euclidean distances is used to measure the similarity in subspaces. The pose estimation is given by the prevailing class label from all resolutions as illustrated in Fig. 2. This gives a single pose as an estimate. We relax the single estimated pose label to a subset of 3 × 3 poses around it for additional robustness. A second-stage is applied thereafter to solve the sub-problem, where only poses in the subset are tackled.

4   Stage 2: Geometric Structure Analysis

The second stage serves to refine the coarse pose estimation. In this section, we use a revised version of the face bunch graph introduced in [17] for this purpose. Face graph is a labeled graph which connects the local image features together with the image's geometric configuration. It exploits the local salient features on a human face, e.g. pupils, nose tip, corners of mouth, and etc. together with their locations.

4.1   Bunch Graph Construction

Each face image constructs a model graph. The model graph is a labeled graph with its nodes corresponding to the Gabor jets at the predefined salient facial features, and its edges labeled by the distance vector between nodes. Gabor jet is defined as the concatenation of the Gabor wavelet responses at an image point. Some examples of the model graphs are show in Fig. 6. Occlusion of the current view determines how many nodes are used. More nodes assert more geometric constraint useful for pose discriminating, however, more identity information could be preserved.

Each view is modeled by one set of bunch graphs from the model graphs of the same pose. The nodes of the bunch graph are the bundles of the corresponding nodes in model graphs. The geometric structure is subject-dependent in a certain degree. Subjects from different race, age group, or different gender possess different geometric configuration. Although a simple average of all the geometric configurations followed by an exhaustive search and match can still be used to find the identity-related fiducial points, this step will also add ambiguity to the global structure between close poses. In the purpose of retrieving the pose information while suppressing the subject identity, we keep every available geometric configuration and use a *semi-rigid* searching for matching, which means only local adjustment is allowed for refine the estimated face graph. Therefore, for each pose, we actually have the same number of bunch graphs as the model graphs. Each bunch graph inherits the edge information from an individual model graph. All the bunch graphs differ only in the edge labels. This is illustrated in Fig. 7. This strategy enables us to avoid large distortions in geometric structure that causes ambiguities between neighboring poses. This offline model construction step gives each pose a set of bunch graphs as the templates.

Fig. 6. Examples of the face model graph. Left: pan: 0° tilt: 0°; middle: pan: −15° tilt: 0°; right: pan: +15° tilt: 0°.

Training images   Model bunch   Bunch graphs as templates
from frontal view   graphs   for frontal view

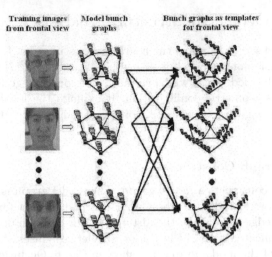

Fig. 7. Construction of the bunch graphs as the template for a single pose. Frontal view is used. The graphs shown here are just for illustration. In actual computation, more nodes are used, hence the graph structure is different from that shown here.

4.2   Graph Matching

Denote the subset of poses confined by the first stage estimation as $\mathcal{P}_s$. Given a test image, every pose candidate in $\mathcal{P}_s$ gives an estimated face graph by searching the sets of nodes that maximize the graph similarity. Graph similarity is determined by both the similarity of the nodes and the distance in edge labels. We use the normalized cross correlation as the nodes similarity metric [17]. Let $\mathbf{J}(i) = (f_1(i), \cdots, f_F(i))$ be the Gabor jet for i-th nodes. Nodes similarity D is given by:

$$D(\mathbf{J}(i); \mathbf{J}(k)) = \frac{\sum_{m=1}^{F} f_m(i) f_m(k)}{\sqrt{\sum_{m=1}^{F} f_m^2(i) \sum_{m=1}^{F} f_m^2(k)}}. \tag{12}$$

The graph similarity S between the estimated face graph $\mathcal{G} = (\mathbf{J}_m, \delta_e)$ and some bunch graph $\mathcal{B} = (\{\mathbf{J}_m^{B_i}\}_i, \delta_e^B)$ is defined as:

$$\mathcal{S}(\mathcal{G}, \mathcal{B}) = \frac{1}{M} \sum_{m=1}^{M} \max_i (D(\mathbf{J}_m; \mathbf{J}_m^{B_i})) - \frac{\lambda}{E} \sum_{e=1}^{E} \frac{(\delta_e - \delta_e^B)^2}{(\delta_e^B)^2}; \tag{13}$$

where λ is the relaxation factor.

Since we have multiple bunch graphs for a single pose, each of them can generate a possible face graph for the testing image. The best matched one needs to be found as the representative face graph for this pose. This best face graph estimate is given by the following steps:

1. Scan the testing image. Each rigid topographic constraint ($\lambda = \infty$) determined by one bunch graph gives a set of matching nodes, and hence a graph $\mathcal{G}_t$. Out of which the best matched one is:

$$t^* = \arg\max_t \mathcal{S}(\mathcal{G}_t, \mathcal{B}_t),$$

with $\lambda = \infty$.

2. The nodes of the best matched estimated graph $\mathcal{G}_{t^*}$ are individually adjusted locally to refine the match.
3. Refined nodes determines the graph.

The best geometric configuration t^* is selected and the graph similarity between the estimated face graph and the t^*-th bunch graph is evaluated by equation 13. The pose with the highest similarity score gives the final pose estimation.

5   Experimental Evaluations

The data set used for evaluating this approach includes 28 subjects. Magnetic sensor is used to provide the ground-truth. Some poses are excluded due to lack of enough samples (see Fig. 3). We include 86 poses. The pan angle spans from $-90°$ to $+90°$; with $15°$ intervals from $-60°$ to $60°$, and then the poses with $\pm90°$ pan angles are also considered. The tilt angle has a consistent interval of $15°$ from $-45°$ to $60°$. 3894 images of size 67×55 and their mirror images are used, so altogether 7788 images included. Each pose has 80~100 images, randomly split into two parts, one for training and one for testing. Some subjects may have multiple samples for one pose, assuming sufficient different facial expressions. We use Viola and Jone's face detector [24] to get the face area. 9 separate detectors are trained for different views. For each image, we manually select one detector according to the ground-truth of the head pose.

5.1   Stage 1: "Coarse" Pose Estimation

Output of the first stage is a $p \times p$ subset of poses. The accuracy is evaluated accordingly: if the true pose does not belong to this subset, it is counted as a false estimate. In our implement $p = 3$ is used if not specially stated. Bigger p gives better accuracy, however, more computational cost will be needed for the second stage refinement. In table 1, the first-stage estimation for different subspaces are evaluated under different p. To better present the error distribution, in Fig. 8 we use a color coded error distribution diagram to show the accuracy for each pose for KDA subspace (evaluated under $p = 3$). Darker color shows more error. All four subspace didn't give a satisfactory results comparable with those reported when $p = 1$, which is actually the accuracy of using subspace analysis alone. This is not a surprise, since the subspace analysis is very sensitive to the data noise, such as background and data alignment. In our data set, the face position is not well-aligned. Also in some images parts of the hair and shoulder appears while not in the other. In such case, the subspace analysis alone is not capable to obtain as good performance. The use of the two-stage framework solves this problem. More experiments validate the advantage of the two-stage framework. We purposely translate the cropping window for the testing face

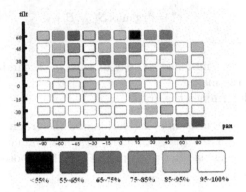

Fig. 8. Color coded error distribution diagram for KDA subspace ($p = 3$)

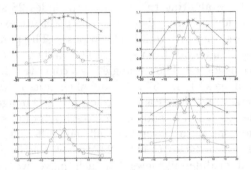

Fig. 9. The performance with the added misalignment ($\pm16, \pm8, \pm6, \pm4, \pm2$) in both directions. Top row: misalignment in the horizontal direction. Bottom row: misalignment in the vertical direction. Left column: accuracy change with misalignment. Right column: relative accuracy change with misalignment. Blue curve with x: evaluated on $p = 3$. Red curve with o: evaluated on $p = 1$.

images by $\pm2, \pm4, \pm6, \pm8, \pm16$ pixels in both directions, which aggravates the misalignment. Use the same KDA subspace obtained in previous step to test the performance. The accuracy is evaluated for both $p = 1$ and $p = 3$, as show in Fig. 9. Experimental results indicate that when using $p = 3$ to evaluate the accuracy, the accuracy is actually quite stable with the aggravating misalignment. However, when $p = 1$, the accuracy keeps stable for small misalignment (<4 pixels), and drops fast with increasing misalignment. Since the second-stage is not affected by the misalignment, if we can get a stable output for the first-stage with increasing misalignment, the overall accuracy would be stable. This shows the advantage of the 2-stage framework.

5.2   Stage 2: Refinement

We only use the best results, which is from KDA subspace analysis, as the first-stage output. The pose estimation accuracy after the refinement is summarized in

Table 2. The overall accuracy (%) using KDA subspace majority voting for the first stage estimation and the semi-rigid bunch graph matching as the second stage refinement. The accuracy is 75.4%.

	$-90°$	$-60°$	$-45°$	$-30°$	$-15°$	$0°$	$15°$	$30°$	$45°$	$60°$	$90°$
60°	16.7	30.8	11.1	50.0	50.0	20.0	30.8	23.1	25.0		
45°	80.5	77.5	65.6	65.4	79.5	88.2	76.7	83.6	58.3	77.8	67.1
30°	80.8	74.7	81.5	73.0	76.3	85.3	71.1	82.2	87.6	83.3	86.6
15°	75.4	71.4	80.5	84.4	94.3	84.0	79.4	82.4	85.7	71.4	87.3
0°	87.5	83.4	77.0	88.8	91.6	86.0	87.9	79.0	83.1	79.6	79.3
$-15°$	67.0	81.2	85.0	78.9	82.5	80.4	89.1	75.9	74.5	84.1	87.0
$-30°$	80.9	84.1	92.2	67.7	89.5	64.7	94.2	75.9	87.0	72.1	76.8
$-45°$	82.9	65.7	77.1	81.6	76.7	65.6	68.8	81.6	71.1	75.0	30.0

Table 3. Comparison of results from different second-stage refinement

KDA +BG	PCA +MDA	MDA +MDA	KPCA +MDA	KDA +MDA
75.4	43.1	44.0	47.3	53.4

Table 2. The accuracy was evaluated by the ratio of samples that were correctly classified. Pose with tilt angle 60° get poor performance. It is because of the severe occlusion. Discarding these poses, the overall accuracy can be improved to 81.3%. For comparison, a second stage refinement by multi-resolution MDA analysis is also performed, using the poses confined by the first stage. The results are shown in Table 3. The comparison shows that by introducing the second-stage structure landmark matching, the estimation accuracy has a markable improvement.

6   Concluding Remarks

In this paper we discussed a two-stage approach for estimating head pose from static images. We use statistical subspaces analysis in Gabor wavelet domain to confine the possible range of the head pose. Semi-rigid bunch graph was used to systematically analyze the finer structural details associated with facial features, so as to refine the first-stage estimate. The combination of statistical analysis on features from entire images with the geometrical topograph driven approach provides a robust way to estimate the head pose in a fine scale. It solves the internal problem of the statistical analysis approach that requires a high-quality data set, as well as introducing the methodology of decomposing a large classification problem into smaller sub-problem, so that template matching is feasible. Experimental results show that better performance can be obtained than statistical analysis alone.

Acknowledgement

Our research was supported by grants from the UC Discovery Program and the Technical Support Working Group (TSWG) of the US Department of Defense. The authors are thankful for the assistance and support of our colleagues from the UCSD Computer Vision and Robotics Research Laboratory, especially Jens M. Pedersen, Pew Putthividhya and Daniel Norgaard. The authors also thank Thomas B. Moeslund for his contributions.

References

1. R. Pappu and P.A. Beardsley. Qualitative approach to classifying gaze direction. In *Proceedings of the IEEE Conf on Automatic Face and Gesture Recognition.*, 1998.
2. R. Stiefelhagen. Tracking focus of attention in meetings. In *Proceedings of the IEEE International Conference on Multimodal Interfaces (ICMI'02).*, 2002.
3. K. Huang, M. M. Trivedi and T. Gandhi. Driver's View and Vehicle Surround Estimation using Omnidirectional Video Stream. In *Proceedings of IEEE Intelligent Vehicles Symposium*, Columbus, OH, pp. 444-449, June 9-11, 2003.
4. B. Braathen, M. S. Bartlett, and J. R. Movellan. 3-d head pose estimation from video by stochastic particle filtering. In *Proceedings of the 8th Annual Joint Symposium on Neural Computation.*, 2001.
5. Y.Li, S.Gong, and H. Liddell. Support vector regression and classification based multi-view face detection and recognition. In *Proceeding of IEEE International Conference on Automatic Face and Gesture Recognition.*, pages 300–305, July 2000.
6. S.Z. Li, Q.D. Fu, L. Gu, B. Scholkopf, Y.M. Cheng, and H.J. Zhang. Kernel machine based learning for multi-view face detection and pose estimation. In *Proceedings of 8th IEEE International Conference on Computer Vision.*, July 2001.
7. M. Cordea, E. Petriu, N. Georganas, D. Petriu, , and T. Whalen. Real-time 2.5d head pose recovery for model-based video-coding. In *Proceedings of the IEEE Instrumentation and Measurement Technology Conference.*, 2000.
8. T. Horprasert, Y. Yacoob, and L. S. Davis. An anthropometric shape model for estimating head orientation. In *Proceedings of the 3rd International Workshop on Visual Form*, 1997.
9. L. Morency, P. Sundberg, and T. Darrell. Pose estimation using 3d view-based eigenspaces. In *Proceedings of the IEEE International Workshop on Analysis and Modeling of Faces and Gestures, in Conjunction with ICCV2003*, pages 45–52, 2003.
10. E. Seemann, K. Nickel, and R. Stiefelhagen. Head pose estimation using stereo vision for human-robot interaction. In *Proceedings of the 6th IEEE International Conference on Automatic Face and Gesture Recognition*, 2004.
11. L. Chen, L. Zhang, Y. Hu, M. Li, and H. Zhang. Head pose estimation using fisher manifold learning. In *Proceedings of the IEEE International Workshop on Analysis and Modeling of Faces and Gestures, in Conjunction with ICCV2003*, 2003.
12. S. Gong J. Sherrah and E. Ong. Understanding pose discrimination in similarity space. In *Proceedings of the The Eleventh British Machine Vision Conference (BMVC1999)*, 1999.

13. Y. Wei, L. Fradet, and T. Tan. Head pose estimation using gabor eigenspace modeling. In *Proceedings of the IEEE International Conference on Image Processing (ICIP2002)*, volume 1, pages 281–284, 2002.
14. S. Srinivasan and K.L. Boyer. Head pose estimation using view based eigenspaces. In *Proceedings of the 16th International Conference on Pattern Recognition*, volume 4, pages 302–305, 2002.
15. M. Potzsch, N. Kruger, and C. von der Malsburg. Determination of face position and pose with a learned representation based on labeled graphs. Technical report, Institute for Neuroinformatik, RuhrUniversitat, Bochum, 1996. Internal Report.
16. V. Krger and G. Sommer. Efficient head pose estimation with gabor wavelet networks. In *Proceedings of the The Eleventh British Machine Vision Conference (BMVC2000)*, 2000.
17. L. Wiskott, J. Fellous, N. Krger, and C von der Malsburg. Face recognition by elastic bunch graph matching. In *Proceedings of the 7th International Conference on Computer Analysis of Images and Patterns(CAIP'97)*, 1997.
18. R. O. Duda, P. E. Hart, and D. G. Stork. *Pattern Classification*. Wiley-interscience, second edition.
19. B. Scholkopf, A. Smola, and K.-R. Muller. Nonlinear component analysis as a kernel eigenvalue problem. *Neural Computation*, 10:1299–1319, 1998.
20. Y. Li, S. Gong, and H. Liddell. Recognising trajectories of facial identities using kernel discriminant analysis. In *Proceedings of the British Machine Vision Conference (BMVC2001)*, pages 613–622, 2001.
21. S. Mika, G. Ratsch, J. Weston, B. Scholkopf, and K. Muller. Fisher discriminant analysis with kernels. In *Proceedings of the IEEE Neural Networks for Signal Processing Workshop*, pages 41–48, 1999.
22. J.MacLennan. Gabor representations ofspatiotemporal visual images. Technical report, Computer Science Department, University of Tennessee, Knoxville., 1991. CS-91-144. Accessible via URL: http://www.cs.utk.edu/ mclennan.
23. J. Ham, D.D. Lee, S. Mika, and B. Scholkopf. A kernel view of dimensionality reduction of manifolds. In *Proceedings of the International Conference on Machine Learning.*, 2004.
24. P Viola and M. Jones. *Robust Real-time Object Detection*, In Proceedings of the Second International Workshop on Statistical and Compu tational Theories of Vision - Modeling, Learning and Sampling. Jointed with ICCV2001.

Gabor-Eigen-Whiten-Cosine: A Robust Scheme for Face Recognition

Weihong Deng, Jiani Hu, and Jun Guo

Beijing University of Posts and Telecommunications, 100876, Beijing, China
{cvpr_dwh, cughu}@126.com, junguo@bupt.edu.cn

Abstract. Recognizing faces with complex intrapersonal variations is a challenging task, especially when using small size samples. Our approach, which obtains state of the art results, is based on a new face recognition scheme: Gabor-Eigen-Whiten-Cosine (GEWC). The novelty of this paper lies in 1) the finding that the same face with complex variations, projected into the Gabor based whitened PCA feature space, is approximately angle invariance; and 2) the experimental studies that analyze the joint contribution of Gabor wavelet, whitening process, and cosine similarity measure on the PCA based face recognition. The new GEWC method has been successfully tested and evaluated using comparative experiments on 3000+ FERET frontal face images with 1196 subjects. In particular, the GEWC method achieves constant 100% accuracy on the 200-subject experiment across illuminations and facial expressions. Furthermore, its recognition rates reach up to 96.3%, 99.5%, 78.8%, and 77.8% on the FB, fc, dup I, and dup II probes respectively using only one training sample per person.

1 Introduction

Face recognition can be defined as the identification of individual from images of their faces by using a stored database of faces labeled with people's identities, which is largely motivated by the need for surveillance and security, human-computer intelligent interaction, telecommunications, and smart environment [1]. The challenge of face recognition comes from the generally similar shape of face combined with the numerous variations between images of the same face, such as changes in facial expression, illumination conditions, age and accessories, etc. The task of a face recognition system is to recognize a face in a manner that is as independent as possible of these image and facial variations [2]. Therefore, a good face recognition methodology should consider representation as well as classification issue to counteract the *intrapersonal variation*.

Discriminating analysis based methods [4][5][6] are widely used to suppress the intrapersonal variation, which define a projection that makes the within-class scatter small and the between-class scatter large to derive compact and well-separated cluster. The drawback of these methods is that they require large and representative training samples to guarantee their generalization. However, many face recognition tasks, such as airport security and law enforcement applications, can only offer small size training

W. Zhao, S. Gong, and X. Tang (Eds.): AMFG 2005, LNCS 3723, pp. 336–349, 2005.

samples. Consequently, the discriminating analysis possibly over-fits to the training data, and fail on future trials using novel (unseen) test data. As evidence in support of our claim, we should draw the attention of the reader to some of the results in the September 1996 FERET competition [7] and those reported by the literature [8].

In general, the difference between two faces can be modeled by three components: *intrinsic difference* [9] that discriminates different face identity; *trained variation*, arising from the different conditions of the same training face (class), such as expression and illumination changes; *novel variation*, which is not characterized by the training samples, such as an unexpected accessory or illumination. Note that the intrapersonal variation consists of both the trained and the novel variation. In the real-world scenario, since one never knows in advance the underlying distributions for the different faces, the novel variation is the most challenge factor. A good face recognition methodology should not only retain maximum intrinsic difference and minimum trained variation, but more importantly, also should be robust to the novel variation.

Our work focuses on developing a robust face recognition scheme from small size sample, namely one or two training samples per person, without discriminant analysis. We first note that PCA is potential to extract discriminating information, because covariance matrix has characterized all the intrinsic difference in the training data. The whitening process is then applied to exclude the trained variation retained by the PCA. Inspired by the Dynamic Link Architecture (DLA) framework [10], we use Labeled-Graph (LG) vector for face representation, instead of the traditional pixel-based representation, to narrow the intrapersonal variation between the probe and corresponding gallery. The features used in the LG vector, based on the 2D Gabor wavelet transform, are expected to be robust to changes in the illumination and facial expression [6][11]. For classification, we newly discovery that the cosine similarity measure is less sensitive to the novel variation in the whitened PCA feature space, which is validated by our extensive experiments.

This paper presents a new face recognition scheme called **Gabor-Eigen-Whiten-Cosine** (GEWC) for face recognition, which integrates the Gabor wavelet representation (Gabor), PCA dimensionality reduction (Eigen), whitening process (Whiten), and cosine similarity measure based classification (Cosine). The effectiveness and robustness of this new method is comprehensively tested using the FERET face dataset. We first conduct a face recognition experiment using 600 FERET frontal face images corresponding to 200 subjects, which were acquired under variable illumination and facial expressions. Furthermore, our method is evaluated against four categories of tasks, following the procedure of the FERET Evaluation. The effectiveness of the GEWC method is shown in terms of the comparative performance against the state of art face recognition methods such as the Eigenface method [3], the Fisherface method [4]. Comparative experimental studies are also performed to illustrate how the four procedures of the GEWC method contribute the face recognition performance respectively.

2 Gabor-Eigen-Whiten-Cosine Scheme

This section details the Gabor-Eigen-Whiten-Cosine scheme for face recognition. Firstly, a Label Graph (LG) vector, which is robust to the illumination and facial expression changes, is derived based on 2D Gabor Transformation. Secondly, PCA is applied on the LG vector to extract a compact feature vector. Thirdly, PCA based features are normalized by whitening process for higher separability. Finally, cosine similarity measure is used at the classification stage to counteract the intrapersonal different between the probes and galleries in the feature space.

2.1 Face Representation

2D Gabor Transform was developed by J. Daugman in 1988, which today is widely applied across computer vision domains [11]. To extract information about object appearance, the image is convolved with a multiple spatial resolution, multiple orientation set of Gabor filters. Specifically, the 2D Gabor filters are usually defined as follow:

$$\psi_{\mu,v}(z) = \frac{\left\|k_{\mu,v}\right\|^2}{\sigma^2} e^{-\left(\left\|k_{\mu,v}\right\|^2 \|z\|^2 / 2\sigma^2\right)} \left[e^{ik_{\mu,v}z} - e^{-\sigma^2/2} \right] \tag{1}$$

where $k_{u,v} = k_v e^{i\phi_\mu}$, $k_v = k_{max}/f^v$ gives the frequency, $\phi_\mu = \mu\pi/8$, $\phi_\mu \in [0,\pi)$ gives the orientation, and $z = (x, y)$. Note that, in equation (1), v controls the scale of the Gabor filters, which mainly determines the center of the Gabor filter in the frequency domain; μ controls the orientation of the Gabor filters. This can be observed intuitively from the visualization of the real part of the Gabor filters. The parameters for the Gabor filters are as follows: $\sigma = 2\pi$, $k_{max} = \pi/2$, $f = \sqrt{2}$, five scales $v \in \{0,1,2,3,4\}$ and eight orientations $\mu \in \{0,1,2,3,4,5,6,7\}$. These Gabor kernels form a bank of 40 different filters and exhibit desirable characteristics of spatial frequency, spatial locality, and orientation selectivity.

In our implement, the Gabor representation for face images is derived as follow: 1) all images are translated, rotated, and scaled so that the center of the eyes are placed on specific pixels, yielding 65×75 pixel cropped and rectified face images (see Fig.1.a); 2) Faces are masked to remove background and hair and histogram

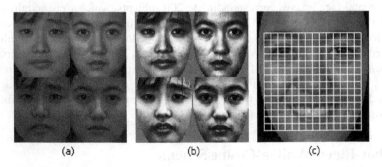

(a)   (b)   (c)

Fig. 1. Illustration of the procedure of the Label graph vector derivation. (a) the cropped and rectified images. (b) the normalized masked images. (c) the settled grid for sampling Gabor features.

equalization is then carried out to smooth the distribution of grey values for the non-masked pixels, making the masked images insensitive to overall level of illumination conditions (see Fig.1.b); and 3) The normalized masked image is convolved with the 40 Gabor filters and the magnitudes of the complex-value filter responses are sampled at 225 points on square grid (see Fig.1.c), which is settled at the core region of the human face. Then the sampled values are combined into a 9000 dimensional Label Graph (LG) vector to form the Gabor representation for a face image.

2.2 Dimension Reduction

As the perceptually meaningful structure of the face representation has many fewer independent degrees of freedoms than its dimensionality, it is natural to pursue dimensionality reduction schemes. A classical technique for dimensionality reduction, particularly in face recognition, is principle component analysis (PCA). In order to produce a compact representation, the LG vector is projected into a lower dimensional feature space found by principle components analysis (PCA).

$$\mathbf{u} = \mathbf{W}_{PCA}\mathbf{x} \qquad (2)$$

The input LG vectors are first transformed by subtracting the mean: $\mathbf{\Phi}_i = \mathbf{x}_i - \mathbf{m}$. The principal components of the training data set are given by the eigenvectors of its covariance matrix $\mathbf{\Sigma} = \frac{1}{n}\sum_{i=1}^{n}\mathbf{\Phi}_i\mathbf{\Phi}_i^T$. Because of the high dimensionality of the LG vectors, $\mathbf{\Sigma}$ is very large; however, there are only $n-1$ nonzero eigenvalues and only the corresponding eigenvectors are relevant for describing the distribution of the training set. In practice, only M ($M < n-1$) eigenvectors having the largest eigenvalues (and, hence, the largest variance in the data set) are kept empirically to form the projection matrix $\mathbf{W}_{PCA}$.

PCA technique is guaranteed to discover the linear projection that maximizes the scatter of all the projected training samples, but this induces its main drawback for the classification purposes: the scatter being maximized is not only due to the intrinsic difference that is useful, but also due to the trained variation that is harmful. Note that in face recognition, the trained variations are usually due to low frequency changes, such as the global variable lighting and similar expression changes of the training samples, which will be retained in leading components. Pentland et al. [13] have empirically shown that superior face recognition results are achieved when the first three eigenvector is not used. It is unlikely that, however, the leading principal components corresponding solely to the trained variation; as a consequence, information that is useful for discrimination may be lost [14]. In the GEWC scheme, we solve this problem using the whitening process.

2.3 Feature Normalization

PCA based feature suffers from two obvious shortcomings: 1) the leading eigenvectors encode mostly for prototypical representational aspects, such as illumination and expression, rather than discriminating information [13]; and 2) Mean-Square-Error (MSE) principle underlying PCA preferentially weights low frequencies [16][17][18], which makes the discriminating information contained in the high frequency components cannot contribute the face recognition. Note that in the Gabor based PCA feature space, the trailing eigenvectors might retain the high-frequency components, which contribute to the fine details required in the identification task, rather than the noise, since the image noise has been suppressed by the Gabor filter.

A straightforward way to counteract these disadvantages is the whitening process, which normalizes the PCA based feature. Specifically, the PCA based feature, $\mathbf{u}$ is subject to the whitening transformation and yields yet another feature set $\mathbf{w}$:

$$\mathbf{w} = \Lambda_M^{-1/2}\mathbf{u} \tag{3}$$

where $\Lambda_M^{-1/2} = diag\{\lambda_1^{-1/2}, \lambda_2^{-1/2}, ..., \lambda_M^{-1/2}\}$. The integrated projection matrix $\Lambda_M^{-1/2}\mathbf{W}_{PCA}$ treats variance along all principle component axes as equally significant by weighting components corresponding to smaller eigenvalues more heavily and is arguably appropriate since our aim is discrimination, rather than representation. Consequently, the negative influences of the leading eigenvectors are reduced, while the discriminating details encoded in trailing eigenvectors are magnified.

2.4 Classification Rule and Similarity Measure

When a face image is presented to the GEWC method, the LG vector of the face image is first calculated as detailed in Section 2.1, and the low dimensional Gabor-based features, $\mathbf{w}$, is derived using (3). Let $\mathbf{m}_k^0, k = 1, 2, ..., L$, be the prototype, the mean of training samples, for class ω_k in the feature space. The GEWC method applies the nearest neighbor (to the mean) rule for classification using similarity measure δ

$$\delta(\mathbf{w}, \mathbf{m}_k^0) = \min_j \delta(\mathbf{w}, \mathbf{m}_j^0) \rightarrow \mathbf{w} \in \omega_k \tag{4}$$

The image feature vector, $\mathbf{w}$, is classified as belonging to the class of the closet mean, $\mathbf{m}_k^0$, using the similarity measure δ.

Popular similarity measures include L_1, L_2, Mahalanobis distance, and cosine similarity measure. In the PCA-based feature space, it is proven that the Mahalanobis distance measure performs the best followed in order by L_1, L_2 distance and cosine similarity measure, because Mahalanobis distance counteracts the fact that simple distance measures, like L_1 and L_2 distance, in the PCA space weight preferentially for low frequencies [6][18]. In our scheme, however, this preference is equalized explicitly by the whitening process, which makes the Mahalanobis distance unnecessary. Instead, we should reconsider the optimal similarity measure according to its invariance with the image changes.

Note that when the novel variation, unseen in the training set, is projected onto the feature space, most energy of it will distribute over all the eigenvectors. This is because such variations are somewhat independent of the variance retained by the feature space. In other words, novel variation, projected into the feature space, is incline to evenly affect the projected scale on each component, and thus take more effect on the L_1 and L_2 distance rather than the vector angle. Therefore, the cosine similarity measure, δ_{CSM}, which is invariant to change in scale, is employed to perform nearest neighbor search in the feature space for face recognition.

$$\delta_{\mathrm{CSM}}(\mathbf{w}_1, \mathbf{w}_2) = \frac{-\mathbf{w}_1^{\mathrm{T}}\mathbf{w}_2}{\|\mathbf{w}_1\| \cdot \|\mathbf{w}_2\|} \tag{5}$$

Although we argue the GEWC method is robust scheme for face recognition, we still bear the burden of establishing our claim with the help of actual data. This we will do in the rest of this paper with the help of a standard testbed: FERET database.

3 Experiments and Analysis

We assessed the effectiveness and robustness of our new GEWC method on the face recognition task using a large scale data set from the The FacE REcognition Technology (FERET) database, which is a standard testbed for face recognition technologies [7]. The FERET facial database displays diversity across gender, ethnicity, and age. To obtain a robust assessment of performance, the GEWC algorithm is evaluated against different categories of images. The categories were broken out by a lighting change, varying expression, and time between the acquisition date of the database image and the testing image.

3.1 Experiments: Recognition Across Illumination and Facial Expression

This experiment involves 600 face images corresponding to 200 subjects and each subject has three images of 256×384 with 256 gray scale level. As the images were acquired during different photo sessions, they display different illumination and characteristics and facial expressions. As two images are randomly chosen for training, while the remaining image is used for testing (see Fig.2), the tested methods have to cope with both illumination and facial expression variabilities.

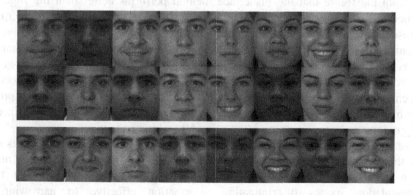

Fig. 2. Example FERET images used in our experiments (cropped and rectified). The top rows show the example of the training images, while the bottom row shows the examples of the testing images.

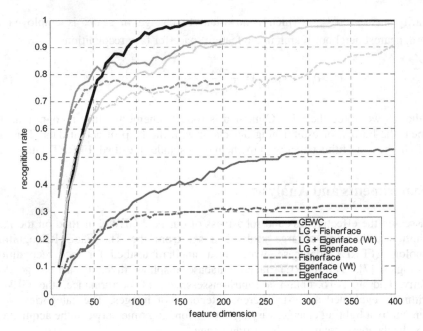

Fig. 3. Comparative performance of the GEWC method and six algorithms. The six include the Eigenface method, the Eigenface method with whitening process (Wt), and the Fisherface method, using two face representations: normalized masked image and Label Graph vector (LG) respectively.

For comparison purpose, we first implemented the Eigenface method [3], the Eigenface method with whitening process, the Fisherface method [4] and tested them using normalized mask images (see Fig.1.b). The comparative face recognition performance of these three methods is shown in Fig.3 by dashed lines, and one can see from the figure that the Fisherface method performs better than the Eigenface method. This shows the superiority of the discriminant analysis method when using representative training data. Note that, however, the whitening process improves the Eigenface method significantly and even brings it a higher accuracy than the Fisherface method. This result indicates that (i) the whitening process suppresses the trained variation encoded in the leading eigenvector, since a 50% increase in accuracy is achieve when whiten the leading 50 features; and (ii) the whitening process effectively explores discriminating information in the trailing eigenvector, since the recognition rate keep increasing when using 50+ whitened features.

We then applied the above three methods on the LG vector, and the results show that the recognition performance improves for all three methods by a large margin when using 50+ feature. These results suggest that (i) Gabor wavelet based representation carries discriminating information effective to narrowing the intrapersonal variation; and (ii) Gabor wavelet takes more affect on the trailing eigenvectors that encode the high frequency information corresponding to local variation, such as local illumination changes, since the benefits of it can only be revealed when using 50+ features.

GEWC method is finally applied and it performs better than all of the other six methods. In particular, GEWC method achieves constant 100% correct recognition accuracy when using 185+ features. The high performance of cosine similarity measure shows that the face and image variations, projected in the Gabor based whitened PCA feature space, are less likely to affect the angle of feature vector rather than its scale. Note that in the PCA based feature space, the superiority of the cosine similarity measure can be revealed only when the whitening process is applied to equalize projected variations. Without the previous whitening process, the cosine similarity measure only achieves equivalent performance to the L_1 and L_2 distance [6][18].

3.2 Experiments: Face Recognition with One Sample Image

In this series of experiments, the GEWC method is evaluated extensively against different categories of image to obtain a robust assessment of its performance. To produce comparable results, we follow the procedure of FERET Evaluation [7], using the same gallery and probe sets.

The gallery images were 1196 **FA** images captured during different photo sessions, with one image per person. The **FB** probes consisted of 1195 images with alternative facial expression; The **fc** probes contain 194 images taken with a different camera and lighting; The **duplicate I** probes involve 722 images with corresponding gallery image taken from on a different day and in a different place, and thus they might contain "unite variation" due to illumination, facial expression, accessories, and aging, etc. The **duplicate II** probes, a subset of duplicate I, is considered the most challenging probe, since they contains 234 images from subjects whose gallery match was taken more than 18 months beforehand. Fig.4 shows some example of these gallery and probe images.

We test the algorithm using different number of training samples randomly chosen from the gallery set. This means that not more than one sample per class is used for training, and the training samples are captured under variable conditions. Although few researchers adopt this methodology of sample selection, this configuration is applicable for real-life face recognition application. Since in the domain of face recognition, one never knows in advance the underlying distributions for different faces [8], representative samples are usually unavailable. In some cases, even a neutral gallery image is hardly available, such as the watch list application.

For comparison, we first implement the Eigenface baseline [7], which improves the standard Eigenface technique using the L_1 distance metric, and its performance for the four tasks is shown in the Fig.5 as function of the number of training samples. As the performance of face recognition varies with the number of features, we reports the best results it obtains. As expected, the Eigenface baseline achieves similar results as those reported in the FERET Evaluation [7]. However, we find that this method does not benefit from the increasing number of training samples. Since the training samples are randomly selected from the gallery images captured during different photo sessions, they display large variations in lighting and expression. The PCA encodes these interpersonal variations from the new training samples, which makes the Eigenface method cannot enhance the recognition accuracy further.

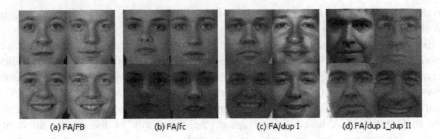

(a) FA/FB   (b) FA/fc   (c) FA/dup I   (d) FA/dup I_dup II

Fig. 4. Example images (cropped and rectified) used in the FERET Evaluation. The top row shows the examples of the FA gallery images, which are also used for training in our experiments. The bottom row shows the four types of probe images. Specifically, (a) illustrates the FB probes, (b) fc probes, (c) & (d) dup I probes, and (d) dup II probes.

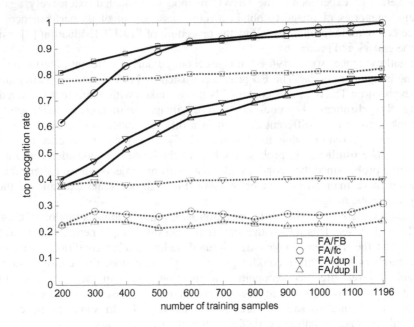

Fig. 5. Comparative performance of the GEWC method (black solid line) and the Eigenface baseline [7] (blue dotted line) as function of the number of training samples for the four face recognition tasks: FA/FB, FA/fc, FA/dup I, and FA/dup II

We then apply the GEWC method, and the performance is improved by a large margin for all the recognition tasks no matter how large the training sample size is. This shows again the superiority of the GEWC method. Furthermore, unlike the Eigenface method, the recognition accuracy increases significantly when using more training samples. This suggests that the GEWC method effectively excludes the interpersonal variations when incorporates the discriminating information from the unused training samples. When using 1196 training images, with one training sample per person, the results of the GEWC method compare well with the best reported results [7], outperforming other systems [4][19][20] by a typical margin of 10–20%. In particular, the GEWC method achieves 96.3% accuracy for facial expression task (FA/FB), 99.5% for illumination task (FA/fc), 78.8% and 77.8% for aging tasks (FA/dup I, FA/dup II) respectively.

3.3 Experiments: Extensive Studies

Actually, Gabor wavelet representation [6][18][19][21], PCA dimensionality reductions [3][4][18], whitening process [6][9][12], and cosine similarity measure [6][19] all are widely used in face recognition literature. However, *it is fire-new knowledge that the GEWC method, which systematically integrates these four techniques, can obtain surprising performance which compare favorably against the state of the art results.* To further reveal and analysis the strengths and weaknesses of these four techniques and the joint contribution of them, we conduct a series of extensive experiments by decomposing the GEWC scheme into four procedures as follows: 1) first apply the standard Eigenface technique [3] on the intensity image; 2)

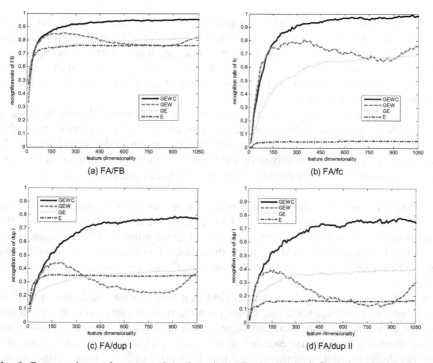

(a) FA/FB

(b) FA/fc

(c) FA/dup I

(d) FA/dup II

Fig. 6. Comparative performance of the four decomposing methods from the GEWC scheme, E (Eigenface method), GE (Eigenface method on the LG vector), GEW (Eigenface method on the LG vector with whitening process), GEWC (GEWC method), for the four recognition task in the FERET Evaluation

apply Eigenface method on the LG vector instead of on the intensity image to evaluate the benefits of the Gabor wavelet; 3) add the whitening process following PCA, and thus the influence of the whitening processing is evaluated by comparing the recognition results with and without the whitening transformation; and 4) substitute the cosine similarity measure for Euclidean distance, the performance improvement achieve by this replacement is evaluated to be the contribution of the cosine similarity measure. In addition, the four steps are applied to the four FERET face recognition task respectively, as described in section 3.2. Fig. 6. (a)~(d) show the comparative results of the four schemes for the four tasks respectively.

Eigenface. The fc probes are most difficult for the Eigenface technique, followed in order by dup II, dup I, and FB probes. One can see that only the leading 150 features could contribute the recognition rate, the low frequency preference of PCA is clearly shown.

Note that in FA/fc task, the Eigenface method is destroyed by the variations due lighting changes, receiving accuracy as low as 5%. This is because the histogram equalization technique can normalize the global illumination level, but the remaining local shines and shadows (see Fig.1.b) could damage the face recognition using the intensity image.

Gabor Wavelet. There is a dramatic improvement by LG vector for the FA/fc test where the recognition rate was increased from 5 percent to 70 percent. These results clearly show that the Gabor wavelet representation, which forms a well regular mapping from pixel space to feature space, is robust to large variation due to local shines and shadows. Moreover, the Gabor wavelet also brings a 20% accuracy enhancement in the dup II task.

On the side, the contribution of the Gabor wavelet is not remarkable in the FB and dup I probes. This because 1) the expression variations are so slight in these images that the equalized gray-level comparison was sufficient to recognize them well [2]; and 2) the discriminating information driven by the Gabor wavelet is concentrate on the high frequency domain which is suppressed by the low frequency preference of PCA.

Whitening Process. The GEW method achieves considerably higher accuracy than the GE method when using the leading 150 features for all tasks. Nevertheless, the performance drops with further increase of the feature number. This is because the interpersonal variation retained in high dimensional components is significantly magnified in whitening, and this "whitening noise" will deteriorate the recognition results.

Comparing Fig.5 and Fig.3, we further find that find that the "whitening noise" is more related to the novel variation, rather than the trained variation or image noise. Note that in Fig.3, although there are large variation in illumination and expression, most of them are trained and encoded in the leading eigenvector. In this case, the whitening does not deteriorate the recognition. However, In Fig.5, most variations are novel due to the non-representative training data. The negative influence of the whitening is shown and becomes more severe when larger novel variation is presented.

Cosine Similarity Measure. The contribution of the cosine similarity measure is highlighted for all four tasks. Specifically, the accuracy increase driven by CSM over the Euclidean distance is up to 10%, 20%, 30%, and 40% for the FB, fc, dup I and dup II probes respectively, clearly showing its robustness to the novel variation in expression, illumination, and aging. The great robustness of cosine similarity strongly supports the supposition that *the novel variation, projected into the whitened PCA space, is likely to change scale of the feature vector rather than its angle.*

4 Conclusion and Discussion

A face is a surface of a three-dimensional solid having partially deformable parts. The images it projects depend upon pose, perspective angle, illumination conditions, age, cosmetics or adornments, and expression. [12]. How to capture the intrinsic variation that discriminates different face identity, and at the same time be invariant to the countless volatile factors that affect the face appearance is crucial for face recognition. In this paper, we propose a GEWC method integrates the four traditional techniques, namely Gabor wavelet for image representation, PCA for dimensional reduction, whitening transformation for feature normalization, and cosine similarity measure for nearest-neighbor classification, to produce a robust and accurate scheme for face recognition. Experiments have verified that the proposed method can suppress trained variation, preserve discriminating information, and be robust to the novel variation.

The feasibility of the GEWC method has been successfully tested on large-scale data sets from the FERET database. Specifically, we used 3000+ FERET frontal images corresponding to 1196 subjects, which were acquired under variable illumination, facial expression, photo sessions, and capture device. The effectiveness and robustness is shown in terms of both absolute performance indices and comparative performance against some popular face recognition schemes such as the Eigenface method and the Fisherface method. In particular, the GEWC method achieves constant 100% accuracy on the 200-subject experiment across illuminations and facial expressions. Furthermore, its recognition rates reach up to 96.3%, 99.5%, 78.8%, and 77.8% on the FERET FB, fc, dup I, and dup II probe using only one training sample per person. In addition, the proposed system also achieves excellent performance on the experiments with another large database, the CAS-PEAL face database [23], which indicates again that the GEWC method is a robust scheme for large-scale face recognition application [24].

The experiments not only show the state of the art results obtained by the GEWC method, but also suggest a number of interesting conclusions: 1) the benefits of the Gabor wavelet comes from its counteraction against local illumination variation; 2) the trailing eigenvectors might encode the discriminating details useful for recognition, which can be revealed by the whitening process; 3) the whitening process can suppress the intrapersonal variation encoded in leading eigenvectors, and thus contribute the face recognition significantly. 4) the Eigenface method cannot profit from the larger training sample size, when the training samples are captured under variable conditions; 5) the same face (class) with complex variations, projected into the Gabor based whitened PCA feature space, is approximately angle invariance.

Acknowledgements

This research was sponsored by NSFC (National Natural Science Foundation of China) under Grant No.60475007 and the Foundation of China Education Ministry for Century Spanning Talent. Portions of the research in this paper use the Color FERET database of facial images collected under the FERET program.

References

1. R. Chellappa, C. Wilson, and S. Sirohey: Human and Machine Recognition of Faces: A Survey, Proc. IEEE, vol. 83, no. 5. (1995) 705–740
2. Y. Adini, Y. Moses, and S. Ullman: Face Recognition:The Problem of Compensating for Changes in Illumination Direction, IEEE Trans. PAMI, vol. 19, no. 7. (1997) 721–732.
3. M. Turk and A. Pentland: Eigenfaces for recognition. Journal of Cognitive Neuroscience, 3(1). (1991) 71–86.
4. W. Zhao, R. Chellappa, and A. Krishnaswamy: Discriminant Analysis of Principal Components for Face Recognition, Proc. Third Int'l Conf. Automatic Face and Gesture Recognition. (1998) 336–341
5. D.L. Swets and J. Weng: Using Discriminant Eigenfeatures for Image Retrieval, IEEE Trans. PAMI, vol. 16, no. 8. (1996) 831–836.
6. C. Liu and H. Wechsler: Gabor Feature Based Classification Using the Enhanced Fisher Linear Discriminant Model for Face Recognition. IEEE Trans. Image Processing, 11(4). (2002) 467–476
7. P. J. Phillips, H. Wechsler, and P. Rauss: The FERET Database and Evaluation Procedure for Face-Recognition Algorithms. Image and Vision Computing, vol. 16, no. 5. (1998) 295–306
8. A. M. Martinez, A. C. Kak: PCA versus LDA, IEEE Trans. PAMI, vol.23, no. 2. (2001) 228–232
9. Xiaogang Wang and Xiaoou Tang: A Unified Framework for Subspace Face Recognition. IEEE Trans. PAMI, vol. 26, no. 9, (2004) 1222–1228
10. M. Lades, J.C. Vorbrüggen, J. Buhmann, J. Lange, C. von der Malsburg, R.P. Würtz, and W. Konen: Distortion Invariant Object Recognition in the Dynamic Link Architecture, IEEE Trans. Computers, vol. 42, no. 3. (1993) 300–311
11. J.G. Daugman, "Uncertainty Relation for Resolution in Space, Spatial Frequency, and Orientation Optimized by Two-Dimensional Visual Cortical Filters. J. Optical Soc. Am. A, vol. 2. (1985) 1,160–1,169
12. J. Daugman: Face and Gesture Recognition: Overview, IEEE Trans. PAMI, vol. 19, no. 7. (1997) 675-676
13. A. Pentland, T. Starner, N. Etcoff, N. Masoiu, O. Oliyide, and M. Turk: Experiments with Eigenfaces, Proc. Looking at People Workshop Int'l Joint Conf. Artifical Intelligence. (1993)
14. P. N. Belhumeur, J. P. Hespanha, and D. J. Kriegman: Eigenfaces vs. Fisherfaces: Recognition using class specific linear projection, IEEE Trans. PAMI, vol. 19, no. 7. (1997) 711–720
15. Laurenz Wiskott, Jean-Marc Fellous, Norbert Krüger, and Christoph von der Malsburg: Face Recognition by Elastic Bunch Graph Matching. IEEE Trans. PAMI, vol.19, no. 7. (1997) 775–779

16. K. K. Sung and T. Poggio: Example-based learning for view-based human face detection. IEEE Trans. PAMI, vol. 20, no. 1. (1998) 39–51
17. B. Moghaddam and A. Pentland: Probabilistic visual learning for object representation. IEEE Trans. PAMI, vol. 19, no. 7. (1997) 696–710
18. Chengjun Liu: Gabor-Based Kernel PCA with Fractional Power Polynomial Models for Face Recognition", IEEE Trans. PAMI, vol.26, no. 5. (2004) 572–581
19. L. Wiskott, J. M. Fellous, N. Kruger, and C. von der Malsburg: Face Recognition by Elastic Bunch Graph Matching, IEEE Trans. PAMI, vol. 17, no. 7. (1997) 775–779
20. B. Moghaddam, T. Jebara, and A. Pentland: Bayesian Face Recognition, Pattern Recognition, vol. 33. (2000) 1771-1782
21. Michael J. Lyons, Julien Budynek, and Shigeru Akamatsu: Automatic Classification of Single Facial Images", IEEE Trans. PAMI, vol. 21, no. 12. (1999) 1357–1362
22. C. Liu and H. Wechsler: Evolutionary Pursuit and Its Application to Face Recognition, IEEE Trans. PAMI, vol. 22, no. 6, (2000) 570–582
23. Wen Gao, Bo Cao, Shiguang Shan, Xiaohua Zhang, Delong Zhou: The CAS-PEAL Large-Scale Chinese Face Database and Baseline Evaluations. technical report of JDL. (2004) http://www.jdl.ac.cn/~peal/peal_tr.pdf
24. Weihong Deng, Jiani Hu, Jun Guo: Robust Face Recognition from One Training Sample per Person, ICNC 2005, Lecture Notes in Computer Science, Vol. 3610. (2005) 915–924.

Two-Dimensional Non-negative Matrix Factorization for Face Representation and Recognition

Daoqiang Zhang[1,2], Songcan Chen[1], and Zhi-Hua Zhou[2,*]

[1] Department of Computer Science and Engineering,
Nanjing University of Aeronautics and Astronautics,
Nanjing 210016, China
{dqzhang, s.chen}@nuaa.edu.cn
[2] National Laboratory for Novel Software Technology,
Nanjing University, Nanjing 210093, China
zhouzh@nju.edu.cn

Abstract. Non-negative matrix factorization (NMF) is a recently developed method for finding parts-based representation of non-negative data such as face images. Although it has successfully been applied in several applications, directly using NMF for face recognition often leads to low performance. Moreover, when performing on large databases, NMF needs considerable computational costs. In this paper, we propose a novel NMF method, namely 2DNMF, which stands for 2-D non-negative matrix factorization. The main difference between NMF and 2DNMF is that the former first align images into 1D vectors and then represents them with a set of 1D bases, while the latter regards images as 2D matrices and represents them with a set of 2D bases. Experimental results on several face databases show that 2DNMF has better image reconstruction quality than NMF under the same compression ratio. Also the running time of 2DNMF is less, and the recognition accuracy higher than that of NMF.

1 Introduction

There is psychological and physiological evidence for parts-based representations in the brain, and certain computational theories of object rely on such representations [11]. For that reason, parts-based learning has received much interest in machine learning, computer vision and pattern recognition [13]. Many parts-based image representation approaches ca be ascribed to a general subspace method, which has been successfully used in many high dimensional data analysis applications. Given a class of image patterns, there are many approaches to construct the subspace. One such method is principal component analysis (PCA) [10], also known as Eigenface method in face recognition [19]. In PCA, any image can be represented as a linear combination of a set of orthogonal bases which form an optimal transform in the sense of reconstruction error. However, due to the holistic nature of the method, PCA cannot extract basis components manifesting localized features [13]. And its two extensions: independent component analysis (ICA) [4], [17] and kernel principal component analysis (KPCA) [18] also have the same problem.

---

[*] Corresponding author.

W. Zhao, S. Gong, and X. Tang (Eds.): AMFG 2005, LNCS 3723, pp. 350 – 363, 2005.

Recently a new subspace method called non-negative matrix factorization (NMF) [11] is proposed to learn the parts of objects and images. NMF imposes the non-negativity constraints in its bases and coefficients. Thus NMF learns localized features that can be added together to reconstruct the whole images, because only additive combination, not subtractive cancellations, are allowed in the reconstruction [11], [20], [6], [9], [5]. The localized, parts-based representation is very different from the holistic 'eigenface' of PCA. And due to its parts-based representation property, NMF or its variations have been used to image classification [1], [7], [8], face expression recognition [2], face detection [3], face and object recognition [13], [14], [15]. However, experiments have shown that when used for image compression and recognition tasks, NMF usually has low image reconstruction image quality and low recognition accuracy. Also NMF needs comparatively more computational costs due to the alternate iterations. To try to overcome those problems, many improved algorithms are proposed including local NMF [13] and sparse NMF [9] which impose extra constraints on the bases. But those methods often need even more iteration time to learn the bases, especially for high-dimensional data such as faces.

In this paper, we present a novel NMF method, called 2-Dimensional non-negative matrix factorization (2DNMF) for image representation and recognition. The key difference between 2DNMF and NMF is that the former adopt a novel representation for original images. In traditional NMF, the 2D image matrices must be previously transformed into 1D image vectors. The resulting image vectors usually lead to a high-dimensional image vector space, where it is difficult to find good bases to approximately reconstruct original images. That is also called the 'curse of dimensionality' problem, which is more apparent in small-sample-size cases. Another disadvantage of NMF is that such a matrix-to-vector transform may cause the loss of some structure information hiding in original 2D images. In contrast to the 1D representation of NMF, we adopt a more natural 2D matrix representation in 2DNMF, i.e. representing 2D images with a set of 2D bases. We first apply NMF on column vectors and then row vectors of original images to obtain the corresponding 1D column bases and 1D row bases respectively, and finally compute the outer-product of those two 1D bases as the 2D bases used in 2DNMF. To evaluate the performances of 2DNMF, a series of experiments are performed on several face databases: FERET, UMIST, Yale and AR. The experimental results demonstrate advantages of 2DNMF over NMF on image reconstruction quality at similar compression ratio, computational efficiency and recognition accuracy.

The rest of the paper is organized as follows: Section 2 first introduces NMF method briefly. This is followed by the detailed description of 2DNMF algorithm in Section 3. In Section 4, experimental results are presented for the FERET, UMIST, Yale, and AR face databases to demonstrate the effectiveness of 2DNMF. Finally, we conclude in Section 5.

2 Non-negative Matrix Factorization

The key ingredient of NMF is the non-negativity constraints imposed on the two factors, and the non-negativity constraints are compatible with the intuitive notion of combining parts to form a whole. Because a part-based representation can naturally deal with partial occlusion and some illumination problems, it has received much attention recently. Assume that the image database is represented as an $n \times m$ matrix V, each column of which contains n non-negative pixel values of one of the m face images. In order to compress data or reduce the dimensionality, NMF finds two non-negative matrix factors W and H such that

$$V_{i\mu} \approx (WH)_{i\mu} = \sum_{a=1}^{r} W_{ia} H_{a\mu} \tag{1}$$

Here the r columns of W are called NMF bases, and the columns of H are its combining coefficients. The dimensions of W and H are $n \times r$ and $r \times m$ respectively. The rank r of the factorization is usually chosen such that $(n+m)r < nm$, and hence the compression or dimensionality reduction is achieved. The compression ratio of NMF is easily gotten as $nm/(nr+mr)$.

To find an approximate factorization $V \approx W H$, a cost function is needed to quantify the quality of the approximation. NMF uses the divergence measure as the objective function

$$D(A \parallel B) = \sum_{i,j} \left(A_{ij} \log \frac{A_{ij}}{B_{ij}} - A_{ij} + B_{ij} \right) \tag{2}$$

NMF factorization is a solution to the following optimization problem:

Problem 1 [12]. *Minimize* $D(V \parallel WH)$ *with respect to* W *and* H *, subject to the constraints* $W, H \geq 0$.

In order to obtain W and H, a multiplicative update rule is given in [11] as follows:

$$W_{ia} = W_{ia} \sum_{\mu=1}^{m} \frac{V_{i\mu}}{(WH)_{i\mu}} H_{a\mu} \tag{3a}$$

$$W_{ia} = \frac{W_{ia}}{\sum_{j=1}^{n} W_{ja}} \tag{3b}$$

$$H_{a\mu} = H_{a\mu} \sum_{i=1}^{n} W_{ia} \frac{V_{i\mu}}{(WH)_{i\mu}} \tag{3c}$$

The pseudo-code for computing the bases W and coefficients H following the above iterative procedure is given in **Algorithm 1**.

```
Algorithm 1: NMF
Input: n×m matrix V, each column of which denotes the
aligned image vector, and rank r
```

Output: $n \times r$ matrix W and $r \times m$ matrix H
1. Obtain initial values for W and H, and set $k \leftarrow 1$
2. While not convergent
3.   update the bases W using Eqs. (3a) and (3b)
4.   update the coefficients H using Eq. (3c)
5. $k \leftarrow k+1$
6. EndWhile

3 2-D Non-negative Matrix Factorization

3.1 2DNMF Algorithm

Let $p \times q$ matrices A_k, k=1, 2, ..., m, denote original training images. In traditional NMF, a 2D image is first transformed into a 1D vector, and then the image databases are represented with an $n \times m$ matrix V, each column of which contains $n=pq$ non-negative pixel values of one of the m face images. In 2DNMF, however, we never transform the 2D images into its corresponding 1D vectors. Instead we will use a more straightforward way which views an image as a 2D matrix.

The procedure of 2DNMF method consists of two successive stages. At first we align the m training images into a $p \times qm$ matrix $X = [A_1, A_2, ..., A_m]$, where each A_k denotes one of the m face images. Similar to NMF, 2DNMF first finds $p \times d$ non-negative matrix L and $d \times qm$ non-negative matrix H such that

$$X \approx LH \tag{4}$$

Here L and H are the bases and combining coefficients respectively. For convenience, we divide H into m $d \times q$ sub-matrices as $H = [H_1, H_2, ..., H_m]$, where H_k denotes the coefficients of the image A_k. Since each column of X corresponds to a column of original images, we also call L as *column bases*. Thus the k-th image A_k can be written as a weighted sum of the column bases L as follows:

$$A_k \approx LH_k, \quad k = 1, 2, ..., m \tag{5}$$

The column bases L can be obtained by solving the following optimization problem:

Problem 2a. *Minimize* $D(X \parallel LH)$ *with respect to* L *and* H, *subject to the constraints* $L, H \geq 0$.

Problem 2a can be solved by performing NMF algorithm on X with rank d. We also call the first stage for computing column bases L as *Column NMF*.

The second stage of 2DNMF involves of computing the row bases. Fom Eq. (5), we construct a new $q \times dm$ matrix $H' = [H_1^T, H_2^T, ..., H_m^T]$. Similarly, 2DNMF seeks a $q \times g$ non-negative matrix R and a $g \times dm$ non-negative matrix C such that

$$H' \approx RC \tag{6}$$

Here R and C are the bases and combining coefficients respectively. And we also divide C into m $g \times d$ sub-matrices as $C = [C_1, C_2, ..., C_m]$, where C_k denotes the coefficients of the matrix H_k^T. Because the columns of H' contains the row information of original images, we call R as *row bases*. Thus H_k^T is formulated as a weighted sum of the row bases R as follows:

$$H_k^T \approx RC_k, \quad k = 1, 2, ..., m \qquad (7)$$

The row bases R can be obtained by solving the following optimization problem:

Problem 2b. *Minimize* $D(H' \parallel RC)$ *with respect to* R *and* C, *subject to the constraints* $R, C \geq 0$.

Similarly, problem 2b can be solved by performing NMF algorithm on H' with rank g. And we call the second stage for computing row bases R as *Row NMF*.

By now we have obtained the $p \times d$ dimensional column bases L and the $q \times g$ dimensional row bases R. By substituting Eq. (7) into Eq. (6), we get

$$A_k \approx LC_k^T R^T, \quad k = 1, 2, ..., m \qquad (8)$$

Let $L = [l_1, l_2, ..., l_d]$, $R = [r_1, r_2, ..., r_g]$, and define the 2D bases of 2DNMF as the outer product between the column base l_i and the row base r_j as follows:

$$E_{ij} = l_i \cdot r_j^T, (1 \leq i \leq d, 1 \leq j \leq g) \qquad (9)$$

Let $D^k = C_k^T$, $k=1, 2, ..., m$, then Eq. (8) turns into

$$A_k \approx LD^k R^T = \sum_{i=1}^{d} \sum_{j=1}^{g} D_{ij}^k E_{ij} \qquad (10)$$

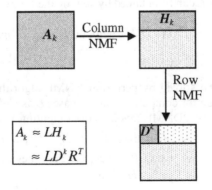

Fig. 1. An illustration for the 2DNMF algorithm

It is easy to verify that the 2D bases E_{ij} s have the following properties:

1) E_{ij} is a 2D matrix with the same size of original image, i.e. $p \times q$.
2) The *intrinsic dimensionality* of E_{ij} is 1.
3) Any training image A_k can be approximately represented with a weighted sum of 2D bases E_{ij} s.

Figure 1 gives a simple illustration for the procedure of 2DNMF. For a $p \times q$ dimensional image A_k, it experiences the Column NMF operation (Eq. (5)) and the Row NMF operation (Eq. (7)) successively. If the ranks d and g are chosen such that $d < p$ and $g < q$, then figure 1 indicates that we can approximately represent the original image A_k with much smaller matrix D^k.

The pseudo-code for computing the column bases L, row bases R, and the 2D bases E_{ij} s is given in part of **Algorithm 2**.

```
Algorithm 2: 2DNMF

Input: pXq matrices {A_k}^m_{k=1}, and rank d, g
Output: pXd column bases L, qXg row bases R, dXg ma-
trices {D^k}^m_{k=1} and 2D bases E_ij
1. Align the m training images into a pXqm matrix X =
[A_1, A_2, ..., A_m]
2. Perform Column NMF on X with rank d: X ≈ LH , obtain-
ing column bases L and coefficients matrix    H = [H_1,
H_2, ..., H_m]
3. Construct qXdm matrix H'=[H^T_1,H^T_2,...,H^T_m]
4. Perform Row NMF on H with rank g: H' ≈ RC , obtaining
row bases R and coefficients matrix C = [C_1, C_2, ..., C_m]
5. For k = 1 to m
6.          D^k ← C^T_k
7. EndFor
8. For i = 1 to d, for j =1 to g
9.          E_ij ← l_i · r^T_j
10. EndFor
```

3.2 2DNMF-Based Image Compression

Suppose we have learned the 2D bases $E_{ij} = l_i \cdot r_j^T, (1 \le i \le d, 1 \le j \le g)$, from the training images A_k, $k=1, 2, ..., m$. According to Eq. (10) each training image A_k can be approximately reconstructed as

$$\hat{A}_k = \sum_{i=1}^{d} \sum_{j=1}^{g} D_{ij}^k E_{ij} \qquad (11)$$

Here $\hat{A}_k$ denotes the reconstructed image corresponding to image A_k.

In Eq. (11), the coefficients D^k are obtained by performing Column NMF (Eq. (5)) and the Row NMF (Eq. (7)) successively. For a test image A which is not contained in the training sets, the values for the coefficients D are unknown. However, we can approximately compute $D \approx L^+AR$ (L^+ is the generalized inverse of L), and then use $\hat{A} \approx LDR^+$ (R^+ is the generalized inverse of R) to get the reconstructed image.

In this paper, we measure the quality of the reconstructed image using the peak signal-to-noise ratio (PSNR), which is defined as follows:

$$PSNR = 10 \log 10 \left(\frac{255^2}{\dfrac{1}{pq} \sum_{i,j} \left(A(i, j) - B(i, j) \right)^2} \right) \tag{12}$$

Here A denotes the original image, B denotes the reconstructed image, and p, q is the size of the image.

Equations (10) and (11) indicate that the $p \times d$ matrix L, $q \times g$ matrix R and the $d \times g$ matrix D^k, k=1, 2, ..., m, can be used to reconstruct the original m $p \times q$ matrices A_k, k=1, 2, ..., m. The memories required for storing L, R and D^k, k=1, 2, ..., m, are $pd+qg+mdg$. So if $pd+qg+mdg < mpq$, the compression or dimensionality reduction is achieved. And it is easy to compute the compression ratio of 2DNMF as $mpq / (pd+qg+mdg)$.

3.3 2DNMF-Based Face Recognition

It contains two steps when using 2DNMF for recognition. One is the feature extraction step and the other is classification step.

In feature extraction step, we first project each training image A_k into the bilinear space as a feature matrix $F_k = L^T A_k R$, for k=1, 2, ..., m, which are then used as the comparing prototypes. A test or query face image A to be classified is represented by its projection onto the space as $F_A = L^T AR$.

In classification step, we calculate the distance based on Frobenius norm between the query and each prototype as follows:

$$d(F_A, F_k) = \left\| F_A - F_k \right\|_F \tag{13}$$

And the query is classified to the class to which the closest prototype belongs.

4 Experimental Results

In this section, we experimentally evaluate the performance of 2DNMF with NMF and local NMF (LNMF) [13] on several face databases. All our experiments are carried out on a P4 1.7 GHz PC machine with 512M memory. For all the three algorithms, the convergence condition is

$$\max_{i,j}\left(\left|W_{ij}^{new}\right|-\left|W_{ij}^{old}\right|\right)\Big/\max_{i,j}\left(W_{ij}^{old}\right)<0.01 \qquad (14)$$

Where W_{ij}^{new} is the value of the bases at the current iteration step while W_{ij}^{old} denotes the value at the last iteration. The maximum iteration steps for NMF and LNMF are both set to 100.

The parameters d (number of column bases) and g (number of row bases) in 2DNMF are both set to 20 in all experiments, if without explicit explanations. The value of r (number of bases) in NMF and LNMF is chosen such that NMF, LNMF and 2DNMF have similar compression ratio in most cases, except for the Yale database where we assure $r=16$ at least. For example, if we set $d=g=20$ on the training set ($m=200$, $p=q=60$, $n=pq=3600$) of the FERET database, the compression ratio of 2DNMF will be $mpq / (pd+qg+mdg)=8.74$. And then we adjust the value of r to make the compression ratio of NMF and LNMF near to 8.74. Here we choose $r=22$, and the corresponding compression ratio of NMF and LNMF is $nm/ (nr+mr)= 8.61$.

4.1 Datasets

We use the following four face databases in our experiments: FERET, UMIST, Yale and AR [16] face database. Table 1 summarizes the statistics of the four datasets (the

Table 1. Statistics of four face databases

Datasets	Size	Dimension	# of classes
FERET[1]	400(200)	60×60	200
UMIST[2]	575(375)	112×92	20
Yale[3]	165 (75)	100×100	15
AR[4]	1400(700)	66×48	100

values in bracket indicate the size of training set). Note that for FERET and AR we only use a subset of the whole datasets. More detailed description of the four face databases can be obtained through browsing the face databases websites, whose linked address are given at the bottom of this page.

4.2 Learning the Bases

In this subsection, we compute the bases of NMF and 2DNMF from the training set. For comparison, we also compute the bases of PCA and its extension 2DPCA [21].

---

[1] http://www.itl.nist.gov/iad/humanid/feret/feret_master.html
[2] http://images.ee.umist.ac.uk/danny/database.html
[3] http://cvc.yale.edu/projects/yalefaces/yalefaces.html
[4] http://rvl1.ecn.purdue.edu/~aleix/aleix_face_DB.html

We do the experiment on the FERET face databases, and 200 **fa** face images are used as the training set.

Fig. 2 plots parts of the bases gotten from the four methods respectively. Fig. 2 (a) and (b) are plotted using the method in [21]. For NMF the first 16 columns of matrix

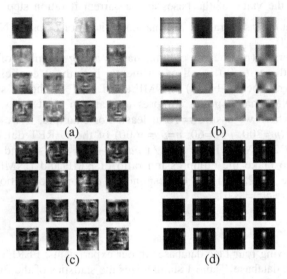

(a)   (b)

(c)   (d)

Fig. 2. Bases obtained from PCA (a), 2DPCA (b), NMF (c) and 2DNMF (d) respectively. (a) and (b) are plotted using the method in [21]. For NMF the first 16 columns of matrix W are retransformed to matrix for plotting, while for 2DNMF the 16 bases E_{ij} ($1 \leq i \leq 4$, $1 \leq j \leq 4$) are directly plotted as images.

W are retransformed to matrix for plotting, while for 2DNMF the 16 bases E_{ij} ($1 \leq I \leq 4$, $1 \leq j \leq 4$) are directly plotted as images.

From Fig. 2, we can see that both the bases of PCA and 2DPCA are global. Compared with PCA, 2DPCA possess of some strip or block like structures. The reason for that is 2DPCA is essentially a kind of line-based PCA [21]. However, the bases of 2DPCA cannot yet reflect any local or part-based features. On the other hand, Fig. 2(c) indicates that although NMF is a part-based algorithm, its bases still take on some holistic property similar to PCA. In contrast we notice from Fig. 2(d) that the bases of 2DNMF are much sparser than those of NMF. It is worth noting that although the base of 2DNMF is sparse, it has no parts-based (like eye, mouth, etc. in face image) features any more due to the essence of 2D methods. That is, 2DNMF is essentially a kind of line-based NMF, so what 2DNMF really learns are some parts of 'line'.

Because each base of 2DNMF can be generated using a p-dimensional column base and a q-dimensional row base, its storing cost ($p+q$) is much less than that of NMF base (which is pq). Thus we can use much more sparse-distributed 2D bases to represent original image, which will be further discussed in the next subsection.

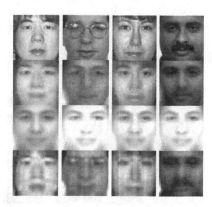

Fig. 3. Some reconstructed training images on FERET database. First row: original images. Second row: images gotten by NMF. Third row: images gotten by LNMF. Bottom row: images gotten by 2DNMF.

Table 2. Comparisons of the performances (PSNR / compression ratio / recognition accuracy) of NMF, LNMF and 2DNMF on four datasets

Data sets	NMF	LNMF	2DNMF
FERET	20.89 / 8.6/ 0.68	7.74 / 8.6/ 0.73	**23.50 / 8.7/ 0.79**
UMIST	21.34 / 24.1/ 0.71	8.08 / 24.1/ 0.67	**24.12 / 25.1/ 0.76**
Yale	22.03 / 4.7/ 0.69	7.16 / 4.7/ 0.68	**23.98 / 22.1/ 0.81**
AR	19.50 / 8.0/ 0.49	5.00 / 8.0/ 0.62	**20.68 / 7.9/ 0.64**

4.3 Image Compression and Reconstruction

In this subsection, we will compare the compression performances of NMF, LNMF and 2DNMF. We carry out experiments on the training set of the four datasets listed in table 1. That is, we only use the training images to learn the bases of NMF, LNMF and 2DNMF respectively. After that we reconstruct the training images or a new image not appearing in the training sets (test images) using the corresponding methods discussed in subsection 3.2.

Table 2 gives the PSNR values of NMF, LNMF and 2DNMF on the four datasets, and the corresponding compression ratios are also given in the brackets of the table. Table 2 shows that 2DNMF has the highest PSNR values on all the four datasets under nearly the same compression ratio except for the Yale database, where even when the compression ratio of 2DNMF is 5 times of that of NMF and LNMF, the former still achieves the best performance.

Fig. 3 shows parts of the reconstructed training images using NMF, LNMF and 2DNMF respectively on the FERET database. From Fig. 3, although the reconstructed images of NMF and LNMF smoother than that of 2DNMF, they don't resemble the

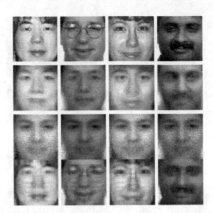

Fig. 4. Some reconstructed test images on FERET database using the same bases as those in figure 3. First row: original test images. Second row: images gotten by NMF. Third row: images gotten by LNMF. Bottom row: images gotten by 2DNMF.

original images any more. That phenomenon is especially severe for LNMF, because it imposes additional constrains on the bases which are useful for recognition but not for reconstruction, as clearly shown in Fig. 3. On the other hand, although there exist some stripping artifacts arising from the use of 2D bases of outer products of 1D row and column bases, 2DNMF reconstruct the original image more faithfully than the other two methods.

Fig. 4 shows some reconstructed test images of the three methods on FERET database using the same bases as those in Fig. 3. Similar as in Fig. 3, the reconstructed images of 2DNMF are most faithful compared with those of NMF and LNMF.

4.4 Face Recognition

In this subsection, we use the learned bases of NMF, LNMF and 2DNMF in section 4.2 for recognition. The detailed method for recognition has been discussed in section 3.3, and the recognition accuracy, which is defined as the percentage of correctly recognized images in test images, is used as the performance measure.

The first experiment is recognizing test images on four face databases without occlusion and noise and the result is given in part of table 2. Clearly, 2DNMF obtains the best accuracy in that case on all the datasets. The second experiment is to test the recognition accuracy of the three methods under partial occlusions or noises. Fig. 5 gives some examples of different levels of occluded images and noisy images (here only the 'Salt & Pepper' noise is considered). Fig. 6 gives the averaged (20 times) results of the three methods on FERET database when occlusions and noises are considered. From Fig. 6, 2DNMF outperforms NMF and LNMF in all cases. And because LNMF learns more localized parts than NMF, it achieves better result than NMF.

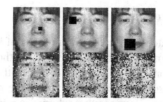

Fig. 5. Some examples of randomly occluded images and noisy images

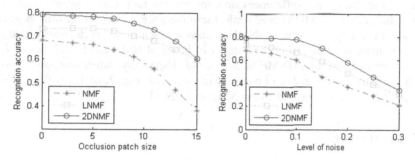

Fig. 6. Comparison of recognition accuracy of NMF, LNMF and 2DNMF under different size of occlusions (left) and different level of noises (right)

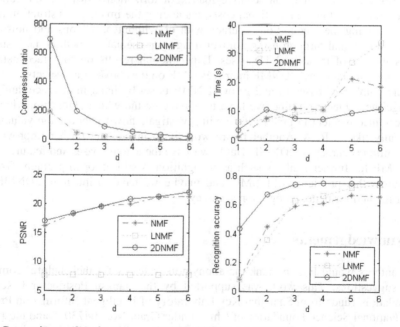

Fig. 7. Comparisons of performances of NMF, LNMF and 2DNMF under different number of bases. For NMF and LNMF, number of bases is $d*d$, while for 2DNMF the both numbers of row and column bases are $2d$.

4.5   The Effect of Number of Bases

In this subsection, we evaluate the effect of the number of bases used in NMF, LNMF and 2DNMF respectively. For NMF and LNMF, we set the number of bases $p = d*d$, and varies d from 1 to 6. For 2DNMF, we set the both the numbers of row and column bases $d=g=2*d$, and also varies d from 1 to 6. The results on FERET database are shown in Fig. 7. From Fig. 7, we see that when d is relatively small (e.g. $d<4$), the compression ratio of 2DNMF is much greater than those of NMF and LNMF, and the recognition of 2DNMF is apparently higher than those of NMF and LNMF. As the value of d increases, the differences on compression ratio and recognition accuracy among the three methods reduce, while the difference on execution time begins to increase. In nearly all cases, 2DNMF achieves much better performance than the other two methods. Remember the number of bases of NMF and LNMF are $d*d$ and the number of bases of 2DNMF is $2d+2d=4d$. Especially, when $d=4$, all the three methods use the same number of bases. However, from Fig. 7, we know that 2DNMF still achieves better performance than NMF and LNMF.

5   Conclusions

In this paper, we have proposed a new method, 2-D non-negative matrix factorization (2DNMF), for face representation and recognition. This work is aimed to improve the performance of original non-negative matrix factorization (NMF) in the following aspect: reducing the computational costs, enhancing the image reconstruction quality and improving the recognition accuracy with or without occlusions and noises. We achieved our goal through using a novel image representation method, i.e. using 2D bases instead of traditional 1D bases. Experimental results on four face databases convince our claim that 2DNMF improves NMF on the above three aspects.

The number of bases (d and g) of 2DNMF is set by hand in advance, and if we change the values each time, we have to re-execute the whole algorithm, which will be very inconvenient in practice. We will investigate how to choose the values automatically like in PCA. Another future work is to investigate further improving the recognition accuracy of 2DNMF. But how to use the learned bases and feature vectors via NMF for further analysis such as recognition is still an open problem. We also encounter that problem in 2DNMF, and maybe we have to integrate 2DNMF with other method for better recognition accuracy.

Acknowledgements

The authors would like to thank the anonymous referees for their helpful comments and suggestions. This work was supported by the Jiangsu Postdoctoral Research Foundation, funds from Shanghai Key Laboratory of Intelligent Information Processing, National Science Foundation of China under Grant No. 60473035 and the Jiangsu Science Foundation under Grant No. BK2004001 and BK2005122. Portions of the research in this paper use the FERET database of facial images collected under the FERET program.

References

1. Buchsbaum, G., Bloch, O.: Color categories revealed by non-negative matrix factorization of Munsell color spectra. Vision Research 42 (2002) 559-563
2. Buciu, I., Pitas,I.: Application of non-negative and local non-negative matrix factorization to facial expression recognition. In: ICPR, Cambridge, 2004
3. Chen, X., Gu, L., Li, S.Z., Zhang, H.J.: Learning representative local features for face detection. In: CVPR, Hawaii, 2001
4. Comon, P.: Independent component analysis- a new comcept? Signal Processing 36 (1994) 287-314
5. Donoho, D., Stodden, V.: When does non-negative matrix factorization give a correct decomposition into parts? In: NIPS, 2004
6. Ge, X., Iwata, S.: Learning the parts of objects by auto-association. Neural Networks 15 (2002) 285-295
7. Guillamet, D., Bressan, M., Vitria, J.: A weighted non-negative matrix factorization for local representation. In: CVPR, Hawaii, 2001
8. Guillamet, D., Vitria, J., Schiele, B.: Introducing a weighted non-negative matrix factorization for image classification. Pattern Recognition Letters 24 (2003) 2447-2454
9. Hoyer, P.O.: Non-negative matrix factorization with sparseness constraints. Journal of machine Learning Research 5 (2004) 1457-1469
10. Jolliffe, I.T.: Principal Component Analysis. Springer-Verlag, New York, 1986
11. Lee D.D., Seung, H.S.: Learning the parts of objects by non-negative matrix factorization. Nature 401(1999) 788-791
12. Lee D.D., Seung, H.S.: Algorithms for non-negative matrix factorization. In: NIPS 13 (2001) 556–562
13. Li, S.Z., Hou, X.W., Zhang, H.J., Cheng, Q.S.: Learning spatially localized, parts-based representation. In: CVPR, Hawaii, 2001.
14. Liu, W., Zheng, N.: Learning sparse features for classification by mixture models Pattern Recognition Letters 25 (2004) 155-161
15. Liu, W., Zheng, N.: Non-negative matrix factorization based methods for object recognition. Pattern Recognition Letters 25 (2004) 893-897
16. Martinez, A., Benavente, R.: The ar face database (Technical Report CVC Tech. Report No. 24).
17. Plumbley, M.D., Oja, E.: A 'nonnegative PCA' algorithm for independent component analysis. IEEE Trans. On Neural Networks 15 (1) (2004) 66-76
18. Scholkopf, B., Smola, A.J., Muller, K.R.: Nonlinear component analysis as a kernel eigenvalue problem. Neural Computation 10 (1998) 1299-1319
19. Turk, M., Pentland, A.: Eigenfaces for recognition. J. Cognitive Neuroscience 3 (1) (1991) 71-86
20. Wild, S., Curry, J., Dougherty, A.: Improving non-negative matrix factorizations through structured initialization. Pattern Recognition 37 (11) (2004) 2217-2232
21. Zhang, D.Q., Chen, S.C., Liu, J.: Representing image matrices: Eigenimages vs. Eigenvectors. In: ISNN, Chongqing, China, 2005.

Face View Synthesis Across Large Angles

Jiang Ni and Henry Schneiderman

Robotics Institute, Carnegie Mellon University, Pittsburgh, PA 15213, USA
{jiangni, hws}@cs.cmu.edu

Abstract. Pose variations, especially large out-of-plane rotations, make face recognition a difficult problem. In this paper, we propose an algorithm that uses a single input image to accurately synthesize an image of the person in a different pose. We represent the two poses by stacking their information (pixels or feature locations) in a combined feature space. A given test vector will consist of a known part corresponding to the input image and a missing part corresponding to the synthesized image. We then solve for the missing part by maximizing the test vector's probability. This approach combines the "distance-from-feature-space" and "distance-in-feature-space", and maximizes the test vector's probability by minimizing a weighted sum of these two distances. Our approach does not require either 3D training data or a 3D model, and does not require correspondence between different poses. The algorithm is computationally efficient, and only takes 4 - 5 seconds to generate a face. Experimental results show that our approach produces more accurate results than the commonly used linear-object-class approach. Such technique can help face recognition to overcome the pose variation problem.

1 Introduction

Face recognition applications often involve pose variations. The gallery may only have the faces under a specific pose, such as the frontal view, but the probe image may be captured under a random pose, sometimes with a large out-of-plane rotation. In order to do face recognition in this scenario, we need to synthesize the new view of the probe face, such that we can compare it with the gallery images.

According to the stereopsis theory in computer vision, to recover the precise 3D geometry of an object, we need at least three images of this object. This is why some approaches use multi-view images [6], or even video sequences [13], to synthesize new views. Although a single image is insufficient to recover the precise 3D geometry, machine learning techniques can apply prior knowledge onto this single image in order to synthesize new views. In particular, Blanz and Vetter pioneered a 3D algorithm based on fitting a 3D morphable model learned from many 3D training examples, to synthesize novel views from a single image [2,3,4].

The drawback of such a 3D approach is its large computational cost of 4.5 minutes for each fitting process [3,4]. This high computational cost limits the approach's applicability to real life applications, such as in airport security. Another drawback is the need for specialized 3D scanning hardware. For practical

W. Zhao, S. Gong, and X. Tang (Eds.): AMFG 2005, LNCS 3723, pp. 364–376, 2005.

systems, it would be more attractive to implement a solution using only 2D images. The linear-object-class method proposed by Vetter and Poggio [12] and its variation [7] hold the promise of such a method. However, our own experiments show that its performance for large out-of-plane rotations, such as 45° and 90° is not satisfactory. In particular, the predicted shapes exhibit significant distortion (Fig. 3, 4, 5).

Vetter and Poggio's linear-object-class method [12] solves a set of linear equations with missing data:

$$\begin{pmatrix} \Phi_1 \\ \Phi_2 \end{pmatrix} \mathbf{y} = \begin{pmatrix} \tilde{b}_1 \\ \tilde{b}_2 \end{pmatrix}, \tag{1}$$

where $\tilde{b}_2$ is the unknown pose and $\tilde{b}_1$ is the known pose of the test example. $\Phi_M = \begin{pmatrix} \Phi_1 \\ \Phi_2 \end{pmatrix}$ is the training set (or vectors formed from a linear combination of the training set, i.e., PCA of the training set) containing the two poses. $\begin{pmatrix} \tilde{b}_1 \\ \tilde{b}_2 \end{pmatrix}$ is represented as a linear combination of the columns in $\begin{pmatrix} \Phi_1 \\ \Phi_2 \end{pmatrix}$. The vector $\mathbf{y}$ contains the parameters describing the linear combination. The linear-object-class method solves for $\mathbf{y} = \arg\min \left\| \Phi_1 \cdot \mathbf{y} - \tilde{b}_1 \right\|^2$, then uses it to predict $\tilde{b}_2 = \Phi_2 \mathbf{y}$. (In the view synthesis problem for faces, shape and appearance are usually analyzed and predicted seperately.)

This method has been discussed in some related problems [8,1,9]. Hwang and Lee [8] use exactly the same method as above in predicting occluded parts of human faces. Black et al. [1] and Leonardis et al.[9] slightly modify the approach, by either excluding [9] or putting less weight [1] on some rows of Φ_1 that they assume are outliers.

We believe that the problems with the linear-object-class method lie with an incorrect assumption: there are no errors inherent in the solution for $\mathbf{y}$ in $\mathbf{y} = \arg\min \left\| \Phi_1 \cdot \mathbf{y} - \tilde{b}_1 \right\|^2$. However, as it is well known, there are measurement errors in the training data due to many factors. These errors will propagate into the solution for $\tilde{b}_2$, using the linear-object-class method. We can improve upon this solution with a probabilistic formulation. This formulation combines "distance-from-feature-space" (DFFS) and "distance-in-feature-space" (DIFS) [10], whereas the linear-object-class solution is purely based on DFFS. By considering DIFS, our method penalizes for points within the subspace, $\begin{pmatrix} \Phi_1 \\ \Phi_2 \end{pmatrix}$, that have low probability. Our representation leads to solutions that have higher probability and, as we will show, significantly better empirical performance.

This paper is organized as follows. In Section 2, a probabilistic model combining DFFS and DIFS is introduced, and the solution for equation (1) is derived. In Section 3, we explain the necessary steps of seperating the shapes from the appearance of faces, and apply the solution in Section 2 to predict a new view of faces. Section 4 shows experimental results of synthetic face images at new views. In Section 5, we discuss this approach and conclude.

2   Probabilistic Modeling

The problem of linear equations with missing data described in equation (1) is restated in the following way:

We have N_T training vectors $\{x_i\}_{i=1}^{N_T}$, each of which is an N-by-1 vector. Usually $N \gg N_T$. A test example $b = \begin{pmatrix} b_1 \\ b_2 \end{pmatrix}$ belongs to the same class defined by the training set. b is N-by-1. We only know b_1, which contains the first N_1 elements of b. The task is to predict b_2, given b_1 and $\{x_i\}_{i=1}^{N_T}$.

2.1   Probabilistic Modeling

Let's first discuss the ideal case that we have enough independent training examples to span the whole N-dimensional space, i.e., $N_T \geq N$.

Here we apply several assumptions:

1. The class defined by the training set is an M-dimensional linear subspace, denoted as F. $M < N$ and determined by PCA from the training set. PCA is computed from the training set $\{x_i\}_{i=1}^{N_T}$, and the M largest eigenvalues of the principal components $\lambda_1 \geq \lambda_2 \geq \cdots \geq \lambda_M$ are the variances along the M dimensions of F.

2. In this subspace F, samples are drawn from an M-dimensional Gaussian distribution with zero mean.

3. If the complete space has N dimensions, there is another $(N - M)$ dimensional linear subspace $\bar{F}$, which is orthogonal and complementary to the eigenspace F (Fig. 1). We assume F and $\bar{F}$ are statistically independent.

4. The samples also contain random noise distributed over all the $(N - M)$ dimensions of $\bar{F}$. Each of the $(N - M)$ dimensions of $\bar{F}$ has approximately equal non-zero variance, i.e., $\lambda_{M+1} \approx \lambda_{M+2} \approx \cdots \approx \lambda_N > 0$.

Under these assumptions, the probability of x is

$$
\begin{aligned}
P(x|\Omega) &= \left[\frac{\exp\left(-\frac{1}{2}\sum_{i=1}^{N}\frac{y_i^2}{\lambda_i}\right)}{(2\pi)^{N/2}\prod_{i=1}^{N}\lambda_i^{1/2}} \right] \\
&= \left[\frac{\exp\left(-\frac{1}{2}\sum_{i=1}^{M}\frac{y_i^2}{\lambda_i}\right)}{(2\pi)^{M/2}\prod_{i=1}^{M}\lambda_i^{1/2}} \right] \cdot \left[\frac{\exp\left(-\frac{1}{2}\sum_{i=M+1}^{N}\frac{y_i^2}{\lambda_i}\right)}{(2\pi)^{(N-M)/2}\prod_{i=M+1}^{N}\lambda_i^{1/2}} \right] \\
&= P_F(x|\Omega) \cdot P_{\bar{F}}(x|\Omega),
\end{aligned}
$$

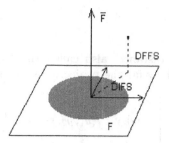

Fig. 1. Decomposition into the eigenspace F and its orthogonal subspace $\bar{F}$. The DFFS and DIFS are also shown.

where Ω denotes the class described by the training set. x is a random point from this class, and its projection onto each dimension is denoted as $\{y_i\}_{i=1}^{N}$. $P_F(x|\Omega)$ and $P_{\bar{F}}(x|\Omega)$ are two marginal Gaussian distributions, in F and $\bar{F}$ respectively.

Since N is very large, we lack sufficient data to compute each $\{\lambda_i\}_{i=M+1}^{N}$ in $P_{\bar{F}}(x|\Omega)$.

Recall the assumption that $\{\lambda_i\}_{i=M+1}^{N}$ are about the same magnitude. Then it is reasonable to use the arithematic average $\rho = \frac{1}{N-M} \sum\limits_{i=M+1}^{N} \lambda_i$ [10] to get an estimation of $P(x|\Omega)$, which is

$$\hat{P}(x|\Omega) = P_F(x|\Omega) \cdot \hat{P}_{\bar{F}}(x|\Omega)$$

$$= \left[\frac{\exp\left(-\frac{1}{2}\sum\limits_{i=1}^{M}\frac{y_i^2}{\lambda_i}\right)}{(2\pi)^{M/2}\prod\limits_{i=1}^{M}\lambda_i^{1/2}} \right] \cdot \left[\frac{\exp\left(-\frac{1}{2\rho}\cdot\sum\limits_{i=M+1}^{N}y_i^2\right)}{(2\pi\rho)^{(N-M)/2}} \right].$$

The distance characterizing the $\hat{P}(x|\Omega)$ is

$$\hat{d}(x) = \left[\sum_{i=1}^{M}\frac{y_i^2}{\lambda_i}\right] + \frac{1}{\rho}\cdot\left[\sum_{i=M+1}^{N}y_i^2\right]. \tag{2}$$

In our problem, we only know the upper part of $b = \begin{pmatrix} b_1 \\ b_2 \end{pmatrix}$, and know it is from class Ω. In order to solve for the unknown part b_2, we want to maximize the likelihood of $\hat{P}(b|\Omega)$ by choosing $\{y_i\}_{i=1}^{N}$, where $(y_1, y_2, \cdots, y_N)^T = \Phi^T (b - \bar{x})$ and $\bar{x}$ is the mean of the training set. We then generate $b_2 = \bar{x}_2 + \Phi_2 \cdot \mathbf{y}$. This optimization depends upon three quantities: $\left[\sum\limits_{i=1}^{M}\frac{y_i^2}{\lambda_i}\right]$, $\left[\sum\limits_{i=M+1}^{N}y_i^2\right]$ and the weight ρ, . Let's look at them one by one.

2.2 $\left[\sum_{i=1}^{M} \frac{y_i^2}{\lambda_i}\right]$: DIFS

This is the Mahalanobis distance, also called the "distance-in-feature-space" (DIFS) [10]. It describes how far the projection of x onto F is from the origin.

Let $\Lambda_M^{-1} = \begin{bmatrix} \frac{1}{\lambda_1} & & & 0 \\ & \frac{1}{\lambda_2} & & \\ & & \ddots & \\ 0 & & & \frac{1}{\lambda_M} \end{bmatrix}$, and $\mathbf{y} = (y_1, y_2, \cdots, y_M)^T$, then

$$\left[\sum_{i=1}^{M} \frac{y_i^2}{\lambda_i}\right] = \mathbf{y}^T \Lambda_M^{-1} \mathbf{y}. \tag{3}$$

2.3 $\left[\sum_{i=M+1}^{N} y_i^2\right]$: DFFS

The residual reconstruction error, also called DFFS [10] is $\sum_{i=M+1}^{N} y_i^2 = \epsilon^2(x) = \|x' - x\|^2$, where x' is the projection of x on F.

The linear-object-class method [12] minimizes the DFFS to find $\mathbf{y}$ in order to predict b_2. Split the eigenvector matrix Φ_M containing the first M eigenvectors into $\Phi_M = \begin{pmatrix} \Phi_1 \\ \Phi_2 \end{pmatrix}$ and split the mean $\bar{x}$ of training data into $\bar{x} = \begin{pmatrix} \bar{x}_1 \\ \bar{x}_2 \end{pmatrix}$, where Φ_1 and $\bar{x}_1$ have the same number of rows as b_1. No matter what method we use to solve for $\mathbf{y}$, since b_2 is defined as $\bar{x}_2 + \Phi_2 \cdot \mathbf{y}$, the residual reconstruction error of resulting $b = \begin{pmatrix} b_1 \\ b_2 \end{pmatrix}$ is

$$\begin{aligned} \sum_{i=M+1}^{N} y_i^2 = \epsilon^2(b) &= \|b - (\bar{x} + \Phi_M \cdot \mathbf{y})\|^2 = \left\| \begin{pmatrix} b_1 \\ b_2 \end{pmatrix} - \begin{pmatrix} \bar{x}_1 + \Phi_1 \cdot \mathbf{y} \\ \bar{x}_2 + \Phi_2 \cdot \mathbf{y} \end{pmatrix} \right\|^2 \\ &= \|b_1 - (\bar{x}_1 + \Phi_1 \cdot \mathbf{y})\|^2 \\ &= \left\| \tilde{b}_1 - \Phi_1 \cdot \mathbf{y} \right\|^2 \end{aligned} \tag{4}$$

where $\tilde{b}_1 = b_1 - \bar{x}_1$. Thus the linear-object-class method [12] solves a least square problem to solve for $\mathbf{y}$:

$$\mathbf{y} = \arg\min \left\| \Phi_1 \cdot \mathbf{y} - \tilde{b}_1 \right\|^2 .$$

2.4 Determining ρ

Moghaddam and Pentland [10] define $\rho = \frac{1}{N-M} \sum_{i=M+1}^{N} \lambda_i$, under the assumption that the number of training examples $N_T \geq N$, and that $\{\lambda_i\}_{i=M+1}^{N}$ are about the same magnitude. However, in practice, N is very large and we have $N_T \ll N$. These N_T training examples can only span an $(N_T - 1)$ dimensional subspace, resulting in that $\lambda_{N_T} = \lambda_{N_T+1} = \cdots = \lambda_N = 0$.

We use the non-zero eigenvalues, $\{\lambda_i\}_{i=M+1}^{N_T-1}$, to guess what $\{\lambda_i\}_{i=N_T}^{N}$ would be like had we been given sufficient training data. Here we add another assumption:

- We assume that the actual values of $\{\lambda_i\}_{i=N_T}^{N}$ will be about the same magnitude as the average of the known eigenvalues $\{\lambda_i\}_{i=M+1}^{N_T-1}$.

Under this assumption, $\rho = \frac{1}{N_T-M-1} \sum\limits_{i=M+1}^{N_T-1} \lambda_i$.

2.5   Solving the Optimization Problem

Given b_1, we want to find b_2 that minimizes $\hat{d}(b)$. Substituting equations (3) and (4) into (2),

$$
\begin{aligned}
\hat{d}(b) &= \sum_{i=1}^{M} \frac{y_i^2}{\lambda_i} + \frac{\epsilon^2(b)}{\rho} \\
&= \mathbf{y}^T \Lambda_M^{-1} \mathbf{y} + \frac{1}{\rho} \left\| \tilde{b}_1 - \Phi_1 \cdot \mathbf{y} \right\|^2 \\
&= \mathbf{y}^T \Lambda_M^{-1} \mathbf{y} + \frac{1}{\rho} \left(\tilde{b}_1 - \Phi_1 \cdot \mathbf{y} \right)^T \left(\tilde{b}_1 - \Phi_1 \cdot \mathbf{y} \right) \\
&= \frac{1}{\rho} \left(\mathbf{y}^T \rho \Lambda_M^{-1} \mathbf{y} + \mathbf{y}^T \Phi_1^T \Phi_1 \mathbf{y} - 2 \left(\Phi_1^T \tilde{b}_1 \right)^T \cdot \mathbf{y} + \tilde{b}_1^T \tilde{b}_1 \right).
\end{aligned}
$$

Letting the partial derivative to be zero,

$$
\begin{aligned}
0 = \frac{\partial \hat{d}(b)}{\partial \mathbf{y}} &= 2\rho \Lambda_M^{-1} \mathbf{y} + 2\Phi_1^T \Phi_1 \mathbf{y} - 2\Phi_1^T \tilde{b}_1 \\
&= 2 \left[\left(\rho \Lambda_M^{-1} + \Phi_1^T \Phi_1 \right) \mathbf{y} - \Phi_1^T \tilde{b}_1 \right].
\end{aligned}
$$

The solution of $\mathbf{y}$ is

$$
\mathbf{y} = \left(\rho \Lambda_M^{-1} + \Phi_1^T \Phi_1 \right)^{-1} \cdot \Phi_1^T \tilde{b}_1. \tag{5}
$$

And the unknown b_2 can be predicted as $b_2 = \bar{x}_2 + \Phi_2 \cdot \mathbf{y}$.

3   Seperating Shape and Appearance

Let's use the above technique to solve the problem of synthesizing new views of human faces. The problem is described as follows. Given a probe face image I under pose 1, we need to synthesize a new image J of this person's face under pose 2. The training set consists of N_T pairs of face images, $\{[I_1, J_1], [I_2, J_2], \cdots, [I_{N_T}, J_{N_T}]\}$. I_i and J_i are faces of the ith subject in the training set. $\{I_i\}_{i=1}^{N_T}$ are under pose 1, and $\{J_i\}_{i=1}^{N_T}$ are under pose 2.

In our approach, we make the common assumption [5,12,7] that the characteristics of shape can be seperated from appearance.

3.1   Shape

On each face image, a set of landmarks are labeled by hand. For the ith training image under pose 1, denote the coordinates of each landmark as (x_j, y_j), $j = 1, \cdots, L_1$, where L_1 is the number of landmarks on the faces under pose 1. Define the shape vector of this ith face image under pose 1 as

$$s_{i,1} = (x_1, x_2, \cdots, x_{L_1}, y_1, y_2, \cdots, y_{L_1})^T.$$

A similar vector $s_{i,2}$ can also be defined in the same way for pose 2. Concatenating these two vectors, we get a vector

$$s_i = \begin{pmatrix} s_{i,1} \\ s_{i,2} \end{pmatrix}$$

as a combined shape vector for the ith subject in the training set.

Thus, for the N_T subjects in the training set, we get a training set of shape vectors $\{s_i\}_{i=1}^{N_T}$.

3.2   Appearance

For each pose, a reference face is chosen, so that every face under this pose is warped to the shape of the reference face, giving a normalized image. The warping is done via a triangulation algorithm with the landmarks [5] assuming that the faces have lambertian surfaces. On each normalized image, only the pixels within the convex hull of the landmarks are kept and all other pixels are discarded. This is done to remove the unnecessary variations of the hair or the background scenery. Let's call the resultant normalized images under pose 1 as $\widetilde{I}_1, \widetilde{I}_2, \cdots, \widetilde{I}_{N_T}$, and those under pose 2 as $\widetilde{J}_1, \widetilde{J}_2, \cdots, \widetilde{J}_{N_T}$. Reshape them into vectors as $\{t_{i,1}\}_{i=1}^{N_T}$ and $\{t_{i,2}\}_{i=1}^{N_T}$ for pose 1 and pose 2 respectively.

For the ith subject in the training set, define

$$t_i = \begin{pmatrix} t_{i,1} \\ t_{i,2} \end{pmatrix}$$

as a combined appearance vector. Thus, for the N_T subjects in the training set, we get a training set of appearance vectors $\{t_i\}_{i=1}^{N_T}$.

3.3   Probe Image and Prediction

Given a probe face image I under pose 1, we need to synthesize a new image J of this person's face under pose 2. With a set of landmarks on I and the reference face under pose 1, we can again decompose I into its shape vector $\hat{s}_1$ and appearance vector $\hat{t}_1$. The landmarks can be obtained using AAM fitting [5]. In our experiments, we hand labeled these landmarks on the probe image I.

If we can predict the shape vector $\hat{s}_2$ and the appearance vector $\hat{t}_2$ of the unknown image J, by warping $\hat{t}_2$ from the reference face under pose 2 back to the shape defined by $\hat{s}_2$, we will be able to get the synthesized new image J.

So the problem turns into: How to predict $\hat{s}_2$, given $\hat{s}_1$ and the training set $\{s_i\}_{i=1}^{N_T}$? And how to predict $\hat{t}_2$, given $\hat{t}_1$ and the training set $\{t_i\}_{i=1}^{N_T}$? They are the same mathematical problem. Using exactly equation (5) that we described

Fig. 2. The 13 poses in CMU PIE database

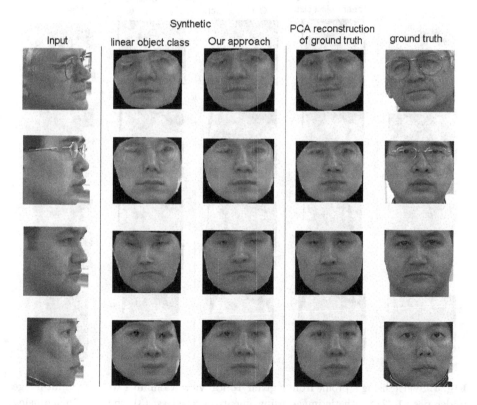

Fig. 3. Synthesizing a frontal view from a given profile. Column 1 to 5: (1) input image under pose 1 (2) synthetic image using linear-object-class. (3) synthetic image using our approach. (4) PCA reconstruction of ground truth of pose 2. (5) ground truth of pose 2.

in Section 2 will predict the unknown shape $\hat{s}_2$ and the unknown appearance $\hat{t}_2$. Then we can combine them to get the synthesized new image J, which is the new view of the probe face under pose 2 .

4   Experimental Results

We tested the performance of this method on the CMU PIE database [11]. The database contains 68 subjects. We chose 64 subjects as the training set, and 4 subjects (04016, 04022, 04026 and 04029) as the test set. Our experiments were performed on the "expression" subset including those images with neutral expressions, and those images containing glasses if the subject normally wears glasses. All images were converted to gray-scale images. The database contains 13 poses, illustrated in Fig. 2. We used combinations of 'c27' (frontal view), 'c37' (45° view) and 'c22' (profile) to test our algorithm. The landmarks were

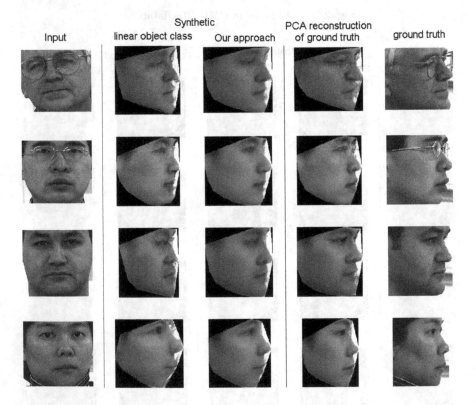

Fig. 4. Synthesizing a profile from a given frontal view. Column 1 to 5: (1) input image under pose 1 (2) synthetic image using linear-object-class. (3) synthetic image using our approach. (4) PCA reconstruction of ground truth of pose 2. (5) ground truth of pose 2.

Input	Synthetic linear object class	Our approach	PCA reconstruction of ground truth	ground truth

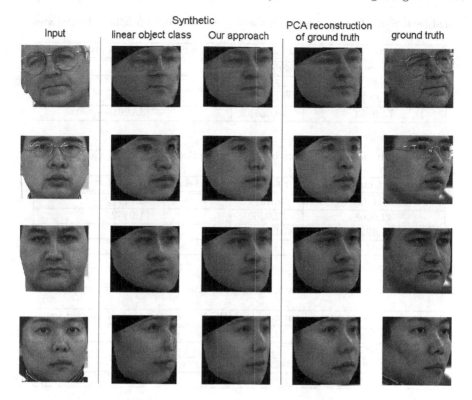

Fig. 5. Synthesizing a 45° view from a given frontal view. Column 1 to 5: (1) input image under pose 1 (2) synthetic image using linear-object-class. (3) synthetic image using our approach. (4) PCA reconstruction of ground truth of pose 2. (5) ground truth of pose 2.

provided courtesy of Ralph Gross [7]. The number of landmarks vary depending on the pose, from 39 landmarks to 54 landmarks.

We performed 3 sets of experiments, including predicting frontal view from profile (Fig. 3), predicting profile from frontal view (Fig. 4), predicting 45° view from frontal view (Fig. 5). These experiments all involve large out-of-plane rotations, such as 90° or 45°. In each experiment, the result of our approach is compared with that of linear-object-class method. We also computed the PCA reconstruction of the ground truth, by projecting the true $b = \begin{pmatrix} b_1 \\ b_2 \end{pmatrix}$ onto the eigenspace, to show the best possible reconstruction under the linear eigenspace assumption. In each experiment, for either the shape or the appearance, we always choose the number of principal eigenvectors that occupies 98% of energy. Each synthesis takes an average of 4 - 5 seconds on a PC with a 3GHz Pentium 4 processor, including predicting shape and appearance and also warping the appearance to the shape. More specificly, the prediction of shape and appearance takes about 0.3 second, and the warping takes about 4 seconds.

Fig. 3 - 5 show how our approach improves upon the results of the linear-object-class method, especially in predicting the shapes and handling large out-

Table 1. Sum of squared errors in shape prediction from profile to frontal view

linear-object-class method	our approach	PCA reconstruction of ground truth
49.5860	36.4763	12.8272
31.8927	27.6268	11.6914
51.8873	34.2422	11.6563
74.9253	49.6667	13.1261

Table 2. Sum of squared errors in shape prediction from frontal view to profile

linear-object-class method	our approach	PCA reconstruction of ground truth
67.1898	38.1367	15.9177
42.6668	32.0460	11.9452
47.4225	31.5215	13.5370
50.4465	28.2523	16.2700

Table 3. Sum of squared errors in shape prediction from frontal view to 45° view

linear-object-class method	our approach	PCA reconstruction of ground truth
46.4735	34.7182	16.0734
42.6817	31.4329	12.1678
56.5308	35.1610	18.0164
65.3341	41.0252	15.2125

of-plane rotations. Although our synthetic images are not perfect replicas of the ground truth, they are similiar to the PCA reconstructions of the ground truth, which are the best possible synthetic images under the linear eigenspace assumption. We performed these experiments using a training set of only 64 subjects. With more training data, the eigenspace would be more accurately described and better results could be expected.

We have also included the numerical comparison of errors for shape prediction in each set of experiments (Table 1, 2, 3). In each table, we compare the sum-of-squared-errors in the coordinates of the predicted shape, using the linear-object-class method, our approach, and the PCA reconstructions of ground truth, respectively. From the numerical errors, we can see our approach is efficient in reducing the errors by at least 30%.

Such technique can be used in face recognition which involves pose variation of large out-of-plane rotations.

5   Discussion and Conclusion

In this paper, we proposed an approach that can efficiently synthesize accurate new views of faces across large out-of-plane rotation, given only a single image. In our approach, we formulate a probabilistic model combining the "distance-from-feature-space" and the "distance-in-feature-space", and minimize the weighted sum of the two distances, in order to maximize the likelihood of the test example with missing data. Experimental results show that our approach produces more accurate results than the commonly used linear-object-class approach which is the basis of many 2D approaches.

Moreover, if compared with the 3D approaches, our method is also attractive in that it is computationally efficient and fast. With no need for a 3D model or 3D training data, it does not construct 3D geometry at all, thus it avoids expensive 3D rendering and fitting. It directly synthesizes 2D images, and requires using only pairs of 2D images. Nor does our approach require correspondence between different poses. Only correspondence between faces under the same pose is used. As a tradeoff, our approach needs the same number of views for each subject in the database, and can only synthesize those views which are in the database.

Pose variations, especially large out-of-plane rotations, make face recognition a difficult problem. Our algorithm of synthesizing new views of a person's face given a single input face image, can enable face recognition systems to overcome the pose variation problem.

Acknowledgements

We would like to thank Ralph Gross for providing us the hand labeled landmarks. We would also like to thank Simon Baker for providing us the CMU PIE database.

References

1. Black, M., Jepson, A., "Eigen-tracking: Robust matching and tracking of articulated objects using a view-based representation," International Journal of Computer Vision, Vol.36, No.2, pp.101-130, 1998.
2. Blanz, V., Vetter, T., "A Morphable Model for the Synthesis of 3D Faces," ACM Siggraph, 1999.
3. Blanz, V., Vetter, T., "Face Recognition Based on Fitting a 3D Morphable Model," IEEE TPAMI, Vol.25, No.9, pp.1063-1074, 2003.
4. Blanz, V., Grother, P., Phillips, P.J., Vetter, T., "Face Recognition Based on Frontal Views generated from Non-Frontal Images," CVPR, 2005.
5. Cootes, T.F., Edwards G.J., and Taylor, C.J., "Active Appearance Models," IEEE TPAMI, Vol.23, No.6, pp.681-685, 2001.
6. Debevec, P., Taylor, C., and Malik, J., "Modeling and rendering architecture from photographs: A hybrid geometry- and image-based approach," Computer Graphics (SIGGRAPH), pages 11-20, 1996.
7. Gross R., Matthews, I., Baker, S., "Appearance-Based Face Recognition and Light-Fields," IEEE TPAMI, Vol.26, No.4, pp.449-465, 2004.
8. Hwang, B-W., Lee S-W., "Reconstruction of Partially Damaged Face Images Based on a Morphable Face Model," IEEE TPAMI, Vol.25, No.3, pp.365-372, 2003.
9. Leonardis, A., Bischof, H., "Robust recognition using eigenimages," Computer Vision and Image Understanding," Vol.78, No.1, pp.99-118, 2000.

10. Moghaddam, B., Pentland, A., "Probabilistic Visual Learning for Object Repre-
    sentation," IEEE TPAMI, Vol.19, No.7, pp.696-710, 1997.
11. Sim T., Baker, S., Bsat, M., "The CMU Pose, Illumination, and Expression
    Database," IEEE TPAMI, Vol.25, No.12, pp.1615-1618, 2003.
12. Vetter, T., Poggio, T., "linear object classes and Image Synthesis From a Single
    Example Image," IEEE TPAMI, Vol.19, No.7, pp.733-742, 1997.
13. Xiao, J., "Reconstruction, Registration, and Modeling of Deformable Object
    Shapes," CMU RI PhD thesis, 2005.

Regularization of LDA for Face Recognition:
A Post-processing Approach

Wangmeng Zuo[1], Kuanquan Wang[1], David Zhang[2], and Jian Yang[2]

[1] School of Computer Science and Technology, Harbin Institute of Technology,
150001 Harbin, China
cswmzuo@163.com
[2] Department of Computing, The Hong Kong Polytechnic University,
Kowloon, Hong Kong

Abstract. When applied to high-dimensional classification task such as face recognition, linear discriminant analysis (LDA) can extract two kinds of discriminant vectors, those in the null space (*irregular*) and those in the range space (*regular*) of the within-class scatter matrix. Recently, regularization techniques, which alleviate the over-fitting to the training set, have been used to further improve the recognition performance of LDA. Most current regularization techniques, however, are pre-processing approaches and can't be used to regularize *irregular* discriminant vectors. This paper proposes a post-processing method, 2D-Gaussian filtering, for regularizing both *regular* and *irregular* discriminant vectors. This method can also be combined with other regularization techniques. We present two LDA methods, regularization of subspace LDA (RSLD) and regularization of complete Fisher discriminant framework (RCFD) and test them on the FERET face database. Post-processing is shown to improve the recognition accuracy in face recognition.

1 Introduction

Over the past thirty years, because of its wide applications in security, human-machine communication, and image retrieval, face recognition has been a focus of research in the areas of biometrics, computer vision and pattern recognition [1]. Among the various methods of face recognition, there are mainly two categories, the geometric-based approaches and the holistic-based approaches.

As a typical holistic-based method, linear discriminant analysis (LDA) has been very successful in high-dimensional pattern classification such as face recognition since the appearance of the Fisherfaces method [2, 3].

When applied to face recognition, LDA always encounters the Small Sample Size (SSS) problem, where the number of the training samples N, is much less than the dimension of facial image. The SSS problem would cause the singularity of the within-class scatter matrix $\mathbf{S}_w$. To date, researchers have proposed a number of ways to alleviate this problem. The most famous approach is Fisherfaces [2, 3], which uses principal component analysis (PCA) to map the original data to a low-dimensional subspace so as to eliminate the singularity of $\mathbf{S}_w$. Other transform techniques, such as

W. Zhao, S. Gong, and X. Tang (Eds.): AMFG 2005, LNCS 3723, pp. 377–391, 2005.

latent semantic indexing (LMI) and partial least squares (PLS), have also been investigated as ways to reduce dimensionality before implementing LDA [4, 5, 6]. Unfortunately, all of these methods discard the null space of S_w, yet the discarded null space contains discriminative information that would be useful in the SSS problem [7, 8, 9]. Recently, some work has been carried out on extracting the discriminative information in the null space of S_w [10, 11]. In this paper, we call this kind of discriminative information *irregular* discriminative information, in contrast with *regular* discriminative information in the range space of S_w. To extract both *regular* and *irregular* discriminative information, Yang presented the theoretical foundation for the PCA plus LDA framework and proposed a complete Fisher discriminant framework (CFD) [12, 13].

The SSS problem would also cause the poor estimation of the scatter matrices, S_w and S_b [21, 22]. The discriminant vectors may be over-fitted to the training set, and are very noisy and are wiggly in appearance [14]. So regularization techniques are investigated to address this [15]. One class of these regularization techniques is subspace LDA method (or the enhanced Fisher linear discriminant model: EFM) [14, 16]. Like Fisherfaces, subspace LDA also adopts a two-phase framework, PCA plus LDA. For subspace LDA, the aim of the PCA projection is to alleviate the over-fitting problem and reduce noise [14, 16, 17], whereas the aim of Fisherfaces is to discard the null space of S_w [2, 3]. Another regularization technique is regularized discriminant analysis (RDA) [18, 19, 20], which can alleviate the poor estimation of S_w [21, 22].

Previous regularization techniques, however, has a number of disadvantages. First, they concentrate only on the regularization of *regular* discriminative information, and ignore the crucial *irregular* discriminative information in the null space of S_w. Second, they all are one-dimensional pre-processing regularization techniques; they adjust the within-class scatter matrix S_w, and neglect of the two-dimensional identity of the discriminant vector. For example, subspace LDA uses PCA projection to modify the dimension of S_w, and RDA regularizes S_w by adding perturbation. Since the aim of LDA is to maximize the ratio of the between-class scatter and the within-class scatter, adjusting S_w will result in the regularization of the discriminant vectors.

In this paper, we propose a post-processing regularization technique to directly modify the discriminant vectors. In Marr's vision theory, the intensity of a pixel is influenced by the surrounding pixels as a Gaussian function of the radial distance. Motivated by this, we consider this influence in the construction of the discriminant vectors. Thus our method first maps a discriminant vector into a 2D image (discriminant image) then use 2D-Gaussian filtering to regularize the discriminant image. Finally, the regularized image is re-mapped to the discriminant vector. Using the proposed method, we present the regularizations of subspace LDA (RSLD) and complete Fisher discriminant framework (RCFD). To evaluate our method, experiments are carried out using the FERET face database. The results show that the proposed method outperforms other methods in term of the recognition accuracy.

The remainder of this paper is organized as follows. In Section 2, we briefly review subspace LDA and the complete Fisher discriminant framework. Section 3 first offers some reasons to study post-processing regularization, then presents the Gaussian filtering approach and our RSLD and RCFD methods, and finally discusses the potential disadvantages of post-processing. In Section 4, the FERET face database is used to evaluate the proposed regularization method. Section 5 offers our conclusion.

2   Subspace LDA and Complete Fisher Discriminant Framework

Various modified LDA methods have been proposed to address the SSS problem. In this Section, we investigate two representative methods, subspace LDA, which use dimensionality reduction to alleviate the over-fitting and eliminates the singularity of S_w, and complete Fisher dicriminant Framework (CFD), which can extract both *regular* and *irregular* discriminative information.

2.1   Subspace LDA

Subspace LDA is based on the PCA plus LDA framework where PCA is used to alleviate the over-fitting and eliminate the singularity of the within-class scatter matrix S_w [14, 16, 17].

In subspace LDA, each image should be previously mapped into a 1D vector by concatenating the rows of the original image. Let $X = \{x_1^{(1)}, x_2^{(1)}, \cdots, x_{N_1}^{(1)}, \cdots, x_j^{(i)}, \cdots, x_{N_C}^{(C)}\}$ be a training set with N_i image vectors for class i. The number of class is C, and $x_j^{(i)}$ denotes the jth image vector of class i. The total covariance matrix S_t of PCA is defined as

$$S_t = \frac{1}{N} \sum_{i=1}^{C} \sum_{j=1}^{N_i} (x_j^{(i)} - \bar{x})(x_j^{(i)} - \bar{x})^T , \tag{1}$$

where $\bar{x}$ is the mean vectors of all training images, and $N = \sum_{i=1}^{C} N_i$ is the total number of training images. The PCA projector $T_{Spca} = [\varphi_1, \varphi_2, \cdots, \varphi_{d_{SPCA}}]$ can be obtained by calculating the eigenvalues and vectors of the total scatter matrix S_t, where φ_k is the eigenvector corresponding to the kth largest eigenvalue of S_t, and d_{SPCA} is the PCA dimension for subspace LDA.

The between-class scatter matrix S_b and the within-class scatter matrix S_w are defined as

$$S_b = \frac{1}{N} \sum_{i=1}^{C} N_i (\overline{x^{(i)}} - \bar{x})(\overline{x^{(i)}} - \bar{x})^T , \tag{2}$$

$$S_w = \frac{1}{N} \sum_{i=1}^{C} \sum_{j=1}^{N_i} (x_j^{(i)} - \overline{x^{(i)}})(x_j^{(i)} - \overline{x^{(i)}})^T , \tag{3}$$

where $\overline{x^{(i)}}$ is mean vector of class i. With PCA projector T_{Spca}, we map S_b and S_w to PCA subspace,

$$\breve{\mathbf{S}}_b = \mathbf{T}_{Spca}^T \mathbf{S}_b \mathbf{T}_{Spca} \text{ and } \breve{\mathbf{S}}_w = \mathbf{T}_{Spca}^T \mathbf{S}_w \mathbf{T}_{Spca} \cdot \tag{4}$$

PCA projection can eliminate the singularity of the within-class scatter matrix. Thus the optimal discriminant vectors can be calculated by maximizing the Fisher's criterion

$$J_F(\mathbf{w}) = \frac{\mathbf{w}^T \breve{\mathbf{S}}_b \mathbf{w}}{\mathbf{w}^T \breve{\mathbf{S}}_w \mathbf{w}} \cdot \tag{5}$$

The discriminant vectors can be obtained by calculating the first d_{LDA} generalized eigenvectors $[\mathbf{w}_1, \mathbf{w}_2, \cdots, \mathbf{w}_{d_{\mathrm{LDA}}}]$ and the corresponding eigenvalues $[\lambda_1, \lambda_2, \cdots, \lambda_{d_{\mathrm{LDA}}}]$ of $\breve{\mathbf{S}}_b$ and $\breve{\mathbf{S}}_w$. Given an image vector $\mathbf{x}$, the discriminant feature vector $\mathbf{z}^S$ is defined as

$$\mathbf{z}^S = \mathbf{U}_S^T \mathbf{T}_{SPCA}^T \mathbf{x} , \tag{6}$$

where $\mathbf{U}_S = [\mathbf{w}_1, \mathbf{w}_2, \cdots, \mathbf{w}_{d_{\mathrm{LDA}}}]$ is the subspace LDA projector.

2.2 Complete Fisher Discriminant Framework

The Complete Fisher discriminant framework (CFD) is a method designed to extract both *regular* and *irregular* discriminant vectors [12, 13]. Like Fisherfaces and subspace LDA, CFD is also based on a two-phase framework: PCA plus LDA. Unlike subspace LDA, PCA is used to reduce dimensionality without losing discriminative information that could be used in CFD.

PCA, also called the KL transform, is used to find the optimal lower dimensional representation by solving the eigenvalue problem of the total scatter matrix $\mathbf{S}_t$. Unlike subspace LDA, CFD chooses eigenvectors corresponding to all positive eigenvalues of $\mathbf{S}_t$ in order to construct the PCA projector $\mathbf{T}_{CPCA} = [\varphi_1, \varphi_2, \cdots, \varphi_{d_{CPCA}}]^T$ and transform the training image vector $\mathbf{x}$ into d_{CPCA}-dimensional PCA space $\mathbf{y}$,

$$\mathbf{y} = \mathbf{T}_{CPCA} \mathbf{x} , \tag{7}$$

where d_{CPCA} is the dimension of the range space of $\mathbf{S}_t$.

In PCA space, the between-class scatter matrix $\mathbf{S}_b$ and the within-class scatter matrix $\mathbf{S}_w$ are defined as

$$\mathbf{S}_b = \frac{1}{N} \sum_{i=1}^{C} N_i (\overline{\mathbf{y}^{(i)}} - \overline{\mathbf{y}})(\overline{\mathbf{y}^{(i)}} - \overline{\mathbf{y}})^T , \tag{8}$$

$$\mathbf{S}_w = \frac{1}{N} \sum_{i=1}^{C} \sum_{j=1}^{N_i} (\mathbf{y}_j^{(i)} - \overline{\mathbf{y}^{(i)}})(\mathbf{y}_j^{(i)} - \overline{\mathbf{y}^{(i)}})^T , \tag{9}$$

where $\overline{\mathbf{y}^{(i)}}$ is the mean vector of class i, and $\mathbf{y}_j^{(i)} = \mathbf{T}_{CPCA} \mathbf{x}_j^{(i)}$. We can then obtain the optimal discriminant vectors by maximizing the Fisher's linear discriminant criterion. However, if $\mathbf{S}_w$ is singular, it is not possible to calculate the generalized eigenvectors directly. To address this, Yang proposed a complete Fisher's discriminant criterion

$$J(\mathbf{w}) = \max(\frac{\mathbf{w}^T \mathbf{S}_b \mathbf{w}}{\mathbf{w}^T \mathbf{S}_w \mathbf{w}}), \text{ if } \mathbf{w}^T \mathbf{S}_w \mathbf{w} > 0 \tag{10}$$

$$J_b(\mathbf{w}) = \max(\mathbf{w}^T \mathbf{S}_b \mathbf{w}), \text{ if } \mathbf{w}^T \mathbf{S}_w \mathbf{w} = 0$$

To solve Eq. (10), we should work out a subspace spanned by $\{\phi_1, \phi_2, \cdots, \phi_{d_W}\}$ in which we can extract all *regular* discriminative information, and a subspace spanned by $\{\phi_{d_{W+1}}, \cdots, \phi_{d_{CPCA}}\}$, in which we can extract all *irregular* discriminative features.

We calculate the eigenvalues and the eigenvectors of $\mathbf{S}_w$,

$$\mathbf{S}_w \mathbf{\Phi} = \mathbf{\Lambda} \mathbf{\Phi}, \tag{11}$$

where $\mathbf{\Phi} = [\phi_1, \phi_2, \cdots, \phi_{d_{CPCA}}]$ is the eigenvector matrix, and $\mathbf{\Lambda}$ is the corresponding diagonal matrix of eigenvalues $\{\lambda_1, \lambda_2, \cdots, \lambda_{d_{CPCA}}\}$. Supposing $\lambda_1 \geq \lambda_2 \geq \cdots \geq \lambda_{d_{CPCA}}$, we choose all eigenvectors corresponding to positive eigenvalues to construct the projector $\mathbf{\Phi}_R = [\phi_1, \phi_2, \cdots, \phi_{d_W}]$. With $\mathbf{\Phi}_R$, we define $\tilde{\mathbf{S}}_b = \mathbf{\Phi}_R^T \mathbf{S}_b \mathbf{\Phi}_R$ and $\tilde{\mathbf{S}}_w = \mathbf{\Phi}_R^T \mathbf{S}_w \mathbf{\Phi}_R$.

We then obtain the *regular* discriminant vectors by maximizing the criterion,

$$J(\mathbf{w}) = \frac{\mathbf{w}^T \tilde{\mathbf{S}}_b \mathbf{w}}{\mathbf{w}^T \tilde{\mathbf{S}}_w \mathbf{w}}. \tag{12}$$

First we calculate the generalized eigenvalues problem of $\tilde{\mathbf{S}}_b \mathbf{w} = \lambda \tilde{\mathbf{S}}_w \mathbf{w}$. Then we choose the eigenvectors $\mathbf{U} = [\mathbf{u}_1, \mathbf{u}_2, \cdots, \mathbf{u}_{d_{LDA}}]$ corresponding to the first d_{LDA} largest eigenvalues. Finally, the *regular* discriminant feature vector $\mathbf{z}^R$ of a image vector $\mathbf{x}$ is defined as

$$\mathbf{z}^R = \mathbf{U}_R^T \mathbf{\Phi}_R^T \mathbf{T}_{PCA} \mathbf{x}. \tag{13}$$

Similarly, we can calculate the *irregular* discriminant vectors. First, all eigenvectors corresponding to zero eigenvalues are chosen to construct the projector $\mathbf{\Phi}_I = [\phi_{d_{W+1}}, \cdots, \phi_{d_{CPCA}}]$. Next, we define $\hat{\mathbf{S}}_b = \mathbf{\Phi}_I^T \mathbf{S}_b \mathbf{\Phi}_I$.

Then, by maximizing the criterion

$$J_b(\mathbf{w}) = \mathbf{w}^T \hat{\mathbf{S}}_b \mathbf{w}, \tag{14}$$

we choose the eigenvectors $\mathbf{V} = [\mathbf{v}_1, \mathbf{v}_2, \cdots, \mathbf{v}_{d_{LDA}}]$ corresponding to the first d_{LDA} largest eigenvalues of $\hat{\mathbf{S}}_b$. Finally, the *irregular* discriminant feature vector $\mathbf{z}^I$ of a image vector $\mathbf{x}$ is defined as

$$\mathbf{z}^I = \mathbf{V}^T \mathbf{\Phi}_I^T \mathbf{T}_{PCA} \mathbf{x}. \tag{15}$$

In [17], the face difference is modeled with three components: intrinsic difference, transformation difference, and noise. From this perspective, the aim of LDA is to maximize intrinsic difference and to reduce both transformation difference and noise. Wang suggested discarding the eigenvectors corresponding to smaller eigenvalues in the projection to the within-class subspace. In the implementation of the CFD framework, we also take this strategy in account. Unlike [12, 13], however, we adjust d_W experimentally to construct $\mathbf{\Phi}_R = [\phi_1, \phi_2, \cdots, \phi_{d_W}]$ rather than choosing all eigenvectors corresponding to positive eigenvalues. We use all other eigenvectors to construct $\mathbf{\Phi}_I = [\phi_{d_W+1}, \cdots, \phi_{d_{CPCA}}]$.

3 Post-processing Regularization Technique

Although little investigated, post-processing regularization technique can be used to further improve the recognition performance of LDA. In this Section, we first describe the characteristics of post-processing regularization. Next we propose our 2D-Gaussian filtering approach for the regularization of LDA, and then present two LDA methods, regularization of subspace LDA (RSLD) and regularization of complete Fisher discriminant framework (RCFD). Finally we discuss the potential adverse effects of the proposed method.

3.1 Advantageous Properties of Post-processing

Post-processing regularization is used to further modify the discriminant vectors after the LDA training. Post-processing technique has four advantageous properties over other regularization techniques, straightforward regularization on discriminant vectors, two-dimensional identity, the complement of other methods, and the capability of regularizing the *irregular* discriminant vectors. First, post-processing is a straightforward regularization technique on discriminant vectors. Other regularization techniques, such as subspace LDA or RDA, modify the within-class scatter matrix $\mathbf{S}_w$ by dimensionality reduction or adding some perturbation on $\mathbf{S}_w$. Obviously, the change of $\mathbf{S}_w$ alters the discriminant vectors.

Second, post-processing regularization allows the use of two-dimensional image processing techniques. Since face recognition is a typical image recognition tasks and the discriminant vector can be mapped to a two-dimensional image, two-dimensional post-processing may be a novel effective regularization technique deserving further investigation. In contrast, both subspace LDA and RDA are one-dimensional regularization techniques.

Third, post-processing is a complement to other regularization techniques and can be used to combine with other methods to further improve recognition performance. For example, subspace LDA modifies the discriminant vectors by adjusting $\mathbf{S}_w$. After LDA training, post-processing can be used to further regularize them.

Fourth, the post-processing technique can be used to regularize the *irregular* discriminant vectors. Other regularization techniques cannot do this. RDA, for example, which adds perturbation on the within-class scatter matrix $\mathbf{S}_w$, cannot modify the *irregular* discriminant vectors. But post-processing still performs well.

3.2 Regularization of LDA Using 2D-Gaussian Filtering

In this Section we propose a post-processing approach, 2D-Gaussian filtering, for regularization of the discriminant vectors. The 2D-Gaussian filter is an ideal filter in the sense that it reduces the magnitude of high spatial frequency in an image and has been widely applied in image smoothing [23]. Since a discriminant vector can be mapped to a 2D image, Gaussian filtering is used to post-process the discriminant images. 2D-Gaussian function is defined as

$$G(x, y) = \frac{1}{2\pi\sigma^2} e^{-(x^2+y^2)/2\sigma^2} , \qquad (16)$$

where $\sigma > 0$, which is the standard deviation. In the implementation of post-processing regularization, we first define a 2D-Gaussian model $\mathbf{M}_g$ according to the standard deviation σ. The window size $[w, w]$ can be determined as $w = 6 \times \sigma$, and the Gaussian model $\mathbf{M}_g$ is defined as the $w \times w$ truncation from the Gaussian kernel $G(x, y)$. Then we calculate the norm of each discriminant vector $\|\mathbf{v}_i\|_2 = \sqrt{\mathbf{v}_i^T \mathbf{v}_i}$, and map $\mathbf{v}_i$ into its corresponding discriminant image $\mathbf{V}_i$. The Gaussian filter $\mathbf{M}_g$ is used to smooth discriminant image $\mathbf{V}_i$,

$$\mathbf{V}_i'(x, y) = \mathbf{V}(x, y) \otimes \mathbf{M}_g(x, y) . \qquad (17)$$

$\mathbf{V}_i'(x, y)$ is transformed into a high dimensional vector $\mathbf{v}_i'$ by concatenating the rows of $\mathbf{V}_i'(x, y)$ together. Finally we normalize $\mathbf{v}_i'$ using the norm of $\mathbf{v}_i$

$$\mathbf{v}_i'' = \frac{\|\mathbf{v}_i\|_2}{\sqrt{\mathbf{v}_i'^T \mathbf{v}_i'}} \mathbf{v}_i', \qquad (18)$$

and obtain the post-processed LDA projector $\mathbf{T}_{pLDA} = [\mathbf{v}_1'', \mathbf{v}_2'', \cdots, \mathbf{v}_{d_{LDA}}'']$, where d_{LDA} is the number of discriminant vectors.

With the proposed post-processing regularization technique, we present two LDA methods, the regularization of subspace LDA (RSLD) and the regularization of complete Fisher discriminant framework (RCFD).

The algorithmic procedure of RSLD is formally stated in Fig. 1.

The algorithmic procedure of RCFD is stated in Fig. 2.

RSLD Algorithm

Step 1. Compute $\mathbf{S}_t$, $\mathbf{S}_b$, and $\mathbf{S}_w$, and calculate the first d_{SPCA} eigenvectors $\mathbf{T}_{Spca} = [\varphi_1, \varphi_2, \cdots, \varphi_{d_{SPCA}}]$ of $\mathbf{S}_t$, then modify $\mathbf{S}_b$ and $\mathbf{S}_w$ by $\tilde{\mathbf{S}}_b = \mathbf{T}_{Spca}^T \mathbf{S}_b \mathbf{T}_{Spca}$ and $\tilde{\mathbf{S}}_w = \mathbf{T}_{Spca}^T \mathbf{S}_w \mathbf{T}_{Spca}$.

Step 2. Calculate the first d_{LDA} generalized eigenvectors $\mathbf{U}_S = [\mathbf{w}_1, \mathbf{w}_2, \cdots, \mathbf{w}_{d_{LDA}}]$ of $\tilde{\mathbf{S}}_b$ and $\tilde{\mathbf{S}}_w$, and compute $\mathbf{T}_{SLDA} = \mathbf{T}_{SPCA} \mathbf{U}_S = [\mathbf{v}_1, \mathbf{v}_2, \cdots, \mathbf{v}_{d_{LDA}}]$.

Step 3. Using 2D-Gaussian filter $\mathbf{M}_g$, regularize each discriminant vector $\mathbf{v}_i$ to $\mathbf{v}_i''$, and construct the LDA projector $\mathbf{T}_{RSLD} = [\mathbf{v}_1'', \mathbf{v}_2'', \cdots, \mathbf{v}_{d_{LDA}}'']$.

Fig. 1. RSLD Algorithm

RCFD Algorithm

Step 1. Compute the total scatter matrix $\mathbf{S}_t$, and choose all eigenvectors corresponding to positive eigenvalues of $\mathbf{S}_t$ to construct PCA projector $\mathbf{T}_{Cpca} = [\varphi_1, \varphi_2, \cdots, \varphi_{d_{CPCA}}]$.

An image vector $\mathbf{x}$ is then transformed to PCA subspace $y = \mathbf{T}_{Cpca}^T \mathbf{x}$.

Step 2. In PCA subspace, construct $\mathbf{S}_b$ and $\mathbf{S}_w$, and calculate all eigenvectors $\{\phi_1, \phi_2, \cdots, \phi_{d_{CPCA}}\}$ of $\mathbf{S}_w$.

Step 3. Calculate the *regular* discriminant vectors: Choose the first d_W eigenvectors of $\mathbf{S}_w$ to construct $\Phi_R = [\phi_1, \phi_2, \cdots, \phi_{d_W}]$, and define $\tilde{\mathbf{S}}_b = \Phi_R^T \mathbf{S}_b \Phi_R$ and

$\tilde{\mathbf{S}}_w = \Phi_R^T \mathbf{S}_w \Phi_R$, then calculate the first d_{LDA} generalized eigenvectors

$\mathbf{U} = [\mathbf{u}_1, \mathbf{u}_2, \cdots, \mathbf{u}_{d_{LDA}}]$. Define the *regular* discriminant vectors

$P_R = \mathbf{T}_{Cpca} \Phi_R \mathbf{U} = [\xi_1, \xi_2, \cdots, \xi_{d_{LDA}}]$.

Step 4. Calculate the *irregular* discriminant vectors: Choose the last $(d_{CPCA} - d_W)$ eigenvectors of $\mathbf{S}_w$ to construct $\Phi_I = [\phi_{d_{W+1}}, \cdots, \phi_{d_{PCA}}]$, and define $\hat{\mathbf{S}}_b = \Phi_I^T \mathbf{S}_b \Phi_I$,

then calculate the first d_{LDA} eigenvectors $\mathbf{V} = [\mathbf{v}_1, \mathbf{v}_2, \cdots, \mathbf{v}_{d_{LDA}}]$ of $\hat{\mathbf{S}}_b$. Define the

irregular discriminant vectors $P_I = \mathbf{T}_{Cpca} \Phi_I \mathbf{V} = [\zeta_1, \zeta_2, \cdots, \zeta_{d_{LDA}}]$.

Step 5. Using 2D-Gaussian filter $\mathbf{M}_g$, regularize each *regular* or *irregular* discriminant vector ξ_i or ζ_j, and construct the *regular* and *irregular* LDA projectors $P_{RR} = [\xi_1'', \xi_2'', \cdots, \xi_{d_{LDA}}'']$ and $P_{RI} = [\zeta_1'', \zeta_2'', \cdots, \zeta_{d_{LDA}}'']$.

Step 6. Extract the *regular* and *irregular* feature vectors of image vector $\mathbf{x}$ by $\mathbf{z}^R = P_{RR}^T \mathbf{x}$ and $\mathbf{z}^I = P_{RI}^T \mathbf{x}$.

Step 7. Classify $\mathbf{x}$ according to the distance $d(\mathbf{z}^R, \mathbf{z}^I; \mathbf{z}_i^R, \mathbf{z}_i^I)$ of feature $(\mathbf{z}^R, \mathbf{z}^I)$ to each template $(\mathbf{z}_i^R, \mathbf{z}_i^I)$: First calculate the distance $d(\mathbf{z}^R, \mathbf{z}_i^R)$, the distance of $\mathbf{z}^R$ and $\mathbf{z}_i^R$, the distance $d(\mathbf{z}^I, \mathbf{z}_i^I)$, and the distance of $\mathbf{z}^I$ and $\mathbf{z}_i^I$. Then normalize them by $d_n(\mathbf{z}^R, \mathbf{z}_i^R) = \dfrac{d(\mathbf{z}^R, \mathbf{z}_i^R)}{\max_i d(\mathbf{z}^R, \mathbf{z}_i^R)}$ and $d_n(\mathbf{z}^I, \mathbf{z}_i^I) = \dfrac{d(\mathbf{z}^I, \mathbf{z}_i^I)}{\max_i d(\mathbf{z}^I, \mathbf{z}_i^I)}$. Finally

define the distance $d(\mathbf{z}^R, \mathbf{z}^I; \mathbf{z}_i^R, \mathbf{z}_i^I) = d_n(\mathbf{z}^R, \mathbf{z}_i^R) + d_n(\mathbf{z}^I, \mathbf{z}_i^I)$.

Fig. 2. RCFD Algorithm

3.3 Discussion

LDA is an optimal statistical analysis technique so post-processing on the discriminant vectors would partially damage this optimality and produce adverse effects such as changing the norm or breaking the orthogonality of the discriminant vectors. In this Section, we'll discuss these adverse effects of post-processing regularization.

While the purpose of LDA is to maximize the Fisher criterion $J(\mathbf{W}_{opt})$, post-processing will produce a lower value of $J(\mathbf{W}_{opt}'')$. Such a decrease in the value of $J(\mathbf{W}_{opt}'')$ will have two contrasting effects. The first, undesirable, is that it would damage the optimality of the discriminant vectors. On the other hand, however, it would at the same time produce the benefits of making the discriminant vectors more robust and of alleviating over-fitting. Similar phenomena are also observed in other regularization techniques such as subspace LDA, where the value of $J(\mathbf{W}_{opt})$ is lowered but the recognition performance is improved, as demonstrated in [14, 16]. Thus experimental evidence is needed to correctly evaluate the post-processing regularization technique.

Post-processing can change the norm of the discriminant vector $\mathbf{v}_i$, $\|\mathbf{v}_i\|_2 \neq \|\mathbf{v}_i'\|_2$. In our post-processing approach, we use a normalization process to pledge the invariance of $\|\mathbf{v}_i\|_2$. We normalize $\mathbf{v}'$ by $\mathbf{v}_i'' = \dfrac{\|\mathbf{v}_i\|_2}{\|\mathbf{v}_i'\|_2} \mathbf{v}_i'$, thus guaranteeing the invariance of $\mathbf{v}_i$'s norm, $\|\mathbf{v}_i\|_2 = \|\mathbf{v}_i''\|_2$.

Post-processing may also break the orthogonality of the discriminant vectors. Generally speaking, the optimal discriminant vectors can be calculated subject to either of two orthogonal constraints, an $\mathbf{S}_t$-orthogonal constraint $\mathbf{v}_i^T \mathbf{S}_t \mathbf{v}_j = 0$ ($\forall i \neq j$) or a simple orthogonal constraint $\mathbf{v}_i^T \mathbf{v}_j = 0$ ($\forall i \neq j$). Previous studies on LDA indicate that the discriminant vectors subjected to $\mathbf{S}_t$-orthogonal constraints exhibit a higher recognition accuracy than those subjected to simple orthogonal constraint [24, 25, 26]. In our LDA methods, the discriminant vectors satisfy the $\mathbf{S}_t$-orthogonal constraint before post-processing. After post-processing, the equation $\mathbf{v}_i^T \mathbf{S}_t \mathbf{v}_j = 0$ ($\forall i \neq j$) may not hold. Like $\mathbf{S}_w$, the total scatter matrix $\mathbf{S}_t$ may also be over-fitted to the training set. Thus the destruction of equation $\mathbf{v}_i^T \mathbf{S}_t \mathbf{v}_j = 0$ may not cause the degradation of the recognition performance, but further experimental evidence is needed to validate this.

4 Experimental Results and Discussion

In this section, we use the FERET face database to test the performance of RSLD and RCFD in face recognition. The FERET face database is a US Department of Defense-sponsored face database that has become a standard face image set used in testing and evaluating face recognition algorithms [27]. For our experiments, we chose a subset of the FERET database. This subset includes 1, 400 images of 200 individuals (each individual has seven images). The seven images of each individual consist of three front images with varied facial expressions and illuminations, and four profile images ranging from ±15° to ±25° pose. The facial portion of each original image was cropped to a size of 80×80 and pre-processed using histogram equalization. Fig. 3 presents the seven cropped images of an individual.

Fig. 3. Images of one person in the FERET subset

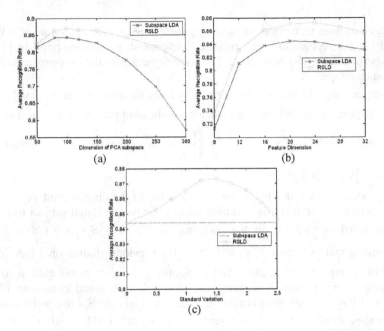

Fig. 4. Illustration of the recognition accuracy over the variation of the RSLD parameters on the FERET subset. (a) Recognition rate vs. the PCA dimension. (b) Recognition rate vs. the LDA dimension. (c) Recognition rate vs. the standard variation.

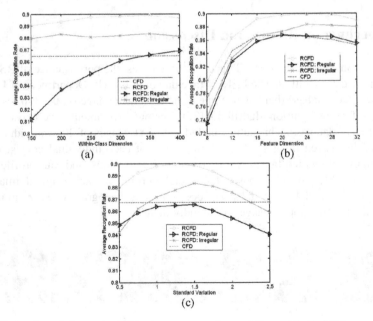

Fig. 5. Illustration of the recognition accuracy over the variation of the RCFD parameters on the FERET subset. (a) Recognition rate vs. the with-class dimension. (b) Recognition rate vs. the LDA dimension. (c) Recognition rate vs. the standard variation.

Using the FERET subset, two experimental schemes are designed to evaluate the performance of RSLD and RCFD. In the first scheme, three images of each person (600 images) are randomly selected for training. These training images are also used as gallery images. The remaining 800 images are used as probe images. In the second scheme, all of the images of 100 persons (700 images) are randomly selected for training. These training images are used to learn the LDA projector. The 100 normal frontal images ("ba") of the other 100 persons in the subset are selected as gallery images, and the remaining 600 images of this group are used as probe images. In both experimental schemes, we use the nearest neighbor classifier to match probe images and gallery images, and the averaged recognition rate (ARR) is used by calculating the mean across 10 runs.

The evaluation of RSLD and RCFD consists two phases, parameter selection and performance evaluation. In the phase of parameter selection, we determine the optimal parameter values for each method. In the phase of performance evaluation, we reevaluate the recognition rates of RSLD and RCFD, and compare them with other methods such as Eigenfaces, subspace LDA and CFD.

The parameter selection of RSLD is to determine the values of three parameters, the PCA dimension d_{PCA}, the LDA dimension d_{LDA}, and the standard variation σ. Since it is difficult to determine these three parameters at the same time, we here adopt a stepwise selection strategy which first finds the optimal PCA dimension d_{PCA} by fixing the other two parameters, and then determine d_{LDA} and σ in the similar way. To determine the optimal value of the PCA dimension, we fix the LDA dimension $d_{LDA} = 20$ and the standard variation $\sigma = 1.5$. Fig. 4(a) shows the recognition rate versus the variation of d_{PCA}. From Fig. 4(a), we determine the optimal PCA dimension $d_{PCA}=100$ which corresponds to the maximum recognition rate. After determining d_{PCA}, we study the recognition accuracy over the variation of the LDA dimension d_{LDA} with $d_{PCA}=100$ and $\sigma=1.5$, as depicted in Fig. 4(b). The maximum average recognition rate is obtained with the LDA dimension $d_{LDA}=24$. Then we explore the recognition rate vs. the variation of σ with $d_{PCA}=100$ and $d_{LDA}=24$, as shown in Fig. 4(c). From Fig. 4, we determine all the optimal values of RSLD parameters, $d_{PCA}=100$, $d_{LDA}=24$ and $\sigma=1.5$, as shown in Table 1.

The parameter selection of RCFD is to determine three parameters, the within-class dimension d_W, the LDA dimension d_{LDA} and standard variation σ. Fig. 5 depicts the effect of d_W, d_{LDA} and σ on the recognition rate. Thus the optimal values of RCFD parameters are determined, $d_W=350$, $d_{LDA}=24$ and $\sigma=1.5$, as listed in Table 1. Unlike RSLD, RCFD extracts two kinds of discriminative feature, *regular* and *irregular*. So the recognition rate of RCFD: *regular* and RCFD: *irregular* are also plotted in Fig. 5.

Table 2 lists the recognition rates obtained using RSLD and RCFD in the parameter selection phase. RSLD can achieve a recognition rate of 87.34%, higher than 84.54%, that obtained using subspace LDA. RCFD can achieve the recognition rate of 89.87%, higher than 86.75%, that obtained using CFD. So the efficiency of post-processing in recognition performance is revealed.

Table 1. The optimal parameters of RSLD and RCFD

Method	RSLD	RCFD: Regular	RCFD: Irregular	RCFD
Parameters	[100,24,1.5]	[400,20,1.5]	[200,24,1.5]	[350,24,1.25]

Table 2. The average recognition rate of RSLD and RCFD across the first 10 tests

Method	RSLD	RCFD: Regular	RCFD: Irregular	RCFD
Recognition Rate (%)	87.34	86.59	88.36	89.87

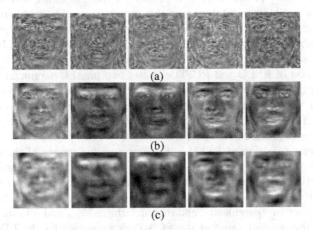

Fig. 6. Illustration of the discriminant vectors of (a) Fisherfaces, (b) subspace LDA and (c) RSLD

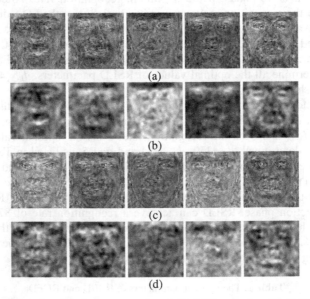

Fig. 7. Illustration of the discriminant vectors of (a) CFD: *regular*, (b) RCFD: *regular*, (c) CFD: *irregular* and (d) RCFD: *irregular*

Table 3. The recognition rates of different methods across the second 10 tests

Method	Eigenfaces	Subspace LDA	RSLD	CFD	RCFD
ARR (%)	25.58±1.0	84.74±1.6	87.30±1.0	87.08±1.1	89.61±1.1

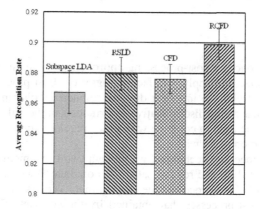

Fig. 8. The average recognition rates of subspace LDA, RSLD, CFD and RCFD across 10 tests with the second experiment scheme

Table 4. The average recognition rate (%) of CFD and RCFD and their standard deviation (std) with the second experiment scheme

Method	CFD	RCFD: Regular	RCFD: Irregular	RCFD
ARR (%)	87.62±0.97	88.32±1.01	87.57±1.46	89.93±1.02

In the phase of performance evaluation, we first show the discriminant vectors of different methods, and then reevaluate the recognition rate obtained using RSLD and RCFD. Fig. 6 shows the discriminant vectors of Fisherfaces, subspace LDA and RSLD. The discriminant vectors of Fisherfaces are very noisy and wiggly. Subspace LDA can visibly improve the smoothness, and RSLD can further smooth the discriminant vectors and make the projection axes more robust. Fig. 7 illustrates the appearance of the CFD and RCFD discriminant vectors. We can see that RCFD can further smooth the discriminant images of CFD: *regular* and CFD: *irregular*.

We reevaluate RSLD and RCFD according to their average recognition rates of another 10 runs. Table 3 lists the recognition rates and standard deviation (std.) obtained using Eigenfaces, subspace LDA, RSLD, CFD and RCFD. The recognition rate of RSLD is 87.30, and that of RCFD is 89.61, both are higher than those of Eigenfaces (25.58), subspace LDA (84.74), and CFD (87.08).

Next we compare the recognition rates of some methods with the second experiment scheme. Fig. 8 and Table 4 depict the average recognition rates obtained by subspace LDA, CFD, RSLD and RCFD. We can see that RSLD has a higher recognition rate

(87.95%) that that of subspace LDA (86.73%), and the recognition rate obtained using RCFD (89.93%) is also higher than that obtained using CFD (87.62%). It is worth noting that, in the first experiment scheme, RCFD: *irregular* (88.48%) is superior to RCFD: *regular* (86.81%) in recognition accuracy, which indicates that *irregular* discriminative feature exhibits a better discriminatory power. But in the second experiment scheme, RCFD: *regular* (88.32%) outperform RCFD: *irregular* (87.57%), which means *regular* discriminative feature has a better generalization capability.

5 Conclusion

In this paper, we propose a post-processing approach, 2D-Gaussian filtering, for the regularization of LDA, and apply it to face recognition. Post-processing differs from other regularization technique in that it directly regularizes discriminant vectors and can be used to regularize the discriminative information in the null space of S_w. Post-processing can also be used to combine with other regularization technique to further improve the recognition performance.

Using the post-processing technique, we present two LDA methods, regularization of subspace LDA (RSLD) and regularization of complete Fisher discriminant framework (RCFD). RSLD post-processes the discriminant vectors obtained by subspace LDA, and RCFD post-processes that obtained by the complete Fisher discriminant framework. Experimental results on the FERET face subset show that post-processing is very effective in face recognition. With three samples of each subject for training, RCFD achieves an average recognition rate of 89.61% on the FERET subset.

Acknowledgment

The work is partially supported by the UGC/CRC fund from the HKSAR Government, the central fund from the Hong Kong Polytechnic University and the NSFC fund under the contract No. 60332010 and No. 90209020.

References

1. Zhao, W., Chellappa, R., Phillips, P.J., Rosenfeld, A.: Face recognition: a literature survey. ACM Computing Surveys, 35 (2003) 399-458.
2. Swets, D.L., Weng, J.: Using discriminant Eigenfeatures for image retrieval. IEEE Trans. Pattern Analysis and Machine Intelligence, 18 (1996) 831-836.
3. Belhumeour, P.N., Hespanha, J.P., Kriegman, D.J.: Eigenfaces versus Fisherfaces: recognition using class specific linear projection. IEEE Trans. Pattern Analysis and Machine Intelligence, 19 (1997) 711-720.
4. Torkkola, K.: Linear discriminant analysis in document classification. Proc. IEEE ICDM Workshop Text Mining (2001).
5. Baeka, J., Kimb, M.: Face recognition using partial least squares components. Pattern Recognition, 37 (2004) 1303-1306.
6. Chien, J.T., Wu, C.C.: Discriminant waveletfaces and nearest feature classifiers for face recognition. IEEE Trans. Pattern Analysis and Machine Intelligence, 24 (2002) 1644-1649.

7. Chen, L.F., Mark Liao, H.Y., Ko, M.T., Lin, J.C., Yu, G.J.: A new LDA-based face recognition system which can solve the small sample size problem. Pattern Recognition, 33 (2000)1713-1726.

8. Yu, H., Yang, J.: A direct LDA algorithm for high-dimensional data with application to face recognition. Pattern Recognition, 34 (2001) 2067-2070.

9. Lu, J., Plataniotis, K.N., Venetsanopoulos, A.N.: Face recognition using LDA-based algorithms. IEEE Trans. Neural Networks, 14 (2003) 195-200.

10. Yang, J., Zhang, D., Yang, J.Y.: A generalized K-L expansion method which can deal with Small Smaple Size and high-dimensional problems. Pattern Analysis and Applications, 6 (2003) 47-54.

11. Cevikalp, H., Neamtu, M., Wilkes, M., Barkana, A.: Discriminative common vectors for face recognition. IEEE Trans. Pattern Analysis and Machine Intelligence, 27 (2005) 4-13.

12. Yang J., Yang, J.Y.: Why can LDA be performed in PCA transformed space. Pattern Recognition, 36 (2003) 563-566.

13. Yang, J., Frangi, A.F., Yang, J.Y., Zhang, D., Jin, Z.: KPCA plus LDA: a complete Kernel Fisher discriminant framework for feature extraction and recognition. IEEE Trans. Pattern Analysis and Machine Intelligence, 27 (2005) 230-244.

14. Zhao, W., Chellappa, R., Krishnaswamy, A.: Discriminant analysis of principal components for face recognition. Proc. Int'l Conf. Automatic Face and Gesture Recognition (1998) 336-341.

15. Bensmail, H., Celeux, G.: Regularized Gaussian discriminant analysis through eigenvalue decomposition. Journal of the American Statistics Association, 91 (1996) 1743-1748.

16. Liu, C., Wechsler, H.: Enhanced Fisher linear discriminant models for face recognition. Proc. 14th Int'l Conf. Pattern Recognition, 2 (1998) 1368-1372.

17. Wang, X., Tang, X.: A unified framework for subspace face recognition. IEEE Trans. Pattern Analysis and Machine Intelligence, 26 (2004) 1222-1228.

18. Dai, D.Q., Yuen, P.C.: Regularized discriminant analysis and its application to face recognition. Pattern Recognition, 36 (2003) 845-847.

19. Chen, W.S., Yuen, P.C., Huang, J., Dai, D.Q.: Kernel machine-based one-parameter regularized Fisher Discriminant method for face recognition. IEEE Trans. Systems, Man, and Cybernetics-B, 35 (2005) 659-669.

20. Pima, I. Aladjem, M.: Regularized discriminant analysis for face recognition. Pattern Recognition, 37 (2004) 1945-1948.

21. Hoffbeck, J.P., Landgrebe, D.A.: Covariance matrix estimation and classification with limited training data. IEEE Trans. Pattern Analysis and Machine Intelligence, 18 (1996) 763–767.

22. Thomaz, C.E., Gillies, D.F., Feitosa, R.Q.: A new covariance estimate for Bayesian classifier in biometrics recognition. IEEE Trans. Circuits and Systems for Video Technology, 14 (2004) 214-223.

23. Pratt, W.K.: Digital Image Processing. 2nd edn. Wiley, New York (1991).

24. Yang, J., Yang, J.Y., Zhang, D.: What's wrong with Fisher criterion. Pattern recognition, 35 (2002) 2665-2668.

25. Xu, Y., Yang, J.Y., Jin, Z.: Theory analysis on FSLDA and ULDA. Pattern recognition, 36 (2003) 3031-3033.

26. Jin, Z., Yang, J.Y., Hu, Z.S., Lou, Z.: Face recognition based on the uncorrelated discriminant transform. Pattern recognition, 34 (2001) 1405-1416.

27. Philips, P.J., Moon, H., Rizvi, S.A., Rauss, P.J.: The FERET evaluation methodology for face-recognition algorithms. IEEE Trans. Pattern Analysis and Machine Intelligence, 22 (2000) 1090-1104.

Linear Programming for Matching in Human Body Gesture Recognition

Hao Jiang, Ze-Nian Li, and Mark S. Drew

School of Computing Science, Simon Fraser University,
Burnaby, BC, Canada V5A 1S6
{hjiangb, li, mark}@cs.sfu.ca

Abstract. We present a novel human body gesture recognition method using a linear programming based matching scheme. Instead of attempting to segment an object from the background, we develop a novel successive convexification linear programming method to locate the target by searching for the best matching region based on a graph template. The linear programming based matching scheme generates relatively dense matching patterns and thus presents a key feature for robust object matching and human body gesture recognition. By matching distance transformations of edge maps, the proposed scheme is able to match figures with large appearance changes. We further present gesture recognition methods based on the similarity of the exemplar with the matching target. Experiments show promising results for recognizing human body gestures in cluttered environments.

1 Introduction

Human body gesture recognition has attracted a lot of interest in recent years because of its potential important applications in surveillance, human-computer interaction and computer animation. Recognizing body gestures is also a challenging problem because of articulated motion of human limbs and bodies and large appearance variations such as the changes of clothing.

In this paper, we study problems where only a single camera is available. We present a gesture recognition method based on a novel linear programming (LP) matching scheme. The proposed LP scheme can be used to solve large scale L_1 metric labeling problems. Target matching in gesture recognition can be formulated as this subclass of labeling problems. Different from standard matching schemes such as the graph cut and belief propagation, the proposed LP relaxation method represents a label space with a much smaller set of basis labels, and is thus more suited for very large label set matching problems. A successive convexification scheme is proposed to solve the labeling problem. Iteratively, the trust region shrinks based on previous relaxation solution and the approximation becomes more accurate when the trust region becomes small. A new aspect of the algorithm is that the cost function is replaced by the lower convex hull at each stage — we re-convexify the cost, while focusing increasingly closely on the global solution. This is novel. The proposed multi-stage relaxation method is found to be more efficient than schemes such as the graph cut or belief propagation for the object matching problem where a large searching range is involved. It can also solve problems

W. Zhao, S. Gong, and X. Tang (Eds.): AMFG 2005, LNCS 3723, pp. 392–406, 2005.

for which traditional schemes fail. Based on the matching scheme, we propose a gesture recognition method which has the following properties: (1) The method works for cases when reliable background subtraction is unavailable, e.g., for still images; (2) It is quite insensitive to the clothing of the figures in the image. In this paper, local features are used because they have less variation than human parts and are therefore more reliable in matching. Unlike global shape features such as shape context [7], local features also enable the proposed scheme to be applicable to matching problems in cluttered environments. To suppress the influence of appearance changes for humans, we propose to match the distance transformations of the edge maps of the template and target images. This representation makes matching figures in different clothing possible. We further present a method to quantify the similarity of the template and the target object and form a reliable gesture recognition system.

Different schemes have been studied for recognizing human body gestures. Background subtraction has been used in gesture recognition. The difficulty with this scheme is that background subtraction is not robust and not always available, and the method cannot distinguish gestures when body parts are covered by silhouettes. One method to solve the problem is by extracting range data for the character in the scene using multiple cameras [1]. But such an approach is more expensive to deploy than monocular systems. A body-part based matching model [2] is presented for human body gesture recognition. As an extension, an SVM body-part matching method [3] is further presented. Mori [4] presents a segmentation based approach for part-based human body gesture recognition. Another method is to match the target as a whole, e.g. the Chamfer matching based method [5] in which tree structured binary templates are used to detect pedestrians. One shortcoming of this approach is that it usually needs many more templates than part-based schemes. Shape matching methods have also been applied for recognition of human actions [6][7]. Shape matching based methods usually need many fewer templates than the Chamfer matching scheme because the template deforms. These schemes work best in relatively clean background settings.

Object matching can be represented as a consistent labeling problem, and is essential for gesture recognition. Consistent labeling is NP-hard in general. Apart from a few cases in which polynomial algorithms are available, approximation algorithms are preferred for image matching. Much effort has been made to study efficient algorithms for these problems. Relaxation labeling (RL) [14] uses local search, and therefore relies on a good initialization process. ICM – Iterative Conditional Modes [9], another widely applied method for solving labeling problem, is greedy and is found to be easily trapped in a local minimum. In recent years, graph cut (GC) [11] and belief propagation (BP) [10] have become popular methods for solving consistent labeling problems. GC and BP are more robust than traditional labeling schemes and are also found to be faster than the traditional stochastic annealing methods. But GC and BP are still very complex for large scale problems that involve a large number of labels. Spectral graph theory based methods [15] have also been studied for matching. The work most related to our proposed scheme are the mathematical programming matching schemes. The early RL methods belong to this class. One of the big challenges in designing mathematical programming based labeling algorithms is to overcome local minima in the optimization process. Different schemes have been proposed. Deterministic annealing schemes [12] have been successfully applied to matching point sets. Convex programming is another scheme for labeling problems. Up to now, methods such as quadratic programming and semidefinite programming can only be applied to small scale problems. Because of its efficiency, linear programming has been successfully applied in vision problems, e.g. estimating motion of rigid scenes [17]. A linear programming formulation [16] is presented for uniform labeling problems and approximating general problems by tree metrics. Another general LP scheme, studied in [13], is similar to the linear relaxation labeling formulation [14]. This LP formulation is found to be only applicable to small problems because of the large number of constraints and variables involved.

2   Gesture Estimation with Matching

In this section, we present a scheme for estimating human body gestures based on visual pattern matching using linear programming. First, we present our novel linear programming matching method, which forms the key component for gesture recognition. Then, we study gesture recognition based on similarity measures.

2.1   Matching by Linear Programming

In L_1 metric space, matching can be stated in general as the following consistent labeling problem:

$$\min_{\mathbf{f}} \varepsilon : \sum_{\mathbf{s} \in S} c(\mathbf{s}, \mathbf{f_s}) + \sum_{\{\mathbf{p}, \mathbf{q}\} \in \mathcal{N}} \lambda_{\mathbf{p}, \mathbf{q}} \|\mathbf{f_p} - \mathbf{f_q}\|$$

in which $c(\mathbf{s}, \mathbf{f}_s)$ is the cost of assigning label $\mathbf{f_s}$ to site $\mathbf{s}$; $\|.\|$ is the L_1 norm and $\mathbf{f}$ are labels defined in L_1 metric space; S is a finite set of sites; $\mathcal{N}$ is the set of non-ordered neighbor site pairs; $\lambda_{\mathbf{p}, \mathbf{q}}$ are smoothing coefficients. In the following discussion, we assume that both S and label sets $\mathcal{L}_\mathbf{s}$ are discrete and $\mathbf{f}$ are 2D vectors. The proposed method can be easily extended to cases where labels have higher dimensionality. We can always convert a discrete labeling problem into a continuous one using the following procedure. First, we interpolate the costs $c(\mathbf{s}, \mathbf{f_s})$ for each site piecewise-linearly such that $c(\mathbf{s}, \mathbf{f_s})$ become surfaces; then we extend the feasible region for $\mathbf{f}$ to the convex hull supported by the discrete labels. The new problem is defined as *continuous extension* of the original discrete problem. To simplify notation, we also use $c(\mathbf{s}, \mathbf{f}_s)$ to represent the continuous extension cost function.

2.2   Approximation by Linear Programing

The above energy optimization problem is nonlinear and usually non-convex, which makes it difficult to solve in this original form without a good initialization process. We now show how to approximate the problem by a linear programming via linear approximation and variable relaxation as outlined in [8] by Jiang et al. To linearize the first term, the following scheme is applied. A basis $\mathcal{B}_\mathbf{s}$ is selected for the labels of each site $\mathbf{s}$. Then the label $\mathbf{f_s}$ can be represented as a linear combination of the label basis as $\mathbf{f_s} = \sum_{\mathbf{j} \in \mathcal{B}_\mathbf{s}} \xi_{\mathbf{s}, \mathbf{j}} \cdot \mathbf{j}$, where $\xi_{\mathbf{s}, \mathbf{j}}$ are real valued weighing coefficients. The labeling cost of $\mathbf{f_s}$ can then be approximated by the linear combination of the basis labeling costs $c(\mathbf{s}, \sum_{j \in \mathcal{B}_s} \xi_{\mathbf{s},j} \cdot \mathbf{j}) \approx \sum_{j \in \mathcal{B}_s} \xi_{\mathbf{s},j} \cdot c(\mathbf{s}, \mathbf{j})$. We also further set constraints $\xi_{\mathbf{s},j} \geq 0$ and $\sum_{j \in \mathcal{B}_s} \xi_{\mathbf{s},j} = 1$ for each site $\mathbf{s}$. Clearly, if $\xi_{\mathbf{s},j}$ are constrained to be 1 or 0, and the basis contains all the labels, i.e., $\mathcal{B}_s = \mathcal{L}_s$, the above representation becomes exact. Note that $\mathbf{f_s}$ are *not* constrained to the basis labels, but can be any convex combination. To linearize the regularity terms in the nonlinear formulation we can represent a free variable by the difference of two nonnegative auxiliary variables and introduce the summation of the auxiliary variables into the objective function. If the problem is properly formulated, when the linear programming problem is optimized the summation will approach the absolute value of the free variable.

Based on this linearization process, a linear programming approximation of the problem can be stated as

$$\min \sum_{\mathbf{s} \in S} \sum_{j \in \mathcal{B}_s} c(\mathbf{s}, \mathbf{j}) \cdot \xi_{\mathbf{s},j} + \sum_{\{\mathbf{p},\mathbf{q}\} \in \mathcal{N}} \lambda_{\mathbf{p},\mathbf{q}} \sum_{m=1}^{2} (f_{\mathbf{p},\mathbf{q},m}^{+} + f_{\mathbf{p},\mathbf{q},m}^{-})$$

$$s.t. \quad \sum_{j \in \mathcal{B}_s} \xi_{\mathbf{s},j} = 1, \forall \mathbf{s} \in S$$

$$\sum_{j \in \mathcal{B}_s} \xi_{\mathbf{s},j} \cdot \phi_m(\mathbf{j}) = f_{\mathbf{s},m}, \ \forall \mathbf{s} \in S, m = 1, 2$$

$$f_{\mathbf{p},m} - f_{\mathbf{q},m} = f_{\mathbf{p},\mathbf{q},m}^{+} - f_{\mathbf{p},\mathbf{q},m}^{-}, \forall \{\mathbf{p}, \mathbf{q}\} \in \mathcal{N}$$

$$\xi_{\mathbf{s},j}, f_{\mathbf{p},\mathbf{q},m}^{+}, f_{\mathbf{p},\mathbf{q},m}^{-} \geq 0$$

where $\mathbf{f_s} = (f_{\mathbf{s},1}, f_{\mathbf{s},2})$. It is not difficult to show that either $f_{\mathbf{p},\mathbf{q},m}^{+}$ or $f_{\mathbf{p},\mathbf{q},m}^{-}$ will become zero and thus $f_{\mathbf{p},\mathbf{q},m}^{+} + f_{\mathbf{p},\mathbf{q},m}^{-} = |f_{\mathbf{p},m} - f_{\mathbf{q},m}|$ when the linear program is optimized. Therefore, the linear programming formulation is equivalent to the general nonlinear formulation if the linearization assumption $c(\mathbf{s}, \sum_{j \in \mathcal{B}_s} \xi_{\mathbf{s},j} \cdot \mathbf{j}) = \sum_{j \in \mathcal{B}_s} \xi_{\mathbf{s},j} \cdot c(\mathbf{s}, \mathbf{j})$ holds. In general situations, the linear programming formulation is an approximation of the original nonlinear optimization problem.

Property 1: If $\mathcal{B}_s = \mathcal{L}_s$, and *the cost function of its continuous extension* $c(\mathbf{s}, \mathbf{j})$ *is convex*, $\forall \mathbf{s} \in S$ *, the LP exactly solves the continuous extension of the discrete labeling problem.* $\mathcal{L}_s$ is the label set of $\mathbf{s}$.

Proof: We just need to show when LP is optimized, the configuration $\{\mathbf{f_s^*} = \sum_{j \in \mathcal{B}_s} \xi_{\mathbf{s},j}^* \cdot \mathbf{j}\}$ also solves the continuous extension of the nonlinear problem. Since $c(\mathbf{s}, \mathbf{j})$ is convex, $\sum_{j \in \mathcal{L}_s} c(\mathbf{s}, \mathbf{j}) \xi_{\mathbf{s},j}^* \geq c(\mathbf{s}, \mathbf{f_s^*})$. And, when the LP is minimized we have $\sum_{\{\mathbf{p},\mathbf{q}\} \in \mathcal{N}} \lambda_{\mathbf{p},\mathbf{q}} \sum_{m=1}^{2} (f_{\mathbf{p},\mathbf{q},m}^{+} + f_{\mathbf{p},\mathbf{q},m}^{-}) = \sum_{\{\mathbf{p},\mathbf{q}\} \in \mathcal{N}} \lambda_{\mathbf{p},\mathbf{q}} || \mathbf{f_p^*} - \mathbf{f_q^*} ||$. Therefore

$$\min \sum_{\mathbf{s} \in S, j \in \mathcal{L}_s} c(\mathbf{s}, \mathbf{j}) \xi_{\mathbf{s},j} + \sum_{\{\mathbf{p},\mathbf{q}\} \in \mathcal{N}} \lambda_{\mathbf{p},\mathbf{q}} \sum_{m=1}^{2} (f_{\mathbf{p},\mathbf{q},m}^{+} + f_{\mathbf{p},\mathbf{q},m}^{-})$$

$$\geq \sum_{\mathbf{s} \in S} c(\mathbf{s}, \mathbf{f_s^*}) + \sum_{\{\mathbf{p},\mathbf{q}\} \in \mathcal{N}} \lambda_{\mathbf{p},\mathbf{q}} || \mathbf{f_p^*} - \mathbf{f_q^*} ||$$

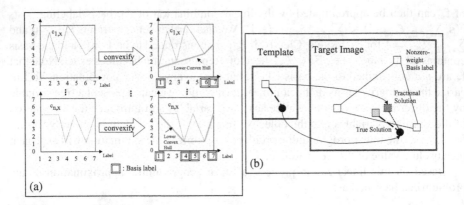

Fig. 1. (a): The convexification process introduced by LP relaxation. (b): An example when the single LP relaxation produces a fractional labeling.

According to the definition of *continuous extension*, $\mathbf{f_s^*}$ are feasible solutions of continuous extension of the non-linear problem. Therefore the optimum of the linear programming problem is not less than the optimum of the continuous extension of the nonlinear problem. On the other hand, it is easy to construct a feasible solution of LP that achieves the minimum of the continuous extension of the nonlinear problem. The property follows.

In practice, the cost function $c(\mathbf{s}, \mathbf{j})$ is usually highly non-convex for each site $\mathbf{s}$. In this situation, the proposed linear programming model approximates the original non-convex problem by a convex programming problem.

Property 2: *For general cost function* $c(\mathbf{s}, \mathbf{j})$, *if* $\mathcal{B}_\mathbf{s} = \mathcal{L}_\mathbf{s}$, $\forall \mathbf{s} \in S$, *the linear programming formulation solves the continuous extension of the reformulated discrete labeling problem, with* $c(\mathbf{s}, \mathbf{j})$ *replaced by its lower convex hull for each site* $\mathbf{s}$.

Its proof is similar to Property 1, by replacing $c(\mathbf{s}, \mathbf{j})$ in the non-linear function with its lower convex hull. Fig. 1(a) illustrates the convexification effect introduced by LP relaxation.

Property 3: *For general cost function* $c(\mathbf{s}, \mathbf{j})$, *the most compact basis set* $\mathcal{B}_\mathbf{s}$ *contains the vertex coordinates of the lower convex hull of* $c(\mathbf{s}, \mathbf{j})$, $\forall \mathbf{s} \in S$.

By Property 3, there is no need to include all the labeling assignment costs in the optimization: we only need to include those corresponding to the basis labels. This is one of the key steps to speed up the algorithm.

Property 4: *If the lower convex hull of the cost function* $c(\mathbf{s}, \mathbf{j})$ *is strictly convex, nonzero weighting basis labels must be "adjacent".*

Proof: Here "adjacent" means the convex hull of the nonzero weighting basis labels cannot contain other basis labels. Assume this does not hold for a site $\mathbf{s}$, and the nonzero weighting basis labels are $\mathbf{j}_{l_k}$, $k = 1..K$. Then, there is a basis label $\mathbf{j}_r$ located inside the convex hull of $\mathbf{j}_k$, $k = 1..K$. Thus, $\exists \alpha_k$ such that $\mathbf{j}_r = \sum_{k=1}^{K} \alpha_k \mathbf{j}_k$ and $\sum_{k=1}^{K} \alpha_k = 1$,

$\alpha_k \geq 0$. According to *Karush-Kuhn-Tucker Condition (KKTC)*, there exists $\lambda_1, \lambda_2, \lambda_3$ and $\mu_{\mathbf{j}}$ such that

$c(\mathbf{s}, \mathbf{j}) + \lambda_1 + \lambda_2\phi_1(\mathbf{j}) + \lambda_3\phi_2(\mathbf{j}) - \mu_{\mathbf{j}} = 0$ and $\xi_{\mathbf{s},\mathbf{j}}\mu_{\mathbf{j}} = 0, \mu_{\mathbf{j}} \geq 0, \forall \mathbf{j} \in \mathcal{B}_{\mathbf{s}}$

Therefore we have,

$c(\mathbf{s}, \mathbf{j}_k) + \lambda_1 + \lambda_2\phi_1(\mathbf{j}_k) + \lambda_3\phi_2(\mathbf{j}_k) = 0, k = 1..K$

$c(\mathbf{s}, \mathbf{j}_r) + \lambda_1 + \lambda_2\phi_1(\mathbf{j}_r) + \lambda_3\phi_2(\mathbf{j}_r) \geq 0$

On the other hand,

$c(\mathbf{s}, \mathbf{j}_r) + \lambda_1 + \lambda_2\phi_1(\mathbf{j}_r) + \lambda_3\phi_2(\mathbf{j}_r)$

$= c(\mathbf{s}, \sum_{k=1}^{K} \alpha_k\mathbf{j}_k) + \lambda_1 + \lambda_2\phi_1(\sum_{k=1}^{K} \alpha_k\mathbf{j}_k) + \lambda_3\phi_2(\sum_{k=1}^{K} \alpha_k\mathbf{j}_k)$

$< \sum_{k=1}^{K} \alpha_k c(\mathbf{s}, \mathbf{j}_k) + \lambda_1 + \lambda_2 \sum_{k=1}^{K} \alpha_k\phi_1(\mathbf{j}_k) + \lambda_3 \sum_{k=1}^{K} \alpha_k\phi_2(\mathbf{j}_k) = 0$

which contradicts the *KKTC*. The property follows.

After the convexification process, the original non-convex optimization problem turns into a convex problem and an efficient linear programming method can be used to yield a global optimal solution for the approximation problem. Note that, although this is a convex problem, a standard local optimization scheme is found to work poorly because of quantization noise and large flat areas in the convexified objective function.

Approximating the matching cost by its lower convex hull is also intuitively attractive since in the ideal case, the true matching will have the lowest matching cost and thus the optimization becomes exact in this case. In real applications, several target points may have equal matching cost and, even worse, some incorrect matching may have lower costs. In this case, because of the convexification process, in a one-step relaxation, the resulting fractional labeling could be not exactly the true solution, as shown in the Fig 1(b). In this simple image matching example, there are 2 sites in the source image and we construct a simple 2-node graph template. There are 5 target points in the target image. In the example, labels are the displacement vectors. We assume that a white rectangle will match a white rectangle with zero cost. And the circles will match with zero cost. Matching between different shape points has large matching cost. The light gray rectangle is in fact the true target for the white one in the source image, but the match cost is a very small positive number because of noisy measurement. By solving the LP relaxation problem, we get a fractional solution as illustrated in Fig 1(b) that has zero cost for LP's objective function but is not the true solution. Adjusting the smoothing parameter will not help because it already achieves the minimal zero cost. A traditional rounding scheme will try to round ξ into 0 and 1. Unfortunately, the rounding will drive the solution even farther from the true solution, in which the rectangle template node will match one of the white points in the target image. Intuitively, we can shrink the searching region for each site based on the current LP solution, and do a further search by solving a new LP problem in the smaller trust region. In the following section, we expand this idea and propose a successive convexification scheme to improve the approximation iteratively.

2.3 Successive Convexification Linear Programming

Here we propose a successive convexification linear programming method to solve the non-linear optimization problem, in which we construct linear programming recursively based on the previous searching result and gradually shrink the matching trust region systematically.

Assume $\mathcal{B}_s^n$ to be the basis label set for site s at stage n linear programming. The trust region $\mathcal{U}_s^n$ of site s is determined by the previous relaxation solution $\mathbf{f}_s^{n-1} = (f_{s,1}^{n-1}, f_{s,2}^{n-1})$, and a trust region diameter d_n. We define $\mathcal{Q}_s^n = \mathcal{L}_s \cap \mathcal{U}_s^n$. $\mathcal{B}_s^n$ is specified by $\mathcal{B}_s^n = \{$the vertex coordinates of the lower convex hull of $\{c(\mathbf{s},\mathbf{j}), \forall \mathbf{j} \in \mathcal{Q}_s^n\}\}$, where $c(\mathbf{s},\mathbf{j})$ is the cost of assigning label $\mathbf{j}$ to site s.

Algorithm 1. Successive Convexification Linear Programming
1. *Set $n = 0$; Set initial diameter $= d_0$;*
2. *FOREACH$(\mathbf{s} \in S)$*
3. *{ Calculate the cost function $\{c(\mathbf{s},\mathbf{j}), \forall \mathbf{j} \in \mathcal{Q}_s^0\}$;*
4. *Convexify $\{c(\mathbf{s},\mathbf{j})\}$ and find basis $\mathcal{B}_s^0$; }*
5. *Construct and solve $\mathcal{LP}_0$;*
6. *WHILE ($n \leq N$ and $d_n \geq 1$)*
7. *{ $n \leftarrow n+1$;*
8. *$d_n = d_{n-1} - \delta_n$;*
9. *FOREACH$(\mathbf{s} \in S)$*
10. *{ IF ($\mathcal{Q}_s^n$ is empty) $\{\mathcal{Q}_s^n = \mathcal{Q}_s^{n-1}; \mathcal{U}_s^n = \mathcal{U}_s^{n-1}; \}$*
11. *ELSE update $\mathcal{U}_s^n$, $\mathcal{Q}_s^n$;*
12. *Reconvexify $\{c(\mathbf{s},\mathbf{j})\}$ and relocate basis $\mathcal{B}_s^n$; }*
13. *Construct and solve $\mathcal{LP}_n$; }*
14. *Output $\mathbf{f}_s^*, \forall \mathbf{s} \in S$;*

Notice that the relaxed LP gives the lower bound of the original problem; It is easy to verify that the necessary condition for successive LP approaching the global minimum is $\mathcal{LP}_n \leq \mathcal{E}^*, n = 0..N$, where $\mathcal{E}^*$ is the global minimum of the non-linear problem. Since the global minimum of the function is unknown, we estimate an upper bound $\mathcal{E}^+$ of $\mathcal{E}^*$ in the iterative process. The configuration of labels that achieves the upper bound $\mathcal{E}^+$ is composed of *anchors* — an anchor is defined as the control point of the trust region for the next iteration. We keep the anchor in the new trust region for each site and shrink the boundary inwards. If the anchor is on the boundary of the previous trust region, other boundaries are moved inwards. A simple scheme is to select anchors as the solution of the previous LP, $\mathbf{r}_s = \mathbf{f}_s^{(n-1)}$. Unfortunately, in the worse case, this simple scheme has solution whose objective function is arbitrarily far from the optimum. In fact, the fractional solution could be far away from the discrete label site. To solve the problem, we present a deterministic rounding process by checking the discrete labels and selecting the anchor that minimizes the non-linear objective function, given the configuration of fractional matching labels defined by the solution of the current stage. This step is similar to a single iteration of an ICM algorithm. In this step, we project a fractional solution into the discrete space. We call the new rounding selection scheme a *consistent rounding* process. Except for $\mathcal{LP}_1$, we further require that new anchors have energy not greater than the previous estimation: the anchors are updated only if new ones have smaller energy. The objective function for $\mathcal{LP}_n$ must be less than or equal to $\mathcal{E}^+$. This iterative procedure guarantees that the objective function of the proposed multi-step scheme is at least as good as a single relaxation scheme. In the following example, we use a simple scalar labeling problem to illustrate the solution procedure.

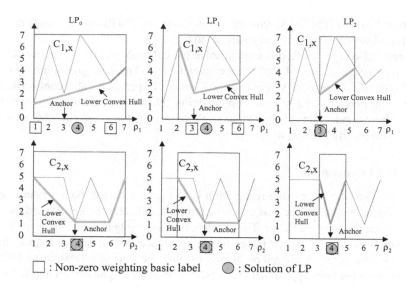

Fig. 2. Successive convexification LP

Example 1. (A scalar labeling problem): Assume there are two sites $\{1,2\}$ and for each site the label set is $\{1..7\}$. The objective function is $\min_{\{\rho_1,\rho_2\}} c(1,\rho_1) + c(2,\rho_2) + \lambda |\rho_1 - \rho_2|$. In this example we assume that $\{c(1,j)\} = \{1.1\ 6\ 2\ 7\ 5\ 3\ 4\}$, $\{c(2,j)\} = \{5\ 5\ 5\ 1\ 5\ 1\ 5\}$ and $\lambda = 0.5$.

Based on the proposed scheme, the problem is solved by the sequential LPs: $\mathcal{LP}_0$, $\mathcal{LP}_1$ and $\mathcal{LP}_2$. In $\mathcal{LP}_0$ the trust regions of sites 1 and 2 are both $[1,7]$. Constructing $\mathcal{LP}_0$ based on the proposed scheme corresponds to solving an approximated problem in which $\{c(1,j)\}$ and $\{c(2,j)\}$ are replaced by their lower convex hulls respectively (see Fig. 2). Step $\mathcal{LP}_0$ uses basis labels $\{1,6,7\}$ for site 1 and basis labels $\{1, 4, 6, 7\}$ for site 2. $\mathcal{LP}_0$ finds solution $\xi_{1,1} = 0.4, \xi_{1,6} = 0.6, \xi_{1,7} = 0, \rho_1 = (0.4*1+0.6*6) = 4$; and $\xi_{2,4} = 1$, $\xi_{2,1} = \xi_{2,6} = \xi_{2,7} = 0$, $\rho_2 = 4$. Based on the proposed rules for anchor selection, we fix site 2 with fractional label 4 obtained by solving $\mathcal{LP}_0$, and search the best label for site 1 in the region $[1,7]$ using the non-linear objective function; we get the *anchor* 3 for site 1. Using similar method, we fix site 1 with its fractional label 4 and search the best label for site 2, and we get its anchor 4. At this stage, using anchor labels we get $\mathcal{E}^+ = c(1,3) + c(2,4) + 0.5 * |3 - 4| = 3.5$. Further, the trust region of $\mathcal{LP}_1$ is $[2,6]$ for site 1 and $[2,6]$ for site 2 by shrinking the previous trust region diameter by 2. The solution of $\mathcal{LP}_1$ is $\rho_1 = 4$ and $\rho_2 = 4$. The anchor is 3 for site 1 and 4 for site 2 with $\mathcal{E}^+ = 3.5$. Based on $\mathcal{LP}_1$, $\mathcal{LP}_2$ has new trust region $[3,5] \times [3,5]$ and its solution is $\rho_1 = 3$ and $\rho_2 = 4$. Since LP achieves the upper bound 3.5 in the trust region, there is no need to further shrink the trust region and the iteration terminates. It is not difficult to verify that the configuration $\rho_1 = 3$, $\rho_2 = 4$ achieves the global minimum. Fig. 2 illustrates the proposed successive convexification process method for this example.

Interestingly, for the above example ICM or even the graph cut scheme only finds a local minimum if initial values are not correctly set. For ICM, if ρ_2 is set to 6 and the updating is from ρ_1, the iteration will fall into a local minimum corresponding to

$\rho_1 = 6$ and $\rho_2 = 6$. The GC scheme based on α-expansion will have the same problem if the initial values of both ρ_1 and ρ_2 are set to 6.

A revised simplex method is used to solve the LP problem. Therefore, an estimate of the average complexity of successive convexification linear programming is $O(|S| \cdot |Q|^{1/2} \cdot (\log |Q| + \log |S|))$, where Q is the label set. Experiments also confirm that the average complexity of the proposed optimization scheme increases more slowly with the searching window size than previous methods such as the graph cut scheme, whose average complexity is linear with respect to $|Q|$.

2.4   Model Generation

The basic idea of body gesture recognition is to match a human body gesture image with different templates; The best matching template indicates the gesture and location of the human object in the image. The problem is challenging because we do not have a segmentation mask in the target image, and therefore we have to deal with strong background clutters. Another difficult problem is to make the algorithm resistant to different clothing and other large appearance changes. For gesture recognition problems, the features selected for the matching process must be insensitive to appearance changes of human objects. The edge map contains all the shape information of an object, and at the same time is not sensitive to color changes. Edge features have been widely applied in Chamfer matching schemes [5]. We propose the use of small blocks, centered on the edge pixels, of the *distance transform* of an image's edge map as the matching feature. A distance transform converts a binary edge map into its corresponding grayscale representation, where the intensity of a pixel is proportional to its distance to the nearest edge pixel. Denoting the square block of the distance transform of I's edge map centered at the edge pixel $\mathbf{x}$ as $\mathbf{d_x}(I)$, the cost of matching is defined as

$$C_{\mathbf{x},\mathbf{y}} = \frac{1}{\Delta^2 \sqrt{\sigma_\mathbf{x} \sigma_\mathbf{y}}} \|\mathbf{d_x}(I_s) - \mathbf{d_y}(I_t)\|$$

where I_s and I_t are the template and target images respectively; $\|.\|$ is the cityblock norm in this paper; $\sigma_\mathbf{x}$ and $\sigma_\mathbf{y}$ are the standard deviations of $\mathbf{d_x}(I_s)$ and $\mathbf{d_y}(I_t)$ respectively; Δ is the size of the square block. The orientation information is now integrated in the proposed feature. For instance, there is now a big difference for two features on orthogonal edges. In this paper, the features are randomly selected on the edges of the template. The neighboring relation $\mathcal{N}$ is defined by the edges of the graph generated by Delaunay triangulation of the feature points on the template. In this problem, source set S contains the feature points on the template, and labels are the displacement vectors of target points to each feature point on the template. Therefore, $c(\mathbf{s}, \mathbf{f_s})$ in the optimization problem equal $C_{\mathbf{s}, \mathbf{f_s}+\mathbf{s}}$.

2.5   Similarity Measures

After finding the matches of the feature points in the template with corresponding points in the target image based on the proposed method, we need to further decide how similar these two constellations of matched points are and whether the matching result corresponds to the same event as in the exemplar. We use the following quantities to measure the difference between the template and the matching object. The first measure is D, defined as the average of pairwise length changes from the template to the target. To compensate for the global deformation, a global affine transform $\mathcal{A}$ is first estimated based on the matching and then applied to the template points before calculating D. D is further normalized with respect to the average edge length of the template. The second measure is the average warped template matching cost M, which is defined as the average absolute difference of the target image distance transform and the warped reference image distance transform in the region of interest. The warping is based on cubic spline. The total matching cost is simply defined as $M + \alpha D$, where α has a typical value from 0.1 to 0.5. Experiments show that only about 100 randomly selected feature points are needed in calculating D and M.

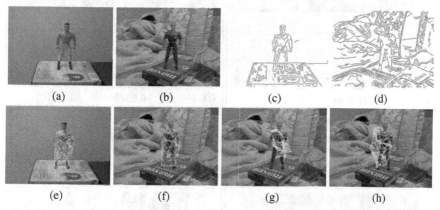

(a)   (b)   (c)   (d)

(e)   (f)   (g)   (h)

Fig. 3. An example where traditional methods fail. (a): Template image; (b): Target image; (c): Edge map of template image; (d): Edge map of target image; (e): Template mesh; (f): Matching result of the proposed scheme; (g): ICM matching result; (h): Graph cut matching result.

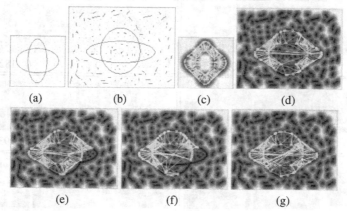

(a)   (b)   (c)   (d)

(e)   (f)   (g)

Fig. 4. Binary to grayscale. (a, b): Template image and target image. (c): Template model showing distance transform; (d): Matching result of proposed scheme; (e): Matching result by GC; (f): Matching result by ICM. (g): Matching result by BP.

Fig. 5. Testing images and their top two matches from four body gestures

(a) Gesture recognition result with template 1

(b) Gesture recognition result with template 2

(c) Gesture recognition result with template 3

Fig. 6. Matching result for Yoga images. The first image in each subfigure is the template and the rest are the top 17 candidate matching images. Numbers show the matching cost.

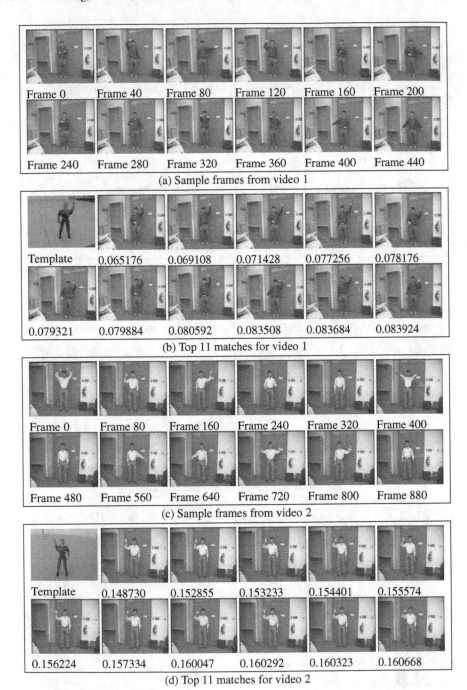

(a) Sample frames from video 1

(b) Top 11 matches for video 1

(c) Sample frames from video 2

(d) Top 11 matches for video 2

Fig. 7. Matching human gestures using flexible toy object template

3   Experimental Results

Fig. 3 shows the advantage of using our deformable matching scheme when we only have one template available. We try to match the distance transform of the template and target images. As shown in this example, greedy schemes such as ICM meet with great difficulty since there are a lot of ambiguities in matching distance transformation images. Comparing with the graph cut scheme, the proposed LP based method can solve the problem more robustly. Fig. 4 shows a comparison result using synthetic binary images. All the methods in the comparison use the same set of energy functions and parameter settings. With a 2.66GHz Pentium IV Linux machine, each LP iteration takes about 1 second for a problem with 100 nodes and 10000 target points. The typical number of iterations is 3 to 4 for most problems.

Fig. 5 shows body gesture recognition results using two articulated objects. Four body gestures are involved. A single template is generated for each gesture using the first object. The region of the object is set for the template object and about 100 features are randomly selected from the edge pixels automatically. Another object with different appearance is used for testing in different background settings. Distance transform images are used in matching to compensate for the appearance changes. A linear combination of the deformation measure D and the matching error M are used to form a matching score. We set the coefficient to be 0.1 for deformation D and unity for matching error M. Top two match candidates and their matching cost are shown in each of Figs. 5 (a) to (p). These experiments show that the proposed scheme can reliably match the target in complex background settings.

In another experiment, we study the following retrieval problem: we use a template image and retrieve the best match in an image data set. The data set is extracted from a video sequence. In this experiment, there is only one human object in the image. The search range is the whole target image. The template images and target images are extracted from different sections of the video, which have a large number of different body gestures and small number of similar body gestures. The character in the image has different clothing and somewhat different size in the template and target image. The test set contains 40 images with about 20 different gestures. Fig. 6 shows retrieval results for 3 different gestures. The matcher is reliable and all the correct matches are located in the first several best matches.

In Fig.7 we conducted experiments to test the performance of the proposed scheme in matching objects with large appearance differences. We use a toy as the template object and search for similar human body gestures in video sequences. Two sequences are used in testing. The first one shown in Fig.7 has 500 frames and the other has 1000 frames. There are fewer than 10% of true targets in the video sequence. The first sequence has a precision of 90% when the recall is 55%; Precision drops to 82% when recall goes up to 100%. The second sequence has a precision of 92% when the recall is 50%; Precision drops to 81% when recall reaches 100%.

4   Conclusion

We propose a novel linear programming method using successive convexification which is more efficient and effective than schemes such as the graph cut or belief propagation methods for the object matching problem where a large searching range is involved. It can also solve problems for which other schemes fail. As well, we propose using distance transformations of the edge maps to match the template and target images. This representation facilitates matching some types of objects with large appearance variations. Experiments show very promising results for human gesture detection in cluttered environments. In future work, we will extend this method to dynamic gesture and human activity recognition problems. The proposed scheme has the potential to be directly applied to general object recognition problems.

References

[1] K.M.G. Cheung, S. Baker, T. Kanade, "Shape-from-silhouette of articulated objects and its use for human body kinematics estimation and motion capture", CVPR, pp. I:77-84, 2003.
[2] P.F. Felzenszwalb, D.P. Huttenlocher, "Efficient matching of pictorial structures", CVPR, pp. II:66-73, 2000.
[3] R. Ronfard, C. Schmid, and B. Triggs, "Learning to parse pictures of people", ECCV, LNCS 2353, pp. 700-714, 2002.
[4] G. Mori, X. Ren, A. Efros, and J. Malik, "Recovering human body configurations: combining segmentation and recognition", CVPR, pp. II:326-333, 2004
[5] D. M. Gavrila and V. Philomin, "Real-time object detection for smart vehicles", ICCV, pp. 87-93, 1999.
[6] S. Carlsson and J. Sullivan, "Action recognition by shape matching to key frames", IEEE Computer Society Workshop on Models versus Exemplars in Computer Vision, 2001.
[7] G. Mori and J. Malik, "Estimating human body configurations using shape context matching", ECCV, LNCS 2352, pp. 666-680, 2002.
[8] H. Jiang, Z.N. Li, and M.S. Drew, "Optimizing motion estimation with linear programming and detail-preserving variational method", CVPR, pp. I:738-745, 2004.
[9] J. Besag, "On the statistical analysis of dirty pictures", J. R. Statis. Soc. Lond. B, 1986, Vol. 48, pp. 259-302.
[10] Y. Weiss and W.T. Freeman. "On the optimality of solutions of the max-product belief propagation algorithm in arbitrary graphs", IEEE Trans. on Information Theory, 47(2):723-735, 2001.
[11] Y. Boykov, O. Veksler, and R. Zabih, "Fast approximate energy minimization via graph cuts", PAMI, Vol.23, pp. 1222-1239, 2001.
[12] H. Chui and A. Rangarajan, "A new algorithm for non-rigid point matching", CVPR, vol. 2, pp. 44-51, 2000.
[13] C. Chekuri, S. Khanna, J. Naor, and L. Zosin, "Approximation algorithms for the metric labeling problem via a new linear programming formulation", Symp. on Discrete Algs. pp. 109-118, 2001.
[14] A. Rosenfeld, R.A. Hummel, and S.W. Zucker, "Scene labeling by relaxation operations," IEEE Trans. Systems, Man, and Cybernetics, vol. 6, no. 6, pp. 420-433, 1976.
[15] B. Luo and E.R. Hancock, "Structural matching using the em algorithm and singular value decomposition," PAMI, vol. 23, pp. 1120-1136, 2001.
[16] J. Kleinberg and E. Tardos. "Approximation algorithms for classification problems with pairwise relationships: Metric labeling and Markov random fields". IEEE FOCS, pages 14-23, 1999.
[17] M. Ben-Ezra, S. Peleg, and M. Werman, "Real-time motion analysis with linear programming", ICCV, pp. 703-709, 1999.

Combination of Projectional and Locational Decompositions for Robust Face Recognition

Fumihiko Sakaue and Takeshi Shakunaga

Department of Computer Science, Okayama University,
Okayama-shi, 700-8530, Japan
{sakaue, shaku}@chino.cs.okayama-u.ac.jp

Abstract. The present paper discusses a method for robust face recognition that works even when only one image is registered and the test image contains a lot of local noises. Two types of facial image decomposition are compared both theoretically and experimentally. That is, we consider both a projectional decomposition, in which images are decomposed into individuality and other components, and a locational decomposition, in which the effects of local noises are suppressed. These two decompositions are simple and powerful and can be applied in collaboration with one another. This collaboration can be realized in a straightforward manner because the decompositions are consistent with one another. They work in a complementary manner and provide better results than when the decompositions are used independently. Finally, we report experimental results obtained using three databases. These results indicate that the combination of projectional and locational decompositions works well, even when only one image is registered and the test images contain significant noise.

1 Introduction

The appearance of the human face changes according to the lighting conditions under which the facial image is captured. However, it is often difficult to control the lighting condition in natural environments. A face recognition algorithm should not be sensitive to the lighting condition in order to realize robust face recognition. Although an eigenface[1,2] can efficiently represent photometric changes, it cannot be constructed appropriately when too few images are available for registration. In this case, photo-insensitive information should be extracted from registered images. In other words, we should decompose the image into individuality and other information. This decomposition is referred to herein as projectional decomposition. This decomposition is a basic and important problem in not only face recognition but also pattern recognition.

Local noises, such as occlusions and shadows, are contained in images and affect the recognition method based on the eigenspace and projection onto the eigenspace. Several algorithms have been proposed[3,4] for robust recognition against various noises. Although these algorithms provide good projection even when an image includes local noises, a great deal of processing time is required.

W. Zhao, S. Gong, and X. Tang (Eds.): AMFG 2005, LNCS 3723, pp. 407–421, 2005.
© Springer-Verlag Berlin Heidelberg 2005

Alternatively, in another approach, the image is regarded as a set of small components [2,5,6,7]. This approach, referred to herein as locational decomposition, does not spread local noises to the entire image and thus can avoid the above-mentioned problem.

In the present paper, we propose a novel method for robust face recognition by combining projectional and locational decompositions. Since projectional and locational decompositions can be used simultaneously, this combination facilitates the realization of a face recognition algorithm that is robust with respect to noises.

2 Definitions

2.1 Normalized Eigenspace

In this section, we present basic definitions and the notation scheme used herein. Since the proposed method is based on eigenspace, this section deals mainly with the concept of eigenspace.

In the present study, all images are normalized as follows. Let an N-dimensional vector $\mathbf{X}$ denote an original image composed of N pixels, and let $\mathbf{1}$ denote an N-dimensional vector in which each element is 1. The normalized image $\mathbf{x}$ of an original image $\mathbf{X}$ is defined as $\mathbf{x} = \mathbf{X}/(\mathbf{1}^T\mathbf{X})$. After the normalization, $\mathbf{x}$ is normalized in the sense that $\mathbf{1}^T\mathbf{x} = 1$. An image space constructed by a set of normalized images is called the Normalized Image Space (NIS).

An eigenspace constructed by mean vector $\overline{\mathbf{x}}$ and m-principal eigenvectors Φ_m in NIS is described as $\langle\overline{\mathbf{x}}, \Phi_m\rangle$. In NIS, an image $\mathbf{x}$ is projected onto eigenspace $\langle\overline{\mathbf{x}}, \Phi_m\rangle$ by

$$\tilde{\mathbf{x}}^* = \tilde{\Phi}_m^+\mathbf{x},$$

where $\tilde{\Phi}_m = [\Phi_m \quad \overline{\mathbf{x}}]$ and $\tilde{\Phi}_m^+ = (\tilde{\Phi}_m^T\tilde{\Phi}_m)^{-1}\tilde{\Phi}_m^T$.

In order to measure the similarity between an input image $\mathbf{x}$ and the eigenspace $\langle\overline{\mathbf{x}}, \Phi_m\rangle$, we define a normalized correlation in terms of NIS, which can be defined by the cosine of an angle when an image $1/N$ is regarded as the origin of the NIS. That is, a normalized correlation C_I between $\mathbf{x}$ and $\langle\overline{\mathbf{x}}, \Phi_m\rangle$ is defined as

$$C_I = C(\mathbf{x}, \tilde{\Phi}_m\tilde{\mathbf{x}}^*) \tag{1}$$

where

$$C(\mathbf{x}, \mathbf{y}) = \frac{(\mathbf{x} - 1/N)^T(\mathbf{y} - 1/N)}{||\mathbf{x} - 1/N||^{1/2}||\mathbf{y} - 1/N)||^{1/2}}. \tag{2}$$

By this definition, a given image $\mathbf{x}$ can be evaluated in terms of NIS without explicit normalization.

2.2 Partial Projection

Let us define an indicator matrix P, which is an $N \times N$ diagonal matrix, each diagonal term of which is 1 or 0, which indicates whether the pixel is effective (1) or ineffective (0) for the projection. Then, $\mathbf{x}$ is partially projected onto $\langle \overline{\mathbf{x}}, \Phi_m \rangle$ with indicator matrix P by

$$\tilde{\mathbf{x}}_P^* = (P\tilde{\Phi}_m)^+ P\mathbf{x}, \qquad (3)$$

where $\tilde{\Phi}_m = [\Phi_m \ \overline{\mathbf{x}}]$ and $(P\tilde{\Phi}_m)^+ = (\tilde{\Phi}_m^T P\tilde{\Phi}_m)^{-1}(P\tilde{\Phi}_m)^T$. A partial residual is defined as

$$\tilde{\mathbf{x}}_P^\sharp = P(\mathbf{x} - \tilde{\Phi}_m \tilde{\mathbf{x}}_P^*). \qquad (4)$$

The last element of $\tilde{\mathbf{x}}_P^*$ is important and is denoted by β_P. β_P is equivalent to the total pixel values estimated by the partial projection. When the cigenspace cannot be constructed because only one image is available, we can regard the image as a 0-dimensional eigenspace. The normalized correlation C_I can be extended to span the partial projection. A partial correlation C_P between $\mathbf{x}$ and $\langle \overline{\mathbf{x}}, \Phi_m \rangle$ within a pixel set indicated by P is defined as

$$C_P = C(P\mathbf{x}, P\tilde{\Phi}_m \tilde{\mathbf{x}}_P^*). \qquad (5)$$

When P is an identity matrix, Eq. (5) is equivalent to Eq. (1).

3   Projectional Decompositions

3.1   Decomposition by Canonical Eigenspace

A facial image contains various types of information, such as head pose, lighting condition, and individuality. In face recognition, it is important to decompose the facial image into the *individuality* and the other information. In the present paper, we refer to this decomposition as a projectional decomposition. In this section, we discuss the projectional decomposition for face recognition.

Principal component analysis (PCA) reduces the dimension of the face space with little loss of representability [1]. Shakunaga and Shigenari[8] proposed an image decomposition by an eigenspace that is constructed from a lot of facial images taken under various lighting conditions. Their method is used as a projectional decomposition in the present paper. We consider an eigenspace constructed from a lot of facial images as the *canonical face space*. The eigenspace is referred to as the canonical space, or CS for short, and the images used for CS construction are referred to as the canonical set. Figure 1 shows examples of the CS. Information that cannot be represented in the CS is regarded as the *individuality*.

The canonical space can be used for decomposing a facial image into the canonical information and the individuality. The former is a projection onto CS, and the latter is the residual of the projection. They are orthogonal to each other.

Fig. 1. Example of CS: Mean vector (leftmost image) and four principal bases

Let $\langle \overline{\mathbf{x}}_{cs}, \Phi_{cs} \rangle$ denote CS. The projection of an image $\mathbf{x}$ onto CS is given by

$$\tilde{\mathbf{x}}^* = \tilde{\Phi}_{cs}^+ \mathbf{x},$$

where $\tilde{\Phi}_{cs} = [\Phi_{cs} \ \overline{\mathbf{x}}_{cs}]$. In the original image space, the projection $\tilde{\mathbf{x}}^*$ is described by

$$\mathbf{x}^\$ = \tilde{\Phi}_{cs} \tilde{\mathbf{x}}^*.$$

The residual $\mathbf{x}^\sharp$ is then expressed as

$$\mathbf{x}^\sharp = \mathbf{x} - \mathbf{x}^\$.$$

The decomposition of $\mathbf{x}$ into $\mathbf{x}^\$$ and $\mathbf{x}^\sharp$ is hereinafter referred to as CS decomposition.

Although the individuality may be represented by only the residual in an ideal environment, it is impossible to completely decompose an input image into the individuality and the other properties in an ordinary environment. Therefore, we simultaneously use both the projection and the residual for face recognition because they are complementary.

A face recognition algorithm is constructed in the conventional way using these two components. In the face registration stage, one eigenspace is constructed from a set of the projections and is denoted by $\langle \overline{\mathbf{x}}^\$, \Phi_m^\$ \rangle$. The other eigenspace is constructed from a set of the residuals and is denoted by $\langle \overline{\mathbf{x}}^\sharp, \Phi_m^\sharp \rangle$. In the recognition stage, a projection $\mathbf{x}^\$$ and a residual $\mathbf{x}^\sharp$ are evaluated independently by

$$C^\$ = C(\mathbf{x}^\$, \tilde{\Phi}_m^\$ \tilde{\Phi}_m^{\$+} \mathbf{x}^\$) \tag{6}$$

and

$$C^\sharp = C(\mathbf{x}^\sharp, \tilde{\Phi}_m^\sharp \tilde{\Phi}_m^{\sharp+} \mathbf{x}^\sharp). \tag{7}$$

Finally, the image $\mathbf{x}$ is evaluated by adding $C^\$$ to $C^\sharp$.

The similarity $C^\$$, calculated in CS, is a variation of the well known distance-in-feature-space [2]. However, the similarity $C^\sharp$ is definitely distinct from the distance-from-feature-space. In the distance-from-feature-space, all of the residual components are simply summed up to L2-norm. In contrast, the similarity

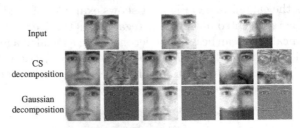

Fig. 2. Examples of CS decomposition and Gaussian decomposition: original images ($\mathbf{x}$) (top row), CS decomposition results ($\mathbf{x}^\$$ and $\mathbf{x}^\sharp$) (middle row), and Gaussian decomposition results ($\mathbf{x}_G^\$$ and $\mathbf{x}_G^\sharp$) (bottom row)

$C^{\sharp}$ is the similarity between the residual $\mathbf{x}^{\sharp}$ and the eigenspace $\langle \overline{\mathbf{x}}^{\sharp}, \varPhi_m^{\sharp} \rangle$ in CS. In other words, $C^{\sharp}$ is the "distance-in-another-feature-space."

Figure 2 shows three examples of the CS decomposition in which input images were not used for constructing CS. The left and center input images, which do not contain an occlusion, are appropriately projected onto CS. Therefore, they are properly decomposed. In the right image, however, an occlusion by a scarf affects both the projection and residual.

3.2   Decomposition by Gaussian Filter

Canonical space decomposition is useful when an appropriate learning set can be prepared for the CS construction. However, often, when a facial image is taken using a different camera under different conditions, CS may not properly decompose the image into the canonical information and the individuality. In addition, when a test image contains numerous noises, such as occlusions, the noises may affect the entire image upon projection onto CS. Furthermore, the test image should be aligned with CS before the CS decomposition. In order to avoid these problems, we consider an alternative method that does not use CS for the projectional decomposition.

Wang et al.[9] proposed a self-quotient image (SQI) that extracts the component that is insensitive to illumination. In their method, a Gaussian filter is used to extract lighting information. The Gaussian filter is used in the proposed method for the projectional decomposition. Let G denote an $N \times N$ matrix that works as the Gaussian filter. Then, the decomposition of image $\mathbf{x}$ into a Gaussian image $\mathbf{x}_G^{\$}$ and its residual $\mathbf{x}_G^{\sharp}$ by the Gaussian filter can be formulated as

$$\mathbf{x}_G^{\$} = G\mathbf{x} \qquad (8)$$

and

$$\mathbf{x}_G^{\sharp} = \mathbf{x} - \mathbf{x}_G^{\$}. \qquad (9)$$

Since the matrix G can be regarded as a projection matrix, $\mathbf{x}_G^{\$}$ can be regarded as a component of the Gaussian space. In this formulation, no a priori knowledge is necessary because $\mathbf{x}_G^{\$}$ can be calculated from only the input image. An input image is simply decomposed into the Gaussian image and its residual. This decomposition is referred to hereinafter as Gaussian decomposition. Figure 2 also shows three examples of Gaussian decomposition. Although the right input image includes an occlusion by a scarf, the effect of this occlusion does not spread to the entire image. [1]

---

[1] In the self-quotient image, each pixel value of the input image should be divided by the corresponding pixel in the Gaussian image in order to cancel the effect of illumination. In the proposed method, however, the Gaussian image is subtracted from the original image in order to calculate the residual. That is, the Gaussian image and the residual are regarded as approximations of illumination and individuality, respectively. This is an alternative method of calculating the self-quotient image, and the computational cost is lower than the self-quotient image because the residual can be calculated by subtraction rather than division.

4 Locational Decomposition

4.1 Parallel Partial Projections

When an input image contains local noises, such as shadows or occlusions, the noises affect the recognition results. First, in the most commonly used method, although images for face recognition are normalized by some method, when the image contains noises, the image cannot be properly normalized. Second, when we use an eigenspace, the effects of noises is spread to the entire image by the projection onto the eigenspace, affecting the face recognition results.

In order to avoid this problem, we utilize local information independently. In this section, we introduce a locational decomposition algorithm, which can utilize local information independently.

A framework of parallel partial projections (PPP) onto an eigenspace is proposed for face recognition under various lighting conditions[5]. This is one method for implementing the locational decomposition, and so local information is treated independently and the spread of noises is prevented. In the present paper, this method is used as the locational decomposition of the image.

Let us describe the j-th partial projection $\tilde{\mathbf{x}}_{P_j}^*$ onto an individual eigenspace $\langle \overline{\mathbf{x}}, \Phi_m \rangle$. Here, we consider a set of partial projections $\{\tilde{\mathbf{x}}_{P_1}^*, \cdots, \tilde{\mathbf{x}}_{P_M}^*\}$, where M is the number of parts indicated by P_j. This can be represented by the backprojected image, which can be calculated as

$$\mathbf{x}^{\$'} = \sum_{j=1}^{M} P_j \tilde{\Phi}_m \tilde{\mathbf{x}}_{P_j}^*.$$

In the discriminant function for PPP, we use a partial correlation. The (partial) correlation is essentially robust with respect to noises because it represents the cosine of the angle between two vectors. The image $\mathbf{x}$ is evaluated by

$$C' = \sum_{j=1}^{M} C(P_j \mathbf{x}, P_j \tilde{\Phi}_m \tilde{\mathbf{x}}_{P_j}^*), \tag{10}$$

where M is the number of P_j and $C(\mathbf{x}, \mathbf{y}) = \mathbf{x}^T \mathbf{y}/(\mathbf{x}^T \mathbf{x} \mathbf{y}^T \mathbf{y})^{1/2}$. Of course, PPP can be used not only for the eigenspace, but also for only one image. When only one image can be registered, the image is regarded as a 0-dimensional eigenspace consisting of the image.

The face recognition algorithm is summarized in Fig 3. Here, local noises are not spread by projection onto the eigenspace.

4.2 Division Scheme

In face recognition using the parallel partial projections, the indicator matrix P can be used to indicate an arbitrary area in the facial image. The image contains some characteristic points such as the eyes, nose and mouth. Several previously

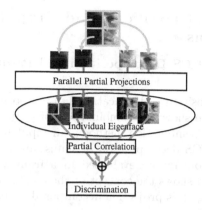

Fig. 3. Parallel partial projections for face recognition

proposed methods have used these characteristic points[2]. Although this method is effective, we do not use characteristic points in the proposed method because correctly determining an effective position for recognition is difficult. Therefore, points that are characteristic points from a human viewpoint may not be characteristic points from the viewpoint of a computer. Furthermore, when the proposed method is applied to the recognition of some other objects, proper characteristic points for the recognition are impossible to conceive of ahead of time.

Therefore, we do not herein consider the optimal placement of P. In the proposed method, images are divided into a set of squares, and experimental results, described later herein, show that the proposed method works well without optimal placement of P.

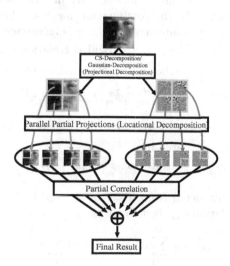

Fig. 4. Combination of projectional and locational decompositions

5   Combination of Locational and Projectional Decompositions

5.1   Combination of CS Decomposition and Parallel Partial Projections

A projectional decomposition and a locational decomposition can be combined in a simple manner. We show two combinations of projectional and locational decompositions. In the combination methods, an input image is projectionally decomposed by either CS decomposition or Gaussian decomposition, and the two decomposed components are evaluated in a framework of the locational decomposition. Figure 4 shows the concept of the combinations.

First, an input image $\mathbf{x}$ is projection decomposed by parallel partial projections onto CS.

$$\tilde{\mathbf{x}}^*_{P_j} = (P_j \tilde{\Phi}_{cs})^+ P_j \mathbf{x} \tag{11}$$

$$\mathbf{x}^{\sharp}_{P_j} = P_j (\mathbf{x} - \tilde{\Phi}_{cs} \tilde{\mathbf{x}}^*_{P_j}), \tag{12}$$

where $\tilde{\Phi}_{cs} = [\Phi_{cs} \ \overline{\mathbf{x}}_{cs}]$. We define $\mathbf{x}^{\$'}$ and $\mathbf{x}^{\sharp'}$ as

$$\mathbf{x}^{\$'} = \sum_{j=1}^{M} P_j \tilde{\Phi}_{cs} \tilde{\mathbf{x}}^*_{P_j} \tag{13}$$

$$\mathbf{x}^{\sharp'} = \sum_{j=1}^{M} P_j \mathbf{x}^{\sharp}_{P_j}, \tag{14}$$

where M is the number of parts. This method realizes the projectional decomposition without any noise expansion because the parallel partial projections onto canonical space do not spread noises. Examples of the decomposition by PPP are shown in Fig 5.

The decomposed images can be locationally decomposed and evaluated in a straightforward manner. In the combination method, the partial correlation should be defined for each component. When an eigenspace constructed from a set of $\mathbf{x}^{\$'}$ is denoted by $\langle \overline{\mathbf{x}}^{\$'}, \Phi^{\$}_m{}' \rangle$, a partial correlation $C^{\$}_{P_j}$ between $\mathbf{x}^{\$'}$ and $\langle \overline{\mathbf{x}}^{\$'}, \Phi^{\$}_m{}' \rangle$ within a pixel set indicated by P_j is calculated by

$$C^{\$}_{P_j} = C(P_j \mathbf{x}^{\$'}, P_j \tilde{\Phi}^{\$'}_m (P_j \tilde{\Phi}^{\$'}_m)^+ P_j \mathbf{x}^{\$'}). \tag{15}$$

In a similar manner, a partial correlation $C^{\sharp}_{P_j}$ between a residual $\mathbf{x}^{\sharp'}$ and an eigenspace $\langle \overline{\mathbf{x}}^{\sharp'} \Phi^{\sharp}_m{}' \rangle$ is calculated by

$$C^{\sharp}_{P_j} = C(P_j \mathbf{x}^{\sharp'}, P_j \tilde{\Phi}^{\sharp'}_m (P_j \tilde{\Phi}^{\sharp'}_m)^+ P_j \mathbf{x}^{\sharp'}), \tag{16}$$

where $\langle \overline{\mathbf{x}}^{\sharp'} \Phi^{\sharp}_m{}' \rangle$ is constructed from a set of the residuals defined in Eq. (14). Then, the total correlation $C_{cs}{}'$ is defined as

$$C_{cs}{}' = w \sum_{j=1}^{M} C^{\$}_{P_j} + (1 - w) \sum_{j=1}^{M} C^{\sharp}_{P_j}, \tag{17}$$

where w is the weight of the projectional components.

Although the locational decomposition provides robustness with respect to local noises, effective information for face recognition does not increase in the entire image. The locational decomposition still requires a sufficient number of registered images for each person because the conventional eigenface method requires a lot of images for the stable recognition. On the other hand, the projectional decomposition often provides stable results even when only a few images are registered. However, the projectional decomposition is sometimes seriously affected by local noises. In the combination method, however, the locational decomposition prevents local noises from spreading to the entire image when the projectional decomposition provides sufficient information for face recognition. Therefore, the combination method works better than the individual decompositions.

5.2   Combination of Gaussian Decomposition and PPP

A combination of the Gaussian decomposition and the parallel partial projections is more straightforward and simpler than the CS decomposition because the Gaussian filter uses only local (independent) information of the input images. In Fig. 5, the right-most images show the results of the Gaussian decomposition, which are similar to the results of the parallel partial projections onto CS using $64(8\times8)$ square subregions as shown in the most upper row. In this method, an input image is decomposed by the Gaussian filter. The Gaussian component and the residual are locationally decomposed and evaluated in a manner similar

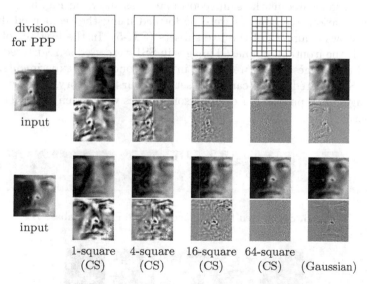

Fig. 5. Examples of the decomposition by parallel partial projections onto CS and the Gaussian filter. The upper row shows the projected images, and the lower row shows the residuals. The first column shows the input images. The second through fifth columns show the images decomposed by the parallel partial projections ($M = 1, 4, 16, 64$) onto CS. The sixth column shows the images decomposed by Gaussian decomposition.

to that described in the previous section. Let $C_{GP_J}^{\$}$ denote the partial correlation between a Gaussian component $\mathbf{x}_G^{\$}$ and an eigenspace constructed in the Gaussian space, and let $C_{GP_J}^{\sharp}$ denote the correlation with the residual. Then, an image $\mathbf{x}$ is evaluated by

$$C_{G'} = w \sum_{j=1}^{M} C_{GP_j}^{\$} + (1 - w) \sum_{j=1}^{M} C_{GP_j}^{\sharp}, \qquad (18)$$

where w is the weight of the projectional components.

6   Experimental Results

6.1   Results for Yale Face Database B

Data Specifications
We performed discrimination experiments on 640 frontal facial images of 10 people, which were taken from the Yale Face Database B [10]. The database includes 65 frontal facial images of each person. Sixty-four of the images were taken under different lighting conditions, and one special image was taken under ambient light. In order to remove the contribution of ambient light, we prepared 64 images of each person with the ambient image subtracted. At the same time, each image was converted to a 64 × 64 pixel image such that the eyes of all of the images are located at the same coordinates, as shown in Fig. 6.

Discrimination experiments were performed using the segmented data set. Figure 7 shows examples of the five subsets (SS1-5). In the first set of experiments, only the frontal illuminated images in SS1 were used as registered images, and all of the images in SS1 were used in the second set of experiments.

The CS is created from a canonical set from our laboratory, which consists of 1,200 images of 50 people. For each person, images were taken under 24 lighting conditions.

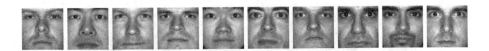

Fig. 6. Segmented facial images in Yale Face Database B

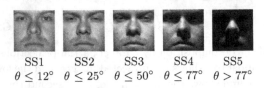

SS1	SS2	SS3	SS4	SS5
$\theta \leq 12°$	$\theta \leq 25°$	$\theta \leq 50°$	$\theta \leq 77°$	$\theta > 77°$

Fig. 7. Example images in subsets 1-5 (SS1-5), where θ is the angle between the light source direction and the camera axis

Discrimination Results

Table 1 shows the discrimination rates for the dataset when only one image is registered from SS1. In the methods that use the PPP, images were divided into sixty-four squares. Among the three single decomposition methods, PPP, the CS decomposition and the Gaussian decomposition, CS decomposition provides the worst results because the method spreads noises by the projection onto CS. Although the PPP provides better results than CS decomposition by preventing the expansion of noises, the results are not sufficient because the method does not include individuality-extraction. Gaussian decomposition provides the best results among the three methods because it can approximately extract individuality without any noise expansion.

The two combination methods, PPP-CS and PPP-Gaussian, work much better than the other methods because they not only extract individuality but also include schemes for avoiding the problems of noises. In addition, in the combination methods, CS decomposition works as well as Gaussian decomposition because CS decomposition does not spread noises by the parallel partial projections.

Table 2 shows discrimination rates when seven images are registered from SS1 for each person. In the experiments, the PPP and the combination methods give the complete discrimination because a sufficient number of images are registered. Two projectional decompositions give slightly worse results than PPP because they cannot sufficiently suppress the noises.

Table 1. Discrimination rates (%) for Yale Face Database B when only one image is registered from SS1. NN denotes the Nearest Neighbor method, PPP denotes the Parallel Partial Projections (locational decomposition), and CS and Gaussian denote the CS and Gaussian projectional decompositions, respectively. In addition, PPP-CS and PPP-Gaussian are combination methods.

Test Class	Method					
	NN	PPP	CS	Gaussian	PPP-CS	PPP-Gaussian
Subset 2	99.2	100	100	100	100	100
Subset 3	74.6	99.2	83.1	99.2	100	100
Subset 4	30.4	78.3	65.9	83.3	98.6	100
Subset 5	12.2	78.3	23.8	44.4	100	100

Table 2. Discrimination rates (%) for Yale Face Database B when seven images are registered from SS1: EF indicates the eigenface method and the other methods are as listed in Table 1

Test Class	Method					
	EF	PPP	CS	Gaussian	PPP-CS	PPP-Gaussian
Subset 2	100	100	100	100	100	100
Subset 3	100	100	100	100	100	100
Subset 4	93.5	100	98.6	98.6	100	100
Subset 5	56.1	100	52.9	74.1	100	100

Table 3. Comparison of the number of parts for each algorithm when seven images are registered from SS1. SS4 and SS5 are used as test sets in the experiment.

# parts	Test Class	Method		
		PPP	PPP-CS	PPP-Gaussian
1 × 1	SS4	93.5	98.6	98.6
	SS5	56.1	52.9	74.1
2 × 2	SS4	96.4	98.6	99.3
	SS5	94.7	90.5	97.4
4 × 4 /	SS4	100	100	100
8 × 8	SS5	100	100	100
16 × 16	SS4	98.6	98.6	100
	SS5	96.3	99.5	99.5

Table 4. Discrimination rates (%) when one image randomly selected from SS4 is registered

Test Class	Method					
	NN	PPP	CS	Gaussian	PPP-CS	PPP-Gaussian
Subset 1	16.7	41.3	39.2	57.8	92.2	96.7
Subset 2	18.4	41.2	36.0	48.3	90.0	93.8
Subset 3	22.0	37.3	33.4	39.2	71.5	78.3
Subset 5	21.4	37.0	25.4	30.2	83.4	84.3

Table 5. Discrimination rates (%) when seven images randomly selected from SS4 are registered

Test Class	Method					
	EF	PPP	CS	Gaussian	PPP-CS	PPP-Gaussian
Subset 1	86.7	99.5	97.6	100	100	100
Subset 2	91.3	99.9	98.6	99.9	100	100
Subset 3	95.5	97.8	98.5	99.4	100	100
Subset 5	70.9	98.1	75.0	87.0	100	100

Table 3 shows the results when the input image is divided to different numbers of image parts. When the number of image parts is too large, the discrimination rate becomes worse because each part can not provide sufficient information for recognition because it is too small. In the experiments, the best result is provided when the number of parts is 4 × 4 and 8 × 8.

Tables 4 and 5 show results when images classified into SS4 are registered. In these experiments, images for registration are randomly selected from SS4. This process was repeated twenty times and the registered images for each person were varied. Most of the results for these experiments were worse than those shown in Tables 1 and 2 because the images in SS4 include more shadows than SS1. However, the results for the combination methods retained high discrimination rates in the experiments.

Table 6. Discrimination rates (%) using other methods: Illumination cone (IC1), illumination cone with cast shadow (IC2), photometric alignment using RANSAC (PA) and segmented linear subspace method (SLS). Note that only one image is registered for PPP-CS and PPP-Gaussian.

Test Class	IC1[11]	IC2[11]	PA[4]	SLS[6]	PPP-CS	PPP-Gaussian
Subset 2	100	100	100	100	100	100
Subset 3	100	100	100	100	100	100
Subset 4	91.4	100	100	100	98.6	100
Subset 5	-	-	81.5	-	100	100

Table 7. Discrimination rates (%) for the AR Database

Test Class	NN	PPP	CS	Gaussian	PPP-CS	PPP-Gaussian
light	40.5	70.1	89.1	82.2	94.8	95.3
scarf	3.7	45.4	37.0	63.7	83.7	84.7

Table 6 shows a number of results reported in the literature[11,4,6]. This table shows that all of the algorithms provide good results when seven images are registered from SS1. However, the proposed methods, PPP-CS and PPP-Gaussian, can provide almost same results with registering only one image from SS1.

In conclusion, the combination methods work better than the individual decomposition methods. In addition, the combination methods have the advantages of both the projectional and locational decompositions and work well even when only one image is registered and the test images or registered images include a significant number of shadows.

6.2   Results for the AR Database

The AR database[12] contains images of 135 people taken under various conditions for each person. For this experiment, we used database images taken under seven different conditions. The example images are as shown in Fig 8. In this experiment, only one image was registered and the other images were used as the test set from which test images were selected.

Under the normal   Under different lighting   Wearing a scarf
condition (registered)   conditions (light-set)   (scarf-set)

Fig. 8. Examples of segmented images in the AR Database

Table 8. Discrimination rates (%) for our database when one image is registered for each person (a) and when all images classified into Classes 1 and 2 are registered (b)

Registered Class	Test Class	Method					
		EF	PPP	CS	Gaussian	PPP-CS	PPP-Gaussian
(a)	Class 2	54.0	83.6	87.1	81.3	95.9	94.4
	Class 3	20.5	70.2	84.2	72.4	86.6	84.3
(b)	Class 3	93.5	93.2	94.0	90.3	99.8	99.7

Table 7 shows the discrimination rates obtained in the experiments. For the light set, CS decomposition and Gaussian decomposition gave better results than the PPP. However, CS decomposition did not work for the scarf set because the test images included a large occlusion. The combination methods worked better than the other methods for both of the individual sets. The results of this experiment indicate that combination methods work well when only one image is registered and the test images include a large occlusion.

6.3 Results for Another Dataset Under the Same Conditions as the Canonical Set

Finally, experimental results are shown for a database that consists of a set of images taken under the same conditions as the canonical set. The database contains images of 50 people taken under 24 lighting conditions for each person. Each image was converted to a 32×32 pixel image. In the methods that use the PPP, images were divided into sixteen squares. The images are classified into three classes. Images classified into Class 1 are frontal illuminated and were used as registered images. Class 2 images, which contain small shadows, and Class 3 images, which contain large shadows, were used as test sets. Table 8 shows the discrimination rates for the database. In the dataset, the two methods that use CS decomposition work better than those that use Gaussian decomposition, because the illumination conditions of the canonical set are identical to those of the test set. The results suggest that the CS decomposition works better when the lighting conditions are similar between the canonical set and the test set.

7   Conclusions

Combination methods of the two types of decomposition, projectional and locational, has been proposed. The projectional decomposition method can extract the individuality from an image. In particular, the Gaussian decomposition can extract the individuality when the image contains noises. The locational decomposition provides robustness with respect to noises when the eigenspace can be constructed properly. The combination methods have the advantages of both of the decomposition methods. The method of combining projectional and locational decompositions works well even when only one image is registered and test images or registered images contain numerous noises, such as shadows or occlusions. We hope that the concept of the proposed method will be useful in solving other problems in image recognition and computer vision.

Acknowledgments

The authors would like to thank A. Georghiades and A. M. Martinez for granting permission to use the Yale Face Database B [10]. and the AR Database[12]. This work was supported by a Grant-In-Aid for Scientific Research (No.15300062) from the Ministry of Education, Science, Sports, and Culture of Japan.

References

1. Turk, M., Pentland, A.: Eigenfaces for recognition. Journal of Cognitive Neuroscience **3** (1991) 71–86
2. Moghaddam, B., Pentland, A.: Probabilistic visual learning for object representation. IEEE Trans. Pattern Analysis and Machine Intelligence **19** (1997) 696–710
3. Black, M., Jepson, A.: Eigentracking: Robust matching and tracking of articulated objects using a view-based representation. International Journal of Computer Vision **26** (1998) 63–84
4. Okabe, T., Sato, Y.: Object recognition based on photometric alignment using ransac. In: Proc. CVPR2003. Volume 1. (2003) 221–228
5. Sakaue, F., Shakunaga, T.: Face recognition by parallel partial projections. In: Proc. ACCV2004. Volume 1. (2004) 1440–150
6. Batur, A., Hayes III, M.: Linear subspaces for illumination robust face recognition. In: Proc. ICCV2001. Volume II. (2001) 296–301
7. Ohba, K., Ikeuchi, K.: Detectability, uniquensess, and reliability of eigen windows for stable verification of partiallo occluded objects. IEEE Trans. Pattern Analysis and Machine Intelligence **19** (1997) 1043–1048
8. Shakunaga, T., Shigenari, K.: Decomposed eigenface for face recognition under various lighting conditions. In: Proc. CVPR2001. Volume 1. (2001) 864–871
9. Wang, H., Li, S., Wang, Y.: Face recognition under varying lighting conditions using self quotient image. In: Proc. IEEE FG2004. (2004) 819–824
10. Georghiades, A., Belhumeur, P., Kriegman, D.: From few to many: Generative models for recognition under variable pose and illuminations. In: Proc. FG2000. (2000) 277–284
11. Georghiades, A., Belhumeur, P., Kriegman, D.: From few to many: illumination cone models for face recognition under variable lighting and pose. IEEE Trans. Pattern Analysis and Machine Intelligence **23** (2001) 643–660
12. Martinez, A., Benavente, R.: The AR face database. Technical Report #24, CVC (1998)

Author Index

Lecture Notes in Computer Science

For information about Vols. 1–3645

please contact your bookseller or Springer